# Key Texts for Latin American Sociology

# Key Texts for Latin American Sociology

Edited by Fernanda Beigel

SSIS SERIES    SAGE STUDIES IN INTERNATIONAL SOCIOLOGY:67

Los Angeles I London I New Delhi
Singapore I Washington DC I Melbourne

Los Angeles | London | New Delhi
Singapore | Washington DC | Melbourne

SAGE Publications Ltd
1 Oliver's Yard
55 City Road
London EC1Y 1SP

SAGE Publications Inc.
2455 Teller Road
Thousand Oaks, California 91320

SAGE Publications India Pvt Ltd
B 1/I 1 Mohan Cooperative Industrial Area
Mathura Road
New Delhi 110 044

SAGE Publications Asia-Pacific Pte Ltd
3 Church Street
#10-04 Samsung Hub
Singapore 049483

Editor: Natalie Aguilera
Assistant editor: Eve Williams
Production editor: Katherine Haw
Copyeditor: Rosemary Campbell
Indexer: Elizabeth Ball
Marketing manager: George Kimble
Cover design: Wendy Scott
Typeset by: C&M Digitals (P) Ltd, Chennai, India
Printed in the UK

**Library of Congress Control Number: 2018964096**

**British Library Cataloguing in Publication data**

A catalogue record for this book is available from the British Library

ISBN 978-1-5264-9026-1
ISBN 978-1-5264-9025-4 (pbk)

At SAGE we take sustainability seriously. Most of our products are printed in the UK using responsibly sourced papers
and boards. When we print overseas we ensure sustainable papers are used as measured by the PREPS grading
system. We undertake an annual audit to monitor our sustainability.

# Contents

About the Editor     ix

About the Contributors     x

Acknowledgments     xxi

**INTRODUCTORY STUDY**

**Latin American Sociology: A Centennial Regional Tradition**     1

Fernanda Beigel (Argentina)

**PART ONE    FOUNDING PROBLEMS**     31

1   **Founding Problems and Institutionalization of Sociology in Latin America**     33

Jorge Rovira Mas (Costa Rica)

2   **Alberto Guerreiro Ramos (Brazil)**
**A Critical Introduction to Brazilian Sociology:**
**Canned Sociology versus Dynamic Sociology**     47

Comment by João Maia (Brazil)

3   **Orlando Fals Borda (Colombia)**
**Theoretical–Practical Experiences: General**
**Working Guidelines on Participatory Action**
**Research (PAR)**     57

Comment by Juan Ignacio Piovani (Argentina)

4   **Aníbal Quijano (Peru)**
**Of Don Quixote and Windmills in Latin America**     64

Comment by Cláudio Costa Pinheiro (Brazil)

5  Edelberto Torres Rivas (Guatemala–Costa Rica)
   On the Pessimism in the Social Sciences                    74
   *Comment by Sergio Villena Fiengo (Costa Rica)*

6  Elizabeth Jelin (Argentina)
   The Foundations of a New Issue: Gender,
   Human Rights and Memory                                    89
   *Comment by Teresa Valdés Echenique (Chile)*

**PART TWO    HISTORICAL AND
CONTEMPORARY DEBATES**                                        103

7  Understanding Historical and Contemporary Debate
   in Latin American Sociology: Enlightening Paths            105
   *Raquel Sosa Elízaga (Mexico)*

8  Sergio Bagú (Argentina–Mexico)
   Building Theory                                            116
   *Comment by Pablo de Marinis (Argentina)*

9  René Zavaleta Mercado (Bolivia)
   The Struggle for Surplus                                   130
   *Comment by Oscar Vega Camacho (Bolivia)*

10  Arturo Escobar (Colombia–US)
    Development (Again) in Question: Trends in
    Critical Debates on Capitalism, Development
    and Modernity in Latin America                            139
    *Comment by Irene Piedrahíta Arcila (Colombia)*

11  Bolívar Echeverría (Ecuador–Mexico)
    The 'American' Modernity (Keys to Its Understanding)       157
    *Comment by Márgara Millán (Mexico)*

**PART THREE    SOCIAL STRUCTURE
AND INEQUALITIES**                                            173

12  Inequality, Inequalities                                  175
    *Nadya Araujo Guimarães (Brazil)*

13  **José Carlos Mariátegui (Peru)**
    **The Problem of Race: Approaching the Issue**                186
    *Comment by José-Carlos Mariátegui Ezeta (Peru)*

14  **Florestan Fernandes (Brazil)**
    **The Weight of the Past**                                    201
    *Comment by Antonio Sérgio Alfredo Guimarães (Brazil)*

15  **Rodolfo Stavenhagen (Mexico)**
    **The Dynamics of Inter-ethnic Relations:**
    **Classes, Colonialism and Acculturation**                    222
    *Comment by Francisco Zapata Schaffeld (Mexico)*

16  **José Nun (Argentina)**
    **Marginality and Social Exclusion (Fragments)**              240
    *Comment by Gabriel Kessler (Argentina)*

17  **Marina Ariza and Orlandina de Oliveira (Mexico)**
    **Households, Families and Social Inequalities**
    **in Latin America**                                          248
    *Comment by Brígida García (Mexico)*

**PART FOUR    IDENTITIES, ACTORS AND**
**SOCIAL MOVEMENTS**                                              271

18  **Latin American Perspectives on Social**
    **Movements Research**                                        273
    *Breno Bringel (Brazil)*

19  **Silvia Rivera Cusicanqui (Bolivia)**
    **Ch'ixinakax utxiwa: A Reflection on the Practices**
    **and Discourses of Decolonization**                         290
    *Comment by Maristella Svampa (Argentina)*

20  **Eder Sader (Brazil)**
    **New Players Came on Stage – São Paulo Workers'**
    **Experiences, Language, and Struggles (1970–1980)**          307
    *Comment by Maria da Glória Gohn (Brazil)*

21 **Virginia Vargas (Peru)**
**Latin American Feminisms and Their Transition**
**to the New Millennium (A Personal Political Reading)** 319
*Comment by Susana Rostagnol (Uruguay)*

22 **Enrique de la Garza Toledo (Mexico)**
**Trade Union Models in Latin America,**
**Before and After** 338
*Comment by Patricia Collado (Argentina)*

**PART FIVE    STATE, SOCIETY AND POLITICS** 353

23 **Politics, State and Society in Latin American Sociology:**
**A Partial Introduction** 355
*Manuel Antonio Garretón (Chile)*

24 **Suzy Castor (Haiti)**
**The Secular Roots of a Difficult Nation-building** 371
*Comment by Patricia Funes (Argentina)*

25 **Ernesto Laclau (Argentina–UK)**
**The Populist Turn and the Center-Left in Latin America** 382
*Comment by Paula Biglieri (Argentina)*

26 **Guillermo O'Donnell (Argentina–US)**
**On Certain Aspects of the Crisis of the State** 389
*Comment by Maria Hermínia Tavares de Almeida (Brazil)*

27 **Bernardo Sorj (Uruguay–Brazil)**
**Political Activism in the Era of the Internet** 404
*Comment by Carlos Ruiz Encina (Chile)*

*Index* 423

# About the Editor

**Fernanda Beigel** is a sociologist and holds a degree in Social and Political Sciences. Principal Researcher at CONICET (INCIHUSA, Mendoza, Argentina), Head Professor in Latin American Sociology and Director of the Doctoral Program at the National University of Cuyo. She has been the director of the Research Program on Academic Dependency in Latin America (PIDAAL) since 2004. Her doctoral studies were fulfilled under the guidance of Arturo Andrés Roig and her postdoctoral studies at the Centre de Sociologie Européenne (EHESS, Paris) with Gisèle Sapiro. Awards include: Bernardo Houssay Award (2003), CLASCO International Essay First Prize (2004) and Mention of Honor for Scientific Value (2017). A specialist in the Sociology of Science and Latin American Sociology, her most recent publications are: *The Politics of Academic Autonomy in Latin America* (Ashgate); 'Publishing from the periphery: Structural heterogeneity and segmented circuits. The evaluation of scientific publications for tenure in Argentina's CONICET' (2014), *Current Sociology*, 62(5): 743–765; 'El nuevo carácter de la dependencia intelectual' (2016), *Cuestiones de Sociologia*, 14: 45–68; 'Peripheral Scientists, between Ariel and Caliban. Institutional Know-how and Circuits of Recognition in Argentina. The Career-best Publications of the Researchers at CONICET' (2017), *Dados–Revista de Ciências Sociais, Rio de Janeiro*, 60(3): 825–865; with O. Gallardo and F. Bekerman, 'Institutional expansion and scientific development in the periphery: The structural heterogeneity of Argentina's academic field' (2018), *Minerva*, 56(3): 305–331; 'Las relaciones de poder en la ciencia mundial. Un anti-ranking para conocer la ciencia producida en la periferia' (2018), *Nueva Sociedad*, 74: 13–28.

# About the Contributors

*Note*: biographies of the authors of the key texts are provided in Comments by specialists.

**Paula Biglieri** holds a Doctoral degree in Political and Social Science from the National Autonomous University of Mexico (UNAM). She is a researcher at the National Scientific and Technical Research Council (CONICET) in Argentina and she is also the Head of the Cátedra Libre Ernesto Laclau of the School of Philosophy and Letters at the University of Buenos Aires. She co-directs the research project 'Theorising Transnational Populist Politics' funded by the British Academy and hosted by the Cátedra Libre Ernesto Laclau and the Centre for Applied Philosophy, Politics and Ethics, University of Brighton. Annually, she leads the graduate seminar on 'Psychoanalysis, Rhetoric and Politics' at the Cátedra Libre Ernesto Laclau. Her theoretical research is mainly focused on the relationship between psychoanalysis and politics, particularly considering the theoretical dimension of populism. She has also studied the cases of the so-called 'last Latin American populist tide'. She has published numerous papers and essays in Argentina, Brazil, Ecuador, Mexico, Slovenia, the UK and the US. She has also co-authored the books, *In the Name of the People. The Emergence of the Kirchnerista Populism* [*En el nombre del pueblo. La emergencia del populismo kirchnerista*] (UNSAM Edita, 2007); and *The Uses of Psychoanalysis in Ernesto Laclau's Theory of Hegemony* [*Los usos del psicoanálisis en la teoría de la hegemonía de Ernesto Laclau*] (Grama Ediciones, 2012).

**Breno Bringel** holds a Doctoral degree from the Faculty of Political Science and Sociology (Universidad Complutense de Madrid). He has been a Visiting Professor at universities in Argentina, Brazil, Chile, Uruguay, Portugal, Spain, France, Switzerland and the UK. He is currently a Professor of Sociology at the Institute of Social and Political Studies at the State University of Rio de Janeiro (IESP-UERJ) where he coordinates the Doctoral Program in Sociology and leads, with José Mauricio Domingues, the Research Group on Social Theory and Latin America. He is the President of the Research Committee on Social Classes and Social Movements (RC-47) at the International Sociological Asssociation (ISA) and Editor of Open Movements, a partnership between Open Democracy and ISA RC-47. His main areas of research are political sociology and Latin American sociology, and his most recent book is *Critical Geopolitics and Regional (Re)Configurations: Interregionalism and Transnationalism Between Latin American and Europe* (Routledge, 2019). In this same ISA Series (Sage Studies in International Sociology) he edited the book *Global Modernity and Social Contestation* (Sage, 2015).

**Oscar Vega Camacho** is an independent Bolivian writer and researcher on philosophy, literature and the arts. He has collaborated in academic journals and magazines, and published *Errancias. Aperturas de vivir bien* in 2011. He was a counselor of the Cultural Foundation of the Central Bank of Bolivia (2011–2016), and Visiting Researcher at the Center for Constitutional Studies of the Bolivian Catholic University 'San Pablo' (2010–2013). He was part of the Presidential Representation for the Constituent Assembly (2007–2008) and is a member of the group *Comuna*.

**Patricia Collado** is a Sociologist and Doctor in Political and Social Sciences. She has a Master's in Social Sciences (FLACSO; Diploma in Political Economy-FLACSO). She is a researcher at CONICET (INCIHUSA, Mendoza, Argentina), Director of the Master's Program in Latin-American Studies (UNCuyo) and Head Professor at the UNCuyo. Her current research projects include: 'Class and political subjectivation. Return to clasic discussion from the changes of contemporary labour'. Her research field is contemporary work studies, trade unionism, social conflicts and social movements. Recent publications include: *Citizenship, Mobilization and Social Conflict*, in collaboration with J.L. Bonifacio and G. Vommaro (PISAC, 2017); 'Recurrent themes, emergent topics, neccesary dialogues in labour studies in collaboration with Montes Cató J' (Revista del CIEP – 2016); 'How is class? A reflection about antagonism labour conflict' (Herramienta 2015), *Conflicts Around Labour. A Comparative Analysis of Mendoza, Córdoba and Buenos Aires* (UNGS, 2015).

**Maria Hermínia Tavares de Almeida** is a Political Scientist and PhD (Universidade de São Paulo and University of California, Berkeley) Senior

Researcher at Centro Brasileiro de Análise e Planejamento (CEBRAP), Professor at the University of São Paulo (retired) and Professor at the Graduate Programs of International Relations and Political Science. She has published the books *Economic Crisis and Organized Interests* (Edusp, 1993) and, with Gian Luca Gardini, *Foreign Policy Responses to the Rise of Brazil – Balancing Power in Emerging States* (Palgrave Macmillan, 2016) and *The Golgen Age – Essays on Democracy in Brazil* (Horizontes, 2019). She holds the Brazilian National Order of Scientific Merit (2006).

**Pablo de Marinis** is a Sociologist (Universidad de Buenos Aires, Argentina, 1991) and holds a DPhil in Philosophy (Universität Hamburg, Germany, 1997). He teaches sociological theory in the Sociology Department of the Facultad de Ciencias Sociales, Universidad de Buenos Aires. He conducts research at the Instituto de Investigaciones Gino Germani, at UBA/CONICET. His main research topics are related to the concepts of 'community' and 'mass/crowd' through the history of sociological theory. He is also concerned with methodological questions of theoretical sociological research and his main publications deal with these issues: www.uba.academia.edu/PablodeMarinis.

**Teresa Valdés Echenique** is a Sociologist (PUC Chile). Between 1981 and 2006 she was a researcher at FLACSO-Chile, where she was a Professor and created the Gender Studies Area, where she conducted a great deal of research. She coordinated the regional projects 'Latin American Women in Figures' and the 'Index of Fulfilled Commitment' (IFC), a strategy for the citizen control of gender equity. She was a researcher at the Center for Studies for the Development of Women (CEDEM) (2006–2012), Visiting Professor at Stanford University (1996–2007) and Professor at various Chilean universities. She was Gender Advisor to the Minister of Health and Head of the Gender Unit of the Ministry of Health (2014–2018). She has published and edited numerous books and articles on gender issues, social participation and citizen control. She received the 'Elena Caffarena' award in 2003 in the category of Women Researcher in Science and Education, awarded by SERNAM-Santiago. Since 2007 she has coordinated the Observatory of Gender and Equity.

**João Maia** is Associate Professor at CPDOC/School of Social Sciences, Fundação Getulio Vargas (Rio de Janeiro, Brazil). He holds a Doctoral degree in Sociology from IUPERJ and a Masters degree from the same institution. His research interests span the history of sociology, social theory and the sociology of science and intellectuals. He co-authored the book *Knowledge and Global Power: Making New Sciences in the South* (Monash, 2018) and 'Negotiating with the North: How Southern tier intellectuals workers deal with the global economy of knowledge' (2017) *The Sociological Review*, 66 (1): 41–57. He also authored 'History of sociology and the quest for intellectual autonomy in the Global South: the cases of Alberto Guerreiro Ramos and Syed Hussein Alatas' (2014), (*Current Sociology*, 62(7): 1097–1115).

**Irene Piedrahita Arcila** is an Anthropologist, Magister in Political Science and Research Professor at the Institute of Political Studies of the University of Antioquia, Medellin, Colombia. She is currently the coordinator of the research group Hegemony, Wars and Conflict. Her work focuses on political anthropology and the State, particularly in ethnographic works, in which she has conducted research on the Colombian peasantry and the connection between memories associated with the armed conflict and the construction of the State. She has published numerous articles and working texts on memory, statehood and peasant communities in protected areas. Her recent work includes: *¿Un Estado Vigilante, Negociador, Ambiguo? Formas en que opera el Estado en el Orquídeas National Natural Park* (2018).

**Raquel Sosa Elízaga** is Doctor in History and Professor at the Center for Latin American Studies (CELA) at the National Autonomous University of Mexico. With a vast academic trajectory, she participates actively in the public debates of the Mexican and Latin American society. Among her recent publications are: 'Pensar con cabeza propia. Educación y pensamiento crítico en América Latina' (Cuadernos del Pensamiento Critico, 2011); *Temas y procesos de la historia reciente de América Latina* (CLACSO 2010); *Encrucijadas Abiertas. América Latina y el Caribe. Sociedad y pensamiento crítico abya yala* (CLACSO, 2018); *Hacia la recuperación de la soberanía educativa en América Latina*, (CLACSO/UNAM, 2010) and *Educación y Exclusión* (Facultad de Ciencias Políticas y Sociales de la UNAM, 2016). She currently conducts a large public university programme in Mexico, Universidades para el Bienestar Benito Juárez García, and is general director of

CREFAL, Centro Regional para la Educación Fundamental en América Latina y el Caribe.

**Carlos Ruiz Encina** is a Sociologist and Doctor in Latin American Studies and a Professor at the Sociology Department and the Doctoral Program in Social Sciences and Latin American Studies (Universidad de Chile). He was Director of the Sociology Department (2014–2018). He is President of Nodo XXI Foundation, an intellectual institute related with the Chilean Frente Amplio. His research areas are state, development studies, conflict and social structure. He participates actively in public debates linked to democracy and development in Chile and Latin America.

**José-Carlos Mariátegui Ezeta** is a scientist, writer and curator working on culture, new media and technology. He studied Biology and Applied Mathematics at Cayetano Heredia University (Lima) and holds both a Master's and Doctoral degrees in Information Systems and Innovation from the London School of Economics and Political Science (LSE). He conceived and curated international original exhibitions and events in new media art and on the history of science and technology. He has published in journals such as *Third Text, The Information Society, Telos* and *Leonardo*. He is founding Director of the José Carlos Mariátegui Memorial Museum (1995–2005) and currently Director of the José Carlos Mariátegui Archive (www.mariategui.org) in Lima. He is currently Editorial Board member for Leonardo Books at MIT Press, Advisory Board member for AI & Society (UK) and of the Bicentenary of the Independence of Peru Committee.

**Sergio Villena Fiengo** holds a doctorate in Studies of Society and Culture and is Professor at the School of Sociology and Director of the Institute of Social Research (IIS) at the University of Costa Rica (UCR). He is a specialist in Latin American sociology and the sociology of culture and arts. His profile and publications can be found at https://ucr.academia.edu/SergioVillenaFiengo.

**Patricia Funes**, PhD, has been Professor of Latin American History at the Social Sciences Faculty, University of Buenos Aires (UBA) since 1999, and, since 2005, Senior Researcher, Consejo Nacional de Investigaciones Científicas y Técnicas (National Scientific and Technical Research Council) at the Gino Germani Research Institute, Social Science Faculty, University of Buenos Aires. Her research topics are related to the history of ideas, political history and memory in

Latin American in the twentieth century. Her current research project is 'Sources, Shapes and Representations of the Recent Past. Personal Archives: History, Memory and Biography'. Her recent books include: *Historia mínima de las ideas políticas en América Latina* (El Colegio de México/Turner, 2014) and *Revolución, dictadura y democracia. Lógicas militantes y militares en la historia reciente de Argentina en América Latina* (Imago Mundi, 2016).

**Brígida García** is Professor–Researcher at the Centro de Estudios Demográficos, Urbanos y Ambientales (CEDUA), El Colegio de México, Mexico City. She holds a Master's degree in Demography from this same institution and a Doctoral degree in Sociology from the National Autonomous University of Mexico (UNAM). Her research areas include family, work and gender in Mexico and Latin America. She has held the post of President of the Mexican Demographic Society (Somede) and in 2015 she was named Emeritus Researcher by the National System of Researchers in Mexico (SNI). Her recent publications cover the topics of households and workers, time use and non-paid work.

**Manuel Antonio Garretón**, is a Sociologist (Universidad Católica, Chile) and has a PhD from the École des Hautes Études en Sciences Sociales (Paris). He has been the director of several academic institutions and a Professor at various national and international universities. His areas of research and teaching are political sociology, transition to democracy, State and society, authoritarian regimes, actor and social movements, political parties, education and the university, public opinion and social demands, education and culture, development of the social sciences, sociological theory and modernity and society in Latin America. He participates actively in political and cultural debates in Chile and Latin America in the intellectual and mass media context. Since 1994 he has been Professor at the Department of Sociology at the Faculty of Social Sciences, Universidad de Chile. He was awarded the Chilean National Prize in Social Sciences (2007) and the Kalman Silvert Award (2015) by the Latin American Studies Association (LASA).

**Maria da Glória Gohn** is a Sociologist and holds a Doctoral degree in Political Science from the University of São Paulo, Brazil (1983) and Post-PhD in the New School of University, New York (1996–97). She is Professor at University of Campinas (UNICAMP) and Visiting Professor at Federal University of ABC (UFABC). She is Researcher 1 A of the

National Council of Research (CNPq) and former Vice-President of the Research Committee 47 of the International Sociological Association (ISA). Her research and teaching fields are: social movements, social theories, urban participatory counsels and social mobilization by NGOs. She has published twenty books on social movements and social participation of the civil society such as: *Manifestações e Protestos no Brasil: Correntes e contra correntes na atualidade* (Cortez, 2017); *Manifestações de Junho de 2013 no Brasil e Praças dos Indignados no Mundo* (Vozes, 2014); *Movimentos Sociais e Redes de Mobilizações no Brasil Contemporâneo* (Vozes, 2014), *Teoria dos Movimentos Sociais* (Loyola, 2014), *Novas Teorias dos Movimentos Sociais* (Loyola, 2014) and *O Protagonismo da Sociedade Civil* (Cortez, 2008).

**Antonio Sérgio Alfredo Guimarães** holds a PhD in Sociology from the University of Wisconsin–Madison (1988). He is a Researcher at CEBRAP–São Paulo, and Senior Professor of Sociology at the University of São Paulo. He held the Simon Bolívar Chair of Latin American Studies at the University of Cambridge (2016–2017), the Chaire Brésilienne de Sciences Sociales Sérgio Buarque de Holanda, Fondation Maison des Sciences de l'Homme (2010–2014), the Lemman Distinguished Chair at the University of Illinois at Urbana-Champaign, and was a Visiting Professor at Princeton University and the Federal University of Bahia, among others. His research field is racial, national and class identities; Black social movements; affirmative action and Black intellectuals. He has published several books, including: *Preconceito Racial – Modos, Temas, Tempos* (Cortez, 2008); *Classes, raças e democracia* (Editora 34, 2002); *Racismo e anti-racismo no Brasil* (Editora 34, 1999; 2e. Edição 2005).

**Nadya Araujo Guimarães** holds the Chair in the Sociology of Work, Department of Sociology at the University of São Paulo. She is also a Senior Researcher associated with CEBRAP (Brazilian Center for Analysis and Planning), and in 2016 was inducted into the Brazilian Academy of Sciences. Nadya Guimarães received her Doctoral degree from the Universidad Nacional Autónoma de México (1983) and carried out post-doctoral studies at the Massachusetts Institute of Technology (MIT) Special Program on Urban and Regional Studies for Developing Areas (1993–1994). She has undertaken research in the following areas: the Brazilian labour market, focusing on economic change and workers' trajectories; comparative studies on unemployment, employment flexibility and labour market intermediaries; gender/race inequalities; and care and care workers. She recently co-authored *Être chômeur à Paris, São Paulo et Tokyo* (Presses de Sciences Po, 2013) and the chapter 'The Future of Work', in *Rethinking Society for the 21st Century* (Cambridge University Press, 2018). She also co-edited *Genre, Race, Classe: Travailler en France et au Brésil* (L'Harmattan, 2016).

**Gabriel Kessler** is a Sociologist and holds a PhD in Sociology from the École des Hautes Études en Sciences Sociales (Paris). He is Principal Researcher at the National Council of Scientific and Technical Research (CONICET), Professor of Sociology at the Universidad Nacional de La Plata (UNLP) and at the Universidad Nacional de San Martín, Argentina. His research focuses on inequality, violence and Latin America social structure. Recent books include: *Controversias sobre la desigualdad* (Fondo de Cultura Económica, 2015), *La sociedad Argentina hoy* (Siglo XXI, 2016) and *Muertes que importan* (with S. Gayol, Siglo XXI, 2018).

**Jorge Rovira Mas** is a Sociologist and holds a Doctoral degree in Sociology From Universidad Nacional Autónoma de México (1980). He was Professor and Researcher at the Universidad de Costa Rica (1970–2013) in the School of Sociology and the Social Research Institute and has been Emeritus Professor since 2016. The author and editor of several books, he has also published numerous articles in specialized journals and contributed with chapters of books in national and international editions. Awards include: Jorge Volio, Cleto González Víquez in National History and Humboldt (2009) from the Deutscher Akademischer Austausch Dienst (DAAD).

**Márgara Millán** is a Sociologist and Social Anthropologist, Professor at the Faculty of Political and Social Sciences, National Autonomous University of Mexico and researcher at the Center for Latin American Studies (CELA, UNAM). Her research areas include: social movements, cultural representations in gender, and the critique of modernity. She was Coordinator of the collection 'Teoría Social Latinoamericana' (1994–1996), along with Ruy Mauro Marini, and Director of the research projects 'Alternative Modernities and New Common Sense' (2011–2014) and 'Political Prefigurations' (2015–2016). Her main articles include: 'Derivas de un cine en femenino' (1999), 'De-centering gender, Re-ordering nation; Zapatism of Indigenous women and its consequences' (2014), and her most recent books are *Modernidades alternativas* (2017) and *Prefiguraciones de lo político* (2018). She is also a founder of

*Con Nosotros*, a civil association that promotes the inclusion of people with disabilities.

**Cláudio Costa Pinheiro** is currently Professor of Asian and African Studies at Rio de Janeiro Federal University, Brazil; Chairman of Sephis Programme, Netherlands; International Scholar, Universität zu Köln, Germany and Visiting Professor for Critical Studies in Higher Education Transformation, Nelson Mandela University, South Africa. His research interests include two main axes: knowledge production and circulation, and structures of power, slavery and forms of dependency, both of which consider the impact and durable effects of colonialism in the institutionalization of power in Western and non-Western societies. He is or has been Visiting Professor or Fellow at the Universities of: (in the US) Wellesley College/Harvard University; (in Europe) Universities of Vienna, Cologne, Humboldt and Free University of Berlin and University of Lisbon; (in India) the University of Calcutta, of Goa, of Delhi, at the Center for the Study of Developing Societies, and at Bukkyo University (Kyoto, Japan). Recent publications include with Schröder, P. and Vermeulen, H. (editors) (2019) 'The German Tradition in Latin-American Anthropology', special issue, *Revista de Antropologia Journal*, 62 (1) 2019; 2018c. *Unhomely Afterlives*, with Williams and Hentschke (eds). *To Be at Home*. Berlin: De Gruyter, 210–218, 2017. Modernity and the artifices of Place-making. AEGS - *Annual of European and Global Studies*, 4, June/July 2017, 51–71.

**Juan Igancio Piovani** is a Sociologist with an MSc in Advanced Social Research Methods and Statistics (City, University of London, UK) and a PhD in the Methodology of the Social and Political Sciences (Sapienza University of Rome, Italy). He is a full Professor of Social Research Methods (Department of Sociology, Faculty of Humanities, National University of La Plata, Argentina) and Principal Researcher of the National Scientific and Technical Research Council (CONICET) at the Institute of Humanities and Social Sciences (IdIHCS). Among his most recent books are *Manual de metodología de las ciencias sociales* (with A. Marradi and N. Archenti, Siglo XXI, 2018); *La Argentina en el siglo XXI. Cómo somos, vivimos y convivimos en una sociedad desigual* (co-edited with A. Salvia, Siglo XXI, 2018) and *¿Condenados a la reflexividad? Apuntes para repensar el proceso de investigación social* (co-edited with L. Muñiz Terra, Biblos-CLASCO, 2018).

**Susana Rostagnol** holds a Doctoral degree in Social Anthropology and is Director of the Department of Social Anthropology (Universidad de la República, Uruguay), and is part of the National Researchers System and coordinator of the Gender, Body and Sexuality Program. Her Research areas include: gender, body and sexuality; gender-based violence, feminist theory and methodology. She has carried out fieldwork in Uruguay and in Andalucía (Spain). Currently she is researching the neoconservative movement and sexual and reproductive rights. She has published several articles and books, the latest include 'Abortion in Andalusia: women's rights and the Gallardón Bill' (*Antropologia*, 5(2), 2018), 'La relación etnográfica en el campo y en el escritorio' (*Disparidades*, 74 (1), 2019) and 'Los meandros políticos de la ciudadanía sexual y los derechos sexuales y reproductivos' (Siglo XXI, Mexico, 2019).

**Francisco Zapata Schaffeld** holds a PhD in Sociology from the University of Paris (1970) and has been a Professor at El Colegio de México since 1974, where he was Chair of the Department of Sociological Studies from 1994 to 2000. He has been a member of the National System of Research since 1984. He teaches courses in the Doctorate Program in Social Science on classical sociology, the sociology of work and the history of the Latin American labour movement. His research areas include: analysis of the class consciousness of striking miners in Bolivia, Chile, Mexico and Peru and the history of Latin American labour. He was Professor at the Yale University Latin American Program (2000) and Fellow at the Kellog Institute of the University of Notre Dame (2002). He has collaborated on various graduate programs at the University of Santiago, Chile (USACH) and the Catholic University of Northern Chile. His most recent publications are: *Ideología y política en América Latina* (El Colegio de México, 2nd edition, 2016); *Historia mínima del sindicalismo latinoamericano* (El Colegio de México, 2013) and 'Ciencias sociales y desarrollo nacional en México', *Antropologías del Sur*, 2: 15–29 (2014).

**Bernardo Sorj** received his PhD in Sociology from the University of Manchester in England. He is the Director of the Edelstein Center for Social Research and Plataforma Democrática, a joint project with the Fernando Henrique Cardoso Foundation. He was Professor of Sociology at the University of Rio de Janeiro, Visiting Professor and Chair at many European, North American and Latin American universities. The author of 30 books and more than 100 academic articles on social theory, international relations, the social impact of new technologies and Latin America political development, he is member of the board of several academic journals, and consultant to governments and international organizations.

**Maristella Svampa** is a Sociologist, writer and researcher. She has a degree in Philosophy from the National University of Córdoba and a PhD in Sociology from the École des Hautes Études en Sciences Sociales., France. She is Principal Researcher at CONICET and Professor in Latin American Social Theory at the National University of La Plata (Argentina). In 2006 she obtained the Guggenheim Scholarship and in 2016 the Kónex Platinum Award in Sociology (Argentina). Among her latest books are: *Latin American Debates. Indianism, Development, Dependency and Populism* (2016); *From the Change of Time to the End of the Cycle. Progressive Governments, Extractivism and Social Movements in Latin America* (2017); *Development in Latin America: Toward a New Future Canada* and *Neo-extractuinism Dynamics in Latin America; Socio-environmental Conflicts, The Territorial Turn and New Political Narratives* (Cambridge University Press). She is also the author of three novels, *Los reinos perdidos* (2006), *Where Our Dead are Buried* (2012) and *The Wall* (2013).

# Acknowledgments

This volume was conceived in the periphery of the periphery: the city of Mendoza (Argentina), in a workshop held in 2012, where the scientific committee discussed the difference between 'classics' and 'key texts'. It is the result of five years of collaboration between many colleagues of 15 Latin American countries that committed to the project and helped with different tasks: the formulation of the project, the translations, queries in archives to confront translation issues, author rights and contacts with heirs or publishing houses. More than half of the volume was slowly translated into English thanks to this collective commitment. The rest of the volume remained untranslated and kept the book waiting for a long time until the International Sociological Association generously funded the rest of the translations. We thank the ISA for their support in broadening the circulation of the knowledge produced in this region. The credit for the collaborations that produced the individual translations are noted where appropriate. The rest (Chapters 8, 10, 11, 18, 20, 21, 23, 24, 25 and 26) were translated by Mariana Donadini, whom we thank for her professionalism.

# Introductory Study

## Latin American Sociology: A Centennial Regional Tradition

*Fernanda Beigel (Argentina)*

The mere mention of French, US or German Sociology refers readers to world renowned disciplinary traditions whose legitimate foundations are beyond doubt. The so-called *founding fathers* of 'international' Sociology (Marx, Weber and Durkheim) and other sociologists from these national fields are conceived as the sources of original and 'universal' theories and methods. However, it is fair to recognize that their circulation and legitimacy are not detached from the material and symbolic power of those nation-states during the period of institutionalization/internationalization of Sociology. In this context, these sociological powers were 'blessed' by the diffusion of their particular *originality* and gifted with an international *universality*. Conversely, the 'universality' and 'originality' of Latin American Sociology has been under scrutiny – either because its production was mainly published in Spanish/Portuguese, thus had scarce circulation outside the region, or because its commitment to social change led to the prejudice that it produced only ideological essays. Sometimes even its own practitioners have felt that they are a retort of concepts and methods elaborated at the 'centers of excellence'. However, Sociology in Latin America has its own local, national and regional traditions.

Unlike the dominating national form of development, the institutionalization of Sociology in Latin America was regional (thus, *international*) from its birth. In fact, the national sociologies evolved in parallel with the appearance of the Latin American Sociology Association (ALAS) in 1950 and other institutions that gave the impulse to a regional research space. The founders of the first Sociology schools took advantage of the material and symbolic stimulus given to the social sciences during the second post-war period. Several regional centers for teaching and research were created and most of them were installed in Santiago de Chile which became the main axis of a *regional academic circuit*. From this platform, Latin American Sociology emerged as a regional tradition with its own path, differentiated from national sociologies, developed through reflection on the continent's main common historical and social problems: colonization, development, dependency, poverty. All this was possible because of the existence of a regional intellectual space with a long and rich history, as we will see next.

Very frequently the center–periphery focus has been introduced to the study of science, assuming that peripheral communities are dependent and marginal while central communities are autonomous and international. In other studies (Beigel, 2013) I have criticized the concept of academic dependency when it is attached to an image of a passive periphery reduced to the role of importer of foreign knowledge, subordinate to an active center considered as the main exporter and producer of 'original' knowledge. Intellectual production is not a simple equation based on economic or political national development, although international circulation is indeed more dependent on material structures and traditional hierarchies. In fact, theories and methods produced outside the mainstream centers have been rarely 'exported' into mainstream circuits, but this is not to imply these are the result of massive imports of central models. Rather the contrary, I argue here that this regional tradition still influences the practice and theory of many sociologists today.

The history of Sociology in Latin America and its different national traditions can be traced back to 1882 when the first chair was created at a university in a capital city. However, Latin American Sociology (LAS), as a specific research field is a centennial tradition born by the mid-1920s and consolidated by the 1960s with the emergence of its own focus and regional institutions. As will be proven by the wide range of key texts contained in this volume, most of them have never been translated into English before, and accordingly they did not circulate in the North, but formed sociologists throughout the whole region, crossing different countries and sociology schools.

In the first part of this chapter I will address a socio-historical account of the development of this regional focus and a field approach to understanding its specific process of institutionalization, as well as the role played by politicization, along with the features of the regional circuit and its external pressures. Secondly, I will analyze the nature of the traditions involved in the construction of its perspective and the weight of the historical-structural method. Thirdly, I will delve into the particular relevance of a conceptual trilogy (nation, class and race) that has been reinterpreted at different historical stages. Finally, I will say a few words on 'critical' sociology and describe the general aims of this editing project and the organization of the volume.

## What is Latin American About Sociology in Latin America?

In his recent book on French Sociology, Heilbron (2015) asks what is French about Sociology in France? He delves into the historical decon- struction of one of the most consolidated and unquestionably 'national' fields and observes the role played by the state structures and national contexts in the institutionalization of Sociology. He recognizes the role played by transnational exchange and international circulation but argues that these were built based on existing national structures. Besides, even if in recent times a de-nationalization of research practices occurred, also national loyalties and specificities were reinforced. He points out that the concept of 'national tradition' is in itself a problematic issue because it can be interpreted as a *national style* or as a mode of thinking attached to the 'character' or 'spirit' of a nation – something impossible to examine empirically or understand sociologically. It can refer to a practice or a way of working that spread beyond the founder of a school and its fol- lowers, acquiring national significance. It can relate to the structure of a given national academic field that comes into play also in producing cer- tain conceptions of social science, in the reception of foreign authors and the selective ways these are incorporated in national debates. Rather than assuming the existence of immutable national minds, Heilbron argues it is more fruitful to identify the social processes that have unified intellec- tual habits or ways of thinking at a national level, particularly values and practices that have been institutionalized, whereas schools play a central role (2015: 220–222).

Indeed, Sociology has developed on the basis of national structures also in a peripheral region such as Latin America, where public universities have been a determinant for the emergence of 'national traditions'. However, the current debates on the internationalization of the social sciences leave aside the incidence of regional intellectual traditions and institutions that long ago called into question the 'national' and pre-existed the 'global'. This research void has to do with a common sense built on the basis of the national path crossed persistently by traditional United States (US) and European academic fields. But it can also be nourished by the experi- ence of European economic integration and its failure to build a regional intellectual space. A comparison with the Latin American experience will be useful at this point.

Sapiro (2017) analyzes the process of formation of the nation-states, focusing on the disintegration of the lettered European community that befell with the abandonment of Latin and the affirmation of vernacular languages. The nationalization of the lettered culture gave an impulse to a process of differentiation of intellectual professions, and these were shaped according with the administrative structures of each country. In a space that was becoming increasingly dominant worldwide during the nineteenth century, the national identity and intellectual field-building process was highly competitive and endogamous. In the midst of the rivalry between the three great powers, France, Germany and the UK, after World War I came the first attempts to create a space for encounters between intellectuals committed to pacification. By 1924 the Institute for Intellectual Cooperation was created with the aim of encouraging internationalization beyond Europe – aside from the fact that the concept of Europe was subject to criticism given the ascent of Nazism. An initial sketch for economic regionalization started with the Marshall Plan in 1949, but the cultural integration was postponed for a long time because of political conflicts coming from bipolarity with communism, rivalries among nations and linguistic barriers. Sapiro argues that Europe was never consolidated as an intellectual space and integration is mainly sustained by experts and officers, not intellectuals. Besides, 'European identity' is not inculcated in school, and this regional space was built within the cultural hegemony of the US (Sapiro, 2017).

If we hold the Latin American space up to a mirror, an inverse image arises. Its regional experience and intellectual exchange is as old as Independence, two centuries already. Costa has argued that this region is not a homogeneous referential unit, but indeed a strongly compelling one (Costa, 2018). With similar colonial structures, the independence revolutions were part of an insurrection that extended beyond national frontiers. The leaders of this military feat were also in charge of the first intellectual reflections on indigenous government, an effort that delved in the opposition between the Spanish rule and the (South) 'American' independent nations, all seen as singular but twinned by history. A continental identity shared by the 'Hispanic-American' new nations was built through different meetings, battles and Congresses, and standing out, Simón Bolivar's Letter of Jamaica in 1815, where one of the main axes of *Latinamericanity* was founded: the idea of Hispanic America as a natural union against a common colonial enemy. As argued by Narvaja de Arnoux (2008), the style of these military-intellectuals was to illustrate battle through a project based on a historical narrative. Politics was conceived as a war and reason/good was believed to be on their side. The colonial rule was a threat for all the continent. The struggle for freedom and the defense against the Spaniards was a collective and sacrificial task.

This Independency narrative is still taught in primary education in most countries, and the schools' patriotic events recreate Bolívar and San Martín's continental battles for colonial liberation. Another traditional celebration, formerly called the 'Day of Race', honoring the date of the colonial discovery of America (October 12, 1492), was also experienced at primary schools. It became part of a regional discussion in 1992, under the 500th anniversary, and currently in most countries it has shifted to the 'Day of cultural diversity' or other such designation. But it is still performed in scholarly events to acknowledge the sacrifice of the original indigenous communities from the whole continent.

Accordingly, *Latin-Americanism* as a cultural, political and intellectual movement is rooted in Independence battles but it has several different phases and designations, starting with the Second Emancipation movement up to the Second Independence intellectuals who were worried by the limits of political independence by the end of the nineteenth century. Economic inequality and intellectual dependency were two main streams of debate when the first organic regional intellectual movement emerged: *Hispanic-American Modernism*. The crossroads between literature and the press was the platform for the development of this reflection, characterized by its opposition to the hegemonic aspirations of the US in conducting a Pan-American alliance and its pledge for a continental identity (Beigel, 1998).

It was only after the second post-war period when Latin-Americanism as such was born. Two main differences with *Hispanic-American Modernism* can be pointed out. The first was the entry of Brazil, formerly alien to the previous processes but playing a central role from the mid-twentieth century until today. The second was the ideological shift that occurred with the displacement of Hispanism as the core of the tradition evoked against Pan-Americanism. A modern regional identity was built, along with the emergence of the Latin American Economic Commission (ECLA) created in 1948. It was in this context that the first attempt to create a common market appeared, the Latin American Association of

Free Trade (ALALC, in its Spanish acronym) in 1961. A new regional philosophy was born, the social sciences received a great impetus and the literary 'boom' emerged. In the next years, this intellectual space became increasingly radicalized, attached to a local path to socialism created by the Cuban Revolution (1959), the guerrilla movements in the 1960s, Allende's democratic socialism (1970), Liberation Theology and the Nicaraguan Revolution (1979). The cultural movements remained and evolved, but the common market never achieved material results.

The questioning of Latin-America as a regional identity was to come during the 1990s from two opposite sides: (a) the neoliberal governments and the new wave of 'open regionalism'; and (b) postcolonial/decolonial studies developed by academic groups affiliated to US universities. The first had its milestone in the North American Free Trade Agreement (NAFTA), signed by Mexico, Canada and the US, and which came into force in 1994, an event that definitively changed the regional landscape. The second evolved in two different theoretical streams, one reinforcing postcolonial perspectives, and the other based on local traditions and developing the concept of coloniality of power.

In spite of this fall from grace, Latin-Americanism was resurrected recently during the leftist turn taken by the governments of Chavez, Kirchner, Lula, Morales and Mujica, as well as the creation of the Union of South American Nations (UNASUR) in 2008. The intellectual space was reinforced and several intra-regional agreements gave an impetus to a number of dynamical cultural, educational and scientific initiatives. Although again, economic integration did not survive the projection stage. A new cyclical phase arrived and is currently in progress after the governmental changes in many countries that seem to have seen the leftist turn move towards a right-wing shift. However, Latin-Americanism as an intellectual platform appears to be vivid and enduring even where commercial or political alliances have been weakened.

At this point, the initial question remains valid: what is Latin American about Sociology in Latin America? I am not referring to its development as a discipline within each national field, but as a specific focus and practice developed in a regional (and, by nature, *international*) research space. The 'Latin-Americanization' of Sociology emerges from the general cultural and political context described above but it has its own trajectory, sustained by specific regional institutions and singular state structures, such as the Chilean government that hosted the process. In previous studies (Beigel, 2010) I have explained how the structure of our regional academic circuit was built and the role played by its particular 'cosmopolis' based in Santiago (Beigel, 2010). The regional research centers such as ECLA (1948), FLACSO (1957), CELADE (1957), DESAL (1960), ILPES (1962) and ILADES (1965) contributed to the consolidation of this research field fueled mainly by the encounter of History, Sociology, Economics and Political Science.

Seeking for regional analogies and structural effects of the colonial heritage, development was addressed as a continental problem by the two regional academic traditions that emerged from this institutionalization process: ECLA Structuralism and Dependency Analysis. Radicalization stimulated the emergence of the latter more as a sociological paradigm than the former, closely linked to economics. The studies by the historians of Colonial Studies on the development of capitalism and the contributions made by the economists from ECLA were critical in the development of the Historical-Structural method that evolved in parallel – but with no contemporary contact – with the school of Annales and the French total History (Beigel, 2006b, 2013). Political dimensions became increasingly stressed by Dependentists as Marxism entered the discussion arguing that heterogeneity was the result of the crystallization of styles of production, social relations and domination mechanisms corresponding to different phases of development but coexisting conflictingly within the nation-states. Other regional research problems came to consolidate Latin American Sociology. Marginality became one of the main concerns and soon Liberation Theology was developed in the midst of the Catholic think tanks at work in Santiago de Chile (Beigel, 2011).

FLACSO played a relevant role in offering Masters' degrees in Sociology to many social scientists from different countries who had graduated as historians, philosophers, lawyers and wanted to become sociologists or were already developing the discipline without holding a specific degree. Between 1957 and 1973, its Latin American School of Sociology formed hundreds of graduates, mainly coming from Chile, Argentina, Brazil and Mexico, strengthening the discipline although reinforcing intra-regional academic inequalities (Beigel, 2009a). Other institutions, such as the Latin American Sociological Association (ALAS) and the regional publishing houses (Siglo XXI and Fondo de Cultura Economica) contributed to the circulation of the new regional traditions. Academic awards, such as Premio Casa de las Americas, established in 1960, delineated a regional intellectual prestige that moved in the orbit of Cuba and its revolutionary project. This circuit of recognition came into play in legitimizing Sociology as a prestigious discipline, but also as a popular 'vocation' for young militants. In 1967, the Latin American Council for Social Research (CLACSO) was created, and its network of research institutes continued disseminating and expanding these traditions through regional research groups, academic competitions and journals until today.

## Latin American Sociology, its History and Laboratories

Sociology in Latin America has a long history, emerging from different paths of development of social knowledge. On the one hand, within the university field, there were the chairs of Sociology first established at the National University of Colombia (1882) and the University of Buenos Aires (1898). These professors were mostly trained as teachers in history or philosophy, or were lawyers who practiced teaching part-time. A second path developed through social essays, which were often published by newspapers or cultural journals. Finally, a third input came from the State: statistical research and reports put together by technicians from the public bureaus of different ministries.

By the mid-1930s there were dozens of sociology chairs in most of the countries of the region. They existed mainly in the areas of Law, History and Philosophy although always as spaces for complementary teaching. In the technical programs, they were grouped within the sections of 'general culture', the 'culture sciences' or 'science of the spirit' (Beigel, 2010). Graduate education did not develop widely during this time. Wherever it existed, the 'academic doctorate' predominated, with a dissertation as the unique requirement. The great exception was the University of São Paulo, which early on developed the first School of Sociology (1934) and the first graduate program.

As an area of academic research, sociology was differentiated during the 1940s, when the first institutes were created in Mexico, Chile, and Argentina. However, the professionalization of research at the universities was slow and fragmented because higher education was institutionally heterogeneous. The first journals helped in this direction: *Sociology*, in São Paulo (1939); *Mexican Journal of Sociology* (1939) from the National Autonomous University of Mexico; the *Inter-American Journal of Sociology* in Caracas (1939); and the *Bulletin of the Institute of Sociology* of the University of Buenos Aires (1942). The collections of specialized books, edited by the publishing houses Fondo de Cultura Económica, Losada, Abril and Paidós were a key element for the diffusion of local research and preceding translation of foreign Sociology texts.

The relationship between the tradition of Latin American Sociology and the 'national sociologies' followed a specific path according to the country observed, but I do not attempt to cover this here. I will only mention one particular national (Argentinian) staging post that has had a relevant incidence in the construction of a regional founding narrative. I am referring to the main dispute that served to institutionalize the discipline: the opposition between 'scientific sociology' as a program of empirical research and 'chair sociology', which rather refers to social or theoretical essays. These denominations and research styles were linked to the trajectory and interests of two scholars based in Argentina in competition for the newly created professional associations, research and teaching institutions: Gino Germani and Alfredo Poviña.

Neither of them was a 'sociologist' in the strict sense, because they had degrees in other disciplines, philosophy and law respectively. Poviña was in charge of the Sociology chair at UBA and the National University of Cordoba. Germani also wanted to be a 'chair sociologist' but could not attain such a position. As Pereyra (2005) recalls, he aspired to teach at UBA but applied unsuccessfully to two teaching positions at the Faculty of Economics and the Faculty of Philosophy and Literature. This stimulated his argument against 'chair sociologists' and the creation of 'scientific sociology' based on the opposition of *social essayism versus empirism*, completed afterwards with the pledge for value neutrality and the separation between science and ideology.

This founding narrative based on the confrontation between 'chair sociology' and 'scientific sociology' was critical for the institutionalization of the discipline, and it was manifest in the birth of the Latin American Association of Sociology (ALAS) in 1950. Too attached to Argentinian references, eventually it reflects the evolution of certain internationalized elite groups while diverse alternative expressions of Sociology were at work in many countries (see among others, Guerreiro Ramos in Part One).

Moving beyond this founding myth and searching for the emergence of LAS as a regional tradition, it is imperative to discuss the contribution of the Peruvian José Carlos Mariátegui (1894–1930), who was not a 'scientific sociologist' nor even a 'chair sociologist' but rather the opposite. An autodidact without formal education, he never taught at any university other than the Popular University González Prada, an informal space of training courses created for workers during the Peruvian University Reform in 1919. Mariátegui's *Seven Essays to Interpret the Peruvian Reality* (1928) involves a rich and critical reading of Marxism and an intense engagement with the locally produced knowledge on the history of Peru and Latin America.

His dialogue with Francisco García Calderón, who published *Le Pérou contemporain* in 1907 in Paris, anticipates the debate between the typical dualism of the sociology of modernization and the Structuralist perspective of the 1960s. Calderón was part of the Société de Sociologie de Paris and participated actively in the journal *Revista de América*, published in France during the first decades of the twentieth century. According to Mejía Navarrete (2005), he inaugurates the 'national studies' and the dualist interpretation of Peruvian society, opposing a modern coast to a traditional and backward mountain range inhabited by indigenous people (2005: 305). A four-fold shift can be pointed out comparing Calderón and Mariátegui, or *Le Perou Contemporain* and *Seven Essays*. First, there was the move from the systemic 'national study' towards the analysis of Peruvian reality as 'the problem of the *Indio*': from Positivism to Marxism. Second, there was the transition from dualism to structural heterogeneity. Third, came the radical change from the academicist writing practised by Calderón, settled in Paris, to that of Mariátegui from Lima, writing in the midst of social movements. Fourth and finally, was the theoretical and practical move from Peru to Latin America as a historical process and as an intellectual community.

Even if Dependency and the Structural-Historical Method were developed analytically between the 1960s and 1970s, these concerns are rooted in the Latin-American Marxism of Mariátegui. In his diagnosis of the local economic formation, he argued that the Peruvian problems were part of the historical continental process initiated by the Colonial Conquest. An incomplete Independence had given birth to a Republic that coexisted with pre-capitalist relations and servitude; accordingly, capitalism had evolved as an overlapping of ancient and new modes of production: (a) the locally powerful *latifundismo* (large estates with autonomous rules and production system); (b) the industrial bourgeoisie; (c) the foreign capital investing in mining and other national resources; and, finally, (d) the indigenous communities which subsisted in the mountain ranges with their ancient social and economic traditions. The three expressions of the dominant groups were articulated by the State. This was why Mariátegui argued that the liberal elite and 'national' bourgeoisie were not dynamic actors for social change. Socialism and nationalism were, thus, complementary because 'nation' was a project yet to be built (Mariátegui, [1928] 1995).

During his life, Mariátegui not only developed studies of structural social problems but also dedicated a great part of his short life to the creation of a regional circuit for the communication of Indigenists and cultural avant-garde groups throughout Latin America. Spearheaded by his journal *Amauta* (1926–1930), he created a publishing network that linked nodes in every country of the region (Beigel, 2006a). Mariátegui found his locus and practice in the midst of the scientific research and politics, a hinge where a new focus was furthered, in dialogue with local–regional–European traditions. Because of his precursory vision of structural heterogeneity, his original Latin-Americanization of Marxism and his contribution to the study of the problem of 'race', I argue that this Peruvian essayist should be considered as the *founding father* of LAS.

In the 1940s important regional studies were published, starting in 1941 with *Historia de la sociología Latinoamericana*, by Alfredo Poviña; then came *Economía de la sociedad colonial. Ensayo de historia comparada de América Latina*, by Sergio Bagú (1949) and *Materiales para el estudio de la clase media en la América Latina*, edited by Theo Crevenna (1950). Germani developed theoretical and methodological studies in his *Sociology of Modernization* (1969). But the Latin-Americanization of Sociology was given further impetus by the new regional centers, faculties and councils promoted by the United Nations and UNESCO after the Second World War. The creation of the ECLA in 1948 was a fundamental milestone in the development of socio-economic knowledge in the region. It systematized statistical information accumulated in public bureaus during previous decades, and it stimulated the national studies and regional offices, as well as the technical training of the officials of the ministries of finance and planning. The Division of Social Studies, led by José Medina Echavarría, furthered the discussion of the social factors of development in his *Consideraciones sociológicas sobre el desarrollo económico de América Latina* (*Sociological Considerations on Economic Development in Latin America*, 1964).

The creation of FLACSO (1957) and the Latin American School of Sociology in Santiago was the result, on the one hand, of Chilean diplomatic proactivity to attract existing foreign aid, and, on the other, of a national State policy aimed at higher education and the development of scientific research. The University of Chile not only provided the infrastructure and some teachers, but also largely financed the operation of this center, exceeding the levels of external contributions and eventually taking charge of the institution after the end of UNESCO's sponsorship (Beigel, 2009a). The *coups d'état* that occurred in Brazil (1964) and Argentina (1966) finally contributed to consolidating the leadership of Chile as a platform for the regionalization of social sciences. Torrents of South American exiles arrived and the regional institutes offered attractive jobs that augured the consecration of a new generation of social scientists. During those years, radicalization was boosted by the famous Camelot scandal (1964–1965) a scientific project funded by the Department of Defense of the United States that aimed to study insurrectionary foci denounced by sociologists as an espionage tool.

In previous studies (Beigel, 2006b, 2010) I have explored the process of academic development that occurred between 1964 and 1973. The regional circuit experienced an exceptional period of productivity, in which new theories and concepts emerged that contributed to the consolidation of indigenous sociological traditions, among them the theories of dependency and the debate on social marginality. These were interdisciplinary debates, traversed by sociology, economics and history. CLACSO played a relevant role as a regional network that favored the development of research groups and performed a determinant role in the regional circulation of the sociological production. During those years Chile became the main laboratory for an endogenous process of knowledge creation, in the context in which this experience generated worldwide attention, first for Christian Democracy, and later for Democratic Socialism.

A series of events completely changed the scenario after the *coup d'état* in Chile, in September 1973, when President Salvador Allende Gossens committed suicide defending Casa de la Moneda (government building). The universities became a target for the military and the schools of Sociology, Anthropology and Journalism were closed. FLACSO was forced to move to Argentina and some of its students were imprisoned or killed. Many Chilean and foreign social scientists – who had supported Allende – were dismissed, exiled or murdered, and a good many of them saw their work opportunities interrupted in a brutally heteronomous academic field. CLACSO played a decisive role in sustaining the regional circuit by supporting the research institutes in the affected countries and creating networks for the movement of the exiled and persecuted social scientists. Systematic aid programs were created, such as the Relocation Program for Social Scientists (PRCS-CLACSO) and the Refugee Program of the World University Service – UK: thousands of Chilean social scientists were transferred to the United Kingdom (Bayle, 2008). Meanwhile, hundreds of private research centers were created with foreign aid and increasingly dependent on external agendas.

Similar military coups quickly occurred in Uruguay and Argentina. The axis of the circuit was moved to Mexico driven by a massive academic exodus escaping from the Southern Cone. According to Agustín Cueva (1988), this situation generated a 'breakthrough' in LAS, which separated the concerns of the sociologists residing in Central America – under the revolutionary environment of the Sandinista Nicaragua (1979) – from the squalid academic fields of South America, decimated by political persecution, unemployment and the absence of academic freedom. In Mexico, heterodox Marxism continued to develop, while in the South critical thinking took refuge in independent academic centers that depended on external aid for their operation. Reflections on democracy, the new social movements, the gender approach and the cultural turn emerged in these years.

In 1989–1991 a great shake-up changed the international configuration and put an end to the world of 'really existing socialism'. The defeat of the Sandinista Revolution through democratic elections in 1990 was a critical local hinge. With the advent of Neo-liberal governments, nation-state came to be considered a 'bad word' and the demise of the two perspectives that had been disputed in LAS until then was decreed: the national approach and class analysis. The research topics of 'critical' sociology began to fade rapidly, along with critical currents of LAS. During the 1990s, LAS survived mostly in the historical research carried out by scholars who were scattered along the continent, had little contact with each other, and achieved the valuable task of dusting off unknown writings and forgotten authors. CLACSO made significant efforts to publish and circulate the accumulation of knowledge produced in the 1960s and 1970s, making this tradition available to young sociologists in a laudable effort to support intellectual history that served as a shelter while awaiting the best times to develop critical social research. While neoliberal-oriented governments were spreading throughout the region and Dependency was losing ground, poverty became one of the main concerns for Sociology. By the end of the twentieth century the regressive effects of those policies highlighted inequality again as the main agenda for LAS, this time along with a broader concern over citizenship.

**Race, Nation and Class Throughout a Sociological Century**

The consolidation of LAS as a research field and regional space was indeed evidenced in the emergence of endogenous traditions based on the historical-structural method, Dependency and Marxism. But also a centennial trajectory can be traced in the sociological studies concerning the trilogy integrated by three analytical categories *race, nation* and *class*. There are some homologies with the developments made by these concepts in the US and Europe, along with transnational dialogues, but also deep differences. Class and nation have been very actively present in LAS and several encounters among them can be seen from 1920 onwards. Conversely, race has been characterized by its erratic intervention in social research during the twentieth century. However, its appearance or absence is relevant to understanding old and new regional debates, as I will attempt to explain in what follows.

For many reasons, *gender* was a subaltern piece in the sociological prism for analyzing inequalities. Firstly, this was because of a structural morphological factor: masculine dominance during the institutionalization and professionalization phases delayed the entrance of women and, accordingly, the emergence of gender studies. The feminization and massification of Latin American universities started around the mid-1950s, thus, the presence of women in teaching and research would increase only after 1960. Secondly, the fact that Marxism and its focus on class was the dominant paradigm also contributed to this direction – women and men were assumed to be equal and the priority was seen to be the class struggle. The process of the de-invisibilization of gender for sociologists was slow and fragmentary. It evolved as an interdisciplinary field deeply linked to the study and the actual evolution of the collective demands of women, which have had a prominent expression in Latin America.

Ciriza and Fernández (1993) argue that the history of the political participation of women includes diverse demands that attempt to include women in citizenship, class struggle and liberation. Three different strands can be observed in the region: the properly called 'feminists', the women formally linked to politics or labor unions, and the more spontaneous women's movements emerging from popular sectors. With diverse demands, points of encounter and mismatches, the feminist movement has developed more consistently since the 1980s, boosted initially by middle-class women linked to Marxism, who confronted the resistance existing in the traditional leftist parties. A broad panorama of the so-called 'second wave' of feminism can be found in Vargas's key text (see Part Four).

A singular trajectory can be traced for the theoretical and practical transition from 'women's' to 'gender' studies in Latin America. Cangiano and Dubois (1993) argue that in the same way as white heterosexual women felt outside the field of power in the central countries during the 1960s, black and indigenous Latin American women felt outside of that kind of 'feminist studies'. Marxism was the dominant tradition for local precursors such as Isabel Larguía, Julieta Kirkwood, Heleieth Saffioti and Eva Giberti (see Jelin's key text in Part One). But a particularly original insight into racism, classism and sexism emerged in Brazil in the late 1970s when the myth of 'racial democracy' was finally faced. Immersed in the Unified Black Movement, Lélia González ([1980] 2018) examined the experience of Black female maids (*mu'kama o ama de leche*) combining Feminism and Psychoanalysis.

Among the spaces that favored feminist dialogue and a regional articulation of local demands were the Feminist Meetings and the UN agency Women, Peace and Development. Some of the most relevant contributions were the studies on dictatorships and the particular marks on bodies along with the studies on the resistance embodied in feminine organizations such as the Madres and Abuelas (mothers and grandmothers) of Plaza de Mayo. It was not until the 1990s that women's studies were firmly tacked on gender studies. The American, Judith Butler had an extensive influence in the expansion of feminist literature in Latin America, together with the arrival of postcolonial debates. Ciriza (2004) analyzes the limits of gender studies that were built through theoretical imports disregarding the local conditions of production and – with higher costs for feminists – without considering the corporeal feature of knowledge itself. The limits of these theoretical imports point then to a local feature of feminism: its materialist perspective and focus on subaltern bodies. More recently, a radical and rooted feminist critique emerged in the midst of the debates on the coloniality of power – struggling against a still resilient indigenous structure of Patriarchy (see Figure I.1).

In sum, during most of the twentieth century gender was a marginal perspective in LAS, although women's demands were an increasing matter of study. Accordingly, the prism for scrutinizing inequality was mainly based on the unstable tripod formed by race, nation and class (RNC), which has a rich history of encounters and disagreements. I am far from even attempting a cartography of this magnitude in this work, but I will try to sketch the main landmarks of the crossroads between RNC in order to present the territory in which the more recent inclusion of gender can be observed. As can be seen in Figure I.1, three historical milestones mark the *encounters* of sociological contributions related to RNC: (1) 1929, (2) 1965 and (3) 2006. In between these dates, bifurcated roads between nation and class prevail, while race transits through an unpaved road mostly mixed with rural issues and studies on peasant movements.

The first RNC encounter was Mariátegui's *Thesis on the Problem of Race* (1929) and his praxis towards the articulation of the indigenes' demands, national development and socialism (see Part Three). As a convinced Marxist, the Peruvian argued that the Indian's problem was not ethnical, but social and economic: related to land tenure. But unlike the rest of his contemporaries, he believed that indigenes[1] were the subject of the socialist revolution in Peru, given their historical life in communitary cooperation and the fact that they formed the majority of the population. Noteworthy is his comprehension of the dominant racial claim. 'When on the shoulders of the productive class weighs the harshest economic oppression added to the hatred and vilification of which it is a victim as a race, it is only a matter of clear and simple comprehension of the situation for this mass to rise up as one man to dump all forms of exploitation' (Mariátegui, 1929, see Part Three).

This thesis was prepared for the Communist Conference to be held in Buenos Aires in June 1929, in a particular context. The official discourse existing in the Komintern was to preserve ethnic identity by conferring national autonomy on non-Russian communities that were part of the Union of Soviet Socialist Republics (USSR). On the other hand, the ideological and scientific struggle against biological racism prevented most Marxists from using the concept of race or stimulating its prevalence. During the conference, the Peruvian delegation presented Mariátegui's argument against considering the problem of the Indio as an ethnic-national issue, but instead as an economic problem, the result of the persistence of feudality. For Mariátegui, the solution was Indo-American socialism and the revolution was a national task: to nationalize meant to de-colonize. However, this did not prevent race from playing a relevant role in preparing for this revolution because only activists from the indigenous milieu, sharing a mindset and indigenous language, were able to achieve consent among their peers (Mariátegui, 1929).[2]

A fair balance of Mariátegui's sociological contributions to the problem of race must be considered in light of two processes that marked

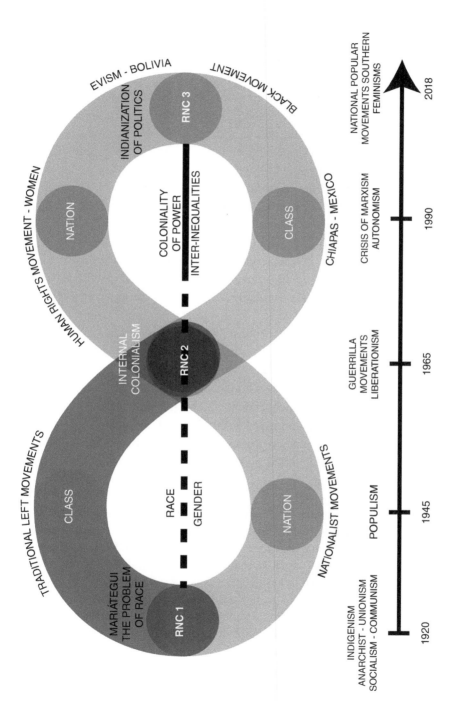

**Figure I.1** RNC: Encounters and disencounters

his itinerary: (a) the context of the major social movement in which he took part, Indigenism; and (b) the shift that occurred along his praxis, from Eurocentric to rooted/creative Marxism. Concerning the first context, Indigenism was a cultural and political movement existent from 1870 until 1970, basically concerned with indigenous redemption but featuring an externality from aboriginal communities. As a part of the socialist trend of Indigenism, Mariátegui participated in the urban movement that attempted to change the social conditions of indigenous people, postulating the project of Indo-American Socialism. Race was, for him, a complementary issue, with class and nation being the main axis for defining 'the problem of the indio'. However, and marking a big difference for his times, Mariátegui acknowledged the 'exteriority' of Indigenism. In one of his *Seven Essays*, he declared that *indigenist literature* did not offer a true image of the indigenes, because it was still a *mestizo* literature. "Precisely that is why it is called indigenist and not indigene. An *indigene literature* is still to come and will arrive in its time. When the Indians themselves are able to produce it' (Mariátegui, 1928 [1995]: 242).

Regarding the second process, in previous studies (Beigel, 2003) I have pointed out that the rooting of Mariátegui's Marxism started in 1925 when he inaugurated his column 'To Peruanize Peru', namely, when he became a sociologist.[3] His main concern was to build and understand the 'primary problem' of his country. And he was already aware that this 'Peruanization' had taken place within himself. When he returned to Peru in 1923, after four years in Europe, he was despised and considered a 'Europeanizing' intellectual by nativists that rejected Marxism. By 1927, he declared that

> Regarding the confluence or alloy of Indigenism and Socialism, nobody attentive to contents and essence can be surprised. Socialism organizes and defines the claims of the masses, of the working class. And, in Perú, the masses – the working class – are four-fifths composed of indigenes. Our Socialism wouldn't be Peruvian – it wouldn't even be Socialism – if it was not based on solidarity, firstly, with the claims of the Indians. In this attitude no opportunism is hidden. Neither artifice, if we give two minutes to a reflection of the meaning of socialism. This attitude is not fake, feigned or clever. It's just socialist. (José Carlos Mariátegui, 'Intermezzo polémico', *Mundial*, 25 February 1927)

After Mariátegui died, the Stalinization process began to gnaw at the potential of this rooted Marxism. The Komintern promoted a cordon sanitaire around Mariátegui's legacy, accusing him of 'populism', and the Peruvian Communist Party adulterated many of his texts in order to canonize him as a Stalinist figure.[4]

As can be seen in Figure I.1, the period 1930–1950 was marked by a disencounter within RNC: the Marxist tradition was inclined to an exclusive focus on class, while populism boosted studies based on the national perspective. Race, for its part, was subsumed by official Indigenist policies, such as the celebration of *métissage* and the Mexican conversion of Aztecas as a 'national symbol', assimilating indigene communities within the process of the consolidation of nation-states. These nationalist Indigenisms attempted to transform the oligarchic foundations of our societies but eventually collaborated in the prevalence of colonial relations. Meanwhile, Indian and Black communities resisted assimilation by different means.

During the 1940s, RNC categories were developed in separated paths, in a sort of division of labor: Sociology was more concerned with class stratification, while Anthropology addressed the racial issues. After the genocide and the catastrophic consequences of the Second World War, the concept of 'race' was seriously revised in the European social sciences and replaced by the category of 'ethnic group'. The elimination of the notion of race, based on the scientific evidence regarding the non-existence of biological differences, was believed by many as a way of evaporating racism itself. One of the first proposals for addressing ethnic discrimination in the public sphere was the idea of defining 'minorities' and granting rights for them. An obvious problem emerged when adopting this type of policy in countries where Blacks and Indians were the *majority* of the population – the simple observation that had boosted Mariátegui's indigenization of Marxism.

Latin American social sciences were not absent in this debate, being present firstly within the new international agencies and later through the concept of 'internal colonialism'. The Brazilian 'racial democracy' was at the center of interest within the unique ambit that became relatively 'international' in the debate towards a consensual, anti-racist, definition of 'race': the United Nations Education, Science and Culture Organization (UNESCO). Several studies (Chor Maio, 2007; Dumont, 2010; Beigel, 2013) have observed that during the 1950s, the Latin American governments played a relevant role within this Organization, and especially Brazil, during the directorship of the Mexican Jaime Torres Bodet (1948–1952). A board of experts was created with the aim of publishing a declaration to sanction racial discrimination. These declarations were the basis for a campaign developed by UNESCO against the apartheid regime in South Africa and racial prejudice in the United States. According to Chor Maio, Brazil was considered as a case of 'harmonious' racial relations and ended up as a key to the anthropological discussion in the boards of experts – four of the nine experts invited to the first meeting in Paris (1949) were Brazilian and others had carried out fieldwork in Brazil. A large group of ethnologists who afterwards would became big names in Sociology, History and Anthropology had arrived in the country in the late 1930s: Claude Lévi-Strauss and Roger Bastide, among others.

In 1950, the UNESCO Division of Racial Studies was created, under the direction of Alfred Métraux, becoming a 'pro-Brazil lobby group' (Chor Maio, 2007: 193) within the Department of Social Sciences, by that time under the direction of the Brazilian anthropologist Arthur Ramos. In 1951–1952, Métraux organized a project to study racial relations in Brazil with Roger Bastide, Florestan Fernandes and a group of students from the Universidade de São Paulo in charge of carrying out a survey. Among the students were Octavio Ianni and Fernando Henrique Cardoso. The report was delivered the following year and the results pointed to the existence of racism and its connection with poverty (The UNESCO Courier, 1952). Surprisingly, this report contradicted the ideal of a Brazilian 'inter-racial paradise', all of which certainly divided local scholars and hastened the withdrawal of Métraux from the Organization.

The next encounter of the RNC conceptual trilogy came during the 1960s, a period of politicization and radicalization in Latin American societies. A broadening of the regional perspective took place through the dialogue with decolonization movements in Asia and Africa, in a new forum christened as 'tercermundismo' after the Bandung Conference of 1955. This context had a particular incidence in the social sciences, and the idea of 'liberation' became the soil for the connection of social demands on class, nation and race. Nelson Mandela's struggles against apartheid, the civil rights movements in the United States and Frantz Fanon's writings circulated profusely in Latin America. Solidarity with the Black movement and the Algerian Revolution was in fact extended but scarcely connected to the demands of Blacks and Indians in Latin America. This state of social movements was reflected in the late interest for race in LAS. A distorted *dejá vú* from Mariátegui's RNC argument was still dominant: class was considered the primary struggle, while racism would be destroyed as a result of the socialist revolution, which, in time, was understood as a national form of liberation from Imperialism.

In this context, a second confluence on RNC can be found in the concept of 'internal colonialism' developed by Pablo González Casanova and Rodolfo Stavenhagen (see Part Three). Both authors were involved in debates and had conceptual differences, but the novelty was to observe the persistence of colonialism through inter-ethnic relations within the nation-states. For Stavenhagen, internal colonies were marked by the *cultural differences* between two sectors of the population. In this case, race appeared in the center of the conceptualization, but its significance was more related to the prevailing notion of ethnic group. On his part, González Casanova argued that internal colonialism included the economic, social and cultural dimensions of domination. The indigene communities were seen as nations that are colonized by the nation-state and suffer a kind of subalternity similar to colonialism or neocolonialism. According to him, they inhabit in a territory without a government of their own. They speak a language and have a culture different from the legitimate 'national' language and culture. They are in a situation of inequality in relation to the elites of the dominant ethnicity who consider this colonized race as inferior or, in the frame of assimilation, as an inert symbol of national identity (González Casanova, [1969] 2006).

Even if the concept of internal colonialism emphasized the racial perspective, it was still hanging between 'nation' and 'ethnic group'. But the main success of this RNC encounter was to overthrow the idea of assimilation as a legitimate course driven by the State – whether or not this was imagined as a 'popular' State. As would be clear afterwards, coloniality was imposed through the naturalization of racial difference and social inequality, but class was the dominant concern throughout rural and urban workers' movements during the process of modernization in Latin America until mid-twentieth century. Whenever class was articulated with the question of nation, it was believed that nationalization under a socialist project was the path for de-colonization. The project of National Liberation or Independence was compatible with the classism existent in these traditional movements, while ethnicity was considered a subordinated matter, dependent on class struggle. Experiences such as the Bolivian Revolution of 1952 tended to consider the Indian as a peasant, with land tenure as their main social problem. Indigenists' 'externalism' was still at work. Accordingly, during the radical phase of the 1960s, perspectives on class and nation found a locus within liberationism, but race and gender still remained as marginal perspectives.

An exception to this path can be found in Brazil, where race relations had been a sociological concern since the 1950s, starting with the UNESCO study mentioned above. According to Araujo Guimarães (see the Introduction to Part Three), Florestán Fernandes came to confront a pattern of accommodation that was interpreted as a 'color gradient', diluting the racial dimension of inequalities, perhaps as the diachronic presence of a past amid capitalist expansion. The sociological contribution of Fernandes and other Brazilian sociologists counteracts the observations made by Bourdieu and Wacquant (1998) in the polemical article 'On the Cunning of Imperialist Reason' – in which they denounced the imposition of an American notion of race into the Brazilian academic field. Racial studies have a long and rooted history in Brazil and racism was far from being solved by the myth of 'racial democracy', as would be evidenced in the next years.[5]

The course of the sociological analysis of race would make a radical turn only by the end of the twentieth century. A silent but consistent process of incarnation of ethnicity was taking place in the local Indian and Black movements but its major manifestations would become regionally visible by the 1990s with the creation of the Pachakutik political parties in the Andean countries, the 1994 insurrection of Chiapas, and the Brazilian Black movement. In previous work (Beigel, 2005b) I examined the process by which ethnicity became a relevant factor of auto-identification within indigenous movements, after being sealed by the communist tradition or misrepresented by urban/mestizo indigenist literature. The idea of an illuminated avant-garde supposedly embodied by leftist parties but generally composed of bourgeois intellectuals contributed to this blindness. A particular form of de-alienation of negative identities was taking place, expressed in the Andean zone, for example in public campaigns such as Ecuador's graffiti 'Amo lo que tengo de Indio' [I love what there is of Indio in me].

Well now, a critical point should be posed here: was the emergence of race as an organizing principle of identification something new, or had it rather been invisible to the social sciences and the leftist political parties? Indeed, it was not really a new process of identification but a combination of ancient and recent memories of subalternity. In which form were these memories re-actualized and by which means was race incarnated in the Latin American social movements is the subject of Part Four of this volume (see the introductory chapter by Bringel). Here I will only point out the fact that the agenda of LAS has evolved behind the morphological changes observed in the social movements.

Segato has argued that until the beginning of the twenty-first century it was rare in Latin America to find reports on the color of the poor, people in prison or victims of police abuse. This was the effect of the 'ethnocide *metissage*' – a forced cancellation of the 'non-white' memory. Race was mostly treated as a cultural feature but not as part of the unequal condition of the population, even if it is a mark of subalternity and domination present since the Conquest (Segato, 2010). The Indigenist movement and State Indigenism contributed greatly in this direction: indigenous communities were analyzed as 'peasants' and Afro-descendants were seen as 'integrated' into an illusionary but persistent *racial democracy* (Wade, 2017).

As a result of the emergence of new Indigene/Black movements by the mid-1970s the 'prosecution' of Indigenism was fulfilled while research on race and gender entered increasingly into the regional sociological agenda. Eventually, it was after the collapse of communism that race came to the forefront. At first sacrificing the nation–class binomial, it was boosted by postcolonial studies and the belief that Latin-Americanism and Dependency Analysis were responsible for a now old perspective centered in the 'nation-state' as a unit of analysis and 'class' as a central principle of identity. The novelty was that the category of *race* became the main axis for the comprehension of domination and social inequality in the capitalist world-system. These debates integrated a dialogue on Eurocentrism that was already taking place in other spaces in the newly baptized 'Global South'. In fact, during these years, class was rephrased into the struggle between South and North, while the displacement of the category of 'nation' was fulfilled. Race gained increasing interest in social research and has been a central issue for intersectional feminism, de-colonial perspectives and studies on inequality.

Actively part of this debate, but from a different side, Quijano (1992) developed his transition from Dependency to Coloniality, articulating class and race into a theory of domination. He argued that *colonialism* is a historical phenomenon that starts with the Conquest of America, Asia and Africa by the European powers and ends with de-colonization revolutions that took place at the beginning of the nineteenth century. Latin America was the first entity/historical identity of the current colonial-modern world system. It was constituted as the 'Occidental Indies', the original space and beginning of a new pattern of power. It was the place of the first classification of the survivors of the colonial geno-cide as *indios* – an 'indigenization' expressed as a 'racialization' that includes at the same time class and racial subalternity. *Coloniality* thus, had proven to be, in the last five hundred years, more profound and lasting than colonialism (Quijano, 2010). This new RNC trilogy fed by postcolonial studies and Quijano's 'coloniality of power' reinforced the place of race-class as causal relations to explain inequalities, but tended to leave aside the national question typically central in the 1960s (see Figure I.1).

After the victory of Evo Morales in the presidential elections of Bolivia (December 2005), a new type of government headed by an Aymaran leader changed the agenda of the social sciences. The 'political instru-ment' that led Morales to power, the Movement for Socialism (MAS), was built in the midst of *cocalero* unionism and the massive demonstrations in defense of water and gas as natural (national) resources against trans-national companies. These two forms of traditional struggle, historically embodied in syndicalism (class) and anti-foreigner movements (nation), arrived now with a sense of novelty. The growth of MAS and the social movements was based on the defense of traditional knowledge, communal justice and indigene organizations.

In 2009 the Bolivian Constitution was completely reformed defining the country as pluri-national and recognizing all indigene nations and languages as official. In parallel, the Bolivian nation was affirmed and a program of nationalizations was performed. A broader relevant change completed the new scenario: the resurrection of Latin-Americanism, starting with the regional initiatives of a pool of presidents such as Hugo Chávez, Néstor Kirchner, Lula da Silva and Evo Morales. In a research agenda with an already consolidated concern for race and class, nation came back on the scene, stirring up postcolonial theories that had based their reflections on the disappearance of nationalism as a collective identity. Several critiques (Svampa, 2016; Stefanoni, 2010) were made of the developmentalist path used by Morales and the limits of de-patriarchalization, but undoubtedly a relevant morphological change took place in the Bolivian social milieu. To be an 'Indio' was considered negative and it was a symbol for subal-ternity in the history of the country. Now, an *indianization* of politics took place: to be an Indio meant having a form of relevant social capital impact-ing rapidly on the composition of the bureaucratic elites. Accordingly, the

Bolivian experience has been a decisive laboratory for a new lens onto inequality, this time reinforcing a new RNC trilogy. Meanwhile, Southern feminisms seem to be preparing the ground, or underground, for the emergence of a RNCG (Race, Nation, Class, Gender) sociology eager to rise.

## What is 'Critical' in LAS?

The founding narrative based on the opposition between 'chair' and 'scientific' sociology was consolidated by Rolando Franco in his well-known article '25 Years of LAS: A Balance', published in *Revista Paraguaya de Sociología* in 1974. The aim was to discuss 'scientific sociology' in order to argue for the validity of 'critical sociology', as the third and contemporary phase of LAS (Franco, 1974). In Spanish, 'critical' meant the contrary to the former program of 'value neutrality', launched by Germani, and a call against the separation between science and ideology. In English, it would be accurate to say that it was critical for this generation of sociologists to engage with politics in order to question established values and unjust structures. In this act, by reinforcing 'critical' sociology, Franco also canonized 'chair', 'scientific' and 'critical' as the three phases of LAS.

The identification between these three phases and the process of institutionalization of national sociologies in the region also contributed to establishing this founding narrative. However, after the process of de-institutionalization experienced in South America and the dismantling of the regional circuit with an axis in Chile, this periodization seemed truncated. More recently, a few studies revised the history of LAS. Svampa (2008) and Roitman Rosenmann (2008) proposed a periodization based more on the central debates of each stage: modernization, dependency/exploitation, dictatorship, democracy and globalization. From a de-colonial perspective, Martins (2012) argues that the constitutive tension of LAS is in the dichotomy between coloniality and anti-coloniality. The first stage would feature a post-independency social thought until 1950, followed by a critical postcolonialist sociology – in his view too attached to Eurocentric perspectives and not finally in breaking from the previous phase. Critical Sociology would have arrived in Latin America in the 1990s, along with the displacement of the center-periphery focus and the new perspectives on discourse analysis. In particular, Martins argues that Dependency Analysis exhibited its limits to explain the relevance of 'cultural' and post-geographical factors in the global era (Martins, 2012: 34).

This periodization attempts to discredit the founding narrative by pushing critical sociology to contemporary times. However, critical sociology is not a phase nor a particular theoretical argument, but a way of practicing the discipline. As Svampa (2008) argues, it is a type of amphibian sociology, in-between academic knowledge and militant engagement – starting with Mariátegui, who was not a 'chair' sociologist and perfectly fits under the label of 'critical' sociologist, with one foot in the social essay and the other in the Indigenist movement. This persistent, historical and regional feature of LAS is radically different from Burawoy's (2005) 'critical' and 'public' sociology. Regarding the first, this regional sociology is not merely academic but involved in social movements. In relation to the second, critical LAS is 'public' – not by intervening in the media debates, but because of its commitment to a particular type of public intervention rooted in the intellectual field. In this sense, critical LAS is not attached to the limits of conceiving social actors as 'audiences' and thus centering its intervention on the mass media. On the other hand, it features by multiple styles of production, combining research and political intervention. More amphibious than academicist and more critical than policy oriented, LAS is a long-standing international platform for global debates.

Although international from birth, the global projection of LAS has been limited by two causal factors on different levels: firstly, the fact that most of its contributions were published in Spanish or Portuguese; and, secondly, the fact that this old regional circuit of recognition has been increasingly subordinated to the mainstream circuit and its high impact on circulation. This volume is aimed precisely at making available our sociological traditions in order to drive global and South–South dialogue. The project was conceived in a workshop held in Mendoza, in 2012, where the scientific committee discussed the difference between 'classics' and 'key texts'. The idea was to broaden the circulation of Latin American Sociology as a tool for today's analysis of our tumultuous world, and not just to translate classical texts that may have already circulated in English. Instead of thinking about regionally or globally *canonized* texts, this workshop stressed the fact that the volume should provide an insight into local contributions to current global debates.

It was also considered relevant to show our diversity in terms of sub-regional traditions – preventing the replaying of existing intra-regional asymmetries, observing gender balance and including authors from as many countries as possible. It was not easy to achieve national diversity under the limits of a single book, but we reached a basic balance. Most of the authors of the key texts have produced their complete work while living and working in Latin America. Only three authors have spent part of their lives in the North (Escobar, Laclau and O'Donnell) due to exile or settlement abroad. In the cases of Laclau and O'Donnell, they decided to return to their homeland in Buenos Aires in the last part of their trajectory. Escobar currently works as a professor partly in the US and partly in Colombia.

Gender balance was a more difficult task. The high levels of masculinization registered in LAS until 1970 cannot/should not be compensated for by an anthology. We decided to give gender debate a relevant space in Parts One to Four and to include a text by the sociologist Suzy Castor in Part Five – whose contribution to the debate on nation-state building has had an even smaller circulation given the fact that she is Haitian, a woman and wrote in Créole or French. The fairest balance was achieved in the six introductory studies, with three written by men and three by women.

Finally, this book is organized in five sections, each one is dedicated to a thematic debate: (1) Founding problems; (2) Historical and contemporary debates; (3) Social structure and inequalities; (4) Identities, actors and social movements; and (5) State, society and politics. The structure of all the parts includes an introductory study, with a selection of key texts followed by brief Comments presenting basic bio-bibliographical data on the author's trajectory.

## Notes

1.   There are serious translation problems when referring to Indigenism, indigeneity and indigenous people or 'Indios' (as used historically by the actors) that must be considered. The concept of indigenous in English remits to autochthony and to native people. In Latin America '*Indígena*'/indigenes refers to aboriginal communities that were called *Indios* by the colonizers during the conquest. For its part, Indigenism is a political and cultural movement developed mainly by middle-class urban *mestizos*, creating an external representation of the *Indios* with no participation of those communities. Indigenism as a movement and as a project can be considered cancelled since the mid-1970s when the indigene movements throughout the region started creating their own political organizations to intervene directly in politics. During the 1920s 'Indio' was extensively used to refer to indigene communities. Currently '*indígena/movimiento indígena*' is the concept academically used in Spanish to refer to aboriginal people. I have chosen to use the term "indigenes" to translate the latter, preserving "indigenous" for meaning autochtonous or rooted.

2.   In several parts of his writings, Mariátegui uses the word Race in opposition to racist uses, advocating in favor of an indigene national project. When he founded his noted journal *Amauta* (Savant in Quechua) he said that this title was an expression of his

'adherence to the Race, his homage to Incaism' (Mariátegui, 1926:1). This alternative concept of race has been in force in the last decades within Latin American movements, and the polemic use by Mariátegui is still interesting for current sociological and anthropological debates.

3. The column titled 'To Peruanize Peru' ('Peruanizar al Perú') was published in the journal *Mundial* from September 1925 until 1930. The first article was titled 'El rostro y el alma del Tawantinsuyu' [Face and Soul of Tawantinsuyu], *Mundial*, Año VI, n 274, 11 September 1925.

4. The return to Mariátegui's texts in Latin America came many decades later, particularly in the 1980s when he became a relevant figure in the debates of the South American exiles in Mexico, together with the renewed interest in Gramsci. Indeed the trajectories of these two intellectuals have similar paths which are incredibly close because of the short and harsh lives they lived, the fragmented writings they left and the issues they developed. But no 'influences' can be pointed out (Beigel, 2005a).

5. For a discussion on Bourdieu and Wacquant's article, see Beigel (2009b).

# References

Bagú, Sergio (1949) *Economía de la sociedad colonial. Ensayo de historia comparada de América Latina* [Economy of Colonial Society. Essay on Comparative History of Latin America]. Buenos Aires: El Ateneo.

Bayle, Paola (2008) 'Emergencia académica en el Cono Sur: el programa de reubicación de cientistas sociales (1973–1975)', *Iconos. Revista de Ciencias Sociales, 30*: 51–63.

Beigel, Fernanda (1998) 'Identificados con un proyecto', *Anuario Mariateguiano, X*(10): 91–106.

Beigel, Fernanda (2003) *El itinerario y la brújula. El vanguardismo estético-político de José Carlos Mariátegui*. Buenos Aires: Biblos.

Beigel, Fernanda (2005a) 'Una mirada sobre otra: el Gramsci que conoció Mariátegui', *Estudos de Sociología*, UNESP, *10*(18/19): 23–49.

Beigel, Fernanda (2005b) 'Las identidades periféricas en el fuego cruzado del cosmopolitismo y el nacionalismo', *Pensar a Contracorriente, Concurso Internacional de Ensayos, Tomo I, La Habana: Editorial de Ciencias Sociales*, pp.169–199.

Beigel, Fernanda (2006a) *La epopeya de una generación y una revista. Las redes editoriales de José Carlos Mariátegui en América Latina*. Buenos Aires: Biblos.

Beigel, Fernanda (2006b) 'Vida, muerte y resurrección de las teorías de la dependencia', in F. Beigel et al., *Crítica y teoría en el pensamiento social latinoamericano*. Buenos Aires: CLACSO, pp. 287–326.

Beigel, Fernanda (2009a) 'La FLACSO chilena y la regionalización de las ciencias sociales en América Latina (1957–1973)', *Revista Mexicana de Sociología, 71*(2): 319–349.

Beigel, Fernanda (2009b) 'Sur les tabous intellectuels: Bourdieu and academic dependence', *Sociologica, 2–3*.

Beigel, Fernanda (2010) *Autonomía y dependencia académica: Universidad e investigación científica en un circuito periférico. Chile y Argentina (1950–1980)*. Biblos: Buenos Aires.

Beigel, Fernanda (2011) *Misión Santiago. El mundo académico jesuita y los inicios de la cooperación internacional católica*. Santiago de Chile: LOM.

Beigel, Fernanda (ed.) (2013) *The Politics of Academic Autonomy in Latin America*. London: Ashgate.

Bourdieu, Pierre and Wacquant, Löic (1998) 'Sur les ruses de la raison impérialiste', *Actes de la Recherche en Sciences Sociales 121–122*: 109–118.

Burawoy, M. (2005) 'For public Sociology', *American Sociological Review, 70*(1): 4–28.

Cangiano, M. and Dubois, L. (1993) 'De mujer a género: Teoría, interpretación y práctica feminista en las ciencias sociales', in M. Cangiano and L. Dubois (eds), *Teoría, interpretación y práctica feminista en las ciencias sociales*. Buenos Aires: Centro Editor de América Latina, pp. 7–16.

Chor Maio, Marcos (2007) 'Un programme contre le racisme au lendemain de la Seconde Guerre mondiale', *60 ans d'Histoire de l'UNESCO*. Paris: Maison de l'UNESCO, pp.189–197.

Crevenna, T. (1950) *Materiales para el estudio de la clase media en America Latina*. Washington: Union Panamericana.

Ciriza, Alejandra (2004) 'Notas sobre los límites de la importación teórica. A propósito de Judith Butler', *El rodaballo, 15*: 58–60.

Ciriza, Alejandra and Fernández (1993) 'Las mujeres y su inclusión en las prácticas políticas', in A. Roig (ed.), *Argentina del 80 al 80*. Mexico: UNAM, pp. 157–182.

Costa, Sergio (2018) 'The research on modernity in Latin America: Lineages and dilemmas', *Current Sociology*, published online, 5 November, DOI: 10.1177/0011392118807523.

Cueva, Agustín (1988) 'Sobre exilios y reinos. (Notas) Críticas sobre la evolución de la sociología sudamericana', *Estudios Latinoamericanos*, Mexico: CELA-UNAM.

Dumont, Juliette (2010) 'From intellectual cooperation to cultural diplomacy: the Brazilian and Chilean experience (1918–1946)', Colloque 'Impacts: Does Academic Exchange matter?', Austrian–American Educational Commission (Fulbright Commission),Vienna, 18–19 November.

Franco, Rolando (1974) '25 años de Sociología Latinoamericana', *Revista Paraguaya de Sociología*.

Germani, G. (1969) *Sociología de la Modernización. Estudios teóricos, metodológicos y aplicados a América Latina*. Buenos Aires: Paidós.

González, Lélia ([1980] 2018) 'Racismo y sexismo en la cultura brasileña' in B. Bringel, and A. Brasil Jr. *Antología del Pensamiento crítico brasileño contemporáneo*. Buenos Aires: CLACSO, pp. 565–583.

González Casanova, Pablo ([1969] 2006) *El colonialismo interno, in Sociología de la explotación*. Buenos Aires: CLACSO, pp. 185–205.

Heilbron, Johan (2015) *French Sociology*. New York: Cornell University Press.

Mariátegui, José Carlos (1926) Presentación de Amauta, *Amauta, 1*: 1.

Mariátegui, José Carlos ([1928] 1995) *Siete ensayos de interpretación de la realidad peruana*. Lima: Sociedad Editora Amauta.

Mariátegui, José Carlos (1927) 'Intermezzo polémico', *Mundial*, Feburary 25.

Mariátegui, José Carlos (1929) 'El problema de la raza', *Amauta, 25*: 69–80.

Martins, Paulo H. (2012) *La decolonialidad de América Latina y la heterotopia de una comunidad de destino soldaría.* CICCUS.

Medina Echavarría, J. (1964) *Consideraciones sociológicas sobre el desarrollo económico en América Latina.* Buenos Aires: Solar/Hachette.

Mejía Navarrete, Julio (2005) 'El desarrollo de la sociología en el Perú. Notas introductorias', *Sociologias,* Porto Alegre, 7, (14): 302–337.

Narvaja de Arnoux, Elvira (2008) *El discurso latinoamericanista de Hugo Chávez.* Buenos Aires: Biblos.

Pereyra, Diego (2005) International Networks and the Institutionalisation of Sociology in Argentina (1940–1963), Doctoral Dissertation: University of Sussex at Brighton.

Poviña, A. (1941) *Historia de la Sociología Latinoamericana.* Mexico: Fondo de Cultura Económica.

Quijano, Aníbal (1992) '"Raza", "Etnia" y "Nación" en Mariátegui: Cuestiones Abiertas', in *José Carlos Mariátegui y Europa: El otro aspecto del descubrimiento.* Lima: Ed. Amauta. pp. 167–188.

Quijano, Anibal (2010) '"Bien Vivir" para Redistribuir el poder. Los pueblos indígenas y su propuesta alternativa en tiempos de dominación global'. In *Informe 2009–2010 Pobreza, desigualdad y desarrollo en el Perú.* Lima: Oxfam.

Roitman Rosenmann, Marcos (2008) *Pensar América Latina. El desarrollo de la Sociología Latinoamericana.* Buenos Aires: CLACSO.

Sapiro, G. (2017) *Los intelectuales: profesionalización, politización, internacionalización.* Eduvim: Cordoba.

Segato, Rita (2010) 'Los cauces profundos de la raza latinoamericana: una relectura del mestizaje', *Crítica y Emancipación,* Año *II* (3): 11–44.

Stefanoni, P. (2010) 'Bolivia después de las elecciones: ¿a dónde va el evismo?', *Nueva Sociedad 225.*

Svampa, Maristella (2008) 'Reflexiones sobre la sociología crítica en América Latina y el compromiso intelectual', *Cambio de época.* Buenos Aires: Prometeo, pp.19–41.

Svampa, Maristella (2016) *Debates Latinoamericanos. Indianismo, Desarrollo, Dependencia, Populismo.* Buenos Aires: EDHASA.

The UNESCO Courier (1952) 'Informe sobre las relaciones raciales en el Brasil', Vol. *8/9.*

Wade, Peter (2017) 'Racism and race mixture in Latin America', *Latin American Research Review, 52* (3): 477–485.

# Part One
# Founding Problems

# 1

# Founding Problems and Institutionalization of Sociology in Latin America[1]

*Jorge Rovira Mas (Costa Rica)*

How did the institutionalization of sociology as a social science discipline in Latin America come about? What relation does this process have with the founding problems of Latin American sociology? This presentation seeks to offer some answers to these questions, while relating to the key texts presented in this section.

Sociology appeared in Europe in a historical and social setting marked by transformations such as those brought about by industrial capitalism, a rapidly growing proletariat and social and political struggles, including socialist ideals. This was the period of the birth and establishment of bourgeois society. In the United States (US), this context had its own variants: the process of urbanization experienced at the end of the nineteenth and beginning of the twentieth century, social problems derived from inequality in the cities, racism and criminality; these issues stimulated social concern and the formation of the first entities devoted to this practice in the US.

As an intellectual practice that conceives itself within the social sciences in a rigorous sense, Sociology is a fruit of modern Eurocentric reasoning. The founding fathers of the first and most eminent sociological schools of thought – Marx, Durkheim and Weber – emerged in the second half of nineteenth-century Europe. The recognition of the discipline and the gradual expansion of its institutionalization in departments at universities came later: in Europe and the US, in the first half of the twentieth century, with a few prior exceptions.

The development of sociology in Latin America began in a historical period with a very different economic, political, cultural and institutional framework. At the end of the nineteenth and beginning of the twentieth century several academic activities preceded sociology's institutionalization. One of these was the presence of courses dedicated to sociology in the faculties of philosophy and law, mostly of a theoretical and speculative nature. The elaboration of studies and institutional diagnostics were carried out by State functionaries – but it was not a usual procedure. More significantly, writers, essayists and philosophers conducted studies on Latin American reality becoming a widespread practice (Solari, Franco and Jutkowitz, 1981; De Sierra, Garretón, Murmis and Trindade, 2007).

In a strict sense, the institutionalization of Sociology as a social science in Latin America, begins in the 1930s and 40s, in countries such as Brazil and Mexico, and finishes only by the mid-1970s, in Central America. Some of the emblematic institutions of this period are: in São Paolo, the Free School of Sociology and Politics (1933) and the journal *Sociología* (1939) (Trindade, 2007); and the Institute of Social Research (1930 and 1939) and the *Revista Mexicana de Sociología* (1939), both in the National Autonomous University of Mexico (UNAM) (Reyna, 2007). Later on came the Central American Program of Social Sciences and the journal *Estudios Sociales Centroamericanos* (founded in 1971–72 by the public universities in the sub-region), and the launch of the Central American Sociology School (1973) at the University of Costa Rica, with a broader regional scope (Rovira Mas, 2007: 68).

The institutionalization of sociology picked up speed after the 1950s, but observed regionally, its development was and continues to be an unequal process in terms of professionalization, quality and temporality. After the Second World War and the creation of the United Nations (UN) in 1945, new topics emerged in the international agenda. One of great relevance, was that of the *development* of the nations. In 1948, the Economic Commission for Latin America and the Caribbean (ECLAC) was created within the UN, with headquarters in Santiago, Chile, led by the prestigious Argentinian economist Raúl Prebisch (1901–1986). His influence was decisive in the generation of an original approach, enriched by Latin American experiences: ECLAC structuralism and its concept of center–periphery as the main dynamic of international economy. With this focus, explanations were sought regarding the factors which influenced the *underdevelopment* of the region and to promote structural changes in these economies. The influence of this perspective on the economy and economic policies committed to *development* lasted at least three decades. Both governmental officials and social science practitioners shared this project throughout Latin America.

In political terms, in the context of the Cold War, Latin American countries oscillated between representative democracies and dictatorships. Mexico was one of the intermediate cases. Meanwhile, cultural and educational institutions – universities included – began to grow quantitatively, with massive student access and a diversification of their curriculum, due in part to the demographic explosion in Latin America. At the beginning their infrastructure was weak and the professionalization of teachers and researchers was incipient, for the aim of the first 'sociologists' was the founding of an academic discipline differentiated from other activities in the social sciences and humanities, led by a group of scholars who would form and settle in the emerging specialized institutions. Fundamental to this process was the new concept of sociological practice which began to gain ground throughout the 1950s: a new appropriation of cognitive resources was required in sociological theory as well as training in systematic procedures to cultivate empirical research – and techniques, including statistics. All of these elements were joined methodologically to generate new knowledge on the local social reality and problems. The disciplinary references were the United States and France, countries considered to be at the vanguard of global scientific developments.

A first conflict generated in this process occurred between the carriers of this modern concept of the discipline on the one hand, and those who defended a practice in which theory was overvalued and research techniques were undervalued or used with poor and outdated skills, on the other hand. The generation of methodologically controlled data collection was disparaged by the latter, where the essay was prevalent in the communication of sociological analysis. In the context of this dispute – with a high profile or diffuse presence depending on the country – the first group was identified as the bearers and representatives of *scientific sociology* and the second as *chair sociology* (Franco, 1979). This conflict was manifest throughout the decade in forums of importance such as the congresses of the Latin American Association of Sociology (ALAS), the first sociological entity of regional scope worldwide, founded in 1950 (Blanco, 2005).

The pledge for scientific objectivity became the organizing principle of those seeking to institute a modern scientific approach to research and teaching. Along with this, the practice of social science became a clear and conscious discipline independent from political inclinations or preferences. This did not entail the scientist quitting, as a citizen, from political participation in society (Franco, 1979: 239–241).

Among the important figures of this *scientific sociology* is the Spaniard José Medina Echavarría (1903–1977), who emigrated to Mexico after the Spanish Civil War, where he performed an outstanding labor of institutionalizing sociology. At the beginning of the 1950s, at the invitation of Prebisch, he moved to Chile to work at ECLAC. He was the first Director (1958–1959) of the Latin American School of Sociology (ELAS) within the Latin American Faculty of Social Sciences (FLACSO) (Franco, 2007), a regional institution, founded in 1957 with support from the Chilean State, along with the United Nations Education, Science and Culture Organization (UNESCO). Apart from contributing to a modern concept of sociology, Medina brought a sociological focus to the issue of *development*, which enriched ECLAC and brought more complexity to its vision.

A second relevant scholar identified with *scientific sociology* and certainly emblematic to this day, is the Italian-Argentine Gino Germani (1911–1979). His work, *The Social Structure of Argentina* (1955), is exemplary of the possibilities for the modern practice of sociology and exerted a powerful influence on the new generations, shoring up the new perspective. He was very influential in the design of the School of Sociology established in 1957 at the University of Buenos Aires, and the renovation of the previously existing Institute of Sociology (1940), which he directed in the 1960s and now bears his name. Germani made use of the sociological theory of modernization, of US origin, to guide his theoretical reflection and empirical research on Argentina and Latin America.

Two prominent Brazilian sociologists during this foundational period were Florestan Fernandes (1920–1995) and Alberto Guerreiro Ramos (1915–1982). The first was influential in the 1950s as a mentor in the group that became known as the Paulista School of Sociology – in which Fernando H. Cardoso and Octavio Ianni were formed, among others. Guerreiro Ramos, while sharing the modernizing ideals of the discipline, raised the need for a style of knowledge production that would reveal the cultural and historical conditions from which sociological practice was to be implemented. This should be rooted in a critical perspective, according to him, on the specific and more pressing problems in Brazilian society.

Another outstanding figure of this period was Orlando Fals Borda (1925–2008), a Colombian, trained at the University of Florida (USA), where he earned his PhD in Sociology in 1955. He was the founder of the Department of Sociology at the National University of Colombia in 1959 and an active part of a generation that renewed and modernized sociology with an approach that recognized the value of empirical research.

However, in the prevailing political climate in his society, of full-fledged poverty, inequality and violence, his research in rural areas of Colombia drove him in the course of the next decade to an approach of sociology explicitly committed to the disadvantaged sectors of society. He further postulated a methodological approach different to the canon prevailing since the 1950s: Participatory Action Research (PAR), one of the key texts included in this volume.

Chile managed to attract a significant number of international institutions of the social sciences that proliferated with the support of the UN, achieving an outstanding institutional presence. The establishment of the ECLAC in Chile – a prominent magnet – and FLACSO has already been highlighted. Others were the Latin American and Caribbean Demographic Center (CELADE, established in 1957), the Latin American Institute for Economic and Social Planning (ILPES, created in 1962), and the regional office for Latin America of UNESCO, among many others. Beigel and her team (Beigel et al., 2010) have studied the dynamics by which a regional academic circuit in the social sciences was generated with some degree of autonomy in the Southern Cone, with its axis in Chile. This autonomy can be larger or smaller depending on the historical and structural context, i.e., determining the *elasticity of the autonomy of the academic fields*. Some features of this process explain the next period of Sociology, ranging from the 1960s up to the early 1970s. The first such feature was a favorable political climate for university education and research, as well as scientific and intellectual debate, in contrast to the process in Argentina and Brazil. A second factor was advances in the formation of educational institutions – mainly universities – led by the elites with State support, seeking to diversify social sciences. These elites were very proactive in bringing international organizations to Santiago, invigorating the conditions of institutionalization of these disciplines, especially sociology and economics. Among the Chilean universities that played a key role during these years, each with international support from other academic networks, were the University of Chile (public) and the Catholic University of Chile (private). Both of these generated numerous academic institutes, teaching staff and researchers (Beigel et al., 2010).

FLACSO played an outstanding role in the founding and support of the modernization/institutionalization of sociology in Latin America, with a regional scope. It excelled in its efforts to promote solid training to young scholars of many countries from the region, who came to Santiago with international scholarships. The program formation lasted two years, the curriculum endeavored to balance theory and techniques of social research, in addition to introducing the sociological perspective of *development*, which would then be complemented by the broad discussion of ideas that prevailed in the intellectual climate of Santiago. Upon returning to their countries, it was intended that these graduates would contribute to the modernization of sociology and social sciences in their academic or professional practice. In the first ten alumni generations from 1958 to 1973, about 250 students from various Latin American countries held FLACSO's diploma, albeit with a high concentration of graduates from Chile, Argentina and Brazil (Franco, 2007). The influence exerted on their country's institutional environments relied heavily on local conditions, dispositions and resources to promote the new skills. An outstanding example was Edelberto Torres Rivas (1930), Guatemalan (fourth FLACSO generation, 1964–1965), for his leadership role in the Central American Program of Social Sciences of the public universities in this sub-region. The institutionalization of sociology in Latin America, partly as an international/regional project, based in a society and academic universe that welcomed it from its own renovating dynamic such as that prevailing in Chile, shows one of the particularities of the modern foundation of Latin American sociology. FLACSO had an outstanding participation but was not the only institution of international character that contributed to this.

The next remarkable period lived by Latin American sociology occurred in the second half of the 1960s. A number of factors built the framework of sociology at this time in the region: firstly, the Cuban Revolution (1959) and the alternative and original projects for social change that came with it it, especially its subsequent socialist orientation; secondly, the failure of the expectations raised by the ideology of Latin American developmentalism; and, thirdly, the coups in Brazil in 1964 and Argentina in 1966 carried out by the military in association with the US government, in addition to the prevailing authoritarian political regimes in other countries. All this resulted in a general questioning of the ideas in vogue on *development* and *industrialization*. The expulsion of Brazilian and Argentinian social scientists, sociologists and economists especially, from the universities and the persecution many of them experienced after the *coups d'état* in their countries, turned Santiago once again into a center of attraction. Talented young individuals, with a very critical view of the evolution that followed in Latin American capitalist societies, joined the various public and international institutions in this city, where the teaching of social sciences proliferated under the new parameters, in an environment in which quality production and intense debate multiplied. Marxism, developed previously by some of the Brazilian sociologists who arrived in Santiago, began to acquire a renewed vitality in this institutional environment.

This is the origin of the debate between the Dependency Theories and the sociology of modernization and structural-functionalism, in the version elaborated by Germani and influenced by the US to conduct research. The scope and limitations of ECLA's structuralism were also questioned, and critically reformulated in some of its most significant contributions. Among these new trends, the historical-structural approach to analyzing the dynamics followed by the international economic system and the relations of subordination between the central and peripheral economies emerged. Similarly, the prevailing positions of the traditional Communist parties in Latin America, which adhered to the guidelines issued by the Soviet Union, were also questioned (Bambirra, 1978). A new diagnosis on 'dependent capitalism' in its different historical and structural contexts in Latin American countries called for empirical research. With Dependency's proposal of an *integrated analysis of development* in various dimensions (economic, social and political), the relations between social classes and groups were placed at the center of the observation — relations both within the dependent societies as well as among these groups with their counterparts in the central societies. According to this approach, these relations affect the possibilities and limitations of the economic and social development of the dependent societies.

The Dependency Theories had the greatest influence in Latin America between the second half of the 1960s and the beginning of the 1980s. The most recognized work, *Dependency and Development in Latin America*, by Fernando H. Cardoso and Enzo Faletto, saw its first edition in Mexico in 1969. The corresponding work for Central America, written by Edelberto Torres Rivas, *Interpretation of Central American Social Development*, initially appeared in Chile in the same year, but it became widespread in Central America after the 1971 edition by a local university press. The Dependency perspective deployed variants, including one clearly linked to Marxism, led by authors such as Theotonio dos Santos, Ruy Mauro Marini, Vania Bambirra and Aníbal Quijano, among others. One of the consequences of this new phase was the criticism and devaluation of some of the contributions provided by the so-called *scientific sociology*. Furthermore, an appeal was made for a sociology explicitly committed to the disadvantaged sectors of society, the popular sectors.

A new dichotomy was forged between empirical research, on the one hand, and the political preferences, on the other. Dependency analysis was methodologically affirmed in the historical-structural analysis of Latin American societies and in interpretive approaches, thus devaluing disciplinary training in techniques of empirical social research, especially quantitative aspects sustained in statistics, as they were 'out of focus due to the paradigm shift' (Cortés, 2006: 52). This, in a context such as the mid-1960s, linked these techniques to the US style of sociological training and its exerted influence on Latin American social science. For many this was seen as an intrusion by the emerging counter-insurgency ideology of the US that sought to use some of the resources and the possibilities of the social disciplines to better identify the prevailing climate of social change in the region and control it.

ECLAC's structuralism and the Dependency Theories have been two of the most important original contributions made by Latin American social science to the production of global knowledge, at the crossroads between economics and sociology. As Beigel and her team have argued, the acceleration of the institutionalization of sociology from its initial version in the 1950s to the next two decades generated a dynamic peripheral circuit of knowledge within the international system of science. This circuit, whose core was located in the Southern Cone of Latin America, acquired a very relevant academic autonomy, transcending the usual boundaries of academic dependency. In turn, it proved very influential, under the regionalization strategy that was part of its own dynamics (Beigel et al., 2010).

The Chilean military's overthrow of Salvador Allende in September 1973 sparked a drastic change in the favorable political and institutional conditions that had been evolving for the development of social sciences – and sociology in particular – in the two preceding decades in Chile and the Southern Cone. Other *coup d'états* in Uruguay, also in 1973, foreshadowing those in Chile several months later and in Argentina in 1976, all created a bleak climate for intellectuality and saw the forced emigration of many social scientists from this sub-region to Mexico and Costa Rica – a tiny democratic oasis in Central America. Military-led authoritarian regimes prevailed in the rest of this area until the Sandinista Revolution triumphed against Somoza in Nicaragua (1979), modifying the trends of social sciences.

Military intervention in the universities, persecution and the disappearance of critical professionals and intellectuals, together with a new general climate of restriction and control of civil rights, and the launch of a neoliberal offensive in economic policies, began to lay the foundations for an unsuspected, long-term transformation of Latin American societies. Two major consequences in the social sciences, will be highlighted here: a new different institutionality came to enable the survival of social sciences under the pervasive sociopolitical conditions, and new issues began to replace *development* (De Sierra et al., 2007). The so-called *independent centers* arose, focusing on different topics with professionals from different disciplines, and were able to provide a refuge for highly experienced and recognized teachers and researchers who were able to remain in their respective societies without extreme risk to continue their work and preserve part of the knowledge they had accumulated. These institutes were independent from the universities, though they almost always received support locally (from religious, social or political organizations) or internationally (from American or European foundations). Beginning in the 1980s, this was also reproduced in Central America (Rovira Mas, 2007).

As for the new emerging themes, social sciences and sociology were now redirected from a primarily *development* preoccupation towards a concern for politics and changing structures, particularly democracy, previously undervalued and under-researched. Observing the restructuring of Latin American societies would also spring from this new core. Attention would be now focused on the question of the State, its historical constitution, authoritarian regimes and their regional particularities, political parties, social movements, factors in the transition from authoritarian regimes to democracy, and the outlook for consolidation of democracy in Latin America, along with the globalized neoliberal environment.

**The Tensions**

From the start, and from the very founding of Latin American sociology, several tensions emerged and have persisted. One of these is the broad, formative education sociologists had to receive in the region's academic institutions – now that their activity was clearly differentiated from the scopes and limitations of social philosophy – in order to develop a solid, creative praxis. There was an oscillation between theoretical formation and training in social research methodology and techniques, both qualitative and quantitative, as well as the strengths to be acquired in social statistics. If the curricula in the 1950s and 60s came close to the versions taught in US universities, especially with regard to technique and methodology, the rise of Marxist and dependency approaches in the following decades was accompanied by political distrust and downgrading of that type of formation. Conversely, in more recent decades, an attempt has been made to recover stronger knowledge and ability in the wielding of instrumental skills, without prejudice to theoretical soundness, a balance projected unequally in Latin American sociological institutions.

A second tension in Latin American sociology has been that of the horizon and meaning of sociological practice. Sociology saw itself very early on as an indispensable factor for building knowledge of the region's social reality and thereby contributing to social change and the development urgently needed by Latin America, regardless of the particular conceptions envisaged for such transformation. The problem offers several angles, one of which is linked to the question of the sociologist's sociopolitical commitment. The conveyors of *scientific sociology* underlined objectivity as one of the core values in the new endeavor and subscribed largely to the Weberian thesis of the axiological neutrality of social science, though this did not mean scientists had to extract themselves from the political life of their community (Solari, Franco and Jutkowitz, 1981). However, in the context of the 1960s and 1970s, the trail of the Cuban revolution led to the ascent of the Third-World Marxism. Sociologists were called to a political commitment against the *status quo* and a questioning of the postulates of *scientific sociology* (Fals Borda, 2015). This meant an ethical obligation to a scientific praxis for the benefit of social change and the exploited and subordinated classes. This original tension with different accents, nuances and a dissimilar scope, has been part of the evolution of Latin American sociology.

A derivative of this was the unfolding of the methodological approach of Participatory Action Research (PAR), a perspective built since 1970 by Orlando Fals Borda, contributing in a similar direction to the critical pedagogy conceived and cultivated by Brazilian educator Paulo Freire (1921–1997). PAR is a call to social research and knowledge generation that takes a primary interest in disadvantaged social sectors, appreciates popular knowhow, involves these groups actively and respectfully in the research process, and commits to sharing the resulting knowledge with them in order to foster a transformation and change of their social conditions (Fals Borda, 2015).

The horizon and sense of sociological practice relates also to the discipline's *ethos*, an issue of particular interest to Edelberto Torres Rivas. The failure of modernization in Latin America that was expected in the 1950s led to the misfortune of the sociology that was self-assumed as the bearer of enlightened reason. The weakness sociology had in anticipating and directing social changes is evident in the effective transformations induced by neoliberal reforms over the past three decades: this is to say, the main contradiction between a free market society that unceasingly leads to marginalization and inequality, and a representative democratic regime that tends to limit itself to elections. Even though democracy was widespread in the region, it lacked a sustaining basis for an aware, participatory and responsible exercise of citizenship. In principle, then, sociology has also lost its original momentum and is threatened by a narrower definition of its task and scope; technical and instrumental knowledge have tended to gain ground and take the lead in its different fields. This is what Torres Rivas calls the picture of pessimism, defined as 'uncertainty about the future or absence of certainty in view of the heterogeneous results' (see Torres Rivas's key text in this section). But despite everything, this should not lead to a radical defeat of the potential of reason and sociology. Its acceptance and recognition is a stimulus to nurture new creativity in the face of reality in the social sciences.

Another fundamental tension is the recurring concern for *academic autonomy* in a broad sense – the questioning of a heteronomous theoretical formation applied with a lack of creativity to local contexts. The concern is, in other words, regarding the prevention of knowledge transfers with a critical assessment, as well as reproduction in the periphery of Northern patterns meant to understand other realities.

As early as the Second Congress of the Latin American Association of Sociology in 1953 in Rio de Janeiro, Guerreiro Ramos (see p. 47) qualified this sociology as 'consular' or 'canned sociology'. In the face of this, he proposes to generate 'an authentic sociology' to foster a sociological attitude to stimulate the senses, reason and theoretical imagination of local sociologists. He calls for a creative way to address research and the production of knowledge, accounting for Latin America's particular social structures.

In the following decade, social science autonomy was part of the project of 'critical sociology' and original concepts were dynamically produced along with an endogenous research agenda (Beigel et al., 2010). Latin American social sciences did an outstanding job of attaining this through ECLAC's structuralism contributions – which Guerreiro Ramos highlights and proposes to his colleagues as an example of the mental decolonization of Latin American economists at that time – and also, beginning in the 1960s, with Dependency theories.

These contributions have lost their influence in recent decades. The cultural offensive involved in the neoliberal modernization of Latin America starting in the 1980s, including its effects on universities and many academic institutions in the field of sociology, has helped foment an underrating of the region's accumulated knowledge production. At the same time, the different productive and reproductive mechanisms of academic dependency fueled the current dynamics of global knowledge circulation and the new features of the post-graduate academic socialization in the region – one of the trump cards of this subordination. Institutions such as FLACSO and the Latin American Council of Social Sciences (CLACSO), founded in 1967, disseminate the region's evolving social sciences production and Latin American intellectual and sociological traditions. They work to bring these contributions out into open debate in the region. But most private and public universities look mainly to the North and its patterns and products.

### The Fundamental Themes

At the heart of Latin American sociology, from the moment it began to institutionalize, a main structural problem was highlighted: the specific nature of Latin American societies in contrast with others classified as 'developed' (such as the United States or Western Europe). The whole problem of diagnosing these societies and how they are to be treated has been one of the most important contributions by Latin American sociology to the creation of a peripheral tradition within international sociology.

This has been accompanied by an interest in social change and *development*, as well as an inclination for a regional or sub-regional analytical perspective. The problem has been dealt with from various theoretical perspectives. Mention has already been made of the sociology of modernization, with its US influence, a perspective Germani used and developed creatively in his typological approach to the processes of transition from traditional to modern society (Germani, 1962). Another attempt in this direction was made by Medina Echavarría, primarily with his Weberian readings and contributions to ECLAC (Medina Echavarría, 1964).

With Dependency Theories, a partial offshoot of ECLAC's structuralism, came an epistemological and theoretical rupture in sociology. They argued that an understanding of Latin American social dynamics, defined up to then as underdeveloped in contrast to developed societies, could only be properly reconstructed when the limited vision of national societies was transcended. It needed to be observed as part of the historical development of international capitalism. Political and economic power factors in the center and periphery relations need to be analyzed; these factors were interpreted as interlinked with the subordination induced by the organized interests of the center societies, structuring and conditioning the dynamics of the dependent societies – those of Latin America, and, in a nutshell, those located in the global South. The key notion of 'internal colonialism', a complex category that spills over into economic, political, social and cultural dimensions – first used for Latin America by the Mexican sociologist Pablo González Casanova (1963) – is another important contribution to this reflection.

An approach which penetrates even more deeply in this same direction (that has been evolving over some 25 years), comes from the work of a well-recognized Dependentist, the Peruvian Aníbal Quijano (1928–2018): the coloniality of power. Eurocentric modernity as a historical construction connects Latin America to Europe from its very sixteenth-century origins, in a movement that has in turn been generating a global society in which Latin America's persistent colonial situation, reproduced in different forms, prevails. This encompasses and projects itself onto all dimensions of social life – but there is one whose relevance is worth noting, the dimension of subjectivity. Eurocentric reason has colonized, and continues to colonize, consciences. Moreover, the social construct of *race* as an early historical product of this modernity, and con-substantial to it, is the backbone of social domination, as Quijano has stated. Thus, Latin American societies – and surely many societies in the South – have a monumental task ahead of them in order to reconstruct their social relations: fighting for the decolonization of power.

**Note**

1. Translated by Isabel Macdonald and revised by Fernanda Beigel.

**References**

Bambirra, V. (1978) *Teoría de la dependencia: una anticrítica*. Mexico: Ediciones Era.
Beigel, F. et al. (2010) *Autonomía y dependencia académica. Universidad e investigación científica en un circuito periférico: Chile y Argentina* (1950–1980). Buenos Aires: Editorial Biblos.

Blanco, A. (2005) La Asociación Latinoamericana de Sociología: una historia de sus primeros congresos, *Sociologías*, *7*(14), 22–48.

Cardoso, F.H. & E. Faletto (1969) *Dependencia y desarrollo en América Latina*. Mexico: Siglo XXI Editores.

Cortés, F. (2006) 'Avatares en la estadística social en América Latina'. In E. de la Garza Toledo (Ed.), *Tratado latinoamericano de sociología* (pp. 45–62). Barcelona: Anthropos Editorial – Mexico: Universidad Autónoma Metropolitana-Iztapalapa.

De Sierra, G., Garretón, M.A., Murmis, M. & Trindade, H. (2007) 'Las ciencias sociales en América Latina en una mirada comparativa'. In H. Trindade (Ed.), *Las ciencias sociales en América Latina en perspectiva comparada* (pp. 17–52). Mexico, DF: Siglo XXI Editores.

Fals Borda, O. (2015) *Una sociología sentipensante para América Latina. Antología y presentación de Víctor M. Moncayo*. Mexico, DF: Siglo XXI Editores; Buenos Aires: CLACSO.

Franco, R. (1979) 'Veinticinco años de sociología latinoamericana. Un balance'. In D. Camacho (Ed.), *Debates sobre la teoría de la dependencia y la sociología latinoamericana* (pp. 232–284). San José (Costa Rica): Editorial Universitaria Centroamericana. There is a commemorative edition from 2015 by San José (Costa Rica): Editorial de la Universidad de Costa Rica.

Franco, R. (2007) *La FLACSO clásica (1957–1973)*. Santiago (Chile): Catalonia.

Germani, G. (1962) *Política y sociedad en una época de transici ón*. Buenos Aires: Editorial Paidós.

González Casanova, P. (1963) 'Sociedad plural, colonialismo interno y desarrollo', *América Latina*, *6*(3), 15–32

Medina Echavarría, J. (1964) *Consideraciones sociológicas sobre el desarrollo económico de América Latina*. Buenos Aires: Solar/Hachette.

Reyna, J.L. (2007) 'La institucionalización de las ciencias sociales en México'. In H. Trindade (Ed.), *Las ciencias sociales en América Latina en perspectiva comparada* (pp. 249–337). Mexico: Siglo XXI Editores.

Rovira Mas, J. (2007) 'El desarrollo de la sociología en Centroamérica: La promesa incumplida', *Íconos. Revista de Ciencias Sociales*, *30*, 65–74.

Solari, A., Franco, R. & Jutkowitz, J. (1981) *Teoría, acción social y desarrollo en América Latina* (2nd edn). Mexico: Siglo XXI Editores.

Torres Rivas, E. (2015) *Centroamérica: entre revoluciones y democracia. Antología y presentación de Jorge Rovira Mas*. Mexico: Siglo XXI Editores; Buenos Aires: Consejo Latinoamericano de Ciencias Sociales (CLACSO).

Trindade, H. (2007) 'Las ciencias sociales en Brasil: Fundación, consolidación y expansión'. In H. Trindade (Ed.), *Las ciencias sociales en América Latina en perspectiva comparada* (pp. 109–192). Mexico: Siglo XXI Editores.

# 2

# A Critical Introduction to Brazilian Sociology: Canned Sociology versus Dynamic Sociology[1]

*Alberto Guerreiro Ramos (Brazil)*

The best way of doing science is by beginning with real life or basing it on the need to respond to the challenges of reality. Following this rule, I propose to deal here with the problems of Brazilian sociology, by expanding the analysis of a case that occurred in the II Latin-American Congress of Sociology, held in Rio and São Paulo, between 10 to 17 July 1953. As Chairman of the Commission of National and Regional Structures, I submitted a document to that event containing the following recommendations:

1. Solutions to the social problems of Latin American countries should be proposed taking into account the effective conditions of their national and regional structures, with the literal transplanting of measures adopted in fully developed countries not being advisable;

2. The foundational planning for teaching Sociology in Latin America should obey the fundamental objective of contributing to the cultural emancipation of students, equipping them with intellectual instruments that will allow them to interpret, in an authentic manner, the problems of related national and regional structures;

3. When exercising advisory activities, Latin American sociologists should not lose sight of the capability of the national revenue of their countries, necessary to support the costs resulting from the measures proposed;

4. In the current state of development of Latin American nations, and due to their increasing necessity to invest in production goods, it is unadvisable to invest resources in research about the minutiae of daily life. Instead, the formulation of generic interpretations of global aspects and partial interpretations of national and regional ones ought to be encouraged;

5. Sociological work should always take into account that the improvement of the living conditions of the population is conditional on the industrial development of national and regional structures;

6.  It is frankly unadvisable for sociological work to directly or indirectly con-
    tribute to the persistence in the Latin American nations of pre-literate cultural
    lifestyles. To the contrary, in relation to the indigenous or Afro-Brazilian
    populations, sociologists should apply themselves to the study and propo-
    sition of mechanisms for social integration that can hasten the incorpora-
    tion of these groups into the current economic and cultural structure of Latin
    American countries;

7.  In the use of sociological methodology, sociologists should take into account
    that demands for precision and refinement result from the level of devel-
    opment of national and regional structures. Therefore, in Latin American
    countries, research methods and processes should be consistent with their
    economic and personnel resources, as well as with the generic cultural level
    of their populations.

However, all of these theses were loudly rejected by 22 votes to 9, made
worse by the fact that the author of this study was openly attacked with
demonstrations of hate and disparagement by one of his opponents. It is
significant to highlight that opinions contrary to those listed above were
coordinated by Brazilian participants of the Congress.

As can be understood from the reading of the recommendations, what
I had in mind was to encourage the practice, in Latin American countries,
of a sociology which reflects on its problems; my intention was to stimulate the cutting of the umbilical cords which have made a discipline an
abortifacient sub-product of European and US sociological thought.

The attitude of the congress towards these theses served to capture the
idea that nowadays, in Brazil at least, two currents, amongst others, of
sociological thought can be clearly distinguished. One can be called, as
I once proposed, 'consular', since it can be considered in many ways an
episode of the cultural expansion of European countries and the United
States; and the other, although it takes advantage of the accumulated experience of universal sociological work, seeks to use this as an instrument
of self-knowledge and for the development of national and regional structures. The theses listed above intended to represent the latter.

The essence of all authentic sociology is, directly or indirectly, a purpose of salvation and social reconstruction.[2] For this reason, inspiration is
taken from the communitarian experience lived by the sociologist in the
function of which meaning is acquired. Disconnected from an effective
human reality, sociology is a ludic activity with the same facile nature.
Whoever talks about life, talks about problems. The essence of life is its
incessant problematics. Thus, to the extent that the sociologist vitally

exercises his discipline, he is forcefully led to intertwine his thought with his own national or regional circumstances.

However, the education of the Brazilian or Latin American sociologist as a rule consists of training for conformism, for the availability of intelligence in light of theories. He learns to receive ready-made solutions, and when faced with a problem of his environment, he tries to resolve it comparing texts, appealing to the recipes which he learned in compendiums.

Trained to think in ready-made thoughts, he frequently becomes, in relation to feelings and volition, a *répétiteur*, in other words he feels pre-formed feelings, and wants because of pre-formed desires, as Péguy would say.

Open our compendiums of sociology. One or another breaks the rule: but in general, each one brings everything, lists authors and systems, without providing the apprentice with guiding criteria for critical thinking. It is as if someone is insinuating: the learner seeks sociological truth, removing a little bit from here, another bit from there. Since these compendiums about which I am speaking, almost all of which are written in these parts, assume this enormity – that there exists an eternal, immutable sociological truth, *au-delá* from the historical contingency, resulting from the aggregate average of all systems[3] – therefore, they incapacitate the student for the functional exercise of a sociological attitude.

On the other hand, another type of mental vice is patent in a large number of our sociological productions. The indigenous sociologist almost always starts from an imported system, to which is given absolute validity, and unconditionally affiliates himself. The harm comes from the origin. We have always had here positivists, Haeckelists, evolutionists and other types of *aficionados à outrance*, and, when one of our contemporary sociologists is introduced to someone, the question soon arises: which school do you follow?

In addition to 'consular', this is a Sociology which can be said to be 'packaged' since it is consumed like a genuine cultural 'fruit preserve'.

Under these conditions, a subservient attitude is assumed among us, in light of the methods and products of sociological work from abroad. Everything that comes from there is orthodox, excellent, imitable. It has still not been noticed yet that the means and the results of sociological work are conditioned by national or regional structures. The immanent effectiveness of transplantations is affirmed. A sociological position is not assumed in the discussion of Sociology. As a result, often debates

or so-called meetings of sociologists are summarized in idolatrous pro-
nouncements and even patriotic intrepidity, such as those which consider
the need to adopt simplified methodological procedures in an underdeveloped country as harming national dignity. I have seen, in a sociology
congress, the fall of a correct sociological proposal because it confronted
the patriotic dignities of those in attendance.

This exemplarism is one of the aspects that can be called the 'infantile
disease' of sociology in colonial countries, a disease which makes the discipline in question a 'gesticulation', empty of meaning, a hollow act, an
illusory action, but capable of satisfying certain individuals.

The 'gesticulator' satisfies himself by pretending to carry out the action
he commits in it, but really does not do it.[4]

In relation to the practices of a large section of sociologists in countries such as Brazil, there is thus a pathology of normality. Since in their
mental postures the culturologically morbid trait is generalized, it comes
to be normal. Among them we have also to take fictions seriously in
order to live in peace. If we dare to be sensible, we are lost, they will not
tolerate us.

This is the infantile disease that is sociology in Brazil. However, I do
not believe it to be incurable. The actual fact of being capable of carrying
out an examination of one's own conscience pushes it towards maturity.
An indication that I am right is what has happened with Latin American
economic thought. Under the auspices of a body such as CEPAL, the
decolonization of the Latin American economist has been achieved, and
the contribution of Brazilians to this change is one of the most illustrious.

**For a Sociology 'With Sleeves Rolled Up'**

Until the present moment, in Latin American sociological thought no
transformation has been discerned correlated to the one led in the economic sector by the Economic Commission for Latin America (CEPAL).

CEPAL's work is characterized by the objective of making the politics and economic thought of Latin American countries functional factors
in their own development. In this way, when proposing solutions to the
problem of development, it starts from the consideration of the resources
available and not idealistically conceived conveniences and necessities.
All the effort of this international body is aimed at the formulation of
principles of an economic strategy whose assimilation will make Latin

American economists more skillful in terms of their advisory activities, so that they can contribute to directing productive factors in each country, in order to accelerate capitalization.

Under these conditions, national revenue becomes the subject of the special attention from economists. It is this which marks the timing, the kind, and the norms of economic policies, which should always seek to aggregate national factors of production in order to achieve the highest levels of profitability. One of the pioneers of this current of ideas, Raúl Prebish,[5] warned in 1951 that the current need for the capitalization of internal activities is often incompatible with the challenge of reproducing, in the less developed countries, the forms of existence of the most developed, notably the United States, because these forms of existence, and the modalities of consumption that they imply as well as the modalities of capitalization, result from costly inputs at which these countries will gradually arrive through the increase of their productivity; and their mere transfusion to the less developed countries, without a deliberate effort of selection and adaptation, provokes tensions which in other times did not arise.

These ideas are perfectly in harmony with one of the recommendations submitted to the II Latin American Congress of Sociology, prepared by the Commission of National and Regional Structures, over which I had the honor to preside. It stated the following:

> In the exercise of advisory activities, Latin American sociologists should not lose sight of the availabilities of national revenue in their countries, necessary to support the costs resulting from the proposed measures.

As I wrote above, I was defeated defending this principle.

Nevertheless, it appears to me that the Latin American sociologist should follow this path. What has hindered us, in this area, is the confinement of sociology within the academic areas defined as belonging to this discipline. The professional thereby loses sight of the economic significance of his work. In a country lacking an organic conscience of its needs, this is a disaster, because to the extent that the sociologist, with this educational deficiency, acquires personal prestige and is listened to or taken seriously, he can induce governmental or private agencies to undertake baneful investments of resources.

What has led Latin American sociologists to obfuscate themselves in relation to this is the fact that they consider identical, in the present phase, the actuality of their own countries and that of the more developed countries. In general, they forget to compare their countries with those that can be considered to be in the same paradigms in terms of phase. On the contrary, their criteria are contiguity and juxtaposition.[6]

A recent episode: a US sociologist advised as a fundamental measure for agrarian reform in Brazil the creation of secondary schools in each municipality in proportion to the number of people, similar to what is found in the US. According to him, the smallest of our municipalities should have at least one secondary school with a minimum of five teachers working full time. He added this observation: any municipality which, after two years of the enactment of this law had not complied with it, should lose the status of municipality.

The suggestion merits criticisms from many points of view, more so because the type of school in question is radically different from what amongst us is given this designation, i.e., a gymnasium or college. Its counter-indication is obvious from the simple point of view of the national revenue of the country. Do the math – how much money would have to be spent in the implementation of this proposition – to see the absurdity which it represents. However let's pretend that in an act of craziness the government resolves to put this into practice. Where will the teachers be found? How do we retain in secondary schools a group of adolescents whose psychology and economic situation constitute factors that prevent their education? Where do we locate secondary establishments in regions with a sparse demographic content, so that each of them functions with the minimum of students technically required? For this and other reasons, observance to the letter of foreign authorities is reckless without taking into account their respective national equations.

Many specialists in Brazil act exactly like this US sociologist, when, for example, they advise that we should spend three dollars per person on health services, that we should have a childcare post for every 10,000 people, a bed for each death due to tuberculosis, five hospital beds for each thousand inhabitants, 60,000 doctors, 100,000 nurses, 165,000 beds for mental illnesses, or when they calculate other institutional necessities in light of the same criteria. For them, social problems are resolved by the 'rule of three'. One of the most spectacular illustrations of this arithmetical conception of social problems is the famous survey carried out about the implementation of Instituto de Serviços Socias do Brasil (ISSB), principally in the part related to health.

By this practice, effects are confused with causes. Actually, high levels of well-being are inseparable from the process that created them. In other words, they are automatic results of a process of development. Therefore, they are factors of this process which must be urgently established here: it is a socio-economic dynamic that ought to be promoted.

It is in the correction of these habits of thinking where the contribution of the sociologist can be most opportune. The sociologist, of all specialists, is the one who is the most qualified, due to the intellectual instruments he possesses, to overcome the divided vision of the needs of the country, replacing it with a unitary vision of its integral context.

A country's development strategy is conditioned by the particular dynamic of its context, which, in each historic phase, presents the specific priorities of development needs. In this way, criteria for social action are not necessarily transferable from one country to another, when those are in different phases of development.

One of the reasons for this non-transferability results from cultural factors. The current transplantations of sociology from US and English centers appears to see only the cultural impediments in this area. However, an important reason for this non-transferability is presented in terms of the available resources.

The basic need of an underdeveloped country such as Brazil is to obtain an optimal combination of its economic factors, with the aim of accelerating the increase of its investment rate in production goods. Imperatives of social accountability impose a selective attitude in the realization of measures. These do not have an absolute value; on the contrary, their efficiency depends on dominant relations at a determined moment in national and regional structures.

Sociological work in a peripheral country, much less than in any other, cannot remain detached from the process of capital accumulation. Like other Latin American nations, Brazil did not reach the minimum annual rate of the net investments to meet the cost of its economic development and could not reach this sum in a spontaneous process. Additionally, awareness of this fact has to be clear enough to focus the scientific work in all its sectors on the national interest.

Oriented in this way, sociological work in our country has before it the path to emancipating itself from this patronage. The true sociologist in Brazil does not need favorable subventions or to commit himself to a perfunctory bureaucracy in order to dedicate himself to his studies. He will be tied to this contingency, if he insists on his academic and academizing tendencies. The demand for specialists in sociology capable of linking their scientific activities to the tasks of promoting of the economic sovereignty of the country is constantly increasing. In other words, sociologists 'with sleeves rolled up' can live today in Brazil from the earnings of their effective work in the effort of national construction.

It is true that, currently, the orientation preached here awakes strong resistance and antipathies, as much as it threatens false positions and false reputations. I recognize that this point of view, due to its pioneering nature, is not the most comfortable. On the other hand, it contradicts powerful invested interests and is configured as incomprehensible, strange and difficult to a legion of sincerely mistaken people. At times a heavy price is paid for ideas. And not everyone is willing to pay this price.

However, none of this should obscure the fact that Brazil is maturing. The level of expansion of its productive forces and the increasingly sharp contradictions between these forces and institutional scenarios in force is making incoercible the qualitative change of Brazilian life in all its aspects.

It is a process. And it is useless to fight against a process.

**Notes**

1.  Published for the first time in Portuguese in 1957 in: *Introdução Crítica à Sociologia Brasileira* (editora ANDES). Translated into English by Eoin O'Neill thanks to the support of João Maia and Fundação Getulio Vargas. Revised by Alberto Guerreiro Ramos.

2.  In confirmation, the scholar can see how, for example, Auguste Comte was led to the idea of sociological science through the mediation of the French problem of his time, and secondarily by the European problem (see the *Course of Positive Philosophy*). Also in relation to this, it can be seen how a renewed position in the field of sociology, such as that of Karl Mannheim, reflects a purpose for those who seek solutions for a crisis.

3.  This way of seeing was in fact proclaimed without hesitation by one of the most important figures of our social sciences, Arthur Ramos, who said: 'I increasingly convince myself that methodological incompatibilities are reduced to the question of nomenclature' (*O Negro Brasileiro*, 3rd Brazilian Edition, 1953). This same conciliatory eclecticism is seen in the work of the most prestigious figure in sociological writing in current Brazil, Gilberto Freyre (see especially *Casa Grande & Senzala*).

4.  I use the term 'gesticulation' in its technical meaning, as used by Lazar and Karl Mannheim. Lazar refers to the type of 'gesticulating child' who is satisfied with gestures while others fight for concrete objectives. Lewin reports the case of an imbecile child who wanted to throw a ball a long distance and, not managing to, is satisfied because he found a substitute in the rigorous movement he made. Determined collective configurations can be favorable to the propagation of this infirmity. In Brazil much intellectual activity is mere 'gesticulation', or the expression of 'gesticulative adults'. For a better development of this, see Karl Mannheim, *Libertad y planificación social* (Fondo de Cultura Económica, 1946).

5. Raúl Prebisch, *Problemas teóricas e práticos do desenvolvimento econômico*, numbers 7 and 8, September and December 1951. See also: Celso Furtado, 'Formação de Capital e Desenvolvimento Econômico', in *Revista Brasileira de Economia*, September 1952.

6. I intended to make a clear application of the phraseology in my studies on child mortality, which contradicts the official point of view of the question. See especially: Guerreiro Ramos 'O Problema da Mortalidade Infantil no Brasil', in *Sociologia*, March 1951.

---

## Alberto Guerreiro Ramos, by João Maia (Brazil)

Guerreiro Ramos (1915–1982) was born in a small town called Santo Amaro, in the state of Bahia, where he started his career working for the local state administration. In 1942, Ramos moved to Rio de Janeiro to study Law and Social Sciences, finishing these degrees in 1942 and 1943. After a frustrated attempt to apply for a post at the university, Ramos got a job in the public services, first in the National Department of Children and then in the Department for Administration and Public Service (DASP). Between 1937 and 1945 Brazil was under an authoritarian regime known as Estado Novo, led by President Getúlio Dornelles Vargas. Vargas launched a program of bureaucratic rationalization and created several federal agencies in order to foster state-led development, and DASP was a leading institution in this process. In the mid-1940s, Ramos trained bureaucratic personnel and conducted empirical research on themes such as administration, housing, nutrition, etc. During these early days as a public servant, Ramos read about not just the European tradition of sociology (mainly Weber and Mannheim), but the North-American one as well. His first articles, published in the *Revista do Serviço Público* (*Journal of Public Service*), reflected this broad intellectual interest.

Ramos became a well-known figure in Brazilian sociology during the late 1940s and 1950s, when he joined the Black movement in Brazil (he worked with Abdias do Nascimento and helped to create the Black Experimental Theater) and authored several articles in Brazilian newspapers on issues such as racism, nationalism and Third-Worldism. In the first half of the 1950s, Brazil was under the democratically elected administration of Getúlio Vargas (the former dictator), who implemented nationalistic policies supported by a broad political spectrum. Ramos worked closely with some of the most prominent advisors of Vargas, and in 1955 he joined the Higher Institute of Brazilian Studies (ISEB), a state-sponsored think tank. This institution would be a major forum on discussion on Third-Worldism, existentialism, liberationism and Marxism.

In 1952, the city of Rio de Janeiro held the II Congress of Latin-American Sociology. Ramos addressed the audience and proposed several ideas to guide the development of Latin American sociology, but most of them were rejected. One of his fiercest opponents was Florestan Fernandes, the head of the so-called 'paulista school of sociology' and one of the leading figures in the development of scientific

*(Continued)*

(Continued)

sociology in Brazil. Ramos maintained that Latin American sociologists needed to work on relevant topics such as development and industrialization, leaving aside monographic works inspired by communities studies that were flourishing in the city of São Paolo under the leadership of other pioneering sociologists in Brazil. Fernandes, in his turn, claimed that the main priority was to improve the methodological skills of Brazilian sociologists so they could achieve a higher standard of scholarship.

Infuriated by the rejection of his thesis, Ramos published several articles in newspapers, presenting his ideas to a broader audience. In these articles, which would be edited in books over the next years, he outlined an intellectual program for younger sociologists. The bulk of this program was a criticism of colonial alienation in Brazilian sociological discourse and a subsequent call for a 'national sociology' based on autonomous thinking. Ramos's program related to broader ideas about autonomous development nurtured in important regional intellectual centers, such as the ECLA (Economic Commission for Latin America).

In 1958, Ramos published his masterpiece, a book titled *Redução Sociológica* (*Sociological Reduction*). Drawing heavily on Husserl and other existentialist writers, he combined nationalism, phenomenology and modern sociology theory. The book aimed to teach sociologists from peripheral countries how to employ the method of *philosophical reduction* in order to recognize and overcome the cultural bias that informed European and North-American sociological theories.

Ramos eventually lost his battle in Brazil. In 1964 the military seized power through a *coup d'état* and targeted figures like him who were deeply involved in parliamentary politics. Ramos was forced to flee to the US in 1966. Until his death in 1982, he taught at the University of Southern California, where he managed to rebuild his ties with theories of public administration. His works and ideas were forgotten in Brazil during the years he was abroad, but since the 1990s a slow but steady flow of theses and dissertations have shed light on Ramos's legacy.

# 3

# Theoretical–Practical Experiences: General Working Guidelines on Participatory Action Research (PAR)[1]

*Orlando Fals Borda (Colombia)*

Not having the space or the humor to make personal proclamations regarding 'who was first or better' or 'who quoted whom', but rather being in favor of recognizing a common methodological task of general application, several ways of working have been expressed or made implicit that can be considered as guidelines for the common ordinary work of *participatory research*. These guidelines can be summarized as follows:

1. It is pointless to seek or determine general *social laws* in our field (as with others like biology, according to Mayr).[2] There will be limited predictable developments as far as time, place and culture go, with effects determined by several specific factors, which are not necessarily linear or irreversible. This does not disallow the adoption of reasonable measures of economic and social policy, nor does it limit the scientific nature of the research experiences. However, it does not authorize *absolute prediction*, due to the plurality of causes and intervening factors.

2. The traditional requirements of logical empiricists for delimiting scientific fields and seeking objective universal laws serve primarily to define *two poles* within the spectrum of sciences: one abstract cosmological and the other focused on participatory, local, relevant, evaluation projects. One cannot compare projects from one pole to another.

3. Research rigor is not judged only by quantitative measures, although these may be necessary in the description and explanation of the work results. Measurements should be complemented with pertinent *qualitative* descriptions that are also valid and necessary. Therefore, in our field it is not convenient to continue blindly imitating research procedures justifiable only for the natural sciences. Our tasks, which are therefore more difficult, must be brought forward with greater competence, seriousness and sense of responsibility compared to other fields of knowledge.

4. Due to the natural fluidity of social, cultural, economic and political phenomena, it is necessary to open the opportunity for a diverse series of *interpretations and reinterpretations* of the same studied phenomena; that is, they must
be seen as processes subject to hermeneutic analysis.

5. All *methods and techniques* in science are legitimate to apply in participatory
research. In fact, as long as they fit within the *reference framework agreed*
by a joint decision within the ABX system[3] and inspired by the participatory
approach philosophy on which the initiative is based – preferably on its
origins – in its grassroots, they are legitimate. Open polls, semi-structured
interviews, group and community work, triangulation of information and
collective workshops have shown to be valid techniques to obtain satisfactory
results on the ground.

6. *Empathy and participant observation* (as in psychoanalysis and ethnography) are among the most appropriate techniques to do research on the
intimate or covert nature of the situations of interest in participatory research
and related experiences. They are especially appropriate for problems of anomie, conflict, violence, drug addiction and other symptoms of social pathology.

7. The *validity* criteria for works on PAR depend not on internal correlation
tests of variables or 'objective' or quantifiable exercises, but on the inductive/
deductive examination of results determined by practice, by the development
of empathic processes felt within the realities themselves, by the weighted
judgment of local reference groups and by common sense. (Even children
can take part in evaluation sessions, as has been successfully tested in the
Barefoot College in Tilonia, India.)

8. The *evaluation* of results is not necessarily carried out at the end of a given
or preset period by the known rhythm of reflection-action, as if it were
a unilinear or unicausal banking procedure in the hands of planners, but
can happen during fieldwork itself, as stimuli to action. The inspiration
needed to continue these tasks is 'fractal'; that is a random, accidental or
spontaneous outcome, which comes from many causes, including intui-
tion and feelings that arise in daily living. (Obviously both this guide and
the previous one make many experts and academics nervous, who feel
their procedures, institutions and schools threatened. We can expect their
growing resistance.)

9. Because of the diversity and contradictions existing in the real world, whose
observation involves focusing on dependent or varied attributes, it is necessary that, unlike planners and logical empiricists, *values, goals and commitments* that encourage the participatory research be transparent. Moreover,
these attributes must be made explicit in the reference frameworks as well as
in the fieldwork.

10. There is no place here for *experimentation* as in the natural sciences, allowing for the repetition of phenomena in controlled contexts: there is only room

for comparative forms of *induction and deduction* subject to a determined space-time. For the same reason, there can be no 'typical cases' or 'pilot projects', but only theoretical-practical interpretations that could be generalized.

11. The breakdown of the researcher/subject dyad to end the asymmetry and to make equal *the relationship* does not mean the intellectual predominance of one pole over another. It means the respectful possibility of mutually fruitful contributions by comparable evidence and facts: the common people are not always right, as neither are the so-called 'doctors'.

12. By receiving and considering *popular wisdom* and *common sense* without prejudice, interdisciplinary academic knowledge can critically promote a holistic or more complete understanding of reality. This enriches and simplifies *forms and styles* of communication with the communities studied.

13. Under certain circumstances it is appropriate to distinguish research *rationality* from political rationality and not to mix them undifferentiatedly: each one will contribute to the inquiry process with that for which it is best prepared or which most satisfies him/her individually or as a citizen.

14. Demonstration techniques in *extension practices* or to induce structural changes, are limited by economic factors and lack of persistence. Since participatory processes are almost always medium to long term, the interested institutions (such as universities and NGOs) as well as the relevant formal provisions, must adapt to them and not the opposite, as still happens.

15. If the fieldwork leads to macro levels of political, social, economic and/or cultural *mobilization*, for example 'countervailing powers' or popular movements, it is important to proceed from the *base* of social structures and up, and/or from the *peripheries* to the centers of the systems involved.

16. The analytical step of participation from a *micro* to a *macro* scale not only can be performed, but also calibrated and correlated with the emergence of social movements, organizational networks and national or international institutional policies, ensuring these cannot be manipulated.[4]

17. Objectivity and subjectivity can coincide in art, in a sensual image and in a literary and aesthetic expression of scientific work, which justifies the creative incursion of the *imagination and expression* in participatory research. This is already a hermeneutical technique.

## Some Hermeneutic Techniques[5]

1. *Relative truth*. It is improper and dangerous to manufacture a truth, because there is not one single truth. In social sciences, according to Agnes Heller, a truth can be the agreement between a researcher and his/her research participant, because knowledge is socially constructed. It is, however, necessary to ensure confirmations of facts and data using triangulation techniques, documentation and archives.

2.  *Credibility and sense.* One can work with verisimilitude as a series of knowledge subject to verification processes, and derive from it the sense of real-life processes. This is the understanding of the action, by giving meaning and context to objects of study such as testimonies of the living or witnesses who have passed away, newspapers, photographs, maps and materials from family archives.

3.  *Historical recovery.* When official or unilateral versions of events and facts exist, it is appropriate to make a critical recovery of history based on family 'trunk' files, interviews with elders with good memory and cross-referencing in order to complement or correct the biases observed. This technique is related to the principle of interpretation/reinterpretation.

4.  *Restitution or knowledge return.* This technique implies respect for the groups from which the information originated, and the adoption of styles and forms of communication adapted to their level of language and literacy so it can be well understood when given back. It can take the form of illustrated booklets, radio-magazines [a type of radio program of general interest that combines information, music, interviews, contests, letters, etc.], videos and socio-dramas. (This technique, as well as the following, involves discarding the usual jargon spoken in literate circles.)

5.  *Symmetrical communication.* This is developed through the verification of information, dialogue or horizontal conversation leading to a credible consensus among researchers and research participants.

6.  *Communicative structure.* The product (written or audiovisual) of the social sciences is composed of two related elements, which must be balanced: a core or skeleton, and a cover or wrapping. The core is built with data from authorized and verifiable sources; while the cover is the elaboration of the same information from particular points of view, with imagination circumscribed by cultural references or with imputations to characters, through which interpretive originality, innovation and creative description are added. This is the *logos mythos* technique that allows writers to gain brilliance and effectiveness in the presentation of their messages and recounting history (see the case of Eduardo Galeano, from Uruguay), which leads to the combination of novel and social science. This was the subject of a dynamic working group in a Congress, coordinated by Rodrigo Parra and Luz Mery Giraldo in Colombia.[6] This structure is responsible also for inducing the construction of multi-vocal or 'stereophonic' works, such as my *Double Story of the Coast*, written in two different but simultaneous channels of communication.

7.  *Communicative balance.* When the core is more elaborated than the cover in a document or communication, it becomes a nomothetic exercise, merely technical and informative, without arousing much interest. If the cover, on the other hand, is excessive, the work can become fiction or ideology and

not science as such or reliable knowledge. The necessary balance between the two elements is acquired with the moderation that comes from *phronesis*, good judgment and communicative practice.[7]

## Notes

1.  This is a fragment of the text originally published in Spanish in *Participación popular: Retos del futuro* (Bogotá, ICFES-IEPRI, Colciencias, 1998, pp. 169–236) and afterwards published in Orlando Fals Borda, *Una sociología sentipensante para América Latina* (Buenos Aires: CLACSO, 2015, pp. 326–332). It was translated by Isabel MacDonald thanks to the support of Jorge Rovira Mas and the University of Costa Rica.

2.  Ernst Mayr, *Toward a New Philosophy of Biology* (Cambridge: Harvard University Press, 1988), p. 19.

3.  An ABX system is one in which the relation between an epistemic subject A and an empirical object B, in a framework of social investigation X, is characterized by the object also being a subject.

4.  At the World Bank, Michael M. Cernea's contribution on this point is noteworthy. Thanks to books such as *The People First (Primero la gente*, Mexico: Fondo de Cultura Económica, 1995) and articles such as 'The Sociological Action-Research of Development: Induced Population Resettlement' (*Romanian Journal of Sociology*, World Bank Reprint Series, No. 480, 1995) and others, for over fifteen years, Cernea and his Working Group on Participation have made relevant changes in the institution's policies. His delegate, Anders Rudqvist, made a successful presentation on this in Cartagena, although with protests from some skeptics who expected greater participative results in the management of the Bank's large projects.

5.  See the comparative article on these techniques, published in *Collaborative Inquiry*, No. 18, 1996, in the case of Agnes Heller and O. Fals Borda in *Double History of the Coast* (*Historia doble de la Costa*, Bogotá: Carlos Valencia, 1978–1986, 4 volumes). The contribution of the *Handbook of Qualitative Research*, a monumental work edited by Norman K. Denzin and Yvonne S. Lincoln (Thousand Oaks, CA: Sage Publications, 1994) has been immense, in particular Part V entitled 'The Art of Interpretation: Evaluation and Presentation'. On truth and authenticity, see Fritjof Capra, *Belonging to the Universe: Explorations on the Frontiers of Science and Spirituality* (San Francisco, CA: Harper, 1993, pp. 144–162).

6.  Proponents of this group were recognized Colombian and foreign writers known for their originality, imagination, style and concern for social issues: Azriel Bibliowicz, J.E. Pardo, Karl Kohut, Claude Fell, Óscar Collazos, R.H. Moreno Durán and Rubén Sierra, as well as Parra and Giraldo. This group has announced the upcoming publication of essays prepared for the Congress.

7.  See David L. Altheide and John M. Johnson, 'Criteria for Assessing Interpretive Validity in Qualitative Research', in N.K. Denzin and Yvonna S. Lincoln (eds), *Handbook of Qualitative Research* (Thousand Oaks, CA: Sage, 1994), pp. 485–499, on metanarratives, style, reflexive ethnography, rhetoric and discourse analysis.

# Reference

Fals Borda, O. (1979–1986). *Historia doble de la Costa*, Vols. 1–4. Mompox y Loba, Bogotá: Universidad Nacional de Colombia/Banco de la República/El Áncora Editores.

## Orlando Fals Borda, by Juan Ignacio Piovani (Argentina)

Orlando Fals Borda (1925–2008) was, arguably, the most distinguished Colombian sociologist. His intellectual contributions to the social sciences, in particular to the field of methodology, and his enduring social and political engagement with deprived peasant communities in Latin America earned him wide respect both in academe and among social movements across the subcontinent.

Fals Borda was born in 1925 in Barranquilla, on the Caribbean coast of Colombia. After completing his secondary education he moved to the United States, where he first studied English literature at the University of Dubuque. In 1953 he obtained a Masters degree in Sociology from the University of Minnesota, with a dissertation later published by the University of Florida Press under the title *Peasant Society in the Colombian Andes*. In 1955 he was awarded a PhD in Sociology from the University of Florida. His thesis, also focused on the peasants' life in his native Colombia – actually in a particular region of the country – was published in Spanish as *El hombre y la tierra en Boyacá: Bases sociológicas e históricas para una reforma agraria* (Ediciones Documentos Colombianos, 1957). Upon his return to Colombia in the late 1950s, Fals Borda initiated a remarkable career that would eventually combine sociological research with institution building, social activism and politics.

According to Gonzalo Cataño,[1] Fals' intellectual trajectory went through three different phases. The first one comprised his sociological studies in the United States and the early stages of his commitment to sociological institution building in Colombia. Apart from his noteworthy contributions to the field of rural sociology, based on research conducted for his dissertations, his graduate studies in Minnesota and Florida gave him a systematic acquaintance with social science's theories and methods, which convinced him of the importance of advancing 'scientific' sociology at home. This was framed within a wider movement that favored the institutionalization of empirical sociology across Latin America. Until then, most university chairs of Sociology in the region had been occupied by academics who were attached to rather essayistic traditions, and whose concepts and approaches were drawn mainly from Law and Philosophy. This was also the case in Colombia, where Salvador Camacho Roldán had started teaching Sociology at the National University in 1882.

As was only to be expected, Fals became a leading figure of this 1950s regional trend in favor of the institutionalization of a 'scientific' and 'empirical' Sociology. Unsurprisingly, his greatest institutional achievement in this period was the establishment – together with the influential left-wing Catholic priest and activist Camilo Torres – of Latin America's first Faculty of Sociology at the National University of Colombia, where he was Dean from 1959 to 1967.

The second phase, from the mid-1960s until his departure from university, was characterized by 'committed sociology', in the words of Cataño. This was a time of political radicalization in Colombia. His close friend and colleague, Camilo Torres, had left the university and the Church in order to join the National Liberation Army, and died in 1966 in Patio Cemento in the midst of an armed combat against the Colombian Army's Fifth Brigade. Fals Borda was no stranger to these historical events and, accordingly, turned his intellectual interests towards politics and the State, reflecting on themes such as power, the ruling class and social movements. In a certain sense, it is also arguable that this period marked a transition in Fals' sociological thought from structural functionalism – which was dominant at American universities when he was a student and which he had 'imported' into Colombia to promote 'scientific' sociology – towards more critical approaches. This is evident both in his major work of the period, later published in English as *Subversion and Social Change in Colombia* (Columbia University Press, 1969), and in his critique of sociological conservatism, which for him tends to reject political involvement in the name of objectivity.

The third phase implied a more radical change in Fals's career: he decided to abandon the university in order to get in closer touch with peasants and social movements so as to combine sociological research with political involvement and the transformation of society. Since the early 1970s, this new approach gave shape to what he called *sentipensante* sociology, which coalesces reason and feelings (through empathy) in the process of knowledge production. This standpoint relies on a particular methodological approach: Participatory Action Research (PAR).

Despite being already a well-known figure within Latin American social sciences, this methodological proposal in particular, which meant that social research should not only produce knowledge about social reality, but also transform it (with a decisive involvement of the social scientists and the local communities) turned him into an unavoidable intellectual reference and a model for committed sociology across the subcontinent and beyond. The text included in this book is part of his attempt to systematize PAR. With sophisticated arguments, Fals engages in some of the most relevant epistemological and methodological debates of the social sciences, proving that his proposal – in the face of all the 'purist' mistrust – was not just about naïve social activism, but was based on a solid – but of course disputable – scientific perspective.

## Note

1. Cataño, G. (2008) 'Orlando Fals Borda, sociólogo del compromiso', *Revista de Economía Institucional*, 10(19): 79–98.

# 4

# Of Don Quixote and Windmills in Latin America[1]

*Aníbal Quijano (Peru)*

What we refer to today as Latin America was constituted together with and as part of the current pattern of power that prevails on a worldwide scale. It is here that 'coloniality' and 'globality' were configured and established[2] as the basis and constitutive modes for a new pattern of power. Such was the point of departure of the historical process that came to define Latin America's historical and structural dependence and that gave birth, in that same movement, to the constitution of Western Europe as the world center for the control of that power. And it was this very same movement that defined the new material and subjective elements at the root of the social existence we now call 'modernity'.

Put in other terms, Latin America was both the original space and inaugural time of the historical period and world in which we now live. In this specific sense, it was the first entity/historical identity of the current colonial/modern world system and of the entire period we refer to as modernity.

Nonetheless, this originating place and time of a historical period, this rich source that produced the basal elements of new world society, was robbed of its centrality, as well as of the attributes and fruits of modernity. Thus, not all of the new historical potential could be fulfilled in Latin America; nor was the historical period and its new social place in the world able to become completely modern. In other words, both were defined at that point and continue to reproduce themselves today as colonial/modern.[3] Why is this so?

Comparing the history of Europe and Japan, Junichiro Tanizaki[4] tells us that the Europeans were fortunate enough to have their history unfold through stages, each deriving from the internal transformation of the last. Yet with regard to Japan, particularly since the Second World War, the course of history was altered from outside by the military and technological superiority of 'the West'.

This type of reflection validates a Eurocentric perspective and the characteristic evolutionary gaze that accompanies it. It can thus be seen as providing testimony of the world hegemony of Eurocentrism as a mode of producing and controlling subjectivity and knowledge. Yet in regard to Western Europe itself, this perspective becomes more of an indication of the late intellectual hegemony of its central-northern regions, and thus can be considered alien and contrary to the legacy of Don Quixote. On the occasion of the 400th anniversary of this foundational masterpiece, we recognize that it is time to return to its legacy. The marvelous scene in Cervantes's masterpiece in which Don Quixote throws himself against a giant and is knocked over by a windmill is, most certainly, the most powerful historical image of the entire period of early modernity. It is the (non) encounter between, on the one hand, an aristocratic ideology – that which marks Don Quixote's own perception – to which social practice now only corresponds in a very fragmented and inconsistent manner, and, on the other hand, new social practices – represented by the windmill – which are en route to generalization, but to which a consistent and legitimating ideology does not yet correspond. And as this familiar image suggests, it is a moment in which the new has not yet been completely ushered in, while the old has not yet truly passed away.

In reality, this (non)encounter shoots through the entire book: the new common sense that emerges with the new pattern of power produced [through] America, with its mercantile pragmatism and its respect for 'the powerful Lord Money' (*Quevedo dixit*) has not yet become hegemonic, nor has it been constituted consistently, although it nonetheless occupies a growing place in the population's mentality. That is, it is already engaged in a dispute over hegemony with the old aristocratic sense of social existence. And the latter, although beginning to yield, is still active, in different forms and shapes – depending on whom we are talking about and where they are located. It continues to inhabit people's subjectivity and resist the surrender of its age-old dominance.

What must be noted, in the specific context of what at that time was the future of Spain, is that neither of these perspectives or meanings can exist, nor take shape, separately or in the absence of the other. This intersubjectivity could be nothing other that a combination – impossible in theory but inevitable in practice – of mercantile pragmatism and chivalrous views.

We are talking about a moment in history in which different times and stories do not come together in any dualistic way or converge on any linear or one-directional evolutionary path, as Eurocentrist doctrines have been preaching since the end of the seventeenth century. Rather, these are complex, contradictory and discontinuous associations between fragmented and changing structures of relationships, senses and meanings, of multiple geo-historical origins and simultaneous and intersecting actions – all of which are, nonetheless, part and parcel of one singular new world that was in the process of constituting itself. It is no coincidence that the windmill itself was a technology that had been inherited from Bagdad, integrated through an Islamic and Judaic world in the southern part of the Iberian peninsula when the former was still a part of Arab hegemony in the Mediterranean; a rich, productive, cultivated and sophisticatedly developed society, center of the world trade in goods, ideas and scientific, philosophical and technological knowledge. 'Chivalry' however was the societal model that the militarily dominant but socially and culturally backwards nobility from the northern part of the Peninsula still attempted to impose – without complete success – upon the remains of the defeated Islamo-Judaic society, subjugating and colonizing the autonomous communities of the peninsula, albeit not with complete success.

This aristocratic regime, dominated as it was by the Counter Reformation and its Inquisition, did not take long to decree the expulsion of 'Moors' and 'Jews' and to impose upon them the infamous 'certificate of pure blood' – the first ' ethnic cleansing' of the entire colonial/modern period. This same archaic aristocratic and feudal model of social existence was also to induce the Crown to centralize its political domination. More than seeking to produce a common (that is, national) identity, it was interested in imposing a regime of internal colonialism upon the rest of the region – one that in fact continues to this day. This was how those in power were able to impede the process of nationalization that unfolded later in North Central Europe, following along the same course and movement as societal *embourgeoisement*.

After America, during a time of rapid capitalist expansion when a growing part of the new peninsular society had fallen under the new pattern of power, even this aristocratic regime could no longer avoid placing its own two feet on mercantilist soil. Yet it continued to hold its head high in the archaic sky of chivalry, which, in its own imagination, still offered equal riches.

Without this infamous (non)encounter that converged with all the disastrous effects that expelling Moors and Jews had on material and cultural production, we would not be able to explain how, with the commercial benefits wrought from the precious minerals and vegetables of the Americas through the non-paid work of servant 'Indians' and 'Black' slaves, Spain had embarked (despite appearances to the contrary) on a prolonged historical course that would lead it from its position at the center of the greatest imperial power to persisting peripheral backwardness within the new colonial/modern world system.

The above-described trajectory renders it evident that aristocratic power, the dominant and immediate beneficiary of the first period of colonial power and modernity, was already too archaic to ride this new, young and spirited horse, guiding it along a route that would benefit its country and the world. Such a power had already demonstrated its inability to turn fully and completely into a bourgeoisie capable of riding the crest of the democratizing wave and the conflicts characteristic of this new pattern of power, and of shaping the heterogeneous population into a nation, as its rivals and successors in North Central Europe were able to do. On the contrary, this archaic dominion had been rotting away over the centuries, caught in an ambiguous feudal-mercantile labyrinth, in an unviable attempt to preserve its power on the basis of an internal colonialism that had been imposed upon the diverse identities of the population, precisely at the outset of world capitalism and in spite of the truly exceptional resources of the coloniality of power.

Where is the difference rooted? The difference, most certainly, is America. The 'Crown', that is, the Hapsburgs, colonial proprietors of the colossal riches that America produced and of the endless supply of free labor from 'Black' slaves and 'Indian' serfs, believed that by having control over these riches they would be able to banish 'Moors' and 'Jews' at no great loss, and in fact, with real gains in terms of control and power. This led the Hapsburgs to use violence to de-democratize the social life of independent communities and foist an internal colonialism and aristocratic rule originating in the Central European feudal model upon other national identities (Catalunyans, Basques, Andalusians, Galicians, Navarrese and Valencians). The well-known result was, on the one hand, the destruction of domestic production and the internal market that it fed, and, on the other hand, the backwards steps taken in relation to secularization and the stagnation of the processes of democratization and enlightenment that colonial modernity had brought – and which, among other things, had given birth to *Don Quixote*.

What impoverished and enslaved the future Spain, and also turned it into the central seat of political and cultural obscurantism in the West over the next four centuries, was precisely that which permitted the emergent central northern part of Western Europe to become rich and secular, and later favored the development of a pattern of conflict that led to the democratization of the regions and countries that made up the latter. And it was just this, the historic hegemony that this pattern made possible, which enabled these countries to elaborate their own version of modernity and rationality, and to make their exclusive appropriation of the historical-cultural identity of the 'West', of the Greco-Roman historical heritage which, nonetheless, had previously and over a long period of time been preserved and worked on as part of the Islamo-Judaic Mediterranean legacy.

All of this took place – and the following point must not be neglected, for it is vital for our understanding of history – at a time when the coloniality of power was still exclusively a pattern of power relations in America and between America and the emergent 'Western Europe' – in other words, at precisely the moment this 'Western Europe' was being produced, linked as it was to America. It is absolutely necessary to recognize such historical implications of the establishment of this new pattern of power and the reciprocal historical production of America and Western Europe as, respectively, a nexus of historico-structural dependence and hub of control from which this new power was wielded.

It is true that, today, capitalism has finally been consolidated in Spain, with the resources and support of the new European Community, under the auspices of the new financial capital. But all trace of the old forms of social order has not yet disappeared. And the current conflicts over autonomy, as well as ETA terrorism, seeking national independence for the Basque country, include the realization that such vestiges remain, notwithstanding the scope of the changes that have taken place. No one has had a clearer perception of this historical (non)encounter than Cervantes – no one, that is, but his very own Cide Hamete Benengeli.

The following represents for us, present-day Latin Americans, the greatest epistemological and theoretical lesson to be taken from Don Quixote: that the historico-structural heterogeneity, the co-presence of historical times and structural fragments of forms of social existence, of varying historical and geo-cultural origins, are the primary modes of existence and movement of all society and all history. Not as in the Eurocentric vision, with its radical dualism paradoxically associated with homogeneity, continuity, unilinearity and one-directional evolution – in a word: 'progress'. For it is power – and thereby power struggles and their shifting balances – that articulates the heterogeneous forms of social existence produced at different historical moments and in distant spaces, bringing them together and structuring them within one and the same world, in a concrete society, into historically specific patterns of power.

This is also precisely the issue regarding the specific space/time that today we refer to as Latin America. Due to its historical and structural constitution as dependent on the current pattern of power, it has been constrained all this time as the privileged space where the coloniality of power plays itself out. And since in this pattern of power the hegemonic mode of production and control of knowledge is Eurocentrism, it is a history replete with combinations, contradictions and (non)encounters that are analogous to those that Cide Hamete Benengeli could identify in his own space/time.

By its very nature, the Eurocentric perspective distorts (when it does not block altogether) perception of our social and historical experience, all the while taking its own time to admit that the latter is real.[5] It operates in today's world, and particularly in Latin America, in the same way that the chivalrous life did in Don Quixote's view of things. As a consequence, our problems cannot be perceived in any other way but through this distorted form, nor can they be confronted and resolved in any way that is not partial or deformed. Thus, the coloniality of power has turned Latin America into a scenario of (non)encounters between our experience, our knowledge and our historical memory.

Within this context, it is not surprising that our history has been unable to enjoy an autonomous and coherent movement, but has, rather, been configured as a long and tortuous labyrinth where our unsolved problems haunt us like ghosts from our past. And this labyrinth cannot be recognized and understood. In other words, we cannot debate and identify our problems if we are not first able to recognize, summon up and engage with our ghosts.

The ghosts from our past, however – like the creature that inhabits the darkness of Elsinore or those which Marx and Engels wrote about in 1848 – have a dark, heavy and matted density. And when they walk onto the stage of history, they tend to bring violent turbulence and often irreversible mutations. In Elsinore, the doubt-ridden Hamlet is in the end transformed into an exasperated hero whose unflinching sword strikes many down, in the most direct attempt to resolve conflicts. In our other example, the furtive ghost that haunted Europe during the mid-nineteenth century later emerges as a central protagonist in the next, with its two world wars, violent revolutions and counterrevolutions, powerful though often dashed hopes, frustrations and defeats, and the lives and deaths of millions that have still not left us. Today, it has the world besieged.

Thus, the ghosts of history cannot be convoked without a cost. Those that belong to Latin America have given ample proof of their ability to provoke conflict and violence, precisely because they represent the product of violent crises and seismic historical mutations whose outcomes remain our unresolved problems. These phantoms still inhabit our social existence, keeping their hold on our memory, upsetting each historical project, erupting frequently in our lives, leaving the dead, wounded and beaten in their wake; the historical mutations that could at last put them to rest are still beyond our reach. Nonetheless, it is not only important that we find a way to do so. It is absolutely imperative. For as these patterns of power reach the apex of their development, at the precise moment in which their worst tendencies are exacerbated through their worldwide dominion, Latin America remains not only a prisoner of the 'coloniality of power' and dependency, but, for this very reason, exposed to the risk of never arriving at the new world the current crisis has prefigured – the deepest and most global crisis of the whole period of colonialism/modernity.

In order to deal with such ghosts and perhaps find some way to have them shed light on our path before they disappear forever, we must free our historical retina from its Eurocentric blindness and re-apprehend our historical experience. Therefore, it is not only desirable but truly necessary that Don Quixote ride forth again, so that he may aid us in undoing the tangled point of departure of our history: the epistemic trap of Eurocentrism that for the past 500 years has left us in the darkness of the coloniality of power, where we are only able to discern the figure of giants – while those who dominate us are able to maintain control and exclusive use of our windmills.

## Notes

1. This is a fragment of the text originally published in Spanish as A. Quijano, 'Don Quijote y los molinos de viento en América Latina' in *Libros y Artes, Revista de Cultura de la Biblioteca Nacional del Perú*, Lima, No. 10, April 2005, pp. 14–16. An extended revised version was published in English in *Estudos Avanzados*, Vol. 19, No. 55, São Paulo, Sept./Dec. 2005.

2. For more on these categories, see Aníbal Quijano: 'Colonialidad del Poder, Eurocentrismo y América Latina', in Edgardo Lander, (Ed.) *Colonialidad del Saber, Eurocentrismo y Ciencias Sociales* (Buenos Aires, CLACSO, 2000, pp. 201 ff). Also by the same author, see 'Colonialidad del poder, globalización y democracia'. Originally published *in Tendencias Básicas de Nuestra Epoca* (Caracas, Instituto de Altos Estudios Internacionales Pedro Gual, 2000, pp. 21–65) and 'Colonialidad y modernidad/ racionalidad', which originally appeared in *Revista del Instituto Indigenista Peruano*, Vol. 13, No. 29, Lima, 1992, pp. 11–20.

3.  Immanuel Wallerstein coined the concept of the Modern World-System in the first volume of his book *The Modern World-System* (Academic Press, 1974, 1980, 1989) as a system of states and regions associated with the expansion of European capitalism. In 1991, Aníbal Quijano introduced the concept of the 'Coloniality of Power' in 'Colonialidad y Modernidad/Racionalidad', (Quijano, 1992) . Both theoretical proposals finally found a common course in the joint publication of both authors, in the text 'Americanity as a Concept or the Americas in the Modern World-System', in *International Journal of Social Sciences*, No. 134, Paris, UNESCO-ERES, November 1992, pp. 617–627. Since then there has been growing use of the concept of the Colonial/Modern World System. See, among others, Walter Mignolo: *Local Histories, Global Designs. Coloniality, Subaltern Knowledges and Border Thinking* (Princeton University Press, Princeton, 2000) and Ramón Grosfoguel's *Colonial Subjects* (Los Angeles, University of California Press, 2003).

4.  *In Praise of Shadows* (New York: Leete's Island Books, 1977).

5.  This issue is discussed in 'Colonialidad del Poder, Eurocentrismo y América Latina', op. cit. and also dealt with in 'Colonialidad del Poder y Clasificación Social', originally in the *Festschrift* for Immanuel Wallerstein and in the *Journal of World-Systems Research*, Vol. VI, No. 2, Colorado, Institute of Research on World-Systems, Summer/ Fall, 2000, Special Issue, edited by Giovanni Arrighi and Walter Goldfrank, Part I.

## References

Bhabha, Homi (1991). 'The world and the home,' *Social Text 31/32* (1992): 141–153.

Clímaco, Danilo (2014). 'Prólogo'. In: *Aníbal Quijano, Cuestiones y Horizontes. De la dependencia histórico-estructural a la colonialidad/descolonialidad del poder*. Buenos Aires: CLACSO.

Quijano, Aníbal (1991). 'Colonialidad y Modernidad/Racionalidad'. In: Heraclio Bonilla (Ed.), '*Los Conquistados*'. Bogotá: Flacso-Tercer Mundo. In English: 'Coloniality and Modernity/Rationality', in: Goran Therborn (Ed.), *Globalizations and Modernities*. Stockholm, Sweden: FRN, 1999.

Quijano, Aníbal & Laguna, Eduardo A. (n.d.). '*Interview: Aníbal Quijano Padre de la teoría de la Colonialidad del Poder*'. Accessed at www.urp.edu.pe/urp/pdf/anibal_quijano.pdf (February 2, 2018).

## Aníbal Quijano, by Cláudio Costa Pinheiro (Brazil)

According to the Indian historian S. Bhattacharya, only small villages give birth to outstanding economists. What, then, to say of sociologists who hail from small places – especially one of today's most influential Latin American scholars? Aníbal Quijano (1928–2018) became widely known for coining 'Coloniality of Power', a concept that articulates notions such as Eurocentrism, race, modernity, colonialism and the exploitation of non-European groups, as issues that combine the

*(Continued)*

(Continued)

historical and present-day conditions for dependency and underdevelopment of Latin America. More recently, *Coloniality of Power* has been expanded to include the epistemic dimension of the political economy of knowledge production in an analysis of this region's relegation to its peripheral condition. The concept initially appeared in 1991 (Quijano, 1991). It had a major impact on intellectuals from across the Global South and made Quijano into an internationally renowned scholar. But he wasn't always recognized as such.

Born in 1928 in Yanama, a small village in the mountains of central Peru, Quijano attended high school in Yungay before moving to Lima to begin his university studies. Yungay would later be destroyed by an avalanche that killed most of its inhabitants, including Quijano's own father. This affected Quijano's emotional landscape and led him to his vision of himself as a displaced individual: 'a person from everywhere, as the place where I lived no longer exists' (Quijano and Laguna, n.d.: 2) – an 'unhomely being' in Homi Bhabha's words (1991). Besides its impact on his life, this event may also have honed an ability to recognize how locally rooted circumstances are equally subsumed by global conditions.

Quijano pursued his academic training in Peru (a Bachelor's degree and PhD, 1964) and Chile (Masters at FLACSO), having a shared background in History, Political Sciences and Law, which explains his interest in the history of political categories and their consequences for the present day. As a professor, he circulated among distinct Latin American universities – mostly in Peru, with stays in Brazil, Puerto Rico, Mexico, Chile, Venezuela and Ecuador – and in institutions in Europe and the United States, where he was professor in the Department of Sociology at Binghamton University (New York), until his death.

Despite his international renown, Danilo Clímaco (2014) argues that Quijano has been a local intellectual for most of his life, and that the global perspective in his work which led to his transformation into an international scholar came much later. Although his international debut dates to the 1960s, Quijano was initially received as a Latin Americanist, confined to themes concerning Peru and its thinkers, the Andean region, Latin American history, development and politics, and so forth. It was not until the 1990s that he was converted into a global thinker when his writings on *Coloniality* as an intrinsic facet of power were appropriated by Latin American scholars' diasporic community in the US, especially by Walter Mignolo, being incorporated into the discussions of *De-colonization, Border Thinking, Exteriority* and *Southern Thinking*.

The fact that Quijano was a local intellectual obviously does not diminish his importance. Ultimately, localism was not unique to the Andean region, as other areas of Latin America were also home to sophisticated thinkers working in a fragile editorial market that limited the reach of their ideas. One should recall that Quijano belonged to an Andean tradition of thought which combined academic participation, political activism and different forms of writing (from essays to poetry and fiction), and included key figures such as José Carlos Mariátegui (Peru, 1894–1930; about whom Quijano wrote extensively), Jorge Cornejo Polar (Peru, 1930–2004) and Silvia Rivera Cusicanqui (Bolivia, 1949), among others.

As a prominent Latin American intellectual, Quijano took part in Marxist and Dependency Theory debates, and joined the Economic Commission for Latin America and the Caribbean (ECLAC). His global approach drew on distinct theoretical frameworks that later conditioned his view of the systemic issues which affected different regions that, like Latin America, also lay on the peripheries of capitalism.

In his text included in this volume 'Of Don Quijote and the Windmills in Latin America' (previously published in Portuguese and Spanish in 2005, 2006 and 2008), Quijano summarizes some of the key themes of his agenda. Written as an essay, it presents a macro-narrative of the tensions stemming from the new patterns of power and conflict established during European colonial expansion, both in the Iberian Peninsula and in the conquered world. Colonialism also consolidated a hegemonic model of society read as an epistemic conquest and as the destruction of other forms of diversity through the subjugation, banishment or extermination of non-European populations. New classifications were created in this process that promoted both 'the first "ethnic cleansing" of the colonial/modern period' and the sociological invisibility of these groups (Moors, Jews, indigenous peoples, Blacks, etc.). For him, race became the first social category of modernity to address new patterns of power and global social domination. He focused on concepts that have characterized his contribution to a historical sociology of power since the 1990s, particularly the articulation of modernity, *Coloniality* and Eurocentrism, in which the production of modernity was an expression of the *Coloniality of Power*. In this context, Eurocentrism refers to the distortion of local narratives through the creation of a new hegemony translated in terms of 'a mode of producing and controlling subjectivity and knowledge'. Throughout this essay, Quijano emphasizes that the Coloniality of Power does not only concern the past, since it gave birth to 'ghosts' that persistently haunt Latin America until today – an image that evokes spectral metaphors common to both Marxism and Latin American magical realism.

One central aspect throughout Quijano's narrative is the conception of Latin America as 'both the original space and inaugural time of the historical period and world in which we now live. In this specific sense, it was the first entity/historical identity of the current colonial/modern world system and of the entire period we refer to as modernity' (see p. 64 in this volume). This statement is as much revealing of his individual trajectory as it is of the capacity of some Latin American scholars to refer to this continent not as an exceptional entity but as part of a process that affected other peripheries equally submitted to the historical and durable effects of colonialism and resonates with the current revival of Global History. Quijano's *Coloniality of Power* has been critical for de-colonial thinking, in dialogue with post-colonial studies, and with some Indian historiography, revealing trends similar to other peripheries affected by European imperialism.

Quijano himself did not connect his own ideas to the debates of other epistemic communities in the Global South: instead, he continued to insist that Latin America was the starting point (the historical socio-genesis) of the entire process. Clímaco is most certainly correct to observe Quijano's localism, given that the Peruvian scholar seems like an apt example of Tolstoy's famous epigraph, 'paint your village and you will paint the world'. He painted his world, represented by the admission of Latin America into the European History.

In whatever way, during the 1990s, along with Enrique Dussell and other Latin American scholars of his generation, Quijano would be metamorphosed into one of the new heroes of the (post)colonial studies. This process led *Coloniality* to be converted into both a (quasi-)theoretical concept as well as a blueprint for the project of de-colonization of knowledge within the social sciences, in its claims to regain universal relevance.

# 5

# On the Pessimism in the
# Social Sciences[1]

*Edelberto Torres Rivas (Guatemala–Costa Rica)*

In the 1950s, the institutionalization of teaching and research in the social sciences slowly began in Mexico, Argentina, Brazil and Chile. This was in the context of the expansion of university enrollment and the professionalization of a group of intellectuals who began to do research, teach courses and publish books and journals on the social sciences. They maintained an attitude of 'modernity' both in relation to what they produced, as well as to the results they expected to obtain, in a cultural and social environment that was not yet prepared for those inputs. This is a reference to a seminal moment that coincided with the perception of development possibilities that were assumed to come about as the awaited time of capitalist modernization, so many times disregarded, apparently dawned.

With a will fed by illusions of development, these intellectuals sought to substitute the traditional agrarian economy with an industrialized one – along with the urbanization of the population and new educational opportunities, the secularization of social life, broader political participation, progress in relation to the rationalization of the State and the establishment of a political democracy. All these are signals of a condition of modernity, attained along a sustained process of modernization. This operational conception of modernity is not casual. We have been formed with a general historic perspective, by a cultural inheritance of modernity, which nourished our lives and hopes. We have been taught that change is propelled by two powerful forces that represent, on the one hand, economic progress, science, technological discoveries and material transformations, that is, *scientific reason at the service of human well-being*; on the other hand, there is the force of secularization that frees us from oppression, cultural backwardness, religious or magical explanations, from the traditional or charismatic powers that make us conscious, autonomous and free men. In other words, *the political reason that modernizes social and political life in community*.

Sociology arose with a rejection of reality, assuming reality to be part of a history of malformations for which its moment of surgery had come. This shame resulted in the development of a moral/intellectual/political commitment in the social sciences, which came about in a moment favored by a euphoric post-war developmentalist environment.

In this end of the century, for reasons that we will not develop here, we live a contradictory experience within the process of modernization, which tries to make liberal democracy a compatible political regime – in the new spaces of modernity – with the free market as a model for development and technical progress. The first drawbacks of this pairing are beginning to be felt, not so much because throughout history we have long experienced this difficult coexistence, but because of rising symptoms of current ambiguity, in which democracy is lived as the administration of an electoral formality, and economic growth as an experience that evermore excludes the majorities. If we were to go deeper into this review, democracy should be supported in a less unequal and more inclusive society. But these results can only be reached through different ways of regulating the market by the State, which would be unbearable if the levels of competitiveness and efficacy are to be maintained. Globalization in poor societies leaves no choices. The liberal democratic edifice is guided by free market logic where political secularization results ultimately in an adversary of economic renovation. *There is already more emphasis on the liberal aspect than the democratic one.*

## Modernization and Modernity: The Triumphant Reason

(A) The sociology of modernization came out first and presented the process of change as a transition born from a conceptual dichotomy, as a movement from traditional society – rural, sacred, analphabetic, authoritarian, prescriptive – to the industrial, modern society – urban, secular, democratic, elective, etc.[2] It was understood that Latin American regional diversity found itself in diverse moments of this transition and that it was possible to hasten it in many of these societies, if they satisfied the variables/requisites more developed societies had satisfied. The key to change was the growing differentiation in the various dimensions of life: in the economy, in the political institutions, in the social roles. Modern complexity is the expression of a large-scale specialization led by reason and carried out by discipline and the will of the State, as well as the innovative acquisition of special actors – the original entrepreneurs from day one.

The set of explanations proposed for Latin America by Germani is based on the implicit conviction of full trust in the rational capacity of the middle classes promoting development. It was just a matter of ensuring the fidelity of the conditions of the historical model, to attain the desired results. Optimism was derived from the example of the consolidated democracies in the prosperous West, reflected on a wisdom that had exhibited its efficacy in the happy example of the big industrialized societies. The final synthesis, in behavioral code, was the importance of introducing changes in the types of predominant social actions which should be converted from a prescriptive (closed, immutable, imposed) into an elective action (rational, open, free). The institutionalization of change as a renewed attitude was also necessary, leaving behind the rigid respect for the traditional, the immutable.

(B) Far from this explanation of change, but still encouraged by a promising horizon as the sociology of modernization, the developmentalist version of change emerged. This was created within an economistic matrix of development, whose starting point was the so-many times proclaimed expansive force of capital, proposed a century ago by Marx. It was said that capitalism was animated by a tendency to expand worldwide as a result of an intrinsic dynamic quality of the productive forces. The vision that needs to be highlighted is that the possibilities for growth on the margins and the inherent inequalities of the global expansion of capital would produce – expressed in topographic language – an interdependent 'center' and a 'periphery' with an asymmetrical bond.

This imminent tendency of the capitalist system to produce and deepen inequalities was perceived in a particularly acute way by Raúl Prebisch, and further elaborated upon, as the starting point of a bold theoretical proposal, corrective of the vices produced by development in the periphery.[3] Prebisch's bourgeois optimism values development as a possibility and a necessity based on a historically viable and theoretically valid set of assumptions. Latin American backwardness is the effect – among other equally important causes – of the nature of unequal commercial exchange and unequal distribution of the fruits of technological progress, all of which is a consequence of backward economic structures. Existing inequalities reproduce, through commerce, the distance between the industrial center and the agricultural periphery.

Accordingly, the answer was to also industrialize the periphery, which would absorb the redundant rural population, create endogenous mechanisms of accumulation and technological innovation and offer goods at lower prices; all of which would produce an active social differentiation and would improve the external unbalances and the terms of international exchange. These results could be anticipated with the appropriate political will of the State and of the actors involved in change.

Modernization projects therefore could be planned and directed by the State. This, while a promoting agent of change itself would build the communications, energy and services infrastructures, facilitated through fiscal and tariff incentives, and would defend the internal market so that young underdeveloped industries could grow in 'greenhouse conditions'. To organize growth requires public policies drawn up for specific purposes, with technical resources made available due to a deliberate will to change. Along with industrialization it was necessary to modify the agrarian structure and the components that accompany the production of large estates and smallholdings. There was also preparation of aspects related to the development of fiscal, monetary and salary policies. As can be seen, this was a long-scope reformist project, arguably the boldest and most thorough during the historical time when it took place, and because of its outcomes.[4] It should be added that in relation to these proposals, the right-wing entrepreneurs distrusted the means and the left-wing workers the ends.

The project of modernization of the periphery developed by Prebisch/ECLAC reiterated the need for directed change, the road to industrialization as a proposal for development planning. It was a proposal for society to implement so-called 'inward development' policies, driven against those directed from the outside and based on external demand. A model of high economic rationality for the benefit of society, especially for local entrepreneurs, was now postulated; a strategy that required extensive State protection – it could almost be said – and a type of politically driven capitalistic growth. Management plans for the economy were needed, implemented by technical authorities and a State capable of implementation.

(C) Through the criticism of ECLA's structuralism and the sociology of modernization a proposal for the interpretation of Latin American history emerged. Based on the refutation of both and making use of a structural perspective, the *notion of dependency* arose (which many elevated to the status of theory, but it was not so). It was developed, in the late

1960s, by an important group of social scientists living in Chile and led by F.H. Cardoso and E. Faletto and then cheered by a generation of intellectuals from around the world in the years to come. In their seminal book,[5] they argue that underdevelopment appeared historically along with the expansion of commercial and later industrial capitalism linked to the same market economies in various stages of productive differentiation, which led them to occupying different positions in the overall structure of the capitalist system.

Hence there is not only a difference of condition in the production system but also a special role within the international order. This implies also a defined structure of dominant relationships. The novelty was to analyze how underdeveloped economies became linked historically to the world market and the ways internal social groups were formed and who defined the relationships towards the outside. The result of this approach involves recognizing that *from a political view there is some sort of dependency implied by underdevelopment.*

Dependency of the less developed countries arises with the economic expansion of the most developed countries, which implies a form of domination manifested in the performance of groups that locally control production. There is a subordination which, in extreme situations, affects decisions made on matters of production and consumption in a dependent society, based on the dynamics and the interests of developed economies (classes). The notion of dependency[6] refers to the conditions regarding the existence and operation of the economic and political system, in its internal and external expressions. The development of a society does not suppose its independence, because *there is no immediate link between the differentiation of the economic system and the formation of autonomous decision-making centers.* Substantially altering the relationship of dependency relies on the political sphere of social behavior. If based on a global interpretation of development, pure stimulus from the market is insufficient to explain growth. In short, it is internal political and social factors (linked to external hegemonic dynamics) that produce policies that take advantage of the opportunities for economic growth. The dependent interpretation on the formation and development of the nation-state requires that the political core of the internal social forces have some autonomy from external economic relations, which nevertheless remain crucial.

The analytical contribution of dependency approach focuses on the fact that dependency is not external, as in the theory of imperialism, but an internal specific expression, as seen in the relationship between classes and groups of power: that is, it implies a situation of dominance that structurally involves a link with the outside. Hence the intentional reading provided by a leftist generation, turning an analytical proposal into a political program: to replace the classes that 'support' dependency, the bourgeoisie, with an alliance that would not act on behalf of the State as the administrative apparatus of foreign domination.

The modernization of the structures of dependency, the strengthening of national decision-making centers, involved the construction of the State as a unifying axis, as the expression of a modern, democratic power. Backwardness is not a structural fatality linked to the condition of dependency. In an *economicist* approach, ECLAC proposed the notion of dependency, arguing for a policy of change: a *politicist* version of economic independence, inspired by both the possible scope of modernity and the affirmation, as common background, of the universalism of reason; technical-bureaucratic in one case, political-cultural in the other.

Of relevance here was to avoid isolation from the cultural models necessarily coming from the center, but to incorporate them into the periphery in the new political conditions favorable to the breakdown of the dependent-structural alliance. The intervention of popular groups as actors in this scenario was a leftist derivation but unavoidable in the notion of dependency.

There was then a convergence between the 'dependency theory' as a plea for the nation, with Marxism theory as the anti-imperialist project. With this interpretative inspiration, a part of the social sciences in Latin America reached its voluntarist climax as an intellectual tool for change; a young generation was indoctrinated, who were mostly political activists rather than social scientists. This Latin American reissue of the so-called 'academic Marxism' in Europe was more an ideological choice than a matter of scientific study. In fact, Marxist theory was always in debt with the reality in most of these countries. Furthermore, the rational root of Marxism was replaced by the emotional experience with a Guevarista tone. And then the commitment to the social sciences was hopelessly mediated with political activism of social scientists.

However, the social sciences found in Marxism a source of symbolic inspiration, a quarry of problematic issues and concepts that enriched the language, although many of them adapted to the uses of an insurrection feeling, or a well-toned cultural reference. In short, Marxism provided an interpretation of the imagined reality and an approach to the theory of revolution. In reality, Marxisms were many (Trotskyists, Althusserians,

*Edelberto Torres Rivas*

pro-Chinese, pro-Soviet communist parties, Gramscians, and a thousand forms of orthodoxies) which, translated into militant language, first provided an unquestioned confidence in the knowledge they 'produced' and then, an overflowing enthusiasm for the possibilities of change.

The illustrated reason for development planning from ECLAC, was paralleled with the enlightened belief in the revolution, aimed at mobilizing militants. As already mentioned, they had in common an optimistic view of the future, which they foresaw as better because it could change. By being moldable it could be improved, because reality is fraught with the rational. Against such possibilities, the roles played by the technician who anticipated in his speech a modern society and the ideologists whose proclamations were inflamed with convictions, and who dreamed of a better world, were key. Nevertheless, at that time nothing was further apart than the expert's discourse on development issues, the energy of which was at the service of the political order that was to be transformed, but within the limits of the system, and the reasoning of the political order, whose strength lay in a new interpretation of reality, seeking to destroy the 'establishment'.

From the 1960s on, but even more in the next decade, with endogenous roots but stimulated by the Cuban revolution, social unrest grew in intensity. This was a peak moment for social and political struggles, encouraged as never before by a desire for revolutionary change. Various forms of Marxism were disseminated and entered strongly into the social sciences. Those were times that schools of social sciences and, in general, the university itself, was the center of an unprecedented political activism. It was never known whether sociology radicalized the young students, or if the radical youth registered as social sciences students.

**Failures of Modernization**

Until the mid-1970s there were periods of important moments in the growth and modernization of Latin American societies. This was neither constant nor widespread but there were socioeconomic changes in quantifiable levels of urbanization, education and installation of industrial parks: an important structural differentiation that left behind agrarian exports as a primary fate in many of these societies. Some other countries were sustained by their powerful agrarian base and it was there, as in Central America, where revolutionary change strategies prospered. Changes in the realm of the economy were not necessarily accompanied by some form

of secularization of democratic life. There has been a suspicious inde-
termination between democracy and growth and, in some countries in
South America, the implantation of bureaucratic-authoritarian regimes – as
O'Donnell (1973)[7] described them – is explained as the bourgeois account
to deepen capitalism and organize its growth. Only in Chile was this
project successful.

Germani himself, in the autumn of his life, was disheartened by the
limited effects of modernization and its visible effects in the constitution of authoritarian regimes. The derivation in the cultural sphere did
not ensure the minimum of social integration for the stability of democratic regimes, because of the regressive force of traditional forms of
legitimation. Pluralism and legitimacy are not easily resolved within
Latin American modernity, as the heterogeneity of society does not provide for the unanimity of popular sovereignty. Germani's fear was the
incompatibility between development and freedom, between modernity
and democracy. When all this happened, the bankruptcy of 'development
planning' assumptions was evident, as the existence of a historical rationality would unlikely be known and manipulated.

In the 1980s, the foreign debt crisis hit all Latin American countries,
forcing the implementation of 'rescue' strategies that privileged the globalized free market and separated the State from its traditional role of
promoter agent of modernization. That is why we say that this was *primarily a crisis of the State and not of the market* as in the 1930s. It was a fiscal
crisis, a devaluation of State intervention in society, a weakening of the
bureaucratic way of public management. That crisis broke the State in all
its forms, from the authoritarian State in Latin America, passing through
the provider State in societies of welfare-capitalism, to the totalitarian
State in the countries with real socialism. Latin American social science at
that time idealized the State. It was uncomfortable with the sociology of
modernization, when the State had to be modernized to oust the oligarchy;
it was a main actor in the planning State of the developmentalist vision,
and also the decisive core in the anti-dependency alliance. The sociological left saw in the State the key institution that had to be controlled in
order to sort out society, as the target of the revolutionary project.

The conservative wave reappraised market functions and placed the
business actors in the center of the social scene. In the midst of the debacle,
it was not difficult to accept the criterion that economic adjustment
policies and liberalization were the only way forward. This logic, represented by the now abandoned Washington Consensus, left no alternatives.

To save what would remain of the post-crisis stage, what seemed reasonable was the free market and a subsidiary State. Throughout the region, the State retreated to its minimum functions of order and control, accounting administrator of social expenditures and disabled agent in the international arena of transnationalized sovereignty.

The energies in the public sphere, the cult of technical reason underlying the optimism of those who aspire to find options for change, faith in an earthly utopia designed by knowledge and sociological imagination, always together, were worn out or vanished. All this happened as a result of a radical transformation in the perceptions of society, of culture, of the imaginary which encouraged the collective wills.

We are living a major revolution focused on communication technologies and genetic engineering. The internet is, at the same time, the archetype and the most powerful tool of that revolution. Under the impulse of these new technologies and flexible forms of organization and management *a new economy and thus a new society* arises, characterized by increased productivity and global competition.[8] The digital society under construction is the society of knowledge, in particular technological knowledge. A general lack of confidence is growing because people perceive the differences in opportunities that globalization offers and the fact that the world, until now divided into rich and poor (which still holds and is indeed aggravated) is showing an even worse gap, between integrated and excluded from the current system of wealth and power.

From this perspective, we should briefly mention what is like writing an agenda of failures on raw flesh: the crisis of Marxism, which occurred more than a decade before the final crisis of 'existing socialism'; the decline of all revolutionary projects; the economic crisis that ended with the usefulness of development plans; the obsolescence of the entrepreneurial State; the end of a historical mode of articulation between society and the market; and the relevance of a deregulated economy with free trade. The fall of socialism and the end of the Soviet Union had not only political but disastrous cultural effects, because we were not living the crisis of some kind of movement, regime or economy, but its end, the end of an era, as stated by Hobsbawm.[9]

The bitterness was worse for the socialists than for the planners. If the technical reason disassociated itself from the political reason, for many it was just a matter of a bureaucratic adjustment of the new priorities, letting the search for options pass by slowly. Technical, managerial and institutional, engineering knowledge was now appearing. For the revolutionary sociologist, the end of socialism left up in the air the roots of any future project of change. The sinking was the end of a personal vital reason as well as the weakening of the strong ideologies and, even more, *the suspicion turned certainty that history does not have an upward direction, but stochastic results*. The image of the social sciences associated with the idea of progress loses its charm and becomes boring.

## Social Sciences and Pessimism

Neoliberalism does not come alone; it goes hand in hand with the followers of Popper, Hayek and Lyotard. It occurs when the market economy becomes the market society, accompanied by the extraordinary success of computers and the world of the internet. At one extreme postmodernists proclaim the collapse of modernity. They refer especially to its cultural foundations, questioning the paradigms in the social sciences. Others recognize the crisis of modernity but are encouraged by a sense of self-regeneration. A first important aspect, we reiterate now, is the crisis of paradigms, which Lyotard qualifies as *the end of meta-narratives*, general categories that have served to interpret reality in the best Enlightenment tradition. Precisely, the contribution of the founding fathers of the nineteenth century, Comte, Marx, Weber, Durkheim, was establishing theoretical categories that integrate and stimulate the processes of knowledge production. They help to interpret reality and to organize it theoretically under concepts like progress, development, upshift, in an optimistic vision that history marches in a certain foreseeable direction. But in the post-modernist view, history is discontinuous, lacking an internal rationality, that is, full of uncertainty about the future. And reality is fragmented and diffuse.

The social sciences continue developing, and to talk about crisis is only valid when referring to the past. It is the outcome of proposing a comparison with nostalgia and with a hurt ego. Today there are more educational institutions, more researchers, more publications, resources and audiences than twenty years ago. And probably there is more information on these societies. But all this happens under another roof. Certainly technological knowledge is privileged over social knowledge; symbolic inputs are sought to explain isolated social processes, information multiplies and there is a renunciation of to need to comprehend the world and society. Intellectual resources are guided by social engineering. In the new political and cultural environment, the profile of the intellectual and researcher blurs to benefit the expert who knows, little or much, but with an immediate utility that has a price. The determinants of the new scenarios are qualified by megatrends reconstituting current society, such as determining market influence, the subsidiary role of the State, the devaluation of politics and public issues, asymmetric international integration, the social segmentation produced by communication technologies, etc.

Thus, knowledge is one more input to be processed. Information is information technology. Surely, twenty years later, *the figure of the intellectual fades and in its place appears the effigy of the technician.* Intellectual excitement gave no opportunity for skepticism, which soon arrived. And that has been replaced by the pragmatism of the functionary who knows that the knowledge offered has immediate utility. Social researchers are professionals whose products now have a new market. Perhaps that fate explains the change of reputation, almost as a reiteration that also in this area, as Say's Law states, demand causes supply.

Today the demands of the production of the social sciences are geared more towards what was called, inside a false dichotomy, applied science. The professionals cluster in *think tanks*, in estuaries of private consultants sometimes of international character, in networks of open technical advice, available to governments, businesses and even non-governmental organizations (NGOs) and social organizations that require certain technical information. This is a manipulated production of knowledge that is sold to those who can 'pay' for the services. Formerly, the academic audience received and studied the result of an investigation, and discussed its possible theoretical value, its contribution to knowledge and its critical value of reality. In the market of information, now the *user* uses it as a confidential document (in the sense of restricted use) and qualifies it according to its applicability or the wisdom of its recommendations, tailored to the demands of a *status quo* that is accepted.

## Pessimism, Yes, But Creative Ones

The offensive of the free market took advantage of postmodern pessimism and accentuated its effects on the social environment in which the social sciences today worked. The absence of a progressive conception of history and criticism of ideologies weakens the roots of utopian thinking. It is important to have some dose of this spiritual food for the emergence of critical thinking, a trait that tends to disappear even though the social scientist does not necessarily sink into cynicism. If the essential task of reason is the intelligibility of the social world, critical relevance does not have to be canceled. It is inherent in this kind of knowledge.

The reproach of the pessimist is that social scientists who have analyzed Latin American history in the last fifty years have not been able to explain why development has been more exclusive, why culture has been more elitist, or to account for the appalling authoritarian period. Reason does not realize the weaknesses of the human capacity to dominate the natural and social realms. The reversibility of socialism and the closure of the revolutionary *ethos* are symptoms of a malaise that turns many into skeptics. This is combined with the evils that the market distributes and inevitably creates a more unequal society with more ecological disaster and an increase in uncivilized forms of social life: fanaticism, intolerance and political arrogance of the strongest kind.

Whatever the truth of all this, *the optimistic/pessimistic consciousness is a Manichaean way of thinking* that has only a temporary meaning. Applied to the effects of a moment in time and qualified as a starting point, one can resume the tasks with more confidence and a less uncertain future. Pessimism in science is not of the same quality as the one that sickens the heart, for it is not a loss of faith but insecurity, uncertainty about the future or an absence of certainty in view of the heterogeneous results. By speaking of pessimism with a positive attitude we place ourselves in a practical perspective, provisional and deductive, because the major premise was an illusion. Disappointed are those who had a dream. It is also a theoretical provision relating to the purposes of human action.

What is really happening in this context for which we have no navigation chart? – (a) the feeling of experiencing a period distinctly different from the past of which we have clear memory; (b) the discovery that nothing can be known with any certainty, because the current basis of epistemology does not appear to be sufficiently reliable; (c) the discovery that history is estranged from itself, without a historicist philosophy and therefore no version of progress can be plausibly defended as future; and (d) the emergence of a new social and political agenda including the issue of environmental protection at the center – the biggest problem for development. New things? What should we do in order to cope with a society in which the responsibility for social integration is no longer formulated by policies and the State but the market?

There are reasons, ultimately, to imagine a better world, given, on the one hand, the gridlock being reached with the negative effects of globalization, and, on the other, the inability of the market to act as a factor of social regulation. The expansion of poverty, but especially the multifaceted nature of inequalities and *pari passu* the failure of policies to counteract them, poses significant challenges to the social sciences. The revaluation of democracy and new forms of making politics, still in germination, points to the consolidation of a culture of citizen participation. The social sciences have new options in the ways of understanding social reality, approaching problems from gestures of dissent, but taking advantage of renewed confidence in reason, able to project a better future, utopian designs, a teleological interpretation. The challenge is to see alternatives, options and paths. From a certain skepticism it will be possible to build certainties. That is the task for the generation that was born with the internet. That is, the generation that has already started walking.

## Notes

1.  Published originally in Spanish in E. Torres Rivas (2001) 'Acerca del pesimismo en las ciencias sociales', *Revista de Ciencias Sociales*, No. 94, IV, pp. 151–167 and in E. Torres-Rivas, *Centroamérica: entre revoluciones y democracia*, pp. 249–281 (Mexico, DF: Siglo XXI Editores; Buenos Aires: CLACSO, 2015). Translated into English by Isabel MacDonald thanks to the support of Jorge Rovira Mas and the University of Costa Rica.

2.  In this climate it was very common to have a dichotomous model, whatever the name given to the initial and final state, as the development that all society should experience. These are the classic formulations of Tönnies, Durkheim, Becker, Redfield and others. This model was used for the first time in the Seminario Latinoamericano sobre Metodología de la Enseñanza y la Investigación en Ciencias Sociales, Facultad Latinoamericana de Ciencias Sociales (FLACSO), Santiago de Chile, September 1958, which marked the birth of this institution.

3.  Although Raúl Prebisch was the inspiration and the most important thinker of ECLAC, an important contingent of economists, sociologists and other Latin American specialists concurred in the decades of the 1950s and 60s, whose contributions were also decisive but are not mentioned here due to the nature of this work.

4.  Intellectual works were numerous, such as the following books of Prebisch: *Hacia una dinámica del desarrollo latinoamericano* (Mexico: Fondo de Cultura Económica, 1963) and *Transformación y desarrollo: la gran tarea de América Latina* (Mexico: Fondo de Cultura Económica – Banco Interamericano de Desarrollo, 1970). Prebisch's thinking became radicalized afterwards, as it appears in *Capitalismo periférico, crisis y transformación* (Mexico: Fondo de Cultura Económica, 1981), which is a terminal plea for the political transformation of capitalism in the periphery. In this work, the optimism no longer appears; rather there is disenchantment in relation to the virtually insurmountable difficulties in achieving development.

5.  F.H. Cardoso and E. Faletto, *Dependencia y desarrollo en América Latina* (Mexico: Siglo XXI Editores, 1969), with numerous editions.

6.  The notion of underdevelopment is different when it refers to a degree of differentiation between the productive system and that of the center/periphery, which refers to the functions performed by underdeveloped economies in the world market.

7.  Guillermo O'Donnell (1973) *Modernization and Bureaucratic-Authoritarianism: Studies in South American Politics*. Institute of International Studies, University of California.

8.  Manuel Castells, 'Tecnologías de la información y desarrollo global', *Política Exterior*, XIV (78), 151–168.

9. Those who believed that the October Revolution was the door to the future of history were wrong. Lincoln Steffens said 'I have seen the future and it works'. It did not work well, but it was not the future either. See E. Hobsbawn, 'Adiós a todo eso' in R. Blackburn (ed.), *Después de la caída del comunismo y el futuro del socialismo* (Barcelona: Crítica/Grijalbo, 1994).

## Edelberto Torres Rivas, by Sergio Villena Fiengo (Costa Rica)

Edelberto Torres Rivas (1930–2018), is a wandering Guatemalan who early on began his long journey across Latin America, when he had to go into exile in Mexico after the coup against the progressive government of Jacobo Arbenz in 1954. He graduated in Law at the University of San Carlos (Guatemala, 1962), with the dissertation: *Social Classes in Guatemala*. His graduate studies in Sociology at the Latin American Faculty of Social Sciences (FLACSO, Santiago de Chile, 1965) strengthened his sociological vocation, while deepening his interest in Latin America. At the Latin American Institute for Economic and Social Planning (ILPES) where Dependency germinated, he wrote his seminal book *Interpretation of Central American Social Development* (1969), a classic of social sciences of this sub-region.

Afterwards he continued with doctoral studies in England and a made a brief stay at the National Autonomous University of Mexico (UNAM). In 1972 he went to Costa Rica and became the Director of the new Central American Program of Social Sciences of the public universities until 1980. He made a notable contribution to the development of the social sciences throughout these years, in which the organization of the XI Congress of the Latin American Association of Sociology (ALAS) and the foundation of the Central American Association of Sociology (ACAS) were decisive. As General Secretary of FLACSO (1985–1993), he continued developing the social sciences along the isthmus, promoting its links with the rest of Latin America. He achieved the creation of new academic headquarters in Guatemala, El Salvador and Costa Rica, as well as in Brazil, Cuba, Bolivia and the Dominican Republic. At the same time, he turned the General Secretariat into a dynamic regional center, generating important projects, such as the *General History of Central America* (1993, six volumes).

He returned to Guatemala in 1996, within the political context of the Peace Accords of that year which ended the armed confrontation between the Government and the Guatemalan National Revolutionary Unity (URNG). He collaborated in the elaboration of the report 'Guatemala, Memory of Silence' (1999), published by the Commission for Historical Clarification. He has been working since then for the United Nations Development Program and has coordinated several Human Development Reports on the Guatemalan society.

His long career has been characterized by his tireless contribution as a voice, researcher, public intellectual, teacher and prolific author. His rigorous contribution to both regional studies and comparative research stands out because he identifies common points between Central America and Latin America, while also showing the particularities and internal complexity of the isthmus. His permanent effort to explain to his Latin American colleagues and those from other latitudes the awe-inspiring Central American history is praiseworthy.

As a sociologist, he has shown a fertile imagination in grasping the uniqueness of Central America, developing his own intellectual tools, among which are the

*(Continued)*

(Continued)

categories: 'low intensity democracies', 'epidermal history' and 'revolutions without revolutionary changes'. A representative selection of his academic texts forms the anthology *Central America, Between Revolutions and Democracy* (CLACSO, 2008), coordinated and presented by Jorge Rovira Mas.

Torres Rivas's valuable contribution to the development, institutionalization, professionalization and international projection of the social sciences in Central America and Latin America has earned him important recognition. Among others, he has received an Honoris Causa Doctorate from FLACSO (2007) and the University of Costa Rica (2015). Other awards include the Kalman Silvert Award (2010) and, for his book *Revolutions Without Revolutionary Changes*, the Iberoamerican Award (2013), both from the Latin American Studies Association (LASA). CLACSO also, in 2014, distinguished him with the Latin American and Caribbean Social Sciences Award.

The text included in this volume, 'On the Pessimism in the Social Sciences' (2001), is a text of maturity and partly a testimonial, elaborated at a very particular moment in global history and that of Central America and the social sciences. It presents a historical account of the optimism/pessimism of Latin American social thought regarding development and democracy in the region. Torres Rivas rejects the denial, more cynical than pessimistic, of the potential of the social sciences, betting on making the 'crisis of paradigms' and 'postmodern disenchantment' an incentive for the creative renewal of Latin American critical thinking, which he considers necessary for the construction of a better future.

Torres Rivas is a worthy heir to a long tradition of intellectuals from Our America. His commited contribution updates the inspiring words of José Cecilio del Valle (1780–1834), a Central American intellectual, who, at the dawn of independent life (1822) stated: '[Latin] America will be my exclusive concern from now on. America by day when I write. America at night when I think. The most worthy object for an American is America'.[1]

## Note

1.    José Cecilio del Valle (1982) *Obra escogida*. Caracas: Ayacucho Library Ayacucho.

## References

Comisión para el Esclarecimiento Histórico (1999) Guatemala, memoria del silencio, Guatemala: Oficina de Servicios para Proyectos de las Naciones Unidas (UNOPS).

Torres Rivas, Edelberto (1971) *Interpretación del desarrollo social centroamericano; procesos y estructuras de una sociedad dependiente*. San José: Editorial Universitaria Centroamericana.

Torres Rivas, Edelberto (1993) (editor general) *Historia general de Centroamérica*, (6 volumes). Madrid: Sociedad Estatal Quinto Centenario-FLACSO.

Torres Rivas, Edelberto (2008) *Centroamérica: entre revoluciones y democracia. Edelberto Torres-Rivas Antología*, compiled and edited for Jorge Rovira Mas. Bogotá: CLACSO-Siglo del Hombre.

# 6

# The Foundations of a New Issue: Gender, Human Rights and Memory[1]

*Elizabeth Jelin (Argentina)*

I propose to trace the conceptual and historical background of the emergence of the concern for human rights, social memory and gender in the social sciences in Latin America. The search, that will take us from the mid-twentieth century until the turn of the century, has the objective of showing that the developments of these fields were not independent of each other; they took place in an interrelated manner, and implied a paradigmatic change that challenged the prevailing perspectives in the social sciences of the region. Furthermore, their origins were not predominantly a process internal to the academic field, but a process guided by social and political struggles. The three share the fact of being interdisciplinary fields, and the three involve institutional, symbolic and subjective dimensions.

This genealogy has a clear autobiographical reference, since it constituted my own intellectual trajectory. I choose to present it as a counterpoint of ideas and paradigms rather than an autobiographical text. It could have been organized around names and networks of colleagues, meetings and debates, and the feelings and anxieties that were present in each moment of the story. No doubt, the autobiographical element is present. Should it be made visible and explicit? Or should it be left hidden behind the cover of scientificity and objectivity? The hypothesis of the linkage between studies of memories and a gender perspective, however, goes beyond the fact that they are intermeshed in the biography of a person.

## The Nineteen Sixties

In the process of consolidating the social sciences in the region, the basic interpretive framework was to understand the economic and social development of 'peripheral capitalism'. The dominant approaches were, on the one hand, views about modernization and development, and a Marxist vision of confrontation and class struggle on the other. The specificity of

Latin America could be seen in two main themes, populism and marginality, which were conceptualized as threats or obstacles, either for the success of modernization processes or for capitalist development and class struggle.

Within these concerns, there was an obvious blindness about the social position of women (there was no talk of gender relations at the time). If women mattered, it was in relation to fertility trends. There was some analysis of the growth of women's participation in the labor force or of the increase of their educational levels, easily interpretable in the modernization key. And high fertility could be 'explained' by the more traditional attitudes of women, or by their religiosity.

However, other processes and other realities were emerging in the region, linked to processes and movements in the international arena. In fact, the second half of the sixties was a period of significant political activation, with new actors and new demands. New social forces emerged in the public space, forces that had not been incorporated in the previously dominant models of analysis, concerned primarily with structural, economic and class determinations. In the dominant paradigms of the time, be it from Marxism or from modernization theories, societal links with the political system were interpreted without the mediation of institutions, actors and social movements – while these were appearing in the socio-political scenario, requiring new capacities and conceptualizations that could allow understanding these struggles in terms of the expansion of citizenship rights.

The last years of the decade also witnessed the emergence of a new feminist wave, first in the core countries and very soon spreading to other parts of the world. This modern feminism had to face a double challenge: to understand and explain the forms of subordination of women and to propose ways of fighting for the transformation of that condition.

A first milestone in this feminist trajectory was the discovery of the *social invisibility of women*: in domestic work, not valued and hidden from public view, in the back of historical struggles, 'behind' great men. The recognition of the value of domestic production and the role of women in the social network that supports and reproduces social existence would become one of the key issues of the seventies. Isabel Larguía and John Dumoulin, from Havana, gave the theoretical keys from a Marxist perspective (Larguía and Dumoulin, 1976). It became mandatory to *make visible the invisible*. Hence the need to conceptualize and analyze the everyday, the anti-heroic, the social fabric that sustains and reproduces.

This debate, so central to the formation of a gender perspective, however, did not penetrate the 'establishment' of the social sciences of the region. It was a development that remained in – or helped to constitute – a segregated space, made up of academic and militant women identified with feminism and the struggle for women's rights.

The theoretical discussion and the practical consequences of the history of patriarchy – a concept that links relationships within the family with broader social relationships, focusing attention on power relations – was an important milestone in the balance of the sixties and seventies. The *liberation* of women implied a transformation of patriarchy as a social system (Valdés, 1990).

## The Seventies: Tragedy and Hope

The seventies witnessed at the same time the bloody dictatorships in the Southern Cone and the mobilization of women, expressed at the First Intergovernmental Conference on the situation of women in Mexico in 1975. Both were previously unknown phenomena, and their manifestation and visibility implied changes in many fields.

State terrorism and illegal repression focused the world's gaze on the region, and stimulated significant changes in the models and frameworks to interpret what was happening. While there were important antecedents in international history, the military coups in the Southern Cone led to the involvement of international networks of activists and organizations linked to human rights. From that time, they became significant players in the protests against repression and state terrorism (Keck and Sikkink, 1998). From the perspective of Latin America, the anti-dictatorial struggle implied the incorporation of the framework of human rights to understanding what was going on and denouncing violations. Until then, domination and social and political struggles were interpreted in terms of class struggle or national revolutions. The incorporation of the Framework 'violations of human rights' was, in that context, a true paradigmatic revolution, since this framework implies defining human beings as bearers of inalienable rights, and incorporates the figure of the victim, demanding special attention. It also assumes the central responsibility of State institutions in guaranteeing the validity and fulfillment of those rights.

Dictatorial repression had special effects on women. From the very beginning, there were women leading human rights struggles. The commitment of many did not come from explicit ideological convictions or from strategic calculations in the anti-dictatorial struggle. It was not a political logic, but a logic of feelings and affection: directly affected women – mothers, grandmothers, relatives of victims – asking for and claiming their disappeared relatives, tortured, dead, incarcerated. The denomination of women's organizations refers to the primacy of the family bond: mothers, grandmothers, widows, *comadres* (godmothers), relatives. There was apparently nothing heroic in that beginning; it was the dramatization, multiplied and expanded, of the female role of caring for the family with love and dedication. What came next was another chapter, namely the transformation of a private demand into a public and political demand for democracy (Schirmer, 1988; Valdés and Weinstein, 1993, among others).

Here, in the practice of the anti-dictatorial struggles, the nascent paradigms of human rights and women converged. Not as an expression of the demands for equality of feminism but as an expression of a traditional familism and maternalism. The distance between the militants in the human rights movement and feminism was considerable, and this led to disagreements and misunderstandings. In fact, the expectation of the feminist movement that, as women, human rights activists would spontaneously express women's 'own' demands hindered dialogue between the human rights movement and feminism. The Mothers of the Plaza de Mayo became a symbol and an emblem: stemming from their pain and suffering, from their traditional role as mothers, they came to subvert the social and political order, highlighting the transformational potential of women. For a feminist perspective, the next question was whether this development out of private pain could transform suffering mothers into women fighting for their rights. Although there are no systematic investigations, the evidence gathered indicates that human rights activists showed the same range and variety of ideological positions as the rest of the women. They were as much or as little feminist as the environment in which they moved.

## The Eighties: Democracy, Citizenship and Social Movements

In 1978, CLACSO (the Latin American Council of Social Sciences) convened a seminar in Costa Rica on 'The Social Conditions of Democracy'. The motivation was clear: the need and urgency felt by academics and intellectuals in the region to imagine conditions and strategies to end the dominant dictatorial regimes (CLASCO, 1985).

Democracy was the project of opposition to authoritarianism and dictatorship; the concept of democracy had to be discussed academically and politically. The sought-after democracy included at its core the defense of the basic rights of the person. This meant concentrating attention around the political system itself, and thus the analysis of the economic conditions and the social structure was not the central concern (Lesgart, 2003). From then on, developments followed the path of 'transition to democracy' and then the ways towards 'consolidation '. The reference to human rights and the assertion of the plea for social participation, in turn, raised the issue of citizenship (Jelin, 1996).

Along with the political scientists who began to reflect and investigate the transformations in state institutions and the democratic forms of participation and articulation of power, another reality was emerging: varieties of social protest and social activism that could not be channeled through the political system and existing institutions, as well as 'new' social movements and forms of collective action, and these began to attract the attention of social researchers in the region. Since the 1970s, both the classic social movements (workers and peasants) and the new movements of women, youth, urban, ethnic, human rights, etc., anchored in more localized and specific goals and demands, have not ceased to be present in the public sphere of the region and in the attention of analysts.

During transition processes in the eighties, the place of social movements in sociopolitical dynamics became more explicit and visible. Several demands of women's and human rights movements were incorporated into the social and political agenda of transitions. Since then, the critical stand of feminism permeated corporate organizations, unions, business organizations, state institutions, and even sectors of the Catholic Church. The issues raised – discrimination against women, demands for policies of equal opportunities (later on the debate on female quotas and the demands for parity in the distribution of State positions), the necessary transformations in the legal structure to attain gender equality – penetrated the social fabric and the public sphere. Over time, there was a growing social and political recognition of certain specific violations of women's rights, such as domestic violence and gender-based violence, trafficking in women for prostitution, and, in the twenty-first century, feminicide. All along, the recognition of sexual and reproductive rights has been gaining ground in the region, and even the issue of the legalization of abortion has been installed in public debate in several countries. In turn, the discourse on human rights was appropriated by vast social sectors, not being restricted or reduced to militant groups with demands linked to recent dictatorships.

From a longer-term historical perspective, the social demands of collective movements have changed their profile (Calderón and Jelin, 1987). Until this time, the Latin American social sciences, preoccupied with power and the quest for political transformation, focused attention on questions of power. Non-institutionalized collective expressions of popular sectors were interpreted as pre-political protests, or as embryos of popular participation to be channeled by a party vanguard. Now, analysts and activists turned their attention to the indicators of societal uneasiness or uneasiness with party politics, discovering inside these movements 'new ways of doing politics' (Lechner, 1982). In these approaches, however, the issue of power remained the organizing principle of interpretive thinking.

The change of paradigm in the analysis of social movements occurred when it was possible to see in them something else: not only new ways of doing politics but also new forms of sociability and indications of changes in patterns of social organization (Evers, 1985). Attention had to be focused on the micro-social processes of reciprocal recognition and on the construction of new collective subjects with identity. This also implied a redefinition of the boundaries between public and private spaces. What mattered was that, grounded in specific and concrete aspects of the most common or even banal aspects of everyday life, the basic principles of social organization were being questioned (Calderón, 1986; Escobar and Alvarez, 1992; Jelin, 1985).

Reflection on and analysis of social movements in the region were not independent of conceptual developments in the central countries. What characterized the Latin American analysis was precisely that these privileged protagonists in the public sphere simultaneously developed new ways of doing politics and new forms of sociability and subjectivity, novel relationships between the political and the social, the public world and private life, in which everyday social practices were to be considered in direct interaction and integration with the ideological and the institutional-political level. The basic concepts and ideas involved – the changing nature of the distinction between public and private, power in microsocial relationships, the construction of subjectivity – were a product of feminist thought.

In the development of a bottom-up perspective, linked to the processes of incipient democratization, a central concept was that of *citizenship.* It had not been a frequently used concept before.[2] Now, a central academic concern was that of the historical expansion (and also reversion) of different types of rights. Latin America showed a different historical development when compared to the model developed by Marshall (1964) for England: the expansion of social rights of the post-war era was not always preceded or accompanied by an expansion of civic and political rights, and even less by citizens' subjectivity. Historically, the formal recognition of labor rights took place earlier than the full recognition of civil and political rights (Collier and Collier, 1991). In turn, the recovery of political rights during transition could be accompanied, as shown in Brazil, by widespread violations of civil rights (Caldeira, 1996).

A short conceptual detour is needed here, to clarify the notion of citizenship that was being built. There is a danger of reifying the concept, identifying the rights of citizenship with a set of observable practices: voting in elections, enjoying freedom of speech, receiving public benefits in health or education, or any other specific practice. Although these practices constitute the heart of the struggles for the expansion of rights in specific historical situations, from an analytical perspective, a necessarily more abstract concept of citizenship refers to conflictive practices linked to power, reflecting struggles over *who* can say *what* in the process of defining what the common problems are and how they will be addressed (Van Gunsteren, 1978). This implies that both citizenship and rights are always in the *process* of construction and change.

This perspective starts from a premise that the basic right is '*the right to have rights*' (Arendt, 1973; Lefort, 1987). Citizenship action is thus conceived in terms of its qualities of self-maintenance and expansion: 'Citizens' own actions are only those that tend to maintain, and if possible increase, the future exercise of citizenship' (Van Gunsteren, 1978: 27; see also Lechner, 1986). The content, policy priorities or areas of struggle may vary, yet in terms of building citizenship they will have consequences insofar as the right to have the rights and the right to public discussion of the content of rules and laws are reasserted.

This was the approach that was being developed in the eighties in the region. In it, the notions of human rights, the consideration of subjectivity and the processes of the constitution of the subjects of law (individual but also collective, a demand especially powerful among indigenous peoples) became central. The issues debated referred to the dilemmas and tensions between individual and collective rights, between equality and the right to difference, between universal rights and cultural pluralism, between the public responsibility of the State and the defense of privacy and intimacy (Jelin, 1993; Jelin and Hershberg, 1996). Here again, the influence of feminist debates was noteworthy. In Chile, the women's movement in opposition to dictatorship carried the banner 'Democracy in the country, in the home, and in the bed', forcefully expressed by Julieta Kirkwood ([1982] 2010). More generally, attention to the paradoxes, tensions, contradictions and gray areas in the analysis of social reality, originally developed in feminism, was slowly and not without difficulty incorporated into the social sciences of the region, previously dominated by the hard core of structural and deterministic thinking.

## The Nineties: Neoliberalism and Beyond

In the nineties, feminist thought and concern for struggles about rights faced a particular historical juncture: the neoliberal boom. In this context and given the ascendance of the framework of neoliberalism, it became necessary to focus attention on the peculiar way in which the articulation of societal actors and the State was taking place. In the case of Brazil, yet with an argument that can be extended to other countries, Dagnino (2004) pointed towards the 'perverse convergence' between the democratizing and participatory wave of post-dictatorial transition and the imperatives of the minimum State posed by the dominant neoliberal mandates in the 1990s, driven by multilateral economic institutions. Both require an active civil society. The perversion of this convergence is that while some actors promote citizens' participation as part of democratic construction, others interpret it as a way to reduce State action and transfer the management of social issues and public goods to 'civil society'. The terminology used by both political projects (the democratizing and the neoliberal) was the same – participation, civil society, citizenship, democracy – while 'their' senses and intentions were clearly different.

Human rights and citizenship, as well as feminism, could be read from a neoliberal perspective. Limiting the actions of the State and waiting for social issues to be solved in civil society, letting market forces act freely, allowing the diversity expressed in multiculturalism, have been well-known features of this period and of this ideology. The concern for the constitution of subjectivity could also fit ideologies centered on individualism.

In the academic and intellectual fields, the reaction to the neoliberal hegemony that proposed uniform prescriptions regardless of context, specific histories and cultural heritages, was to work on an analytical approach that placed special emphasis on the historicity of social phenomena: looking at the present as a process than encompasses past experiences and horizons of expectations towards the future, to use Koselleck's terminology (Koselleck, 1993). In more concrete terms, the subjective constitution of citizenship and rights, as well as the dynamics of social demands, require rising above conjunctural analyses, addressing issues that embody multiple temporalities. Towards the future, the questions raised referred to the challenges posed by the construction of democracy and equality – in the mechanisms of institutional functioning, in egalitarian substantive matters and in the processes of social empowerment. Towards the past, it was about finding ways to overcome and settle accounts with discriminatory and excluding social structures and mechanisms of domination, as well as with the recent terrorist and repressive states. The idea that linked both issues was the belief that one cannot build a democratic future with impunity for the past. It is at this point that the consideration of social memories enters the scene.

The concern with social memories emerged in the Southern Cone during the post-dictatorial transitions of the eighties. At that time, facing the legacies of the very recent past became urgent. The usual instruments of democratic political institutions did not seem to be enough. The 'private' sufferings and pains overflowed the intimate arena and invaded the streets. The human rights movement began to claim the recognition and legitimacy of the memories of the dictatorial past. And here – as in other conjunctures – the demands of the movement dictated the new research agenda of the social sciences. Thus, inquiries and interventions to open up the field of research and debate on the memories were initiated. In this context, a group of social scientists proposed an intervention aimed at installing such new topics and questions of research, reflection and citizens' political action in the region. The task was to develop a conceptual apparatus and to rigorously investigate the recent and ongoing processes regarding the memories of the recent past. The aim was to train a group of young researchers and to support the establishment of networks and nuclei that would work on this field, defined very loosely as 'studies on memories', yet with a clear emphasis on the fact that memories are never linear, they are always plural, and involve struggles among actors who present different understandings of the past (Jelin, 2002, 2003, 2017).[3] From that moment on, this academic-intellectual field, rooted in ethical and political commitments, developed with strength. Faced with the effervescence of social demands and the presence of activists in the countries of the region, committed intellectuals could not stop paying attention to these developments, and social memories became a recognized and legitimate area of study.

## Historical Convergence, Convergence of Perspectives

The themes discussed here emerge in the Latin American social sciences in an interrelated manner. They involve new interpretative frameworks that break disciplinary traditions (law and psychoanalysis, sociology and political science, anthropology and history). They call for the recognition of subjective processes and cultural frames of action. To relate the institutional level with the cultural patterns of meanings and with the processes of actors' subjectivity transcends the usual framework of any single discipline of social research.

Other more paradigmatic considerations bring together the study of memories and feminism. Both are rooted in the recognition of ambiguities, tensions and contradictions in the social world. Primo Levi, speaking of life in the Nazi concentration camps, referred to 'gray areas' where univocal, explicit, absolute or categorical criteria are suspended. There is no way to delve into memories without recognizing this ambiguous and gray reality. At the same time, contemporary feminist thinking incorporates the approach to the dilemmas and paradoxes that constitute gender relations as a central issue. That women claim equal rights based on their specificity and gender identity entails an irresolvable paradox, which is permanently re-established in the history of social struggles (Scott, 1996). Feminist thinking recognizes ambiguity, contradiction and paradoxes (Fraser, 1997; Scott, 1996), and this is shared by memory studies. This is also present in the analysis of other tensions between demands for equality and difference, fundamentally those anchored in race and ethnicity, thus expanding the horizon of social reflection (Jelin, 1993; Jelin and Hershberg, 1996). In these spaces of debate and construction (that of temporality and memory, that of the paradoxes of equality and difference), other historical periods (the Conquest and indigenous genocide, for example) and other social actors are incorporated as topics of analysis, thus paying attention to actors silenced and hidden in the 'official stories' constructed by the winners of the battles of history.

## Notes

1.   Written in English especially for this volume. Some of these ideas are part of the book published in Spanish: E. Jelin (2017) *La lucha por el pasado*. Buenos Aires: Siglo Editores XXI.

2.   In his review of the subject, Bryan Roberts registered a dramatic increase in the number of publications dedicated to citizenship in Latin American social science. Between

1966 and 1973, in the catalogue of the Benson Collection at the University of Texas (perhaps the most important Latin American library in the world) only three titles in Spanish and Portuguese registered the keyword 'citizenship'. Between 1993 and 2000, the number was 139 titles (Roberts, 2005: 137).

3. The Program, organized and sponsored by the Latin American Committee of the Social Science Research Council, was called 'Collective Memory and Repression: Comparative Perspectives on the Process of Democratization in the Southern Cone of Latin America', a title that expressed the perspective with which we addressed the issue at that time. Years later it would be revisited and revised (Jelin, 2017). From 1998 to 2003, about sixty young fellows from six countries – Argentina, Brazil, Chile, Paraguay, Peru and Uruguay – were trained and did their own research projects on memories. The result was a series of twelve books, *Memorias de la represión*. A critical analysis of the Program from an epistemological perspective is found in Cruz (2016).

# References

Arendt, Hannah (1973). *The Origins of Totalitarianism*. New York: Harcourt, Brace and World.

Caldeira, Teresa (1996). 'La delincuencia y los derechos individuales: redefiniendo la violencia en América Latina', in Elizabeth Jelin and Eric Hershberg (eds), *Construir la democracia: derechos humanos, ciudadanía y sociedad en América Latina*. Caracas: Nueva Sociedad.

Calderón, Fernando G. (ed.) (1986). *Los movimientos sociales ante la crisis*. Buenos Aires: CLACSO.

Calderón, Fernando and Elizabeth Jelin (1987). *Clases y movimientos sociales en América Latina: perspectivas y realidades*. Buenos Aires: CEDES.

CLASCO (1985). *Los límites de la democracia*, 2 vols. Buenos Aires: CLACSO.

Collier, Ruth B. and David Collier (1991). *Shaping the Political Arena*. Princeton: Princeton University Press.

Cruz, María Angélica (2016). 'La investigación en memorias de las dictaduras militares del Cono Sur como conocimiento situado', in A. Bello, J. González and O. Ruíz (eds), *Historias y memorias. Diálogos desde una perspectiva interdisciplinaria*. Temuco: Universidad de la Frontera.

Dagnino, Evelina (2004). 'Confluência perversa, deslocamentos de sentido, crise discursiva', in Alejandro Grimson (ed.) *La cultura en las crisis latinoamericanas*. Buenos Aires: CLACSO Libros.

Escobar, Arturo and Sonia E. Alvarez (eds) (1992). *The Making of Social Movements in Latin America: Identity, Strategy and Democracy*. Boulder: Westview Press.

Evers, Tilman (1985). 'Identidad: la faz oculta de los nuevos movimientos sociales', *Punto de Vista*, 25: 31–41.

Fraser, Nancy (1997). *Justice Interruptus: Critical Reflections on the 'Postsocialist' Condition*. New York and London: Routledge.

Jelin, Elizabeth (ed.) (1985). *Los nuevos movimientos sociales*, 2 Vols. Buenos Aires: CEAL.

Jelin, Elizabeth (1993). *About Women, About Human Rights*. Lima: Entre Mujeres.

Jelin, Elizabeth (1996). 'La construcción de la ciudadanía: entre la solidaridad y la responsabilidad', in Elizabeth Jelin and Eric Hershberg (eds), *Construir la democracia: derechos humanos, ciudadanía y sociedad en América Latina*. Caracas: Nueva Sociedad.

Jelin, Elizabeth (2002). *Los trabajos de la memoria*. Madrid and Buenos Aires: Siglo XXI de España Editores / Siglo XXI de Argentina Editores.

Jelin, Elizabeth (2003). *State Repression and the Labors of Memory*. Minneapolis: University of Minnesota Press.

Jelin, Elizabeth (2017). *La lucha por el pasado. Cómo construimos la memoria social*. Buenos Aires: Siglo Veintiuno Editores.

Jelin, Elizabeth and Eric Hershberg (eds). (1996). *Construir la democracia: derechos humanos, ciudadanía y sociedad en América Latina*. Caracas: Nueva Sociedad.

Keck, Margaret E. and Kathryn Sikkink (1998). *Activists Beyond Borders*. Ithaca and London: Cornell University Press.

Kirkwood, Julieta ([1982] 2010). *Ser política en Chile. Las feministas y los partidos*. Santiago: LOM.

Koselleck, Reinhart (1993). *Futuro pasado: para una semántica de los tiempos históricos*. Barcelona: Paidós.

Larguía, Isabel and John Dumoulin (1976). *Hacia una ciencia de la liberación de la mujer*. Barcelona: Cuadernos Anagrama.

Lechner, Norbert (1982). ¿Qué significa hacer política?. In Norbert Lechner (ed.), *¿Qué significa hacer política?* Lima: DESCO.

Lechner, Norbert (1986). 'Los derechos humanos como categoría política'. In Waldo Ansaldi (ed.), *La ética de la democracia*. Buenos Aires: CLACSO.

Lefort, Claude (1987). 'Los derechos del hombre y el Estado benefactor', *Vuelta*.

Lesgart, Cecilia (2003). *Usos de la transición a la democracia. Ensayo, ciencia y política en la década del ochenta*. Rosario: Homo Sapiens.

Marshall, T.H. (1964). *Citizenship and Social Democracy*. New York: Doubleday.

Roberts, Bryan (2005). 'Citizenship, Rights and Social Policy'. In Charles Wood and Bryan Roberts (eds), *Rethinking Development in Latin America*. University Park: Penn State University Press, pp. 137–158.

Schirmer, Jennifer (1988). 'Those Who Die for Life Be Called Dead: Women and Human Rights Protest in Latin America', *Harvard Human Rights Yearbook, 1*, pp. 41–76.

Scott, Joan W. (1996). *Only Paradoxes to Offer: French Feminists and the Rights of Man*. Cambridge: Harvard University Press.

Valdés, Teresa (1990). 'Mujeres y derechos humanos: "menos tu vientre", Documento de Trabajo', *Serie Estudios Sociales*, No. 8, Santiago: FLACSO.

Valdés, Teresa and Marisa Weinstein (1993). *Mujeres que sueñan. Las organizaciones de pobladoras en Chile*, 1973–1989. Santiago: Libros FLACSO.

Van Gunsteren, Herman (1978). 'Notes on a Theory of Citizenship'. In Pierre Birnbaum, Jack Lively and Geraint Parry (eds), *Democracy, Consensus, and Social Contract*. London: Sage.

# Elizabeth Jelin, by Teresa Valdés Echenique (Chile)

Elizabeth Jelin (1941–), born in Argentina, PhD in Sociology and Senior Researcher at CONICET, has made countless contributions to the Latin American and global social sciences – uncountable for their scope and permanent renewal with new generations of researchers.

These contributions were made both through academic production and through the creation or strengthening of research and teaching institutions: the CEDES (Center for Studies of State and Society) (1975–1993); the Gino Germani Social Research Institute – Faculty of Social Sciences, University of Buenos Aires (1993–2003) and the Economic and Social Development Institute (IDES) (1997– today). She also created research programs that have allowed the formation of generations of researchers throughout the region. Prominent among them is the Sociocultural Research Program in Mercosur, the Research and Training Program for Young Researchers on Collective Memory and Repression and the Postgraduate Program in Social Sciences of the National University of General Sarmiento (UNGS) and IDES. In addition, she was Visiting Professor at numerous universities in first world countries.

Jelin participates in international academic networks and associations and has been a member of directive boards such as the International Association of Sociology, the Latin American Studies Association (LASA) and the Research Network on Interdependent Inequalities in Latin America (Berlin). She has also served on the board of the Social Science Research Council (SSRC), the United Nations Research Institute for Social Development (UNRISD), the World Commission on Culture and Development of the United Nations (UNESCO) and the Wissenschaftskolleg zu (Berlin), and has collaborated with foundations linked to Latin America such as the Ford Foundation and the Inter-American Foundation.

For her scientific contributions, she has been recognized in Argentina with the Konex 2006 Award for Humanities, the Houssay Award for Research in Social Sciences given by the Argentine government (2013) and the Doctorate Honoris Causa by the Université Paris-Ouest, Nanterre La Defense (2014).

Jelin's academic work includes a variety of topics, such as family, social movements, gender, democracy, citizenship, integration, human rights and memories of repression. However, the originality of her contribution has to do with a point of view, an entrance to social phenomena in which subjectivity and the microsocial dimension are not separated from structural, economic, political and social processes. Her research reveals that it is not enough to examine demographics if the daily lives of families and women are not understood, thus revealing a gender order that subordinates them, or if the dilemmas of child care and the sexual division of labor are not tackled. For Jelin, it is not possible to understand the social movements that flourished in the region in the seventies and eighties, especially the women's movement, regardless of the relation between individual identity and collective participation, thus deepening the notion of citizenship. Thus, her contributions to Latin American social sciences are essential in the conceptualization of the "new social movements", which allowed questioning the traditional political view of social

*(Continued)*

(Continued)

movements towards an understanding from the perspective of culture and the construction of democracy; likewise, in the reconceptualization of citizenship exercised by these movements, which promote solidarity, responsibility and human rights.

In another stream of her research, she argues that it is not possible to understand the barriers and difficulties of regional integration proposed by Mercosur and to value its contributions without knowing and recognizing cultural dynamics and local identities, and the valuable exchanges already built from the integration. Her research incorporates in the foreground the question of the way in which gender order plays within the dynamics of family, social movements and human rights, as well as in the memories of repression.

This look at the socio-political processes of the region entails a methodological option that approaches anthropology, with life stories and in-depth interviews with the actors, the use of photographs and images where the interviewees identify themselves, but also her committed participation in the processes and social movements investigated. An acute and rigorous observer, Jelin asks about her own role in these processes meanwhile analyzing them.

Her experiences of military dictatorships and exile gave rise to her pioneering research and political commitment to the memories of dictatorship and repression in Latin America. More than twenty years were dedicated to observing the forms and contents of memories, in Argentina, Chile, Uruguay, Brazil and Paraguay, as well as the case of Peru. Jelin not only created a field of knowledge but also contributed to the formation of several generations of researchers in different countries of the region, which resulted in numerous publications.

Her most recent book *Las luchas por el pasado. Cómo construimos la memoria social [Struggles Over the Past. How We Build Social Memory]* (Siglo XXI Editores, Buenos Aires, 2017) collects the work of those twenty years. It deals not only with the experience of the human rights movements in Argentina and the Southern Cone, but also with the similar memory processes experienced in other parts of the world when the meanings of the past elaborated by social actors are updated and reinterpreted in confrontation and fight against silences and public erasures, against policies of forgetting crimes, torture, repression, violence. Once again, it highlights the subjective and intersubjective dimension of the memory and political processes, and the intergenerational transmission of social memories linked to dictatorships and violence, an issue tremendously in force in the scenario of several countries in the Latin American region.

# Part Two
# Historical and Contemporary Debates

# 7

# Understanding Historical and Contemporary Debate in Latin American Sociology: Enlightening Paths

*Raquel Sosa Elízaga (Mexico)*

Latin American Sociology has been transformed by the rhythm of regional experience: it is full of sudden assaults due to continuous political and economic instability; frequently overwhelmed by constant crises induced both by business associations and government practices; permanently dominated by foreign interests; and questioned by the growing pressure of populations that accumulate grievances and disagreements. Our region is torn by constantly repeated and aggravated tensions: basically, those resulting from its submission to economic policies dictated by international corporations and organisms, from which very small and authoritarian elites of power benefit. Almost the entire logic of governments, barely and sporadically concerned with potential loss of legitimacy, is built upon the principle of the control and minimization of peoples' needs and rights. Corruption, manipulation and repression have become the basic tools to silence nonconformity, and they stand in order to prevent the exercise of true democratic participation and intervention in public affairs. But as these *analgesics*, strong as they may be, have only temporary effects, new threats of ruptures and alternatives to the existing order reappear and open ways to a cyclic revitalization of a precarious stability, which is kept and prolonged on the verge of its exhaustion.

Likewise, scientific productions and main academic debates have revolved in one way or another around processes of polarization, confrontation and erosion that re-emerge at each step, in the face of long-unresolved problems. Let us remember that Fernando Mires reconstructed the dramatic history of some of the region's main crises during the twentieth century and called them 'permanent rebellions' (Mires, 1989).

Sociology marked its professional institutionalization in the international arena during the 1950s, with the simultaneous foundation of the International Sociological Association and the Latin American

Sociological Association (ALAS). Its organizational efforts – later strengthened by initiatives such as the Latin American Council for Social Sciences (CLACSO), the Faculty of Latin American Social Sciences (FLACSO), among others – have long been recognized for systematically promoting debates about development, dependency, sustainability, productive regimes, poverty, inequality, social movements, the State, power, democracy, political authoritarianism, and cultural, social, ethnic and gender diversity, among many others, all over the region. From its foundation as a university discipline and up to the present, Sociology has been consistently influential through the proposal of a necessary and thorough reconstruction of the material foundations, the forms of socialization and representation, the options of inclusion and diversity, the revaluation of cultures and identities, the interpretation of history and the future perspectives of Latin American societies. Highlighting the keys to understanding such mandatory reconstruction is the purpose of our contribution to this anthology on Latin American social thought.

## Latin America From its Roots

One of the characteristic features of Latin American Sociology has been its urge to explain, confront and contribute to overcome the fundamental historical and contemporary dilemmas of our region. During this process, it has faced the need for a critical analysis of the thoughts, models, methodologies and professional practices built in countries that have exercised colonial domination over vast areas of our subcontinent. The fact that these orientations have indeed managed to prevail through the continuous dispossession of resources and territories, but also by influencing or determining peoples' beliefs, fears, aspirations and behavior has represented a major challenge to truly committed social research. Nevertheless, this endeavor has also counted on the presence and knowledge legitimated by innumerable experiences of struggle and resistance that have faced the challenge of finding possible and potential means to transform social reality. Many of these experiences have also left a shared concern about the need for rearticulating diverse and meaningful concepts, proposals and practices in order to be ready to face present and future challenges. And this has led to the serious undertaking of reinterpretation, reorientation, fusion and even reinvention of purposeful approaches and actions in order to truly overcome the order imposed by colonial establishments.

An expression of this continuous tension is that which confronts *Latin Americanism* with what could be known as a *Specialism* originated and cultivated in the world's dominant theoretical and professional circles. Societies that have never been completely freed from colonial domination often manifest doubts about whether they will actually be able to successfully overcome or at least propose something original to the scientific establishment. This may explain why alternative routes need to be based on a wider scope, and seen through as many lenses as can be grabbed hold of. The incorporation of diverse and frequently contradictory methods, concepts and practices used by what have been known as disciplines (Sociology, Anthropology, Philosophy, Economics, etc.), together with the use of popular and traditional knowledge, and of course, the recognition of regional approaches, memory and history, become crucial, as nothing can be left behind or on the side if one really wants to reach adequate conclusions and formulate adequate options of social knowledge for our own side of the world.

The need to confront and solve grievances caused by multiple foreign invasions and the constant siege of mental and practical colonialism, demands that true and consequent acts of knowledge acquire the quality of becoming both acts of survival and of sovereignty. The context of a region like ours incorporates the following features: societies built on the forced coexistence of human beings extracted from their original land, enslaved, thrown into these unknown places; the mingle of original peoples with their treasures' predators, forced to live within the social order created and imposed by them; the combined intervention of merchants, landowners, entrepreneurs and bureaucrats of all kinds, as if coming from different historical ages but sharing the same reality through every stage; the use of mercenaries, smugglers, pirates as means to reinforce public office; sudden owners of others' lands, riches and enslaved workers, who, in order to survive, find ways in hybrid, mixed cultures and contradictory social interactions; impoverished migrant workers, refugees and the displaced, brought about by violence and wars; sages, poets and singers, utopians and mystics. A reality such as this cannot be understood by applying tools created for the so-called modern or occidental societies, and will definitely be subsumed under a one-and-only disciplinary view. In terms of the Latin American, African and Asian main historical and contemporary social problems, the theory and practice of what we refer to as *specialism* can only mean the assumption of a narrow point of view built upon the insistence in maintaining the past and present hegemonic order.

Latin American societies have had their own, peculiar history of sur-vival. Authoritarian regimes co-exist with libertarian populations, while over-exploited territories stand close to ecological reserves, where enor-mous biodiversity is defended by peoples who refuse to surrender or renounce their space, their air, their water, their right to live. It is thus not possible to pretend to reconstruct the trajectory of both social development and Sociology without fully understanding the meaning of the continuous presence of these confrontations. Thus, as we navigate turbulent waters in order to try to unveil the identity and routes followed by Latin American Sociology, we will seek to decipher some fundamental keys to our his-torical and contemporary social and sociological debate. And for that, in this introductory essay, we will follow the guidance of authors who have illuminated the complex reflections with which the social thought of our region is woven.

## Learning to Observe

Our journey begins with the Argentine historian and sociologist Sergio Bagú, an extraordinary human being, who developed some of the most significant, vast and rigorous scientific views, keen-edged observations and wide social perspectives that Latin America could have known in the twentieth century. By the end of the 1950s he had already outlined from an original perspective the complex and contradictory historical articulations between Latin American communalist societies and the Spanish monar-chical regime at the time of the Conquest. He was particularly interested in uncovering the disruption suffered by Spain after the Arab invasion and occupation of its territory, while also engaging himself in understanding the process and consequences of the Crusades, as well as those of the Reconquest. Nearly four centuries of Spanish history may well account for the building of one of the most powerful military and religious cultures in world history, which certainly explains and in a certain way prefigures the essence of what would be its colonial rule and heritage. In his book *Economy of the Colonial Society* Bagú introduced us to the understanding of forced entanglements, unforeseen consequences, impossible minglings and amazing unravelings, which became characteristic Latin American historical features upon the Spanish invasion (Bagú, 1949).

Years later, in *Time, Social Reality and Knowledge* (Bagú, 1970), this cosmopolitan author, like very few others, managed to synthesize the way in which a knowledge horizon and its epochal view are constituted.

Considering the compulsory ways in which European cultural traditions and their universalistic pretensions were generalized in America, Bagú clearly pointed out that those human beings placed under Spanish rule on conquered territories, after continuous fierce repression, were supposed to restrict themselves to believing, accepting and behaving according to Spanish orders. However, as historical evidence proves, they were nevertheless prone to maintaining and reproducing their previous conceptions and practices, even when they were forced to deny, challenge and destroy everything they had previously believed in. Bagú stated that this particular trait, the contradictory condition of surviving by being able to live in at least two different social and cultural worlds, long remained after Latin America's Independence from Spain, left its print after different and successive invasions, wars, dictatorships and other authoritarian regimes, and still persists to the present times.

Drilled to obey and comply with the principles and ways of the new order, and forced to erase any memory of their own cultures and times, the natives of Latin America were also obliged to experience conviviality with Asian and African slaves, with peoples from all over the world, and in a significant and unique manner, not only resisting the rigidity and hardships of the life imposed on them, but also developing their own humanity and social experience. Considered permanently unfit, excluded and frequently expelled from the imposed social order, they also became experts in looking for and finding ways of communicating with and understanding others alike or different from them, in their newly shared territories.

Confronted in his own time by an equally rigid and exclusive scientific perspective, which has systematically refused to recognize the vastness, diversity and complexity of societies outside Europe and North America, Bagú dared to question his colleagues by asking them why is it that they perceived only part of social reality, and not the whole, even if evidence of its existence could be found everywhere. And he gave strong examples: more than forty years ago, he referred to the importance of massive migrations and the economic weight of drug smuggling, at a time when neither of these phenomena had been incorporated into official statistics and dealt with as major trends and social problems in our contemporary societies.

To assume the contradictory, the denied or unrecognized, to *learn to observe* the hidden, occult and visible forms of relationships among human beings, its ways and expressions in Latin America, and to open our minds and broaden our views and horizons became the *leitmotiv* of Bagú's work. And after his teachings, whenever we acknowledge the limits of what we initially perceive or believe as true, we have to remember that, in order to give a sensitive explanation of social realities we need to go beyond established facts and constructed data and reach the highest point of observation and understanding. However, we must also be humble enough to accept that we will never have definitive answers to our questions, and that every era will renew both questions and findings. So it was with Bagú, who never ceased to search for further explanations and continued to propose original interpretations of different issues, each one of which gave clear examples of how to interrogate and deconstruct dominant social views, both in Latin America and the rest of the world.

Thus, almost at the end of his life, he delivered an extraordinary text, *Social Theory and Political Catastrophe*, where he referred with great accuracy to the theoretical and practical lessons we can extract by understanding human reactions to social and political catastrophes, taken as critical examples of confronting dominant and epochal views, after which they are conceived as historical symbols, with full and enduring meanings (Bagú, 1997). Bagú not only acquired new knowledge and broadened his perspective through the teachings of the past, but he also projected his explanations onto the future, as these experiences determine our interpretations of the world we live in, both the one we face and the one we imagine, so that we can simultaneously crave our past and foresee our future social involvement. The reconstruction of extreme situations, in which the survival of humanity is placed in serious danger, allows us to visualize untold mass responses that have – most of the times without any previous sign of agreement, perhaps for reasons difficult to unravel – has forced millions of human beings to confront, with unparalleled courage, the most dangerous challenges to human and social survival, as happened during the battle of Leningrad, during World War II. This is what Bagú calls the *anonymous heroism of the masses*. And it is through these historical dilemmas – the way in which they are faced, dealt with and solved in real history – that we may find a great anchor on which to pin our hopes for the formidable powers of resistance and striving for life that vastly organized populations have accomplished during their time. Of course, in Latin America, such examples abound.

## Learning to Think Critically

In his own and also unique manner, René Zavaleta Mercado, an incomparable Bolivian sociologist, found that it is precisely in times of crisis when we may be able to fully perceive the conflicts faced by societies. Identifying the social and political subjects of these crises may also allow us to unravel the sense of tragedy involved in their individual and collective decisions, as well as the consequences and the horizons that they have contributed to amplifying or canceling for the future. A text published after his death reunited his unfinished notes and writings of more than twenty years of research on Bolivia from different historical archives, as well as his own research of possible meaningful keys to unravel the main trends of his country's processes of transformation. He thus viewed victories and defeats in the light of his own theoretical, political and militant experience in both his own country and the rest of Latin America. *Lo nacional-popular en Bolivia* (1986) is a formidable synthesis of his proposed method to decipher the keys and codes of what he calls *constituent* moments or episodes in history.

He gets to a point where he re-elaborates episodes in which a nation and its people may happen to deny the possibilities open to them to broaden or 'exploit' their own visibility horizons and thus became absent – in real and figurative senses – from their own history, unable to understand the meaning of what was being decided, and alien to the decisions that others made about them. This happened to Bolivia, during the Pacific War, when tragic events resulted in, among other things, the loss of its sea ports. If peoples are not aware of their own history, it is most probable that future generations will suffer the consequences (Zavaleta, 1986). The cycle opened in Bolivia with the Pacific War was in an equally dramatic way closed, fifty years later, with the Chaco War, with still another important loss of its territory. This country's *constituent* moments were thus explained by Zavaleta as a fatal combination of unbridled and blind ambition on the side of holders of power, and the isolation, passivity and subordination of an absent or not fully conscious people. An armed defeat to which poor peasants were taken as an unwilling part of the army with no voice, preceded, according to Zavaleta, the cancellation of the viability of Bolivia as a country for a very long time. The anguish, human misery and social decay that resulted from this tragedy, not only marked that epoch, but also seriously limited Bolivia's future options, even to this day. What contemporary authors like Piotr Sztompka call *social traumas*, that is, events that leave their tragic trace – paralyzing or deviating historic courses and also forcing the denial or hiding of shameful or painful episodes in societies' accumulated experience (Sztompka, 2004) – reappear years or even decades and centuries after as the fundaments of the explanation for certain transformation initiatives that have not succeeded or prospered. These traces will also accompany the continuous rebirth of social and political motives and initiatives for the rupture of an irrational and unjust established order.

## Caring for, Defending, Enriching Our Territory

The Colombian academic and intellectual Arturo Escobar formulated in *The Invention of the Third World* (1996), a profound critique of the impact and consequences of external interventionism in countries subordinated to the main contemporary powers. After thorough research, Escobar explains the strong influence of concepts and categories that penetrated academic and public sectors after the brutal reorganization of international geopolitical fields at the end of the Second World War. The facts reaffirmed the European and North American conviction that *development* should be relaunched in the peripheries, as well as on the borders that separated East and West, North and South, in order to block new threats of destruction against an order that was perceived as both precarious and indispensable. The building of a new model of what we could call *Cold War societies*, as the Catalan historian Josep Fontana suggests in his masterful study *For the Empire's Well Being* (Fontana, 2011), updated and deepened the old colonialist pretension. By virtue of the Marshall Plan and the American prestige following the Nazi defeat, this model was transformed into a paradigm aimed at disregarding and delegitimizing any pretense of questioning the capitalist order, as based on the predominance of cities and industrialism, and associated from then on with *modernity*. As a consequence, a new *order* was imposed under the protection and vigilance of the United States and its powerful corporations.

The paradigms of *development* and *modernity* refused to accept and recognize the real evolution of countries in which different transformation processes had occurred. And this not only happened in regard to China, India or the USSR, but also manifested itself in a demented ignorance of other peoples' experiences in Africa, Asia and Latin America. Whatever social or ethnic differences existed, along with the impact of poverty, the lack or lack of well-being or even the importance given by the people to cultural identity or national sovereignty, were dismissed as mere expressions of a condition of historical, social and cultural inferiority.

The deconstruction of the concept of *development* elaborated by Escobar was decisive in reopening the debate on sustainable alternatives in Latin America, Asia and Africa, especially in the context of the recurrence and worsening of economic, social, political and cultural crises in the world by the imposition of the neoliberal scheme, from the eighties and nineties in the past century (Escobar, 1996).

Escobar's subsequent work has allowed us to establish significant modes of articulating disciplines and areas of knowledge, starting from the recognition of the centrality of *place* in social practice. His contribution, by conceiving new forms of territoriality, or what he calls a *political ecology*, has opened up new horizons to our understanding of the relationship between organized human beings and nature, and has broadened our views on the importance of considering land and its subsoil, water and air, as well as the living creatures on them as dependent on each other and in perpetual movement, in order to improve their conditions and ensure their well-being. His findings can be considered more as a path to open new searches than as unsurmountable determinations in human history, while they have clearly helped us to put aside the pretensions of a *universalist* colonialism.

To confront the reality of a seemingly boundless growth of business interests, particularly of transnational corporations, with the consequences of systematic violence of communities' rights to determine their life, is a truly necessary exercise to understand Latin America's options and potentialities in the world today (Escobar, 1999, 2014).

## The Originality of the Baroque

Few thinkers as deep and original as Bolívar Echeverría has our America produced. His passage through complex societies, such as the Ecuadorian, German and Mexican, his approach to the world through the eyes of the *philosophy of praxis*, and his constant contact with political and social practice for the transformation of the world were the basis of his work, which he deployed from a deep knowledge of the variegated historical evolution of capitalism in the world (Echeverría, 1998).

The baroque studied by Echeverría is an insurmountable synthesis of combined superimposed, amalgamated, identities, which at the same time eagerly express, at the same time, a rebellion against the dominant world and its own being – an identity alien to the complacencies and complicities obliged by the unbearable imposed order. Our Latin American baroque is, from his perspective, a way of assimilating, denying, reinventing the form, the background and the perspective of a social knowledge as complex and full of nooks and crannies, as surprising. What has been produced in Latin America, in a unique way, is not for him an exclusive result of coloniality, nor can it be solely explained by the previous existence of native or Afro-descendant peoples. It is, rather, the expression of a constant movement of creation, resistance and search to save hidden areas of manifestation of the self that our peoples have developed in contexts where compulsory relations with the world have been built after the expansion of capitalism.

In a certain way, what Echeverría is interested in is precisely reaching a full contradictory conscience and acting it out through what he calls *subjectiveness*, that is, a moment when we are able to decide by ourselves, both theoretically and practically, and become empowered, not in the sense of immediately able to surmount the visible obstacles to a true liberation of our collective being, but in the sense that we can fully display and express our feelings, needs and urge for creation. Our acceptance of both our weaknesses and difficulties, particularly including the way in which we have internalized the relationship between dominants and dominated in our own selves, is essential to our recognition of the true fundaments of our condition as alive beings and also as part of a force beyond our individual selves. This is, he would say, the essence of the *baroque modernity* that defines us.

The brief synthesis of these key authors' understanding of the complexity of social reality and social thought in Latin America is meant to motivate readers to engage themselves in the kind of search that they, among many others, have accomplished in order to give a full meaning to our place and mind about our world today. These authors clearly propose transversal ways of addressing major social problems in complex societies, based on the Latin American experiences of this and the past century. Their original theoretical perspectives, as well as the experiences that rooted them, are now starting to be recognized throughout the world. We hope that reading these very small parts of their work will encourage readers to make the most of it translated into different languages, and nurture other views of a social world in urgent need of further understanding and change.

## References

Bagú, Sergio (1949). *Economía de la sociedad colonial. Ensayo de historia comparada de América Latina*. Buenos Aires: El Ateneo.
Bagú, Sergio (1970). *Tiempo, realidad social y conocimiento*. Mexico: Siglo XXI.

Bagú, Sergio (1997). *Catastrofe politica y teoria social.* Mexico, Siglo XXI Editores.

Echeverría, Bolívar (1998). *La modernidad de lo barroco.* Mexico, Ed. Era.

Escobar, Arturo (1996). *La invención del tercer mundo. Construcción y deconstrucción del desarrollo.* Bogotá, Norma.

Escobar, Arturo (1999). *El final del salvaje: Naturaleza, cultura y política en la Antropología Contemporánea.* Bogotá, Instituto Colombiano de Antropología.

Escobar, Arturo (2014). *Sentipensar con la tierra.* Bogotá, Colección Pensamiento Vivo.

Fontana, Josep (2011). *Por el bien del imperio: una historia del mundo después de 1945.* Barcelona, Ediciones de Pasado y Presente.

Mires, Fernando (1989). *La rebelión permanente. Las revoluciones sociales de América Latina.* Mexico, Siglo XXI Editores.

Sztompka, Piotr (2004). *Sociología del cambio social.* Madrid, Alianza Editorial.

Zavaleta, René (1986). *Lo nacional popular en Bolivia.* Mexico, Siglo XXI Editores.

# 8

# Building Theory[1]

*Sergio Bagú (Argentina–Mexico)*

In science, as in life itself, what is known and what is ignored are linked by a dynamic bond. As knowledge boundaries expand as a result of scientific advancement, the ability to discover and understand what is still ignored improves, and it becomes easier to read the dynamics of the portion that was already known. Furthermore, the view of substantial matters broadens, adding a chapter – or at least a paragraph – to theory.

The methodology of sciences of societies cannot introduce experimentation as a procedure; instead, it relies largely on experience. The activity required for scientific construction is selective; it does not hinge on the mechanical addition of the footprint of experience but on the incorporation of an intelligent analysis of that experience, based on the basic research objectives.

Sciences of society and sciences of behavior/personality share vigorous relationships and clearly defined boundaries. It proves useful to ratify these ties and limits, as, although obvious today, they used to seem blurry at one point in time. If these sciences focus on human beings, where do the boundaries lie? Psychology, psychoanalysis and psychiatry all examine human personalities. Their object of study are individuals. History, sociology, economics, cultural anthropology and human geography study mankind's society. Clearly, both groups of sciences share a close complementarity, providing each other with direct, ongoing feedback. Knowing where they come close and where they draw apart, society sciences are constantly enriched by personality sciences' findings and ponderings, and vice versa.

The human mind has an intrinsic dynamic. It cannot remain static, and, when scientific obsession takes hold of it, the mind thinks even when it is not thinking.

Many years ago, I read a text by John Dewey which today is impossible for me to cite with fidelity. With a paradoxical style and a hint of humor, he stated that reactionary people are right because, when the thinking starts, it is impossible to predict where it will go; safety can only come from banning thinking. I hope I am not betraying the idea expressed by an author whose work I profoundly respect.

Dewey's reflection points to the core of scientific creation itself. Its development may be conditioned, but the goals, guidelines, conclusions and the pace of conceptual creation can be neither foreseen with any certainty nor imposed as a norm.

This holds true for all types of sciences, but its principle becomes even more complex in the fields of personality and human sciences, as researchers in these areas are part of the reality studied. In human society sciences, building theories involves summarizing what we already know, but also imagining formerly unsuspected or barely intuitively perceived basic dynamics. Creative imagination is ubiquitous in every kind of work associated with science. Absolute empiricism does not exist in scientific creation, even when researchers strive to consistently remain on the paths indicated by experience.

The notion of structure – a set of elements, with each acquiring logical and functional validity as an organic part of a whole – is often used as a synonym for *system*. In practical terms, the word 'system' refers to large networks that may even encompass the entire world. The terminology allows for an organizational scaling that faithfully addresses contemporary reality, as the world today shows increasingly complex micro and macro structures, as well as micro and macro *systems*. It should be noted that the term 'system' is commonly used to refer to organizational macro-types, such as the capitalist *system* and the socialist *system* – which portray realities, albeit with some imprecision regarding their boundaries.

Three processes build the reality of the *system* in human societies. One is the integration of the elements characterizing the system. Another is the establishment of physical boundaries for the system, while the third refers to how time penetrates the system and, therefore, all its subordinate structures.

## 1. The Heterogeneity of Homogeneity

When we use the term 'system' to refer to an integrated set of social relations, we feel strongly tempted to identify a specific system with a rigorously outlined, clearly homogenous organizational type. The common terminology often used by social scientists currently reveals that approach in very perceptive traits. Indeed, since the break up of the Soviet Union, the spreading of the capitalist system around the world seems a universally accepted fact today. This expression comes with the idea of a very specific type of social relations.

The truth, however, takes other paths. When capitalism had yet to dawn in history, and throughout its long-lasting consolidation, the world did not feature a wide range of organizational types. The opposite happens nowadays. Within the realm of global capitalism, organizational types have grown substantially in number, both in terms of the nature of social structures as well as life conditions and cultural scales.

This reality is so universal today that it is even present in every large metropolis in the capitalist world. For instance, it seems hard to find a more differentiated range of socio-organizational types within national borders than the one featured in the United States, a country where the most exuberant wealthy lifestyles coexist side by side with extreme poverty.

More examples, while less striking, can be found quite easily. It is noteworthy that what we now call globalization has yielded a humankind that has never, through millennia, displayed such an extraordinary heterogeneity as it does now. In other words, after the Soviet Union's fall, the world has become both more homogenous and more heterogeneous than ever before.

The possibility to overcome this basic contradiction lies in recognizing that what has become universal in recent years is a single distributive mechanism for basic functions that causes striking inequalities. There is an obvious, intrinsic contradiction in this, but where does it reside? In the terminology, in the approach, or in reality itself? The answer is complex: reality is not contradictory – it's real. Then, our approach and our terminology do not entirely suit reality. They tend to fragment it, breaking it down and, every so often, rebuilding it as a static whole.

Our analytical deficiency comes as a result of our cultural training, which, in turn, follows a view of the world that we typically call 'Western' and rests on, among other things, the belief that it is the only possible expression of human rationality. This viewpoint has been stated by several European and US authors.

Many of the values currently analyzed by social sciences have been translated into quantitative terms and are now commonly used in economic, demographic and sociological arguments. To the extent that this quantitative expression can truthfully convey a reality, this proves highly commendable. Yet, it is unacceptable to undermine the searches and conclusions that can only be stated qualitatively. Science – good science – consists of both quantities and qualities.

This observation applies entirely to cultural values. Coexistence principles, the scales in which relationships among individuals and groups unfold, the emotional universe, the recognized types of knowledge and their respective means of acquisition, how important knowledge is considered, and the social scope of ethics all seem unable to fit into a mathematical construct, and, yet, they serve as a sort of backbone to human societies, an invisible order of substantial values whose total absence can only be endured briefly by a social organization, but cannot be introduced as a permanent organizational guideline. A cultural construction in crisis lies at the core of every – actual or potential – political catastrophe in this century analyzed here. Nowadays, human society sciences provide a wide array of efficient analytical tools, but there are some conceptual gaps and methodological shortcomings that impair our observation and critical analysis capabilities in processes of such magnitude.

## 2. Deep Roots

Initiated centuries ago, the diversification of society sciences has slowly heightened in Western culture since the 1600s, but thoughts on the nature and dynamic of human society date much farther back, with roots in every great culture – even by means of religious grounds and philosophical pondering.

Without a doubt, the developments experienced by the generations preceding original thinkers and the events they witnessed in their own lifetime directly encourage scientific thinking, but the dose of immediate experience required by creative minds to produce science may prove lower than the input of their imaginations. Adam Smith analyzed the free-competition-based capitalist system when the first industrial revolution was barely dawning. Karl Marx examined advanced industrial capitalism before the second industrial revolution, which is why he wrote his seminal work by hand, as typewriters had not been invented yet, and under a gas lamp, as there was no electricity back then.

Truth be told, geniuses often enlighten times that are not entirely dark. When Adam Smith was alive, England already boasted workshops looking for ways to enhance labor efficiency by improving tools, and, in the multiple European countries visited by the young philosophy professor before writing his classic piece, waged labor was largely concentrated in single workshops with no machinery. To rebuild the industrial society dynamic, Karl Marx did not need to wait for typewriters or electric lighting. Some industrial society features – though not all, of course – were present in his time, with the basic traits still remaining in today's new technological revolution age.

This reconstruction does not aspire merely to applaud the genius's contribution, but it does intend to serve as a reminder that historical breakthroughs often have older, deeper roots than those perceived in common historical recreations.

Thoughts on the so-called economic phenomena have been fragmentarily exposed for many centuries. Some economic endeavors, such as trade and loans, worried the Catholic Church for centuries, as it judged them from a theological and ethical standpoint. However, in the early Modern Age, when Portugal and Spain built their colonial empires, and as sea and land trade expanded while banking emerged, reflections on economic phenomena became more organic. Schumpeter (p. 95) believes that St Antonine, in fifteenth-century Florence, was the first author to present a broad view of the economic process. Still, Schumpeter also records several works by sixteenth-century Spanish authors that reveal 'an elevated Spanish economic theory' at that time (p. 165).

## 3. Antiquities

Remembering the past in a human community is one of the oldest, most significant purposes of culture. From olden times, communities have tried to preserve their collective memories, with this task relying, at some point, on a community member, a long time before writing was invented. These memory bearers probably combined truths and myths in their recollections. In any case, members in charge of memory transfers started to enjoy great respect in some communities.

Ultimately, collective memories serve to promote community cohesion and as identity drivers. Nowadays, national histories also serve that purpose – albeit, of course, with very different specialized elaboration conditions.

Herodotus, a Greek thinker who lived in the fifth century BC, has been credited as the father of history. His works account for an advanced phase in past memory preservation. Aristotle, in the fourth century BC, was one of the most fruitful thinkers of all times. Some of the many topics addressed by his systematic thinking may be regarded as the first chapter in political science history.

The antiquity that can be assigned to thinking on human societies stems from its very subject, following the discovery that the human community is a reality with its own features. Along the extended history of religious thinking, the relationship between individuals and their divinity is complemented, at an early cultural development stage, by the relationship between the divinity and a clearly defined human community.

The ideas that have led to society sciences in the European Western world can be traced back to Rome quite accurately. Roman Law – possibly Rome's most significant construction – proves a testament to a society where private property gathered momentum, including the ownership of human beings. It should be noted that Roman Law continued to serve as an acknowledged source of Private Law until the twentieth century in several European countries and in Latin America.

In Europe's Western countries, the Middle Ages are closely associated with the history of the Catholic Church and its official theology, with its theological notions changing slowly over time and supported by an ethics applicable to relationships among humans. In this latter approach, the first activities that announced the dawn of a new economy – characterized by trade, currency and interest-based loans – were ruled not by laws but by theology, Christian morality and the Church's commands.

The great transformation of society sciences started to take a clear form in the fifteenth and sixteenth centuries. I am revisiting this known background to remind us that the systematic thinking about human community is ancient and has been conveyed by the most diverse cultural means. This account also helps to point out the existing parallelism between the developement of capitalism and social research diversification in specialities.

## 4. Beginnings [Gestation] in Modern Times

Economic theory developed as the capitalist system expanded, with a prologue of some three centuries – from the fifteenth to the eighteenth century – and gathering momentum in the latter century, when the industrial revolution – across its various stages – supported the expansion of the colonial system and international trade. The rest of the story becomes even more familiar.

Sociology started to take shape as a specialty, driven by class structure transformations, in the first half of the twentieth century, leaving a number of introductory chapters in earlier centuries and in several countries.

Cultural anthropology – also known as social anthropology in England – became a recognized university study field, encouraged by colonial expansion, as the European metropolis slowly came to understand that populations dominated in other continents featured cultures and social organizations that should be examined rather than just caricaturized. Demographics started when rural populations began to migrate to cities – a phenomenon regarded as peculiar and threatening – as capitalism advanced into their traditional domains. By the second half of the nineteenth century, the boundaries of demographics became clearer, when census surveys turned into a regular activity and the need to analyze the quantitative data gathered was perceived.

Human geography is largely a refined cultural product, as it came to life in the late nineteenth century to link migratory streams, human settlements, soil conditions, natural resources, and cycles of weather.

## 5. Hierarchization

This account of highly repeated facts should highlight something that has been rather neglected: the hierarchies progressively acquired by social specialties.

Several aspects of this process may be pointed out – the rise of historiographical specialties, the quick shift towards mathematics experienced by demographics, the great importance awarded to social values in cultural anthropology. Yet, the decisive trend has hinged on how economic theory has prevailed among all other social sciences, standing as a paradigm of scientific reasoning, especially during the twentieth century.

Two virtues have been attributed to economic theory, expressly or tacitly. First, economic theory is conveyed mathematically, which proves its accuracy and undeniable scientific hierarchy. Second, its study subject overshadows all others – it is argued – in terms of importance for human societies, as, virtually by itself, economic theory reveals the roots of civilized coexistence and even the fate of humankind.

Little by little, over a hundred years, economic theory rose to the hierarchy of benchmark for all social sciences. Resembling economic theory gradually became the yardstick for true scientific value to judge history (so imprecise), sociology (so discursive), cultural anthropology (so obsessed with non-capitalist societies), and human geography (attempting to analyze seasonal paces in organizational forms but relying on just a small amount of quantitative data).

Economic thinking took a parallel path. Theoretical reflection continued in the West, but it did not become dominant, nor was it granted a higher category. The distribution criteria followed by the Nobel Prize in Economics – the only one awarded to any society science – a few years after its creation in 1969 proved quite clear: it does not reward theoretical contributions, but the technical ingenuity used to enhance business organizations and to secure greater profits for large private companies.

This shift from theory to technique runs parallel to the central purpose of greater business efficiency. Oddly enough, the Soviet Union's economic development did not draw away from this trend, underscoring it instead. Economic policy was considerably developed in that country, particularly program techniques, but the theory remained untouched – or, rather, it moved backwards.

A science that, after becoming a paradigm for all other social sciences, turns its theory into a productivity technique favors all conceptual deviations, even the most far-fetched. At a debate on the fate of contaminating industries located in central countries, Lawrence H. Summers (at the time Chief Economist of the World Bank), a World Bank economist, offered a very original solution: moving them to poor countries. This outburst of technological ingenuity at the heart of industrial capitalism immediately prompted, fortunately, extreme sarcasm within the economic profession itself. London's *The Economist* used the following headline for its report, 'Let Them Eat Pollution,' while the same city's *Financial Times* broadened its critical view to encompass the entire profession, heading its article with the cry, 'Free Planet Earth from Economists' (*Le Monde Diplomatique*, Paris, March 1992, p. 7).

## 6. Critical Attitudes

Some reactions from the core of contemporary economic thinking prove smarter and calmer. Over thirty years ago, the United Nations Economic Commission for Latin America and the Caribbean (ECLAC), at that time headed by Raúl Prebisch, realizing that the economic development plans it had formulated for several Latin American countries had failed to serve their purpose, decided to create the Social Studies Division. José Medina Echavarría, a Spanish sociologist with a long track record in his field and a broad cultural acumen, was appointed to head it. The new Division would start sociological studies in parallel with economic studies in order to introduce social elements into Latin America's economic planning.

Many years later, Shahid Javel Burki, the World Bank's Vice-President for Latin America, admitted that the free-market-based development strategy promoted by that agency had failed, as it was applied to the poorest 20% of the world's population. In 1973, he recalled, 750 million lived in extreme poverty, and that number has doubled by today. The first step proposed by Burki consists of increasing the number of social scientists working at the Bank. Currently, there is one social scientist for every 28 economists (correspondent in Washington, D.C., *La Jornada*, Mexico, June 26, 1996).

Over thirty years, two important international bodies operating in the same area – Latin America – have witnessed the same failure of economic knowledge and offer the same solution: complementing it with sociological knowledge. Whether this is the most appropriate path to advance development goals remains a topic for contemporary debate.

It is still possible to find other reputable testimonies intended to weigh the real contribution that economic research with the highest institutional credentials receives from economists for understanding contemporary capitalism in central countries.

Edmond Malinvaud, a renowned representative of France's mathematical economics, concludes that the concrete knowledge on true economics is very scant (Combemale, 1990: 113).

As regards the written production on economics, Maurice Allais, Economics Nobel Prize winner in 1988, believes that economic theory has become, over the past 45 years, a succession of dogmatic, unrealistic theses that have been forgone one after another – a set of pure sophisms based on unattainable mathematical models that cannot forecast – let alone explain – events (*Le Monde Diplomatique*, Paris, May 1992, p. 3).

Moving to the United States and standing at the White House, it is worth remembering that an impressive team of mathematical economists work there, with all kinds of readily available data on their country and the world, as well as state-of-the-art computers. It would be impossible to gather a more sophisticated set of technologies and data than that which is at the disposal of such a rigorously selected group of mathematical economists – graduates from the best schools in the country. However, in 1985, their failure to issue a short-term forecast on economic recovery, the value of the US dollar, and other basic metrics of their domestic economy became an acknowledged fact in official circles, eventually leaking to the press and even prompting a sarcastic remark by President Ronald Reagan (R.D. Hershey, in *Excelsior*, Mexico, January 19, 1985).

## 7. The Unacceptable

Nothing in this chapter should be construed as an attempt to invalidate any of the human society sciences. It is unacceptable, however, to condition the validity of a scientific field to on a single analytical method.

In any case, the entire set of society sciences, as they are practiced today, leads to consider a context of global scale. Western Europe's social theory is strongly influenced by the development of the capitalist system, but it has also introduced some very significant heterodox tenets.

The Soviet system was not a capitalist variant, but a socialist variant that only allowed for a very limited development of social theory. As a result, it curtailed the likelihood of its own survival as a system.

None of the social sciences – as they have developed thus far – is poised to guide the cultural process involved in understanding social dynamics as a whole. The prevailing role conquered by economic theory over the past century is a typical outcome of the capitalist system and stems from the illusion that a single, rather elementary key has been found to decipher everything happening to humankind.

The human social process is so intrinsically complex, and it unfolds in so many ways, that all contributions from all social sciences prove indispensable. It is clear today that personality sciences can contribute significantly to society sciences and vice versa.

It should be noted, nonetheless, that ethics, which, since the dawn of capitalism, has been alienated from all attempts to explain social matters, should make a comeback as a valuation tool, and also as a means to explain human social issues.

## 8. A Substantial Scheme

No formula can encompass the entire reality of human beings and their society. This does not mean that the basics of such a reality will always escape the mind's reach. It means that, at this point in our scientific knowledge, we should exercise modesty in our effort – deployed by all great cultures in history – to discover universally valid tenets. However, there is enough knowledge to rebuild some organizational schemes that, while never fully comprehensive, are ubiquitous – that is, they are found in every type of social organization.

One of these schemes – noticed by some authors, including Fossaert (1994: 13) – rests on three capabilities: producing, organizing and

reasoning. The first one refers to producing what contemporary economists call goods and services, which may also be referred to as things
and activities. The second one hinges on organizing human actions within
communities. Finally, reasoning points to thinking about mankind's reality
and the phenomena surrounding it. These three capabilities are supported
by an inseparable simultaneity and complement each other –none of them
can exist without the other two. However, throughout history, large dis-
similarities have characterized their development.

The ability to produce has advanced at an extraordinary pace in the
contemporary world, but it is very unequally distributed. The ability to
organize creates very sharp discrepancies in any of the fields that are currently perceived as somewhat autonomous – economics, politics, culture.
Out of the three capabilities, reasoning ability shows the greatest gaps
among human groups, as philosophers' reasoning bears no resemblance
whatsoever to that of professional politicians in consolidated contemporary democracies; neither does the reasoning of great business leaders in
capitalist economy hubs resemble in any way that of impoverished farmers in Northeastern Brazil, who relocate to São Paulo to avoid starvation
in their homeland.

Our historical knowledge and our theoretical aptitude enable us to
reconstruct multiple past and present processes framed by this three-prong
scheme, and that theoretical effort can better afford us an understanding
of some basic dynamics. Yet, it is paramount to remember a fundamental
truth: human beings' collective reality can never be truly encompassed
by that trilogy. Much of what constitutes the bulk of human personality is
not covered by those three steps, as I have noted earlier. Neither love, nor
aesthetic inspiration and scientific reasoning before their translation into
works, nor the religious values incorporated to the human mind outside
the institutionalized practice that we also call religion, are included there.
Still, that trilogy serves as a sort of basic organizational principle – a substantial scheme that historians and sociologists find in any development
stage and any type of social organization.

**Note**

1.   Originally published in Spanish, in Sergio Bagú (1997) *Catástrofe política y teoría
social*, VI: Construir teoría, Siglo XXI Editores, Mexico. Translated by Mariana Donadini
and revised by Fernanda Beigel.

# References

Bagú, Sergio (1997) *Catástrofe política y teoría social*, Siglo XXI Editores, Mexico.

Combemale, P. (1990) 'Ce qui se sait vraiment en l'économie', *La Revue du Mauss*, Paris, 8, Segundo trimestre.

Fossaert, Robert (1994) *El mundo en el siglo XXI. Una teoría de lossistemas mundiales*, traducción de Elaine Cazenave-Tapie Mexico, Siglo XXI. First edition published in French, 1991.

## Sergio Bagú, by Pablo de Marinis (Argentina)

Sergio Bagú (1911–2002) was born and spent his formative years in Argentina, although his career was developed in several countries (Uruguay, Chile, Peru, Venezuela, the United States) and especially in Mexico – the country that welcomed him generously when he left for his last exile in 1974 until his death in 2002. He is a true representative of the 'Latin American intellectual' and his biography embodies in an exemplary form a way of life and work that, frankly, is now in decline around the world. As an 'intellectual', he made the activity of thought, teaching and research the main purpose for his life, also putting those efforts at the service of normative values, with a strong political-ideological drive (university autonomy, anti-fascism, democracy, socialism). He transcended the boundaries of the social and human sciences (in particular, history, economics, sociology, philosophy and political science), using their different contributions but avoiding disciplinary narrowness. As a 'Latin American', his manner of exercising his thought never meant a renunciation of understanding 'the universal'. Always in the context of a strongly self-reflexive attitude, Bagú was concerned not to succumb to cultural colonialism and/or to ephemeral intellectual fashions. But, in turn, he distanced himself from a parochialism that he also judged as pernicious and sterile. Throughout his work, Bagú's perspective focused on the region as a whole and on some of its countries, but also served as a kind of pretext for thinking about the world, the human condition and our fundamental civilizational options. He defined his research as: 'the conquest of the right to own opinion, respectful of the background but liberated from all inhibitory reverence' (1970: 1).

Books such as *Economía de la sociedad colonial* (1949) and *Estructura social de la colonia* (1952) anticipated in two decades the arduous debates (scholarly, but also with strong political implications) that would take place around the feudal or capitalist nature of the economic structures in the region. Other works, such as *La idea de Dios en la sociedad de los hombres* (1989) and *Time, Social Reality and Knowledge* (1970) are good examples of that permanent concern with 'the universal' pointed to above, which, on the other hand, is not absent either in studies of a more national or regional scope.

His text 'Building Theory' is a good example of this. It is a chapter of his last book published in 1997. In a kind of retrospective look at the entire twentieth

*(Continued)*

(Continued)

century, in its first part he analyzes and reconstructs various 'catastrophes' from a historical perspective of long duration and not merely '*événementiel*'. Precisely for that reason, he carefully uses conceptual categories in the style of the best sociology. Thus, in this exercise, he firstly deals with the phenomenon of war (with particular emphasis on modern and contemporary wars), and then of fascism (in its different historical variants). Afterwards, he delves into the Soviet Union and the United States, highlighting some possible reasons for the collapse of the former, and exploring some of the profound contradictions that were running through the latter. The first part of the book concludes with a chapter in which he reviews a number of dramatic experiences of the twentieth century (e.g., the uprising of the Warsaw ghetto), out of which emerged the creative ability, genius and inventiveness of 'anonymous crowds'. If all the experiences analyzed in the previous chapters cast a gloomy light on mankind and its future, Bagú finds here valid reasons to still harbor some hope.

The second part of the book consists of four chapters and contains mostly theorizing efforts to understand the dynamics of the 'catastrophes' mentioned above, but also includes valuable, broader contributions to the theoretical and epistemological debates of the social sciences, in the face of their current challenges. As in the rest of his work, the simplicity of Bagú's prose contrasts here with the density and height of his arguments.

The first chapter of the second part is the one selected for this volume, a piece of enormous theoretical and epistemological richness. It tackles basic concepts of the social sciences, such as structure and system, the relations between macro and micro instances of social life, and also globalization as a phenomenon involving both tendencies to homogenization and to heterogenization. There are also historical reviews of the emergence of the different social sciences, and the tendency to dominance of economic theory within the social sciences, consolidated throughout the twentieth century – and deplored by Bagú. This text includes an incisive critique of the 'Western' view of the world, questioning its hegemonic ambition to represent the unique possible expression of human rationality, thereby leaving open the possibility of a 'different thought', and anticipating thus much of what the post-colonial/ decolonial literature would later present as an absolute novelty.

In the second part of the book he introduces general questions of the same kind, including the necessary balance between production and consumption and the historical variations of that relationship, or the relations between capitalism and democracy. In a style of questioning that is very reminiscent of Zygmunt Bauman's, because of his ability to connect events that at first glance seem largely diverse, Bagú compares drug trafficking with slavery, or wonders whether there will soon be a collapse of the US as the last imperial power in history. The book closes with a hopeful message: if in other critical moments (before the rise of fascism, or before the imminence of a nuclear war) humanity could climb to new heights, it could well do so again. Within this context Bagu argues that social sciences can play an important role: 'for the human being, to know more about their own society means being able to better solve the current problems and to anticipate more sharply the new ones that will always arise' (1997: 150).

## References

Bagú, Sergio (1949) *Economía de la sociedad colonial. Ensayo de historia comparada de América Latina*, Librería y Editorial El Ateneo, Buenos Aires.

Bagú, Sergio (1952) *Estructura social de la colonia. Ensayo de historia comparada de América Latina*, Librería y Editorial El Ateneo, Buenos Aires.

Bagú, Sergio (1970) *Tiempo, realidad social y conocimiento. Propuesta de interpretación*, Siglo Veintiuno Editores, Mexico DF.

Bagú, Sergio (1989) *La idea de Dios en la sociedad de los hombres. La religión: expresión histórica, radicalidad filosófica, pauta de creación social*, Siglo Veintiuno Editores, Mexico DF.

Bagú, Sergio (1997) *Catástrofe política y teoría social*, Siglo XXI Editores, Mexico.

# 9

# The Struggle for Surplus[1]

*René Zavaleta Mercado (Bolivia)*

Our claim is that the three countries involved in the conflict[2] obstinately shared the same myth of the surplus.[3] We have also claimed that not all surplus generates receptivity, although it is indeed a favourable element in its production. What interests us, then, is receptivity and not the surplus; receptivity, moreover, only as it relates to the question of the constitutive moment.

This is a concept that will have to be used repeatedly over the course of this exposition. [Alexis de] Tocqueville defined it almost ingenuously: 'Every people bears the mark of its origin'. 'The circumstances that surround its birth and aid its development also influence the subsequent course of its existence' (De Tocqueville, [1835] 2004: 31). The concept is more complex than this, but this definition will do for now. If it's true that men cannot experience anything without making it into a representation, or experience a representation without translating it into a discourse, this means that the 'conception of the world' is an instinct. Ideology is essential and it is durable. No one is willing to sacrifice his conception of the world except when he is compelled to do so by a momentous and imposing force. Of course, there may be people with more diffuse constitutive moments than others, more syncretic and weaker. Still, there are certain profound events, certain unfailing processes, even certain instances of collective psychology that found the mode of being of a society for a long period of time. An interpellative event at a moment of general receptivity, at a constitutive moment, is destined to survive as a kind of unconscious or substrate of that society.[4] This is the tragic role of the past in history; in a way, one can only ever do what has already been foreseen. Great epidemics and famines, wars and, in our time, revolutions, are the classic moments of general receptivity: men are prepared to substitute the universe of their beliefs. This role was fulfilled by the constitution of space – by agriculture – in the Andean world, by the Arauco War in Chile, and by the Conquest with its attendant demographic catastrophe and the chimera of gold in all the Latin American countries (Cook and Borah, 1977; Ribeiro, 1972; Sánchez Albornoz, 1973). It can therefore be said that the delusion of surplus led to a confrontation of social formations governed by very different constitutive moments. The constitutive moment refers to the ultimate source of each society, to its deep genealogy, as Hegel said, to its orginary essentiality.

To continue along this line of reasoning, according to the general understanding of the problem (that of the surplus), it has been determined that development can take place only where a constant and substantial economic surplus exists. The history of Latin America itself, however, has provided concrete examples of what we might call the infecundity of the surplus (or at least its relative infecundity). Even Potosí emphatically proved that it is not the surplus that matters but who appropriates it and for what. Great surpluses like that of Argentina in the last third of the nineteenth century and the first of the twentieth, that of Chile's nitrates and copper, even that of Venezuela's oil and Cuba's heyday, attest to the absolutely supplementary role of this factor (Cortés Conde, 1969; Malavé Mata, 1974: 203; Zanetti, 1975).The history of the period immediately prior to the war shows how a great surplus, that of the guano boom, had not sufficed for the construction of a nation. On the other hand, Mexico in the period between 1910 and 1920 and then in the 1930s produced a very high level of state receptivity without the benefit of a large surplus. Here receptivity was the result of the activity of the society. Even Chile ultimately had demonstrated that state receptivity is one thing and the surplus is another. Indeed, when Chile took hold of an immense surplus, its social optimum was impoverished and it clearly had previously had a considerable level of state accumulation on the basis of a rather modest surplus.[5]

From all this it should be clear that the concept of the surplus is not to be privileged a priori. In a tentative analogy, it could be said therefore that the surplus refers to absolute profit and to formal subsumption, while receptivity is connected to real subsumption or the internal or essential reorganization of the productive act. The significance of the surplus here, however, derives from the fact that it is a requirement of large-scale reproduction, which, in turn, contains the whole logic of the new experience of time. Since it is as if men today live many days in the space that used to occupy a single day, since they have taken hold of time and concentrated it, they must construct far more elaborate mechanisms so that this precarious agglutination does not explode. A separate excursus would certainly be in order regarding the relation between surplus and receptivity, and of both to the structure of the state, the expansion of the state, and the theory of mediations (Marramao, 1982: 80). The form in which the surplus exists and the form of its absorption, then, determine the very succession of modes of production. On the other hand, capitalism itself is the history of the construction of its state or, in other words, the history of the capitalist state is that of the production, distribution and application of the surplus. To be precise, it is clear that the surplus does not have an autonomous function because the optimum is composed, in reality, of the relation between surplus and receptivity. Where there is no receptivity, the surplus has no function. The greater the degree of receptivity, the more we must take into account the datum of the surplus. Receptivity, as we have seen, can ultimately exist even with a meagre surplus, although with a greater degree of material social erosion.[6]

This is the basis on which we can define the formal character of the state, that is, its degree of development on the basis of the division of surplus value.[7] The model of circulation of surplus value determines the type of capitalist state. Although we cannot embark here upon a technical analysis of the problem, it is one thing if, for example, surplus value is largely absorbed in an essentially non-productive moment, which is that of luxury consumption, and another if the consumption of surplus value is fundamentally directed towards the erection of the general capitalist, and, on the whole, we could say that appropriation primarily by the general moment of the state or the total capitalist and by the productive moment itself tends to coincide with a more rapid rotation of capital, which has its own significance. It is within these parameters that we must understand that it is not by chance that representative-democratic structures were established in areas where there was a greater retention of the global surplus because this also applies to the global logic of surplus value.

This has to do with the function of the optimum. We will consider the national problem in greater detail below. For now, it would be fair to say provisionally that the nation expresses the degree of cohesion, interpenetration and intensity of civil society, while the state is political power in action (politics understood in its practical relation to power and not as pronouncement or deliberation), whose force in society can be either dependent upon democratic process or arbitrary, of systemic stalemate or omnipotent. In any case, the contemporary notion of the state cannot convincingly be reduced to the classical model of the political state because there is a politics of society and a politics of the state and, furthermore, there is no doubt that the state must act as a person in civil society to assert its autonomy or separation.[8] The modern state must then adapt to expanded reproduction or perpetual mobility and, on the other hand, also to the totalization of society, that is, general circulation (or the generalized social market). In the binary or transfigurative movement that things in this structure tend to have, it could be said that, perhaps as a result of the accumulation of time, a much more decisive measure of organic solidarity or subjective interpenetration emerges here, as well as far more structural forms of contradiction, contestation and counterhegemony. Solidarity, therefore, as well as dissent or resistance, are inscribed with the mark of their provenance from men who command the use of their own will. The work of interaction modifies subjects in relation to one another; they are reformed by one another. This necessarily produces, at least in its prototype, a particular mode of totalization that constitutes the unequivocal specificity of the phenomena of the nation and the state in capitalism.

The very sense of time, the idea of the provisionality of the world, that is, the expansion of circulation and generalized interaction, because the old particularity has been destroyed and one cannot take refuge within what no longer exists but only in the particularity proper to the collective (no one acts for himself and the self ultimately resides in the first person plural) (Zavaleta Mercado, 1975), would have translated into the simple suppression of capitalism if here the originary construction of ideology in its new form, that is, the superstition of the indestructibility of the state, had not taken place. The establishment of consent, whether by means of an impression of power of the state or through the seduction of a new culture, is only the extension of the real subsumption of labour under capital. There is an element of gratification that comes with the institution of the forms of mediation without which totalization itself or the generalization of capitalism would do itself in. To invite men to be free and to interact among themselves without mediation would be an act of self-destruction. Hence the far more actively conservative function that we expect of the capitalist state (Offe, 1972: 85). It must, in other words, move within a world of uncertainty – a world uncertain but cognizable. Mediations, in turn, like enclaves or bunkers of the state within society and of society in the state, belong to the common expenses (and the degree to which they are taken on as such reveals the extent to which a bourgeois mentality has been assumed) of the circulation of surplus value, and this, at least at its initial moment, is the function of the surplus. Rentier profits can guarantee a few years of prosperity, but then the *raison d'état* is accidental.[9] No investment is ever so successful, on the other hand, as an investment in total capital.[10]

The surplus, therefore, is in principle a transmitter of ideology but it could not operate as such if at its base there did not exist a certain receptive appetite or desire, which is proper to material events that are or are deemed to be supreme. Societies cannot live without gods and there are certain events or dogmas that give each society its deities. On the other hand, given that the surplus is remitted primarily to the ruling class and only in a secondary way to the oppressed, it cannot be thought of as something that acquires effective validity except where it can produce a culture and knowledge linked to a system of mediations, a system that is always local. Institutions generally belong to the sphere of a national (and not a global) view of history. In all cases, as we have seen, the powerful idea of the surplus blurs into the vague but fundamental idea of receptivity. There is a relation of species to genus and of appearance to essence between them.

The surplus is not spontaneously transformed into the substance of the state. If this were the case, advanced states would exist wherever a surplus existed. Potosí possessed a surplus that it was incapable of appropriating and the same could be said of Spain, in an intermediary position in the chain (Vilar, 1972). The surplus is conditioned by what for Marx is an element of value: a moral-historical dimension.[11] We must now consider the importance of the fact that the quantitative limit of the economy is a non-economic factor in an indirect way. In essence, this is a certain quality of the social, a kind of relation between the overdetermined or the moment of the state, and the self-determined or democratic. It is therefore something dynamic, something that must be formulated, that must evolve by trial and error. A sudden material discovery (which is what every Latin American, because he is an 'eldoradianist', ultimately longs for) surely generates a surplus and one that is not always used in a sensible way. However, a surplus can also be generated through the redistribution of the existing product, which is the path of reform; this is feasible too but at a higher cost. Reforms excite or move people in a way that is even more dangerous than revolutionary measures. Finally, especially at decisive political moments, new moral-historical principles can be generated, that is, there can be a moral act that founds a new surplus. Even the abuse of these principles, in what can be called the negative formation of ideology, the justification of self-plunder, can be conceived as a foundational event.[12]

# Notes

1. Fragment of the text originally published in Spanish in René Zavaleta Mercado, *Lo nacional-popular en Bolivia* (Siglo XXI Editores, Mexico, pp. 21–34, 1986). Translated by Anne Frieland in: *Towards a History of the National-Popular in Bolivia* (2016, pp. 64–77). Published by Seagull Books, London.

2. See the explanation of the conflict in the Comment by O. Vega Camacho.

3. Paul A. Baran takes up Bettelheim's definition, which says that 'the economic surplus ... is constituted by a portion of the net social product appropriated by the non-working classes' (*Excedente económico e irracionalidad capitalista* [Economic Surplus and Capitalist Irrationality] [Mexico City: Cuadernos de Pasado y Presente, 1980], p. 75). Here we use the concept in the sense of the difference between the product of labour and the non-confiscated portion of the goods produced.

4. For the concept of interpellation, see Louis Althusser, 'Ideology and Ideological State Apparatuses' in *Lenin and Philosophy' and Other Essays* (Ben Brewster trans.). London: New Left Books, 1971, pp. 127–88.

5. In fact, given that the railways did not yet compete with maritime transport, California was closer to Chile than to the eastern United States, which proves how relative the concept of space is. This was surely a decisive factor in Chile's weak boom of the middle of the nineteenth century. Based for the most part on wheat and grains, trade with Chile in California rose from US$250,195 in 1848 to US$1,835,466 in 1849 and US$2,445,868 in 1850 (Jobet (1982), p. 35). In other words, the rapid growth of the Chilean economy during the decades prior to the war ensured that the crisis that followed it was experienced as something intolerable. 'From 1848 to 1860 trade figures tripled', 'the urban population increased by 50 per cent' (Jobet, 1982: 42). Chile was the world's top producer of copper even before the conquest of the great Bolivian deposits (Chuquicamata). In 1869, Chile already produced 61% of the world's copper (Jobet, 1982: 55).

6. Peru was a typical example of a surplus that could not be made into accumulation, while Chile paradoxically degraded its margin of receptivity with the conquest of an immense surplus. The Meiji represented a case of great receptivity and a precarious surplus, at least at first.

7. In theory, indeed, the circulatory model of surplus value should determine the extent to which the total capitalist exists, which has to do with the totalization of the bourgeois class. Without totalization or identity neither the expansion of the state nor organized capitalism is possible. In any case, the state can be tax-based, as the Spanish state was, and have little pretension to totalization; the retention of surplus value in its most general moment or that of the state does not in itself indicate a primacy of accumulation.

8. In truth, the more organic the insertion or inclusion of the state in society, the more consistent its autonomy founded on distance. This should not be confused with the state that has not differentiated itself from the units of society, that which has no choice but to act as a faction that governs arbitrarily.

9. Peruvians like Pardo used the guano surplus to abolish indigenous tribute, which was like an attempt to win Peru its independence from the Indians. Around 1830, indigenous and casta tribute in practice made up half of all tax revenues (Ernesto Yepes del Castillo, *Perú 1820–1920: Un siglo de desarrollo capitalista* [Peru, 1820–1920: A Century of Capitalist Development] [Lima: IEP, 1972], p. 43). The surplus conquered in the Pacific,

on the other hand, enabled the 'Chilean experts' [duchos de Chile] (the expression is Matte's) to 'win their independence' from the state (Jobet, 1982: 67–68).

10. The history of the relation between the Bolivian state and the tin barons, who in practice never contributed anything, is an example of absolute non-contribution to total capital and its consequences. They were ruined by their own greed.

11. Both Marx and Gramsci use the term 'moral', in the sense of 'moral-historical' or 'intellectual and moral reform'. This does not refer merely to the theft of man's labour power in the first case, or the internal form of valorization of conduct in the second. It seems to us that in both cases it involves the principle of action according to ends, the transformation of which ought to be in daily life and the hegemonic internalization of the present foundations of the social.

12. On the authoritarian construction of hegemony, see the work of Erich Fromm; Hubert Bacia, 'La predisposición autoritaria' [The Authoritarian Personality] in Wolfgang Abendroth et al., *Capital monopolista y sociedad autoritaria: La involución autoritaria en la R.F.A.* [Monopolistic Capital and Authoritarian Society: The Authoritarian Involution in the RFA] (Barcelona, Fontanella, 1973), p. 209; Oskar Negt, 'Hacia una sociedad autoritaria' [Towards an Authoritarian Society], in Abendroth et al., *Capital monopolista y sociedad autoritaria*, p. 237.

## References

Antonio, R.J. (1976). *Pierre Vilar, A History of Gold and Money 1450–1920*. London: New Left Books.

Cook, S.F and Borah, W.W. (1977). *Essays in Population History: Mexico and the Caribbean*. Mexico: Siglo XXI.

Cortés Conde, Roberto (1969). 'The Argentine "Boom": A Missed Opportunity?'. In T. Halperín Donghi et al. (eds), *The Fragments of Power: From Oligarchy to Argentine Polyarchy*. Buenos Aires: J. Álvarez, pp. 217–241.

De Tocqueville, Alexis ([1835] 2004). *Democracy in America* (Arthur Goldhammer trans). New York: Library of America.

Jobet, Julio César (1982). *Desarrollo social de Chile: ensayo crítico*. Mexico: Casa de Chile (Centro de Estudios del Movimiento Obrero Salvador Allende).

Malavé Mata, H. (1974). *Historical Formation of Venezuela's Anti-Development*. Havana: Casa de las Américas.

Marramao, Giacomo (1982). *Lo político y las transformaciones*. Mexico: Cuadernos de Pasado y Presente (No: 95).

Offe, Claus (1972). *Strukturprobleme des kapitalistischen Staates*. Frankfurt: Suhrkamp.

Ribeiro, Darcy (1972). *American Historical-Cultural Configurations*. Montevideo: Centro de Estudios Latinoamericanos.

Sánchez Albornoz, Nicolás (1973). *The Population of Latin America: From Pre-Columbian Times to the Year 2000*. Madrid: Alianza.

Vilar, Pierre (1972). *Oro y moneda en la historia, 1450–1920*. Barcelona: Ariel [translators: Armando Saez Buena y Juana Sabater Borrell, revised by: Jordi Nadal Oller].

Zanetti, Oscar (1975). 'Foreign Trade in the Neocolonial Republic'. In Juan Pérez de la Riva et al. (eds), *The Neocolonial Republic: Yearbook of Cuban Studies*, Vol. 1. Havana: Ed. de Ciencias Sociales, pp. 45–126.

Zavaleta Mercado, R. (1975). 'Class and knowledge'. *Historia y Sociedad*, No. 7.

# René Zavaleta Mercado, by Oscar Vega Camacho (Bolivia)

René Zavaleta Mercado (1937–1984) was a Bolivian lawyer and politician who had a very intense and brief life, interrupted by a fatal disease, leaving a quite extensive written body of work in terms of books, essays and journal articles. As a young man, he was elected congressman and Secretary of State. He later joined the Communist Party of Bolivia (PCB), and because of military dictatorships he spent the last years of his life in exile, mostly in Mexico City. It was in this context in which he came to be involved in academic activities, becoming one of the founders of FLACSO (Facultad Latinoamericana de Ciencias Sociales) in its Mexico headquarters. His unfinished and most remarkable book, *Towards a History of the National-Popular in Bolivia*, was published posthumously in 1986.

Zavaleta Mercado's thought intersects the national question, not only in Bolivia but also in Latin America as a whole. This led him to work on economic, social, cultural, political and historical issues. He did this by taking up one of Gramsci's notions that grasps the perspective of national popular struggles, such as those fragments of unofficial history or a counter-history that could potentially modify radically the idea we have of nation, country and social subjects. Such flashes of memory coming from social struggles shaped a landscape of societies in search of their national identity, through political-economic self-determination and social democratization within the structural formation of a desired nation-state.

In the fragment selected for this volume, taken from 'The Struggle for Surplus', the first chapter of the book, he uses this title figuratively to refer to the War of the Pacific (1879–1884), a confrontation between an alliance of Bolivia and Peru against Chile. It was an armed conflict based on a territorial dispute over the immense guano deposits in the Pacific coast, ending with Chile's victory and the usurpation and occupation of extensive territory of the other two countries. The greed for guano, at that time, was because of its extreme desirability as fuel in spinning mills and also for its properties as a fertilizer, especially in England during its economic expansion, thus causing this country to play an active role in promoting the war.

Zavaleta Mercado's interest in the War of the Pacific caused him to outline the reasons behind this historical conflict that compromised national interests, such as the particular interference of foreign interests and each country's capacity to face war in terms of their army and supplies, of their state affairs and of their economies, territorial administration and communications. But mostly to show how society faces conflict and how it responds. He begins his historical inquiry by trying to understand the differences between these countries in terms of their nation-state formation and their capacity to confront war, by comparing their particular economic interests and the desired national image of growth. But goes on to subvert this modern syllogism of state, society and economy, displacing the problematization by asking: what kind of state, what or who makes up society, what is the state's territorial occupation, what is the national interest, what is the nation and for whom?

Zavaleta Mercado concentrates on analyzing the conformation of *state-form*, not only to study whether the state has the capacity to produce economic surplus, but also because of the importance of knowing what is the state's ability to absorb the surplus. And he points out that none of the three countries involved in this war had

*(Continued)*

(Continued)

any interest in the surplus from the point of view of the state, nor did they attempt to withold it or use it to regenerate the nation instead of letting it go abroad to metropolitan centers. They all lived with the illusion of the 'magic of surplus', his literal words, because it was abundant naturally in these lands of conquest and dispossession.

But his main research concerned those remaining fragments of national popular struggles. Trying to understand the state's process of formation as a set of forces at play, not only considering the interests of the ruling class, but, primarily, the implications of the relations of force that the dominant class had to put into effect over the dominated classes and thus finding the traces of resistance and struggle displayed by the subjugated classes to change their condition.

The state form is a social relation, as Marxists would say. This is where he introduces two decisive categories in the analysis of the national state-form: the social equation or optimum and the state's disposition to manage a situation. Bringing up Gramsci's notion of optimum is one of strategic value for political action, because it is not enough to make an analysis of the nation-state since it cannot serve as a comparative tool in relation to other states; it requires a historical examination that can disembowel the dense and complex accumulation of motley structures and processes that are at work. The optimum will be the particular equation established between state and society, a relational quality of a society for its reproduction on a large scale, that is at the level of the superstructures – ideology, law and state – by working the mediations, structures and support frameworks by means of which civil society existed before the state and the *political state* confronting civil society.

The state's disposition is a specific category for understanding the modern conditions of political construction. As Zavaleta Mercado demonstrates, what we usually take up as political and public decisions of free will are mostly constrained by external circumstances and determinations (interest in guano, for example) and this is especially true for the world of the periphery, a world coveted for their surpluses (guano, silver, oil). So this doesn't mean that there is no margin for decision, or that there is not a certain ability for self-determination; rather, it mostly entails the construction of a capacity for self-knowledge and the assessment of modes of dependency. To create national political decisions in the world of the periphery entails self-determination, and having an understanding that for democratic participation to prevail it is necessary to foster citizenship in terms of equality and human rights. This would mean a social and cultural emancipation, opening the paths for the formation of a national popular horizon.

# 10

# Development (Again) in Question: Trends in Critical Debates on Capitalism, Development and Modernity in Latin America[1]

*Arturo Escobar (Colombia–US)*

For more than sixty years, Latin America has experienced – possibly enjoyed and suffered – significant twists and turns regarding the thought and practice of 'development'. Although this has largely been ascribed to economic, cultural and knowledge production processes in metropolitan coutries (before: core countries; today: the Global North), 'development' has always undergone its own shifts and reinvented itself in our continent. Not much has changed today, although, as we will see, it could be said that the last five years have marked a true reinvention of the discourse of 'development' and has opened paths to go beyond it.

The beginning of the 'development' era is often rhetorically identified with President Truman's well-known inaugural address on January 20, 1949, when he announced to the world the new 'Fair Deal' doctrine for those regions that came to be known as 'underdeveloped areas'. According to his famous Point Four Program, the conditions necessary to replicate worldwide the features of advanced societies (high levels of industrialization and urbanization, agricultural technicalization, rapid growth of material production and living standards, and widespread adoption of 'modern' education and values) lay in a wise combination of capital, science and technology. Within a few years, this dream was universally embraced by those in power and, during several decades, it came very close to becoming hegemonic in the economic, social and cultural life of many people (Esteva, 1992; Escobar, 1996). Today, this era seems finally to have come to an end.

The first part of this paper briefly reviews academic (and, to a lesser degree, political) discussions on 'development' and 'post-development'. The second part provides an analysis of several salient aspects of the current juncture as background. The third part addresses the five trends in the critical studies of 'development' in Latin America over the past years which I believe are the most novel. These include: decolonial thinking; alternatives to 'development'; transitions to post-extractivism; crisis and change of the civilizing model and several interrelated perspectives focused on 'relationality' and 'communal' models. The fourth part offers some brief final reflections on certain topics (modernity, the invisibility of Afro-descendants and gender, and sustainability).

## From 'Development' to Post-development': The Genealogy of 'Development' (1951–2000)

From the point of view of the genealogy of thought and the sociology of knowledge, the era of 'development' may be divided into four major stages. Over the first fifty years (1951–2000), the conceptualization of 'development' in the social sciences underwent three main moments corresponding to three contrasting theoretical approaches: the modernization theory in the 1950s and 1960s, with its allied theory of economic growth; dependency theory and related perspectives in the 1960s and 1970s; and critiques of 'development' as a cultural discourse in the 1990s. A fourth stage could be added: a phase defined by the supremacy of a neoliberal vision of economy and society, which, more than a new stage in itself, contributed to a partial loss of interest in 'development' as such. Let us briefly consider each of these stages.

The modernization theory inaugurated a period of certainty in the minds of many theorists and world elites under the premise of the beneficial effects of capital, science and technology. From this view, 'development' was sure to happen if countries met the requirements laid down by large institutions such as the World Bank and if they worked hard to apply the flows of knowledge that, starting in the 1950s, were produced within First World universities and, later, within its peripheral counterparts. During the 1950–1960 period, the category of 'modernization' primarily referred to the induced transformation of 'traditional societies' into 'modern societies' (the American way). At the end of the story, we would all be rich, rational and happy.

This certainty suffered a first blow with dependency theory, which argued that the roots of underdevelopment were to be found in the connection between external economic dependence (the dependence of periphery countries on core countries) and internal social exploitation (particularly class exploitation), not in the alleged lack of capital, technology or modern values. For dependency theorists, the problem was not so much with 'development' as with capitalism: that is, 'development' and modernization would result from the transformation of capitalist societies into socialist societies'.[2] In the 1980s and particularly the 1990s, a growing number of cultural critics in many parts of the world started to question the very concept of 'development'. They analyzed 'development' as a 'discourse' (the trending category by then) of Western origin that operated as a powerful mechanism for the cultural, social and economic production of the Third World: that was the third moment.

These three moments may be classified according to the root paradigms from which they emerged as: liberal, Marxist and post-structuralist theories, respectively. For liberals, the key question was (and still is, albeit with economic actors that differ from the State and have acquired a more central role than the State): how can society develop through a combination of capital, technology, and State economic and social policies? Marxists asked: how had 'development' served as dominant ideology and how could it be separated from capitalism in order to pursue a socialist (or at least social-democrat) 'development' The question the post-structuralists asked was very different: how did Africa, Asia and Latin America come to be defined ('invented') as 'underdeveloped'? How has the 'development' discourse shaped the reality of these countries in particular ways? In other words, how has 'development' served as a strategy for cultural, social, economic and political domination? The implications of the twist in this last question will prove to be, as we will see later, deeper than the previous questions.[3]

It will prove useful to give a brief account of the arguments advanced by this last school, since the notion of post-development that seems to be regaining strength today emerged directly from the post-structuralist critique. Its main elements can be summarized as follows:

- As a historical discourse, 'development' emerged in the early post-World War II period, even if its roots lie in deeper historical processes of modernity and capitalism. It was in this period that 'development' experts started to focus massively on Asia, Africa and Latin America, giving reality to the construct of the 'Third World'.
- 'Development' enabled the creation of a vast institutional apparatus through which the discourse became a real, effective social force, transforming the economic, social, cultural and political reality of the societies in question. This apparatus included a wide range of organizations, from Bretton Woods institutions (the World Bank and the International Monetary Fund) and other

international organizations (the UN system), to planning and development national and local-level agencies.

- It could be said that the 'development' discourse operated through two main mechanisms: the professionalization of 'development problems', including the emergence of expert knowledge and wide areas of knowledge to deal with every aspect of 'underdevelopment'; and the institutionalization of 'development' and the vast network of organizations mentioned above. These processes could be seen as systematic mechanisms for linking knowledge and practices (forms of knowledge and types of power) with particular projects and interventions.
- Finally, the post-structuralist analysis pointed to the exclusion of the knowledge, voices and concerns of those who, paradoxically, 'development' was supposed to serve: the poor in Asia, Africa and Latin America.[4]

## Post-development as a Concept and a Social Practice (1991–2010)

Imagining the end of 'development', one way or another, was the natural corollary of the deconstructive task of the 1990s. However, the post-development concept, albeit controversial, has proven to be long lasting and seems to be making a comeback in this decade. Let's take a look at it. As already mentioned, post-development emerged from the analysis of discourses and practices of 'development' that had a profound impact on the ways in which Asia, Africa and Latin America came to be considered 'underdeveloped' and treated as such.

In this context, post-development was meant to identify at least three interrelated objectives: first, the need to decenter 'development'; that is, to displace it from its central position in discussions and representations of social realities in Asia, Africa and Latin America. A corollary of this first goal was to open up the discursive space to other forms of describing those realities, less mediated by 'development' premises and experiences. Second, in displacing 'development's' centrality from the discursive imaginary, post-development suggested that it was indeed possible to think about the end of 'development'. In other words, it identified alternatives to 'development', rather than 'development' alternatives (such as participative, sustainable, human-scale 'development', which, from the post-development perspective, were considered part of the same discursive universe) as real possibilities. Third, post-development emphasized the importance of transforming the particular configuration of expert knowledge and power. To this end, it proposed that the more useful ideas about alternatives could be gleaned from the knowledge and practices of social movements rather than from the newly qualified experts from the most prestigious universities in the world.

It is fair to say that post-development's trajectory and repercussions in Latin America beyond academic and intellectual circles were limited, with the partial exception of Mexico and Colombia. However, initially formulated in the early 1990s and disseminated through a number of texts in the continent, it has not passed totally unnoticed.[5] This concept could be yet another case in Latin American intellectual history of the famous debate posed by Brazilian scholar Roberto Schwartz in the early 1970s (which was more confined to literary and cultural circles than to the social sciences). The post-development notion could provide an interesting possibility to debate about ideas that may have little application at the moment and which may disappear or re-emerge in the future.

What, then, can we say about the notion of post-development after this, perhaps too hasty and partial, brief review of academic trends? There are a few issues that can be highlighted concerning the notion's usefulness at present. I believe that the notion's core is still valid, that is: the need to decenter 'development' as a social descriptor; the questioning of 'development' knowledge practices; and post-development critiques of the ideas of growth, progress and modernity. That said, one of the main implications of post-development remains seemingly unsolved by this approach: the notion of alternatives to 'development'.

Not only does the 'development' project go on, it seems to have become stronger since the mid-1990s. As Esteva, one of the more lucid and strong critics of 'development' stated in his most recent analysis: 'development has failed as a socio-economic endeavor, but the development discourse still contaminates social reality. The word remains at the center of a powerful but fragile semantic constellation' (2009: 1). Yet a series of crises, emerging discourses and concrete cultural-political challenges seem to play in favor of keeping the imaginary of alternatives to 'development' alive. To this possibility I will devote the rest of this essay.

## A New Framework for Critical Perspectives on Development: The Crisis of 'Globalization'

In Latin America, the 1980s are known as the 'lost decade'. This decade represented the most virulent period of market reductionism and its concomitant political-economical technologies, such as: structural adjustment, privatizations, market liberalization and the dismantling of social policies. As is well known, almost all countries in the region followed, one way or another, the so-called 'Washington Consensus' policies until the end of the 1990s.

During this time, interest in development seemed to have vanished in favor of market actions, although, as Gudynas and Acosta indicated, under the neoliberal market reforms, 'the basic development core persisted and was accentuated' (2011: 74). Much has been written about these two decades, especially from a Marxist political economy perspective. This critique is still relevant, although it is not enough to account for the new trends in social practice and in the field of ideas. Although the 1980s and the 1990s ushered in the era of 'globalization' and the liberal and Marxist analyses of it, accepting the fact that such globalization and its diverse imaginaries are in crisis now seems unavoidable.

The world has changed greatly since the mid-1990s. As far as development studies are concerned, as I see it, the five most salient factors in this transformation have been: In the first place is the tremendous role assumed by China and, to a lesser extent India and Brazil, or in general, the BRICS nations (Brazil, Russia, India, China and South Africa) in the global economy. The second factor is the realignments in global geopolitics following the attacks on the World Trade Center in New York City on September 11, 2001 and the subsequent invasion of Iraq in March 2003. The third factor is the end of the so-called Washington Consensus, that is, the set of ideas and institutional practices that had ruled the world economy since the 1970s, more commonly known as neoliberalism (now replaced by the so-called 'Commodities Consensus', which will be discussed later). The dismantling of really-existing socialism and of centrally planned economies could be cited as a fourth factor, given that, although it started in the 1980s, it became irreversible in the 1990s. The fifth factor has been the environmental crisis, eventually brought into the spotlight in national and world debates by the UN conferences on global climate change and scientific convergence around the findings of the Intergovernmental Panel on Climate Change (IPCC). The ecological crisis alone, if not taken seriously, has the potential to destabilize any and all presently existing 'development' frameworks. This is actually happening now in several places in Latin America.

There have been, of course, many other important changes in the world economy, geopolitics and global conscience since the 1990s, some of which have become more visible in recent years. The explosion of connectivity enabled by digital information and communication technologies (ICT) – firmly established as a scholarly theme by Castell's trilogy on the 'Information Society', published in the second half of the 1990s (see especially Castells, 1996) – has become a mandated reference point for much 'development' work and social movements, despite the fact that the majority of the world population lacks access to such goods and services. The economic crisis that started in 2007 and caused the collapse of financial institutions, the real estate bubble and the downturn in stock markets, mainly in the North, had important global consequences in terms of slowing down economic activity, credit availability and international trade. Many countries in the Global South saw a significant increase in poverty and unemployment and a resulting decline in economic growth (Latin American countries with progressive governments being a partial exception).

Whereas for some critics the crisis spelled the end of financialized capitalism, institutions like the World Bank have engaged in debates to rethink globalization after the crisis, largely based on conventional strategies to boost exports' competitiveness, particularly in the case of Africa. It is clear that the main international lending institutions do not have any new ideas for dealing with 'development' issues after this crisis, as evidenced by the ongoing Eurozone crisis. The increase in religious fundamentalisms in many regions of the world, including the United States, should also be cited as among the most significant transformations: in some countries it involves resistance to post-9/11 policies and the rejection of Western-style modernity.[6]

## The Opening of the Spaces for 'Decolonization'

While the 1980s represented the lost decade in social and economic terms, the 1990s was marked by a great upsurge in critical knowledge production in the field of 'development'. Many authors have argued that academies in the region seemed to have adjusted to the realities of globalization posed by the markets and, in general, to the neoliberal model during the period. The late 1990s and the first decade of the new millennium seemed to have witnessed a reactivation of the space of critical thinking in the region and, to a certain extent, a radicalization of the social practice, particularly with social movements and, to some degree, progressive governments as the main impetus behind them.

As is well known, Latin America was a global epicenter of critical perspectives in previous decades (e.g., ECLAC's critical developmentalism in the 1950s and 1960s, as well as Dependency Theory, the Theology of Liberation, participatory action research, and popular education and communications under the influence of Freire and Fals Borda, in the 1960s and 1970s). At the outset of the millennium and after two 'lost' decades, the continent seems to have strongly re-emerged as the most distinctive source of counter-hegemonic or alternative thought at the global level. Conditions and themes are certainly different, but there is a significant degree of continuity.

It is a peak moment, which Gudynas and Acosta (2011), two of the most active exponents in the debates on 'development', characterize as one of significant renewal. Whereas Acosta (2010) highlights that, with *Buen Vivir* (BV, by its initials in Spanish) or Good Life, albeit an 'opportunity to construct', we would be setting off on the road to post-development, Gudynas emphasizes the most resolute questioning of the alternatives to 'development', 'that is, alternatives in a deeper sense, aiming to break away from the cultural and ideological bases of 'development', bringing forth other imaginaries, goals and practices' (Gudynas and Acosta, 2011: 75). For Svampa, environmental and social struggles around extractivism, 'have helped resurface a set of nodal debates that cut across Latin American critical thinking with regard to the concept of progress, the view of nature', the role of indigenous people and the national-popular identity in the process of national and continental construction (2012: 25).

This effervescence over concepts and social practices, which was palpable in various spaces associated, one way or another, with 'development', is clearly reflected in the above-mentioned authors, in many other authors represented in the valuable collection published by Massuh (2012), and in the numerous works co-published by Acosta and Martínez for Abya-Yala since 2009 (2009a, 2009b). Equally relevant are the books published with the collaboration of CLAES (Centro Latin Americano de Ecología Social) and Gudynas, some of which will be reviewed later; and the rich Bolivian production on the subject.

## Five Trends in Major 'Development' Studies (and Beyond)[7]

It would be impossible to fairly summarize the many different perspectives, actions and trends that have arisen in this last period. Taken as a whole, and once again from the perspective of the genealogy of critical thinking and the sociology of knowledge, five innovative areas and two fundamental changes in the epistemic conditions of critical knowledge production can be highlighted.

The most interesting areas, according to this author, include the following: a consistent, strong theoretical framework, known as the modernity, coloniality and decoloniality perspective (MCD), especially its emphasis on epistemic decolonization; a theoretical and political imaginary, with alternatives to 'development' along with the conceptualization of *Buen Vivir* (Good Living) as the most clear expression of that emerging imaginary; a theoretical and practical proposal for economic and social transformation and transitions to post-extractivism; a seemingly old discourse albeit in a process of renewal and materialization, the crisis of the civilizing model; and, finally, a theoretical stance – which nonetheless gains resonance in the political practice of movements – articulated around relationality and 'the communal', including the perspectives of the 'pluriverse'.

Epistemic decolonization; alternatives to 'development' and *Buen Vivir* (BV); transitions to post-extractivism; civilizing crises and alternatives to modernity; communal logics, relationality and the pluriverse: these five emerging areas, which are interrelated in a variety of ways that we will not analyze here, are charting their intellectual and political path through the epistemic and social (cultural and political) intricacies of the continent, weaving a landscape of thinking, fields of study, and political and cultural processes that differs from the one that prevailed a few decades before.

Two changes in the conditions for producing knowledge target this new landscape. The first change has to do with the fact that the range of knowledge producers has expanded well beyond academia. Today, a growing number of researchers, activists and intellectuals outside academia are heeding the urge to provide alternative interpretations of the world, including of 'development'. In this sense, the complex conversations in which many types of knowledge producers are engaging worldwide are in themselves a hopeful condition for the critical analysis of 'development' at the present time. This urge involves the need to transform not only the places and contents of theory, but its very form. This trend is particularly acute in the field of social movements and in transition studies, where activists' own research and knowledge production are becoming central to understanding what social movements are, why they mobilize and what kinds of worlds they wish to build.

The second change is related to the first one but it is more likely to go unnoticed by academics: that contemporary social theory is falling short of imagining both the questions that should be raised concerning today's key issues and their possible answers. Already visible are the rifts and limitations of modern social theory, even in its more 'enlightened' versions, as is the case with popular French and Italian theorists, however interesting they may be, and their *criollo*[8] followers. The most important corollary of these two changes is the need to establish new conditions and conversation spaces among critical academia, independent intellectuals/ artists, and social movements' intellectuals/activists. Actually, the latter group seems to be leading this project, a fact that adds up to a very promising condition for today's knowledge production.

Before briefly outlining each of these five areas, it is worth noting that there are obvious differences between them, since they are different kinds of entities that respond to various dynamics and interests. Some (MCD) could be defined as research programs, others (transitions to post-extractivism) as research-action programs/projects in the sense that they emerge and largely aim at transforming imaginaries and concrete social practices (particularly in the mining sector). A third type would fall in between them (for example, communality and the pluriverse), while the civilizational debate appears to be, up to now, more a political-cultural positioning than a research or research-action program in itself, although some steps have been taken in this regard. Sociologically speaking, the picture is somewhat messy and confusing; however, far from being an obstacle, this reflects the dynamics in question and what is at stake. What does seem clear to me is that a sustained dialogue between these two trends could prove useful at present, both to clarify and enrich their respective positions and to create synergies.

Would it be possible to argue that, taken as a whole, the new trends and epistemic conditions constitute what was once referred to as 'post-development', especially in terms of displacing 'development', on the one hand, and changing the epistemic conditions for the debate, on the other? Obvious though it may seem, this question may be relevant. Let's listen again to Gudynas and Acosta: 'Buen Vivir represents an alternative to development, and thus constitutes a possible response to substantive post-development critique' (2011: 78). Svampa identifies a useful typology in the 'development' debate: 'neo-liberal neo-developmentalism, progressive neo-developmentalism and the post-development perspective' (2012: 26). This reveals 'a fracture in critical thought' (Svampa, 2012: 25), where post-development positions 'agglutinate a diversity of currents with decolonizing ambitions, targeting at the dismantling and deactivation – through a series of categories and limit-concepts – of the apparatuses of power, myths and imaginaries that are at the basis of the current development model' (Svampa, 2012: 51).

Whatever the case, the present moment seems to be one of true 'reinvention', to return to Gudynas and Acosta's dictum – although many of the possible paths to attain it are clearly uncertain. It is worth clarifying that these epistemic disputes tend to go hand in hand with actual struggles carried out by different groups. At the social level, names like Bagua, Conga, Santurbán and Marmato, La Toma (the paradigmatic struggle of the Afro-Colombian community against large-scale mining in Northern Cauca, Colombia), Tipnis, Yasuní, etc., reverberate throughout the continent with new shades (where anti-capitalism resonates as much as environmentalist, cultural, communal, and even civilizational and spiritual movements), without forgetting, of course, Porto Alegre and the repeated summits oraganized by Indigenous and Afro-descendant organizations, as well as around food sovereignty and environmental issues (Rio + 20) during the last ten years.

## The Modernity–Coloniality–Decoloniality Perspective

Fifteen years after its emergence, there are already many genealogies, maps, characterizations and critiques of what I have herein called the 'The Modernity/Coloniality/Decoloniality Research Program' or MCD, or decolonial thought. This is not an appropriate space to review the various maps of MCD, or its critiques.[9] Suffice it to say, from a critical academic perspective, MCD has probably been the most visible interpretive framework that has emerged in the 2000s in that space. Largely associated with names like Aníbal Quijano, Walter Mignolo, Enrique Dussel, Mariá Lugones, Catherine Walsh and Edgardo Lander, MCD somehow represents a classic example of the emergence of a new perspective or paradigm and its dissemination through a network of authors, formal and informal publications, conferences, internal and external debates, the introduction of a lexicon or set of categories, and individual and collective positionings. It may be considered a consistent, elegant framework, once again, from the sociology of knowledge, with foundational categories such as: coloniality of power, coloniality of knowledge and of being, epistemic decolonization, the modern/colonial world-system, as well as an innovative characterization of the long history of the continent (re-interpretation of the Conquest) and of Eurocentrism as the knowledge form of that world-system. Although rooted in the big wave of the already mentioned intellectual production in the continent in the 1960s and 1970s, it also differs from it in several key aspects: (a) it addresses the concept of 'modernity' in an innovative, critical and determined fashion; (b) it identifies epistemic decolonization (from the space of knowledge production) as a crucial domain of struggle and world transformation; and therefore, (c) it makes a worthwhile effort to go beyond intra-European and intra-modern

perspectives about modernity and reality, that is to say, to overcome
Eurocentrism. In short, MCD can be considered a strong social framework
with a firm cultural and epistemic orientation. Over the years, decolonial
thinking has opened up to other issues that had been disregarded in the
first decade: gender, nature, interculturality and coloniality beyond Latin
America. As a new generation of decolonial authors has expanded and a
generation of intellectuals and young activists enters into the picture, new
orientations emerge and some critiques get answered. Still, it is appropriate to say that the lack of a direct relationship with struggles and concrete
situations, with a few exceptions – and the academicist language that still
characterizes the bulk of its texts – remains one of the most solid critiques
of this perspective. However, the conceptual corpus created by this group
has somehow permeated the other four perspectives we will examine next,
and has found echoes in some social movements.

## Alternatives to 'Development'

The notion of an alternative to the very idea of 'development' (although,
as explained before, it has been under construction in critical thinking for
some time now), appears to be emerging as a strong proposal, particularly
in the work carried out by Gudynas and Acosta and their collaborators in
Ecuador, Peru and Uruguay, although the concept is currently under discussion in academic and intellectual-political circles in many other countries such as Colombia, Mexico and Bolivia. *Buen Vivir* – including its
role in the Ecuadorian and Bolivian constitutions – has been, no doubt,
the major trigger for this discussion, closely followed by the debates on
the rights of nature (RN). Each of these topics (*BV*, RN and alternatives to
'development') deserve a separate chapter (whole books have been written on the first two of them).

   We will restrict ourselves here to mentioning that this trend suggests
a radical questioning of the hard core of ideas associated with 'development' (growth, progress, market reforms, extractivism, competitiveness,
an excessive increase in individual material consumption, anthropocen-
trism, etc.); it feeds on analyses based on indigenous knowledge and
movements; it identifies the need to go beyond Western knowledge
(therefore, it implies a critique of European modernity, albeit somehow
mild, as compared with MCD and the discourse on the crisis of the civilizing model); and discussions are resumed about BV and RN as a 'political
platform to develop alternatives to development' (Gudynas and Acosta,

2011: 73). Rather than isolated interventions, BV and RN must be considered in the context of a whole range of pioneering innovations, including the rethinking of the State in terms of plurinationality, and of society in terms of interculturality, a comprehensive and integral notion of rights and an improved 'development' model the goal of which is precisely the realization of *BV*. All these innovations must be considered multi-cultural, multi-epistemic, and as deeply negotiated and often contradictory political construction processes (Gudynas and Acosta, 2011).

It is clear, however, that *BV* constitutes a challenge to long-standing notions of 'development'. This return of 'alternatives to development', in other words, speaks of alternatives 'in a deeper sense' (Gudynas and Acosta, 2011: 75). Appealing to the coloniality of knowledge, this deeper sense is to be found in the domains of culture, imaginaries and ideas. Through a detailed and scholarly analysis of the unfolding of BV and RN in Ecuador and Bolivia, on the other hand, authors find support for their main theses in rationalities, proposals and struggles of indigenous movements, and in the sophisticated proposals of their intellectuals (in addition to drawing from a variety of eclectic theoretical sources, including ecology).

It is important to highlight the emphasis placed by this group on the relationship between theoretical discussion and social practice; that is to say, the fact that conceptual alternatives must contribute to providing answers to the urgent issues that are not being resolved by current developmentalism. Its proposal of alternatives to 'development' is both 'a critique of developmentalism and an attempt at alternatives' (Gudynas and Acosta, 2011: 82), which is a truly commendable effort to overcome epistemological practices of academicism, avant-gardism, etc. The next section, which is also associated with this group and deals with alternatives to extractivism, actually targets this issue.

**Transitions to Post-extractivism**

A hallmark of most contemporary transition discourses (TDs) is the fact that they posit a cultural and institutional transformation that implies a *transition to an altogether different world.*

Thus, although TDs originate in many parts of the world and different knowledge domains and operate through different social practices, there is a clear difference between the transition discourses emerging in the North and their counterparts in the Global South. In the North, the most prominent include 'Degrowth', but there is a variety of transition proposals and imaginaries worth considering such as: 'The Great Turning' (by Joana Macy, scholar of Buddhism and general systems theory), 'The Great Transition Initiative' (Tellus Institute), or 'The Great Work or Transition to an Ecozoic Era' (inspired by theologist and ecologist Thomas Berry), among others. Also included are several inter-religious dialogues, some UN processes, the concept of anthropocene, etc.

In the Global South, TDs boast a different emphasis; a particularly important one in South America involves 'transitions to post-extractivism' (TPs; see Escobar 2014 for an extended discussion). I would like to stress the importance of building bridges between transition narratives in the North and in the South, not only to gain perspective but to disseminate TDs with a radical politics of transformation. Although there can be no single or general framework for the political practice of transitions, these bridges between different forms of activism for transitions are currently crucial, given the global character of many of the prevailing processes.[10]

## Notes

1. This is a fragment of the chapter published in Spanish: 'El desarrollo (de nuevo) en cuestión: algunas tendencias en los debates críticos sobre capitalismo, desarrollo y modernidad en América Latina' in Arturo Escobar, *Sentipensar con la tierra: nuevas lecturas sobre desarrollo, territorio y diferencia* (Editorial Universidad Autónoma Latinoamericana UNAULA, Colección Pensamiento Vivo, 2014), pp. 25–65. Original translation by Mariana Donadini, revised by Fernanda Beigel and Arturo Escobar.

2. The dependency approach was undoubtedly more comprehensive than the modernization perspective, in the sense that its analysis of 'structural dependency', following the Marxist orientation, required not only a global analysis but an analysis of economic, social and political interrelationships. It may prove useful to read Chapter 2 of Cardoso and Faletto's 1969 classic framework for *An Integrated Analysis of Development*, from this perspective. Amin (1975) has also written an important body of work on the topic, from outside the continent.

3. For a more in-depth discussion of 'development' stages and the post-development concept, see Escobar (2005).

4. As happens with modernization and dependency, it is difficult to outline the main works of post-structuralism and the differences between them. I will point out that the poststructuralist critique comprises a large and heterogeneous group of authors (as was the case with the other two schools) of which only a few could be considered post-structuralists. Many considered themselves cultural critics. Most of them came from countries in the Global South, especially South Asia (Nandy, Kothari, Shiva, Vishvanathan) and Latin America. Several of them were linked to Illich's work (Esteva, Sachs, Rahnema and Robert) or were connected with social movements. For a discussion

of this approach and bibliography, see Sachs (1992) and Escobar (1996). If we were to consider the field of social theory as a whole, we would say that, in addition to Foucaldian post-structuralism, this third school had links with anticolonial and postcolonial theory, cultural studies and a certain post-Marxism, such as Laclau and Mouffe's (1985).

5. According to *Postdevelopment Reader*'s publishers (Rahnerna and Bawtree (eds) 1997), the word 'post-development' was first used in 1991 in an international colloquium held in Geneva. The author of this article first used the term that same year in Caracas at a conference on Latin American critical thinking, organized by, among others, Edgardo and Luis Lander and Margarita Lopez Maya. See Escobar (1992). There are several books in Spanish on this topic, particularly from Colombia, Mexico and Spain.

6. For more details on this section, see the Preface to the second edition of *La invención del desarrollo* (Escobar, 2011).

7. The presentation and analysis of each section are brief, as well as their bibliographical references, which are vast in all cases (with the partial exception of the last topic treated). The journal *América Latina en movimiento* (www.alainet.org) is an important source of activist orientation for these debates.

8. Translator's note: '*criollo*' is a Spanish word used to refer to a person of Spanish descent born in Spanish Colonial America.

9. A recent chronology by a group from Patagonia can be found at: www.ceapedi. com.ar. It is quite similar to the one recently suggested by some of the leading members of the group, Mignolo (2010). The book, published by Lander (2000), remains the most cited collective work by this group. See especially the Introduction.

10. The movement around the idea of '*decroissance*' or 'degrowth' has grown and has differentiated itself dramatically from other movements since it was initially formulated by Serge Latouche in France.

## References

Acosta, A. (2010). *El buen vivir en el camino del post-desarrollo. Una lectura desde la Constitución de Montecristi*. Quito: Fundación Friedrich Eber, Fes-Ildis.

Acosta, A. and Martínez, E. (eds.) (2009a). *El buen vivir. Una vía para el desarrollo.* Quito: Abya-Yala.

Acosta, A. and Martínez, E. (eds.) (2009b). *Derechos de la naturaleza. El futuro es ahora.* Quito: Abya-Yala.

Amin, S. (1975). *Unequal Development*. London: Monthly Review Press.

Cardoso, F.H. and Faletto, E. (1969). *Dependencia y desarrollo en América Latina*. Mexico, DF: Siglo XXI.

Castells, M. (1996). *The Rise of the Network Society*. Oxford: Blackwell.

Escobar, A. (1996). *La invención del tercer mundo. Construcción y deconstrucción del desarrollo*. Bogotá: Norma.

Escobar, A. (2005). 'El posdesarrollo como concepto y práctica social'. In: D. Mato (ed.). *Políticas de economía, ambie4nte y sociedad en tiempos de globalización*. Caracas: Universidad Central de Venezuela. (pp. 17–32)

Escobar, A. (2011). 'Prefacio'. In: *La invención del desarrollo* (2nd edn.). Popayán: Universidad del Cauca.

Escobar, A. (2014). *Sentipensar con la tierra: Nuevas lecturas sobre desarrollo, territorio y diferencia*. Editorial Universidad Autónoma Latinoamericana UNAULA, Colección Pensamiento Vivo.

Esteva, G. (1992). 'Development'. In: *The Development Dictionary*. London: Zed Books.

Esteva, G. (2009). *What is Development?* Unpublished paper, Oaxaca: Universidad de la Tierra.

Gudynas, E. and Acosta, A. (2011). 'La renovación de la crítica al desarrollo y el buen vivir como alternativa'. *Utopía y Praxis Latinoamericana, 16*(53): 71–83. Available at: www.gudynas.com/publicaciones/GudynasAcostaCriticaDesarrolloBVivirUtopia11. Pdf

Laclau, E. and Mouffe, C. (1985). *Hegemony and Socialist Strategy*. London: Verso.

Lander, E. (ed.) (2000). *La colonialiad del saber: Eurocentrismo y ciencias sociales. Perspectivas latinoamericanas*. Buenos Aires: CLACSO.

Massuh, G. (ed.) (2012). *Renunciar al bien común. Extractivismo y (pos)desarrollo en América Latina*. Buenos Aires: Mardulce.

Mignolo, W. (2010). 'Introduction: Coloniality of Power and De-colonial Thinking.' In: W. Mignolo and A. Escobar (eds). *Globalization and the Decolonial Option*. London: Routledge. (pp. 1–20)

Sachs, W. (ed.) (1992). *The Development Dictionary*. London: Zed Books.

Svampa, M. (2012). 'Pensar el desarrollo desde América Latina'. In: G. Massuh (ed.), *Renunciar al bien común. Extractivismo y (pos)desarrollo en América Latina*. Buenos Aires: Mardulce (pp. 17–58).

## Arturo Escobar, by Irene Piedrahíta Arcila (Colombia)

Arturo Escobar (1952–) born in Manizales (Caldas, Colombia) and academically trained in the United States, has profoundly influenced the academic and political discussions around development in the social sciences and also contemporary anthropology in Colombia. His research on development, poverty, inequality, and social and political mobilizations, has reshaped the way these problems have been thought about in sociology, as well as placing ethical and political reflections around the construction of scientific knowledge.

Escobar began his studies as a chemical engineer at Universidad del Valle (Valle del Cauca, Colombia), and later traveled to the United States to pursue a PhD in the Philosophy, Policy and Planning of Development at the University of California. There, Escobar took classes with Michel Foucault, one of the academics who most influenced his work. Such an influence can be traced from the way Foucault understands power and discourse, conceived not only as that which is spoken, but also as that which unfolds, namely practice. This is why in many of his texts these are key concepts to analyze reality and understand cultural phenomena through a political lens. In addition, his work has been fueled by the discussions he has had with the Modernity/Colonial group led by Edgardo Lander, and by the multiple experiences he has had as a visiting professor in the United States, Latin America and Europe.

One of his most influential works is *Encountering Development: The Making and Unmaking of the Third World* (1995), which derives from his doctoral thesis 'Power and Visibility: The Invention and Management of Development in the Third World', written in 1987. This work is a milestone in the criticism of economic development theories, not only because it demonstrates the unfulfilled promises of this discourse, but because it establishes a political position from the academic arena that invites us to question the geopolitical divisions North/South, West/East, developed/underdeveloped. In fact, the genealogical process that Escobar builds throughout the chapters of this book evidences a deep insight on the idea of the Third World itself and the infantilization that for decades these territories have been subjected to. This is what Escobar calls a regime of representation.

Another of his books, *El final del salvaje. Naturaleza, cultura y política en la antropología contemporánea* (1999), has served to rethink the problems that concern local anthropology. In the 1990s, Colombian anthropology experienced a theoretical and methodological crisis due to the changes in the objects of study, the new theoretical frameworks and questions that emerged from the historical and socio-political events that the country was going through. This led to the reformulation of the disciplinary work from what some have called a 'deindiologization' of Colombian anthropology. In this context, *El final del salvaje* brought new lines of work and analysis (based on new theoretical proposals to studying social movements from a cultural perspective), environmental processes and conflicts through political ecology, and new forms of understanding of the modern project from the critics to the theories of economic development and the production of scientific knowledge.

Criticism is a constant element in Escobar's publications. However, he has also been concerned with transcending such criticism and positioning other forms of thinking for the emergence of new concepts with which to understand the world. The alternatives proposed by Escobar can be traced to works such as *Más allá del Tercer Mundo. Globalización y diferencia* (2005a), *El 'postdesarrollo' como concepto y práctica social* (2005b), and *Sentipensar con la tierra* (2014): the concepts to understand and name development must change.

Escobar's research has an additional potential. Although his works contain deep theoretical reflections, his work draws on constant conversations with communities and social movements in the country, especially those located in the Colombian Pacific, near to where he is an Associate Researcher, at the Universidad del Valle, Cali. For this reason, in his works the reader will find direct references to the experiences of these communities, as well as to the analysis of the processes and reflections that these groups make. His position-taking embodies the maxim that indicates that the academic is also political, even when his work is developed in the United States. Hence, in recent years, his opinion has been consulted to understand and analyze events such as the peace process with the FARC, what will happen to the territories in the post-conflict scenario, and the impact of contemporary capitalism and the government policies that sponsor mining and energy exploitation in the country as the main source of wealth.

*(Continued)*

(Continued)

**References**

Escobar, A (1987). Power and Visibility: The Invention and Management of Development in the Third World. PhD dissertation, University of California, Berkeley.

Escobar, A. (1992). 'Imagining a postdevelopment era? Critical thought, development, and social movements'. *Social Text, 31/32*: 20–56.

Escobar, A. (1995). *Encountering Development: The Making and Unmaking of the Third World*. Princeton: Princeton University Press.

Escobar, A. (1999). *El final del Salvaje: Naturalerza, cultura y política en la antropología contemporánea*. Bogta: ICANH.

Escobar, A. (2005a). *Más allá del Tercer Mundo. Globalización y diferencia*. Bogotá: Instituto Colombiano de Antropología e Historia.

Escobar, A. (2005b). 'El "postdesarrollo" como concepto y práctica social'. In: Daniel Mato (ed.), *Políticas de economía, ambiente y sociedad en tiempos de globalización* (pp. 17–31). Caracas: Facultad de Ciencias Económicas y Sociales, Universidad Central de Venezuela.

Escobar, A. (2014). *Sentipensar con la tierra: nuevas lecturas sobre desarrollo, territorio y diferencia*. Editorial Universidad Autónoma Latinoamericana UNAULA, Colección Pensamiento Vivo.

Rahnema, M. and Bawtree, V. (eds) (1997) *The Postdevelopment Reader*. London: Zed Press.

# 11

# The 'American' Modernity
# (Keys to Its Understanding)[1]

*Bolívar Echeverría (Ecuador–Mexico)*

The "Americanization" of modernity during the 20th century is a general phenomenon: in fact, all aspects of 20th-century civilized life exhibit, one way or another, an overdetermination on which "Americanism" or the "American identity" has somehow left its imprint. This phenomenon has not restricted itself, as one would expect, to societies in Northern America, where it was born in the 18th century, but has spread, since the late 19th century, throughout the entire world.

"American" modernity has expanded beyond its original boundaries not only or preferably to relatively recent postcolonial contexts – as in Asia or Africa, where European modernity was regarded as a separate movement, viewed as something foreign or embraced by the elites; it has particularly reached long-established modernity situations in Europe or Latin America.

Also at this turn of the century, as throughout modern history, societies and non-European countries, such as Far East nations, for example, pay the price of a greater or lesser degree of "Westernization" of their lifestyle in order to get access to the advantages of modernization. However, at present, such "Westernization" has reduced itself to an "Americanization". In the era of "globalization", "Americanism" has imposed itself as a "common identity" or at least as a universal identity that must be shared by all people insofar as they seek to become adequate consumers of modern goods and to participate in "civilized" life.

Several facts and tendencies contribute to determining that which is distinctly "American" in contemporary modernity: the process of decline of economic, social and political life in the last fifty years – that seems to set world history towards a catastrophe of extreme, unprecedented magnitude-follows the development pattern defined by one of the many versions of capitalist modernity: the "American" version. Any attempt to stop, reverse or even survive to such a process of decline and its consequences must first assess the resources available in current modern civilization to make it feasible. It would be wrong to assume that current resources are the same as or similar to those available to modern civilized life in the past century to counteract its abominations, and which were wasted with catastrophic effects. The differences between last century's modernity ("European") and current modernity ("American") at all levels (technical, social and political) seem obvious at first glance, but are actually unclear. It is necessary to describe them precisely and examine them critically in order to recognize the specificity of the latter below the surface of its apparent similarity to the former, thus detecting in it new resources that may be used to adequately fight it.

1. Capitalist modernity is a "civilizing project" that developed spontaneously in the practical life of European societies at the beginning of the second millennium of our era. Its purpose has been to reconstruct human life and its world by adjusting and developing the possibilities offered by a widespread technical revolution emerging at the time. The peculiarity of this modernity project resides in the way it approaches this civilizing reconstruction, endowing it with a particular meaning: to give "another turn of the screw" to the already millennial commoditization of human life and its world, initiated eight or nine centuries BC; to radicalize the "subsumption" or subordination of the "natural form" of that life to its "double", "the value form", resulting from a commoditized life. To transform that subsumption from a mere external or "formal" fact into a "real" or "technical" fact; into a fact that "internalizes" or incorporates the particular capitalist way of reproducing wealth into the composition itself of the instrumental field, of society's machine system, thus strengthening exploitation of labor in its salaried/proletarized scheme. The process of conducting to the generalization the telos of the valorization of value, prompted by the capitalist way of reproducing social life, is, undoubtedly, the dominant process in the history of European modernization, but is far from being the only one. Other proposals of modern life that reassert the telos of the "natural form" of human life keep coming up and challenging it. However, up to date, they have failed to succeed.

2. The civilizing project of capitalist modernity was implemented, in concrete historical terms, in the first place, by invading the pre-existing figures in European civilization and imposing itself on them or even replacing them and, second, by suppressing civilizing pre-figurations resulting from other non-capitalist, up-to-date versions of the technical revolution. Therefore, the actual historical reality of modern civilization

in Europe can only be understood if we figure it out as the execution of the civilizing project brought about by the capitalist mode of social reproduction which involves crushing the resistance presented by several pre-modern civilizations and multiple non-capitalist approaches to modern civilization. In the struggle or confrontation triggered by this resistance, the winning side, the capitalist side, is able to succeed only due to a dynamic set of commitments that it has to enter into with these already established civilizations and civilizing proposals. Such commitments enable the latter to repurposefully reproduce certain essential features of the "natural form" of social life and to force the capitalist side to divert its self-affirmation and to delay it. Particularly in the Mediterranean world, and as a result of a millennial history, the "formal subsumption" imposed by merchant's capital and usurer's capital (which Marx called "antediluvian" forms of capital) on Western civilization had already evolved in social life into a rich fabric of traditions and customs, into a wide and complex set of identities zealously cultivated on a daily basis. Thus, going from the prevalence of "antediluvian" capital to the prevalence of "productive capital" – the kind of capital which consummates the "real subsumption" of social life under capitalism – turned out to be a considerably difficult move that actually took place in mid-18th century. In fact, it was so difficult as to enable the opening of a new historical era following the French Revolution: the period of the "actuality of revolution" (as Georg Lukacs called it), in which an alternative modernity project, the communist project, managed to jeopardize the capitalist option that was trying to improve itself. (Fernand Braudel reports the difficulty of this move when he speaks of the "strangeness" and "clumsiness" of capital in the face of production issues.)

3. In the 17th century, the history of modern-capitalist civilization branches off into two overlapping, parallel and adjacent but autonomous development lines: the European branch, clearly the main, predominant line, and the apparently secondary branch, the "(North) American" line.

What distinguishes these two branches from one another is the degree of commitment between the execution of the capitalist civilizing project and the already civilized (pre-modern and modern) reality to be taken into account. The European line of modern civilization is an "impure" line due to its high degree of commitment. This line progresses slowly and meanderingly, re-functionalizing a "pagan" social identification endowed with a consistency and dynamic of its own and which forces the capitalist "value form" to accommodate itself to a multiple and complex set of "natural" or concrete forms of life, some still pre-modern and others already modern.

On the other hand, the "American" line is an almost "pure" line, on account of its weak commitment between the capitalist and the "natural". This line follows an almost straight path, along which it unfolds without major setbacks, amidst a civilized life quite flat or elementary in which the "natural" identification of life to be re-functionalized reduces itself, quintessentially, to an ardent faith in the Judeo-Christian Holy Scriptures and blind obedience to moral guidelines derived from them.

4. Behind the seemingly purely doctrinal differences between the European Christians and the Puritan colonists who would create the American branch – differences that led to the latter being "expelled" to America – lie other more decisive differences related to the "elaborated" (miscegenated) or the "elementary" (pure) part of civilized life that each of them represented in the modernization process. European modernity is essentially a Southern European or Mediterranean modernity while "American" modernity rather derives from a Northwestern European modernity. Here, the geographical difference points to an identity difference which played an important role in consolidating the capitalist mode of social wealth reproduction. The former is a "Catholic" modernity; the latter, a "Protestant" modernity, although not in the theological sense of the terms but in an identity-political sense, that is, with regard to the degree of radicalization of Christianization of everyday life, the extent to which the Christian religious assembly itself, the ecclesia, had managed to put itself in the place of or to replace the community or the polis as a socializing, identifying instance of singular and collective individuals.

European Catholic or Mediterranean modernity featured a relatively low degree of Christianization since it resulted from an evangelization process whose destructive effects on pagan identities and cultures in Mediterranean societies had faced strong resistance, forcing it to adopt a peculiar "strategy" in order to integrate or mix them into a Christian identity and culture which had to be relativized and "loosened up" to that purpose. European Protestant or Northwestern modernity, on the other hand, featured a high degree of Christianization because it had stemmed from an evangelization process whose devastating effect had progressed without major obstacles along the ruins of North European identities and cultures (Celtic and Germanic) and, without the need to compromise its principles, without going into the intricacies of miscegenation, had replaced those identities and cultures with an ecclesiastic, purist Christian identity.

5. "American" modernity, as an extension of the particular North European modernity, comes along to complete something which Christianity seems to have had the task of preparing: a sociality endowed with an "ethos" that enables it to offer a positive, "realistic", acquiescent and docile response to the "spirit of capitalism" (Max Weber); to its requirement of a certain kind of human being able to accommodate himself/herself to actions that subsume human life under capital; of certain humanity that displays an ethical-anthropological "whiteness" as a basic feature of its behavior and appearance.

In the exaggeratedly North European "American" line of capitalist modernity, the commodification of life and its world, the subsumption of the "natural form" of life under its "value form" takes place in a context in which the former displays extreme weakness and very few possibilities of resisting the action of the latter. It is a "natural" life whose creativity is hindered by and stuck in inertia or repetition. There is nothing or almost nothing in the practical experience of social individuals that enables them to perceive a contradiction between producing and consuming objects as "earthly goods", or as commodities, "heavenly goods", or pure economic values. The gradual but consistent development of the "natural form" subject to capital in "(North) American" modern life explores beyond all limits the potential for quantitatively increasing goods produced/consumed. On the other hand, however, it imposes a repetition without substantial alterations of the ancestral qualitative consistency of such goods. Thus, new use values must be discovered in the projected demands – on the basis, in principle, of nature's inexhaustible availability – from money – rich private owners who are unable to collectively break away from the established system of needs. This process differs from the one unfolding in European modernity, where the new use values discovered have been re-functionalized by the capitalist value but without invalidating the social-natural "logic" or blocking the creativity that results from a spontaneous collective interaction with nature, a specifically identified interaction that always proves problematic since it includes a review of the inter-human and human-natural "contracts" objectified in the qualitative consistency of the life world.

Considered at the essential level of the history of modernity, the "Americanization" of modernity in the 20th century will undoubtedly be a culmination point that marks the closest degree of interconnection between the consolidation of the technical revolution in the productive forces and the capitalist procedure to update it. It would be the attainment of the highest degree of subsumption of "natural" logic or use value logic of modern social life under the capitalist logic of the self-valorization of mercantile value, an almost complete identification between them.

On the contrary, if we take into account the history of the concrete, formal consistency of modern life, the Americanization of modernity would bring along a radical impoverishment: in fact, it implies, in the first place, a sharp break with pre-modern past, both pagan and Christian; a past without which modernity, as "determined negation" of other previous civilizing forms, is severely diminished in its historical substance. Secondly, it also involves a systematic elimination, in daily life, of competition among multiple life proposals or different possible "ethe" in capitalist modernity. Indeed, it tends to ensure the monopoly of the capitalist way of being for one of them in particular, the "realistic" ethos ("Protestant" or "Puritan").

6. The two branches of modern history, the European and "(North) American" branches, will converge in the second half of the 19th century, three centuries after their divergence. By then, while the former has led capitalist modernity to a state of self-denial, the latter has steered it to full realization. The former, "European" modernity – challenged by the communist project – is in the midst of a crisis, having failed to satisfactorily conclude the task of completely subordinating the "natural form" (neither in its traditional version nor in its new versions). The latter, on the other hand, the American modernity, is growing and expanding rapidly, pleased to have completed the task.

Communicating vessels between both versions of capitalist modernity will not be at the service of a "return", a reintegration of the "American" version into the "European" version, but will rather favor an invasion of the latter by the former, whereby it will try to absorb it and replace it during a slow and probably incomplete process throughout the 20th century.

7. This symbiosis revitalizes and injects new blood into "European" modernity, particularly in the second European post-war period of the 20th century. However, it is a transfusion only geared towards those aspects that "American" modernity considers "worth salvaging". In the process, this symbiosis opens up a division in European modernity between its re-defined version the "American" way and its pure or "authentic" version, true to the traditional "European" identity, a version which, by the way, undergoes a deep crisis. Today, "being modern in the European way" implies recognizing, as Jean Baudrillard, that an "American truth" had always been waiting, like a destiny to be fulfilled, in the European horizon, and it implies validating, at the same time, that that against which any capitalist

modernity turns, the specific historical substance – that which is "dispensable" in the "American" perspective – is the only thing that legitimized and granted specificity to "European" modernity. For its part, the historical "(North) American" branch of capitalist modernity also experiences significant changes as a result of this symbiotic reunion. These changes are, in fact, even more crucial than the ones taking place in the European branch, serving to complete "American modernity" and to make it what it is today, the American way of life.

8. Perhaps the main historical-empirical key of "American" modernity lies in the casual – providential, if you will – coincidence of a peculiar community life project, the Christian Puritan Project, with an equally peculiar natural fact: the relative abundance of natural means of production; in the unexpected convergence of a morality that seeks eternal salvation (celestial) through compulsive dedication to productive work (our present "workaholism") with a natural situation that exceptionally favors maximizing work productivity.

The significance of this "foundational" convergence in redefining "American modernity" cannot be overestimated: a moral behavior framework devised to ensure survival in situations of "total threat" to human survival, designed and enhanced during thousands of years under conditions of "absolute" scarcity, is all of a sudden put to the test, after a "second exodus of the people of God", this time to America, in a radically different situation, where only a relative scarcity prevails (that is, a certain degree of abundance, acceptance and non-rejection of the human by the natural).

The facts of the "New World" in themselves challenged this framework of moral behavior, seeking to prove that the earth inhabited by man is not necessarily, as most Europeans in the very place of origin of modernity seemed to believe, a "valley of tears", a "place for testing and trials". They were particularly determined to prove that earthly wealth is not only the result of man's sacrifice in war or at work, that it does not consist in pure economic value, that is, the materialization of that sacrifice; they demonstrated that wealth is only a partial result of human effort (as Karl Marx reminded social democrats) since nature contributes its part "free of charge"; they showed that social wealth is an objectification of human activity, but not as a projection on an empty or insensitive foundation, merely for free, but as a "collaboration" with it, as an action that completes or "complements" a "natural action" that is always in process by itself.

However, the "American" modernity project – which does not seek to improve society but to attain capitalist profits – thought it more convenient to cling to the security afforded by faith; it kept away from the political adventure involved in questioning the supernatural foundation of public affairs or social things. It reaffirmed the belief in the Puritan scheme, with its central concept of sacrifice: it is preferable to continue paying the debt owed to Jesus Christ with renunciation to pleasure, with blood and "the sweat of the brow" in order to ensure salvation, at least in "the hereafter", to continue living a life of sacrifice, than to interact directly, with no divine warranty of any kind, with a nature whose abundance will always be unreliable, unpredictable, uncertain. The founders of "American" modernity minimize the active contribution of nature to building concrete wealth, they despise it. In reaffirming the pure human origin of social wealth they invalidate, in the "naturalness" of use value, everything casual or fortuitous that will not serve as immediate basis for mercantile value. Nature is reduced to a menu of "opportunities" and the individual entrepreneur will find, after a hard, initiatory search, the one opportunity "reserved" for him/her (as it is well known, territorial appropriation will advance into the Western territory of North America eliminating, devastating and exterminating everything which does not serve hic et nunc and directly as "raw material", be it "pseudo-human" indigenous people, forests or herds).

Under the capitalism that supported European modernity, the concept of "land rent" that paid for the excesses of the "leisure class" (Thorstein Veblen) also exalted, in its own way, the precious character of nature. Under the 20th-century capitalism that supported "American" modernity, the "rent of technology", that is, of the objectification of human cleverness, displaced the "rent of land". Nature was functionalized as relatively "superabundant" and its value consequently declined, losing the precious essence it had always boasted and minimizing its devastating abuse.

9. An empirical verification seems to lie at the basis of "American" modernity: that America has a "manifest destiny" given by God to the community of godly divines or Puritans (Calvinists, not Quakers) recently arrived on the Mayflower and its descendants. This destiny is manifest in the fact that God had supposedly given neo-English colonizers a natural Lebensraum to conquer freely, extending from the Far West to infinity.

Far from leading to prove that this ethics lacks foundation and to question it, the unusual and exaggerated multiplication of the "visible saints" – due to the unfolding of the productivist puritan ethics under unexpected conditions of a relative natural abundance – empirically "over-legitimized" that ethics. The natural exuberance of the "New World" – the "promised land" – brought forth an unusual generosity in the "invisible hand" of the market, an ironically excessive validation of the ethics of the elect or "visible saint". The exception almost became the rule: the winner or the one God had chosen to become the "normal" human type or the majority of humans in (North) American society, while the loser, the white trash, was the anomalous minority that proved the rule. As an assembly of "visible saints", the parochial community of farmers and the community of communities, the WASP (White Anglo-Saxon Protestant) "nation", felt that God had favored it with a "destiny of salvation".

10. The most characteristic and decisive transformation experienced by the "American" capitalist modernity is without doubt the introduction of what could be called the "American hybris", which consists in what many authors describe as the "artificialization of the natural" or the "naturalization of the artificial".

The "natural form" of human life, with its subjective self-affirmation project, confers necessity or "naturalness" to the objects in the world. Therefore, it could be said that a certain quality of life or its world is "artificial" when it results from the fortuitous combination of other qualities, from a mere quantitative increase of them or their number; that is to say, when it does not arise from a "project" or intention and lacks the "necessity" or "naturalness" discovered/determined by a subject. To put it in historical terms: when it is the result of a simple enhanced realization of the economic value of a commodity, and not of a concrete "inner" transformation, "agreed upon in a certain kind of democracy", of life and its world or a set of its use values.

The hybris or absolute excess of "American" modernity consists in its claim of having finally achieved a total subsumption of the "natural form" of human life and its world under the "value form". This subsumption has not only repurposed life "from within and without" but has completely invalidated the "natural form" in it. It manifests itself in practical life through the tacit opposition to "naturalness" as the foundation of the life world; through the recognition, inherent in that practice, of the self-sufficiency of its "artificiality". By contrast, the respect displayed in European modernity towards social and historical "naturalness" seems to be the very cause of its crisis and decadence.

"American" modernity may signal the emergence of a new "artificial naturalness", a naturalness characteristic of the value of commodity-capital, a value able to not only self-valorize regardless of the "natural" use values but to promote, by itself – the ghost of a great pretender – the emergence and creation of substitute use values. "American" modernity avoids the basic, "natural" task of any concrete civilizing project of creating, in a simultaneous and coordinated manner, in human life, a sufficient subsystem of social production capabilities and a satisfactory subsystem of social consumption needs. For "American" modernity, the increase in production capabilities, however infinite its growth possibilities, will never meet – as a result of an asymptotic parallelism – the ever indefinite openness, the constitutive, metaphysical insatiability of consumption needs.

The fundamental misconstruction of use value to which the great modern industry technically or "naturally" tended to – misconstruction that, in the 16th century, turned it from an instrument to liberate workers into an instrument of their organic slavery – serves as the basis for the "design" of use value that the capitalist mercantile economic value brings on production with the mere act of imposing its self-valorization in the random game of the market. It is an outrageous use value by definition: useful, certainly, but not to nurture life but to achieve human suicide and the annihilation of nature where human life unfolds.

11. It is hardly surprising that, until recently, this claim of "American modernity" has encountered a positive, even enthusiastic welcome, particularly among a wide layer of European intellectuals.' The "(North) American" civilization has been able to celebrate itself as self-sufficient, as owner of an "artificial naturalness" that will enable it to do away with life's ancient and modern "naturalness", facilitated by the conditions of a radical and widespread civilizing crisis. Besieged in its "small continent" (Braudel), "European" civilization, which respects the "natural" use value but withholds it in its purism, experiences a decline that drives it to the edge of automatism, while in the rest of the wide world other "natural" civilizations fail to find a way to attune their own inclination to create a modernity to the fundamentalist defense of a substantialized identity. In this fragile scenario, "American" modernity has managed to hold this "validity" and to overlook, and make others overlook, its untenable hybris, its absolute excess: the devastation it implies for human life and the nature that makes it possible.

12. Upon examining that which distinguishes "American" modernity from European modernity – of which the former is an independent historical extension – its distinctive feature seems to lie in its total or unrestricted willingness to assume the fact of progress, that is, the realization of the productivist drive for "production for the sake of production", typical of

capital accumulation, and favored by the "invisible hand" of the market (Adam Smith); in its inclination to accept the rapid-paced changes that this abstract productivism introduces in practical life and social reality.

Thus, "Americanism" or the "American identity" presents itself, at a first empirical level, as a progressivism – a general feature of capitalist modernity – but radicalized or taken to extremes: a progressivism that has eliminated the identity-related ("cultural"), social and political obstacles that hindered it in European modernity.

"American progressivism", with its total surrender to progress, can be described as a peculiar way to build the temporality of social life world, and as a particular way of updating the politics of that social life. In the face of its impact upon these two elements of the construction of the life world, "American progressivism" presents itself, first, as "presentism" and, second, as "apoliticism".

According to this, "American progressivism" would essentially imply a systematic closure of everyday experience in the face of past and present determinations of a society perceived as a supra-tribal or republican collectivity. In other words, it would lead to an indifference both towards historical commitments objectified or crystallized in the life world shared by all, and towards future expectations projected from the present life of society as a whole. "American progressivism" would thus create a phobia of any political body that seeks to "impose", from its polis or its urban time-space, significant or meta-private-scope determinations on a social life always lived in a series of presents of countless "tribes" or ad hoc communities composed of private individuals, committed to carry out a particular enterprise.

The eruption and limitless acceleration of progress was only possible within "American" modernity, wherein the resistance of "use value" to mercantile "value" is completely dismantled. After centuries of Germanic subjugation, the Roman-Christian colonization had managed, in certain cases, to massively shape individuals whose distinctive characteristics or "natural" identity reproduced itself in very basic terms. This was the case of the Calvinist and Puritan communities that had arrived to colonize New England and to assume, as its European counterpart, the "historical task" of capitalist modernization.

To replace a technique with other "more efficient" one, or a satisfier (a good produced) with a "better" one is a characteristic feature of progress. In prevailing modernity, the efficiency of the former and the quality of the latter must be defined, in principle, with reference to a human identity figure already commoditized in terms of its productive and consumptive potentialities; it must respond to a life world design in which the telos of valorization of the mercantile value of things prevails over that of their "natural form". The "more efficient" or the "best" must be determined in relation to the criteria of a human being interested only in the abstract productivity or "value productivity" exhibited both in his/her own activity and in the objects he/she makes use of. (Moreover, this productivity legitimizes each individual's effective membership and belonging to the community).

Although the idea of progress in the American Dream aims "to improve" the individual and his/her world, it actually "improves" or increases subjugation of the "natural form" to the "value form".

13. The use value of 20th-century city, 20th-century countryside and 20th-century channels of communication is a distorted use value, in which the telos of valorization seems to have definitively replaced the telos that modern society can democratically contemplate. The use value of an individual car (from Ford's T model and the Volkswagen onwards) does not answer to "natural" transportation needs, that is to say, to socially concrete needs that the modern human being decides to experience in a sovereign manner; on the contrary, it is a use value that "anticipates his/her desires" and creates a need which is not his/hers but a need developed by capital to satisfy its own accumulation need through it. The same applies to the use value of household and household appliances seemingly "essential to the modern housewife"; as well as the use value of an individual's body (as an instrument of work and consumption) and the products and items he/she uses to satisfy his/her food, health, hygiene and care needs; the use value of entertainment media, etc.

Globalized, omnipresent, the "American modernity" floods markets worldwide with goods with a use value designed and driven by value self-valorization needs; it overwhelms with goods that, for this reason, do not offer the liberating delight – endowed with that "weak Dionysian strength" – that lies in every delight prompted by the "natural form" of life, but only the satiation that results from abundant consumption enabled by availability of certain amount of money, the representative of any good. Thus, "American modernity" is a modernity that necessarily promotes the "consumerism" phenomenon, that is, a quantitative compensation for the failure to achieve a qualitative delight in satisfaction. This consumerism is clearly exemplified in the "Give me more!" of the pornography industry and in diminished sexual pleasure amid overproduction of orgasms.

14. The success of "American modernity" and the demonstration of the American way of life's superiority over other modern ways of life within capitalism has been facilitated by an ongoing "civilizing negotiation" process which becomes particularly noticeable in the "cultural industry's" effort (Max Horkheimer and Theodor W. Adorno) worldwide to put society's festive and aesthetic creativity at the service of self-praise, a practice in which the establishment needs to engage on a daily basis. The "cultural industry" promotes the emergence of an overwhelming "profusion of forms" in the universe of goods produced, a fact that is visible both in the rapid succession of changes in fashion (in car, home and self-presentation design) as in the hectic world of show business. This profusion of forms intrudes upon the singular and collective human experience in an uncontrollable way, expressing, beyond its exaggerated self-presentation – through Hollywood movies and stars, rock music and its by-products, and, above all, television and its encouragement of passive addiction to sports and its heroes, and pseudo-interactive videogames – a deep dynamic, the conflicting and ambivalent dynamic of a reality that is a civilizing imposition. In fact, within this imposition process – particularly in the "miscegenation" of forms in New York and other large American cities, on which "American" WASP turns its back as if they were Sodom and Gomorrah – there is no way to know to what extent capital, with its peculiar "will of form", simply uses and abuses (traditional and modern) "natural forms" as means for its self-promotion, and to what extent these "natural forms" blend with capital-prompted forms in order to resist and survive precisely through their "distortion".

15. There is no doubt that the distinct nature of WASP significantly contributes, at the rhetorical level, to the "American" modernity that has prevailed during the past one hundred years. However, just as "the German nature" is not enough to causally explain Nazism, "the American nature" is not enough to account for a historic figure of modern capitalism which, far from having derived from it, rather uses it as an instrument of its own historical consolidation.

Thus, rather than the idiosyncrasy of an empire, "Americanism" is the empire of an "idiosyncrasy" of a human being shaped in the image and likeness of commodity-capital. "Americanism" is not a feature of the American national identity imposed by the United States worldwide but, rather, a peculiar way of civilized life that casually "availed" itself of the North American history to achieve universalization, imbuing itself in the process with certain "natural" behavioral characteristics of its people.

In fact, it could be said that the 20th century, the century of "American modernity", has mainly been the century of the counterrevolutionary restoration of the dictatorship of capital after having languished during the "European modernity" with its "socialist deviation".

## Note

1. Fragment of a text originally published in Spanish in Bolívar Echeverría, *Modernidad y blanquitud, Ediciones Era*, Mexico, 2010, pages 87–114. Rights reserved © Bolívar Echeverría's heirs. Original translation by Mariana Donaldini, revised by Fernanda Beigel.

---

### Bolivar Echeverría, by Márgara Millán (Mexico)[1]

Bolívar Vinicio Echeverría Andrade (1941, Riobamba/Ecuador – 2010, Mexico City) was an Ecuadorian philosopher, educated in Germany in the 1960s and resident in Mexico City from 1971. His solid background identifies him as one of the most interesting and creative Latin American Marxists. Defining very broadly two periods of his trajectory, we could point to, firstly, an accusative reading of *Capital* (1974–1986) and a second phase focused on a critique of capitalist modernity, from which emerges an acknowledgement of the American (US) modernity as an exacerbation of the realist ethos ('La modernidad Americana'). From the first phase emerges *The Critical Discourse of Marx* (Editorial Era, 1986). This book is a first synthesis of the methodology proposed by Echeverría, which is based in his notion of *criticality*. In this book we find the first schemes of Echeverria's reading of the social dialectic, where the process of material reproduction as well as the process of communication or cultural dimension that accompanies it are a pre-condition. Thus, the process of physical reproduction is at the same time metaphysical.

The long duration of modernity, in which historicity we are still immersed, is based on the emergence of a neo-technical revolution that occurred around the eleventh century. Since then, and even today, this revolution has presented itself as a challenge for modernity in establishing itself, for the first time in the history of humanity, under the principle of a horizon of 'relative scarcity'. It is that challenge that has been solved repeatedly in its capitalist configuration. Accordingly, Echeverría distinguishes between modernity and capitalism. In other words, between potential modernity (the possibility of a collective form and concrete individuality based on the challenge that new technologies constitutes for the complete reproductive process) and its factual reality, modernity 'really existing', that is, between modernity as power and capitalist modernity.

The telos of the valorization of value has been historically triumphant until today, shaping modernity and spreading first in Europe and afterwards in America. The problematization of the value of use as a contradiction is distinguished in Echeverría's development of the critique of political economy. In other words, the value that underpins the process of capital reproduction as an abstract entity, and the value of use as the vital and singular reference of the concrete world of qualitative life. Value being valued as a substitute or automatic subject of the process of social reproduction in capitalism is the basis of human alienation on all levels. The community that emanates from this order is an apparent community, which is imposed on 'the economy' as an unchangeable externality.

Echeverría describes at least four ethoses of capitalist modernity, that is, four behaviors and attitudes in the face of the inviable contradiction that underlies the type of modernity that we inhabit. These are: the realist ethos, the classical ethos, the romantic ethos and the baroque ethos. The quadruple ethics of modernity is recognizable in its geographical historical unfolding in the Mediterranean, the Nordic, the Western and the Central European areas. The difference would reside, in qualitative terms, in the greater or lesser resistance of the different pre-modern civilizations as well as in multiple non-capitalist sketches of modern civilization in the face of the overwhelming force of capitalism to reduce, disintegrate and subsume them (Echeverría, 2008: 20).

The realist ethos unfolds in North European modernity denying the contradiction between value/value of use. It is in this aspect of modernity that the ethos is constructed as acquiescence and docility towards the 'spirit of capitalism' pointed out by Weber. However, it was in its 'Americanization' that what had already appeared on the north European side, *whiteness*, was reinforced – what we know as 'the American way of life'.[2] From the seventeenth century onwards there are two parallel lines of development in capitalist modernity, the European (with its internal nuances) and the (North) American, and what differentiates them is precisely the density of the commitments that each one must establish between the capitalist civilizing project and the already civilized reality that it confronts and seeks to cancel.

The realist ethos (Protestant or puritanical) in its American context is developed as an absolute excess. Thus, Echeverría will speak of the American hubris, present in 'the American way of life', which consists of having completely folded the 'natural form' of human life and its world into the 'value form', to such a degree that the first one is annulled. This excess establishes a new naturalness, the 'artificial naturalness' of commodity-value, but this time without any resistance, unleashed and narcissistic.

Progressivism as a destiny, as an end in itself, finds its maximum expression there. The notion of progress of the American Dream seeks to 'improve' the human being and his world (when) what really 'improves' or increases is the degree of submission of the 'natural form' of life under its 'form of value' (Echeverría, 2008: 36). It is thanks to the cultural industry that the seduction of this idea of progress works. Creativity at the service of the administration of forms, innovations and fashion seduces and subsumes qualitative life in hyper-consumerism.

*Whiteness*, already present in Western North-European modernity, is based on the US identity, on the identity of the WASP (White Anglo-Saxon Protestant). However, what is essential, what is at the heart of what Echeverría calls the Americanization of modernity, is the radicalization of capitalist identity, the affirmation of a total or absolute capitalist modernity, which has undoubtedly been nourished by certain features of the North American population.

*(Continued)*

(Continued)

**Notes**

1. Translated into English by Maximiliano Salatino and revised by Fernanda Beigel.

2. In 'The modernity of Barroco, and other essays' (1998), Echeverría delves into the Baroque ethos, the one that emerged in Mediterranean Europe and spread strongly in Our America, in the long seventeenth century of the Hispanic colony, and which persists to this day as a founding feature of Latin American cultural diversity.

**References**

Echeverría, Bolívar (1986). *El discurso crítico de Marx*. Mexico: Era.

Echeverría, Bolívar (1998). *La modernidad de lo barroco*. Mexico: Era.

Echeverría, Bolívar (2008). "La modernidad Americana". *(Claves para su comprensión), en La americanización de la modernidad*, Compilación de B. Echeverría. Mexico: Era.

# Part Three

# Social Structure and Inequalities

# 12

# Inequality, Inequalities

*Nadya Araujo Guimarães (Brazil)*

The subject of inequality has rightfully challenged Latin American sociology from its beginnings. After all, how can we build an understanding of social structure in countries marked by the experience of colonial domination based on the submission of indigenous or enslaved ethnic and racial groups without tackling this debate? For this very reason, authors have returned to the subject time and again in an attempt to comprehend the specificities of Latin America.

This omnipresence of the subject of inequalities on the Latin American agenda was however unable to advance the gaze of sociology to preferential status. For a long time, the preeminent place belonged to economists, who reduced the matter to its monetary dimension: unequal income distribution indexes were the measure of inequality. Dimensions relevant to sociological analysis usually appeared as independent variables whose power of determination with regard to patterns of inequality and the intensity of iniquity should be tested. Elsewhere, they appeared as effects of the unequal appropriation of income – the latter being the true object.

Indeed, the simplicity of measurements of a monetary nature, the potency of econometric demonstrations and the perfect international comparativeness afforded by the monetary indicator, rendered a propensity to measuring our inequalities with tools for an economic approach irresistible; particularly so in the eyes of the principal international agencies and organisms. Furthermore, the high levels of iniquity documented by the profusion of the popular Gini coefficient, of particular gravity in some of our countries, nourished the interest of those organisms in monitoring their dynamics across different contexts.

Thus, over the course of the last decades, assessments of the state of *income* inequality in Latin America were disseminated and always very well received. Through them, economists (occasionally in partnership with sociologists) sought to investigate that which took place within contexts as distinct as those of the structural adjustment to which the region's most important economies were submitted during the 1980s–1990s (Lustig, 1995; Tokman and O'Donnell, 1998); or they attempted to understand the behavior of income disparities under inclusion policies, rights expansion and cash transfers to the poor put into practice by left or left-of-center governments during the course of the 2000s, following processes of re-democratization (López-Calva and Lustig, 2010).[1] Reviews conducted by sociologists and anthropologists are much more recent (Gootenberg and Reygadas, 2010). In them, the emphasis placed on the multidimensional nature of inequality is noteworthy, as much as the effort to capture its subjective dimension. In short, it might be said that the field of inequalities in Latin America has traveled a long road, during the course of which sociology has succeeded in establishing its place as a legitimate provider of relevant explanations.

Furthermore, it is curious that the recurrent presence of the subject on the agenda of Latin American sociologists did not lead the matter of inequality to gain, in the local history of sociological thought, the centrality attributed to other subjects. Indeed, when it comes to understanding the dynamics of its social structure, as is the case here, it was the debate on the roots and correlatives of (under)development that occupied pride of place prior to that on inequalities.[2]

It catalyzed the interest of Latin American thinkers, particularly from the 1950s to the 1970s, during the consolidation of sociology's institutionalization in our countries. Such a movement had several effects. Thus, and on one hand, its recognition as an autonomous scientific subject and the consensus regarding the professional formation of new generations of sociologists required adhesion to a transnational disciplinary canon; after all, the plea for the existence of a science of society should be based upon the idea of universality of science. As previously highlighted by Beigel (in the introductory study to this volume), the formation of the first generations of 'scientific' sociologists was anchored to an array of European or US authors led by Durkheim, Marx and Weber.

Nevertheless, and during this same period, among those who produced knowledge and/or were already active on the front lines of social movements, the intellectual debate (marked by increasingly anti-capitalist reflections) strengthened criticism of Eurocentric (and often linear) interpretations of the transformation of Latin American social structures; indeed, this was the time of a conjoining of multiple movements of a popular and/or revolutionary nature, the most important of which (the Cuban Revolution) had occurred in the region. Thus, and against the current of the previous trend, a fertile ground has been nurtured for the challenge to the classic lineages, or, at least, to reinterpretations of these. Significant examples may be found in criticism[s] of the theory of modernization, powerfully inspired by Weber, or in the discomfort produced by the formulations of orthodox Marxists regarding the accumulation and structuring of the labor market, or among the relations between capitalist development and non-(pre?)capitalist forms of the organization of social work relations.

Within the region, authors such as Raúl Prebisch, Celso Furtado, Aníbal Pinto, Fernando Henrique Cardoso, Enzo Faletto, Caio Prado Jr, Octavio Ianni, André Gunder Frank, Ruy Mauro Marini, Theotonio Dos Santos, José Nun and Aníbal Quijano distinguished themselves as they engaged in the debate regarding the specific challenges that faced Latin American development, gaining indisputable international recognition. Some of their works became obligatory references in the intellectual trajectory of a soci-oeconomics of development and made appearances in academic debates on varieties of capitalism that took place outside Latin America (Gereffi, 1990, 1994; Trigilia, 2002). As Quijano (2012: 17) rightly recognized:

> Development was, especially in the Latin American debate, the key term of a political discourse associated with an elusive project of relative de-concentration and redistribution of the control of the industrial capital in the new geography that was configured in the Global Colonial-Modern Capitalism, at the end of the World War II.

These authors tackled the subject of inequality via a special place of entry, to wit: the debate on underdevelopment, dependency and marginality. One path (following Quijano's aforementioned hint) attempted to produce answers to the chances of our exiting the crisis to which modern capital-ist society succumbed during the Second World War without increasing the disparities between intra and internationals; that is, within a macro perspective, the gaze upon development proposed to account for the ine-qualities that established themselves among the economies of the distinct countries. This concern had already flourished in the immediate post-war period, with the diagnosis of the Economic Commission for Latin America and the Caribbean (CEPAL) about the commercial gap that marked rela-tions of exchange between countries, reducing the chances of growth and expanding inequalities on an international scale. Nearly a quarter of a cen-tury later, in the late 1960s, with the so-called 'theory of dependency', the debate gathered strength, with new contours and academic echoes beyond Latin America (Cardoso and Faletto, 1969).

The centrality that this reflection acquired, as well as its international repercussions, would be incomprehensible were we to lose sight of the fact that the end of the war represented the beginning of a wave of economic growth that would extend until the 1970s under the direction of corporate strategies of transnational companies with strong impacts upon peripheral economies. At that moment, the response of Latin American intellectuality was, at once, pertinent and creative. In light of previous explanations that sought to determine new trends outside national societies whose transformation they attempted to comprehend,[3] Cardoso and Faletto pointed out a need to reflect on the varieties of inter-relationships between national societies and the international economy. In this sense, they emphasized the importance of social classes (and of a class theory) *in dependent societies* to unravel the forms by which the relationship of dependency had established itself in each country. Embedded inside this focus was a theory of Latin American development that stated the importance of understanding the unequal form of the constitution of the national elite and the local implantation of international links.[4]

Amid such debates on the specificity of Latin American capitalist development, intellectuals from the golden years of sociology's institutionalization in Latin America (the 1960s and 1970s) provided us with another conceptual product of tremendous vigor for comprehending inequalities – the theory of marginality. In their approach to the way by which the integration into internationalized capitalism occured among us, some authors provided continuity to the effort of rethinking social classes in Latin American countries in which the process of industrialization was underway.[5] José Nun (1969) and Aníbal Quijano (1970) advanced towards unraveling the impacts of our process of development, focusing on the structure of the labor market and the new inequalities reproduced in it. This was a strategic dimension to understanding poverty and the integration of the working class into the project of substitutive industrialization and internationally integrated capitalist growth that the post-war period had revealed for Latin America.

In doing so, Nun and Quijano challenged important interpretations that we inherited from the classics. They specifically confronted Marx's formulation regarding labor use, production of value, capitalist competition and the offer of labor force, highlighting its limited applicability to what was happening in Latin American labor markets, a reality dependent upon monopolistic capitalism. In order to overcome such a difficulty, they emphasized the coexistence of two economic circuits in our countries: the oligopolized (and internationalized) and the competitive (and local) circuit.

The subject of social inequalities was at the core of the interest and formulation proposed, given that the key question that drove Nun and Quijano referred to the mode of inclusion in (and the forms of exclusion from) regular work in each of these circuits. Thus, unlike the position formulated by Marx in his influential analyses on the formation of competitive capitalism in the Northern hemisphere, they declared that, in dependent Latin American capitalism, a significant number of workers did not fulfill the employability requirements in effect in the oligopolized circuit. For this very reason, they reproduced themselves as socially marginal; contingents face to face with the dynamic of sectors integrated into the international economy. Among us, only one part of the working class was to preserve the characteristics of what Marx had conceptualized as a 'reserve army'; these individuals could be incorporated into the firms in moments of economic recovery and expansion of productive activity. This, however, did not happen with the entire contingent of workers. For this very reason, in order to understand the inequalities and poverty manifest in our urban centers, there would have to be a specific theorization about the important mass of marginal workers who have their chances restricted, at best, for inclusion in the economy's competitive circuit. In other words, local interpretative canons needed to be established, ones that were able to produce a plausible response to the phenomenon of economic, social and spatial segregation that manifested itself in the '*favelas*', the '*villas miséria*' and '*callampas*', that populated the Latin American world.

And yet, even as the movement of globalization intensified, the process for substituting importations showed its limitations among us, while growth strategies of the 'export-oriented' variety, such as those of the Asian countries ('tigers' and 'new tigers') began to leave their marks on the facts, in managerial agendas and in academic literature. The new reality drew attention to the so-called 'externalization' of the activity of global corporations upon the quality and quantity of jobs, both in developed countries and in developing ones. Competitiveness came to be based on links of interdependency between these two groups of countries. In the 1990s–2000s, this rekindled a debate similar to that which had taken place during the 1960s: could it be that these growing links of interdependency would contribute to a reduction of poverty in countries such as Latin American or Asian ones, permeated by global chains of production? Kaplinsky (2000) borrowed from Bhagwati (1958) the suggestive idea of 'immiserizing growth' to refer to the coexistence of a remarkable level of international economic activity and a decreasing economic gain by workers who were integrated into these new chains of value.

The debate on 'winners' and 'losers' in the new order was open – a debate that involved not only the tensioned 'North–South' axis (as in the early days of economic internationalization and of the mode of theories of imperialism), but which now had before it the challenge of the disjunctive 'inclusion vs. exclusion' debate that permeated social structure in all capitalist, central or peripheral societies. These were challenged by the restructuring of companies, by the reduction of manual work and direct production, by the emergence and stabilization of high levels of long-term unemployment, which affected even the most inclusive and successful 'welfare regimes'. The weakening of ties, the deterioration of working conditions, the loss of rights and the reduction of state protection pointed to new forms of 'social fractures' that opened up the (political and academic) debate on the challenge of facing the dilemma of the choice between competitiveness and equity; could these variables be related in zero-sum form?

What the Latin American experiment and the ideas of the interpreters of its inequalities could bring to the understanding of what now disturbed capitalist societies in the so-called 'First World', to wit, the deep social asymmetries that had emerged as a result of the global economies, especially by fracturing the political (of citizenship), social (of opportunities) and cultural (of the celebrated uniformity that was behind the idea of nationhood) foundations?

Our unequal (iniquitous) social structure was sufficiently different in its social history and politics to be able to provide academic reflection with alternative agendas or configurations; our (Latin American) variant of capitalism could, thus, operate as a sort of (perverse) foreshadowing of this new 'social fracture' that challenged the First World. But, and at the same time, our cultural history placed us close enough for the analogies to be rendered plausible. Not without reason, the intellectual creation of our 'local classics', in response to the understanding of the inequalities that transcended Latin reality, early on animated the production of categories in the mainstream of the sociology of the North. I draw attention to two suggestive examples: the concept of 'peripheral Fordism', coined in the late 1980s by Alain Lipietz (1987), during the course of the French debate on forms of Fordism, and the idea that 'the West' was undergoing a process of 'Brazilianization', formulated by Ülrich Beck (2000), amid the European debate on the crisis of welfare states, diminished employment and individualisation in so-called 'risk society'. In both formulations an explicit dialogue was established with Latin American thinkers who had studied our social inequalities, seeking to understand their specificities. Such examples witness a reciprocal fertilization, captured in its course in the very process of producing and questioning established canons in distinct intellectual communities, when they see themselves challenged to explain the advance of inequalities in their societies.

However, if properly observed, the contribution of thinkers on inequalities in Latin American sociology shows new facets of the wealth and refinement of the arguments deployed. To illustrate this, in a sort of opposite reading inspired by Jelin (2014), we have selected a few works produced at different moments in different countries and in diverse intellectual environments. In examining them, the reader will verify how these seminal authors considered the complex and multifaceted nature of the phenomenon, as it was theorized by contemporary sociology (Tilly, 1998). Thus, in the texts that make up this section, we shall see them leaving clues or even, occasionally, explicitly pointing out (i) the diverse and multidimensional nature of the phenomenon obliging the interpreters to allude to 'inequalities' (in plural) instead of 'inequality' (singular): (ii) the consubstantial intersection between its multiple dimensions; (iii) the strength of the subjective processes associated with the experience of these varied forms of inequalities; in addition to, last but not least (iv) the remarkable durability that characterizes our inequalities, that seems to challenge, in their troublesome persistence, the important process of structural change through which Latin American societies have passed.

One point of departure permeates the different jobs: in Latin America, the process of the production of inequalities would have combined two movements of appropriation of resources, simultaneous and coexisting, spoliation and capitalist exploitation.[6] In either of these senses, the market, as distributor and structurer of inequalities, would establish itself along the crucial analytic-explicative axis (Jelin, 2014: 13) – hence the central place occupied by class structure in all the texts. The position occupied in the market may be associated (and often is) with other dimensions, such as race or ethnicity, whether as the diachronic presence of a past amid capitalist expansion (Florestan Fernandes, in his consideration of the integration of Brazilian Blacks within a competitive social order), or through the inexorable prominence that values such as merit tended to acquire, as opposed to origin ('achievement' vs. 'adscription', inspired by the thinking of Talcott Parsons). But social rank can equally be the result of processes of spoliation; so long as they were useful to capitalist accumulation, they would be based on feudal forms of control over the access to land in large agricultural property systems (as Mariátegui thought, and we shall soon read, about the so-called 'indigenous problem' in Latin America, and in Peru especially).

In the words of Stavenhagen (2013) (see Chapter 15), written forty years after the document prepared by Mariátegui for the Komintern Conference of 1929, in Buenos Aires, are an example of how sophisticated the argument became. In the texts that are included in this section we shall see how ethnic discrimination, residential segregation, economic submission, social subordination, juridical incapacity and political dependency operate as intersected mechanisms (to use a concept that would not be formulated for quite some time). Colonial, class and ethnic domination, and internal colonialism are exercised throughout this intersection:

> Colonial relationships and class relationships underlay ethnic relationships. In terms of colonial relationships, the Indian society as a whole confronted colonial society. Primary characteristics of the colonial situation were ethnic discrimination, political dependence, social inferiority, residential segregation, economic subjection, and juridical incapacity. … Expansion of the capitalist economy during the second half of the nineteenth century, together with the ideology of economic liberalism, once again transformed the quality of ethnic relationships between Indians and Ladinos. We consider this stage as a second form of colonialism, which we might call internal colonialism. Indians of traditional communities found themselves once again in the role of a colonized people: they lost their lands, were forced to work for the 'strangers', were integrated against their will into a new monetary economy, and fell under new forms of political domination. This time, colonial society was national society itself, which progressively extended its control over its own territory.

> Now there were not only isolated Indians who, abandoning their communities, joined the national society; but Indian communities themselves, as a group, were progressively incorporated into expanding regional economic systems. To the extent to which national society extended its control, and capitalist economy dominated the area, relations between colonizer and colonized, between Ladino and Indian, were transformed into class relationships.

But multiple inequalities may also be found, as indeed they were, at the micro-social level. In it, when we observe the dynamics of transformations in families, using domiciles as units of observation, class inequalities would appear to reinforce inequalities of gender. Marina Ariza and Orlandina de Oliveira's text, which closes this section, shows how creative the dialogue has been between Latin American sociologists and demographers. The multiplicity of the forms of inequality and their patterns of intersection are once again revealed, albeit in new plumage, as previously underscored, when it befit sociology to dialogue with history and anthropology.

Taken as evidence, new forms of intra- and inter-inequalities between households not only contributed to a better comprehension of the structure of Latin American societies; they questioned theoretical and methodological points of departure from the functionalist perspective which, for a long time, supplied the canons for studies in the field of relations between family and society. As Brígida García emphatically states in her commentary, analytic precedence hitherto conferred upon the nuclear family and its dynamic needed to make room for a recognition of the relevance of the multiple connections and networks that link relatives and neighbors, family life and community life. Indeed, the singular notion of 'family', as a universal configuration, had to surrender to the evidence that ethnic distinctions matter and social differences mark the configuration of the sexual division of labor as well as power relations between men and women. In this sense, reflection on the production of inequalities intra- and inter-households, notably in economic contexts marked by instability in the growth of opportunities, allowed us to highlight both the multidimensionality that marks such inequalities and the specific structural and symbolic dynamics that constitute them in our countries. In so doing, sociological thought found itself forced, with no loss of attention to theoretical formulations produced in more developed capitalist countries, to revise such expectations, building new analytic apprehensions.

To sum up, and in light of the group of texts that follow, the coexistence of two distinct trends is remarkable, like veritable power lines that have stoked Latin American sociology's considerations of inequalities on a two-way street: on one hand, the remission of thought to key texts that established disciplinary canons; on the other, the need to confront such canons, challenging them with the specifics of the iniquitous Latin American social structure.

# Notes

1. It should still be underscored that income inequality as described in these assessments took only *work* income into consideration. Today, international literature (Piketty, 2013; Piketty and Saez, 2014) as well as Latin-American analysis (Souza, Medeiros and Castro, 2015) contains abundant evidence regarding the importance of other earnings (other than those of labor) to more precisely measure the extent of the distance, notable in Latin America, between the part of income appropriated by the rich in comparison with the remainder of the population and the poor especially.

2. Even though, and as we shall see ahead, the two subjects are clearly imbricated, it is 'development' and not 'inequality' that constitutes the most important of the debates and marks the presence of Latin American intellectual production on the international academic scene.

3. Those explanations appealed either to 'theories of imperialism', to organizational studies of company strategies, or to explanations regarding the effects of the deterioration of international trade relations.

4. Contrary to this understanding, many critics of this interpretation, including Latinos, stressed (like Francisco Weffort, 1971) that we did not exactly stand before a 'theory' of dependency, (1969) (challenging the pretense of generality that came with Cardoso and Faletto's formulation. Others, like Ruy Mauro Marini, argued (following Andrew Gunder Frank (1967) and foreshadowing what Immanuel Wallerstein would later elaborate) that economic transformation left limited degrees of freedom to the 'native' social classes, which dependency theory did not account for. In so doing, Marini also disbelieved its pretense of generality, drawing attention to the fragile theory of capitalism that sustained it; to him, the dialectics of dependent development did not descry a historical horizon greater than that of the 'development of underdevelopment', to paraphrase Frank's idea that had caused such a furore in the early 1970s.

5. Indeed, Cardoso (1964) had already given us a fine, seminal reflection on elites and developmentalism in his also classic *Industrial Entrepreneurs and Economic Development in Brazil [Empresário Industrial e Desenvolvimento Econômico no Brasil]*. Drawing on the Schumpeterian argument, he has sought to equate links between modernization, growth, innovation and innovators (these above all); his style found resonance in studies on the elites and ruling classes conducted by authors in Argentina and Mexico; not to mention the Latin Americanist analyses of Colombia and Venezuela.

6. A specific combination of the structure and the history of this Latin American capitalist order. For this very reason, the reading of the texts [in this section] highlights the assurance that, for these authors, the inspiration of European thought would have to be maintained, since it established the subject's canon, *without losing sight of* the need to adjust such a canon to the specificities of the historical construction of the social structure to be analyzed. Recreated categories and mid-range formulations became constantly deployed tools.

# References

Beck, Ü. (2000). *The Brave New World of Work*. Cambridge: Polity Press.

Bhagwati, J. (1958). 'Immiserizing growth: A geometrical note'. *Review of Economic Studies 25*, (June): 201–205.

Cardoso, F.H. (1964). *Empresario industrial e desenvolvimento econômico*. São Paulo: Difusão Européia do Livro.

Cardoso, F.H. and Faletto, E. (1969). *Dependencia y desarrollo en América Latina; ensayo de interpretación sociológica*. Mexico: Siglo XXI Editores.

Frank, A. G. (1967). *Capitalism and Underdevelopment in Latin America*. Monthly Review Press.

Gereffi, G. (1990). *Manufacturing Miracles: Paths of Industrialization in Latin America and East Asia*. Princeton, NJ: Princeton University Press.

Gereffi, G. (1994). 'The International Economy of Economic Development'. In: N. Smelser and R. Swedberg (Eds.), *Handbook of Economic Sociology*. New York: Russell Sage Foundation, chap. 9, pp. 206–233.

Jelin, E. (2014). 'Desigualdades de clase, género y etnicidad/raza. Realidades históricas, aproximaciones analíticas'. desiguALdades.net Working Paper Series 73, Berlin: desiguALdades.

Kaplinsky, R. (2000). 'Globalisation and unequalisation: What can be learned from value chain analysis?', *Journal of Development Studies 37*(2): 117–146.

Lipietz, A. (1987). *Mirages and Miracles: The Crisis in Global Fordism*. London: Verso.

López-Calva, L.F. and Lustig, N. (Eds.) (2010). *Declining Inequality in Latin America. A Decade of Progress?* Washington, DC: Brookings Institution Press.

Lustig, N. (Ed.) (1995). *Coping with Austerity: Poverty and Inequality in Latin America*. Washington, DC: The Brookings Institution.

Marini, R. M. (1969). *Subdesarrollo y revolución*. Mexico, DF: Siglo XXI.

Nun, J. (1969). 'Superpoblacion relativa, ejército industrial de reserva y masa marginal'. *Revista Latinoamericana de Sociología, 2*.

Piketty, T. (2013). *Le Capital au XXIᵉ siècle*. Paris: Éditions du Seuil.

Piketty, T. and Saez, E. (2014). 'Inequality in the long run', *Science, 344*(6186): 838–842.

Quijano, A. (1970). *Redefinición de la dependencia y proceso de marginalización en América Latina*. Santiago: Centro de Estudios Socio-Económicos, University of Chile.

Quijano, A. (2012). '"Live Well": Between the "Development" and the Descoloniality of Power'. In: A.L. Bialakowsky et al. *Latin American Critical Thought: Theory and Practice*. Buenos Aires: CLACSO, pp. 15–27.

Reygadadas, L. and Gootemberg, P. (eds) (2010). *Indelible Inequalities in Latin America. Insights from History, Politics, and Culture*. Durham, NC and London: Duke University Press.

Souza, P.H.G.F., Medeiros, M. and Castro, F.A. (2015). 'Top Incomes in Brazil: Preliminary Results', *SSRN Electronic Journal 35*(2): 998–1004.

Stavenhagen, R. (2013). 'Class, Colonialism, and Acculturation'. In *The Emergence of Indigenous Peoples*. Heidelberg, New York, Dordrecht and London: Springer and El Colegio de Mexico, pp. 3–44.

Tilly, C. (1998). *Durable Inequality*. Berkeley: University of California Press.

Tokman, V. and O'Donnell, G. (Eds.) (1998). *Poverty and Inequality in Latin America*. Notre Dame: The University of Notre Dame Press.

Trigilia, C. (2002). *Economic Sociology: State, Market and Society in a Modern Capitalism*. Oxford: Blackwell Publishers.

Weffort, F. (1971). 'Notas sobre a "teoria da dependência": teoria de classe ou ideologia nacional', *Estudos CEBRP, 1*(1–24).

# 13

# The Problem of Race: Approaching the Issue[1]

*José Carlos Mariátegui (Peru)*

Among other things, the problem of race in Latin America acts through bourgeois intellectual speculation to conceal or ignore the true problems of the continent. Marxist criticism has a vital duty to address this problem in real terms, ridding it of any specious or pedantic misrepresentation. Economically, socially and politically, the problem of race, along with that of the land, is, at its root, the problem of ending feudalism.

Because of the servitude imposed on them since the Spanish conquest, the Indigenous races in Latin America find themselves in a resounding state of backwardness and ignorance. The interests of the exploiting class, first the Spanish and later the Creole, have invariably tended, and under various guises, to explain the condition of the Indigenous races on the basis of their inferiority or primitivism. By posing the national domestic issue in this manner, this class has done little more than reproduce the reasoning of the white race with respect to the treatment and tutelage of the colonial population.

The sociologist Vilfredo Pareto, who considers race just one of several factors that determine the course of a society's development, has condemned the hypocrisy of the idea of race as it appears in the imperialist and enslaving policies of white nations. In his own words:

Aristotle's theory of natural slavery is the theory put forward by modern civilized peoples to justify their conquests of peoples whom they consider 'racially inferior' and their dominion over them.[2] Aristotle said that some men are naturally slaves and others masters, and that it is proper for the former to obey and the others to command, which is just and of benefit to all concerned. So say the modern peoples who decorate themselves with the title 'civilized'. They assert that there are people – themselves, of course – who were intended by nature to rule, and other peoples – those whom they wish to exploit – who were no less intended by nature to obey, and that it is just, proper and to the advantage of everyone concerned that they do the ruling and the others the obeying.

Whence it follows that if an Englishman, a German, a Frenchman, a Belgian or an Italian, fights and dies for his country, he is a hero; but if an African dares defend his homeland against any one of those nations, he is a contemptible rebel and traitor. So the Europeans are performing a sacrosanct duty in exterminating Africans in an effort to teach them to be civilized, as in the case of Congo. Nor is there any shortage of those who piously admire this work 'of peace, progress and civilization'. With a truly admirable hypocrisy, these blessed civilized people claim to be acting for the good of their subject races in oppressing and even destroying them; indeed, so dearly do they love them that they would have them 'free' by force. So the English freed the Hindus from the 'tyranny' of the rajahs. The Germans freed the Africans from the tyranny of their black kings. The French freed the Madagascans and – to make them freer still – killed not a few of them and reduced the rest to a condition that is slavery in all but the name. So the Italians freed the Arabs from the oppression of the Turks. Such talk is uttered in all seriousness, and there are even people who believe it. The cat catches the mouse and eats it; but it does not pretend to be doing so for the good of the mouse. It does not proclaim any dogma that all animals are equal, nor lift its eyes hypocritically to heaven in worship of 'the Father of us all'. ([Pareto], *Trattato de Sociologia General*, Vol. II)[3]

The exploitation of the Indians in Latin America is also justified under the pretext that it serves the cultural and moral redemption of the oppressed races.

On the contrary, it is easy to prove that the colonization of Latin America by the white race has had a retarding and depressing effect on the lives of the Indigenous races. The natural evolution of the Indigenous has been stunted by the vile oppression of the white man and the mestizo. Peoples such as the Quechuas and the Aztecs, who had reached an advanced degree of social organization, regressed under colonial rule to the status of scattered agricultural tribes. What elements of civilization that remain in Peru's Indigenous communities are, above all, the surviving elements of an ancient autochthonous organization. Subjecting agriculture to a feudal system, the white civilization has not created centres of urban life, nor even, in every case, industrialization and mechanization. In the latifundios [large landed estates] of the mountain range, with the exception of a few cattle ranches, white domination does not represent any type of progress with respect to the aboriginal culture, not even in terms of technology.

We define the 'problem of the Indio' as the feudal exploitation of the natives within the large agrarian landholding system. The Indio, in ninety percent of cases, is not a proletarian but a serf. Capitalism, as an economic and political system, is unable in Latin America to build an economy free of feudal impediments. Regarded as an inferior race, the Indigenous people are thus suitable for the maximum possible exploitation; and the capitalist system, benefiting itself as it does, is unwilling to forfeit this advantage. In agriculture, the establishment of wages and the adoption of machines do not erase the feudal character of large-scale landholdings. They simply perfect the system of exploitation of land and the peasant masses. A good part of our bourgeoisie and '*gamonales*' warmly embrace the thesis of the Indio's inferiority: the 'problem of the Indio', according to this view, is an ethnic problem whose solution depends on mixing the Indigenous race with superior foreign races. The persistence of a feudal-based economy stands in irreconcilable conflict, however, with a sufficient immigration pattern capable of producing such a transformation through interbreeding. The wages paid in the coastal and highland haciendas (when the wage system is in fact adopted) eliminate the possibility of employing European immigrants in agriculture. Immigrant peasants would never agree to work under the conditions that the Indios face; only the promise of becoming small landowners would be enough to attract them. Except for the black slave or the Chinese 'coolie', the Indio has proven irreplaceable in the coastal hacienda. Plans to colonize with European immigrants are, for the time being, only being considered in the forested eastern region known as Montaña. The thesis holding that the problem of the Indio is an ethnic one does not merit discussion. But it is worth noting the extent to which the proposed solution is at odds with the interests and capabilities of the bourgeoisie and *gamonalismo*, among whom one finds its proponents.

For Yankee or English imperialism, the economic value of these lands would be much less if, in addition to its natural resources, there were not also a backward and miserable Indigenous population that, with the assistance of the national bourgeoisie, it was possible to exploit in extreme. The history of the Peruvian sugar industry, now in crisis, shows that their profits have rested, above all, on the cheapness of labour; that is, the misery of the workers. Technically, this industry was never in a position to compete with other countries in the world market. The industry's distance from the consumer market and the costs of transport were offset by a cheap labour force. The labour of enslaved peasant masses, housed in abominable hovels, deprived of freedom and basic rights, subjected to a toilsome workday, placed Peruvian sugar planters in a position to compete with other countries who better cultivated their lands, benefited from protective tariffs or a geographical advantage. Foreign capital uses the feudal class to exploit these peasant masses to its advantage. Nevertheless, the *latifundistas* are sometimes incapable of acting as the heads of capitalist enterprise (due to inherited prejudice, arrogance and medieval caprice), such that foreign enterprise has to undertake the administration of large estates and sugar mills. This is the case for the sugar industry, which, in the Chicama Valley, is entirely monopolized by English and German companies.

Above all, race carries a particular relevance where the issue of imperialism is concerned. But it also has a distinct role that prevents the struggle for national independence in Latin American countries with a high percentage of Indigenous population from being equated with other situations in Asia or Africa. Our feudal and bourgeois classes feel the same disdain for the Indio, blacks and mulattos as the white imperialists. This racism of the ruling class favours imperialist penetration. Neither the native landowner nor the creole bourgeoisie has anything in common with their coloured peons. Class solidarity is compounded by racial solidarity, turning the national bourgeoisie into docile instruments of Yankee or British imperialism. And this prejudice is extensive throughout much of the middle class, which, despite their own evident miscegenation, imitates the aristocratic and bourgeois contempt for the coloured plebe.

Imported into Latin America by the colonizers in order to enhance their power over the Indigenous American race, the black race has passively fulfilled their colonialist role. Harshly exploited, the black race reinforced the Spanish conqueror's oppression of the Indigenous race. More miscegenated, with a greater familiarity and harmony in the colonial cities, the blacks became an auxiliary to white dominance, notwithstanding the occasional outburst of ill-temper or rebelliousness. Working as artisans or domestic servants, the black or mulatto composed a plebeian class more or less unconditionally at the disposal of the feudal class. Industry, factories and unions offer the blacks redemption from domesticity. By erasing racial boundaries between proletarians, class consciousness has historically elevated the morale of the blacks. Unions provide the definitive break with the servile habits that otherwise would keep blacks in the condition of artisans or servants.

The Indio, in their capacity to embrace progress and modern production techniques, are in no way inferior to the mestizo. On the contrary, they are generally superior in doing so. The idea of racial inferiority is so discredited today that it hardly deserves the honour of a rebuttal. With regard to the perceived inferiority of the Indio, white prejudice, like that of the creole, is lacking in any factual basis worthy of scientific study. The Indigenous race's addiction to the coca leaf and their alcoholism, while exaggerated by commentators, are the consequence and result of white oppression. *Gamonalismo* encourages and exploits these vices, which in a sense feed off the need to resist the physical pain that is particularly alive and active among subjugated people. The Indio in ancient times only drank '*chicha*', a drink made with fermented corn, whereas, with the introduction into the continent of sugarcane production, the Indigenous now drink alcohol. The production of alcohol from sugarcane is one of the more secure and profitable businesses for large landholders, in whose hands also lies the production of coca in the warm mountain valleys.

The Japanese experience has long shown the ease with which people of races and traditions distinct from the European can appropriate Western science and adapt themselves to using their productive techniques. In the mines and factories of the Peruvian highlands, the Indigenous peasant confirms this experience.

Marxist sociology has summarily dispatched racist ideas, all of which are product of the imperialist spirit. Bukharin writes in 'The Theory of Historical Materialism':

In the first place, the race theory is in contradiction with the facts. The "lowest" race, that which is said to be incapable, by nature, of any development, is the black race, the Negroes. Yet it has been shown that the ancient representatives of this black race, the so called Kushites, created a very high civilization in India (before the days of the Hindus) and Egypt; the yellow race, which now also enjoys but slight favor, also created a high civilization in China, far superior in its day to the then existing civilizations of white men; the white men were then children as compared with the yellow men. We now know how much the ancient Greeks borrowed from the Assyro-Babylonians and the Egyptians. These few facts are sufficient to show that the "racial" explanation is no explanation at all. It may be replied: perhaps you were right, but will you go so far as to say that the average Negro stands at the same level, in his abilities, as the average European? There is no sense in answering such a question with benevolent subterfuges, as certain liberal professors sometimes do, to the effect that all men are of course equal, that according to Kant, the human personality is in itself a final consideration, or that Christ taught that there are no Hellenes, or Jews, etc. (See, for example, Khostov, *Theory of the Historical Process*, p. 247: "it is extremely improbable that … the truth is on the side of the advocates of race equality"). To aspire to equality between races is one thing; to admit the similarity of their qualities is another. We aspire to that which does not exist; otherwise we are attempting to force doors that are already open. We are now not concerned with the question: what must be our aim? We are considering the question of whether there is a difference between the level, cultural and otherwise, of white men and black men, on the whole. There is such a difference; the "white" men are at present on a higher level, but this only goes to show that at present these so called races have changed places.

This is a complete refutation of the theory of race. At bottom, this theory always reduces itself to the peculiarities of races, to their immemorial "character". If such were the case, this "character" would have expressed itself in the same way in all the periods of history. The obvious inference is that the "nature" of the races is constantly changing with the conditions of their existence. But these conditions are determined by nothing more nor less than the relation between society and nature, i.e, the condition of the productive forces. In other words, the theory of race does not in the slightest manner explain the conditions of social evolution. Here also it is evident that the analysis must begin with the movement of the productive forces.[4]

Where some maintain the inferiority of the Indigenous race, others favour the opposite extreme: the idea that the creation of a new [Latin] American culture will be essentially the result of autochthonous racial forces. To subscribe to this thesis is to fall into the most naïve and absurd mysticism. It would be senseless and dangerous to oppose the racism of those who, despising the Indio, uphold the absolute superiority of the whites, by asserting a racism that overestimates the Indio, entrusting his figure with a messianic faith in the racial mission of an American renaissance.

The odds for the Indio to elevate themselves materially and intellectually depend on changes in socioeconomic conditions. These are not determined by race, but by economics and politics. Race alone has not inspired, nor will it ever inspire an understanding of the emancipatory idea. Above all, it will never acquire the power to impose that idea and carry it out. What ensures the Indio's emancipation is the dynamism of an economy and a culture that bears the seeds of socialism. The Indian race was not defeated in the wars of conquest by an ethnically or qualitatively superior race; it was defeated by a technology superior to that of the aboriginal communities. Gunpowder, iron and cavalry were not racial advantages; they were technical advantages. The Spaniards reached these remote areas because they possessed the navigational means to cross the oceans. Shipping and trade later allowed them to exploit the natural resources of their colonies. Spanish feudalism was superimposed onto Indigenous agrarianism, leaving partially intact the latter's communitarian forms; but this very adaptation created a static order, an economic system whose stagnancy guaranteed Indigenous servitude. Capitalist industry upsets this equilibrium; it disrupts this stagnation by creating new productive forces and new relations of production. The proletariat gradually begins to grow at the expense of artisanship and servitude. The nation's economic and social evolution enters into an era of activity and contradiction that, on an ideological level, leads to the emergence and development of socialist thought.

In all this, the influence of the racial factor is clearly insignificant compared to the influence of economic factors – production, technology, science, etc. Without the material elements that make modern industry possible – capitalism, if one prefers – would it even be possible to design a plan, much less the aspiration, for a socialist state based on the emancipation of the Indigenous masses? The dynamism of this economy, this framework, that destabilizes all relationships and through classes presents opposed ideologies, all of this makes possible the resurrection of the Indios, determined on the plane of economic, political, cultural and ideological forces, and not racial forces. The republic's dominant class is above all guilty of a lack of any liberal, bourgeois sense of its capitalist mission, its failure to hasten the economic transformation from a colonial to a capitalist economy. Feudalism, with its stagnation and inertia, hinders emancipation, the Indigenous insurrection; Capitalism, with its conflicts and instruments of exploitation, forces the masses to raise their demands, obliged to join in a struggle where they are trained materially and mentally to lead a new order.

The problem of race is not present in all Latin American countries, and where it is, it is present to varying degrees and with different qualities. In some Latin American countries it is regionally isolated and lacks a palpable influence on social and economic processes. But in countries where the Indigenous people comprise the major part of the population, like Peru and Bolivia, and to a lesser degree Ecuador, the Indio's demands are the dominant popular and social ones.

Race is so deeply intertwined with class in these countries that revolutionary politics cannot but be taken into consideration. The Quechua or Aymara Indio sees their oppressor in the 'misti', the white man. Among mestizos, only class consciousness is capable of destroying the widespread contempt and loathing felt for the Indio. It is even common to find this prejudice among those in the city who proclaim themselves revolutionaries, who remain reluctant to recognize this very prejudice as part of an environmental inheritance.

A language barrier stands between the Indigenous peasant masses and the white or mestizo revolutionary workers.

However, through the work of Indio propagandists, the socialist doctrine, by the very nature of its demands, will begin to take root among the Indigenous masses. What has been lacking up to this point is the systematic preparation of these propagandists. The literate Indio, corrupted by the city, ends up collaborating with those who exploit their race. But in the city, among revolutionary workers, the Indio has already begun to embrace the revolutionary idea, to make it his own, to grasp its value as an instrument for the emancipation of his race, oppressed, as he is, by the same class that exploits his class brother, the worker in the factory.

The realism of a confident and exact socialist politics, one that grasps and utilizes the basic facts of these nations, this realism can and should transform the race factor into a revolutionary factor. The current situation in these countries is based on the alliance between the feudal landholder class and the mercantile bourgeoisie. Having defeated this *latifundista* feudalism, urban capitalism will be powerless to resist the rising tide of worker strength. Its representatives are a weak, mediocre bourgeoisie, nurtured by privilege, lacking in organizational and combative spirit, ever losing its hold over the fluctuating intellectual milieu.

Socialist critique in Peru has introduced a new approach to the problem of the Indio by denouncing and repudiating the bourgeois or philanthropic temptation to consider the problem as an administrative, legal, moral, religious or educational one.[5]

### The Indian Struggle Against *Gamonalismo*[6]

When speaking of the Indio's attitude towards their exploiters, a common assumption suggests that the debased and downtrodden Indio is incapable of any form of struggle or resistance. However, the long history of Indigenous insurrection and revolt, along with the subsequent repression and massacre, suffices to refute that impression. In most cases, Indio rebellions began with a violent incident that compelled them to revolt against authority or the landholder. But in other cases they could not be limited to a local mutiny. There, the rebellion followed a less incidental path and was extensive to an entire region. In order to repress these rebellions, the government has resorted to stronger measures and unleashed veritable massacres. Thousands of Indian rebels have spread terror among the *gamonales* in more than one province. One recent uprising that attained extraordinary proportions was that commanded by Major Teodomiro Gutiérrez, a highland mestizo, going by the name Rumimaqui, who boasted a high percentage of Indigenous blood and who proclaimed himself the redeemer of his race[7]. Major Gutiérrez had been sent by President Billinghurst to the Puno department, where he was meant to conduct an investigation and report back to the government following Indigenous complaints that the *gamonalismo* system was raising excessive levies. Gutiérrez established close contact with the Indios. When the Billinghurst government was overthrown, he became convinced that the legal path was useless and he threw himself behind revolt. Several thousand Indios followed him, but, as always, disarmed and defenceless before the troops, they were condemned to death or dispersal. Following this uprising came those of La Mar and Huancané in 1923 and other, smaller ones, all bloodily repressed.

In 1921, delegations from various community groups attended an Indian congress convened under government auspices. The congress was meant to discuss the demands of the Indigenous race. In Quechua, delegates delivered strongly worded accusations against the *gamonales*, the authorities and the priests. The Committee for Tawantinsuyu Indigenous Rights was created. The congress was held annually until 1924, when the government began to persecute revolutionary elements among the Indigenous leaders, intimidating the delegations and undermining the spirit and purpose of the assemblies. The 1923 congress saw the passing of a number of resolutions – the separation of church and state; the repeal of the Law of Highway Conscription – that proved unsettling to *gamonalismo* and posed a danger to the establishment, where groups of Indigenous communities from different regions could establish contact and coordinate their actions. That same year saw the formation of the Regional Indian Workers Federation, a short-lived and ultimately frustrated attempt to organize the Indios along the lines of anarcho-syndicalist principles and organizational methods. Nevertheless, it represented a revolutionary reorientation of the Indian vanguard. With two of the organization's Indio leaders exiled and others intimidated, the Regional Indigenous Workers Federation was soon reduced to a mere name. And in 1927 the government dissolved the Tawantinsuyu Committee under the pretext that its leaders were mere exploiters of the race they purported to defend. This committee never established any importance beyond its affiliation with the Indigenous congresses, and composed as it was of leaders with scant ideological and personal value, it regularly organized demonstrations in defence of the government, which it regarded as pro-Indio. Notwithstanding, for some *gamonales* it remained an instrument of agitation, a remnant of the Indigenous congresses. The government, for its part, guided its policies so as to imply an association with pro-Indigenous statements, promises of redistributing land, etc., in an attempt to deflect Indigenous agitation, encouraged by revolutionary groups or those susceptible to revolutionary influence.

The penetration of socialist ideas and the expression of revolutionary demands among the Indigenous have continued despite these fluctuations. In 1927, a pro-Indigenous action group called Grupo Resurgimiento [Resurgence Group] was founded in Cuzco. Composed of several intellectuals, artists and workers from Cuzco, it published a manifesto denouncing the crimes of the *gamonalismo*. Soon after its creation, one of its leaders, Dr Luis E. Valcárcel, was arrested in Arequipa. His imprisonment lasted only a few days, but the Grupo Resurgimiento was dissolved by the Cuzco authorities.

## Conclusions on the Problem of the Indio and the Tasks Involved

The problem of the Indio is identified with the problem of the land. The ignorance, backwardness and misery of the Indians are, as we said, nothing more than the consequences of their servitude. Feudal *latifundistas* maintain the exploitation and absolute domination of the Indigenous masses. The Indian struggle against the *gamonales* invariably rests on the defence of their lands against absorption and dispossession. Therefore, there exists an instinctive and deep-seated Indigenous demand: the demand for land. Our active duty consists in organizing, systematizing and defining this demand.

Those 'communities' that have demonstrated a truly remarkable resistance and tenacity in the face of the harshest oppression also represent a natural condition for the socialization of the land in Peru. The Indio has deep-seated habits of cooperation. This is so even when communal property enters into individual ownership, and not only in the highlands but also on the coast, where higher concentrations of mestizos counteract Indigenous customs; even under those circumstances, cooperation endures and heavy labour tends to be collaborative. With minimal effort, the community can become a cooperative. Reallocation of *latifundio* land for the communities is the solution to the agrarian problem in the highlands. On the coast where property is omnipotent and communal ownership has disappeared, the inevitable tendency is towards the individual distribution of land ownership. The harshly exploited sharecroppers, known as *yanaconas*, must be supported in their struggle against the landowners. The *yanaconas* have a natural claim to the land they work. The struggle is different on large estates where owners directly exploit peon labour recruited in part from the highlands. The demands we must pursue are: freedom of association, abolition of the '*enganche*' system,[8] improved wages, the eight-hour workday and compliance with labour protection laws. Only when the peons on these estates have achieved these demands will they be headed towards their definitive emancipation.

Only with great difficulty can union propaganda reach the haciendas. Each hacienda, whether on the coast or the highlands, is a fiefdom. No associations except those patronized by the owners and administration are tolerated, such as sport or recreational associations. But with the increase in automobile traffic, a gap is slowly opening in the barriers that had previously isolated the estates from external propaganda – hence the importance for the class-based movement in Peru to organize and actively mobilize transport workers. When the peons in the haciendas learn that they can count on the fraternal solidarity of the unions and have grasped their value, the desire to join in the struggle that is today lacking will be aroused again, as it has been in the past. The core union activists, as they gradually begin to cohere in the haciendas, will serve to explain their rights to the masses, to defend their interests, to represent their grievances and encourage their organization as the circumstances permit.

For the progressive ideological education of the Indigenous masses, the worker vanguard can draw on those militants of the Indian race, in the mines or especially the urban centres, who engage with trade union and political movements. They assimilate its principles and are schooled to play a role in the emancipation of their race. Workers from an Indigenous milieu often return temporarily or permanently to their communities. Their knowledge of Indigenous languages facilitates their mission as instructors of their racial and class brothers. Indigenous peasants will only truly understand those individuals close to their environment who speak their own language. They will always regard whites and *mestizos* with distrust, and, in turn, whites and *mestizos* can hardly assume the difficult task of approaching the Indigenous milieu and introducing class propaganda.

Methods for self-education, the regular reading of the brochures produced by the organs of the Latin American workers' movement, correspondence with comrades in urban centres, these will be the means by which the Indigenous activists fulfil their educational mission.

The coordination of Indigenous communities by region, the defence of those who suffer legal or police persecution (the *gamonales* prosecute those who resist them or whose lands they wish to appropriate), the defence of communal property, the organization of small libraries and centres of study; all these activities must be led by the Indian members of our movement, with the dual purpose of imparting class-based guidance and education to serious Indian leadership, and to prevent the influence of misleading elements (anarchists, demagogues, reformists, etc.).

The organization and education of the mining proletariat is, together with that of the agricultural proletariat, one of the most pressing issues in Peru. The mining centres, the largest of which is on its way to becoming the largest profit centre in South America (La Oroya), are advantageous sites for class propaganda. Apart from representing substantial proletarian concentrations under salaried conditions, these centres draw Indian workers into contact with urban industrial workers who contribute their class spirit and principles. The Indios in the mines are still largely peasants, and thus adherents recruited from among their ranks are also militants won from the peasant class.

The task will be in every way a difficult one; but progress will depend fundamentally on the ability of those militants who perform this task and who possess a precise and concrete assessment of the objective conditions of the Indio issue. The problem is not racial, but rather social and economic; however race plays a role therein and in the means to confront the problem. For example, only militants drawn from the Indigenous milieu, with a similar mentality and language, can achieve an effective and immediate influence over their companions.

A revolutionary Indio consciousness will perhaps need time to take shape, but once the Indio takes hold of the socialist idea, with discipline, tenacity and strength that few proletariats from other environments will be able to surpass.

## Notes

1.  Originally published in Spanish in the journal *AMAUTA*, No. 25, Lima (Peru), July–August 1929, pp. 69–80. Translated by Fernanda Beigel and revised by Nicolas Allen. We thank José-Carlos Maritágeui Ezeta for his collaboration in contrasting original archives for this difficult endeavor.

2.  Mariátegui alters the original text of Pareto, adding "race": "to jusfiy their conquests of people whom they call inferior".

3.  Translation note: Pareto's original in English was preserved except for the passages in which there is a difference in Mariátegui's translation. N. Allen. Cfr. Vilfredo Pareto, *The Mind and Society: A Treatise on General Sociology* (New York: Harcourt Brace, 1935), pp. 626–27.

4.  Nikolai Ivanovich Bukharin, *Historical Materialism: A System of Sociology* (New York: International Publishers, 1925), pp. 127–128.

5.  The Indigenous uprising of 1915 took place in the department of Puno.

6.  See Mariátegui, José Carlos ([1928], 1995) *Siete ensayos de interpretación de la realidad Peruana* (Lima: Sociedad Editora Amauta).

7.  Due to space limits, we have left aside a fragment entitled "The Socioeconomic Situation of the Indigenous Population in Peru" which offers a summary of demographic and economic data on the Indigenous population in the1920s.

8.  A particular form of exploitation created in the Latin American colonies, the "enganche" implied a continuous relation of indebtedness with the landholder.

---

## José Carlos Mariátegui, by José-Carlos Mariátegui Ezeta (Peru)

José Carlos Mariátegui (1894–1930) is considered one of the most influential intellectuals of the twentieth century in Latin America, whose significance accrues and evolves over time. Within his brief life-span of 35 years, he successfully defined his distinctive character as a thinker and a producer of an original and fundamental corpus of work that reflects on Peruvian reality from a global perspective. Mariátegui experienced a childhood of hardships. Due to a chronic illness, he was deprived of a formal education – both at school and at university. However, an early stimulating environment made him into an autodidact as he transformed his lack of studies into an advantage. He developed a self-teaching capacity, which made him a voracious reader of everything he had at hand, contributing to his maturing quickly, as he would later say, from an 'ephemeral childhood' to a 'premature adolescence'.

His work at the newspaper *La Prensa* began humbly, starting as messenger, before moving on to become a linotypist's assistant and then proofreader, making his way to the news room and becoming an acclaimed and respected columnist before the age of twenty. His writing as a journalist covered literary, artistic, social and political topics which allowed him a vast mature interpretation of social reality. Such a comprehensive journalistic practice also gave him a deep understanding of work practices on editorial and journalistic enterprises, which he later developed for his own endeavours, such as with the journal *Nuestra Epoca* (1918) and the newspaper *La Razón* (1919). Being an uncomfortable figure to Augusto B. Leguía's government, in 1919, he was obliged to travel to Europe as a propaganda agent for the Peruvian government in Italy; a subtle form of deportation. He lived first in Italy and then in Germany, where he immersed himself in the systematic study of Marxism while also understanding the dynamics of fruitful editorial-intellectual enterprises, such as Gramsci's *L'Ordine Nuovo*, Gobetti's *La Rivoluzione Liberale* or Barbusse's *Clarte*. His time in Europe also helped him to develop a characteristic literary style to communicate his ideas, less rhetorical than that of his youth, marked by an elegant and distinctive prose.

Mariátegui returned to Peru in 1923 with the idea of founding a newspaper. Although this project did not materialize, a few months later, in October, he assumed the interim direction of the *Claridad* journal, and in November he started to advertise what would later become *Amauta*, one of the greatest journals of Latin America (1926–1930). *Amauta* gave an account of the work of the young Peruvian and Latin American intelligentsia in literature, social sciences and art, as well as international contributors.

The facet of José Carlos Mariátegui as a cultural entrepreneur is relatively unexplored. These activities summed up his editorial practice, through the publication of books and journals, which he channeled in various directions, seeking to complement them with cultural, educational and political projects which could prompt a true social, ideological and cultural transformation in Peru. Fundamental to this pursuit was the establishment and articulation of a network across the country, even in small localities, which formed an extended 'capillary tissue' of collaborators and distributors that allowed him to understand the true national reality directly from its actors: intellectuals, educators, workers, among others. Thus, Mariátegui's work covered all aspects of editorial work, from the act of writing all the way up to printing and circulation. For Mariátegui, intellectual autonomy required the development of an integral editorial and production infrastructure. Along with his brother, Julio César, he founded the Minerva Publishing House in 1925, dedicated to the edition and publication of scientific, literary and artistic books, and acquired a printing press that allowed him to carry out his editorial endeavours with few restrictions.

Marxism for Mariátegui was a tool for the analysis of Peruvian reality that allowed him to maintain intellectual autonomy. Without a pretense of orthodoxy, he returns to the writings of Marx, Engels and Sorel, in an open manner, far from the dogmatic rigidity that characterized most of the left in Latin America at that time. Such an overt perspective on socialism proclaimed a bottom-up approach – a socialism that comes from organized social groups, or as Gramsci stated, 'a socialism over capital'. Mariátegui's views on Marxism reflect an active practice that engaged with theory through all his endeavours: as a writer, as a political philosopher, as a social activist and as a cultural entrepreneur. Mariátegui was one of the first intellectuals to produce a post-colonial critique that remains valid to this day, questioning the different existing forms of modern dominance and how its system governs people's lives. The colonizing scheme in Latin America was not only intolerant of understanding the 'other', but sought to appropriate the evolution of what the local population had already developed within their own system. However, this did not

*(Continued)*

(Continued)

mean the replacement or incorporation of technologies that would allow a modernization nor did it enable a dialogue with traditional knowledge that may have created
new production models. Such a critique is particularly relevant today as there is still
a persistent struggle for global domination, especially among the new world powers, regardless of their ideological line, markedly abusive and exploitative in their
capacity, and by new types of colonization, manifested not only in geographical
usurpation, but by the new global information and consumerist capital.

During his life he only published two books, mainly comprising a selection of
his articles published in local magazines at that time. *The Contemporary Scene [La
escena contemporánea]* was published in 1925 and gave a global perspective of
his European experience by bringing together thoughtful analyses of the key world
actors and historical events at that time. *Seven Interpretive Essays on Peruvian
Reality [7 ensayos de interpretación de la realidad peruana]*, is considered the most
important contribution to the social study of Peruvian reality to this day, portray-
ing an original way of applying and thinking of the Marxist method from a local
perspective. During this prolific time, he also founded the Socialist Party and the
General Workers' Confederation of Peru (CGTP).

Thus, Mariátegui may be considered as a visionary, not only because he was
at the same time an activator, an analyst and an interpreter of both local and world
reality, but also because he understood how intertwined intellectual autonomy and
intellectual production are, and how important it is to generate a vast network of
collaborators. This happened at the heart of his public life, in a moment of intellectual fertility, a few months before his intended move to Buenos Aires, tired of
the adverse working conditions under the government of Leguía, at the same time
making it evident that he could contribute to political thought not only in his own
country but also internationally.

However, as has been with the case with other renowned intellectuals such as
Gramsci or Gobetti, the active life of Mariátegui was cut short, and he died on the
16th of April 1930, a few months before reaching his thirty-sixth year, succumbing
to the chronic ill health that had dogged him since childhood. Several articles that he
left as editorial projects were published after his death as anthologies, and the books
written about him add up to more than six hundred in more than twenty languages.
Mariátegui was an exceptional man. Perhaps we must see him not just through his
successful enterprises in his short lifetime, but more significantly as a man of
brilliance who had the intellectual and executive strength to guide a new epoch in
the ideological evolution of Peru and Latin America, becoming a milestone in his
own right in the history of ideas of the twentieth century.

**References**

Mariátegui, J. C. (1925) *La escena contemporánea.* Lima: Minerva.
Mariátegui, J. C. (1928) *Siete ensayos de interpretaciónd e la realidad peruana.*
    Lima: Sociedad Editora Amauta.

# 14

# The Weight of the Past[1]

## *Florestan Fernandes (Brazil)*

Brazil lives simultaneously in a number of historical-social epochs. Some scenes recall the relations of the colonizers and conquerors with the natives; others abound in the turbulent activity of an industrial civilization with all the characteristics – both national and foreign – associated with it. Against this backdrop, ethnic or racial relations and the significance of color in human life manifest themselves in different ways. The Brazilian racial dilemma may be characterized most succinctly by the situation of the Negro or Mulatto[2] in the city of São Paulo. Although the percentage of Negroes and Metis in São Paulo is among the lowest in the urban centers of Brazil, the city is significant for other reasons. On the one hand, it is situated in the last region in Brazil where slavery played a constructive role in the long cycle of economic prosperity that began with the production and export of coffee. On the other hand, it was the first Brazilian city that exposed the Negro and the Mulatto to the vicissitudes of life that are characteristic of and unavoidable in a competitive economy in the process of expansion. It, therefore, permits one to analyze objectively and under almost ideal conditions why the old racial order did not disappear with the abolition and legal interdiction of the caste system, but spread out into the social structure that emerged with the expansion of free labor.

## Racial Inequality and Social Stratification

The Brazilian racial dilemma, as seen in the example of São Paulo, has its origins in phenomena of social stratification. The major historical-social transformations that have taken place since the 1800s have benefited only the white population. Their world has been profoundly changed by the economic expansion and social progress that originated with the production and export of coffee and was afterwards linked to accelerated urbanization and industrialization. The world of the Negroes has remained essentially outside these socio-economic processes.

The disintegration and the end of slavery did not immediately modify the relative positions of the racial groups in São Paulo's social structure. Legally the caste system was abolished; in practice, the Negro and the Mulatto population did not rise above the social situation they had known earlier. Instead of entering en masse into the social classes that were in the process of formation and differentiation, they found themselves incorporated into 'the plebs' – as if they were destined to become a class that was socially dependent and condemned to a disguised 'caste' condition. The asymmetric model of traditional social relations that assured white supremacy and Negro inferiority found in São Paulo the material and moral conditions to survive intact.

São Paulo's geographical and socioeconomic development is not typical of other Brazilian cities, for the latter owed their expansion to the early exploitation of slave labor. It was not until the last quarter of the nineteenth century that São Paulo underwent the changes that transformed it into a city comparable to the other urban agglomerations of Brazil. Only after coffee started being produced in the western part of the province and exported in increased quantities did São Paulo, in fact, cease being a rural area and begin to enjoy economic prosperity.

That São Paulo participated only belatedly in Brazil's colonial economy worked to the disadvantage of the Negro and Metis population and the emancipated slave. The beginning of São Paulo's economic expansion coincided with the influx and concentration of an increasing number of immigrants of European origin and with a crisis in the system of slavery itself. Few Negroes and Mulattos were able to take advantage of the facilities that would have been available to them under different circumstances and that would have permitted them to become artisans or merchants. With the abolition of slavery, they were drawn into the least desirable and low-yielding occupations, inasmuch as the most interesting occupations were taken over by and became the monopoly of the immigrants.

The movement on behalf of the abolition of slavery and the whole process of the disintegration of the system of slavery appeared – as was inevitable – to be a revolt of the whites against slavery and the seignorial order. These slavery regime institutions interfered with the socioeconomic development of the prosperous regions of the country and stifled the expansion of capitalism. The abolitionist movement, even though seemingly inspired by humanitarian motives, advocated rather against the impediment to social and economic interests that slavery represented.

The Negroes and the Mulattos were merely an 'object' and a 'mass for maneuvering' in the revolt. They could give expression to neither their deep-seated aspirations nor their immediate needs. With rare exceptions, they were relegated to a secondary role. What may be termed the 'abolitionist conscience' was more than anything else the patrimony of the whites. They led, organized, and, at the same time, contained the revolt within the limits defined by the preponderant race.

In the acute stage of transformation, the control of the process passed into the hands of the most conservative elements, who were anxious to take charge of the social, economic and political interests of the large landholders. They not only refused to indemnify the landholders for the financial losses they had suffered as a result of abolition, but also totally ignored the problem of applying measures that would assure a minimum of protection to the slave or the freedman. They focused their principal effort on elaborating a policy that would guarantee the rapid replacement of slave manpower. At the close of the Empire and the beginning of the Republic, governmental policy was, consequently, directed primarily towards encouraging immigration by all possible means.

The Negroes took no active part in the 'bourgeois revolution'. Its development centered on two types of persons: the coffee producers and the immigrants. The sociological and economic position of the coffee producers underwent a vast change along with the economic growth stemming from the coffee trade and the expansion of the cities and towns. The immigrants tenaciously seized upon every opportunity in the new country and forced the Negroes out of the few worthwhile positions they had been able to obtain in the skilled trades and in small-business activities. Victims of a negative process of selection, the Negroes had to accept what came to be considered 'Negro service' – uncertain and degrading work, as hard as it was badly paid. While prosperity favored all other elements of the population, they struggled with very great difficulties in holding – or even obtaining – the humblest and most undesirable positions.

The Negroes had not been prepared in advance – either as slaves or as freedmen – for the socioeconomic role of independent workers. They had neither the technical training nor the mentality and discipline of a wage earner. Having formerly had no status in the social order, the Negroes were unable to evaluate correctly the nature, obligations and limitations of a work contract. They suspected that a labor contract was a trick intended to enforce slavery by other means. They felt that if a man sold his muscles and his work, he was selling himself.

Seeing and feeling themselves free, the Negroes wanted to be treated like men or, as they saw it, like those who were masters of their own lives. A fatal lack of adaptation on the part of the Negroes and Mulattos resulted. The attitude and behavior of the former slaves, who conceived of their freedom as being absolute, irritated white employers. The Negroes assumed that since they were 'free', they could work when and where they pleased. They tended not to show up for work whenever they had enough money on hand to live for a while without working; they especially did not like to be remonstrated with, warned or reprimanded.

On the pretext that they were 'free' and that 'slavery was a thing of the past', they wanted a kind of independence entirely incompatible with any system of employed labor. This misunderstanding could, of course, have been gradually corrected. Since there was, however, a comparative abundance of labor owing to immigration, the employers were intolerant of the Negroes and Mulattos. They did not attempt to understand them, considering them irresponsible and too difficult to handle outside slavery.

The abundance of qualified labor available as a result of intensive immigration led to a rapid change in the thinking and the attitude of employers, even in the choice of field workers. The Negroes had formerly been considered the only possible field labor, at least for the kind of work previously done by slaves. The employers had been comparatively tolerant of the Negroes' defects and had a real desire to help them improve as much as possible. As it became evident that the Negroes could be replaced – even quite easily in the more prosperous areas – and that the replacements were 'more intelligent' and more efficient, this indulgence on the part of employers disappeared. The Negroes, consequently, passed without transition from the category of privileged workers to that of third-class laborers, at the very same time that they were increasing their own demands and becoming more exacting. Almost automatically, they were relegated to the lower edge of the productive system – to undesirable, poorly paid, and socially degrading occupations.

Slavery had despoiled the Negroes of almost every vestige of their own cultural heritage. It allowed them only a very limited share in the social order. They developed their personality under the shadow of a slave or former slave status. Abolition thrust them into the 'freeman's world' without the social and institutional resources that would have enabled them to adapt themselves to their new position in society. They were ignorant of, and thus could not practice, any form of organized life normally enjoyed by the white people – including family life and all forms of cooperation and mutual assistance based on the family. In order to make real use of his rights as a free man, it would have been necessary, first, for the Negro to shed his second nature – formed during the times when he was a slave or a recently freed slave – and to assimilate the social customs that constituted the white man's world. This lack of a definite sociocultural background was an insurmountable handicap for the Negroes who settled in São Paulo, a city whose rapid growth and great industrial development caused intensely keen competition among all classes and strata of the social order.

The Negro population became extremely mobile after the abolition of slavery. Negroes and Mulattos migrating to the city found space as best they could by huddling into the caves and the overpopulated sections of the metropolis. Many Negroes, poorly adapted to city life, moved towards the interior of the state of São Paulo or towards the parts of Brazil where they had first lived, most often the northeast and the north. In general, the movements into and away from the city balanced one another, but there was a definite concentration of a rural population in an urban area.

Ill-adapted to urban life by nature and lacking the 'mental or moral qualities' necessary to earn wages and to meet economic competition, three-quarters of the Negro and Mulatto population lived in a hand-to-mouth way. They crowded into hovels – those caves cannot be called anything else – and there was actually not room enough for them all. The abandonment of children, the sick and the old, unmarried mothers, alcoholism, homeless wandering, prostitution, occasional or organized crime – all these were the normal results of a human drama unprecedented in the social history of Brazil.

The only members of this population assured of earning a wage were the women, who could always find work as household servants. The women immediately became the support of the family groups. They provided the living, either entirely or partially, for the home, supplying the men with money for food and clothing and even for their minor expenses. The idleness of the men, at first due only to circumstances and endured as a kind of dignified protest, soon became transformed in many cases into an ill-disguised and sociopathic form of exploitation of one human being by another.

Under these conditions, the Negroes had nothing on which to base any hopes for the present or for the future. The future took on, in fact, a still more negative aspect because the white people looked upon this situation, and explained it, from a racial standpoint. Reading about these people in the newspapers or observing scenes of depravity, they accused the Negroes themselves of being responsible for their condition since they 'had no ambition, did not like to work, were naturally inclined towards crime, prostitution and drunkenness, and were incapable of controlling themselves without the domination of the white people'. The tragedy of the Negroes' condition had little emotional effect upon the whites. They did not exercise any direct or indirect social control to improve that condition. The victims became, consequently, ever more degraded.

The Negroes and Mulattos did not have any organized methods that would have enabled them to lift themselves out of that phase of degraded collective life. Nor could the city authorities do anything since they lacked social services comprehensive enough to solve such serious human problems. Demoralization went hand in hand with material degradation. The Negroes abandoned themselves to their fate with a feeling of profound frustration and an apathy they could not overcome. A defeatist state of mind took possession of them and made them think that 'the Negro was born to suffer', 'a Negro's life is like that' and 'there is no use trying to do anything about it'. The only point on which the Negroes would not yield was on their stubborn desire to remain in the city.

No human group could support with total inertia a situation like that faced by the Negro and Mulatto population in São Paulo. Before long, a few timid attempts to protest and to defend themselves began to appear and to grow in importance. These attempts became more substantial between 1925 and 1930 and began to bear their first fruits. A Negro press started a campaign to make the Negroes conscious of the racial situation in Brazil and of the 'abandonment of the Negro'. Organizations joined in the campaign to lend practical effectiveness to the 'Negro protest'. For the first time in the history of the city, Negroes and Mulattos joined together to protect the economic, social and cultural interests of the race. They sought to create forms of unity and of organized social activity that would result in the re-education of the Negro, the progressive increase of his earnings and his standard of living, his participation in the political activities of the community, and, consequently, the possibility of his becoming a real citizen according to all social standards.

These social movements succeeded, however, in attracting only a small fraction of the Negro and Mulatto population of São Paulo. The Negroes' conformism, apathy and dependence on white people prevented the successful conclusion of these attempts to affirm Negro independence. By exposing the dominant racial ideology, however, these movements set up a counter-ideology that enlarged the Negroes' zone of perception and consciousness of the racial reality in Brazil. Moreover, by stressing certain basic trends of equality, they encouraged the Negroes to wave the flag of racial democracy and to demand a fair share of the earnings, the standard of living, and the prerogatives enjoyed by other classes of the community. As these claims were manifested in a peaceful manner, they did not lead to any measures of racial segregation and did not provoke any tensions or racial conflicts. To that extent, they were constructive from the social point of view. They disseminated new ideas about the Negroes, gave a new dimension to their method of solving problems, and constituted an effort to assimilate the social methods and to profit from the economic facilities enjoyed by the white people. They answered exactly the requirements of the competitive economy and revealed themselves to be the only means by which the colored population of São Paulo was attempting to adapt itself collectively to the historic-social demands of the times.

These movements and the objectives towards which they were directed did not meet, however, with any constructive reaction on the part of the white people. The latter remained indifferent to them, raising a wall of incomprehension that deprived the movements of their practical effectiveness. Moreover, the more influential circles, with their traditionalist attitudes and judgments, considered the social movements arising from the Negro community to be a danger and a threat – as if it had been these movements that had introduced the racial problem into the country.

When the 'New State' was set up, these movements were legally prohibited and the principal organization that appeared during this period, the Brazilian Negro Front, was suppressed. With the disappearance of the New State, between 1945 and 1948, there were some attempts to reorganize the protest. All failed completely because the Negroes who were reaching a higher level in society preferred a selfish and individualistic strategy for the resolution of the Negro problem. Lack of machinery for racial unity deprived the Negro community of the loyalty and altruistic support of the rare elements that arose from it. The contribution that the social movements could have made to the modernization of the traditional system of racial relations was repressed and nullified. The adaptation of that system to the historic-social situation prevalent in the city now depends, if no change takes place, on the slow and indirect effects of the gradual assimilation of Negroes and Mulattos into the present social order.

In the period immediately following the abolition of slavery, the economic facilities of São Paulo were monopolized by the white people of the former dominant classes and by the immigrants. A census conducted in the city in 1893 clearly demonstrates this. Of 170 capitalists, 137 were Brazilians (80.5 per cent) and 33 were foreigners (19.4 per cent). Of 740 property owners, 509 were Brazilians (69 per cent) and 231 were foreigners (31 per cent). In some of the leading professions that had traditionally been controlled by the local elite, there were few foreigners. This was the case, for example, with the judges and lawyers. In professions more closely connected to technical progress, foreigners appeared in significant proportions. There were, for example, 127 Brazilian engineers to 105 foreign; 23 Brazilian architects to 34 foreign; 10 Brazilian surveyors to 11 foreign; and 274 Brazilian teachers and professors to 129 foreign. Among those listed as 'personnel of the industries', immigrants appeared to be the privileged workers.

Unlike the agricultural occupations, in which the native element predominated (1,673 Brazilians or 68 per cent as compared with 783 foreigners or 32 per cent), urbanization actually amounted in the other sectors to Europeanization, as shown by the following important examples: 5,878 natives (41.6 per cent) in domestic service against 8,226 foreigners (58.3 per cent); 774 natives (21 per cent) in manufacturing activities against 2,893 foreigners (79 per cent); 1,481 natives (14.4 per cent) in skilled trades or handicrafts against 8,760 foreigners (85.5 per cent); 1,988 natives (18.9 per cent) in transportation and affiliated occupations against 8,527 foreigners (81 per cent); 2,680 natives (28.3 per cent) in commercial activities against 6,776 foreigners (71.6 per cent). The average for these activities shows that 71.2 per cent of the jobs were held by foreigners.

Since other sundry information shows that the participation of the Negro was very low in terms of percentage, especially for skilled or semi-skilled work, there is an indirect but very significant indication that the later economic development of the city corrected only negligibly the Negroes' economic participation rate. In fact, it was not until after 1935, with the intensification of internal migration, that the need for manual labor greatly increased the employment possibilities of the Negro and Mulatto population. Even this change was more a matter of quantity than of quality. A larger number of Negroes succeeded in earning a living wage, although at the more unskilled and badly paid types of work.

A census taken in 1951 shows that the activities of Negroes were beginning to reach a level that could have existed at the time of abolition had it not been for the competition provided by the immigrants. Sample statistics, selected at random among men and women, show that 29 per cent of the Negroes and Mulattos were working in skilled trades and 21 per cent were employed in domestic service. The following figures of the percentage of Negroes employed in specific activities give a clear idea of the situation: 9 per cent in public service, including principally ushers or court messengers, servants and bookkeepers; 8 per cent in industry, mostly skilled or semi-skilled work; 7 per cent in office work, including a small number as stenographer-typists, file clerks, and bookkeepers; 4 per cent in business, a few of them employed as salesmen or heads of sections. On the whole, the picture has changed, but not greatly. The Negroes, still in a very unprofitable situation in the scale of occupations, have little possibility to advance or improve themselves in the near future. In this connection, figures from the census of 1940 should be noted; by collecting only the most significant indications from this, Table 14.1 was compiled.

**Table 14.1**  Distribution according to employment situation of men and women, age 10 and above, city of São Paulo, census of 1940

| Situation | Whites | Negroes | Mulattos | Orientals | Totals |
|---|---|---|---|---|---|
| Employer | 15,261 | 51 | 72 | 342 | 15,726 |
|  | 97.04% | 0.32% | 0.46% | 2.17% | 100% |
| Employee | 323,997 | 15,114 | 10,925 | 2,317 | 352,353 |
|  | 91.95% | 4.28% | 3.10% | 0.66% | 100% |
| Independent | 74,448 | 2,051 | 1,595 | 1,577 | 79,671 |
|  | 93.44% | 2.57% | 2.00% | 1.98% | 100% |
| Family member | 4,644 | 80 | 56 | 565 | 5,345 |
|  | 86.88% | 1.50% | 1.05% | 10.57% | 100% |
| Situation unknown | 4,393 | 356 | 325 | 44 | 5,118 |
|  | 85.83% | 6.96% | 6.35% | 0.86% | 100% |
| Population | 1,203,111 | 63,546 | 45,136 | 14,074 | 1,326,261 |
|  | 90.71% | 4.79% | 3.40% | 1.06% | 100% |

*Note:* Including individuals whose color was not given.

In spite of the pessimistic conclusions that must be drawn from these statistics on the whole, the changes that had taken place are significant. The Negroes and the Mulattos had succeeded in obtaining reliable sources of earnings, regardless of the employment situation in which those earnings were obtained. This enabled them to integrate themselves into the employment structure, creating, thereby, a situation favorable to the gradual acquisition of the social techniques formerly the monopoly of the white people. Moreover, the Negroes and the Mulattos had simultaneously reached a level, as regards the classification of occupations and competition with the white man, that opened to them certain possibilities of vertical mobility from the sociological standpoint. 'A part of the system', the Negroes and Mulattos could struggle to elevate themselves, to improve their position in the system. Although still not very strong, the colored elite or the colored middle class stood forth as a new reality and would have a chance to increase continuously if socioeconomic conditions continued as they were.

## Prejudice and Discrimination in Racial Relations

Insofar as the integration of the white race into the system of social relations is concerned, only the class system fully applies in São Paulo. In the case of the Negroes and Mulattos, however, both the caste and the class systems combine in variable forms. Archaic influences are always free to act and to cause them to live over again to a large extent a racial order that should now be more than a relic of the historic past. This configuration of the caste and class systems favors the persistence and, under some aspects, the renewal of the traditionalist and asymmetric model of racial relations. This model maintained itself practically intact in São Paulo until about 1930 – that is, for a half century after the abolition of slavery. Even today one cannot say that the abolition is irreversible or that the old model is entirely obsolete. It still clings to the past in part and is continually strengthened by the extreme inequality in the economic situation and the social destiny of the two races.

The final disappearance of the old model of racial relations will not become historically concrete in São Paulo until the entire Negro and Mulatto population reaches class situations equivalent to those enjoyed by the white population. The old model will not disappear until the competitive social order is freed in the economic, social and cultural fields of the distortions that result from the tendency to concentrate income, social privilege and power in the hands of a single race. Generally speaking, the Brazilian racial difficulty resides more in the lack of equilibrium between racial stratification and the current social order than in specific ethnocentric and irreducible influences.

Prejudice and discrimination appeared in Brazilian society as unavoidable consequences of slavery. The Catholic mores condemned the enslavement of man by man. They imposed upon the master, moreover, the fundamental obligation of providing the slave with religious instruction and faith, making slave and master equal before God. In order to escape or neutralize such obligations, the masters resorted to an extravagant sociocultural rationalization that converted slavery into an apparently pious and merciful relationship. The slave was assumed to be a brutish, pagan and animal-like creature, dependent for his existence and survival upon the responsibility so generously assumed by his master. The condition of being a slave became inseparable from total degradation, both biologically and psychologically.

These rationalizations, so painfully demanded by the religious mores, were strongly reinforced by arguments borrowed from Roman law, which did not recognize the slave as having the status of a person and conferred almost unlimited power upon the master. Uniting these two tendencies, the prejudice against the Negroes and their descendants, the half-breeds (*mestiço*) or Mulattos, took the form of a moral sanction from the social standpoint. A person's status was thought to be transmitted by the mother (*partus sequitur ventrem*). Racial marks or features played a secondary role in this context, since they merely served to show ostensibly, as if they were a stigmata, those who were in the degrading and infamous situation of having been a slave and later a freed slave. This prejudice became racial, however, by the contingency of the slaves' biological origins.

Discrimination, in its turn, was considered an institutional condition made especially necessary by the relations between master and slave, and by the corresponding social order. Since the basis of the distinction between master and slave rested upon the social situation (and consequently upon their respective positions), discrimination was established mainly as a means for the social separation of coexisting racial categories. It determined the relationship between master and slave living closely together. Words, gestures, clothing, housing, food, occupations, entertainment, ambitions, rights and duties – everything was subjected to a process that transformed cohabitation and coexistence into total separation, rigid and irremediable, of the two social categories which were at the same time two different races.

Because the slaves formed the bulk of the population, a majority that could become dangerous and uncontrollable, they were rated as enemies of the public and private order. To keep slaves under the master's yoke, increased violence in repression, discipline and control was considered necessary. The bodily substance of the slave was ignored as being part of a 'person'. It became an inflexible habit to put the slave in his place and to keep him there, to force him with violence or gentleness to obedience and passivity.

Prejudice in Brazil served to confer legitimacy upon morally outlawed behavior and institutions, while discrimination served to regulate the coexistence and cohabitation between the races by a truly inflexible code of ethics intended to maintain the economic, social and cultural distance existing between master and slave. From their most distant origins, prejudice and discrimination had two aspects: one, structural and dynamically social; the other, racial. On the one hand, master and slave were in close relationship, but opposed to each other as social categories. Both prejudice and discrimination were basically linked to the structure and operation of a caste society in which racial stratification corresponded to principles of economic and sociocultural integration in the social organization. On the other hand, the masters were of the white race, and, for the sake of their interests and their social values, they exercised a social domination that was at the same time a racial domination. This applied conversely to the slaves who were, by selection, Negroes or Mulattos.

Social stratification presupposed, therefore, a racial stratification that it covered and concealed. Because the one was inherent in the other, the existence of a basic parallel between color and social situation could be admitted. The history of São Paulo illustrates the different and successive steps of this parallelism – from the final disintegration of the old system to the formation of a class society. Leaving aside the age of slavery, one faces three clear-cut periods. In the first, the transitional phase, the traditionalist and asymmetric model of racial relations remains unchanged. The second shows what occurred when the social rise of the Negro caused a break in the parallelism between color and the social situation. The third poses the question of the probability or improbability of this parallelism being incorporated into the class system, which would mean the absorption of racial inequality into an expanding competitive economy.

The first period can be illustrated by what happened in São Paulo between 1888, the date of the abolition of slavery, and 1930. Under living conditions that excluded the Negro and Mulatto population almost entirely from the active economic life of the city, this population remained essentially in a status equivalent to that of the freedman or former slave in the slaveholding and seignorial social order. The traditionalist and asymmetric model of racial relations maintained itself almost completely in the new historic-social situation, as if the change in the legal status of the

Negroes and Mulattos were not to be reflected in their social prerogatives. The traditionalist model of racial relations was, however, not the only die-hard process. The entire social structure on which it was based, the racial ideology that gave it its meaning, and the social customs that it fulfilled remained intact.

These facts are truly significant from the sociological point of view. They bring out two essential truths. First, changes affecting the integrated model of the social order are not necessarily reflected directly, immediately and deeply upon racial relations. Where traditionalism persists in Brazil, it is inevitable that the parallel between color and social situation should be more or less vigorously maintained, even if the human beings concerned deny that reality. Secondly, prejudice and racial discrimination do not appear as historical by-products of the legal chain of the social status of the Negro and the Mulatto. On the contrary, the persistence of this prejudice and discrimination constitutes a phenomenon of cultural backwardness. The old social regime's attitudes, behavior and values concerning racial relations are maintained in historic-social situations, in which they are in open conflict with the economic, legal and moral foundations of the prevailing social order. In this connection, the mani-festations of racial prejudice and discrimination have to do neither with the competition or rivalry between Negroes and white people nor with the real or possible aggravation of racial tensions. They are the expression of mechanisms that actually perpetuate the past in the present; they represent the continuation of racial inequality as it prevailed under the old caste system. Wherever traditionalism remains intact in racial relations – even if the contrary tendency is announced – it implies a tacit survival of the parallelism between color and social situation.

The second phase deserves still greater attention. Under certain circum-stances, Negroes and Mulattos could emerge from their condition in the slaveholding and seignorial society. It was necessary, however, for them either to be incorporated into the legal nucleus of the white family that granted them its favor or to be accepted as the protégés of that family. In such a case the individual would to some extent lose his racial identity and acquire the social identity of the family to which he owed his freedom. It cannot be claimed, as many have thought, that an alternative of this kind amounted to a complete and definite correction of color or whitening '*branquea mento*' by social situation. Although the sphere in which the colored person was accepted and could act in the white environment was sometimes quite large, he had to know how to keep up appearances, how to remain in his place, and how to practice towards his white benefactors a policy of sympathetic appeal and unconditional obedience.

These were cases of social upgrading that could actually be called social infiltration. By favoring a talented Mulatto or a remarkable Negro, this process of social elevation deprived the colored population of its elite in a continuous and inexorable manner. Moreover, because it concerned only a small number of persons, this mechanism did not help to change the racial situation or to alter the white man's conception of the Negro. The individuals selected for their particular gifts were considered to be the exception that confirmed the rule. Their abilities did not benefit their race, but were thought to result from the influence or the psychobiological and social heritage of the whites. People would say in speaking of them: 'He is a Negro with a white soul', 'he is black only on the outside', 'he is white on the inside' or 'he doesn't seem to be a Negro at all'. On the other hand, if they failed in any way or showed an unexpected weakness of any kind, people would say: 'I told you so', 'when a Negro doesn't mess things up on his way in, he will do it on his way out', 'once a Negro, always a Negro', 'what could you expect of a Negro?' The substantial possibilities for employment and increased earnings and for social eleva-tion offered in a competitive economy – especially during the last twenty years – have, however, made it possible for many of the so-called colored elite or colored middle class to reclassify themselves socially without recourse to white patronage for vertical social mobility.

Confronted by the 'New Negro', the white man finds himself confused and in an ambiguous position. The 'New Negro' is already a relatively complex human being. His mentality has adapted to the times and to city life. He is not afraid to compete freely with the white man, and, above all, he intends to succeed in life at all costs. Refusing to live with poor Negroes, he breaks the material bonds or the moral ties that united him and his original environment; he does not want to live on a low scale and does not respect the unity that would make the rich Negro a defense-less victim of his needy friends and relatives. He despises the careless Negro whom he considers the cause of the degradation of the race; he opposes social movements of a protest character, maintaining that these movements could stimulate illusions among the Negroes and animosity among the white people. He assimilates the white mentality, exaggerating and taking the white man as a model for his ambitions. He often practices a naïve but severe kind of puritanism that he thinks will protect him from criticism and purify him from any external cause of moral degradation.

He deliberately cultivates refinement and amiability, not only to tone down his attitude of self-assertion but also to express himself, his thinking and his evaluation of human importance. Furthermore, he will not listen to any white people who attempt to put him in his place by applying the traditional model of race relations. If he yielded on this score, he would lose all gains he had so far achieved. The 'New Negro' appears to be the chief human agent in modernizing racial relations in the city of São Paulo. He is, in fact, the active and constant expression of the rejection of the traditional manifestation of racial prejudice and discrimination.

Three essential conclusions can be derived from a study of the 'New Negro'. First, when the Negro breaks with the stereotyped conditions and the dissimilated proprieties of the past and gains a social position by his personal merits, his wealth, or his prestige, the polarization that served to camouflage the parallelism between color and social situation inevitably disappears. The lines of resistance to color itself then appear in comparatively clear-cut profile. Prejudice and racial discrimination are unmasked. Restrictions that seemed in a confused way to be linked to social situation manifest themselves in terms of color alone. Moreover, when the white man finds himself in competition with the Negro, he is finally obliged to resort, more or less openly, to attitudes and behavior that are incompatible with the tradition of dignity and to appeal to ethnocentrism or racial intolerance as a medium of self-defense.

Secondly, an opposite reaction is also clearly made manifest, although in an apparently more superficial and less prevalent form. White people who really believe in tolerance and equality seek to protect this 'New Negro'. They defend him against indirect pressure and encourage him to realize his ambitions. Their attitudes may be more or less ambiguous or insincere, and they may have a distorted concept of racial reality. Still, these white people do declare their hostility to the Pharisees of prejudice and racial discrimination in disguise. At the same time, they try to lend a helping hand to the deserving Negro, as they express it, even if they are not always successful. In this way, following the advent of the 'New Negro' and as a result of the strength of his personality and his success, some sectors of the white population have committed themselves more deeply to a modernization of the existing standards and customs of racial relations.

A third aspect is that the Negroes themselves do not react in a uniform way to the success of the 'New Negro'. His friends and relatives on the same social level may be enthusiastic and offer sympathy and moral help, serving as a kind of sounding board and a source of encouragement to the Negro concerned. But evil tongues are often at work even in his own social environment. His pretensions and accomplishments are sneered at or ridiculed. Negroes, especially those of a lower social level, are just as apt to react to his achievement with resentment as with satisfaction. Success ultimately leads to social elevation, and that results in a break with his former circles. This is why relatives and friends are anxious and, by a strange reaction of affection, condemn those they love.

Aside from relations of personal character, success is pointed to with enthusiasm. The most prevalent feeling is that what one Negro can do, another Negro can also do. A kind of folklore is constructed about the Negro who makes his way in the world and who serves as an example to encourage others who have the same ambitions. Nevertheless, the heroes of this folklore abandon their old environment, isolate themselves from their origins, and endeavor laboriously to forge the prestige of the 'good Negro' who has a social situation and who is 'somebody'. This more or less characteristic reaction separates the leading Negro figures from the environment of the great colored masses and induces them to ignore the vital importance of movements, which could succeed in accelerating the democratization of racial relations.

The third problem places before one an enigma. It is impossible to know how Brazilian racial relations will evolve in a distant future. It seems probable that dominant trends will lead to the establishment of an authentic racial democracy. In the immediate future, however, certain repeated events cause one to fear the success of these trends. A spontaneous socioeconomic development was the real cause of certain significant changes in Brazil. Up to the present time, this development has, however, obviously been insufficient to bring about an adaptation of the social order, inherited from the past, to the demands of the class society. In many social environments, there exists a very clear-cut tendency to accept and to practice old discriminatory procedures. Some people are afraid they will lose their social standing by 'accepting the Negro'; others accept the Negro only under conventional circumstances and reject him when it is a question of a true friendship or communion of sentiments. Still others defend certain archaic positions at all costs and reject any possibility for the Negro to reach positions of management or leadership. Mixed marriages meet with almost insurmountable resistance as things now stand.

Facts of this kind show the danger that is beginning to appear. The concentration of income, social privilege, and power in the hands of one single race, the weakness of the efforts that could be capable of correcting the necessarily negative efforts of this concentration, and ethnocentric and discriminatory attitudes may facilitate the gradual absorption of the parallelism between color and social standing into the class system. There is no doubt about the existence of this threat. The worst aspect of it is that only a fully conscious and organized effort can successfully fight against it.

Under present conditions, it is very unlikely that this kind of reaction on the part of society could be definitely established. What is vital for the white sectors of the population is not the fate of racial democracy but the continuity and the rhythm of expansion of the competitive social order. Democracy at the political level does not even appear to them to constitute a problem. Negro and Mulatto circles, for their part, do not possess the elements that would enable them to spread and generalize a state of mind necessary for a conscious, systematic and organized defense of racial democracy. The poor sectors lack the appropriate means; the successful Negroes or 'colored elite' either do not feel the necessity of this defense or do not consider it advantageous to commit themselves to such objectives, which concern the future of the community rather than their own personal situation. Racial democracy is, consequently, abandoned to its fate without having any champions to defend it as an absolute value. If in the formation and spontaneous development of social classes racial inequality were confused with the inequality inherent in the competitive social order, racial democracy would then be fatally condemned and would continue to be nothing but a beautiful myth, as it is now.

Men and the societies they form do not always modernize themselves entirely. Archaic elements and factors sometimes continue to exist and to have an active effect long after their own historical period. They exercise negative influences on the development of personality, of culture, and of society itself. This seems to be the case with São Paulo, even though it is the most modern and the most highly developed city in Brazil. It is still held in the clutches of the past in the field of racial relations. It has plunged in an indecisive way into a period of transition that is being indefinitely prolonged, as if the Negroes had to wait for the spontaneous advent of a second abolition in order to become the equals of the whites.

These aspects of reality raise two major problems. One concerns the kinds of men who 'make history' – the social classes from which they arise, and the economic, social or political interests and the concepts of ideology, nation or race to which their leadership is applied. In São Paulo these men have been of very diverse social origins. They represent, respectively, the former privileged classes or their descendants, the immigrants or their descendants, and selected elements among the national migrating populations. All have had the same deeply rooted desire to enrich themselves, to achieve success and to exercise power. For them, the ideal values of the competitive social order have had no charm. They have been content to make use of those values as a means of achieving their own success in a rational, rapid and sure manner. They have 'made history', but they have neither known nor cared about the people and their human problems. They have banished equity from their cultural horizon. They have had, therefore, no perspective from which to form an appreciation of the human tragedy of the Negro – or other tragedies just as poignant and as worthy of 'history-making action'. The Negro ceased to count in the process of discovery – as if he were excluded from the common social life. And, even worse, democracy, which constituted the legal and political foundation for the competitive economy and, at the same time, was its only means of moral control, actually ceased to be the source of inspiration for those who were 'making history'.

The other problem concerns modernization, particularly its repercussions in the field of racial relations. It is very difficult for modernization to reach balanced proportions and to be extended thoroughly to all levels of organized social life. Modernization goes hand in hand with the relative power and vitality of those groups that are interested in certain sociocultural changes. It progresses in accordance with their ability to establish these changes definitely in the course of history. Although the city of São Paulo underwent a rapid transformation in its urban physiognomy and in its economic organization, it remained more or less a prisoner of the past in other fields, including those of human relations and the development of its institutions. This is especially true of its racial relations, which have revealed themselves to be an astonishing and dangerous pool of stagnation.

In order to change this situation, the human groups directly concerned must become conscious of the situation and make an organized effort to change it – as has happened in other spheres of social life that have become rapidly modernized. The Negro himself must launch the initial challenge provoked by the Brazilian racial problem. He must achieve one immediate objective – a more equitable share in the benefits of the competitive economy. He must strive for a long-term objective – the building of real racial democracy in the community. If he strives towards this goal, he will lead the white people of the various social classes to defend this cause, on which a balanced operation and development of the competitive economy largely depend.

From this perspective, the extent to which the modernization of racial relations is linked to the faculty of rationalization and to the capacity for social action of certain human groups can be better understood. So long as the Negro is limited by the racial ideology set up by the white people and governed only by the desire to 'belong to the system' – that is, to identify himself as much as possible with the white people themselves – he will remain historically neutral. He thus becomes the principal victim of an invisible chain that results from the weight of the past. He becomes incapable of measuring up socially and positively to the demands of the present. He does not assert himself as strongly as he could in the shaping of his own future in humanity.[3]

## Notes

1.  Originally presented by F. Fernandes as a speech in the Conference Race and Color, organized by The American Academy of Arts and Science and the Congress for Cultural Freedom, Copenhagen, 11 September, 1965. Published in Florestan Fernandes (1967), *Daedalus*, Vol. 96, No. 2, 560–579. More recently in (2008), Dominación y desigualdad. El dilema social latinoamericano. Florestan Fernandes. *Antología*, pp. 81–111, CLACSO, Consejo Latinoamericano de Ciencias Sociales Siglo del Hombre Editores.

2.  The terms 'Negro' and 'Mulatto' were widely used in the sixties in Brazil. Florestan used these terms in his book published in 1971 in the United States, *The Negro in Brazilian Society* (New York: Atheneum).

3.  Interested readers will find in the following two works the empirical foundation and the interpretation of the sociological considerations developed herein, together with further bibliographical references to other publications on the subject: Roger Bastide and Florestan Fernandes, *Brancos e Negros em São Paulo* [Whites and Blacks in São Paulo], São Paulo, 1959; Florestan Fernandes, *A Integracao do Negro a Sociedade de Classes* [The Integration of the Negro in a Class Society], São Paulo, 1964).

## Florestan Fernandes, by Antonio Sérgio Alfredo Guimarães (Brazil)

Sociology, as an empirical discipline, practiced and taught at university institutions, was introduced in Brazil in 1933 (ELSP), 1934 (USP) and 1935 at the Universidade do Distrito Federal, in Rio de Janeiro, at the Free School of Sociology and Politics (ELSP) and at the University of São Paulo (USP) (Candido, [1959] 2006). Two

*(Continued)*

(Continued)

themes then dominated research: education and race relations. A graduate of the ELSP, Florestan Fernandes, was admitted to USP as an assistant of Roger Bastide and would become a leading figure in the new directions that sociology then took in Brazil. His *Weight of the Past* is a relevant text where he condenses his interpretation of the articulation between racial prejudice and capitalist development in Brazil. He had drafted the thesis in the research on race relations in São Paulo, carried out in Brazil between 1950 and 1953 by UNESCO's Department of Social Sciences. Later, he reworked his analysis in the 1960s for his Professor of Sociology's dissertation (Professor Chair) at the University of São Paulo.

Until the 1960s, studies of race relations in Brazil were carried out predominantly in the Northeast of Brazil, where a pattern of racial accommodation smoothly led to the transformation of the racial caste of slavery into the social classes of post-abolition, with the absorption in the middle strata of a large contingent of colored people. This pattern of accommodation became known internationally as color gradient, or pigmentocracy, where color (the racial appearance defined by phenotypic features) was almost perfectly associated with socioeconomic status, diluting the original races from colonization. Freyre (1938) spoke of ethnic democracy to praise what would be, in the words of Bilden (1929), a laboratory of civilization in the tropics. The interpretation of Brazil as a *racial democracy* won increasing diffusion in the world during the 1950s. It is against this backdrop that one must understand Fernandes's analysis of race relations.

São Paulo was his research field, a city where modern industrial capitalism was founded against the pattern of racial accommodation typical of cities in the Northeast, Minas Gerais and Rio de Janeiro, where a mestizo middle class of civil servants, merchants and craftsmen had established themselves. On the contrary, the capital of São Paulo had been formed in the displacement of Black and mestizo populations with a rural base by the wave of European immigration that had occurred between 1880 and 1940. This new pattern of racial relations was more conflictive and ethnic, developing in the midst of an accelerated development of capitalist labor relations. In Fernandes's view, this would be the future pattern of race relations that would prevail in Brazil, replacing that of the Portuguese colonization of sugar plantations, tobacco, cotton, or mineral extraction.

Fernandes however did not believe that competitive capitalism should develop on a racial basis. On the contrary, the capitalist regime, based on the extraction of labor surplus value, would only perfect itself without those obstacles. His task as a sociologist was, therefore, to explain how the substitution of Blacks and Mulattoes by European immigrants in the São Paulo labor market had taken place, and how the racial prejudice that he considered proper to the slave regime persisted in São Paulo. His response appears clearly outlined in this short text: Black displacement would have been an unintended consequence of the behavior of Afro-descendants themselves, informed by the status-role of slavery. While the permanence of racial prejudice was due to the narrow imagination of the elites, resulting from the slave order, the elites unable to complete the 'bourgeois revolution'. In his intellectual production, Fernandes develops the historical-structural method, aiming to explain the forms of action where socio-economic orders do not update social behavior adequately, although performed by socialized agents. This sociological method became, in the years that followed, the hegemonic method of sociology in Latin America.

For a long time, until the 1980s, Fernandes's analysis of the subaltern position of Blacks in Brazil was the only one to counter the Freyrian interpretation of racial harmony and democracy, and to recognize the persistance of racial prejudice and the responsibility of dominant groups for the curtailment of social rights in Brazil. It was, therefore, a widely used analysis for the political mobilization of Blacks that followed the authoritarian regime established in 1964. The new generation of Black intellectuals that emerged in the 1960s was deeply influenced by Fernandes's analysis.

His dialogue with the sociology of Germani in Argentina seems clear today if we focus on explanations for the diverse emergence of subaltern classes and the industrial proletariat in Latin America. However, his silence on the role Afro-descendants played in social mobilizations during the formation of the Brazilian state has obscured other potential comparative studies, such as the great similarities between Brazil, Colombia, Venezuela and Cuba.

Fernandes's analysis lost pre-eminence with the great development of sociological research on modern capitalism and the coexistence of various forms of surplus value extraction seen as normal and not as an exception to this pattern of development. This opened a contemporary historiography of slavery and the post-abolition period that produced primary data on the everyday life of foreign immigrants, slaves and freedmen between 1880 and 1920 in the São Paulo region, as well as their role in the formation of the nation.

## References

Bilden, R. (1929) Brazil, laboratory of civilization. *The Nation*, 128 (3315): 71–74, New York.

Candido, A. ([1959] 2006) A sociologia no Brasil. *Tempo Social*, 18 (1): 271–301.

Freyre, G. (1938) *Conferências na Europa*. Rio de Janeiro: Ministerio da Educacao e Saúde.

# 15

# The Dynamics of Inter-ethnic Relations: Classes, Colonialism and Acculturation[1]

*Rodolfo Stavenhagen (Mexico)*

Let us pull together the different threads in this essay and attempt a general formulation of the system of relationships between Indians and Ladinos.[2] Our historical point of departure will be the Spanish Conquest, although we do not deny the importance of pre-Hispanic social processes in the subsequent character of the Mayan region. The Spanish Conquest was a military enterprise and part of the political and economic expansion in post-feudal and mercantilistic Europe. The Conquest was fundamentally influenced by commercial factors (the lust for gold and spice). As a military enterprise the Spanish Conquest was a violent confrontation of two societies, two different cultures. The weaker one – the Indian – succumbed. The Indians received from the conqueror the treatment accorded since ancient times to the vanquished: looting, dispossession, slavery, even extermination. Yet the Conquest of the New World was not like preceding ones. In Spain, deep transformations were taking place due to the Reconquista. The American continent would perform an essential role in Europe's economic development, and were ascribed to the native populations specific functions in this development. For different political and economic reasons, destruction and enslavement of native populations had to come to a stop. The military conquest was transformed into a colonial system. Just as other colonial systems which the world has known since then, this one was managed over three centuries on behalf of the interests of certain powerful social classes of the metropolis, and that of their representatives in New Spain. The Crown's policy reflected these changing and often conflicting interests. At first Indian chiefs and Indian aristocracy were kept in their positions, which suited the colonial administration's realpolitik. But towards the end of the sixteenth century Indian communities had become socially and economically homogeneous. Their internal social differentiation was no longer in the interests of the colonizer. Residential segregation of Indians (through settlements of 'converted' Indians and other mechanisms) and the *encomiendas* (lands which the Crown granted as trusteeship to the conquistadores) were the first instruments used by the conquistador to levy taxes and services. Part of the Indian society's wealth was simply transferred to the conquering society. Indian communities were transformed into labor reserves of the colonial economy. Systems of serfdom and forced labor in plantations, mines and workshops constituted the basis of the economic system.

Colonial society was the product of mercantilist expansion: of the dawning of the bourgeois revolution in Europe. Its structure still retained much of the feudal era, especially in the character of human relationships. Some researchers even affirm that feudalism grew stronger in America after it had begun to decline in Spain, and that America 'feudalized' Spain once again (Parlem, 1952). Exploitation of the Indian population constituted one of the main goals of colonial economic policy. In order to maintain this labor reserve, it was framed by a complex of laws, norms, restrictions and prohibitions which kept accumulating during three centuries of colonialism, and which resulted in the corporate 'folk' communities. All things were determined for the settler's benefit: the land tenure of the Indian community, its local government, technology, economic production, commerce, residential pattern, marriage norms, education, dress styles, and even its idiom and use of language. In Spain, nobles, landowners, commercial bourgeoisie and petty bourgeoisie were at times fighting, at times co-operating in the struggle for their respective interests. But in Spanish America a rigid social hierarchy based upon centralization of political and economic power and validated in the legislation of Indians kept the natives in their position of inferiority with respect to all of the other social levels.

The colonial system worked on two levels. The restrictions and economic prohibitions which Spain imposed upon her colonies (and which were to foment the Independence movements) were repeated, often aggravated, in the relations between the colonial society and the Indian communities. The same commercial monopolies, the same restrictions on production, the same political controls which Spain exerted upon the Colony, the colonists imposed upon Indian communities. As Spain was to the Colony, so the Colony was to Indian communities: a colonial metropolis. Since then mercantilism penetrated even the most isolated villages of Spanish America.

The social groups in Spanish America which took part in the processes of economic production and distribution that sustained the Spanish

Empire also participated in the class structure of the colonial system. In the same way, the Indian population participated in the class structure of the Colony. Colonial relationships and class relationships underlay ethnic relationships. In terms of colonial relationships, the Indian society as a whole confronted colonial society. Primary characteristics of the colonial situation were ethnic discrimination, political dependence, social inferiority, residential segregation, economic subjection and juridical incapacity. In the same way, class structure was defined in terms of labor and property relations. These relations were not defined in ethnic, political, social or residential terms. Only juridical coercion (supported by military power) as well as other economic and extra-economic pressures intervened in the establishment of labor relations. Labor relations were not between two societies, but only between two specific sectors within them. Colonial and class relationships appear intermixed throughout this period. While the former primarily answered to mercantilist interests, the latter met the capitalist ones. Both kinds of relationships were also opposed to each other: the development of class relationships came into conflict with the maintenance of colonial relationships. Indian communities were constantly losing members to the developing national society. Despite tutelary legislation, the biologic and cultural mixing was a constant process which kept producing new problems for colonial society. Those Indians who for various reasons were absorbed by the larger society, therefore, quit the aforementioned colonial relationships to become integrated simply in a class structure. In consequence, they were no longer Indians.

These two kinds of socio-economic relationships in which the Indian ethnic groups were involved received moral sanction with the rigid social stratification in which the Indian (biologically, culturally and juridically defined) was always at the bottom (with the exception of the slave). From these conditions there emerged the corporate community and the formation of indo-colonial cultural characteristics, which we today call Indian culture. Ethnic relationships of the period thus presented three main aspects: two kinds of relationships of dependence and one kind of relationship of order.[3]

The dynamics of these systems of relationships were varied. The colonial relationships between Indian communities and the larger society tended to strengthen the Indian communities and foment their ethnic identity. The subordinate group usually reacts to a dominant–subordinate relationship of the colonial kind with a struggle for liberation (at the most diverse levels). Colonialism produces nationalism and struggles for independence. The colonial period was not devoid of native rebellions. Conversely, class relations contributed to the disintegration of the Indian community and its integration into the larger society. Both kinds of relations complemented each other in terms of the Indian's oppression. But the opposed tendencies which they engendered explain why certain Indian communities survived, while others were transformed into peons' or squatters' enclaves in the haciendas which displaced the *encomiendas* of the sixteenth and seventeenth centuries. Colonial relationships usually dominated class relationships. Although colonial relations were only one aspect of a world-wide system of mercantilist class relations, the more narrowly defined class relationships between Indians and Spaniards (including *criollos*, Spaniards born in the Colony) usually appeared in the form of the colonial relations described above. This was essentially due to the nature of colonial economy.

Finally, social stratification, which has sometimes, because of its rigidity, been called a caste system, reflected more the colonial character than the class character of the Indian's subjugation. The stratification system, in turn, exerted its own influence upon the development of class relationships.

Political independence in Spanish America did not basically change the relationships between Indians and the larger society. Despite the legal equality of all citizens (including Indians), various factors joined to maintain the 'colonial' character of these relations: first, internal struggles which lasted many decades; and second, the economic depression during the first half of the nineteenth century. Both kinds of factors helped to keep Indian communities marginal, isolated from the outside world, and increasingly corporate. Another reason should also be taken into account. At the beginning of the colonial period tutelary laws were established because it was considered that Indians were inferior beings. But by the end of three centuries of colonialism, these laws had served to maintain and fix that inferiority. In consequence, when legal equality was declared, the Indian was effectively in a condition of inferiority to the rest of the population, in every area of economic and social life.

The first effective changes occurred during the second half of the nineteenth century: first with the Reform laws and later with the introduction of new cash crops (principally coffee) into the Indian region. Both phenomena, of course, are closely related to one another. Legal equality and disamortization of communal land had two immediate consequences:

the Indian could now freely dispose of himself in the labor market, and the land he held could become private property. In fact, this did not take place in the abstract, but in the specific situations that have already been mentioned: extension of commercial farming; penetration by Ladinos into communities inhabited by Indian ethnic groups; appropriation of land by Ladinos; the formation of great latifundia and the Indians' wage labor on these properties and haciendas. Coffee plantations became working centers for a considerable mass of Indians, legally or illegally recruited from their communities. At the same time the first products of industrialization penetrated into the more distant villages of the Indian region in the form of goods carried by Ladino traders. In this way new economic relationships were established between the Indians and the rest of the population.

Expansion of the capitalist economy during the second half of the nineteenth century, together with the ideology of economic liberalism, once again transformed the quality of ethnic relationships between Indians and Ladinos. We consider this stage as a second form of colonialism, which we might call internal colonialism. Indians of traditional communities found themselves once again in the role of a colonized people: they lost their lands, were forced to work for the 'strangers', were integrated against their will into a new monetary economy, and fell under new forms of political domination. This time, colonial society was national society itself, which progressively extended its control over its own territory.[4]

Now there were not only isolated Indians who, abandoning their communities, joined the national society; but Indian communities themselves, as a group, were progressively incorporated into expanding regional economic systems. To the extent to which national society extended its control, and capitalist economy dominated the area, relations between colonizer and colonized, between Ladino and Indian, were transformed into class relationships.

The corporate community has been characteristic of colonial society in Indian America. Corporative social structure has an ecologic and economic basis. When colonial society is transformed into 'underdeveloped' society, when the economic structure of the corporate community is modified (loss of lands, wage labor, commercialization of agricultural produce, etc.), then it is rather unlikely that the corporate quality of the community's internal social relationships would survive for long. As we have seen, some of the Indian's cultural characteristics are bound to the highly structured corporate community. If this structure should progressively disappear, these cultural characteristics would become weaker.

Ethnic stratification in the region is the result of this historical evolution. It reflects the colonial situation which has been maintained till present times. Behind inter-ethnic relationships, which show themselves as a stratification system, there is a social class structure. When an Indian works for a Ladino, the main point is not the inter-ethnic relationship but the labor relation. During the decade of the thirties, the Indians of Chiapas organized to defend their working conditions in the coffee plantations; not as Indians, but as workers. During the years 1944–1954 there were also labor unions of Indian agricultural workers in Guatemala. They have become organized in their struggle for land, under the agrarian reform programs but as landless peasants. These relationships sometimes assume cultural shapes. The struggle for land, for instance, is carried on in the name of the restitution of communal and clan lands. At times there have also emerged messianic movements against Ladinos. Yet it was always a matter of structural changes within the traditional community.

Inter-ethnic stratification no longer completely corresponds to new class relationships which have developed along with a monetary economy. 'Colonized' Indians are not a social class. We are not saying that Indians and Ladinos are simply two social classes. This would be over-simplifying a deeply complex historical situation. During the course of economic development (or more precisely, of the development of economic underdevelopment, as a result of colonial economy), various new social classes emerge. They are not yet totally formed, because 'colonial' relationships still determine the social structure at different levels. The Indian participates in various kinds of socio-economic relationships.

He holds various occupational roles at the same time. He may be a small farmer in the communal lands, an ambulant trader, a salaried worker during different periods of the year, or during the course of his life. This situation may last as long as the regional economic structure allows it. But this structure is suffering rapid changes: the monetary economy is expanding, capitalist labor and trade relations are becoming generalized, regional communications are developing, and local industrialization is getting started. These different kinds of class relationships contribute to separating the individual from his corporate community. The community's corporate structure is breaking up. Should it disappear, inter-ethnic stratification will have lost its objective basis.

Nonetheless, the inter-ethnic stratification system, which, like every stratification system, is deeply rooted in the values held by the members of the society, is an essentially conservative force within the social structure.

While it reflects a situation of the past (the clear dichotomy between Indians and Ladinos in every area of social, economic and political life characteristic of the colonial situation), it curbs the development of new class relationships. We should not forget that the landless peasant and the salaried worker are also Indians. Even though relations of production will be determinant of future transformations in the region, ethnic consciousness may weigh heavier than class consciousness. Thus, exploited or poor as a Ladino may be, he feels privileged as compared to the Indians, even those who may have a standard of living higher than his own. Indians, on the other hand, tend to attribute all of their misfortunes to the Ladinos as such (a position which, by the way, is shared by certain romantic indigenous intellectuals), an attitude which contributes to the concealment of objective relationships between classes. This range of problems has been little studied in the region and it represents, in my opinion, an interesting field of research.

To the extent to which class relationships become more clearly defined, there emerges a new stratification, based on socio-economic indices. This stratification already exists among Ladinos, and is progressively expanding to the Indians. The status symbols of the Ladinos are beginning to be valued by the Indians too. It is no longer sufficient – or even desirable – that the Indian should become 'ladinized'. Young Indians, particularly those who now work for the government, without ever breaking ties with their communities, are buying dark sunglasses, pens, watches, etc., wearing them ostentatiously as symbols of prestige. The situation will have radically changed when social stratification includes Ladinos and Indians independent of their ethnic characteristics. Ideally this would mean the maintenance of Indian cultural identity independent of stratification. To what degree this situation is workable depends on many special factors. It has been noted that in Quetzaltenango (Guatemala) something of the sort is taking place, and this also seems to be the case in Mexico among the Maya of Yucatan, the Zapotec of Oaxaca, and the Tarascans of Michoacan.

This also depends on the attitudes and reactions of Ladinos, whose position is not stable within the class society. Ladinos have always accepted (at least from one generation to the other) the admission of acculturated Indians into their group. It is difficult to foresee the reactions of the Ladino community faced with two hypothetical alternatives of the interethnic stratification system's evolution: on the one hand, the complete assimilation of Indians (which is rather unlikely); and on the other, a general economic rise of the Indian ethnic group as such (which would be a challenge to Ladino superiority). The development of a class society leads in the direction of either of these hypothetic situations. The final result will depend on how class conflicts are solved. Indian-Ladino acculturation is a process operating on several levels. Adams foresees the ladinization of Guatemala, while in Mexico there is some talk about the integration of Indians into the Ladino culture. Yet it is necessary to study which aspects of Indian culture will be transformed in this process. Here it is convenient to distinguish structural from cultural. Those cultural elements intimately associated with the corporate structure of the community and with inter-ethnic stratification will surely disappear with the transformation of the colonial situation into a class situation. In this sense, the Indian will stop being an Indian (or will only be so in a cultural sense, and no longer in a social or structural sense). Tax has pointed out that in Guatemala social relations are 'civilized', while the world view remains 'primitive' (Tax, 1956).

There may also exist a class culture, and many 'Indian' cultural elements will accompany the development of class society as elements integrated into a new structure. One author has recently suggested that the 'Indian' culture of Chiapas is nothing but a rural culture, similar to rural cultures in other parts of the world (Goldkind, 1963).

The system of inter-ethnic stratification can only be understood as referred to the corporate structure of the Indian community and its cultural characteristics. This structure, in turn, can only be explained in terms of its colonial past. The colonial situation has become progressively transformed. The Indian thus finds himself in the midst of diverse and contradicting situations: at times he is 'colonized', and at times he is a member of a class (in the sense that he is in a typical class situation).[5] In other words, not only does the Indian perform various roles (as everybody else), but he also participates in dichotomized role systems, which are historically and structurally conflicting.[6] Nor does the Ladino escape ambiguity: at times he is the 'colonizer', at times the bearer of 'national culture' and a member of 'national society', and at the same time he finds himself in most diverse class situations, in confrontation with Indians and other Ladinos.

Until now our analysis has mainly focused on corporate community as a prototype of one of the poles of inter-ethnic relationships. This position is obviously inadequate. It overlooks, at the cultural level of inter-ethnic relationships, those 'cultural' Indians who are not incorporated into a corporate community; that is, those 'modified', 'Latinized', 'acculturated' categories referred to by anthropologists. Nonetheless, this approach finds its justifications in the fact that the analysis was not carried out on the cultural but rather on the structural level. On the other hand, it has been stressed that two main structural units are involved in the structure of inter-ethnic relations: the corporate community and society as a whole (in its diverse manifestations). The task now remains to approach the problem from the point of view of the total society.

Contemporary inter-ethnic relations partly result from colonial policy. They also represent the disintegration of that policy and are a function of present economic and class structures. As has been shown by various economists, underdeveloped economies tend to polarize into areas of growth and structurally related areas of stagnation. The Maya region of Chiapas and Guatemala constitutes such an area, as do other Indian areas of Mexico. The 'marginal' populations inhabiting these areas are growing in absolute numbers, despite national economic development (González Casanova, 1962). If this happens in Mexico, despite accelerated economic growth in recent years, then in Guatemala, where there has been no such development, it must surely happen with greater intensity. During the colonial period, colonial relations in the Indian regions served the interests of a well-defined dominant class which in turn subdued the colonial society as a whole to its own interests, insofar as relations with Spain would permit. In the situation of internal colonialism (which might be called the endo-colonial situation) class relationships within the whole society are more complex. The regional dominant class, represented by Ladinos, is not necessarily the dominant one in the national society. In Guatemala, since the defeat of the nationalist bourgeoisie in 1954, these two groups became identified. There is no contradiction between landowners, the commercial bourgeoisie (particularly coffee growers) and foreign capital (Diaz Rozzotto, 1958; Adams, 1960).

In Mexico the situation is different. National power is held by a bureaucratic, 'developmentist' bourgeoisie, a product of the 1910 Revolution. This bourgeoisie has displaced latifundists on a national level, but in more backward regions, such as Chiapas, it tolerates them while seeking the support of a new rural bourgeoisie composed of traders, neo-latifundists and public employees (Stavenhagen, 1963). In both Mexico and Guatemala the regional dominant class is composed of 'power brokers' – to use Wolf's term (1959) – of mestizo origin who have come to fill the power vacuum left by the old feudal landowning aristocracy. In Guatemala the endo-colonial situation is stronger than in Mexico, where latent contradictions between the 'developmentist' bourgeoisie in power and its weak shadow in the Indian hinterland contribute to a rapid development of class relationships to the detriment of colonial relationships, and have allowed the development of a structural development–underdevelopment dichotomy. Thus, inter-ethnic relations at the level of total society may be considered as a function of the development–underdevelopment structural dichotomy (in its social aspect of internal colonialism), and of the dynamics of national class structure. For the purposes of analysis, four elements may be isolated in the inter-ethnic situation: colonial relationships, class relationships, social stratification, and the acculturation process. These four elements constitute interdependent variables, and with them we may attempt to build a hypothetic model of inter-ethnic relations.

**Colonial Relationships**

These relationships are a function of the structural development–underdevelopment dichotomy and they tend to be in force for as long as the dichotomy persists. As long as there are areas performing as internal colonies in underdeveloped countries, the relationships characterizing their inhabitants tend to take the form of colonial relationships. These are strengthened where there exist, as in the Maya region, marked cultural differences between two sectors of the population, leading to a rigid stratification defined in cultural and biologic terms (which is sometimes called caste). Colonial relations tend to limit and impede acculturation and cultural ladinization, and to maintain a rigid stratification. There exists an obvious interest on the part of the dominant ethnic group (Ladinos) in maintaining colonial relations, especially when their predominance depends on the existence of cheap and abundant labor. This is the case when the possibilities for expansion of the economy are few; when agriculture has a low level of productivity and when the labor–capital relation in agriculture is high; when local or regional industrialization is weak or nonexistent; and when the region's internal market is poorly developed. Therefore, the maintenance of colonial relations is rather a function of the degree of development of the national economy than of local or regional decisions.

In contrast to Ladinos, the Indians – the subordinate ethnic group – derive no benefit from the colonial situation and may try various forms of reaction to it. The first is withdrawal into the corporate community, both physically and socially. As Wolf pointed out (1959), this has happened on various occasions in the history of the region, and it represents on the part of the Indian ethnic group a latent tendency which becomes manifest when the economic and political situation allows it. In association with this withdrawal, the Indians also react to the colonial situation in terms of 'nationalism'. This form of reaction may have as its objective the strengthening of the Indian government (regional council), and possibly the struggle for the Indians' national political representation. It also becomes manifest through measures adopted to encourage education in the Indian language and development of Indian culture. It particularly becomes manifest through an extreme anti-Ladinism and resistance to Ladinization. Here there also intervene other counter-acculturative factors such as messianism and, on certain occasions, armed upheavals and other violent manifestations. Finally, there is a third form of reaction to the colonial situation, and this is assimilation. It is an individual process which, as has been seen, represents a separation from the corporate structure of the community. From a cultural point of view it represents Ladinization. From a structural point of view it means that the individual becomes integrated into the class structure, no longer as an Indian (that is, a colonized person), but simply due to his relationship to the means of production. Ladinization, as we have seen, may be the result of upward mobility in the scale of socio-economic indices. But generally it only means the proletarianization of the Indian.

Of the three main forms of reaction to the colonial situation, the first, simple withdrawal, does not seem to have many adherents at present. Among those who are still clinging to it we find a few traditionalistic elders. But other members of the community know that there are better ways to combat the harmful effects which colonial relations have upon Indians. The reaction which we have called 'nationalism' (for lack of a better term) assumes diverse shapes. Some of them are spontaneous and circumstantial (such as armed upheavals and messianic movements); others have been induced by external agents (such as education in the Indian language); and still others may be the consequence of a political consciousness of Indian communities (such as the election of a person participating in the corporate civic-religious political structure to a position in the constitutional municipal government). At present, the main forms of 'nationalistic' reaction are promoted – at least in Mexico – by the national government's specialized agencies. Measures such as literacy in the Indian language and adequate political representation of the Indians show that those responsible for Indianist policy are conscious of the colonial character of inter-ethnic relations, despite the fact that the problem has never been formulated in those terms by the ideologists of *indigenismo*. Yet paradoxically, these measures are only taken as a means to an end which represents its absolute negation, that is, the incorporation of the Indian into Mexican nationality, in other words, the disappearance of the Indian as such. The paradox, nonetheless, has a practical justification: national integration can only be achieved if contradictions inherent in colonial relations are overcome. This can be done either by suppressing one of the terms of the contradiction, or by a qualitative change of content in that relation. By encouraging measures of a 'nationalistic' kind, Indianist policy is committed to the second of these alternatives. Yet if the contradiction inherent in the colonial relation between Indians and Ladinos is solved, there would be a greater contradiction solved at the same time: that which exists between those colonial relations and national integration (since the existence of the former represents an obstacle to the latter). In other words, national integration may be achieved, not by eliminating the Indian, but only by eliminating him as a colonized being.[7] Mexican Indianism has admitted this timidly and not without some ambiguities. But in this respect it is much more advanced than the rest of the national society. Indianism certainly does not escape the contradictions of national society when, for instance, it is stated that literacy in the Indian language in Chiapas only serves to facilitate the teaching of Spanish, and a series of 'assimilationist' measures (particularly the action of 'acculturation agents' or 'promoters of cultural change') are simultaneously put into practice.

## Class Relationships

We cannot over-emphasize that the class character and the colonial character of inter-ethnic relations are two intimately related aspects of the same phenomenon. They are separated here only for the purpose of our analysis. Class relationships have developed parallel to and simultaneously with colonial relations and tend to displace them more and more. But the colonial character of inter-ethnic relations impresses particular characteristics upon class relations, tending to stop their development. In this context, class relations mean mutual interactions between persons holding opposed economic positions, independent of ethnic considerations. These relations develop together with the region's economic development. As agricultural production increases, as the market for industrial products expands, as the monetary economy develops, and as the labor market expands, colonial relations lose their importance and give way to the predominance of class relations. The latter's development also depends, to a great degree, upon structural factors of national economy and is not the result of decision-making at the regional or local level. At any rate, this development tends to impress upon the class relations between Indians and Ladinos a char-acteristic mark while the 'feudal' or 'semi-feudal' aspects, so frequently indicated in the literature, tend to disappear.

Consequently, measures for local or community development such as improvement of agricultural techniques, establishment of production co-operatives, etc., may change colonial relations into class relations, but not necessarily so. This transformation can only take place if such devel-opments are accompanied by the parallel development of the regional economy as a whole, and particularly of its Ladino metropolis. If such is not the case, the likelihood is that the fruits of local development will enter the traditional socio-economic circuits without modifying the regional structure.

It has already been seen that on certain occasions Ladinos are interested in maintaining colonial relations. There also exist circumstances in which they are interested in strengthening class relationships to the detriment of colonial relationships. This happens particularly with the development of the productive forces: when Ladinos are presented with new opportunities for investment, when they need seasonal labor which can only be obtained through monetary incentives, or when they require non-agricultural labor (for certain manufacturing industries or for construction work in the cities or on the roads); finally, when they need to develop new regional markets and the strengthening of the Indians' demand for manufactured products. The Ladinos' interest in the development of class relations also arises when the agrarian reform manages to really break the land monopoly and when the possession of his own land can turn the Indian back to subsist-ence farming. In this case, class relations develop particularly through the marketing of crops and the agricultural credit structure.

Under certain circumstances Ladinos may have an interest towards curbing the development of class relations: for instance, when their inter-ests are affected by the establishment of plantations by foreign companies, which modifies the status quo by attracting a certain amount of labor and paying higher wages than those which are usual in the region, etc. This has happened in Guatemala. Or, for example, when economic develop-ment of the region contributes to the liberation of labor, thus increasing its emigration or at the least its capacity to demand higher salaries, in which case the Ladino latifundists are forced to invest a greater amount of capital in agriculture, and this capital they do not possess.

Indians are also interested in the development of class relationships because these imply the existence of better economic opportunities and of wider alternatives for action. On the other hand, they may be interested in curbing the development of class relations because they tend to destroy the subsistence economy, because they contribute to economic and psychological insecurity and encourage the proletarianization and disintegration of Indian culture.

The development of class relations involves new forms of sociability and social organization; there emerge new social categories and new groupings and social institutions. The development of these relations tends to destroy the rigidity of social stratification, to modify its bases (from ethnic characteristics to socioeconomic indices) and to encourage the Ladinization of the Indian.

## Social Stratification

Insofar as the regional system of social stratification has only two strata based essentially on ethnic characteristics it tends to maintain the appearance of a colonial situation. At the same time, it tends to change into a clearly defined socio-economic stratification. The already existing stratification among Ladino ethnic groups tends to become extensive to both ethnic groups. Perhaps the day will come when both ethnic groups – independent of their cultural characteristics – will be included into a single stratification system, based exclusively on socio-economic criteria. The old stratification system, based on ethnic characteristics (sometimes called castes) tends to conflict with the development of class relations and the socio-economic stratification based on them. Thus, for instance, an Indian trader or landowner receives discriminatory treatment from Ladinos who are in a socio-economic situation inferior to his own, while Indian day laborers tend to receive smaller wages than the Ladinos who are in the same position. Among the Ladinos there exists an obvious concern over maintaining the bases of ethnic stratification; especially among the lower strata of the Ladino population, who in this way avoid competing with mobile Indians. This is the same phenomenon as that of the poor whites in the south of the United States and other such cases in other parts of the world.

Social stratification, as we have seen, comprises two aspects: inter-ethnic stratification reflects its colonial past, while Ladino socio-economic stratification, in which Indians are increasingly participating, reflects the development of new class relations, devoid of their ethnic content. The Indians' upward vertical mobility in the socio-economic scale is accompanied by a certain degree of Ladinization, but, as has already been pointed out, not all of the aspects of Indian culture change at the same rate. The development of class relations tends to facilitate the Indian's upward mobility, since an ascent in the socio-economic scale renders the conservation of a low status based upon exclusively ethnic criteria more precarious. Upward mobility, as much in the socio-economic scale as in the shift from the Indian to the Ladino ethnic group, is a function of the transformation of the colonial situation into a class situation.

## Notes

1. Published first in Spanish in 1963 "Clases, colonialismo y aculturación", AMERICA LATINA, Centro Latinoamericano de Pesquisas en Ciencias Sociales, Rio de Janeiro, Año 6, No. 4, October–December, pp. 63–104; in English in R. Stavenhagen (2013), *The Emergence of Indigenous Peoples*, pp. 30–43, Springer.

2. In Mexico 'Ladino' is used to refer to the mestizo population.

3. On the concepts of relation of dependence and relation of order and their application to the study of class structures, see S. Ossowski, *Class Structure and Social Consciousness* (London, 1963).

4. Considered within González Casanova's general approach. See his study, 'Internal Colonialism and National Development', in *Studies in Comparative International Development*, 1, 4 (1965).

5. We use the term 'class situation' not in the sense given by Max Weber (cf. H.H. Gerth and C.W. Mills (Eds.), *Max Weber: Essays in Sociology* (New York: Oxford University Press, 1946: 181), but in the sense that the individual who finds himself in such a situation participates with others in a kind of relations that has the character of class relations.

6. See S.F. Nadel, *The Theory of Social Structure* (London, 1957), especially chapter 4. It would be interesting to do a formal analysis of the roles of inter-ethnic situation here described. Nadel's model, nonetheless, does not seem to include a situation like that which is brought about between Indians and Ladinos when they face each other as colonizer and colonized and as belonging to opposite classes simultaneously. In other words, the same process of interaction between individuals and groups may be understood at different levels of an analysis of roles and in varying conceptual terms. Nadel's concept of 'summation' comes closest to this situation.

7. The term 'national integration' is very ambiguous. The way it is used by Myrdal, for example, referring to its economic aspects, it simply means equality of opportunities (cf. G. Myrdal, *Solidaridad o desintegración* (Mexico, 1956)). When Aguirre Beltrán in *El*

*proceso de aculturación*, speaks of 'intercultural integration' at the regional level, he rather refers to the homogenization of the cultural differences between Indians and Ladinos, that is, to the predominance of the mestizo culture, which is why we affirm, differing from Aguirre Beltrán, that national integration may be achieved without the disappearance of the 'cultural' Indian.

## References

Adams, Richard N. (1960) *Social Change in Guatemala and U.S. Policy*. New York: Social Change in Latin America Today.

Diaz Rozzotto, Jaime (1958) *El character de la revolución guatemalteca, ocaso de la revolución democrático-burguesa corriente*. Mexico. Ediciones Revista Horizonte.

Goldkind, V. (1963) 'Ethnic relations in Southeastern Mexico: A methodological note', *American Anthropologist*, 65, 2.

González Casanova, Pablo (1962) 'Sociedad plural y desarrollo: el caso de México', *América Latina*, 5, 4.

Parlem, Angel (1952) 'Notas sobre la clase media en México'. Washington: *Ciencias Sociales*; No. 14–15 and 16–17 (Reproduced in: *Las clases sociales en México*, s.f. (1960)).

Stavenhagen, Rodolfo (1963) 'La réforme agraire et les classes rurales au Mexique', *Cahiers Internationaux de Sociologie*, 34.

Tax, Sol (1956) *La Visión del mundo y las relaciones sociales en Guatemala*. Guatemala: EME. Cultura Indígena de Guatemala.

Wolf, E.R. (1959) *Sons of the Shaking Earth*. Chicago: The University of Chicago Press.

## Rodolfo Stavenhagen, by Francisco Zapata Schaffeld (Mexico)

A Mexican of German origins (1932–2016), Stavenhagen undertook studies in anthropology and sociology in the United States (Chicago, 1949–1952), Mexico (1952–1956) and France (Paris, 1959–1962). He acquired a multidisciplinary training that played an important role in his career because it enabled him to analyze various interrelated social problems. In the 1950s, and still in his training period, he worked in the National School of Political and Social Sciences at the National Autonomous University of Mexico (UNAM-Universidad Nacional Autónoma de México) under the direction of Pablo González Casanova.

In 1953 he became a researcher at the recently created Instituto Nacional Indigenista (INI) [National Indigenist Institute), where he started to study the problems of the Indian population of Mexico under the direction of Gonzalo Aguirre Beltrán, a renowned anthropologist. He focused on aboriginal communities in the states of Chiapas, Oaxaca and Veracruz. His link to INI was crucial to the definition

*(Continued)*

(Continued)

of his vocation. Indeed, many themes discussed in his *Seven Erroneous Theses about Latin America* (1965) and especially in his PhD dissertation (1964) were inspired by the studies made of these communities that illustrated the impact that the INI's 'modernizing strategies' had imposed upon the Mexican indigenous world.

His formal training culminated in 1964 with the defense of his doctoral thesis in sociology, at the University of Paris under the direction of Georges Balandier, a renowned professor at the École Pratique des Hautes Études (EPHE). It was titled 'Essai comparatif sur les classes sociales rurales dans quelques pays sous-développés' [Comparative essay on the rural social classes in some underdeveloped countries]. The originality of the dissertation rested on the comparative dimension of the problem of social class in agrarian societies in Africa and Latin America. In this work Stavenhagen revealed his permanent concern for the analysis of the interaction between rural and urban, traditional and modern, pre-industrial and industrial societies.

In 1965, Stavenhagen became the Secretary General of the Latin American Center of Social Research (CLAPCS) in Rio de Janeiro (Brazil), while Manuel Diegues was its Director. He undertook the publication of the journal *América Latina* and supervised various research projects, such as the study of social stratification in Latin America with Gino Germani and others. He enriched the debate on the characterization of the Latin American process of development with that of dependency, focused on the critique of structural dualism, developmentalism and modernization theory. Together with Pablo González Casanova, he questioned the conceptions that assumed the existence of a polarity where two social and economic systems coexisted without interconnections, the modern pole being defined as the positive one, as the manifest destiny of the continent. Both authors contributed to the enrichment of dependency theory through the analysis of the links between class and race in the specific context of colonial societies, which became the foundation of the concept of 'internal colonialism'.

Their respective points of view indicate their underlying their differences. In González Casanova (1963, 1965, 1967) one finds the view that places the center–periphery relation at the same level as the subordination of the backward to the advanced elements within national society. In countries where exploitation was dominant, there exists a dual character for national society, but in a different sense from the conception of structural dualism. Both poles are connected by economic relations (natural resources, work, market, investment), by political relations (integration to a specific domination and to a territorial organization) and by social relations (the plurality of groups that maintain power relations among them). This connection is predominantly cultural and is identified with the existence of inequalities and discrimination among them. Nevertheless, one should not assimilate these relations to class exploitation. This is where González Casanova follows a different view from that of Stavenhagen in underlining that this link is a relation of domination by an entire population and its various social classes to another population and its various social classes. That is to say, if we translate this in terms of dependency theory, we can recognize the subordination of the periphery to the center in global terms. Therefore, the phenomenon of 'internal colonialism' includes the economic, social and cultural dimensions of domination and is not restricted to the exploitation of one class by another. For González Casanova, 'the internal colonial structure, internal colonialism, is different of the class structure and different from rural–urban relations, enough to analyze them as a specific analytical instrument' (1963).

On his part, Stavenhagen (1963, 1967), conceives the origin of 'internal colonialism' as a situation where domination exerted by the colonial power hides class domination. Therefore, 'internal colonialism' is 'an organic structural relation between a growing, dynamic pole and an internal colony, backward, underdeveloped and increasingly underdeveloped' (1963). Given the fact that ethnic groups remain in the same place and given that there is no development of a free labor market, the weight of the colonial relation tends to subsist. There is a permanent tension between these two dimensions. The contrast between these two poles of the colonial relationship is expressed as a tension between developed and underdeveloped regions of national society. Those tensions are not only manifested in economic terms but they also include cultural aspects. Therefore, 'internal colonialism' is 'an organic structural relation between a growing, dynamic pole and an internal colony, backward, underdeveloped and increasingly underdeveloped'. If the developed pole has dynamism, it is difficult for internal colonialism to survive. It is possible that gradual national integration can take place and that ethnic groups that succeed in maintaining their identity become assimilated into national society. Thus, inter-ethnic relations are transformed into class relations and internal colonialism would tend to disappear.

The piece through which Stavenhagen gained notoriety in Mexico and in Latin America, was titled *Seven Erroneous Theses About Latin America*, a text that contributed to making him a reference point in the critical reflections on the dynamics of inter-ethnic relations, class, colonialism and acculturation.

## References

González Casanova, Pablo (1963) 'Sociedad plural, colonialismo interno y desarrollo', *América Latina*, 3.

González Casanova, Pablo (1965) 'Sociedad plural y desarrollo: el caso de México', in J. Kahl (ed.), *La industrialización en América Latina*. Mexico: Fondo de Cultura Económica.

González Casanova, Pablo (1969) 'El colonialismo interno', *Sociología de la explotación*, Mexico: Siglo XXI Editores.

González Casanova, Pablo (1976) 'Les classes sociales au Mexique', *Cahiers Internationaux de Sociologie*, 39, July–September.

Stavenhagen, Rodolfo (1963) 'Classes, colonialismo y aculturación: ensayo sobre un sistema de relaciones interétnicas en Mesoamérica', *América Latina*, 4.

Stavenhagen, Rodolfo (1967) 'Las relaciones entre la estratificación social y la dinámica de clases', in Anthony Leeds (ed.), *Estructura, estratificación y movilidad social, Organización de Estados Americanos*. Washington.

Stavenhagen, Rodolfo (2012) 'Siete Tesis equivocadas sobre América latina', in Carlos Illades (ed.), *México como problema. Esbozo de una historia intelectual*. Universidad Autónoma Metropolitana – Siglo XXI Editores, pp. 307–326.

# 16

# Marginality and Social Exclusion (Fragments)[1]

*José Nun (Argentina)*

In 1969, I proposed the concept of marginal mass in an article I wrote for the *Revista Latinoamericana de Sociología* that generated profuse controversy. Thirty years later, in 1999, I updated some aspects of my thesis in a paper that appeared in *Desarrollo Económico*. Shortly thereafter, this second text was translated into English to be published in *Latin American Perspectives* and into Portuguese in *Novos Estudos CEBRAP* which gave rise to new debates, especially in Brazil. In its own way, this resumes a discussion that, for quite different reasons, Fernando Henrique Cardoso started there in the early 1970s.

However, those who approach these questions now often encounter a problem: the older materials (including my polemic with Cardoso) are not only dated but have become difficult to access. Hence the idea of bringing them together in this volume, along with the most recent of the studies mentioned.

The main purpose of this introduction is to place the reader briefly in the theoretical-ideological climate in which the notion of marginal mass arose as well as the debate around this concept. A good part of the argument has not lost its relevance and furthermore I wish to underline the connections between the problems of marginality in Latin America and those of social exclusion in Europe. I conclude with a couple of remarks aimed at correcting the economic bias that is usually inherent in the raising of this kind of questions.

> It was in the framework of this confrontation of paradigms that the problem of marginality emerged in Latin American socio-political literature. As I said then, it appeared full of good feelings and bad conceptualizations because marginality is one of those signifiers that seduces with traps. It tempts use because of its apparent simplicity when, strictly speaking, its meaning is always complex because it refers to another item that gives it its meaning: it so happens that one is only marginal in relation to something else.[2]

After the Second World War, peripheral urban settlements (*villas miseria, callampas, favelas, rancheríos*, etc.) were called marginal. The ecological references of the term were quite clear: it designated dwellings located on the edge of cities and lacking some minimum requirements of habitability. It thus implied two other meanings: an urban center in relation to which the peripheral was defined and whose average housing conditions were considered normal.

It was precisely this last aspect that led to the almost immediate extension of the use of the concept, upon realizing that non-peripheral shelters (*conventillos, cités*, alleyways, neighborhoods, etc.) suffered from deficiencies equal to or worse than peripheral urban settlements. Therefore, the physical location of the dwelling was relegated to the background and marginality began to refer to the negative features of the lodgings.

Defined in this way, this was presented primarily as a technical problem. Urban planners, architects, economists and social workers were summoned to eradicate a transitory problem, the product of a circumstantial (though presumably inevitable) disequilibrium in the development process. Some typologies of marginal dwellings were elaborated, ambitious construction programs were announced and a hyper empiricist approach to the question was stimulated, which, as it was formulated without further explanation, gave a great impulse to uncontrolled generalizations.

Marx said that Britons usually confuse the manifestations of a phenomenon with its causes. Something similar happened here and from the recurrent failure of these efforts arose the concern of the dominant sectors, who increasingly perceived the marginal areas as a propitious terrain for subversive and revolutionary preaching. The technical problem became a social problem and now the dwellings were of much less interest than their occupants. It was now the time for social psychologists, political scientists and sociologists, who were joined by numerous anthropologists whose research topics also migrated from the countryside to the city.

It is clear that, having lost its initial anchorage, marginality began to oscillate as a signifier between several possible meanings. Thus, a simplifying 'social engineering' took an unacceptably deterministic leap and started considering as marginal all the inhabitants of a marginal dwelling. And this despite the fact that the best studies available highlighted, if anything, the great heterogeneity of the world of urban poverty.

This was also the starting point of an approach advocated by sectors of the Catholic Church, which gained rapid relevance. According to them, marginality was a manifestation of the internal disintegration of social groups affected by family disorganization, anomie, ignorance, etc. It was claimed that this was the main reason preventing such groups from intervening in collective decisions and that this lack of *active* participation led, in turn, to their very low *passive* participation as recipients of 'the constitutive goods of the global society' (see, e.g., DESAL, 1966: 4).

From this standpoint, the 'marginals' ceased to be necessarily urban because phenomena such as these occurred with equal or greater intensity in rural areas. In this way, 80 per cent of the Latin American population was considered marginal, which could be good for catechetical purposes but took away all specificity from the category and left open the question of whether, in that case, the remaining 20 per cent could not be better called marginal.

It should be pointed out that this vision of the problem took on special importance in the field of politics since, in countries such as Chile or Venezuela, it was the ideological basis for the Campañas de Promoción Popular (Popular Promotion Campaigns) advocated by the Christian-Democratic governments. On the other hand, it was easily adapted to the functionalist interpretations of modernization that were still in vogue in several places.

As usual, the meaning of the term marginality referred back to the implicit concept that gave it meaning. In this case, the referential scheme was evident: it was the 'urban-modern' pole of society, whose system of norms and values continued to be considered as the bearer of a development project capable of absorbing the marginal sectors, after subjecting them to an adequate preparation. In this way, the groups excluded from participation ceased to bear witness to an exploitative structure in order to express, above all, their own psychological or cultural deficiencies. It is true that only a naïve romanticism could ignore that poverty fuels such deficiencies; but what was at stake was the causal order of the whole process.

Thus, the theme of marginality entered the territory of myth to announce the message of a possible incorporation into all the advantages of development in the context of a social harmony guarded by the elites. Social scientists, as revolutionaries of a single revolution – that which separates the traditional from the modern – were called on to pave the way for such transformation, preserving the bases of the established society. It is not that in so doing they did not denounce some of the deprivations and sufferings of the marginalized sectors. In the rhetoric of the bourgeois myth, Barthes (1957) explained, the figure of the vaccine plays a key role: 'the accidental evil of a class institution is acknowledged in order to better hide the main evil'. Thus, 'the collective imagination is immunized with a small inoculation of the recognized evil and is thus defended against the risk of a generalized subversion' (Barthes, 1957).

It was precisely with the intention of shedding a little light on that 'main evil' and to give another use to the term 'marginality' that I tried to reformulate the problem by introducing the notion of marginal mass. To do this, I placed myself in the field of historical materialism, proposing a re-reading of several texts of Marx that seemed and still seem important to me. In addition, I made use of some methodological contributions by Althusser that helped me to organize the reflection, even though – I must say – I never participated in the 'Althusserian vogue', as I warned in a footnote at the time. I leave to the readers the task of assessing for themselves the extent to which my works of thirty years ago were based on something more than the revolutionary rhetoric characteristic of the time.

It is worth making at least a brief reference to the most common critique that the notion of marginal mass received at that time. As I explain in detail in the first of the following articles [within the compilation from which this text is taken], the concept of a reserve industrial army was used by Marx to designate the functional effects of relative overpopulation in the phase of capitalism he studied. I proposed, instead, to give the title 'marginal mass' to the part of the relative overpopulation that, in other contexts, did not have those functional effects.

But in those years a leftist hyper functionalism dominated a good part of Latin American social thought. As Wilbert Moore once pointed out, the American functionalists themselves (as Moore himself) had never gone that far: they maintained that many things were functional for the reproduction of capitalism, not that everything was functional for it. This was, instead, what some leftist critics of the notion of marginal mass did, insisting that even the last of the landless peasants or street vendors in our cities were not only functional but also decisive for capitalist accumulation. For this reason, their objections were often unfair or excessive, the fact that some of them have helped to illuminate other aspects of the problem notwithstanding.

In the first place, I make continuous references to the diverse forms that the processes of unequal, combined and dependent development have assumed in Latin America, subordinating in varying degrees pre or proto-capitalist forms of production (see Murmis, 1969; Nun, 1989). In other words, such partial contributions to the accumulation of capital in different places (the provision of cheap food, distribution circuits in deprived areas, precarious jobs, etc.) were contemplated in my argument although they were not central to it – as incidentally, they were not central to Marx either when he dealt with these questions.

Secondly, it was not and is not plausible to argue that the relative over-population as a whole is functional in all its dimensions (even if it may be so in some) nor does this mean that the functional patterns that observers detected were necessarily the most convenient or profitable for the hegemonic capitalist sectors.[3] It seems almost obvious that where such functionality operates, for example in the goods market, it is just because this market has not yet become attractive for those capitalist sectors. This is because, as Godfrey observes, 'as soon as small producers have developed a market of some interest, the larger firms seize it, with the help of the state if necessary' (Godfrey, 1977: 65).

The discussion therefore lost sight of the crucial difference that separates the processes of conservation and dissolution of pre-existing productive and commercial forms in a given economy and the no-less important fact that the course, complexity and intensity of such processes changes according to the specific context in question. In order to defend the alleged general functionality of the relative overpopulation, my critics concentrated almost exclusively on situations marked by conservation processes, without realizing that the contribution made by those situations to the central scheme of accumulation was so low that it did not reach the thresholds required for the dissolution processes to be triggered.

Nonetheless, I must emphasize again that the matter was never strange to me (how could it be given the chosen field of study?) and is, for example, the subject of my hypothesis about the peculiar mechanisms of system integration and social integration that, in many regions, have been characteristic of the dependent pattern of capitalist development. The disagreement lies in the fact that where my critics emphasized the functionality derived from conservation processes, I thought that this apparent functionality concealed a much deeper phenomenon: the need to neutralize non-functional population surpluses which, otherwise, ran the risk of becoming dysfunctional since they could not be incorporated into the hegemonic productive forms. This truly political management of such surpluses escaped the horizon of most of my critics, at the same time that it was one of the focuses of the concept of marginal mass.

All this was congruent with my double conjecture. On the one hand, I believed that, fostered by transnational monopoly capital, the processes of dissolution I mentioned were expanding and intensifying. On the other hand, I thought that these processes tended to be led by economic agents that generated fewer and fewer good quality jobs. In spite of foreseeable spatial and temporal variations, it seems legitimate to affirm that this double conjecture has proved to have a high level of validity, which the neoliberal economic policies of the last decades have only increased.

That said, I will add a marginal note that some discussions indicate that is less obvious than I assumed. Introducing and substantiating a concept such as marginal mass is not the same as arguing that it is always and everywhere applicable. Not only do my collaborators and I distinguish from the beginning between different types of marginality, but the prevalence (or not) of the effects of a 'reserve industrial army' or 'marginal mass' in concrete situations is an empirical question, for the treatment of which – and this is the problem – it is necessary to have the appropriate analytical instruments.

## Notes

1.   Published originally in Spanish as an introduction to the book *Marginalidad y exclusión social*. FCE: Buenos Aires, 2000. Translation revised by José Nun.

2.   This [the original] text includes revised fragments of my presentation to the special issue of *Revista Latinoamericana de Sociología*, No. 2, 1969, pp. 174–7.

3.   In those days, a question that my critics refused to answer was why, for example, Robert McNamara, President of the World Bank, was committed to diffusing the use of the anti-contraceptive pill in Third World countries – in order to stop population growth. All of which indicated that surplus populations were not as functional as imagined.

## References

Barthes, Roland (1957) *Mythologies*. Paris: PUF.

DESAL (Instituto de Desarrollo Economico y Social) (1966) *Seminarios de Promoción Popular*. Mimeo.

Godfrey, Martin (1977) 'Surplus population and underdevelopment: Reserve army or marginal mass?', *Manpower and Unemployment Research*, X, 1: 63–72

Murmis, Miguel (1969) 'Tipos de marginalidad y posición en el proceso productivo', *Revista Latinoamericana de Sociología*, 2: 413–421.

Nun, José (1989) *Crisis económica y despidos en masa*. Buenos Aires: Legasa.

## José Nun, by Gabriel Kessler (Argentina)

Born in 1934, José 'Pepe' Nun's work is one of the richest and always topical contributions to Latin-American Sociology and Political Science. Nun was first trained as a lawyer and later completed graduate studies in Sociology and Political Science in France, as a student of Alain Touraine. In parallel, he became involved with US Political Science, particularly with David Apter. During his formative years he also showed a strong interest in philosophy and economics. Throughout his career he has worked on central issues such as populism, the social question, the transition to democracy, the role of social movements, and more recently, theories on democracy and inequalities. He has been a professor and researcher in several foreign universities and has collaborated with the founding and administration of Latin American academic institutions and editorial projects dedicated to spreading the contributions of social sciences. He is also a public intellectual: he served as Argentina's National Secretary of Culture (2003–2007) and throughout his career he always wrote in newspapers on issues of political and social relevance (see Svampa and Pereyra, 2016).

Throughout his trajectory, Nun has managed to combine the contributions of Marxist theories with other contributions from political science, economics and analytical philosophy, in an original way. In his different studies he has built important concepts for interpreting Latin America's reality. One of his main contributions, and the subject of this article, is related to the concept of *marginal mass*. This concept is framed in a discussion about the particularities of Capitalism in the region that was developed among social scientists from the mid-twentieth century. In the midst of a debate on an 'incomplete' capitalist development and the doubts concerning the existence of traditional social classes, one of the main issues in under discussion was the features of the population masses that were not formally part of the economy. This is how the concept of marginality made its appearance in the debate of the social sciences – an issue that is still relevant given that it remains unsolved in Latin American societies.

Nun's contribution was part of the debate that occurred in a group which included authors like Miguel Murmis, Fernando H. Cardoso, Aníbal Quijano, among others, who took part in a project financed by the Ford Foundation in 1966. This group moved in two directions. Outwardly, it distanced itself from the existing idea of marginality at the time, which was linked to Christian Humanism and was explained by a moral deficit; therefore, education was seen as the solution. Internally, there was a productive debate, which pondered whether that marginal population was functional or not to Latin American capitalism. Was it, in Marxist terms, a 'reserve industrial army' keen to enter the labor market that influenced the persistence of low wages pressuring to enter the labor market? Or, as Nun argued, was it a marginal mass, an overpopulation excessive to Latin American capitalism? In modern terms: Were these marginal people excluded from the dominant social structure, with no place in it? Time proved Nun's position to be correct, and his contribution gained serious relevance in the 1990s, when Robert Castel coined the concept of disaffiliation. Nun was a pioneer of a new perspective within Marxism attempting to understand the particularities of Latin American capitalism. I believe that the issue was remarkable because it raised not only academic, but also political interest.

In effect, determining if a group was or wasn't 'working class' was a way of pondering whether or not it had revolutionary potential. If, instead, it was closer to being a lumpen-proletariat, its revolutionary potential was nearly null, when not –always following Marx – counter-revolutionary.

In the next decade, the transition from dictatorships to democracies in the region found Nun, along with his generation of fellow intellectuals, rethinking the democratic question. Two books stand out in that regard: in *The Choir's Rebellion* (1989) based on Gramscian and Wittgensteinian concepts he interpreted new social movements, by analyzing everyday life; followed by *Essays on the Democratic Transition*, in which he establishes an important difference for Latin American social sciences, which is between the social accumulation regimen and the political regimen of government (see Svampa and Pereyra, 2016). These concepts are key to understanding different forms of transition. His interest in democracy and the social question has not faded, and in recent years he has carried out a reflection centered on the role of tax systems in diminishing inequality (a central issue in Latin America, where these are completely regressive), and in a book published in 2015 he reflects on theories about democracy.

Throughout Nun's work several topics have concentrated his attention: unemployment and class consciousness, the military dictatorships and their relationship with the middle classes, the role of agrarian corporations. His work is part of the best of the Latin American intellectual tradition, as it combines various disciplines and analytic horizons. Some of his main books are: *A Latin American Phenomenon: The Middle Class Military Coup* (1966), *Essays on the Democratic Transition in Argentina* (1987), *Economic Crisis and Mass Firings* (1989), *The Rebellion of the Chorus* (1989), *The Alfonsín Administration and Agrarian Corporations* (1991); *Democracy – Government of the People or Government of the Politicians?* (2000); *Marginality and Social Exclusion* (2001), *Inequality and Taxes* (2011), *Common Sense and Politics* (2015).

## Reference

Svampa, M. and Pereyra, S. (2016). Entrevista a José Nun. *Cuestiones De Sociología*, (14), e010. https://www.cuestionessociologia.fahce.unlp.edu.ar/article/view/CSn14a10.

# 17

# Households, Families and Social Inequalities in Latin America[1]

*Marina Ariza and Orlandina de Oliveira (Mexico)*

The evolution of household social inequalities in Latin America over the past decade reflects both the effect of socio-economic processes and the secular trends associated with demographic change. The context of recurrent economic crises, moderate growth and increased income concentration that has accompanied the economic model currently underway in the region has forced families to intensify the utilization of their labour supply. Women's labour force participation constituted a crucial household strategy to obtain additional economic resources for family survival. Nevertheless, the deterioration of employment opportunities and gender inequalities (occupational segregation and gender discrimination) prevailing in the labour market make it difficult for women to obtain enough resources to aid their families to cross the poverty threshold (González de la Rocha, 1994). In fact, extended families headed by women share the highest level of poverty in the region.

In an economic context characterized by the reduction of job opportunities to absorb the growing population of active ages, international migration has also played a central role in families' survival. Yet although international remittances constitute additional resources for a significant number of households, their capacity to offset the high levels of poverty and rising income inequalities generated by current structural economic changes in the region, varies across countries. Their impacts depend on the countries' level of development, their initial inequality, and segments of the income distribution where 'remittances-receiving households' are concentrated (Fajnzylber and López, 2008).

Our purpose in this work is twofold. First, to single out the consequences that the structural economic transformations, brought about by the restructuring of production and the liberalization of the economy, together with secular demographic changes, have had on households' inequalities. Special attention is paid to changes in household composition and sexual division of labour. Second, to show one of the more dramatic costs of the structural economic reforms for families: the still high poverty levels prevailing in various types of household in the region. By comparing three different sets of countries, we seek to demonstrate that a favorable demographic scenario, together with household coping strategies, are no substitute for economic and social policies designed to reduce poverty and social inequalities.

It is worth recalling that households are residential groups comprising a set of persons – who may or may not have kinship links – that share a dwelling, a common budget and a series of services and activities that are essential to the everyday reproduction of its members. In contrast with households, families are only constituted on the basis of kinships links, whether or not these are legally sanctioned. Despite this analytical difference, family and domestic units are concepts that necessarily overlap and complement each other.

By emphasizing inequalities in families and households we assume that the family itself is a prominent trait of social stratification inasmuch as kinship ties are the foundation of solidarity as well as the initial (and perhaps most durable) basis of hierarchy and reciprocity. The family plays a central role in terms of reproducing and compensating for the various forms of inequality that characterize a society's stratification system (Jelin, 1998).

Despite the general trend towards growing socio-economic inequity and high poverty levels, Latin American countries display sharp socio-economic divergences and also differ as regards the advance of the demographic transition; aspects that should be borne in mind in the study of family inequalities prevailing in the region. The underlying methodological purpose of selecting countries for comparison was threefold: first, to highlight inter-regional inequalities; second, to posit that higher levels of socio-economic development are not necessarily related to lower levels of social inequality, and finally, to show that economic crises may partly offset the benefits of demographic transition. At the beginning of the twenty-first century, the countries we compare are marked by significant variations in the levels of socio-economic development, the extent of social inequality and poverty and the degree of progress of the demographic transition (CEPAL, 2003, 2004).

*Argentina and Uruguay*, countries with high levels of social and economic development, and a more advanced stage of demographic transition, are facing new economic and social challenges resulting from the drastic contraction of their economy at the beginning of this century. The increase in unemployment and in poverty levels has been acute particularly in Argentina. Due to its lower concentration of income and social policies aimed at benefiting retirees and pensioners, Uruguay has partly offset the effects of the economy's poor performance in household poverty levels. Although recent data show an unheralded increase in poverty, Uruguay is still distinguished by having the lowest levels of poverty and inequality in the region. Likewise, the fact that in 2002, 13% of urban households in this country received remittances from abroad, undoubtedly helped to partially contain the trend towards an increase in poverty.

*Brazil and Mexico* show how the low rate of expansion of the economy in a context of liberalization, together with sharp income differences, may make it difficult to take advantage of the so-called 'demographic bonus' resulting from the expansion of groups of an active age and the reduction of demographic dependency rates. Neither country has achieved the economic growth required to create the amount of jobs required to absorb the growing labour force.

Finally, *Honduras and Nicaragua* show how economic and demographic lags interact to increase household poverty levels. Given the extremely high levels of demographic dependency, relatively high fertility rates and lower levels of urbanization, these countries are faced with daunting economic and social challenges that are extremely difficult to overcome in a context of low economic growth and high unemployment levels, particularly in the case of Nicaragua (CEPAL, 2003, 2004).

## Socio-economic and Demographic Changes Affecting Households' Characteristics

As a heterogeneous, unequal region, Latin America has been characterized by marked structural transformations. Within the space of a few years, most of the economies in the region have been obliged to undertake profound processes of productive restructuring, putting an end to the development model centered on the growth of the internal market, characteristic of the import substitution years, and focusing more on liberalizing the economy, tourism and attracting transnational capital as the basis of accumulation (CEPAL, 2003, 2004).

Labour markets show profound transformations derived from the processes of globalization and productive restructuring. The so-called quiet labour revolution[2] is expressed in a series of trends experienced by all Latin American countries: the increase of part-time work, under-employment and unemployment, the loss of job security, the growing polarization of the labour market, deregulation processes, job flexibility, the depreciation of qualifications and the general increase in the precariousness of jobs (Pérez Sáinz, 2000).

In Latin America, the process of economic restructuring was preceded by the implementation of stabilization and adjustment policies as a strategy for coping with the recurrent economic crises that had plagued the region since the 1980s. Since then, workers' living conditions had deteriorated as a result of high inflation levels, salary control and the reduction of services provided by the state. The increasing precariousness of the labour market resulting from the more flexible nature of jobs was accompanied in some countries in the region (such as Argentina, Brazil, Nicaragua and Uruguay, for example) by high unemployment levels and in others, such as Mexico, by the expansion of informal activities (including self-employment, small businesses and unpaid work.) The proliferation of informal businesses in small-scale commerce and services and the increase of piece work linked to the sub-contracting practices of large firms, together with the expansion of export industries and service and commercial activities affected the trend towards the feminization of the labour market observed in recent decades, another facet of the process of the flexibilization of work on a world scale (Standing, 1999).

Women's growing incorporation into economic activity outside the household has been precipitated by a series of social transformations. The increase in educational achievement has undoubtedly played a significant role, as have tertiarization and the recent crises and economic re-structuring undergone by the region, as previously pointed out.[3]

The increasing rate of women's economic participation has had important repercussions upon household domestic organization. Actually, each of the development strategies implemented in Latin American has involved, through the sexual division of labour, a particular relationship between the labour market and the family that directly affects the internal distribution of domestic and extra-domestic roles. Whereas the import substitution model was based on a polarized system of role distribution, in which the householder-provider, through his work, managed to support a numerous family which was the object of attention of the wife-housewife, the growth strategy focused on liberalization, the recurrent episodes of economic crisis, linked to the expansion of the service economy and the new demographic conditions, exerted pressure on traditional family roles to make them more flexible.

The globalizing economic dynamic is also responsible for the extraordinary scope and intensity of the international migratory movements of recent years (Portes, 1996). International migration has had marked consequences for the composition of households in the places of origin, contributing to the formation of extended families and those headed by women, as we will see. It is also worth noting that the remittances sent by immigrants to their countries of origin have become one of the main sources of foreign currency and a factor in balancing current account deficits, even though they are not always sufficient to counteract the perverse effects of the model of accumulation ongoing in the region.

The last quarter of the twentieth century was also a time of secular socio-demographic tendencies that, at different rates and at different times, have created more favorable conditions for economic and social development, and changed family life. The continuous decrease in mortality levels led to an increase in life expectancy at birth and the ageing of the population, particularly in countries that had begun demographic changes several decades ago, prolonging and in some cases modifying the duration of family roles. At the same time, the reduction of fertility rates, permitted by contraceptive use, coupled with greater life expectancy at birth, has reduced the total time women spend in the sphere of socio-biological reproduction (pregnancy, childbirth and child-raising, and socialization), although the ageing of the population has increased family duties linked to the care of the elderly. At the same time, the prolongation of schooling has extended the period of adolescence, delaying the division of the family nucleus among the middle class. This set of transformations (reduction of fertility and mortality, increased life expectancy at birth, ageing of the population, reduction of households' dependency rates),[3] together with the increase in women's labour force participation, and internal and international migration trends, have had decisive consequences for households' characteristics and internal dynamics (CEPAL/CELADE, 2005; García and Oliveira, 2011).

## Household Composition: Continuities and Changes

Economic and demographic transformations, jointly with the recurrent economic crises, affect the economic and social aspects of family life, altering its kinship composition and internal organization, and encouraging the participation of other members to cope with the decrease in income and the lack of job security (Ariza and Oliveira, 2005). As for household composition, it is worth noting that figures show a clear interrelationship between type of family arrangements and the households' income level (see Table 17.1). This illustrates the impact of the marked social inequalities prevailing in Latin America on households' composition; certain arrangements are less economically vulnerable than others. Actually, *one-person households* and *nuclear families without children* enjoy a certain amount of economic self-sufficiency; they are not usually found in the lowest deciles of income distribution. In contrast, *nuclear two-parent families with children* are concentrated in the lowest deciles of income distribution in the various countries (except in Nicaragua); the same occurs with *extended and compound* households; and the percentages of *single-parent households* are also highest in the poorest deciles, except for Mexico.

*One-person households*, concentrated in the richest income quintile, have increased particularly in countries at an advanced stage of demographic transition, due to the ageing of the population, as in the case of Uruguay and Argentina. This trend had already begun to emerge some time earlier, with the rise in life expectancy at birth, accompanied by the possibility of marital dissolution, either through widowhood or separation (due to greater exposure to risk by the simple fact of spending more years together as a couple); aspects that increase the probability of creating one-person households.[5]

Taken as a whole, *nuclear households* continue to constitute a majority in the region, although they have been experiencing clear transformations in their internal composition in the last decade; their presence is larger in Brazil and Mexico. The most frequent traditional family model in previous eras (two-parent nuclear households with children) became less important in all countries (Table 17.2). This loss of importance of the *normative family model* is due to economic and demographic factors. The socio-economic vulnerability of this household arrangement, that is concentrated in the poorest income quintile, has been increasing in an economic context characterized by enormous labour market deterioration. The expansion of other household types (one-person households and those with female headship) and the progressive changes in the family life cycle play an important role as well.[6]

**Table 17.1** Types of urban households in Latin America by household per capita income level (6 countries), 2002 (percentage of total number of households)

| Country | Types of households | | | | | | | | | | | | | | |
| --- | --- | --- | --- | --- | --- | --- | --- | --- | --- | --- | --- | --- | --- | --- | --- |
| | One person | | | Nuclear two-parent with children | | | Nuclear single parent[a] | | | Nuclear, no children | | | Extended and compound | | |
| | Income quintiles | | | | | | | | | | | | | | |
| | 1 | 3 | 5 | 1 | 3 | 5 | 1 | 3 | 5 | 1 | 3 | 5 | 1 | 3 | 5 |
| **GROUP A** | | | | | | | | | | | | | | | |
| Argentina[b] | 2.8 | 18.1 | 24.5 | 51 | 37.4 | 35.1 | 15.5 | 9 | 9.2 | 3.8 | 14.4 | 21.2 | 26.8 | 21.2 | 10 |
| Uruguay | 1.7 | 15.3 | 37.4 | 52.2 | 31.8 | 22.1 | 11.3 | 10.1 | 8.6 | 4.2 | 20.3 | 21.9 | 30.6 | 22.5 | 10 |
| **GROUP B** | | | | | | | | | | | | | | | |
| Brazil[c] | 3.6 | 13.2 | 17.5 | 56.5 | 42.3 | 38.5 | 13.6 | 10.7 | 10 | 3.6 | 11.3 | 17.5 | 22.6 | 22.6 | 16.5 |
| Mexico | 1.2 | 3.7 | 15.8 | 56.3 | 54.4 | 42.3 | 10.3 | 11.9 | 12 | 2.9 | 7.2 | 16.8 | 29.3 | 22.8 | 12.9 |
| **GROUP C** | | | | | | | | | | | | | | | |
| Honduras | 2 | 3.1 | 12 | 42.4 | 38.9 | 34.3 | 14.3 | 11.1 | 12 | 1.9 | 3.7 | 7.2 | 39.5 | 43.2 | 34 |
| Nicaragua[c] | 2.1 | 3.4 | 9.2 | 36.9 | 41.4 | 38.4 | 13.1 | 12.1 | 9 | 1 | 1.9 | 9.3 | 47 | 41.2 | 34.1 |

*Source: Anuario estadístico de América Latina y el Caribe 2004 (2005) Santiago de Chile: Naciones Unidas, CEPAL.*

*Notes:*

[a]Household income is classified by quintile, based on per capita income. Quintile 1 is composed of the poorest household; quintile 5 corresponds to the richest.

[b]Thirty-two urban agglomerations.

[c]Refers to 2001.

**Table 17.2** Distribution of households by type, urban zones in Latin America (6 countries), 1990–2002 (percentages)

| Country | Year | Total households | One person | Household without marital bond | Nuclear families | Nuclear no children | Nuclear two-parent with children | Nuclear single parent – man | Nuclear single parent – woman | Extended and compound |
|---|---|---|---|---|---|---|---|---|---|---|
| **GROUP A** | | | | | | | | | | |
| Argentina (Greater Buenos Aires) | 1990 | 100 | 12.5 | 4.2 | 69.9 | 15.5 | 46.8 | 1.2 | 6.4 | 13.5 |
| | 2002 | 100 | 15.3 | 3.9 | 66.7 | 14.1 | 41.7 | 2.4 | 8.5 | 14 |
| Uruguay | 1990 | 100 | 13.9 | 5.6 | 64.3 | 17 | 38.9 | 1.3 | 7.2 | 16.2 |
| | 2002 | 100 | 17.7 | 5.4 | 61.3 | 16.3 | 34.8 | 1.6 | 8.6 | 15.6 |
| **GROUP B** | | | | | | | | | | |
| Brazil | 1990 | 100 | 7.9 | 3.9 | 71.1 | 10 | 51.6 | 1.2 | 8.4 | 17.1 |
| | 2002 | 100 | 9.8 | 4 | 68.7 | 10.7 | 46.5 | 1.3 | 10.2 | 17.5 |
| Mexico | 1989 | 100 | 4.6 | 4.1 | 71.6 | 6.3 | 57.6 | 1.2 | 6.4 | 19.7 |
| | 2002 | 100 | 6.5 | 3.2 | 70.8 | 8.3 | 51.7 | 1.5 | 9.4 | 19.4 |
| **GROUP C** | | | | | | | | | | |
| Honduras | 1990 | 100 | 4.2 | 5.9 | 57 | 4.5 | 41.8 | 1.2 | 9.6 | 32.8 |
| | 2002 | 100 | 5.1 | 5.8 | 55.4 | 4.3 | 38.9 | 1.5 | 10.7 | 33.6 |
| Nicaragua | 1993 | 100 | 5.2 | 4.2 | 54.5 | 3.5 | 40 | 1.4 | 9.5 | 36.2 |
| | 2001 | 100 | 4.1 | 4.3 | 53.3 | 3.7 | 37.7 | 1.1 | 10.8 | 38.3 |

*Source:* CEPAL, based on special tabulations of data from household surveys conducted in the respective countries.

In contrast, *extended families* (parents and children and other relatives) and *compound families* (including the presence of non-relatives) have increased or maintained their presence in all the countries analyzed; they achieved greater pre-eminence in the poorest countries, accounting for over a third of all households in Honduras and Nicaragua. The persistence of extended families is usually interpreted as the result of economic household strategies and cultural practices characterized by the prevalence of consensual unions and matri- or patri-local residential patterns. Countries with a greater presence of complex households also have high percentages of consensual unions (De Vos, 1995: 25).

A great deal has been written in Latin America about the formation of this type of household as a response by sectors of the population to situations of crisis or relative deprivation. The improvement in living standards that an extended domestic unit would offer its members would basically be due to the incorporation of people (relatives) that have skills to offer the job market or extra hands among which to distribute the tasks of domestic reproduction, leaving others free to join the labour force.

It is also worth noting the inevitable influence of emigration and of the displacement of the population as refugees on the increase of extended households. Both aspects influenced household composition and size, thereby encouraging the formation of compound or extended households or altering the balance in the distribution of these types of families. The increase in *woman headship* is other consistent feature throughout the region. Data for the beginning of this century indicate that over 30% of households in Honduras, Nicaragua and Uruguay have female headship; the figure for the other countries analyzed (with the exception of Mexico) is around 28% (see Table 17.3).

Various factors are involved in the formation of households with female headship. The deterioration of male opportunities in the labour markets due to the expansion of unemployment and decreasing wages is an important aspect to take into consideration; given the difficulty of maintaining their household in certain contexts the male provider prefers to abandon their family rather than depend on women's work. Factors linked to countries' levels of socio-economic development, such as the degree of urbanization, schooling and economic participation of the female population, also exert a major influence in a variety of ways by promoting favorable conditions for the autonomy and individualization of women. In these cases, headship may be more the result of individual choice than of social or family imposition. In other cases, it may constitute a space of authority at an advanced phase of the life cycle (García and Oliveira, 2011).

**Table 17.3** Proportion of urban households headed by women in Latin America (6 countries), 1990–2002 (percentage of total number of households)

| Country | Year | Total households | One person | Nuclear two-parent | Nuclear single parents | Nuclear no children | Extended and compound |
|---|---|---|---|---|---|---|---|
| **GROUP A** | | | | | | | |
| Argentina | 1990[a] | 21.1 | 68.6 | 0.9 | 84.1 | 0.7 | 31.9 |
| | 2002[b] | 28.6 | 64.9 | 3.2 | 81.3 | 4.3 | 38.2 |
| Uruguay | 1990 | 25.2 | 70.6 | 0.8 | 85 | 1.9 | 35 |
| | 2002 | 32.3 | 63.5 | 6.5 | 84.6 | 8 | 42.1 |
| **GROUP B** | | | | | | | |
| Brazil | 1990 | 20.1 | 55.9 | 0.7 | 87.6 | 1.4 | 32.5 |
| | 2002 | 27.6 | 52.6 | 4.5 | 89.5 | 6.1 | 42.6 |
| Mexico | 1992 | 16.6 | 50.6 | 0.4 | 88.9 | 1.6 | 25.6 |
| | 2002 | 21.4 | 47.8 | 1.9 | 86.5 | 2.2 | 34.2 |
| **GROUP C** | | | | | | | |
| Honduras | 1990 | 26.6 | 40 | 1.9 | 89 | 1.5 | 37.6 |
| | 2002 | 31.4 | 45.3 | 3.1 | 87.7 | 7 | 42.8 |
| Nicaragua | 1993 | 34.9 | 44.5 | 8.4 | 87.1 | 8.5 | 48.3 |
| | 2001 | 34.2 | 44 | 6.2 | 90.3 | 3.1 | 46 |

*Source:* CEPAL, based on special tabulations of data from household surveys conducted in the respective countries.

*Notes:*

[a]Metropolitan area.

[b]Thirty-two urban agglomerations.

The increasing importance of international migratory flows in the recent economic context also affects household structure in many ways. It is a well-known fact that massive male emigration processes promote the formation of families with female headship and/or matrifocal ones, or extended households, altering the balance of the marriage market and even modifying age at marriage.

Others socio-demographic aspects are relevant too. Nuptiality patterns have a decisive influence on the degree of prevalence of female headship, since a greater presence of consensual unions is associated with high conjugal instability and therefore with a growing likelihood of the formation of single-parent or extended families. Families with female headship account for nearly 90% of single-parent nuclear households and over 40% of extended and compound families in Brazil, Honduras and Nicaragua (Table 17.3). Uruguay too has high percentages of female headship among the group of extended families.

The increase in life expectancy at birth makes the occurrence of women headship at later stages of the life course more likely, when the dissolution of marriage occurs as a result of widowhood or separation. In addition to this, there are socio-cultural behaviors that determine the lower frequency of remarriage among widows or women that are separated or divorced than among their male peers. Thus, for example, in countries with a more advanced demographic transition, the percentage of one person households with female headship rises to 65% (see Table 17.3). Finally, the presence of the population of African origin and the frequency of teenage pregnancy must be taken into account in the explanation of female headship (De Vos, 1995).

## The Loss of Importance of the Male Breadwinner Family Model

Changes in the organization of everyday reproduction[6] are closely linked to the repeated episodes of economic crisis that have accompanied the implementation of the new development model, together with policies of reduced protection and work flexibility, which have had a long-term negative impact on salary levels and the population's purchasing power. Several of these episodes have had a more negative effect on male labour.

As we have already emphasized, families have responded by increasing the utilization of their labour supply. Thus, and in different ways, we are gradually moving away from a system of family organization with a predominance of a single male provider, whose salary was sufficient to support the family, with a housewife spouse, to a system of two or three multiple providers.

In effect, in all the countries analyzed, the relative importance of two-parent nuclear families with children in which the wife does not participate in the labour market fell significantly, although at the beginning of the twenty-first century, this type of nuclear family continues to be the most common family model in the region. The greatest predominance of this traditional model of family organization occurs in Mexico (44%) while the lowest prevalence occurs in Uruguay where it is only the case in 28.2% of all nuclear households. The second most common type of organization in nuclear households, in all the cases analyzed, consists of couples with children, in which the wives work; in Brazil, Honduras and Nicaragua, this accounts for over 30% of nuclear households (Table 17.4).

Through their participation in the labour market and by supporting their families, many sectors of Latin American women have undoubtedly managed to redefine their social roles beyond domesticity.[7] However, the increase in female economic participation has not been followed by the reorganization of domestic roles. Data for Mexico and other countries in the region show that in most social sectors, the wife continues to be responsible for the supervision and/or undertaking of domestic tasks. On the few occasions when it does take place, male domestic participation occurs sporadically (at weekends, on vacation, or in the event of illness) and more regularly when the female spouse engages in paid, extra-domestic employment. Male domestic participation is more common between the ages of 30 and 39, among those with higher educational attainment and urban socialization. Household repairs, car maintenance and administrative paperwork are the tasks habitually assigned to men in the domestic sphere. Another recurrent aspect in various countries is that men participate more in child care than in household tasks as such (i.e., dishwashing, cooking, ironing, shopping, cleaning, laundering and ironing) (García and Oliveira, 2011).

In the current context of the state's reduced role in providing social services, families are forced to cope with greater economic and domestic responsibilities. Assuming virtually all the responsibility for administering and performing household tasks and having to obtain economic resources to share the everyday support of the family has created an extra workload for the female population (Arriagada, 2004; García and Oliveira, 2011).

**Table 17.4** Types of nuclear families and women working in urban zones in Latin America (6 countries), 1990–2002

| Country | Year | Nuclear two-parent No children Wife works | Nuclear two-parent No children Wife doesn't work | Nuclear two-parent Children Wife works | Nuclear two-parent Children Wife doesn't work | Nuclear monoparental Woman works | Nuclear monoparental Woman doesn't work | Nuclear single parent man | Total |
|---|---|---|---|---|---|---|---|---|---|
| **GROUP A** | | | | | | | | | |
| Argentina (Greater Buenos Aires) | 1990 | 6.4 | 15.8 | 23.5 | 43.4 | 5.4 | 3.8 | 1.7 | 100 |
| | 2002 | 7.5 | 13.6 | 26.9 | 35.5 | 7 | 5.8 | 3.6 | 100 |
| Uruguay | 1990 | 7.7 | 18.8 | 27.4 | 32.9 | 5.6 | 5.6 | 2 | 100 |
| | 2002 | 8.3 | 18.4 | 28.6 | 28.2 | 7.5 | 6.5 | 2.6 | 100 |
| **GROUP B** | | | | | | | | | |
| Brazil | 1990 | 5.3 | 8.7 | 27.2 | 45.3 | 6.4 | 5.3 | 1.7 | 100 |
| | 2001 | 7 | 8.5 | 32.3 | 35.4 | 8.5 | 6.4 | 1.9 | 100 |
| Mexico | 1989 | 2.4 | 6.4 | 20.7 | 59.8 | 5.3 | 3.6 | 1.7 | 100 |
| | 2002 | 4.8 | 6.9 | 28.9 | 44 | 9 | 4.3 | 2.1 | 100 |
| **GROUP C** | | | | | | | | | |
| Honduras | 1990 | 2.6 | 5.3 | 25.7 | 47.6 | 11 | 5.7 | 2 | 100 |
| | 2002 | 3.5 | 4.4 | 30.3 | 39.8 | 12.8 | 6.4 | 2.7 | 100 |
| Nicaragua | 1993 | 3.2 | 3.3 | 31 | 42.4 | 12.3 | 5.1 | 2.6 | 100 |
| | 2001 | 4.4 | 2.6 | 35.2 | 35.6 | 14.5 | 5.6 | 2.1 | 100 |

*Source*: CEPAL, based on special tabulations of data from household surveys conducted in the respective countries.

## Households' Poverty Levels: the More Vulnerable Family Arrangements

Despite the discrepancy in poverty levels between countries, there is a considerable degree of homogeneity in the households in each country that are experiencing a more critical situation. The households' economic inequalities are clear: extended households, two-parent nuclear families with children and single-parent households with female headship are the poorest. Although the poverty level varies by country, *extended units* account for the largest share in all countries. The economic situation of extended households is dramatic in Honduras and Nicaragua, where the incidence of poverty exceeds 60%, and in Argentina, where it accounts for almost half of all households. In the other countries, with the exception of Uruguay, figures for the incidence of poverty fluctuate, accounting for approximately 35% of extended households (Table 17.5).

Given these results, we wondered how much the formation of extended households could be seen as an *effective* strategy in the fight against poverty. Although the information presented here does not question whether these factors can be found in the origin of extended households (without excluding the close link between family cycle and household formation), it denotes that despite this, the situation of extended families leaves much to be desired. Although necessity may unite them, it does not help them escape poverty. The question we have so far been unable to answer is how much greater the poverty levels of these household members would have been if they had not lived together or the extent to which extended households and poverty reinforce each other. It is extremely likely that the extension of the family nucleus will increase the human and material resources of household members, preventing them from falling into even more critical situations; although there is obviously a ceiling effect for the possibilities of relative well-being they can achieve, given both the limited structure of opportunities available to them and their scant resources in terms of social and human capital.

### Two-parent Nuclear Families with Children

The traditional household model of two-parent nuclear families with children displays considerable levels of poverty as well. Honduras and Nicaragua are distinguished, once again, by the highest levels, followed closely by Argentina (see Table 17.5). Bearing in mind the fact

**Table 17.5** Poverty incidence by type of households, urban zones, Latin America (6 countries), 1990–2002 (percentages)

| | | | Non-Family households | | Family households | | | | | | | |
| | | | | | Nuclear families | | | | | Other types of family | |
| Country | Year | Total households | One person | Households without marital bond | Subtotal: nuclear families | Nuclear no children | Nuclear two-parent with children | Nuclear single parent – man | Nuclear single parent – woman | Extended | Compound |
|---|---|---|---|---|---|---|---|---|---|---|---|
| **GROUP A** | | | | | | | | | | | |
| Argentina (Greater Buenos Aires) | 2002 | 31.6 | 10.8 | 16.6 | 33.5 | 16.0 | 38.9 | 26.5 | 38.2 | 49.3 | 48.9 |
| Argentina | 2002 | 34.9 | 11.0 | 25.0 | 37.1 | 17.6 | 41.9 | 27.6 | 44.5 | 52.8 | 51.3 |
| Uruguay | 2002 | 9.3 | 0.4 | 4.9 | 10.4 | 1.7 | 14.4 | 7.2 | 1.5 | 16.0 | 24.3 |
| **GROUP B** | | | | | | | | | | | |
| Brazil | 2002 | 27.4 | 8.6 | 17.1 | 29.1 | 10.2 | 32.9 | 22.5 | 32.5 | 33.7 | 30.9 |
| Mexico | 2002 | 26.0 | 5.3 | 21.5 | 25.5 | 11.1 | 28.0 | 5.4 | 27.3 | 35.8 | 33.2 |
| **GROUP C** | | | | | | | | | | | |
| Honduras | 2002 | 60.4 | 29.2 | 47.8 | 61.8 | 41.3 | 64.2 | 54.0 | 62.2 | 67.6 | 58.6 |
| Nicaragua | 2001 | 57.8 | 35.0 | 47.3 | 55.8 | 25.0 | 57.2 | 48.5 | 62.4 | 63.9 | 71.2 |

*Source*: CEPAL, based on special tabulations of data from household surveys conducted in the respective countries.

that two-parent nuclear households with children account for the largest volume of the population, it is clear that much of the population in the countries analyzed (except for Uruguay) is experiencing acute economic shortages. It is worth recalling that in the current socio-economic context, the normative family model – the two-parent household with children – is being attacked on two flanks: on the one hand, by the incipient reduction of its prevalence due to the emergence or strengthening of non-traditional households and family life cycle changes, and on the other by their limited capacity to guarantee the full reproduction of their members as a result of wages contraction, increasing unemployment and the precarization of the available employment. In fact, this last aspect has been reflected in recent years by the reduction of the number of households depending on the income of a single breadwinner, usually the male householder-provider, as we have already pointed out. Nevertheless, the increasing utilization of the available labour force, mainly women and young people, does not offset the structural trends toward increasing poverty.

**Units with Female Headship**

Women-headed households have elicited an enormous amount of discussion on their social vulnerability as a group and their relative suitability for becoming a means of identifying the urban poor. The information available shows that poverty and female headship continue to be closely linked in several Latin American countries. This affects the majority of single-parent nuclear households headed by women in Honduras and Nicaragua and almost half these households in Argentina (Table 17.5). According to the data from Mexico and Central American countries, women-headed extended households are still poorer than nuclear women-headed households. Figures for 1994 show the same trend for the five countries analyzed (Table 17.6).

Despite the unequivocal nature of these data, research on the link between female headship and poverty in Latin America over the past few decades has yet to reach a consensus (García and Oliveira, 2011). Recent analyses tend to highlight their heterogeneity. There are countries such as Mexico where researchers have reached the conclusion that these households are not necessarily the poorest (Gómez de León and Parker, 2000). As García and Oliveira (2011) point out, the link between female household headship and poverty tends to be based on an analysis of job-related income. Subsequent studies question the suitability of this indicator for

**Table 17.6** Poverty incidence in nuclear and extended households headed by men and women, urban zones, Latin America (5 countries), 1994 (percentages)

| Household type | | | | | |
|---|---|---|---|---|---|
| | Single parent headed by women | | | Single and two-parent headed by men | |
| Country | Nuclear | Extended and compound | Country | Nuclear | Extended and compound |
| Argentina | 14.6 | 16.9 | Argentina | 11.8 | 9.8 |
| Uruguay | 7.9 | 12.3 | Uruguay | 6.1 | 8.3 |
| Brazil | 45.7 | 53.9 | Brazil | 39.3 | 45.2 |
| Mexico | 27.3 | 37.8 | Mexico | 29.2 | 39.6 |
| Honduras | 78 | 79.5 | Honduras | 69.1 | 69.5 |

Source: Arriagada (1997)

describing the level of relative well-being in these households. Thus, the study by Gómez de León and Parker (2000) shows that, at least in the case of Mexico, what prevents women-headed households from experiencing higher levels of poverty is the contribution of non-job-related income such as remittances, which are not found as commonly in other types of household. All these factors have made more complex the analytical dimensions involved in the study of female household headship, ranging from strictly economic aspects to those of intra-familial dynamics, including an evaluation of patterns of internal authority and solidarity, family violence, children's status and women's domestic workload, all of which are intended to assess the quality of family life offered by these households (García and Oliveira, 2006).

**Final Considerations**

Throughout this work, we have compared countries with very different socio-economic and demographic features in order to explore the complex inter-relationships between macro-structural transformations and the persistence of sharp household[8] inequalities in Latin America. We gave special attention to families' composition and households' well-being. We have argued that the recurrent economic crises that have struck Latin American since the1980s, together with the restructuring of production, the liberalization of the economy and the deterioration of labour conditions have exacerbated the already existing household social inequalities.

As for household composition, the research confirms the internal differences in the region in terms of the greater relative importance of one-person households in Argentina and Uruguay, nuclear families in Brazil and Mexico and the enormous prevalence of extended and compound households in Honduras and Nicaragua. This last aspect is closely related to the high frequency of consensual unions and migration in these countries. The contrasts between the countries are also reflected in the different proportions of women-headed households, the highest levels of which are found in Honduras, Nicaragua and Uruguay.

Despite this initial heterogeneity, the tendencies towards change are very similar in all the countries, albeit with varying degrees of intensity. Thus we have a scenario characterized by an incipient *diversification of family itineraries* caused by the availability of a range of options to the detriment of the traditional normative household. Indeed, two-parent nuclear families with children are becoming less important whereas women-headed and one-person households are increasing in all the countries analyzed.

The traditional family model (two-parent nuclear family with children) has lost relative force, not only because of the demographic changes noted, but also because of their decreasing economic self-sufficiency, at least in terms of the model of the single male provider. The recent socio-economic changes caused by the growth strategy underway have eroded families' capacity for reproduction, encouraging the participation of women as other household members. The high percentages of poverty experienced by these households – ranging from a quarter to over half in all countries except Uruguay – leave no room for doubt. If we bear in mind the fact that although these families are not the poorest ones, those being extended families, they account for the largest volume of the population, which shows the precariousness of a considerable sector of Latin American families nowadays.

Once again, the most vulnerable family contexts in the various countries have more similarities than differences. Extended units are in a truly critical condition, which of course, is far more accentuated in countries with less relative well-being: Nicaragua and Honduras. In Central American countries, the widespread, high levels of poverty tend to make households far more homogeneous; all of them have extreme shortages. Previous studies show that among extended households, those with female headship are in a worse relative position; one-parent nuclear families headed by women, increasing in nearly all countries, also show high poverty levels.

Finally, we would like to draw attention to the heterogeneous, selective nature of the possible favorable consequences of socio-economic and demographic changes on family life. In Latin America, changes in families' characteristics, strategies and relations have taken place at varying rates between different social sectors and ethnic groups, as well as between countries and between regions within the same country. The coexistence of enormous social inequalities is a distinctive feature of the region which has been accentuated by globalization. The greatest benefits of the processes of socio-economic transformation have been concentrated in the areas of the greatest relative development, in the cities and in the most privileged social sectors. These sectors have had access to the available educational opportunities and better employment prospects; they have also been the protagonists in specific changes such as the increase in extra-domestic work, the delay in age at marriage, the greater use of birth control and the reduction of fertility rates. In turn, these sectors are more likely to seek a redefinition of the sexual division of labour. The consequence of these sharp differences between social sectors has been the reinforcement of class and gender inequalities. The increase in poverty levels and social vulnerability reaffirms the types of family relations marked by inequities between men and women.

## Notes

1. Published originally in Spanish in: M. Ariza and O. Oliveira, (2007), in 'Familias, pobreza y desigualdad social en Latinoamérica: una mirada comparativa', *Estudios Demográficos y Urbanos*, (22) 1: 9–42. Translated to English and revised by the authors for this volume.

2. Although, because of the radical nature of the change, this transformation is more obvious in the Western European countries for which the term was coined, it has found eloquent expression in Latin America.

3. It is estimated that over half the growth of non-manual sectors that took place between 1960 and 1990 in Latin America was due to female employment.

4. The diminishing of the population under 15 years old and the increase of those in active ages contributed to reducing households' dependency rate – an aspect that alleviates the pressure on household economic resources.

5. Given the different mortality rates by sex, it is highly likely that a large number of these households consist of women over the age of 60.

6. The earlier family stages crucial to socio-biological reproduction decrease while the later stage of dismemberment increases and starts the so-called empty nest stage (Arriagada, 2004).

7. The organization of everyday reproduction involves obtaining resources (both monetary and non-monetary) through the engagement of family members in economic activity and the production of goods and services for the market or self-consumption; in addition to the undertaking of a wide range of domestic activities, the administration of the family budget and the establishment of support networks.

8. According to CEPAL data for 1994, spouses' contribution in the form of job-related earnings to the family income ranged from 28% in Mexico and Uruguay to nearly 39% in Argentina and Honduras.

## References

Ariza, M. & de Oliveira, O. (2005). Families in transition. In C.H. Wood & B. Roberts (Eds.), *Rethinking Development in Latin America* (pp. 233–247). University Park, Pennsylvania: The Pensylvania State University Press.

Arriagada, I. (1997). 'Politicas sociales, familia y trabajo en la America Latina de fin de siglo'. *Políticas Sociales 21*, (54p). Santiago de Chile: CEPAL/ Naciones Unidas.

Arriagada, I. (2004). 'Estructuras familiares, trabajo y bienestar en América Latina'. In I. Arriagada & V. Aranda (Eds.), *Cambio de las familias en el marco de las transformaciones globales: Necesidad de políticas públicas eficaces* (pp. 43–73). Serie: Seminarios y Conferencias 42. División de Desarrollo Social. Santiago de Chile: CEPAL/Naciones Unidas.

Comisión Económica para América Latina y El Caribe, CEPAL (2003). *Panorama social de América Latina, 2000–2003*. Santiago de Chile.

Comisión Económica para América Latina y El Caribe, CEPAL (2004). *Balance preliminar de las economías de América Latina y El Caribe, 2003*. Santiago de Chile.

Comisión Económica para América Latina y El Caribe and Centro Latinoamericano y Caribeño de Demografía, CEPAL/CELADE (2005). *Dinámica demográfica y desarrollo en América Latina y el Caribe*. Serie: Población y Desarrollo, *58*, Santiago de Chile.

De Vos, S.M. (1995). *Household Composition in Latin America, The Plenum Series on Demographic Methods and Population Analysis*. Madison, WI: Springer.

Fajnzylber, P. & López, J.H. (Eds.) (2008). *Remittances and Development. Lessons from Latin America*. Washington: The World Bank.

García, B. & de Oliveira, O. (2011). 'Family changes and public policies in Latin America'. *The Annual Review of Sociology*, *37*, 613–633.

Gómez de León, J. & Parker, S. (2000). 'Bienestar y jefatura femenina en los hogares mexicanos'. In M. P. López & V. Salles (Eds.), *Familia, género y pobreza* (pp. 11–45). Mexico: Miguel Ángel Porrúa.

González de la Rocha, M. (1994). *The Resources of Poverty: Women and Survival in a Mexican City*. Cambridge, MA: Blackwell Publishers.

Jelin, E. (1998). *Pan y afectos. La transformación de las familias*. Mexico: Fondo de Cultura Económica (Col. Popular, 554).

Pérez Sáinz, J.P. (2000). *Labour Market Transformations in Latin America*. Paper presented for Social Science Research Council (SSRC) Conference, Latin America Labor and Globalization Trends Following a Decades of Economic Adjustment: A Workshop, July. Flacso-Costa Rica.

Portes, A. (1996). 'Transnational Communities: Their Emergence and Significance in the Contemporary World-system'. In R.P. Korzeniewwicz (Ed.), *Latin America in the World-economy* (pp. 151–168). London: Greenwood Press.

Standing, G. (1999). 'Global feminization through flexible labor: A theme revisited'. *World Development*, *27*(3), 583–602.

## Marina Ariza and Orlandina de Oliveira, by Brígida García (Mexico)

During the last decades, Latin American sociologists and social demographers have been particularly critical of the theoretical and methodological foundations of the functionalist perspectives on family studies. One important aspect that has been questioned is the importance given in that frame of reference to the isolated nuclear family and its dynamics; in contrast, the relevance of the multiple connections and networks among relatives and neighbours which characterize family and social life in our national contexts have been pointed out. In this way of thinking, the prevalence of extended family units in Latin America has been emphasized, as well as the relevance of social heterogeneity and inequality among domestic units of different social strata and ethnic groups. In synthesis, the idea has been to break away from the notion of the universal family, and to give more importance to the production system, to social classes and their relationship to household organization.

The economic context, as well as traditional social inequality, are often taken into consideration as the crucial dimensions that establish the limits and possibilities for individual action. However, the households, families or domestic units are seen as mediating institutions, with their own dynamics and effects, which in some circumstances can accentuate or lessen the possibilities that are generated at the macrosocial level. Within this frame of reference, during the economic crisis of the 1980s and the decades of economic restructuring that have followed, a central topic of research has been the strategies or actions implemented by families or households in their struggle to counteract economic and social hardship. At the beginning of this line of research, the solidarity aspects of the domestic group were the most emphasized; however, with the introduction of the gender perspective, conflicts were introduced more explicitly, as was the role of women in daily reproduction.

Economic participation, the diversification of labor activities and the intensification of working time are central aspects of family actions or strategies. Also, as one can notice in the work of Ariza and Oliveira, it is very important to take into account the interaction of socio-economic and demographic aspects, including the needs of households and the availability of family labour. This work is an excellent example of Latin American family research and provides information on the extent and depth of the situation of poverty in several Latin American countries and the diversity of situations that arise in terms of the composition of families when economic and demographic transformations are taken into account. One of its main contributions is the analysis of changes in women's work and poverty levels in different types of households in the 1990s and the beginning of the twenty-first century. The authors explore the heterogeneity of situations and call attention to the fact that poor families, especially if they are extended, have not been able to counteract the perverse effects of economic policies on their quality of life.

Marina Ariza and Orlandina de Oliveira have profuse trajectories regarding the study of families, work and gender in Mexico and Latin America. They have written extensively on these subjects and are based at the National Autonomous University of Mexico (UNAM) and El Colegio de Mexico, respectively. One of their main research interests has been the relationship between family formation and women's economic participation, as well as the historical and cultural comparison among different types of families in Mexico, the Caribbean, and Northern Europe. They have stressed the place of the domestic units in the reproduction of social inequalities – as they have done in the text published in this book – and also considered the family as a symbolic reference and as a producer of values and meanings in different societies.

# Part Four

# Identities, Actors and Social Movements

## 18

# Latin American Perspectives on Social Movements Research

*Breno Bringel (Brazil)*[1]

Social movements have historically played a central role in Latin America (LA) both in developing practices of resistance and creating alternative and integrationist imaginaries in the region. They are often confused with particular organizations or specific struggles, but social movements are not limited to one *actor* or one *action*. They are a broader part of a complex action system (Melucci, 1989). Rather than a strictly defined object of study, as they have been largely perceived by hegemonic theories in the United States, Latin American sociology has primarily regarded social movements as a valuable heuristic tool to understand societal transformations and the possibilities and uncertainties of social change.

In other words, instead of incorporating social movements into a relatively defined field of study on collective behavior (Blumer, 1951), resource mobilization (McCarthy and Zald, 1977), collective action (Tilly, 1978) or contentious politics (Tarrow, Tilly and McAdam, 2001), the Latin American debate has viewed them as part of more comprehensive interpretations of society, politics, culture and/or economy. This feature brings the Latin American sociological discussion closer to the European debate, particularly to cultural and Marxist approaches that seek to understand social movements vis-à-vis changes in society.[2]

From this perspective, social movements develop themselves in tune with major societal shifts (such as urbanization, industrialization, displacements in social structure, the emergence of new information and communication technologies) while simultaneously influencing them. They act as 'thermometers' of society, giving visibility to its main conflicts and concerns, and exposing the limits of the forms of domination and the various types of cultural and sociopolitical agreements. They dispute over cognitive and political meanings through actual and symbolic battles, creating myths and symbols, constructing discourses and identities, forging worldviews and mobilizing resources and social energy.

Therefore, addressing social movements in LA entails moving beyond the boundaries of narrow disciplinary and epistemic definitions and breaking with spatio-temporal, rigid images to proceed along a dynamic field of continuous struggles and recreations. While striving to construct themselves as subjects of their time, they look to the past to experience the present and build the future, as Aymara sociologist and historian Silvia Rivera Cusicanqui demonstrated when she suggested, in the selected key text in this section, that the indigenous rebellion is driven by superimposed memories going back to different, highly complex and not merely linear times, ranging between the short and the long term.

In spatial terms, the defense of the territory, culture and the common goods has shaped deeply territorialized resistance practices. These local(ized) roots have long been considered as a synonym of localism and provincialism, that is, as a symptom accompanying the development of closed, isolated communities excluded from modernity. Developmental and modernization theses which reinforced this argument – while at the same time becoming the seminal basis of criticism of Latin American sociology during its institutionalization period in the mid-twentieth century – interpreted many of the Latin American historical social movements as expressions of tradition, rural life and backwardness. Hence it was most surprising to learn that in recent decades, Latin American peasant and indigenous movements had become key actors in internationalized and global struggles. Continental articulation is not new, but ongoing regionalization of resistance has enabled, in the past three decades, the development of transnational networks and convergence spaces that have facilitated resistance to several initiatives and policies and provided feedback and synergies that impacted on the political and institutional domain, serving as the keystone of a new political cycle at the turn of the century that has recently come to an end.

The aim of this text is not to analyze specific *authors* and their contributions (and their legacies to the Latin American debate), nor particular *actors* involved in struggles (and their strategies), but rather seeks to offer an overview of Latin American social movements, sensitive to the cultural, historical, economic and sociopolitical regional context. In addition to this brief introduction, this text consists of four parts.

The first part addresses the origins and history of Latin American social movements, drawing attention to possible interpretations of collective actors in peripheral contexts that transcend hegemonic theories and

Eurocentric visions. The second part deals with classic, political-ideological matrices, which, despite their changes over time, still serve as the main discursive and political affiliations normatively guiding the action of social movements and political actors in the region. The third part delves into the geopolitical dimension of Latin American social movements in an attempt to reflect on the effects of these paradigms on territorial struggles, regional imaginaries and development disputes. Finally, the fourth and last part ventures into a more recent field associated with the turn of the century in order to identify continuities and ruptures, and examine the more significant and transversal axes of social conflict and the social movements resulting from them.

## Modernity, Coloniality and Resistance

There has always been resistance, but social movements – in a strict sense – are often associated in academic discussions with the emergence of modernity and the creation of a world of nation-states (Tarrow, 2011: part I). Locally oriented struggles, disturbances, riots, uprisings, revolts or insurgencies would be related phenomena, but not synonymous with social movements, whose social and historical construction dates back, in the specialized literature, to a specific time-space: the rise of industrial society in mid-nineteenth-century Europe. As a result, the labor movement appears as the privileged subject, the capital–labor axis constitutes the central conflict in society, and national boundaries serve as demarcation lines of the field of action. Moreover, in this movements' imagination, class identity – highly centered – is confused with the privileged territory – the factory and, in a more general way, the urban space – and, by and large, with a major element in the repertoire of collective action: the strike.

This interpretative scheme repeats itself endlessly in practically all historical and theoretical books on social movement theory. However, how do peripheral societies – such as Latin American ones – who underwent a 'delayed', uneven spread of industrialization, fit into this scheme? What can history and mainstream social movement theory tell us about societies facing different axis of conflict and where labor movements lacked the centrality they enjoyed in Europe? What has Latin American sociology contributed to this topic and what has it kept for itself?

A large share of Eurocentric, restricted views of modernity and social movements not only hid, from the nineteenth century on, several social and political experiences and trajectories but also contributed to building a strong mirror of political and normative horizons. Emancipation, autonomy, democracy, rights, citizenship and development seemed key notions, laden with teleology and a universal horizon expressed from a particular *locus*. In the same line, notions, categories and concepts used by the various 'social movement theories' arising in the 1960s and 1970s in the United States (the resource mobilization theory and the political process theory) and Europe (post-Marxism and the theory of the new social movements) were mainly built upon European and North American experiences[3] and not on the widespread anti-colonial struggle in Africa or anti-imperialist movements in Latin America during that same period (Bringel, 2011).

This diagnosis has triggered numerous proposals in the region for decolonizing Eurocentric modernity, historicizing social struggles and recovering experiences silenced by colonial wounds and epistemic violence (Bringel and Domingues, 2015; Cairo and Grosfoguel, 2010; Mignolo, 2007). In fact, the last decades have witnessed the emergence of several proposals associated with postcolonial and decoloniality studies, as well as with an 'indigenous', 'Southern', 'global', 'endogenous', 'autonomous' sociology, among other labels, that has constantly sought to challenge hegemonic Western narratives. While not a new or homogeneous intellectual movement, it has gained strength in recent years, revisiting foundational issues of Latin American sociology,[4] and disputing differing modernity perspectives and their effects.

Social movement theories also seek to break with an international labor division between Northern producers and Southern consumers. Foweraker (1995) very explicitly emphasizes that there are many social movements in LA but little theoretical literature on them, thus accounting for the strong influence of North American and European theoretical paradigms. The same applies to other peripheral countries, where the great majority of studies on the topic boasts a very descriptive and appreciative character. This does not mean that the issue is unaddressed from the peripheral context, but, rather, that social movements in the global periphery have not been developed as autonomous fields of discussion, as was the case in the core regions. In fact, the theme was treated in a transversal manner, within broader theoretical proposals. Despite this and some important recent developments in the international debate (Cox, 2017; Cox, Nilsen and Pleyers, 2017; Ellis and van Kessel, 2009; Fadaee, 2016, 2017; Singh, 2001), there is still a long way to go in the search for more robust analytical constructions to better understand social movements in LA and the rest of the Global South.

Upon attempting to systematize contemporary critique of the debate on modernity and social movements, several major contributions and common themes emerge: questioning of the different legacies of colonialism (cultural, historic and geographic) and their forms of persistence to this day; an attempt to capture 'alternative epistemologies' that challenge the patriarchal, racist, capitalist and Eurocentric character of modernity and its forms of knowledge; the recovery of silenced experiences; re-setting a subtler boundary between the object (of study) and the (political) subject; and greater openness of other *loci* of knowledge production beyond universities (Bringel and Domingues, 2017). However, part of this debate seems to focus primarily on the epistemic and discourse levels, revealing difficulties in breaking away from 'destituting' critique towards a more 'instituting' theoretical construction. In other words, we still need more useful approaches to theoretical interpretations that will enable us to associate, for example, Latin American social movements with the historical social struggles in the region.

Several studies analyze the extent to which a significant number of social actors in the region undertake a relentless search for the articulation of various short-, long- and medium-term temporalities and memories, signaling their historicity and collective subjectivity. This is done by creating diverse mediations and through existing inheritances, narratives and references that provide feedback to social struggles. In an effort to go beyond the short-term perspective, some authors have recently tried to outline the relations between social movements and their normative orientations, turning towards the grammars of collective action in the region and its sedimentation in social struggles. Thus, the political language of contemporary movements is the result of situational changes and an available 'political and conceptual repertoire' that is reinvented and redefined over time, assigning new meanings to classic themes of thought and transformative political action in LA, such as, for example, anti-imperialism or decolonization.

This is a major contribution – albeit not always systematized – of Latin American sociology to the social movement debate. Argentinean sociologist Maristella Svampa hints at the importance of reconstructing political-ideological matrices of confrontation, understood as 'those guidelines that organize the way of thinking politics and power, as well as the concept of social change' (Svampa, 2010: 8). Svampa revisits a relevant notion from Latin American sociology that had already been used in several ways – either to analyze political traditions like the 'national-popular matrix' (Argumedo, 1993), or to refer to relationship patterns between the State and society and their mediation approaches (Garretón, 2001, 2009).

In a direct line from this debate, I define political-ideological matrices as relatively stable political and discursive affiliations normatively guiding collective action and social movements' contentious politics. While my definition does not differ too much from Svampa's, I advance a different typology more convergent with the transversality of historical conflicts, resistance to coloniality and social struggles in the region. I identify six classic political-ideological matrices that appear intertwined in various ways throughout the history of the region, affecting past and current social movements. They are: the indigenous-community matrix; the black and anti-racist resistance matrix; peripheral nationalism; agrarianism; socialism; and feminism.

## Social Movements and Latin American Political-ideological Matrices

In the first place, the indigenous-community matrix emerges as the cornerstone of the struggle against colonialism and coloniality. Resistance to colonial extermination and genocide is a milestone of this matrix sustained by indigenous people and marked by a strong relationship between culture, nature and territory. Many initial narratives are in dispute over this matrix, ranging from pre-Columbian collective records to descriptions of evangelization efforts in letters and chronicles by Spaniards such as Bartolomé de las Casas; oral stories, commentaries and research by *mestizos* like the Inca Garcilaso de la Vega; and descriptions and drawings by 'translators' (Bringel and Cairo, 2019) such as indigenous chronicler Guamán Poma de Ayala. Despite the dispersion of records and struggles, many references assert that this matrix constitutes the basis for what would later be defined as *indigenism* and *indianism*. An emblematic historical example is the Tupac Amaru movement in the eighteenth century, with its rebellious character and anticolonial resistance. While this matrix had its epicenter in the Andean region, with a major presence in some countries of Central America and Mexico, its influence has spread throughout the subcontinent. In the late nineteenth and early twentieth centuries, creative cultural and intellectual movements joined the secular resistance, shaping the construction of an indigenous activist field that expressed itself both through direct action and subversive writing.

Peru sees the emergence of Manuel González Prada's 'indigenous libertarian' movement, which heavily influenced Mariátegui (1978 [1928]) and his Indo-American socialism, enhancing the role of the indigenous as revolutionary subject and largely contributing to rejecting the ideology of progress and a linear perspective on universal history. Traces of this matrix are still evident today in the public emergence of prominent indigenous movements as political subjects in recent decades in Bolivia or Ecuador.

The second political ideology matrix that gears collective action of Latin American social movements is that of black and anti-racist resistance. In the Americas, slavery led to the trafficking of slaves from sub-Saharan Africa as well as a racialization, which, as Quijano states (2000a), established the idea of 'race' in its modern meaning by reference to the phenotypic differences between conquerors and conquered. However, developing a social classification criterion that defines power positions and structures in society according to the belief that a particular racial group is inferior to the others was not passively accepted. Initial black insurgencies and uprisings were linked to the liberation struggle and, later, to anti-racism, which still has a deep impact on the debate on the decolonization of power and being. In addition to several isolated experiences in American territories, it is worth highlighting the slave revolution in Haiti in 1804 that made it the first nation to gain political independence in Latin America and the Caribbean and, also, the first to abolish slavery, representing a major milestone for this matrix. The slave revolution became a reference for various movements of this matrix, thus reconstructing a transnational history through the diaspora and re-territorialization. Unlike the previous indigenous-communitarian matrix that attempts to articulate its worldviews with a strong identity-territorial meaning, this matrix rather focused on reconstructing ties and worldviews in alien territories that served as liberation and resistance spaces, such as *'palenques'* in Colombia and Cuba, *'cimarrones'* in Venezuela, *'maroons'* in Jamaica and Haiti, or *'quilombos'* in Brasil.[5] Finally, it could be said that the deepening of historical, ever-present relations between race, class and gender has helped black and Afro-descendant movements regain presence in LA in recent decades, both in the public space and social discussion, with a diverse agenda centered on land ownership, intercultural education, racism, and ancestral memory.

Haiti pioneered the century-long political Independence process in LA, while Cuba brought it to an end. This process forges another of the classic Latin American political-ideological matrices: the peripheral nationalism. Initially associated with the dream of emancipation and a project to create a 'nation of nations' and to build continental unity, this notion sparked several disputes over the ownership of the nationalist and independent narrative that local aristocrats often put above popular movements (Abelardo, 2011). Hence, the endless struggle over the meanings of 'national question' in the periphery (Beigel, 2005) has prevented political independence from settling the problems of the colonial period, since far from breaking with the basis of the previous order, it strengthened it and made it more complex, reinforcing many of the capitalist development dictates and establishing relations of internal colonialism (Casanova, 1969; Stavenhagen, 1963). In the course of its conflicts with liberalism and positivism and with deeper ties between the region and the rest of the world, peripheral nationalism gradually merges with anti-imperialism, forging a revolutionary nationalism in several countries, and sometimes also with populism, shaping a middle-class nationalism that reached its peak in the first half of the twentieth century, inspiring subsequent movements that influenced, and still influence the configuration of many trade union movements and workers' struggles.

The fourth political-ideological matrix, agrarianism, despite its much earlier roots, also largely consolidated itself during the transition between the nineteenth and twentieth centuries, often in relation to the nationalist matrix. It has secular roots, because the phenomena of land expropriation and land concentration in the hands of major landowners, albeit reinforced by independence, are a hallmark of the colonial period (Chonchol, 2003). In fact, it is probably one of the most lasting signs of continuity of the regional social structure in the past five centuries, despite the mid-twentieth century accelerated demographic transition, resulting in the urbanization of practically all countries in LA. Political-identity boundaries between indigenous and peasants were weak and had often changed over time; however, this line of demarcation became stronger when the 'agrarian question' gained weight as a specific guideline associated with land concentration, *haciendas*[6] and feudalism, thus marking, according to André Gunder Franck, in open disagreement with Ernesto Laclau, the character of dependent capitalism in Latin America (Frank, 1966, 1967; Laclau, 1971). The struggle for agrarian reform played a pivotal role in autonomizing this matrix in the fields of action and thought, as well as the Mexican revolution in 1910, a major milestone and, also, albeit through different means, the Bolivian revolution of 1952. If we take a look at the region as a whole during the last century, this matrix strongly underpins all demands for agrarian reform, land struggles and agrarian references guiding social movements throughout LA, many of them regionally articulated around La Vía Campesina, and strongly influenced by Brazil's Landless Workers' Movement (Bringel and Vieira, 2015).

A fifth political-ideological matrix involves socialism. Although it features a variety of possible insights, types and characteristics, we refer here to a broad field of the socialist, utopian, anarchist and Christian left in LA, nurtured by a strong relationship with European modern practices, ideas and ideologies, often giving rise to combinations with some of the political ideology matrices we have previously addressed. The strength of this matrix at the global level in the nineteenth and twentieth centuries should prevent us from falling into a mere Eurocentric diffusionism. Despite some fairly orthodox alignments, for the most part, ideas and grammars were not received passively but rather creatively, prompting, for example, original proposals for developing a community, Indo-American socialism. The feedback effect between movements, trade unions and communist and socialist parties translates into numerous social struggles throughout the twentieth century, ranging from those which triggered revolutions, such as the Cuban revolution, to more localized experiences zeroing in on direct insurgent guerrilla action in the 1960s and 1970s and, later, cooperativism, production and popular education.

Last but not least, feminism should also be treated as a specific political-ideological matrix in LA forging collective action and social movements in the region in a secular way. Despite its autonomous significance, this matrix was rendered invisible for a long time and regarded as a transversal element and/or an integral part of broader, successive 'waves' originating in Europe and the United States. Such waves would gradually arrive in the region either through black women's struggles against slavery, for suffrage or, later, against gender inequality. Even 'Latin American thinking' contributed to this lack of visibility by naming movements after male figures.

We all know Túpac Katari, San Martín, Simón Bolívar, Emiliano Zapata and Che Guevara well. However, who knows Bartolina Sisa, Gregoria Apasa, Juana Álvarez, María Josefa Guelberdi, Juana Azurduy, Nísia Floresta, Flora Tristán, Juana Paula Manso de Noronha, Juana Rouco Buela or Adelaida Velasco? And there are more. Many women have helped lead struggles against colonization and patriarchy, and for political independence, recognition of women's participation in politics, libertarian education, liberation, socialist construction and women's emancipation. This is not about simply reversing the equation and coming up with women's names, but to collectively register references, resistances and dissenting readings that make up a Latin American feminism, related to historical struggles in the region and the previous political-ideological matrices herein mentioned. The superb anthology organized by Gargallo (2010), as well as various recent efforts also by Gargallo (2014) and Ciriza (2015) allow us to reconstruct records, voices, trajectories and, above all, epistemics that have inspired in recent decades communitarian, indigenous, black, and lesbian women feminisms as well as other women's struggles rooted in Latin America and the Caribbean. As stated by Virginia Vargas in one of the key texts included in this section of the book, Latin American feminist movements have thrived in the midst of diversity for decades, in meetings and knowledge exchange spaces that have facilitated political articulation and knowledge production, two key elements in Latin American social movements, characterized by their pedagogic and formative character.

## Latin America from Below: Territory, Regional Imaginary and Disputes Over Development

The matrices previously discussed may merge, split themselves, or even create new ones. However, they are considered 'structuring' because they have gradually become basic orientations of collective action, sociopolitical practices and ideas that may spark social movements. In addition, they denote three central, recurring elements in Latin American sociology.

The first of them is that *Latin American social movements have been and are essentially territorial in nature.* Part of the broad contemporary discussion on the 'return' of the territory ends up disregarding the historicity of a constitutive dimension of social movements in the region. This is obviously a result of colonial territorial occupation and the region's peripheral position, its insertion in and relation to the world economy, but also of particular social and cultural, and political-ideological trends. In recent decades, territorial dynamics have become more complex on account of increasing spatial and temporal acceleration and intense transnational flows. Therefore, territory should be considered not only as a material basis where collective action unfolds, but also as a place laden with power/knowledge/resistance relationships that help shape senses of belonging and recreate social ties, and where territorialities are disputed.

Secondly, the political-ideological matrices previously analyzed also point to the historical importance of the construction of broader and more comprehensive imaginaries that transcend action, residency and socialization spaces in territorialized social struggles and movements. This implies taking into consideration a geopolitical dimension in social movements that articulates regional scales and imaginaries (Bringel and Cabezas, 2014; Bringel and Falero, 2008). In other words, *political-ideological matrices can be linked to the historical construction of diverse, alternative, regional imaginaries forged by social movements*. For example, the indigenous-communitarian matrix has advocated for centuries the construction of '*suyus*' (regions) with different names, some of which, like 'Abya Yala' have been revived in recent years by contemporary indigenous movements. In a like manner, the peripheral nationalist matrix has generated different regional imaginaries that go back to the initial moments of political independence with the idea of 'The United States of South America' and, later, with Marti's idea of 'Nuestramérica'. Finally, it can also be said that even though the idea of 'Latin America' came from outside, it was disputed and redefined in practice as a unit of continental resistance. Several political-ideological matrices – such as the agrarian, socialist and nationalist – and various recent struggles have collaborated in this direction, creating a Latin American sense not only in speeches, but also in the generation of converging sociopolitical and formative exchanges and practices.

Lastly, *Latin American political-ideological matrices are deeply intertwined with the question of development*. Quijano (2000b) precisely recalls how development trajectories of the global pattern of capitalist power affects countries and regions in different ways. While development was associated with the modern and with 'advanced capitalist' nations, this dominant power pattern became universal and 'natural' in the periphery. Its relation with social movements and the different matrices was often ambiguous. Various social movements related to socialist and nationalist matrices adopted the developing imaginary and its contradictions. Others, linked to the agrarian matrix, for example, largely emphasized the need for development alternatives. However, the subjects related to the indigenous-community matrix especially attempted to break with the 'development ghost', searching for alternatives to it, as it reflected on current proposals around the '*Buen vivir*'[7] formula (Bringel and Echart, 2015, 2017).

## Final Reflections: Axes of Social Conflict and Social Movements in the New Century

The matrices, influences, imaginaries and scenarios discussed so far have driven us to the contemporary Latin American scenario anchored in history and regional (geo)politics. In fact, over the past three decades, following the fall of the Berlin Wall, social movements in the region started to increasingly traverse the borders of the nation-state, raising their voices more autonomously. The Zapatista uprising, development of transnational networks, resistance to the Free Trade Area of the Americas (FTAA) and the creation of regional convergence spaces have led to the construction of practices and narratives with a strong Latin American character. Though localized, struggles are not limited to the local scale and appeal to a strong regional and global meaning. However, in opposition to this integration, Latin American sociology appears much more fragmented, perhaps due to the current trend towards ultra-specialization and greater levels of development of the social sciences in different countries.

As a result, in recent times, social movements, rather than academia, have produced more critical and relevant knowledge on the Latin America reality, understanding Latin America as a diverse unit. The need to know the other and his/her specificities while trying, at the same time, to forge intelligibility between struggles, has enabled us to identify common and transversal elements in the region. Faced with these dynamics, studies not only *on* social movements, but also *with* and *from* movements allow us to determine some of the main axes of social conflict in the region in the twenty-first century, providing feedback to Latin American sociology from a broader perspective (Bringel and Falero, 2016: 36–38), as follows.

### Work-related Struggles

Led by trade unions or trade union movements, these struggles adopt a basic format inherited from the twentieth century, though frequently renovated. They usually have a close relationship with the socialist matrix or the nationalist revolutionary one, where urban conflict prevails. Struggles for fair wages and labor rights coexist in this field, together with struggles for employment and social protection and new forms of struggle associated with worker-recovered companies and agricultural cooperatives, among others. It also includes precarious struggles and struggles linked to non-employment, that is to say, those which gave rise to movements of the unemployed (such as the *piquetero*[8] movement in Argentina) in several countries of the region, within the framework of a deep (regional and global) restructuring of the labor conflict, as exposed by de la Garza Toledo in another key text in this section.

### Struggles Related to State Form Transformation

These struggles go beyond electoral logics and particular political reforms, and can be associated with the constituent power. This is the case with past plebiscites and referenda in Uruguay (although it is also used by right-wing politics linked, for example, to public safety) and such struggles have recently re-emerged within the Latin American political cycle in Bolivia and Ecuador, deriving from actions carried out by indigenous movements that raise the flag of decolonization and the structural transformation of the hegemonic State form in modernity. These struggles are usually accompanied by an insurgent cycle which, in turn, gives way to instituting dynamics that propel new political constitutions, obtaining feedback from diverse political ideologies.

### Struggles Over Territory and Natural Resources

An essential part of contemporary LA, these territorial disputes revolve around conflicts associated with biodiversity, mining, neo-extractivism, water and infrastructure claims. In their defense of common goods, these struggles more explicitly dispute development meanings and models, involving a wide range of actors and diverse transnational interests. Transnational companies' activities, for example, and different logics of capital and State direct intervention in territories tend to become hotbeds of confrontation, with struggles for land and territory (typical of the agrarian matrix), while, at the same time, spawning resistance from communities *affected* by hydroelectric dams, specific companies or mining activities, as well as participation in more articulated movements in the cultural domain. Special attention should be given to the role of the feminist matrix in this conflict axis, particularly of 'communitarian feminism' and its forms of resistance to resource plunder.

### Social Rights-related Struggles

These include all the fundamental struggles for the claim of basic rights (education, health, housing, etc.) and are targeted at strengthening Latin

America's political and social democratization process. They bear a strong, public and democratizing imprint faced with increasing attempts at the commodification of rights. Student movements in Chile, for example, are an emblematic case, but there are many others in the region. If we look at the other struggles from a transversal perspective, we see new types of rights arising, such as, for example, the right to food and food sovereignty, which redefines the role of agrarianism, cross-cutting the classic matrices. Whatever the case, everything seems to point to a significant transformation of this axis, taking into account its shift from a proactive and affirmative role since political re-democratization following military dictatorships in the region (brilliantly exposed by Eder Sader in his key text) to its more defensive, reactive, current role after the rise of conservative governments and forces.

### Struggles for the Reproduction of Life, Memory and Identity

In parallel, and sometimes converging with the previous axis, these struggles involve a wide range of cultural movements and actions for truth and justice, associated with human rights organizations and all questions related to recovering memory, recognition and identity rights, including sexual identity and all matters related to demands, among others, for same-sex marriage and women's right to the voluntary interruption of pregnancy.

The axes set out above highlight some of the main trends and characteristics of social conflict in LA in the twenty-first century. Political-ideological and structuring matrices are dynamically deployed and redefined by various actors and diverse meanings. Thus, persistence of social movements and their key role in creating regional, developmental, alternative imaginaries are not simply the result of the emergence of specific social organizations but, also, of broader configurations of societal and geopolitical disputes.

### Notes

1.  The author recognizes the comments of Fernanda Beigel, along with the permanent intellectual collaboration of Alfredo Falero in several issues discussed in this chapter.

2.  See the intellectual proposal of the Research Committee on Social Classes and Social Movements (RC-47, ISA): www.isarc47.org/sample-page/

3.  In particular, the student struggles of 1968, the inflections of the workers' movement and the feminist struggles, the anti-military and ecologist movements in Europe, along with the civil rights movements in the US.

4.  See Part One of the present volume.

5.  '*Palenques*', '*cimarrones*', '*maroons*' and '*quilombos*' are terms used to refer to villages, settlements or communities inhabited by direct descendants of African slaves.

6.  '*Haçienda*' is a term used to refer to a large landed estate in Spanish America. A traditional institution of rural life, it originated in the colonial period.

7.  '*Buen Vivir*' is a term used to refer to a culture of life based on the ancestral knowledge of indigenous peoples that strives for harmony and aims to strike a balance between humans and nature, and which foresees a return to a way of life that had been suppressed by colonization.

8.  The term mainly refers to the Argentine unemployed workers' movement that unites impoverished workers in repeated waves of protest involving blocking and barricading roads.

## References

Abelardo, J.R. (2011). *Historia de la nación latinoamericana*, Ediciones Continente/Peña Lillo, Buenos Aires.

Argumedo, A. (1993). *Los silencios y las voces en América Latina: notas sobre el pensamiento nacional y popular*, Colihue, Buenos Aires.

Beigel, F. (2005). 'Las identidades periféricas en el fuego cruzado del nacionalismo y el cosmopolitismo', in: Pensar a Contracorriente I, La Habana: *Editorial de Ciencias Sociales*, pp. 70–100.

Blumer, H. (1951). 'Collective behavior', in: A.M. Lee (Ed.) *New Outline of Principles of Sociology*, Barnes and Noble, New York.

Bringel, B. (2011). 'El estudio de los movimientos sociales en América Latina: reflexiones sobre el debate postcolonial y las nuevas geografías del activismo transnacional', in: Yamandú Acosta et al. (Eds.) *Pensamiento Crítico y Sujetos Colectivos en América Latina: perspectivas interdisciplinarias*, Ediciones Trilce, Montevideo, pp. 35–55.

Bringel, B. and Cabezas, A. (2014). 'Geopolítica de los movimientos sociales latinoamericanos: espacialidades, ciclos de contestación y horizontes de posibilidades', in: Preciado, J.C. (Ed.), *Anuario de la Integración Latinoamericana y Caribeña*, University Press of the South/Ediciones de la Noche, New Orleans/Guadalajara, pp. 323–342.

Bringel, B. and Cairo, H. (2019). 'Interregionalism from below: cultural affinity, translation and solidarities in the Ibero-American space', in: Heriberto Cairo and Breno Bringel (Eds.) *Critical Geopolitics and Regional (Re)Configurations: Interregionalism and transnationalism between Latin America and Europe*, Routledge, London, pp. 161–177.

Bringel, B. and Domingues, J.M. (2015). *Global Modernity and Social Contestation*, Sage, London.

Bringel, B. and Domingues, J.M. (2017). 'Social theory, extroversion and autonomy: dilemmas of contemporary (semi)peripheral sociology', *Method(e)s: African Review of Social Sciences Methodology*, 2, 1/2, CODESRIA/Routledge, pp.108–126.

Bringel, B. and Echart, E. (2015). 'Movimientos sociales, desarrollo y emancipación', in: Sotillo, J.A. (Ed.), *Antología del Desarrollo*, Los libros de la Catarata, Madrid, pp. 579–675.

Bringel, B. and Echart, E. (2017). 'Imaginarios sobre el desarrollo en América Latina: entre la emancipación y la adaptación al capitalismo', *Revista Española de Desarrollo y Cooperación*, *49*, pp. 9–24.

Bringel, B. and Falero, A. (2008). 'Redes transnacionais de movimentos sociais na América Latina e o desafio de uma nova construção socioterritorial', *Caderno CRH*, *21*, 53, pp. 269–288.

Bringel, B. and Falero, A. (2016). 'Movimientos sociales, gobiernos progresistas y Estado en América Latina: transiciones, conflictos y mediaciones', *Caderno CRH*, *29*, especial 3, pp. 27–45.

Bringel, B. and Vieira, F.B. (2015). 'Movimientos internacionalistas y prácticas de cooperación sur-sur: brigadas y experiencias formativas del Movimiento de los Sin Tierra de Brasil y La Vía Campesina', *Revista Española de Desarrollo y Cooperación*, 36, primavera-verano, pp. 65–80.

Cairo, H.C. and Grosfoguel, R. (2010). *Descolonizar la modernidad, descolonizar Europa: un diálogo Europa – América Latina*, IEPALA, Madrid.

Casanova, P.G. (1969). *Sociología de la explotación*, Siglo XXI, Mexico DF, pp. 223–250.

Chonchol, J. (2003): 'La reforma agraria en América Latina', in: Vargas, J. (Ed.) *Proceso Agrario en Bolivia y América Latina*, CIDES-UMSA, La Paz, pp. 205–222.

Ciriza, A. (2015): 'Construir genealogías feministas desde el Sur: encrucijadas y tensiones', *Millcayac – Revista Digital de Ciencias Sociales*, *II*, 3, pp. 83–104.

Cox, L. (2017). 'The multiple tradition of social movement research: theorising intellectual diversity', *Fondation Maison des Sciences de l'Homme*, Working Paper 2017–128, pp. 1–19.

Cox, L., Nilsen, A. and Pleyers, G. (2017). 'Social movement thinking beyond the core: theories and research in post-colonial and post-socialist societies', *Interface: A Journal for and about Social Movements*, *9*, 2, pp. 1–36.

Ellis, S. and van Kessel, I. (2009). *Movers and Shakers: Social Movements in Africa*. Brill, Leiden.

Fadaee, S. (Ed.) (2016). *Understanding Southern Social Movements*. Routledge, London.

Fadaee, S. (2017). 'Bringing in the South: towards a global paradigm for social movement studies', *Interface: A Journal for and about Social Movements*, *9*, 2, pp. 45–60.

Foweraker, J. (1995). *Theorizing Social Movements*, Pluto Press, London.

Frank, A.G. (1966). 'The development of underdevelopment', *Monthly Review*, *18*(4), pp. 17–31.

Frank, A.G. (1967). 'Capitalism and Underdevelopment in Latin America: Historical Studies of Chile and Brazil', *Monthly Review Press*, New York.

Gargallo, F. (Ed.) (2010). 'Antología del Pensamiento Feminista Nuestroamericano', *Tomo I (Del Anhelo a la Emancipación)*, Biblioteca Ayacucho, Caracas.

Gargallo, F. (2014). *Feminismos desde Abya Yala*, Editorial Corte y Confección, Mexico.

Garretón, M.A. (2001). 'Cambios sociales, actores y acciones colectivas en América Latina', *CEPAL – Serie Políticas Sociales*, Santiago de Chile, *56*, pp. 1–45.

Garretón, M.A. (2009). 'Transformación de la matriz sociopolítica y desarrollo en Chile', *Diplomacia, Estrategia y Política*, *9*, pp. 45–71.

Laclau, E. (1971). 'Feudalism and capitalism in Latin America', *New Left Review*, *I/67*, May–June, pp. 19–38.

Mariátegui, J.C. (1978 [1928]). *Siete ensayos de interpretación de la realidad peruana.* Ediciones Era, Mexico DF.

McCarthy, J. and Zald, M.(1977). 'Resource mobilization and social movements', *American Journal of Sociology*, *82*, pp. 1212–1241.

Melucci, A. (1989). *Nomads of the Present: Social Movements and Individual Needs in Contemporary Society,* Temple University Press, Philadelphia.

Mignolo, W. (2007). *La idea de América Latina*, Gedisa, Barcelona.

Quijano, A. (2000a). 'Colonialidad del poder, eurocentrismo y América Latina', in: E. Lander, (Ed.) *La colonialidad del saber: eurocentrismo y ciencias sociales. Perspectivas Latinoamericanas*, CLACSO, Buenos Aires.

Quijano, A. (2000b). 'El fantasma del desarrollo en América Latina', *Revista del CESLA*, *1*, pp. 39–55.

Singh, R. (2001). *Social Movements, Old and New*, Sage, New Delhi.

Stavenhagen, R. (1963). 'Clases, colonialismo y aculturación en América Latina', *Revista América Latina – CLAPCS*, *4*, pp. 63–104.

Svampa, M. (2010). 'Movimientos sociales, matrices sociopolíticas y nuevos escenarios en América Latina', Working Paper 01/2010, Universitat Kassel.

Tarrow, S. (2011). *Power in Movement: Social Movements and Contentious Politics*, Cambridge University Press, Cambridge (updated and revised 3rd edition).

Tarrow, S., Tilly, C. and McAdam, D. (Eds.) (2001) *Dynamics of Contention*, Cambridge University Press, Cambridge.

Tilly, C. (1978). *From Mobilization to Revolution*, McGraw-Hill, New York.

# 19

# Ch'ixinakax utxiwa: A Reflection on the Practices and Discourses of Decolonization[1]

*Silvia Rivera Cusicanqui (Bolivia)*

The colonial condition obscures a number of paradoxes. Throughout history, the modernizing efforts of the Europeanized elites in the Andean region resulted in successive waves of recolonization. One example is the Bourbon reforms that both preceded and followed the great cycle of rebellion from 1771 to 1781. Although it is true that modern history meant slavery for the indigenous peoples of America, it was simultaneously an arena of resistance and conflict, a site for the development of sweeping counterhegemonic strategies, and a space for the creation of new indigenous languages and projects of modernity (Thomson, 2003). The condition of possibility for an indigenous hegemony is located in the territory of the modern nation – inserted into the contemporary world – and is once again able to take up the long memory of the internal colonial market, of the long-distance circulation of goods, of networks of productive communities (waged or unwaged), and of the multicultural and multicolored [abigarrados] urban centers. In Potosí, the large market of coca and silver was called 'El Gato' ('the cat', a Castilianization of the indigenous *qhatu*), and the *qhateras* (merchants) were emblematic of indigenous modernity. They were the last link in the production and sale of these goods that were fully modern and yet grounded in indigenous technologies and 'knowledges' (Numhauser, 2005). The bustling colonial space was also the site that linked the indigenous leaders Tupaq Amaru II, Tupaq Katari, and Tomás Katari to long-distance mercantile circulation.[2] And it was the experience of the Spanish Crown's commercial levying – not only the royal fifth, the checkpoints, and tithes or other tax burdens, but also the monopoly on coca, the forced distribution of goods, and the coercive recruitment of porters and shepherds [*llameras*] – that unleashed the fury of rebellion. Against the financial and predatory forms of coercive taxation, the Katari-Amaru project was the expression of indigenous modernity in which religious and political self-determination signified a retaking of their own historicity – a decolonization of imaginaries and of the forms of representation.

Such actions demonstrate that we indigenous were and are, above all, contemporary beings and peers, and in this dimension [*aka pacha*], we perform and display our own commitment to modernity. Cultural postmodernism, imposed by the elites and reproduced by the state in a fragmented and subordinate way, is alien to us as a tactic.[3] There is no post or pre in this vision of history that is not linear or teleological but rather moves in cycles and spirals and sets out on a course without neglecting to return to the same point. The indigenous world does not conceive of history as linear; the past–future is contained in the present. The regression or progression, the repetition or overcoming of the past is at play in each conjuncture and is dependent more on our acts than on our words. The project of indigenous modernity can emerge from the present in a spiral whose movement is a continuous feedback from the past to the future – a 'principle of hope' or 'anticipatory consciousness' – that both discerns and realizes decolonization at the same time (Bloch, 1977, 1995).

The contemporary experience commits us to the present – *aka pacha* – which in turn contains within it the seeds of the future that emerges from the depths of the past [*qhip nayr uñtasis sarnaqapxañani*]. The present is the setting for simultaneously modernizing archaic impulses, for strategies to preserve the status quo and others that signify revolt and renewal of the world: *Pachakuti*. The upside-down world created by colonialism will return to its feet as history only if it can defeat those who are determined to preserve the past, with its burden of ill-gotten privileges. But if the preservers of the past succeed, the past cannot escape the fury of the enemy, to paraphrase Walter Benjamin.[4]

Who really are the archaic and conservative groups and classes in Bolivia? What is decolonization, and what does it have to do with modernity? How can the exclusive, ethnocentric 'we' be articulated with the inclusive 'we' – a homeland for everyone – that envisions decolonization? How have we thought and problematized, in the here and now, the colonized present and its overturning?

In 1983, when Aníbal Quijano still spoke of the movements and uprisings of the Andean peasantry as 'pre-political' (in a text that I fittingly criticized) (Cusicanqui, 1981), I was writing *Oppressed but Not Defeated*, which provided a radically different reading of the significance and relevance of the indigenous protests in the Andes to the struggles of the present. In this text, I argued that the Katarista-Indianista uprising of 1979 made clear for Bolivia the necessity of a 'radical and profound decolonization' in its political, economic, and, above all, mental structures – that is, the country's ways of conceiving the world (Cusicanqui, 1987).

The book's conclusion resulted from a detailed analysis of different historical moments of domination in our country: the colonial, liberal, and populist horizons that not only reversed the legal and constitutional orderings but also recycled old practices of exclusion and discrimination. Since the nineteenth century, liberal and modernizing reforms in Bolivia have given rise to a practice of conditional inclusion, a 'mitigated and second-class' citizenship (Guha, 1988). But the price of this false inclusion has been the archaism of the elites. Recolonization made the reproduction of feudal and rentier modes of domination possible, modes based on the privileged ascriptions granted by the colonial center of power. Today, the rhetoric of equality and citizenship is converted into a caricature that includes not only tacit political and cultural privileges but also notions of common sense that make incongruities tolerable and allow for the reproduction of the colonial structures of oppression.

Bolivian elites are a caricature of the West. In speaking of them, I refer not only to the political class and the state bureaucracy but also to the intelligentsia that strikes postmodern and even postcolonial poses, and to the US academy and its followers who built pyramidal structures of power and symbolic capital – baseless pyramids that vertically bind certain Latin American universities – and form clientelist networks with indigenous and black intellectuals.

The cultural studies departments of many North American universities have adopted 'postcolonial studies' in their curricula with an academicist and culturalist stamp devoid of the sense of political urgency that characterized the intellectual endeavors of their colleagues in India. Although the majority of the founders of the journal *Subaltern Studies* formed part of the Bengali elite in the 1970s and 1980s – many of them graduated from the University of Calcutta – their difference was located both in language, in the radical alterity that it represented to speak Bengali, Hindi, and other languages in India, and in a long tradition of written culture and philosophical reflection. Yet, without altering anything of the relations of force in the 'palaces' of empire, the cultural studies departments of North American universities have adopted the ideas of subaltern studies and launched debates in Latin America, thus creating a jargon, a conceptual apparatus, and forms of reference and counter-reference that have isolated academic treatises from any obligation to or dialogue with insurgent social forces. Walter Mignolo et al. have built a small empire within an empire, strategically appropriating the contributions of the subaltern studies school of India and the various Latin American variants of critical reflection on colonization and decolonization.

Domestically, the Bolivian elites have adopted an official multiculturalism that is riddled with references to Will Kymlicka and anchored in the idea of indigenous people as minorities. Across Latin America, massive protests were triggered against neoliberal policies in Venezuela (1989), Mexico (1994), Bolivia (2000–2005), and Argentina (2002) that alerted the technocrats of the necessity to 'humanize' structural adjustment. The immediate consequence of this was an ornamental and symbolic multiculturalism with prescriptions such as 'ethno-tourism' and 'eco-tourism', which draw on a theatricalization of the 'originary' condition of a people rooted in the past and unable to make their own destiny.

In 1994, in an effort to hide the business of 'capitalization', Bolivian President Gonzalo Sánchez de Lozada adopted the culturist agenda of indigeneity, through his symbolic vice president (Víctor Hugo Cárdenas), municipal decentralization, and constitutional reform. Whether it was for fear of the rabble or to follow the agenda of their financiers, the elites were sensitive to the demands for recognition and political participation of indigenous social movements and adopted a rhetorical and essentialist discourse centered on the notion of 'original people'. This recognition – truncated, conditional, and reluctant – of indigenous cultural and territorial rights allowed for the recycling of the elites and the continuation of their monopoly on power. What did this reappropriation mean, and what were its consequences? The Kataristas and Indianistas, based in the western Andes, had a schematic view of the eastern peoples and spoke of 'Aymaras', 'Qhichwas', and 'Tupiguaranís' or simply of 'Indians'. Simultaneously, the notion of origin refers us to a past imagined as quiet, static, and archaic, which allows us to see the strategic recuperation of indigenous demands and the neutralization of the decolonizing impulse. A discussion of these communities situated in the 'origin' denies the contemporaneity of these populations and excludes them from the struggles of modernity. They are given a residual status that, in fact, converts them into minorities, ensnaring them in indigenist stereotypes of the noble savage and guardians of nature. And so, as the indigenous people of the east and west are imprisoned in their *tierras communitarias de origen* (original communal lands) and are NGO-ized, essentialist and Orientalist notions become hegemonic, and the indigenous people are turned into a multicultural adornment for neoliberalism.[5] The new stereotype of the indigenous combines the idea of a continuous territorial occupation, invariably rural, with a range of ethnic and cultural traits, and classifies indigenous behavior and constructs scenarios for an almost theatrical display of alterity. Rossana Barragán calls this strategy cholo-indigenous ethnic self-affirmation, as an 'emblematic identity' (Barragán, 1992).

But the multicultural discourse also conceals a secret agenda to deny the ethnicity of the multicolored [*abigarradas*] and acculturated populations – the settlement areas, mining centers, indigenous commercial networks in the internal and black markets, the cities. This agenda allowed the elites and the technobureaucracy of the state and the NGOs to comply with the dictates of empire: 'zero coca' forced eradication and closure of legal markets in the tropics of Cochabamba, intellectual property laws, tax reform, and the liquidation of contraband.[6] The term 'original people' affirms and recognizes but at the same time obscures and excludes the large majority of the Aymara- and Qhichwa-speaking population of the subtropics, the mining centers, the cities, and the indigenous commercial networks of the internal and black markets. It is therefore a suitable term for the strategy of depriving indigenous peoples of their potentially hegemonic status and their capacity to affect the state.[7]

The official multiculturalism described above has been the concealing mechanism par excellence for new forms of colonization. The elites adopt a strategy of cross-dressing and articulate new forms of cooptation and neutralization. In this way, they reproduce a 'conditional inclusion', a mitigated and second-class citizenship that molds subaltern imaginaries and identities into the role of ornaments through which the anonymous masses play out the theatricality of their own identity.

What, then, is decolonization? Can it be understood as only a thought or a discourse? I think that this question is another central point that has been barely alluded to in contemporary debates. Modernizing discourse, such as that of the liberals at the end of the nineteenth century, could have existed only if it had been accompanied by liberal practices, by genuine operations of equality and coparticipation in the public sphere. By recognizing what was only an ill-intentioned and rhetorical equality for the Indians, the Ley de Exvinculación of October 5, 1874, canceled the liberal reforms and formalized, after the fact, an aggressive recolonization of indigenous territories throughout the country, resulting in a massive expansion of large estates through the expropriation of communal lands.

Meanwhile, the elites were engaged in rent-seeking activities, long trips to Europe, and above all, speculative investment in land and mining concessions. The 'illustrious' people at the time, such as the 'scientists' of the Mexican Porfiriato [the much-hated rule of Mexican President Porfirio Diaz 1876–1911], constructed, with strong support of the state apparatus (the army, in particular) a rentier and aristocratic class that was not only more colonial than that of the Spanish aristocracy but also more archaic and pre-capitalist. In effect, the nineteenth-century oligarchy remained aloof from the commercial and industrial activities that characterized their sixteenth-century ancestors and was instead dedicated to the usurpation of land, speculation, and import–export trade. The exploitation of materials, primarily under the control of foreign capital and long-distance internal markets (which includes very large cross-border spaces in all the neighboring countries), fell into the hands of indigenous and mestizo populations with large urban–rural networks and links to the expanded reproduction of capital. It was, therefore, the practice of the diverse productive collectives – including those who 'produced' circulation – that defined the modern condition, while the modernizing discourse of the elites only served to mask their archaic processes of cultural and political conservatism, which reproduces and renews the colonial condition throughout society.

There can be no decolonization discourse, no theory of decolonization, without a decolonizing practice. The multiculturalism discourse and the hybridity discourse are essentialist and historicist interpretations of the indigenous question. They do not address the fundamental issues of decolonization but instead obscure and renew the effective practices of colonization and subalternization. Their function is to supplant the indigenous populations as historical subjects and to turn their struggles and demands into elements of a cultural reengineering and a state apparatus in order to subjugate them and neutralize their will. A 'change so that everything remains the same' bestows rhetorical recognition and subordinates, through patronage, the Indians into purely emblematic and symbolic functions – that is, a sort of 'cultural *pongueaje*' [a free domestic service required of indigenous tenants] at the service of the spectacle of the multicultural state and mass communication.

The *gatopardismo* [the policy of changing everything so that everything remains the same] of the political and economic elites is reproduced in miniature in the social sciences that study the Andean region. Here we find a typical structure of 'internal colonialism' as defined by Pablo González Casanova in 1969.[8] The arboreal structure of internal colonialism is articulated with the centers of power of the Northern Hemisphere, whether they be universities, foundations, or international organizations. I refer to this crucial theme – the role of the intellectuals in the domination of empire – because I believe that it is our collective responsibility not to contribute to the reproduction of this domination. By participating in these forums and contributing to the exchange of ideas, we could be, unwittingly, providing the enemy with ammunition. And this enemy has multiple facets, both local and global, situated both in the small corners of 'tiny power' in our universities and pauperized libraries and in the heights of prestige and privilege. It is from these 'palaces' (the universities of the North) that, following [Gayatri Chakravorty] Spivak, dominant ideas emanate, and it is also there that the 'think tanks' (suggestive of a war) of the imperial powers are located. The arboreal structure of internal–external colonialism has centers and subcenters, nodes and subnodes, which connect certain universities, disciplinary trends, and academic fashions of the North with their counterparts in the South.

Let us take the case of Duke University. Walter Mignolo, jointly appointed to romance studies and the Program in Literature, emigrated from Argentina in the 1980s and spent his Marxist youth in France and his postcolonial and culturalist maturity in the United States. At one point, Dr Mignolo got the urge to praise me, perhaps putting in practice a saying we have in the south of Bolivia: 'Praise the fool if you want to see [her] work more'. Taking up my ideas about internal colonialism and the epistemology of oral history, he regurgitated them entangled in a discourse of alterity that was profoundly depoliticized.[9] Careful to avoid more polemical texts such as 'Andean Colonial Mestizaje', he took on, out of context, ideas I had put forward in 'The Epistemological and Theoretical Potential of Oral History', when the Andean Oral History Workshop was in its infancy and had not yet passed through the severe crisis that we are overcoming only today (Cusicanqui, 1989). It was, therefore, an overly optimistic vision, which in many ways has been reworked in my most recent texts. But the North American academy does not follow the pace of our discussions; it does not interact with the Andean social sciences in any meaningful way (except by providing scholarships and invitations to seminars and symposia), and so Mignolo ignored these aspects of my thinking.

The fashion of oral history then spreads to the Universidad Andina Simon Bolivar in Quito, where the Department of Cultural Studies, led by Catherine Walsh, a disciple and friend of Mignolo's, offers a course of graduate study completely based on the logocentric and nominalist version of decolonization. Neologisms such as decolonial, transmodernity, and eco-si-mía proliferate, and such language entangles and paralyzes their objects of study: the indigenous and African-descended people with whom these academics believe they are in dialogue. But they also create a new academic canon, using a world of references and counter-references that establish hierarchies and adopt new gurus: Mignolo, Walsh, Enrique Dussel, Javier Sanjinés. Equipped with cultural and symbolic capital, thanks to the recognition and certification from the academic centers of the United Sates, this new structure of academic power is realized in practice through a network of guest lectureships and visiting professorships between universities and also through the flow – from the South to the North – of students of indigenous and African descent from Bolivia, Peru, and Ecuador, who are responsible for providing theoretical support for racialized and exoticized multiculturalism in the academies.

Therefore, instead of a 'geopolitics of knowledge', I propose the task of undertaking a 'political economy' of knowledge (Mignolo, 2002). Not only because the 'geopolitics of knowledge' in the decolonial sense is a notion that is not put into practice (it rather raises a contradiction through gestures that recolonize the imaginaries and minds of intellectuals of the South), but also because it is necessary to leave the sphere of the superstructures in order to analyze the economic strategies and material mechanisms that operate behind discourses. The postcolonial discourse of North America is not only an economy of ideas, but it is also an economy of salaries, perks, and privileges that certifies value through the granting of diplomas, scholarships, and Master's degrees, and through teaching and publishing opportunities. For obvious reasons and as the crisis deepens in public universities in Latin America, this kind of structure is well suited to the exercise of patronage as a mode of colonial domination. Through the game of who cites whom, hierarchies are structured, and we end up having to consume, in a regurgitated form, the very ideas regarding decolonization that we indigenous people and intellectuals of Bolivia, Peru, and Ecuador have produced independently. And this process began in the 1970s – the rarely quoted work of Pablo González Casanova on 'internal colonialism' was published in 1969 – when Mignolo and Quijano were still militants of a positivist Marxism and a linear vision of history.

Here is an anecdote. Some time ago I wrote a political critique of the Bolivian Left for a seminar organized by an academic foundation in Mexico. The article, titled 'On the Problems of So-Called Leftists', was meant to criticize the way that the elites of the Marxist Left in Bolivia, because of their enlightenment and positivist vision, had overlooked the issue of Indian identity and the problems of decolonization, applying instead a reductionist and formulaic analysis that allowed them to facilely reproduce the cultural domination exercised by their class origin and by their proficiency in the legitimate language and Western thought. It was obvious that to do so, and to proclaim themselves spokespeople and interpreters of the demands of indigenous people, it was necessary to use obfuscating discourses. My article used the notion of 'internal colonialism' extensively in order to analyze this superiority complex of middle-class intellectuals with respect to their indigenous peers and all the implications of this fact. The irony is that later the editors of an English-language journal suggested that I correct my sources. They indicated that I should cite Quijano's concept of 'coloniality of knowledge' to make my text accessible to an audience completely unaware of the contributions of González Casanova and the Andean Oral History Workshop. I responded that I was not at fault if in 1983 Quijano had not read us – we had read him – and that my ideas about internal colonialism in terms of knowledge-power had come from a trajectory of thought that was entirely my own and had been illuminated by other readings, such as that of Maurice Halbwachs about collective memory, Frantz Fanon about the internalization of the enemy, Franco Ferraroti on life histories, and above all from the experience of having lived and participated in the reorganization of the Aymara movement and indigenous insurgency of the 1970s and 1980s (Fanon, 2004; Ferraroti, 1982; Halbwachs, 1992).

The vertical structure of this baseless pyramid that is produced by the academies of the North in their relations with the universities and intellectuals of the South expresses itself in multiple ways. For example, Quijano formulated the idea of coloniality of power in the 1990s, and Mignolo in turn created the notion of 'colonial difference', thus reappropriating Quijano's ideas and adding nuances. It is through these processes that the notions of the 'coloniality of knowledge' and the 'geopolitics of knowledge' arose. In his book about the communal system, Félix Patzi in turn relies extensively on Quijano and Mignolo, ignoring the Kataristas' ideas regarding internal colonialism, which were formulated in the 1980s and had their origins as far back as the late 1960s in the pioneering work of Fausto Reinaga (Patzi, 2004; Reinaga, 1969).

Ideas run, like rivers, from the south to the north and are transformed into tributaries of major waves of thought. But just as in the global market for material goods, ideas leave the country converted into raw material, which become regurgitated and jumbled in the final product. Thus, a canon is formed for a new field of social scientific discourse, postcolonial thinking. This canon makes visible certain themes and sources but leaves others in the shadows. Thus, Javier Sanjinés could write a whole book on mestizaje in Bolivia and completely disregard the entire Bolivian debate on this topic (Sanjinés, 2004). Thus we have cooptation and mimesis, the selective incorporation of ideas and selective approval of those that better nourish a fashionable, depoliticized, and comfortable multiculturalism that allows one to accumulate exotic masks in one's living room and to engage in absurd discussions about the future of public sector reforms. Can you believe that even the names of the ministries in the government reform of the first government of Sánchez de Lozada – including his symbolic adoption of the indigenous Vice President Cárdenas – emerged from the offices of the United Nations Development Programme and the gatherings organized by Fernando Calderón [the Bolivian 'decolonial' sociologist]?

I believe that the multiculturalism of Mignolo et al. neutralizes the practices of decolonization by enthroning within the academy a limited and illusory discussion regarding modernity and decolonization. Without paying attention to the internal dynamics of the subalterns, cooptations of this type neutralize. They capture the energy and availability of indigenous intellectuals – brothers and sisters who may be tempted to play the ventriloquist of a convoluted conceptualization that deprives them of their roots and their dialogues with the mobilized masses.

The title of this paper is 'Ch'ixinakax utxiwa'. The world of *ch'ixi* also exists.[10] Personally, I don't consider myself *q'ara* (culturally stripped and usurped by others), because I recognize my fully double origin, Aymara and European, and because I live off my own efforts. Because of this, I consider myself *ch'ixi* and consider it the most appropriate translation of the motley mix that we, who are called mestizas and mestizos, are. The word *ch'ixi* has many connotations: it is a color that is the product of juxtaposition, in small points or spots, of opposed or contrasting colors: black and white, red and green, and so on. It is this heather gray that comes from the imperceptible mixing of black and white, which are confused by perception, without ever being completely mixed. The notion of *ch'ixi*, like many others (*allqa, ayni*), reflects the Aymara idea of something that is and is not at the same time. It is the logic of the included third. A *ch'ixi* color gray is white but is not white at the same time; it is both white and its opposite, black. The *ch'ixi* stone, therefore, is hidden in the bosom of mythical animals like the serpent, the lizard, the spider, or the frog; *ch'ixi* animals belong to time immemorial, to *jaya mara*, *aymara*, to times of differentiation, when animals spoke with humans. The potential of undifferentiation is what joins opposites. And so as *allqamari* combines black and white in symmetrical perfection, *ch'ixi* combines the Indian world and its opposite without ever mixing them. But *ch'ixi's* heteronomy also alludes in turn to the idea of muddling, to a loss of sustenance and energy. *Ch'ixi* is firewood that burns very fast, that which is feeble and intermingled. It parallels, then, this fashionable notion of cultural hybridity lite conforming to contemporary cultural domination.

The notion of hybridity proposed by Néstor García Canclini is a genetic metaphor that connotes infertility (García Canclini, 1995). Yet, hybridity assumes the possibility that from the mixture of two different beings a third completely new one can emerge, a third race or social group with the capacity to merge the features of its ancestors in a harmonic and as yet unknown blend. But the mule is a hybrid that cannot reproduce. The notion of *ch'ixi*, on the contrary, amounts to the 'motley' [*abigarrada*] society of René Zavaleta and expresses the parallel coexistence of multiple cultural differences that do not extinguish but instead antagonize and complement each other. Each one reproduces itself from the depths of the past and relates to others in a contentious way.

The possibility of a profound cultural reform in our society depends on the decolonization of our gestures and acts and the language with which we name the world. The reappropriation of bilingualism as a decolonizing practice will allow for the creation of a 'we' as producers of knowledge and interlocutors who can have discussions as equals with other centers of thought and currents in the academies of our region and also of the world.

The metaphor of *ch'ixi* assumes a double and contentious ancestry, one that is denied by the processes of acculturation and the 'colonization of the imaginary' but one that is also potentially harmonious and free if we liberate our half-Indian ancestry and develop dialogical forms for the construction of 'knowledges'.

The metaphor of hybridity suggests that we can 'enter and leave modernity,' as if it were a stadium or a theater, instead of a constructive process – simultaneously objective and subjective – of habits, gestures, modes of interaction, and ideas about the world. The Indian commitment to modernity centers itself on a notion of citizenship that does not look for homogeneity but rather for difference. But at the same time, as a project in pursuit of hegemony, it has the ability to translate, in practical terms, the fields of politics and of the state, supposing a capacity to organize society in our image and likeness, to build a lasting cultural fabric, and to set legitimate and stable norms of coexistence. This implies the construction of a homeland for everyone. Eduardo Nina Qhispi, linked to the *movimiento de caciques-apoderados* from the 1920s and 1930s, formulated his utopia of the 'reinvention of Bolivia' in a context of the colonial deafness of the oligarchical elites and of ready warriors, who, on the internal front, dismantled the leadership of the communities. In this desirable society, mestizos and Indians could live together on equal terms, by adopting, from the beginning, legitimate modes of coexistence based on reciprocity, redistribution, and authority as a service. Further, in this society the Indians would expand and adopt their culturally patterned ideas of democratic coexistence and good government and admit new forms of community and mixed identities, or *ch'ixi*, and thus enter into a creative dialogue in a process of exchanging 'knowledges', aesthetics, and ethics.

In this vein, the notion of identity as territory is unique to men, and the forms of organization that were adopted by the indigenous people of Bolivia are still marked by the colonial seal of the exclusion of women. It is a project of reinvention in Bolivia that will overcome the official multiculturalism that confines and stereotypes us and that would also return us to the macho logocentrism that draws maps and establishes belonging. The notion of the identity of women, however, is similar to a fabric. Far from establishing the property and the jurisdiction of the authority of the nation – or the people, the autonomous indigenous – the feminine practice weaves the fabric of the intercultural through women's practices as producers, merchants, weavers, ritualists, and creators of languages and symbols capable of seducing the 'other' and establishing pacts of reciprocity and coexistence among different groups. This seductive labor, acculturated and surrounding women, allows for the complementing of the territorial homeland with a dynamic cultural fabric that reproduces itself and spreads until it reaches the mixed and frontier areas – the *ch'ixi* areas – and there contributes its vision of personal responsibility, privacy, and individual rights associated with citizenship. The modernity that emerges from these motley relations and complex and mixed languages – Gamaliel Churata called them 'a language with a homeland' (Churata, 1957) – is what builds the Indian hegemony to be realized in spaces that were created by the cultural invader: the market, the state, the union. In doing so, we create our own project of modernity, a more organic one than that imposed by the elites, who live through ventriloquizing concepts and theories and through academic currents and visions of the world copied from the North or tributaries from the centers of hegemonic power.

Decolonizing thinking will allow us to create a different Bolivia that is genuinely multicultural and decolonized, and part of the affirmation of this is our bilingualism, multicolored and *ch'ixi*, which projects itself as culture, theory, epistemology, and state policy and also in new definitions of well-being and development. The challenge of this new autonomy is in constructing South–South links that will allow us to break the baseless pyramids of the politics and academies of the North and that will enable us to make our own science, in a dialogue among ourselves and with the sciences from our neighboring countries, by affirming our bonds with theoretical currents of Asia and Africa – that is, to confront the hegemonic projects of the North with the renewed strength of our ancestral convictions.

## Notes

1.   Originally published in *South Atlantic Quarterly*, Volume 111, no. 1, pp. 95–109. (c), 2012, Duke University Press. All rights reserved. Republished by permission of the copyright holder, Duke University Press. www.dukeupress.edu (original Spanish published by Tinta Limon Ediciones, 2010, Buenos Aires).

2.   These were the heroes and martyrs of indigenous resistance against colonialism. Tomás Katari was an Aymara appointed as cacique to the indigenous people of Potosí, Bolivia, by the Spanish Crown. He advocated for peaceful resistance against the Spanish that could lead to a series of reforms and the establishment of a utopic Aymara society. Katari was eventually executed for his beliefs and for the actions of his followers. Tupac Amaru II (born José Gabriel Condorcanqui) was the leader of an indigenous/mestizo uprising against the Bourbon Reforms of the Spanish in 1780 in and around Cuzco, Peru (he was executed shortly thereafter). By early 1781 news of Tupac Amaru's uprising had spread to what is now Bolivia, where Julian Apasa Nina (taking the name Tupac Katari in honor of Tomás Katari and Tupac Amaru II) along with his wife, Bartolina Sisa, and Tupac Amaru's brother, Diego, laid siege to the city of La Paz for nearly six months (after which he, too, was captured and executed). For a wonderful account of the scope and context of these uprisings, see Thomson (2003), *We Alone Will Rule*. For an account of how these uprisings continue to influence contemporary Andean movements see Forrest Hylton and Sinclair Thomson, *Revolutionary Horizons: Past and Present in Bolivian Politics* (New York: Verso, 2007).

3.   Partha Chaterjee, *Our Modernity* (Rotterdam: South–South Exchange Programme for Research on the History of Development, 2007).

4.   Walter Benjamin, 'Thesis on the Philosophy of History', in *Illuminations* (New York: Schocken, 1969), 253–64.

5.   Edward Said, *Orientalism* (New York: Vintage, 1979).

6. Zero coca was a coca eradication program implemented under President Hugo Banzer Suárez.

7. This lecture was given at a time when a rupture with the crisis of the state – such as the one produced on December 18, 2005, which ended with the triumph of Evo Morales's MAS [Movimiento al Socialismo] – and the formation of the first modern government in the Americas in the hands of an indigenous person was not even thought possible.

8. Pablo González Casanova, *Sociología de la explotación* (The Sociology of Exploitation) (Mexico City: Grijalbo, 1969). Although there is no existing translation of González Casanova's book into English, an article in which he explores similar themes was published in English as 'Internal Colonialism and National Development', *Studies in Comparative International Development* 1, No. 4 (1965): 27–37.

9. Walter Mignolo, 'El potencial epistemológico de la historia oral: Algunas contribuciones de Silvia Rivera Cusicanqui' ('The Epistemological Potential of Oral History: Some Contributions by Silvia Rivera Cusicanqui'), in *Estudios e outras práticas intelectuales Latinamericanas en cultura e poder* (Studies and Other Latin American Intellectual Practices in Culture and Power), ed. Daniel Mato (Caracas: CLASCO, 2002), 201–12.

10. The following section of this paper was developed by Cusicanqui from a conference presentation that she gave in Aymara. The lack of translation for Aymara words in the following paragraphs is accounted for by the fact that she is attempting to give non-Aymara speakers a summary of the concepts that she develops. – Trans.

# References

Barragán, R. (1992) 'Entre polleras, lliqllas y ñañacas. Los mestizos y la emergencia de la tercera república' ('Between Chicken Farmers, lliqllas and ñañacas: The Mestizos and the Emergence of the Third Republic') in *Etnicidad, economía y simbolismo en los Andes*, Vol. 2, Congreso Internacional de Etnohistoria, Coroico (Ethnicity, Economy, and Symbolism in the Andes, Vol. 2, International Ethnohistorical Conference, Coroico), Silvia Arze et al. (eds) (La Paz: Hisbol-IFEA- SBH/ ASUR).

Benjamin, W. (1969) 'Thesis on the Philosophy of History', in *Illuminations*. New York: Schocken, 253–64.

Bloch, E. (1977) 'Nonsynchronism and the Obligation to Its Dialectics', trans. Mark Ritter, *New German Critique*, *11*: 22–38.

Bloch, E. (1995) *Principle of Hope*. Boston: MIT Press.

Chaterjee, P. (2007) *Our Modernity*. Rotterdam: South–South Exchange Programme for Research on the History of Development.

Churata, G. (1957) *El pez de Oro* (The Golden Fish). Cochabamba: Editorial Canata, 14.

Cusicanqui, RS. (1981) Rebelión e ideología ('Rebellion and Ideology'), *Historia Boliviana 2*: n.p.

Cusicanqui, R.S. (1987) *Oppressed But Not Defeated: Peasant Struggles Among the Aymara and Qhechwa in Bolivia*, 1900–1980. Geneva: United Nations Research Institute for Social Development.

Cusicanqui, R.S. (1989) 'El potencial epistemológico y teórico de la historia oral: De la lógica instrumental a la descolonización de la historia' ('The Epistemological and

Theoretical Potential of Oral History: From Instrumental Logic to the Decolonization of History'), *Temas Sociales 11*: 49–75.

Fanon, F. (2004) *The Wretched of the Earth*. New York: Grove Press.

Ferraroti, F. (1982) *Histoire et histoires de vie* (History and Histories of Life). Paris: Presses Universitaires de France.

García Canclini, N. (1995) *Hybrid Cultures: Strategies for Entering and Leaving Modernity*. Minneapolis: University of Minnesota Press.

González Casanova, P. (1969) *Sociología de la explotación*. Mexico: Grijalbo.

Guha, R. (1988) 'The Prose of Counterinsurgency', in *Selected Subaltern Studies Reader*. Oxford: Oxford University Press, 12–40.

Halbwachs, M. (1992) *On Collective Memory*. Chicago: University of Chicago Press.

Hylton, F. and Thomson, S. (2007) *Revolutionary Horizons: Past and Present in Bolivian Politics*. New York: Verso.

Mignolo, W. (2002) 'The geopolitics of knowledge and the colonial difference', *SAQ 101*, No. 1: 57–96.

Numhauser, P. (2005) *Mujeres indias y señores de la coca. Potosi y Cuzco en el Siglo XVI* (Indian Women and the Men of Coca: Potosi and Cuzco in the 16th Century). Madrid: Ediciones Catedra.

Patzi, F. (2004) *Sistema comunal. Una alternativa al sistema liberal* (The Communal System: An Alternative to the Liberal System). La Paz: CEEA.

Reinaga, F. (1969) *La revolución India* (The Indian Revolution). La Paz: Ediciones PIB.

Said, E. (1979) *Orientalism*. New York: Vintage.

Sanjinés, J. (2004) *Mestizaje Upside Down: Aesthetic Politics in Modern Bolivia*. Pittsburgh, PA: University of Pittsburgh Press.

Thomson, S. (2003) *We Alone Will Rule: Native Andean Politics in the Age of Insurgency*. Madison: University of Wisconsin Press.

## Silvia Rivera Cusicanqui, by Maristella Svampa[1] (Argentina)

The work of Silvia Rivera Cusicanqui (1949–), Bolivian thinker, historian and sociologist with Aymaran roots, is without doubt fundamental in Latin American studies. Even if her theoretical position could be defined as a radical subalternism, her critical gaze and her iconoclastic and irreverent style escape any attempt at labeling her with an academic classification. Together with other colleagues, around 1980, Cusicanqui founded the Workshop on Andean Oral History/Taller de Historia Oral Andina (THOA), a space to analyze the social struggles by indigenes, communitary and anarchist groups. Her book *Oppressed but Not Defeated: The Struggle of Aymara and Qhichwa Peasants, 1900–1980*, (1984), became a classic of unmissable reading for anyone who seeks to cross the threshold into the indigene struggles in Bolivia. Especially relevant are the analyses of the CSUTCB (Confederación Sindical Unica de Trabajadores de Bolivia) and the emergence of Katarismo, a powerful political and intellectual movement that reinterpreted the relationship between ethnicity and social classes. Here she also introduces an analysis of collective social agents, in terms of different temporalities and memories. While the

Aymara forces of the Altiplano are seen as returning to the long memory of the struggles (the insurrection of Tupac Katari in the eighteenth century), the forces of the Quechua-mestizo peasantry of the valleys are seen as related to the short memory of the mid-twentieth century, linked to the national and agrarian revolution (MNR's nationalist populism). This focus has been recurrently used by several researchers who seek to analyze the axis of the historical account present in Bolivia.

Among other works, 'Lxs artesanxs libertarios y la ética del trabajo'/The libertarian artisans and work ethics (1988) should be highlighted – she not only reconstructs the trade union history in the 1920s, but above all gives an account of the leading role played by women's unions. This perspective was deepened in 'Bircholas: women's work, capitalist exploitation or colonial oppression among Aymara migrants from La Paz and El Alto' (2002). Later came the books *Las fronteras de la coca: epistemologías coloniales y circuitos alternativos de la hoja de coca: el caso de la frontera boliviano-argentina* (2003), as well as *Sociology of the Image: A Vision from Andean History* (2009), and more recently, a very interesting compilation of articles entitled *Violence (Re)covered in Bolivia* (2010).

Gifted with a multi-faceted talent, Rivera has also produced videos and films, both documentary and fiction. With regard to her academic career, for two decades she was a Professor of Sociology at the Universidad Mayor de San Andrés (UMSA) in the Bolivian capital city of La Paz. She was also a visiting professor at numerous universities (Columbia and Austin, USA), UNAM (Mexico), Simón Bolívar (Quito, Ecuador), the National University of Jujuy and UNSAM (Argentina). In 1990, she received the Guggenheim Scholarship and since 1993 she is has been Professor Emeritus at UMSA.

In recent years, Rivera became a South-South network weaver, especially for post-colonial studies. Together with the Bolivian historian Rosana Barragán, she published the first compendium in Spanish on the subject, entitled *Post Colonial Debates: An Introduction to the Studies of Subalternity* (La Paz, 1997), which brings together essays by Hindu historians Ranajit Guha, Partha Chaterjee and Dispesh Chakrabarty, among others. As both authors wrote: 'It begins with the erasures and silences of the official discourse, but it advances to a reading of the insurgency from within, that is, from the notion of the insurgent community' (Cusicanqui and Barragan, 1997: 18).

Certainly Rivera's texts focus on domination, as well as the need to articulate decolonizing discourses with practices. In the analysis of this domination-insurgency dialectic, she reinterpreted a key concept: internal colonialism. Which is defined not simply as a presence throughout history, but rather as a structure of domination, that expresses itself through different configurations: 'ethnic oppression, contradictions in the processes of *mestizaje [metissage]*, the channeling and partial articulation of the democratic demands of the excluded groups through new political formations'. From a long-term perspective, internal colonialism is understood as 'a structuring framework of identities', a mode of domination, a kind of habitus internalized in subjectivity (Cusicanqui, 2010: 118).

This reformulation of internal colonialism, which operates by structuring internal subjectivity and colonial practice, appears in the brief text 'The Other Bicentennial', where she immerses us in the long memory of the struggles through

*(Continued)*

(Continued)

the figure of Tupac Katari, whose evocation is projected on the most recent cycle of popular struggles – making possible the emergence of a new government, under the leadership of Evo Morales. The long memory is reactivated and reinterpreted through the different cycles of rebellion: in 1781 defeat 'builds symbols of lasting domination in painting, through theatre, in the oral tradition'; in a short period of years (2003–2005) there was a reversal of history, that is, the victory of the rebels. In short, Cusicanqui eloquently synthesizes one of the great Latin American issues for the academy and politics: the criticism of the recurrent misrecognition of popular movements, the reluctance to consider the subordinates as full actors, and therefore, the need to think of history from below, from our specific categories.

## Note

1.    Translated by Maximiliano Salatino and revised by Fernanda Beigel.

## References

Cusicanqui, R.S. (2010) *Violencias (re) encubiertas en Bolivia*. La Paz: La mirada salvaje/Editorial Piedra Rota.
Cusicanqui, R.S. and Barragán, R. (1997) *Post Colonial Debates: An Introduction to the Studies of Subalternity*. La Paz.

# 20

# New Players Came on Stage – São Paulo Workers' Experiences, Language, and Struggles (1970–1980)[1]

*Eder Sader (Brazil)*

## Two Images

I started this study wondering about the meaning and scope of the changes that occurred in popular classes' behavior in the country's political life, particularly in São Paulo. First, I looked at some facts that I deemed evident: the number of votes that the MDB[2] received in every election since 1974 (Lamounier, 1980; Lamounier and Cardoso, 1978), the diffusion of popular movements' characteristics in neighborhoods surrounding the Greater São Paulo area, the creation of the so-called 'Cost-of-Living Movement',[3] the increase in union groups protesting the ministerial tutelary structure, the emergence of grassroots communities, and the inception of the Workers' Party. These developments all pointed to a collective protest movement against the current social order.

All these events created an image that sharply contrasted with the one commonly associated with workers. To clarify this view, I will just take advantage of some easily collected references, starting with a statement made by Fiat Brazil's general manager in the early 1970s:

> Brazilian workers' discipline, dedication to work, and enthusiasm mark a deep contrast with the outbursts and turmoil that currently besiege all developed countries in the capitalist area...[4]

This idyllic picture seemed to stem from workers' integration in the social order. In exchange for their dedication, workers enjoyed the advantages of well-being. The following statement appeared in an interview published by *Jornal do Brasil* in 1976 and was quoted by J.F. Rainho (1980:13):

> ... more concerned about having the amenities of their own homes, replacing the libertarian and propaganda meetings that they themselves [sic] organized

at the turn of the century, the television, today's Brazilian workers have joined consumer society and no longer think like the Italian pioneers – largely anarchists – who worked at factories until 1930 and took pride in their historical role.

The lightness of these generalizations deserves no comment. However, this passive and conformist image rests on a deeply rooted tradition of Brazilian political thinking – a historical montage of a paradigm that establishes the criteria used to understand the worker's mindset. Starting with Oliveira Vianna, workers' internal heterogeneity, dispersion, and fragmented behavior, showing their inability to universalize their goals, were shaped by the intrinsic characteristics of the historical building of Brazil's society, its State, and its industrialization. The results of historical experiences were viewed as developments marked by Brazil's own social structure. Therein lies the origin of this image of a class with an inability for autonomous action (Paoli and Sader, 1986).

Firstly, the defeats suffered by the workers' movement in 1964 and 1968 reinforced this image of powerlessness. For some time, Francisco Weffort's work on the strikes at Osasco and Contagem, which states that 'the workers' movement should not be considered only as something that depends on social history but also as a subject of its own history' (Weffort, 1972: 10), remained rather neglected regarding the roots of these movements. Ultimately, the military regime's consolidation in the early 1960s followed the obliteration of and silence imposed on social movements. The narratives and interpretations of that time provide nearly no information on the procedures carried out by workers. In a society propelled by the pace of capital accumulation, economists' speeches occupy the spotlight, featuring workers only as production drivers. As an example clearly illustrating the disappearance of workers from the speeches of the time, I remember a brave book entitled *A industria automovilística e a 2ª Revolução Industrial no Brasil*, written by Ramiz Gattá, a businessman who managed to delve into everything associated with that subject – industry origins, the role of several governments, banking policy variations, public debates with 'anti-industrial circles', ANFAVEA's creation,[5] arguments with FIESP,[6] clashes with farmers – without ever feeling the need to devote at least a few of those 500 pages to talk about workers.

In the meantime, decisive changes happened throughout that decade, but they unfolded with such subtlety that it would take quite some time to show them in full. In small events, until then viewed as insignificant or as repeated signs of powerlessness, new connotations started to surface.

Demonstrations that seemed unable to affect the state's institutionalization – formerly regarded as signals of political immaturity – began to take on new value as expressions of resistance, autonomy, and creativity. I believe these changes accounted for a delayed, deeper effect of the defeats in the 1960s, revealing a crisis in the political and analytical milestones that outlined the social notions on State and society in our country. Against the backdrop of this crisis, academic or activist intellectuals ceased to view the State as a privileged enclave or instrument for social changes and started to underscore a sharp division – Manichean at times – between civil society and State. Once again, I turn to Weffort:

> The increasingly generalized disappointment with the State, starting in 1964 [military coup] and particularly after 1968 [strengthening of the regime], paved the way to discovering civil society. Actually, the realization that other things, in addition to the State, mattered in politics began with the simpler facts on the life of persecuted people. In the toughest times, they had to rely on those they found around them. There no longer were there political parties to turn to or courts to trust. In hard times, the first shelter was provided by family members, followed by friends, and, in some cases, workmates. If there was any chance to defend oneself, one needed to rely on the help of a brave attorney – generally, a young, new graduate who had engaged in politics at university. What are we talking about here if we are not referring to civil society, even in its 'molecular' form of interpersonal relationship? The Catholic Church stood as the only institution with enough strength to welcome those who were persecuted. (Weffort, 1984: 93)

From this tense 'State terrorism' experience, Weffort draws the elaboration of civil society and the change in the way to approach political matters:

> We wanted to have a civil society; we needed it to defend ourselves from the monstrous State we faced. This means that if it didn't exist, we would have to invent it; it turned out to be too small, we would have to expand it […] Clearly, when I talk about 'invention' or 'expansion', I am not using these terms in the same way as false propaganda. I construe these notions as signs of values present in political action, infusing it with meaning because it sought to make them a reality. (Weffort, 1984: 95)

We found ourselves in the kind of critical times that change our own questions and the viewpoints that our society adopts to challenge itself. This is the 'invention' Weffort refers to, pointing to the realm of insights, where theoretical speculations stem from. As a result of this experience, the State ceased to be regarded as a standard to measure the relevance of every social expression (Telles, 1984).

Questions started to be raised about the potential power of social movements that could only unfold outside the State's institution. As Weffort noted, this is no longer an exclusively intellectual movement. Ideas here belong to the emergence of new collective practice models. This new appreciation of 'civil society' conveyed a change of positions and meanings in society, which took place both in thinking categories as well as in social action orientations.

If we examine the ideas formulated about workers' practices and existence conditions, we will notice a significant difference between the notions elaborated in the early and late 1970s in Brazil. In the first half of that decade, the working classes were regarded as completely subordinated to the capital rationale and to the domination of an all-powerful State. The working classes were divided by their competition in the labor market and business strategies (Bacha, 1976; Conceição Tavares, 1974; Singer, 1972), as well as fragmented by their status of rural migrants who lose their cultural bearings in the city (Berlinck, 1977; Menezes, 1976; Rodrigues, 1974), depoliticized by the actions of a State that casts aside or represses representation mechanisms (Cardoso, 1977), blindsided and subjected to massification by communication media (Chucid, 1977; Sodré, 1981). Even their survival strategies seemed to derive from capitalist proliferation: self-build, a mechanism used by the poorest population to solve its housing problem, lowered the reproduction costs of labor, enabling the reduction of real wages (Oliveira, 1987). Professional development – viewed by workers' families as a means for social mobility or just to protect themselves in a highly competitive labor market – was disseminated to such an extent that it ended up reducing qualified workers' real salaries (Paiva, 1980; Romanelli, 1978). These observations made in the field of social sciences about workers' social habits – influenced or shaped by the capital and its State rationale – match the statements by workers and activists.

By the end of that decade, several works started to describe the emergence of popular labor movements that arose with a sense of autonomy and protest against the establishment. This 'new union movement' strove to remain independent from the State and political parties (Paoli, Sader and Telles, 1984); 'new neighborhood grassroots movements' rose as a result of self-organization, reclaiming rights without the favor exchanges of the past (Caccia Bava, 1980; Evers, 1982; Singer and Brant, 1980; Telles, 1981). This 'new sociability' surfaced at grassroots associations, with solidarity and mutual support opposing the values of an inclusive society (Betto, 1981; Boff, 1979; Perani, 1978; Singer and Brant, 1980); these 'new social movements' politicized areas formerly silenced in the private sector (Paoli, 1985). New collectives seemed to emerge, creating their own space and requiring new categories to be understood (Paoli, 1982).

This calls for a broader discussion. However, for the purpose of this chapter, where I just try to outline the circumstances and characteristics of the set-up of my study subject, this description should suffice to understand why, half way through the first formulation, I realized that this was *a transition from order legitimization models to contentious schemes*. I would be unable to explain that phenomenon as such because I was not looking just at a breakthrough in order legitimization models. Indeed, I was witnessing *the emergence of a new popular class set-up on the public stage*. In other words, the late 1970s saw the rise of a new class configuration – not only as compared to the models in place at the beginning of that decade but also, and mostly, as compared to earlier historical periods. Taking into account the places where these social actors emerged; their issues, values, and language, as well as the characteristics of the social actions that served as their cradle, it seemed clear that this was *a new type of workers' expression*, contrasting with previous mo(ve)ments in Brazil: the libertarian one of the early decades of the twentieth century (Fausto, 1976; Foot Hardman, 1983; Simão, 1976) and the populist approach that arose after 1945 (Rodrigues, 1966; Weffort, 1975). My research should explain then the nature of this new set-up.

## Some Considerations

Social movements that took the public stage (and changed it) in the late years of the 1970s brought new schemes for popular classes' living conditions and social expression. Their common traits make it possible to talk about a new class configuration, which stands out if compared to the prevailing scheme before 1964.

The experience of the authoritarian period and self-organization practices bred a profound distrust of any institutionalization escaping the direct control of the people involved, as well as a deep, renewed appreciation of the autonomy of every movement. As a result, the diversity of movements, produced by the different conditions engulfing every one of them, translated into a resolve to maintain that autonomy.

The condemnation spurred by the instituted form of political practice, regarded as tampering, found its reverse side in the willingness of people to 'own their own history'. This means mainly taking command of the decisions that shape their living conditions. Thus, they broadened their own notion of politics, as they politicized multiple areas of daily activities.

Relying on the values of justice, as opposed to the inequalities prevailing in society, solidarity among the oppressed, workers, and the poor, as well as dignity, built with their own struggle in order to recognize their value, they turned the affirmation of their own identity into a value that precedes rational calculations to secure concrete goals. The strikes at the end of the decade were the key developments in the elaboration of their history, which provided a sense of social transformation. At the same time, they instituted the conception that their rights would only be conquered by social struggle.

However, we have noted earlier that diversity is a key feature of these social movements. It proves hard, therefore, to consider a homogenous model or a scheme that represents them and serves as a paradigm of popular classes' imaginary. The identities developed in mothers' clubs, factory groups, 'true unions', health commissions – while variable and mutually influential – preserved their diversity. The decisive events where they found each other and which became 'merging moments' (Kowarick, 1982) created new collective identity forms that provided broader common references and stronger ties.[7] Basically, this is what happened in the 1979–1980 strikes. Yet, the singularity of the multiple movement formats did not vanish on this account.

Thus, in this new set-up of popular classes, we find different expressions that are linked to other stories and experiences. This can be illustrated from the cases I've followed in depth, which serve as empirical elements of my work. At mothers' clubs, women's practices conveyed the appreciation of primary relationships and their own affirmation of sisterhood conquests. In the case of health commissions, there was an appreciation of the achievements made in the spaces of public services. In the unions' opposition, we saw the growing value of factory-based organization and struggle. In fact, São Bernardo's union movement showed the valuation of unions' recovery as a public labor space and the acknowledgement of strikes and meetings as political forms of assertion.

Popular classes organize themselves in a very large array of levels: according to people's living or working place or around a community principle that brings them together. Every organization scheme features an obsessive expression of its own autonomy. This is conveyed in different ways, but 'direct actions' stand out as a means to express their wills. As a result, they are very intermittent, changing, flexible, and unstable.

Social movements were one of the main elements of the political transition that unfolded between 1978 and 1985. They illustrated deep trends in society, underscoring the ground lost by the established political system. They showed the huge distance separating established political mechanisms and social life forms. They stood as much more than that, fueling the crisis and driving a social transformation. They held the promise of a radical political life renewal.

These movements also pointed to a new politics, built on daily-life situations and heralding a new notion of politics based on stakeholders' direct engagement. They reclaimed democracy, linking it to social life domains, where the working population is directly involved: in factories, unions, public services, and neighborhood administrations. They clearly showed that there were actually dark places, neglected by usual discourses and remarkably absent at the established stages of public life. These movements provided a public space that went beyond the political representation system. With their organization and fighting schemes, these movements pushed the boundaries of politics. They reflected the autonomy of collective actors seeking the control of their living conditions, opposing the established power institutions.

Today, when the country's political transition takes place, what used to be a promise has become history. The issues at stake were somehow resolved. Blurred aspirations of social justice and democracy – present in society – were addressed and formulated in a different way by the Democratic Alliance that built the so-called 'Brazilian New Republic'. Starting in 1982, with the establishment of the first PMBD state governments,[8] a new State approach began to work on recognizing the legitimacy of popular organizations, incorporating them into its own dynamics.

This is not the place to analyze the new regime and its contradictions as regards the preservation of an authoritarian system and the already accomplished liberalization. Neither is it the time to look at its stance when it comes to the proclamation of social justice goals and the predominance of large capitals, which leads to a policy of sacrifice for workers. Suffice it to say that, one way or another, this project won the decisive political battles waged between 1982 and 1984. Delving into these battles would become the topic of another story.

What matters here is that, in this regard, the political project implied by the late 1970s' social movement suffered a defeat. As a result, nowadays, its promises are often viewed as illusions, mystifications, or assessment errors. Truth be told, every past representation involves 'illusions', as, sharing the time frame of the events it represents, it cannot account for them entirely, for these developments continue to unfold, and the needs for action leads it to assume a general notion of their meaning. Indeed, while we may no longer harbor any of the 'illusions' of several years ago, we cannot erase the fact that, in fact, those movements did hold those promises and carry those meanings as possibilities in an ongoing scenario.

These projects led to decisive confrontations when they were barely turning into political agents. The rhythm of their history differed from that of established politics, and the latter established the terms of the debate. Driven to political battles before their time, they showed their immaturity as power alternatives in the political representation realm. Nonetheless, the political movements that emerged in the 1970s, with the expression that meant that they established themselves, became a component of the country's political life. Their promises, imprinted in the collective memory, can be updated. In fact, they are a condition for the existence of an effective democracy among us.

## Notes

1.   Fragment from the book published in Spanish: Eder Sader (1988), Cuando nuevos personajes entraron en escena: experiencia, lenguaje y luchas de los trabajadores del Gran São Paulo (1970–1980), in Gerónimo de Sierra (Ed.) (1994) *Democracias Emergentes en América del Sur*, Mexico: UNAM. Translated by Mariana Donaldini, revised and annotated by Breno Bringel.

2.   [Note from reviser: the Brazilian Democratic Movement (Movimento Democrático Brasileiro, in Portuguese) is a Brazilian centre-right political party. Founded in 1965, one year after the military coup in Brazil, it was in its origins a kind of catch-all party which served as an institutional and formal umbrella for opponents of the military regime, ranging from liberal conservatives and Christian democrats from parties like the Christian Democratic Party and the Social Democratic Party to former labourists, socialists and communists.]

3.   [Note from the reviser: the Cost-of-Living Movement was created in 1973 from the confluence between Mothers Clubs and Basic Ecclesial Communities (BECs) of the Catholic Church in the southern suburbs of São Paulo. Among its main claims were: an increase in wages above the increase in the cost of living; the freezing of prices of basic products; and an immediate emergency salary bonus for all categories of workers.]

4.   Quoted in the Resolutions of the First Congress of Metallurgical Workers of São Bernardo do Campo in 1974.

5. [Note from the reviser: founded in 1956, the National Association of Motor Vehicle Manufacturers is the entity that brings together motor vehicle and agricultural machinery manufacturers with industrial facilities and production in Brazil.]

6. [Note from the reviser: FIESP is the Federation of Industries of the State of São Paulo, the largest professional association in Brazilian industry. Founded in 1931, it encompasses over 130 trade unions that represent over 150,000 Brazilian companies.]

7. I use the concept of 'merging moments' in the sense given by Lucio Kowarick, as 'conjunctural estuaries' where parallel struggles flow, as diversities that temporarily present agglutinating elements. This concept 'is not a mere compendium of previous experiences. Their moment of fusion represents something new when social forces are redefined, generating spaces for future developments' (Kowarick, 1982, p. 25).

8. [Note from the reviser: The Brazilian Democratic Movement Party (PMDB) was founded in 1980 as a successor to MDB – see Note 2 above.]

# References

Bacha, E. (1976) *Os mitos de una década*, Paz e Terra, São Paulo.

Berlinck, M. (1977) *Marginalidade social e relações de clase em São Paulo*, Vozes, Rio de Janeiro.

Betto, F. (1981) *O que é comunidades eclesial de base*, Brasiliense, São Paulo.

Boff, L. (1979) 'A influência política das comunidades eclesiais de base', *Religião e Sociedade*, n. 4.

Caccia Bava, S. (1980) '*Movimientos reivindicativos urbanos na Grande São Paulo: um estudo de caso*', Relatorio à Fapesp, São Paulo.

Cardoso, F.H. (1977) *O modelo político brasileiro*, Difel, São Paulo.

Chucid, S. (1977) *Televisão e consciência de classe*, Vozes, Rio de Janeiro.

Conceição Tavares, M. (1974) *Da substituição de importações ao capitalismo financiero*, Zahar, Rio de Janeiro.

Evers, T. (1982) 'Movimentos de bairro em São Paulo: o caso do "Movimento de Custo da Vida"', *Alternativas populares da democracia*, Vozes, Rio de Janeiro.

Fausto, B. (1976) *Trabalho urbano e conflicto social*, Difel, São Paulo.

Foot Hardman, F. (1983) *Nem pátria, nem patrão*, Brasiliense, São Paulo.

Gattás, R. (1981) *A indústria automobilística e a segunda revolução industrial no Brasil: origens e perspectivas*. São Paulo: Prelo.

Kowarick, L. (1982) '*Os caminos do encontro – reflexões sobre as lutas sociais em São Paulo*', CEDEC.

Lamounier, B. (ed.) (1980) *Voto de desconfiança*, Vozes, Rio de Janeiro.

Lamounier, B. and Cardoso, F.H. (eds.) (1978) *Os partidos e as eleições no Brasil*, Paz e Terra, São Paulo.

Menezes, C. (1976) *A mudança: análise da ideologia de um grupo de migrantes*, Imago, Rio de Janeiro.

Oliveira, F. (1987) *O elo perdido*, Brasiliense, São Paulo.

Paiva, V. (1980) 'Estado, Sociedade e educação no Brasil', in: *Encontros com a civilização Brasileira*, n. 22.

Paoli, M.C. (1982) 'Os trabalhadores urbanos nas falas dos outros', *Comunicação*, n. 7, Museu Nacional UFRJ.

Paoli, M.C. (1985) 'Mulheres: o lugar, a imagen o movimiento', in: *Perspectivas antropológicas da mulher*, n. 4.

Paoli, M.C. and Sader, E. (1986) 'Sobre "clases populares" no pensamento sociológico brasileiro', in R. Cardoso (ed.) *Aventura antropológica*, Paz e Terra, São Paulo.

Paoli, M.C., Sader, E. and Telles, V.S. (1984) 'Pensando a classe operária: os trabalhadores sujeitos ao imaginário acadêmico', *Revista Brasileira de História*, n.6.

Perani, C. (1978) 'CEBs: alguns questionamentos', *Cadernos do CEAS*, n. 56, Salvador.

Rainho, L.F. (1980) *Os peões do grande ABC*, Vozes, Rio de Janeiro.

Rodrigues, L.M. (1966) *Sindicalismo e conflicto industrial no Brasil*, Difel, São Paulo.

Rodrigues, L.M. (1974) *Trabalhadores, sindicatos e industrialização*, Brasiliense, São Paulo.

Romanelli, O. (1978) *História da educação no Brasil, 1930/1973*, Vozes, Rio de Janeiro.

Simão, A. (1976) *Sindicato e Estado*, Ática, São Paulo.

Singer, P. (1972) 'O Milagre Brasileiro: causas e consequências', *Cadernos Cebrap*.

Singer, P. and Brant, V.C. (1980) *São Paulo: o povo em movimento*, Vozes, Rio de Janeiro.

Sodré, M. (1981) *O monopolio da fala*, Vozes, Rio de Janeiro.

Telles, V.S. (1981) 'Movimientos populares nos anos 70; formas de organização e expressão', *Relatorio à Fapesp*, São Paulo.

Telles, V.S. (1984) '*A experiência do autoritarismo e práticas instituinte*', Universidade de São Paulo (USP), Masters Thesis.

Weffort, F. (1972) 'Participação e conflicto industrial: Contagem e Osasco – 1968', *Cadernos Cebrap*, n.5.

Weffort, F. (1975) *Sindicato e política, Tese de libre docência*, USP, São Paulo.

Weffort, F. (1984) *Por que democracia?*, Brasiliense, São Paulo.

# Eder Sader, by Maria da Glória Gohn (Brazil)[1]

Eder Simão Sader (São Paulo, 1941–1988) was an activist and vital intellectual in Brazil from his student days. During the military regime (1964–1984) he participated in the creation of POLOP (Marxist Revolutionary Organization – Labor Policy). Always in the countercurrent of dominant tendencies on the Brazilian Left, Sader questioned centralism and orthodoxian Marxist approaches that saw politics as a reflex of the structural determinations of capitalism. Persecuted by the military regime, he was exiled in Chile and France (where he taught at the University Paris VIII), between 1971 and 1979. Upon the general amnesty, he was allowed to return to Brazil in the late 1970s, when he participated in the founding of the Workers' Party (PT) and taught at the University of São Paulo (USP).

The text included in this volume, taken from 'When New Players Come on Stage', is the result of his doctoral dissertation at the USP, written colloquially and, at the same time, with great theoretical and methodological rigor. The field of observation selected by Sader includes a crucial period in the Brazilian history of the twentieth century, the 1970s and 1980s, a moment of resistance against the military regime. His focus fell on the city of São Paulo and its surroundings, where new groups emerged in the struggle for the re-democratization. The saga of popular movements is portrayed along an original thread, in terms of sociological interpretation. For him, these movements created a new social and historical subject, collectivity, from the political and social practice.

The collective actions are analyzed according to the reconfigurations of the collective actors, focusing on their trajectory, articulations, and 'discursive matrices'. In doing so, light was shed on the new configurations in the struggles of workers and the inhabitants of peripheral regions. The daily life of these workers is observed according to the dimensions of their way of living in the workplace and in the neighborhood, organized within associations, unions and religious institutions. On the other hand, the process of social reproduction is analyzed in the struggle for housing, in public spaces and in the re-socialization of migrants. These processes are not seen as a mere reproduction of determinations of capitalist structures already given, but rather as the construction of strategies of resistance, given by the formulation of new notions of law and social justice. Hence, Sader presents us with a new way of looking at Brazilian politics, through the politicization of daily life, the construction of collective identities and the possibilities of building democracy from these processes.

It is interesting to observe that, in the presentation of the book, Sader mentions in gratitude, the importance of previous studies published in the journal *Desvios*[2] between 1982 and 1985 where 'the theme of social movements was often associated with issues of autonomy, institutionalization, possibilities of a new political practice and the pathways of the Brazilian transition' (Sader, 1988: 22). This indicates that his work was the result of a collective debate where themes and propositions were debated highlighting the very notion of subject and autonomy – which he uses in the sense given by Castoriadis. The autonomous subject is the one capable of reworking external determinations in view of what he defines as his will. In this sense, these subjects are agents of the construction of new meanings attributed to their living conditions – fundamental interpretation exercises for social and individual change.

Eder's contribution is the main bibliographical reference on the studies on the so-called 'movement era' of the 1970s–1980 in Brazil and in Latin America. It is a watershed in the field, and a theoretical-methodological new paradigm for thinking about reality from the experience of the subjects on the scene. Its relevance is not only as an interpretation of a past time. It is extremely topical to understanding current Brazil, especially after June 2013, when the 'newest' players came on stage, with languages, representations, ideologies and practices different from what had existed until recently. After Sader's work, social movement studies in Latin America expanded its focus, with diverse discursive matrices as well as new theoretical-methodological possibilities to think about social change and the emergence of collective actors.

## Notes

1.   Translated by Marcia Rangel and revised by Fernanda Beigel and Breno Bringel

*(Continued)*

(Continued)

2.     Eder Sader was one of the founders of the journal *Desvios*, which in its first issue presented an article discussing '11 Thesis on Autonomy'. The focus of reflection in the journal in those times was the analysis of the new popular social movements with an autonomous dynamic. The journal pledged for the need to rethink the contemporary theoretical and political references that evidently were unable to explain phenomena like the new popular associativism in peripheral neighbourhoods, and the new unionism of the São Paulo ABC region (Santo André, São Bernardo do Campo and São Caetano do Sul).

## Reference

Sader, Eder (1988). *Quando novos personagens entraram em cena: Experiências e lutas dos trabalhadores da Grande São Paulo 1970–80*. Rio de Janeiro: Ed Paz e Terra.

# 21

# Latin American Feminisms and Their Transition to the New Millennium (A Personal Political Reading)[1]

*Virginia Vargas (Peru)*

## A Glimpse at the Feminist Process in the Region: Actors, Strategies and Performance Spaces

Second-wave feminist movements have probably been the most significant subversive phenomena of the twentieth century, strongly questioning the monolithic and hegemonic thought on human relations and the sociopolitical, economic, cultural and sexual contexts in which they developed. Latin American feminisms have been a key and active part of this process in the region.

Latin American feminisms largely progressed at different paces at the end of the 1970s, becoming widespread in all countries of the region during the 1980s. Their emergence paralleled the expansion of a large, heterogeneous, popular women's movement, representing the different forms in which women were beginning to understand, connect and perform with regard to their subordinate and excluded status. Within this heterogeneity, during the early years of the movement's expansion, several basic branches particularly managed to convey the specific, different ways in which women constructed identities, interests and proposals. One was the feminist stream, in the strict sense of the term, which initiated a fast-paced process that challenged women's position in sexual and social arrangements, leading to a subsequent struggle to change the conditions of women's subordination and exclusion, both at the public and private spheres. The second branch included poor urban women who entered the public space through politicization of their traditional roles, confronting them and expanding their content to question the private sphere. The third stream were women in more traditional and formal political participation spaces such as political parties and trade unions, who prompted a comprehensive questioning process and pursued autonomous organization within these traditional spaces of male legitimacy. In the 1990s, these branches multiplied in many other spaces.

Each of these offshoots developed its own objectives alongside interaction and confrontation dynamics. They also outlined diverse, sometimes conflicting interests, albeit at times largely converging. This plurality of processes adopted different dynamics and strategies, in response to the specific contexts in which they unfolded. Their interaction also underwent changes. Initial defensive and tight relationships became more flexible and diversified so that militants often felt themselves part of or represented by more than one space. An early lesson learned from this flexibility involved recognizing that feminist struggles may take different starting points to question women's subordination and create movements.

The feminist branch, drawing on previous streams and expanding itself with them while keeping its own development forms and spaces, extends unequally but consistently in the region. It initially gained ground in Brazil, Mexico, Peru, Colombia, Argentina, Chile and Uruguay, as well as in the Spanish-speaking Caribbean, particularly the Dominican Republic and Puerto Rico and, later, Cuba. By the middle of the decade, it found an echo in Ecuador, Bolivia, Paraguay and Costa Rica and, towards the end of the decade, it had expanded to other Central American countries. Thus, towards the end of the 1980s, it had reached all the countries in the region with varying degrees of intensity. While trying to respond to the particular and heterogeneous characteristics of the different Latin American nations, it has managed to develop certain shared features and dynamics: at the outset, it comprised mainly women from a broad middle class; plus a significant portion were left-wing, who quickly challenged the former for their resistance to take a more complex view on the multiple forms of subordination of people and, specifically, of women.

Of these initial influences, feminisms, now without 'categorization' – socialist, popular or revolutionary were the early labels – retained a subversive, long-term transformation perspective and a commitment to unite struggles for transforming female subordination with demands for social and political transformations. It was not always easy. Seeking and constructing a discourse of its own always poses a challenge to a movement, since it responds to context-specific potentialities and limitations. These searches were reflected in the content of feminisms' struggles, in their articulations with large popular women's movements and their increased knowledge production, raising awareness of new 'knowledges' from a personal and collective experience. They also translated into an early differentiation, within the feminist nuclei, expressed as 'two forms of existence': feminist work centers and as part of a broad, informal, mobilized, street feminist movement. Thus, two distinct dynamics of 'feminist identity' converged: professional activists and militants of a movement in the process of formation. Both dynamics largely consolidated their forms of existence and gave rise to collectives, networks, dates, regional encounters, feminist calendars, rituals, symbologies and subjectivities, increasingly shared by all feminisms in the region. The subsequent impact on academia, through 'gender studies' and 'feminist studies', drew from and boosted feminist strategies and the production of knowledge on women's reality, their insertion in society and their increasingly broad forms of resistance.

Throughout this process, the Latin American and Caribbean Feminist Encounters held since 1981 – every two years at first and, then, every three years – were meeting points of crucial importance for new knowledge production and to reinforce the new paradigm by linking experiences and strategies, making them collective, and communicating advances, tensions, conflicts, ideas and knowledge arising from the different feminist searches in the region. Thus, feminism as an organization and a theoretical-political proposal expanded at the national level, while, at the same time, a regional articulation developed that strengthened strategies and discourses and emphasized the historical international character of first-wave feminism.

Knowledge production and 'new knowledge' creation was a substantial part of feminist development. Since its inception, the movement not only attempted to draw attention to the reality of women's subordinate status, but, in doing so, this led to, as Mary Carmen Feijoo puts it, a set of epistemological ruptures and the creation of new paradigms and new interpretative guidelines around reality. This resulted in the development of new worldviews 'which, rather than add women's issues to the traditional fields of thought begin to deconstruct and reconstruct the field of knowledge from a feminist perspective' (Feijoo, 1996: 229). This particular form of production of knowledge or 'knowledges', from the militant experience and from subjectivity, expresses what Richards calls a pluridimensional feminist theory which crosses the construction of objects (knowledge production) with subject formation (new subjectivity policies that are reinvented around the difference), multiplying their intervention paths (Richards, 2000: 236).

From the beginning, feminisms advanced proposals that linked women's struggles with the struggle for democratic 'requalification' and/or recovery. More specifically, in the struggles against dictatorships, feminisms started linking the absence of democracy in the public arena with their conditions in the private sphere. It is not by chance that the slogan used by Chilean feminists in their struggle against dictatorship, 'democracy in the country and at home', was fervently adopted by all Latin American feminist movements, since it articulated the different dimensions it sought to transform and expressed the political nature of the personal, a fundamental contribution of second-wave feminism.

The main concern of the feminist movements of the eighties basically aimed to recover the difference of what it meant to be a woman in an oppression experience, to reveal the political nature of women's subordination in the private domain, its persistence and its effects on their presence, visibility and participation in the public domain. By politicizing the private, feminists acknowledged 'the discomfort of women' in that space (Tamayo, 1997: 1), creating new categories of analysis, new visibilities and even new languages to name what until then had remained unnamed: domestic violence, sexual harassment, rape in marriage, feminization of poverty, etc., which were some of the new signifiers that feminism placed at the center of democratic debates. Hence, feminists of the 1980s, as Nancy Fraser would put it (referring to violence against women, but with wider validity), questioned the established discursive limits, politicized issues until then depoliticized, and created new audiences for their discourses and new spaces and institutions in which these opposing interpretations could develop to reach wider audiences (Fraser, 1994).

These processes were accompanied by the development of a strong identity politics, a driving factor of feminist strategies in this first stage. An early and significant recognition of the political autonomy of the movement placed an emphasis on the defense of its own space and discourse, an emphasis that was characteristic of and necessary for a developing movement with weak negotiations with the State, strong tensions with political parties, and which defended itself from invisibilization attempts and sought to impact the social arena with its own discourse. However, this identity politics was constantly interspersed with the search for new, more flexible forms of inclusion and interaction with social reality. This identity politics became more flexible and complex as more complex and relational definitions of autonomy gained ground.

The 1990s posed new and intricate scenarios that influenced the development of feminisms and their transformation strategies. These scenarios were marked by the globalization process, with its ambivalent and contradictory effects, and the more negative dynamics of which were reinforced and accelerated in the context of neoliberal policies, while its more positive and articulatory dynamics were favored by the new democratic recovery–transition–construction scenarios in the region. Economic, political, social and cultural globalization, with its tremendous threats and promises (Waterman, 1998), opened up new fields of action for social movements and feminisms and new landscapes of struggle for citizenship rights, exposing the transformations of the nation-states and increasing penetration into global spaces. These dynamics unfolded in the new scenarios resulting from globalization and drew both on the global dynamics driven by social movements and the global space opened by the United Nations, which developed new global agendas throughout the 1990s in its Summits and World Conferences on topics relevant to contemporary democratic life. A significant sector of feminist organizations was active in 'disputing' content and perspectives at each of these international conferences. Thus, feminists became fundamental actors in the construction of democratic spaces in regional and global civil societies.

At the same time, at the regional level, the spread of democracy as a system of government instead of dictatorships, the attempts at modernization of nation-states and reassessment of existing democracies created, by the end of the 1980s, a new cultural and political climate. In the process of completing the unfinished project of modernity and faced with the demands of transactional powers to include women in this modernization, governments made women's 'recognition' a pivotal part of their domestic policies. However, this recognition did not translate into the redistribution either of power or resources.

Many feminist expressions took up the fight for the expansion of democracy, with women included, as a key strategy, broadening the spectrum of their alliances with civil societies and social movements with similar strategies and, unprecedently, also with the State. However, they had different perspectives (or at least they attempted to, without always succeeding). For civil society – and feminists within it – the democratic perspective and the focus on rights appeared as a conflicting terrain of dispute, as 'interpretation wars' (Slater, 1998) between civil society and the State, faced with the latter's hegemonic, partial and still exclusionary discourses. Feminisms sought, at least theoretically, not only access to equality but also recognition of diversity and difference, access not only to existing rights but also to the process of permanently discovering and expanding the contents of these rights through the struggle of male and female actors. The struggle for the recognition of sexual and reproductive rights, as not only women's rights but also as a constitutive part of the construction of citizenship, illustrates this process.

## Continuity and Change

All these processes and rapid changes in regional and global dynamics strongly impacted feminisms. In the 1990s, they became more diverse, extending their presence and influences, and expanding to: '... a broad, heterogeneous, polycentric, multifaceted and polyphonic field of discourse and action. The spaces multiplied where women who called themselves feminists acted or could act ... caught up not only in classically politi-cal struggles, but also simultaneously involved in disputes over mean-ings, definitions, in discursive struggles, and in essentially cultural battles' (S. Álvarez, 1998: 298).

During the 1990s, feminisms were thus 'in transition' towards new forms of existence that expressed themselves in varying spaces and with different dynamics. A first approach to these involves the spaces from which discourses were shaped and feminist strategies deployed: civil soci-ety, interactions with States, participation with other political spaces or movements, academia, and the so-called 'cultural sector'. Some groups expressed themselves from an identity perspective: as black, lesbian, indigenous, or young women. Yet others focused on specific themes, creating nuclei and movements, and regional thematic networks (health, human rights, violence, among the most developed). These variations of feminist approach spread at local, national, regional and/or global levels.

The terrain from which interactions within the social public sphere and the political public arena unfolded also changed, along with the changes in context and the modification of feminist organizations' forms of existence. Many of the organizations that, in the 1980s, had managed to combine movementism activism with the creation of work centers or 'non-governmental organizations' (hereinafter NGOs) began to emerge as feminist 'institutionality'. Its extension and visibility in relation to other feminist dynamics and institutions has been critically pointed to by vari-ous authors (S. Álvarez, 1998; Lang, 1997), as the 'NGO-ization' process of the feminist movement.

Another significant change was the professionalization of some feminist issues, such as reproductive health and reproductive and sexual rights. Violence against women, including domestic and sexual violence, has been acknowledged by all states in the region. Women raised their voices regarding other current, critical topics, such as human rights. Many feminists, through their NGOs and regional networks, assumed a profile as experts in the rights' perspective, which usually oriented their interventions in the political public sphere, creating specific movements and a new institutionality around this and other issues.

In short, this 'institutionality' deeply modified the dynamics and perspectives of the work centers/NGOs of the 1980s. Initially developed in an atmosphere of solidarity and proximity to social organizations, collective mobilizations and collective pressure actions related to the issues 'in dispute', changes in social and economic contexts and cultural climates during this period also influenced their orientation and dynamics, giving way to a more efficient, effective institutionalized form of existence. This led to improved proposals and professionalization as well as a certain influence on the State, albeit without reaching – according to some – 'macro' spaces and issues and thus losing in the process – according to others – the creative, innovative and bold attributes of street protests that marked their existence and visibility in previous decades.

During the 1990s, these processes, which contain multiple meanings, began to be perceived exclusively and in a polarized way as the tension between 'the autonomous' and 'the institutionalized'. Indeed, an a priori approach could reveal two major, apparently opposite trends. The matter in dispute between them is the content of feminist autonomy as movementism expression, while the tension point lies in the institutionalization of important sectors of feminisms either working in feminist organizations or supporting the institutionalization of women's gains. The first trend is determined on the grounds of primitive feminist practices, fostering a strong identity politics, rejecting the possibility of negotiating with the political public sphere, whether at national or global level. The second, along a continuum full of doubts, seems to assume the importance of negotiating with society and the State. Referring to Chile, but with a broader scope, Richards defines this process as the retreat of militant feminism from political mobilization spheres towards two main areas of institutionalization of practices and knowledge gained by women: NGOs and gender studies programs at universities.

However, they are not unambiguous processes. The conflicting diversity of feminist strategies is also reflected within the wide 'institutionalized' spectrum. Hence, while some favor the relationship and outline their visibility in relation to their negotiation capability with the State or their ability to assume the execution of governmental plans and programs; others shape it with regard to their ability to influence monitoring and accountability processes; and yet others according to the possibility of strengthening a feminist pole from within civil society, able to raise challenging perspectives to actually existing democracies and reinforcing articulations and alliances with other expressions of democratic and identity movements. In addition, many others seek to maintain the difficult balance between two or more possibilities.

Both positions – autonomous and institutional – additionally pose their own risks. While one of them entails the risk of isolation, the other carries the risk of what many female authors have considered the depoliticization of feminist strategies, by making the professional displace and replace the militant and by the operative becoming more important than the discursive (Richard, 2000: 230). Ungo acknowledges this when he states that 'these two opposite politics clearly and tensely coexist within the feminist movement, but they are not the only ones, and the debate is a complex thing now that there is a risk of new authoritarianisms shutting down all communications' (Ungo, 1998: 184). These stances and tensions still manifest themselves in the new millennium, albeit in less antagonistic ways, slowly clearing the way for the recognition of more complex dynamics and realities, and of the risks respectively involved in both perspectives.

To support democracy and institutionality placed feminisms at the center of a historical tension that was already a long-time concern of Tilman Evers that arose from the recognition that movements are permanently facing the dilemma of gaining certain power spaces within dominant structures at the risk of remaining subordinated, or of autonomously sustaining an identity without negotiating, while also running the risk of remaining weak and marginal (Evers, 1984). This tension marked the feminist movements of the nineties in a more concrete and complex way and its extent has additionally unveiled the ambivalent and contradictory content of feminist strategies.

This tension has been analyzed from a number of different viewpoints. María Luisa Tarres (1993) describes it as a difficult balance between ethics and negotiation. For her part, Schild highlights the ambiguous and contradictory character of feminist strategies (Schild, 1998), which, on the one hand, are oriented towards effecting transformations that bring women closer to equality within actually existing democracies while, at the same time, attempting to subvert, expand and radicalize democratic systems. In reference to the Chilean case, this author analyzes how feminist strategies can simultaneously confront and reproduce dominance concepts when articulating with the hegemonic project of social and economic modernization that promotes a particular conception of citizenship: as an individual access to the market and within minimal conceptions of citizenship.

The impact of this tension or power 'knotty point' (Kirkwood, 1985) has translated into a certain 'technification' of feminist agendas – the result of which was that the most dealt-with feminist issues often facilitated negotiations with the public sphere, weakening contents seeking to strengthen democratic civil societies and effecting cultural political transformations.

This may account for the fact that one of the most analyzed or ideologized aspects within this tension centers around the (autonomous) relationship with the State and the contents of feminist agendas. In this regard, we once again find different and varying positions at both ends, ranging from those that regard with suspicion any governmental effort to take up a proposal on the feminist agenda to those who demand the 'subsequent' incorporation of the entire agenda. The more radical stances reject any interaction with the State, claiming loss of control over feminist agendas by allowing the use of feminist knowledge and of the work carried out by women's organizations, in what is considered an undeniable process of system integration (Lidid, 1997), giving way to an 'experts' feminism' that has allowed that 'a large part of the feminist movement is losing strength, entering into agreements with power structures, with the subsequent weakening of its rebellious nature' (E. Álvarez, 1997: 34), concluding that 'our fight to change the world, must now prove to be acceptable and legitimate within the established order' (Bedregal, 1997: 51). Pisano is much more categorical: 'Those who view women within power structures as a sign of progress and change are not taking into account that the dominance system remains unaffected and that women's access to power from within the feminine does not modify it. Gender relations may change, but this does not imply a change in the patriarchal system' (Pisano, 1997: 65).

Many other critical stances, while not rejecting the possibility of interaction with public spaces, caution against the risks of an 'amorphous' relationship with the State that fails to take into account, as stated by

Tamayo, the ambivalence and adverse effects of disciplining and censoring women and their movements with regard to key feminist and democratic issues, without practices which ensure their essential rights and freedom, and with no citizenship mechanisms to control and effectively influence State activity (Tamayo, 1997: 2). According to this author, this has contributed to generating a number of agents who become involved in disciplinary orientations of women's lives. In this regard, Barrig points out:

> if it is a matter of identifying a line (between civil society and State) it would be drawn higher up than feminists' position regarding national states, because we would be dealing with a deeper and maybe more dangerous shift of a renovated feminism and, on certain occasions, almost hegemonic, towards a technocratic vision and action which lack the political mark which the persistent feminist memory insists on recovering. (Barrig, 1999: 25)

Similarly, in their analysis of the Brazilian case, Shumaher and Vargas argue that:

> if we refer to public policies in the strict sense, understanding it as a series of interlinked measures that represent direct government actions in particular areas which aim to intervene in specific social realities, then we must accept that the agenda of the Councils was limited to targeted interventions and localized actions that did not lead to the implementation of public policies. (Shumaher and Vargas, 1993: 14)

Feminists Vargas and Olea in 1998, Abrcinskas in 2000, Birgin in 1999, Guerrero and Ríos in 2000 and Montaño in 1998 also reflected on these contradictions.

Thus, it would seem that, as indicated by Barrig and Vargas in the case of Peru, but with a broader scope, a certain spontaneous pragmatism has prevailed in feminist strategies, and the places and positionings from which feminists influence, agree or collaborate with governments have sometimes been uncertain. Apparently, without a transition between the feminist collective identity and its 'contra-cultural' proposals, the level of debate proved insufficient. There seems to be a narrow margin for maneuver to attain the capacity to influence government policies while, at the same time, maintaining autonomy for critique and mobilization (Barrig and Vargas, 2000). Or, as Valenzuela notes, there will be no systematic, consistent and explicit politics to create channels enabling the population to control public management (Valenzuela, 1997).

This would explain why, for example, in the 1990s, crucial issues on feminist agendas such as those relating to sexual rights dwindled steadily and no strategies were unfolded – either towards or from civil societies – to put pressure on the States for their recognition. Or why feminisms or democratic civil societies in Chile did not fight passionately enough for causes that are central to modernity and open maneuvering space for women, such as divorce; or why the defense of democratic rights and the historical triumph of modernity that led to the rise of secular States, without the strong confessional characteristics dominant in Latin American countries, were not always assumed with intensity. It would also account for the fact that the struggles for expanding female citizenship have more strongly impacted on the civic-political dimension than on the socio-economic dimension, producing a certain kind of civil schizophrenia that has replaced the meaning of rights in economic terms with 'charity', as Fraser and Gordon would put it (Fraser and Gordon, 1997), with the consequent risk of manipulation and patronage, still so rooted in Latin American political cultures. Or why important feminist sectors in Peru fell into the temptation of isolating the advances in women's citizenship from the persistent democratic fight waged against Fujimori's dictatorial government.

That is, during this last period, feminisms have progressed over dangerous ground. The major risk has probably been the blurring of powers, responsibilities and autonomous interrelationships between civil society and the State, neglecting dispute contents or interpretation fights through which civil society shapes its democratic proposals and adopts a political perspective that, in the words of Beatriz Sarlo, is an 'oppositional perspective, always on the lookout for de-programming the pre-agreed upon by the ritualization of order moving closer and displaying before such order the scandalous difference, the scandal of multiple perspectives' (Sarlo, cited in Richards, 1993: 43).

We insist, however, that these are complex processes that entail ambivalences, uncertainties, searches, risks and no univocal realities. And they are not exclusive to feminist movements, since they also respond to the dramatic and rapid changes brought about by globalization, which have led some authors to speak of a 'change of era' and not simply of an era of intense changes, with the subsequent impact on people's subjectivities. In addition to the mentioned transformations, these dynamics accentuated the trend towards a growing fragmentation and individuation of movements' collective action. According to Lechner:

civic organizations' sphere of action is limited by the changes undergone both by the public and the private domains. Ongoing economic reforms not only restrict State actions but promote a vast 'privatization of social behaviors' ... In the 'consumer society', even valid for marginalized sectors, individuals assess and estimate differently the time, emotional energy and financial expenses they invest in public activities. Any invocation of solidarity will be abstract as long as this 'ego culture', which makes people afraid of engaging in collective commitments, is disregarded. (Lechner, 1996b: 29)

Thus, besides feminist militants' willpower, social, cultural, economic and political changes at the end of the millennium also contributed to these transformations. Of course, stages of movement development were also relevant to the extent that social movements' dynamics of expression are consistent with the effects of the visibility and consolidation of some of their proposals, and the changing forms of interaction, economic, social and cultural dominance, and the new opportunities and political limitations they face. And, although Offe (1992) argues that movements are ill-equipped to deal with the problem of time, she also notes that social movements (not only feminisms) never altogether decline. Some cycles come to an end, leaving behind significant modifications or finding new ways of expression. New processes begin, within a movement or as a result of new spaces and new male/female actors who denounce exclusions – both old and new – differently, including gender exclusion, around more specific domains, with more value-related, cultural, innovative, and plural contents, expressing discrimination beyond the individual level, as part of broader democratic concerns. There is, for example, a very interesting indigenous movement, more visible and powerful in certain countries of the region, where indigenous women are advancing, albeit with difficulty, in terms of their ability to make proposals and gain visibility; there are strong and varied rights movements, which include, amidst conflict and tension, women's rights movements; there are active feminists in environmental movements, movements regarding consumer rights, democratic defense, local power, new expressions of student movements led by women leaders, etc. There is a movement of young women, but also a significant generational divide. These young women bring in new leaders, new proposals and new abilities to analyze reality. However, a connection between old feminists and new activists is lacking, with the former expecting the latter to 'join' the increasingly blurred and indistinct feminist domain without taking into account their positioning or contributions. These relevant movements expressing partial aspects of the construction of citizenship and permeated by gender conflicts have opened up new grounds for feminist fighting and expression.

## As a Conclusion

Every feminist process and movement over the last two decades has contributed a theory corpus and practical experience that have proved extremely enriching. However, the profound transformations of this 'change of era' have posed new possibilities as well as new risks and challenges to social movements. Moreover, they have facilitated ambivalent searches that seek to answer uncertainties and identify political position-takings in order to meet the new demands and dynamics brought about by a globalized world.

Uncertainty has settled not only in practice but in theory, to the extent that changes in our interpretative codes do not always follow changes in reality. These new contexts require new thinking and new proposals, based on the new sensitivities, new insights and new global, regional and national horizons that are promoting the development of citizenship practices but which still fail to position or define themselves as new courses of action of the feminist movement. Once again Feijoo adequately summarizes the situation, stating that feminists find themselves in a plight, much like an individual who lives off of the interest from his/her savings and, in doing so, however, rapidly reduces his/her capital (Feijoo, 1996). That is, the ability to elaborate new questions to challenge this new reality and our own 'truths' is of fundamental importance. We cannot use past codes to analyze current reality, nor only exclusively with regard to the most functional needs of modernity. Therefore, as Valenzuela points out, while it is necessary to produce knowledge that is functional to the State, it is also central to maintain the externality of the knowledge production process and its link with global issues. Hence, 'an independent, defiant and denunciation knowledge' is required (Valenzuela, 1997: 157), which places knowledge production at the level of the needs for action. However, as Lechner used to say, practices precede theory (Lechner, 1996a). In many ways, the feminist practice of the new millennium is denoting new trends.

Although the feminist plurality includes multiple dynamics, perspectives and discourses, one of them is the tendency to activate movementism dynamics, expressing a new cycle. Many feminist expressions, coming from different spaces or standpoints, are reassuming the more radical and transgressive themes and outlooks, additionally readopting an autonomous perspective and seeking to establish a different vision of the future, based on the new conditions caused by the changes brought about by the globalized world. There is an attempt to respond to new risks, new exclusions, and new rights emerging therefrom.

We can briefly identify some of the most promising trends: (1) the recognition of diversity not only in women's lives but in relation to societies' multicultural and multiethnic features. These features have been tinged by inequality for centuries, constituting an inescapable commitment undertaken by the feminist movement. As Black, Brazilian, feminist Leila Gonzales told me years ago, the feminist movement has been racist not by commission but by omission. This view on diversity and its close relationship to exclusion has also fostered the emergence of new male/female authors, representing new social movements. (2) There has also been an incursion into new themes and dimensions, in an effort to expand to a macro perspective, particularly in relation to the macroeconomic dynamics sustaining poverty and inequality and regarding democratic governability, searching for strategies to empower women in those spheres. This has implied recovering the partly forgotten agenda, thus closing the gap between the political dimension and the social dimension of female citizenship. Gender justice and social justice are being integrated into feminist strategies, and there have already been valuable reflections in this regard, such as the recovery of cultural subversion and subjectivity as a long-term strategy for transformation, and a transgressive subversion that modifies common, traditional values and meanings, and challenges authoritarian political culture in our societies, bringing fresh air to democracies. This shift to politics and culture has prompted new questions regarding our historic struggles, such as violence against women, which nowadays seems to find its clearer boundary not only in this State-based authoritarian culture but also in civil society itself. It has also driven new strategic struggles at the global level, negotiating with nation states new regulations regarding rights neglected in national spheres, such as the mobilization led by the Latin American and Caribbean Committee for the Defense of Women's Rights (CLADEM, by its initials in Spanish) and supported by many feminist organizations and NGOs in the region requesting the creation of a Convention on Sexual and Reproductive Rights at the Organization for American States (OAS) that would perform the same role as the Belem du Para Convention with regard to violence against women.

Throughout this process, the autonomy of feminism somehow begins to disperse and expand; in addition to unpostponable 'own agendas' and the necessary autonomy to negotiate and/or establish them, many feminist streams have also taken up the fight for civil society's autonomy as a fundamental part of their positioning. They have also broadened their alliances with other social movements that fight for the expansion of human rights. It would seem that, within this positioning process, a perception arises: that women's affairs should be recognized as first-order, democratic, political and cultural issues, involving both men and women, and that democratic issues at the cultural, social, economic and political levels should be issues falling under women's scope and part of their agenda. There is also the additional understanding regarding the unpostponable need to articulate feminist agendas with democratic agendas. These new trends widen the scope of feminist action and enable feminism to move forward, from the struggles for the democratization of gender relations to anti-racist and anti-homophobic struggles, struggles for economic justice, a healthy planet, symbolic and cultural transformations, etc. This growing tendency to recover this view of gender as transversal and cross-cutting within the multiplicity of other democratic, political and cultural struggles that not only women but also countless other social movements are waging is becoming one of the most profound and promising changes that are currently taking place.

## Note

1.   An extract from the article published in Spanish as 'Los feminismos latinoamericanos en su tránsito al nuevo milenio (Una lectura político personal)' in Daniel Mato (ed.) (2002). *Estudios y otras prácticas intelectuales latinoamericanas en cultura y poder.* CLACSO: Caracas, pp. 388–399. Translated by Mariana Donaldini.

## References

Abrcinskas, Lilian (2000) 'El aborto ¿da o quita votos?', *Cotidiano Mujer III Epoca*, No 31, November 1999, March 2000 (Montevideo).

Álvarez, Elizabeth (1997) *Ponencia en el VII Encuentro Feminista Latinoamericanos y del Caribe* (Cartagena – Chile: Edición de la Comisión Organizadora).

Álvarez, Sonia (1998) 'Latin American Feminisms Go Global: Trends of the 1990s and Challenges for the New Millennium'. In: Sonia Alvarez, Evelina Dagnino and Arturo Escobar (eds) *Cultures of Politics Politics of Cultures re-visioning Latin American Social Movements* (Westview Press).

Barrig, Maruja (1999) 'La persistencia de la memoria. Feminismo y Estado en el Perú de los 90'. In: *Documento del Proyecto Sociedad Civil y Gobernabilidad Democrática en los Andes y el Cono Sur* (Fundación Ford – Departamento de Ciencias Sociales de la Pontificia Universidad Católica del Perú, Lima).

Barrig, Maruja and Vargas, Virginia (2000) 'Una agenda feminista: el rescate de la utopía'. In: Ivonne Macassi and Cecilia Olea (eds) *Al Rescate de la Utopía* (Lima: Flora Tristán).

Bedregal, Ximena (1997) 'Ponencia'. *Presentada en el VII Encuentro Feminista Latinoamericano y del Caribe* (Cartagena – Chile: Edición de la Comisión Organizadora).

Birgin, Haydee (1999) 'De la certeza a la incertidumbre'. *Fempress* (Red de comunicación alternativa de la mujer. Santiago de Chile).

Evers, Tilman (1984) 'Identidade: a fase oculta o movimientos sociaes'. *Novos Estudios*, Vol. *2*, No. 4. (Brasil).

Feijoo, Maria del Carmen (1996) 'La influencia de los referentes teóricos y de los contextos sociales en la fijación de las agendas de investigación sobre las relaciones de género'. In: Virginia Guzmán and Eugenia Hola (eds) *El Conocimiento como un hecho politico* (Santiago de Chile: Centro de Estudios de la Mujer).

Fraser, Nancy (1994) 'La lucha por las necesidades: esbozo de una teoría crítica socialista-feminista de la cultura política del capitalismo tardío'. *Propuestas Documentos para el Debate* (Red 'Entre Mujeres': Lima).

Fraser, Nancy and Gordon, Linda (1997) 'Contrato versus caridad. Una reconsideración entre ciudadanía civil y ciudadanía social'. *CON/TEXTOS*, No. 2.

Kirkwood, Julieta, (1985) *Ser política en Chile. las feministas y los partidos.* Santiago de Chile: FLACSO.

Lang, Sabine (1997) 'The NGOization of Feminism'. In: Joan W. Scott, Cora Kaplan, Debra Keates (eds) *Transitions, Environments, Translations. Feminism and International Politics* (New York and London: Routledge).

Lechner, Norbert (1996a) 'Los limites de la sociedad civil'. *Revista Foro*, No. 26. Bogotá: Foro Nacional por Colombia.

Lechner, Norbert (1996b) 'La problemática invocación de la sociedad civil'. In: *Los Límites de la Sociedad Civil*. Revista Foro No. 28. Bogotá: Foro Nacional por Colombia.

Lidid, Sandra (1997) *Ponencia en el VII Encuentro Feminista Latinoamericano y del Caribe* (Cartagena – Chile: Edición de la Comisión Organizadora).

Montaño, Sonia (1998) 'Actuar por Otras: la representación política de las Mujeres'. In: Thomas Manz and Moira Zuazo (eds) *Partidos políticos y representación en América Latina* (Caracas: Editorial Nueva Sociedad).

Offe, Claus (1992) 'Reflexiones sobre la auto transformación institucional de la cultura política de los movimientos: un modelo provisional según estados'. In: Russel J. Dalton and Manfred Kuechler (eds) *Los Nuevos Movimientos Sociales* (Spain: Alfons el Magnanim, Generalita Valenciana, Diputación provincial de Valencia).

Pisano, Margarita (1997) *Ponencia en el VII Encuentro Feminista Latinoamericano y del Caribe* (Cartagena – Chile: Edición de la Comisión Organizadora).

Richards, Nelly (1993) 'En torno a las diferencias'. In: Manuel Antonio Carretón, Saul Sosnowski and Bernardo Subercaseaux (eds) *Cultura, Autoritarismo y Redemocratización en Chile* (Chile: Fondo de Cultura Económica).

Richard, Nelly (2000) 'La problemática de los feminismos en los años de la transición en Chile'. In *Estudios Latinoamericanos sobre Cultura y Transformaciones sociales en tiempos de Globalización* (Venezuela: Daniel Mato compilador, CLACSO-UNESCO).

Schild, Veronica (1998) 'New subjetcs of rigths? Women's movements and the construction of citizenship in the "new democracies"'. In: Sonia Alvarez, Evelina Dagnino and Arturo Escobar (eds) *Cultures of Politics Politics of Cultures: Re-visioning Latin American Social Movements* (Westview Press).

Shumaher, M. Aparecida and Vargas, Elizabeth (1993) *El Lugar en el Gobierno: Alibí o conquista?* (Río de Janeiro: Separata).

Slater, David (1998) 'Rethinking the spatialities of social movements: questions of (b) orders, culture, and politics in global times'. In: Sonia Alvarez, Evelina Dagnino and Arturo Escobar (eds) *Cultures of Politics Politics of Cultures: Re-visioning Latin American Social Movements* (Westview Press).

Tamayo, Guilia (1997) 'La Maquinaria Estatal: Puede Suscitar Cambios a Favor de las Mujeres?'. In *Separata de la Revista Socialismo y Participación*, No. 79 (CEDEP. Lima)

Tarres, María Luisa (1993) 'Hacia un Equilibrio de la ética y la negociación'. *Debate Feminista*, March (Mexico).

Ungo, Urania (1998) 'Dilemas del pensamiento feminista: del nudo a la paradoja'. In: Cecilia Olea (ed.) *Encuentros, (des) Encuentros y Búsquedas: El Movimiento Feminista en América Latina* (Lima: Flora Tristán).

Valenzuela, María Elena (1997) 'Las mujeres y el poder: la acción estatal desde una perspectiva de género en Chile'. *Seminario La participación social y política de las mujeres en Chile y Latinoamérica.*

Vargas, Virginia and Olea, Cecilia (1998) 'El proceso hacia Beijing: es desde adentro'. In: Virginia Vargas, *Caminos a Beijing* (Lima: UNICEF, IFEM. Ediciones Flora Tristán).

Waterman, Peter (1998) *Globalization, Social Movements and the New Internationalism* (London and Washington: Mansel).

## Virginia 'Gina' Vargas, by Susana Rostagnol (Uruguay)[1]

Virgina Vargas (1945–) is a relevant figure in Latin American feminism, which cannot be understood without taking her contributions into consideration. As Vargas herself has pointed out, building the feminist movement was the goal that her generation was committed to. There were no models to follow, so they had to create a path of their own. Throughout her life, she has combined sociological analysis of the movement and committed activism, both aimed at advocacy as a key component of women's emancipatory process.

In 1979, she founded the Flora Tristán Center for Peruvian Women, whose mission is to 'fight the structural causes that restrict women's citizenship and/or affect its exercise. It advocates for broadening women's citizenship as well as for encouraging development policies and processes which lead to equity and gender justice'[2]. Vargas

*(Continued)*

(Continued)

has been the center's coordinator for several years. The center has been a place from which much of her academic and activist work has developed – 'that uncomfortable fulcrum between knowledge and action', as she calls it elswewhere in this article, where reflection draws on subjectivity and emotions, while action thrives on theory. Her concerns have always focused on the feminist movement as political practice.

In 1985, Vargas made an incursion in party politics, running as a candidate for Izquierda Unida (United Left Party) alongside other feminists. The party's slogan was 'woman, vote for you'. She was not elected and has continued participating in non-party politics, through civil society organizations. She has expressed disappointment regarding the disagreements between feminism and the Left, particularly in Peru, where the murder of María Elena Moyano attests to this troubled relationship.[3] In the years that Fujimori ruled the country, Vargas voiced her conviction that the expansion of feminist ideas had to go hand in hand with the 'fight for a full and radical democracy as a way of life rather than just a form of government'.

Both in her academic work and her activist practice, Vargas has repeatedly stressed the importance of considering the different currents of the feminist movement, its agreements and discrepancies, and the tensions it comprises. As she mentions elsewhere in the article included in this volume, 'an early comprehension of this flexibility and diversity was the realization that women's struggles may have different starting points, each of them leading to question their subordination and to build movements'. It may have been that vision of feminism, along with her leadership skills, which led her to be designated by civil society organizations to coordinate feminist NGOs in Latin America and the Caribbean in their preparations towards the Fourth World Conference on Women, held in Beijing in 1995. Without losing sight of her concerns regarding Peruvian reality, Gina Vargas has displayed an internationalist vocation, where the paths of the Latin American and Caribbean feminist movement have been – and continue to be – fundamental, devoting a good deal of her energies to it. She claims that feminisms have maintained a subversive perspective and a commitment to unite the feminist struggle with social and political transformations. The article included in this volume begins with the assertion that feminist movements have possibly been the most subversive force of the twentieth century. Nevertheless – without implying any contradiction – other works authored by Vargas focus on her concerns about the difficulties of maintaining the radical character of feminist thought and action while entering the public space in the negotiation of women's agendas. In a 1999 article, co-authored with Maruja Barrig[4], she expressed her disillusionment with the growing institutionalization of Peruvian feminism, which was 'diluting activism in lobbying actions'. The result of this move, she claimed, has been a feminist activity aimed at having an impact on the state apparatus, neglecting the process of strengthening the exercise of citizenship.

Her analysis of the movement is based on reflection about the regional feminist meetings: she describes those held in the 1980s as 'the conquest of autonomy and the assaults on diversity'; the meetings held in the 1990s as 'the myths of the threatening diversity'; and those celebrated in the current millennium as 'the challenge of new subjects and new contexts'. She locates the Beijing–Huairou process as a watershed, defining it as 'a process of "rebellious dispute" … between the currents of global civil society and the currents of transnational official spaces'[5]. Critically tracing the history of the feminist movement has been a constant aspect of her intellectual work. She has delved into the disparities and contradictions within the feminist movement – something at which she works particularly hard throughout the article included in this volume. The disputes between autonomous and institutionalized feminists have strained the movement in its definitions of ethics and negotiation. When referring to the 1990s, she claims that feminisms have travelled a risky path, where complex processes imply ambivalence, bewilderment and queries rather than univocal realities. The search for alternative strategies to fight for substantive social change in the condition of women has not been an easy task for the movement. The article reflects on the uncertainties of shifting times when social and political change could not be addressed by the usual paradigms.

Throughout her work, Gina Vargas has exposed the intimate link between praxis and theory, prioritizing action as the main force for change, and hence claiming that 'social and political movements take praxis as the site for questioning political, anthropological and sociological theory, and for moving towards the construction of new paradigms, as they make visible the existence and possibility of diversity' (2005). She has insistently highlighted that feminism constitutes a 'particular way of knowledge production which starts from activist experience and subjectivity', and implies an epistemological breakaway from the traditional forms of producing sociological knowledge.

## Notes

1. Translated by Sabrina Yáñez (INCIHUSA, CONICET, Argentina).
2. See http://www.flora.org.pe/web2/index.php?option=com_content&view=article&id=197&Itemid=120
3. "La lucha por la democracia. El feminismo y la izquierda en Perú: trágicos desencuentros", *A María Elena Moyano, Report of the Americas. The Latin American Left: A painful rebirth.* (NOCLA), 15 (5), 1992; "Mi amiga María Elena", Institute of Social Studies, La Haya (Holanda), 1992.
4. "A feminist agenda: rescuing utopia", paper presented at the Seminar 'Reflections for a feminist agenda', Centro Flora Tristán-Woman Kind, Lima, 1999.
5. "The construction of a regional feminist internationalism", in Vargas 2008: 162–185.

## References

Barrig, Maruja & Vargas, Virginia (1999) '"Una agenda feminista: el rescate de la utopía", ponencia presentada en el Seminario 'Reflexiones para una agenda del feminismo', Centro Flora Tristán-Woman Kind, Lima.

Vargas, Virginia (2002) 'Los feminismos latinoamericanos en su tránsito al nuevo milenio. (Una lectura político personal)', In: Daniel Mato (ed.), *Estudios y otras prácticas intelectuales latinoamericanas en cultura y poder.* Caracas: CLACSO.

Vargas, Virginia (2005) 'Los feminismos latinoamericanos en su tránsito al nuevo milenio. Una lectura político-personal', In: Daniel Mato (ed.) *Cultura, política y sociedad. Perspectivas latinoamericanas,* CLACSO, Consejo Latinoamericano de Ciencias Sociales. Available at: http://biblioteca.clacso.edu.ar/clacso/gt/2010091 2053709/cultura.pdf

# 22

# Trade Union Models in Latin America, Before and After[1]

*Enrique de la Garza Toledo (Mexico)*

Trade unions in Latin America have been affected in the first place by neoliberalism because wage policy has been managed to contain inflation. Overall, wage increases have been lower than inflation growth, with the exception of 2000 and 2001, in order to also attract foreign direct investment. This is also due to a decrease in social security policies aimed at wage earners and its replacement by those focusing on extreme poverty. Trade unions also have less influence over governments and economic policy, and unions' influence in parties is lower than before. In addition, a significant part of large collective employment contracts have been flexibilized (de la Garza, 2001).

Secondly, trade unions have been affected by productive restructuration – even if focused on a limited group of large companies, its impact has been important for employment and production. However, dominant productive models[2] oscillate between Taylorist-Fordism and a precarious Toyotism[3] defined by partial applications of 'total quality' and strategies 'just-in-time', with a division of labor that leads to segmentation – assigning to technicians and engineers the conception of the activities while leaving to workers the executive tasks, having greater responsibility but limited to the position, with low salaries, little investment in training and high external personnel rotation (de la Garza, 1993); that is to say, a Toyotism based on low wage and high intensity of work with new organization rules. Productive restructuring has mainly affected the central core of the working class in Latin America, including exports, the industrial sector, modern services and trade.

Thirdly, trade unions have also been affected by the growth of the informal employment sector, self-employment and micro-establishments employment. This is a hard segment to be organized, not only because labor laws commonly establish a minimum number of workers to set up a trade union, but also because within these small businesses' wage relations are confused with family cooperation, seen as survival strategies rather than the creation of companies and businesses (de la Garza and Neffa, 2001).

A fourth factor is that neoliberalism and the opening of the economy together with productive restructuration created a new younger working class that, compared to the previous one, has a high presence of women and no identification with work, the company or the union, who rotate frequently and establish family life strategies far from the needs of the collective working class.

In Latin America until the 1980s, one of the most comprehensive trade union typologies classified them as *corporative* or *classist*. Corporative unions would highlight the dominant experiences of trade unionism in Mexico, Argentina (CGT), Paraguay, Brazil and Venezuela (CTV), just like Bolivia, Peru and Colombia during specific periods. And classist unions refer to dominant trade unions in Chile (before the 1990s), Uruguay and Bolivia (in the 1952 revolution period), as well as some of the central ones in Ecuador, Peru, Colombia and Central America. These classifications relate to a more general concept: the *trade union model*.

A *trade union model* should consider the structure and internal functioning of the union, work and the links with work and the companies, as well as the State and society (including other unions, NGOs and social movements), as follows.

(1) *Union structure and internal functioning.* This level should contain representativeness problems, legitimacy and democracy in leaders' elections and decision-making, as well as bureaucracies' establishment and relationship within the union, taking into account consensus, coercion, power and domination. Legitimacy in a trade union can be achieved in several ways, not only by respecting democratic rules. Alternatives like charismatic leadership, clientelism or patrimonialism, even terrorism and gangsterism could become legitimate. Democracy could be delegated or direct. Also it is possible to find bureaucratization processes, concentrations of power in a layer of union officials, oligarchic formations keeping power by holding knowledge and skills, as well as relations or influences, by demonstrating themselves as irreplaceable for proper union functioning. The organizational structures of trade unions can certainly be complex, with few or many levels of authority being subject to simple or detailed regulations.

Structures such as operating modes, concentration, exercise of power and domination are not alien to union culture, which implies ways of giving meaning to unions, as well as leaders and decision-making processes.

In this sense, trade union cultures can be democratic, caudillist, clientelist and patrimonial, terrorist and gangsterist. It is democratic insofar as peoples' convictions are maintained with respect to statutes and rotation of leaders – if they do not fulfill the base expectations – and the vote is that which decides (Lipset, 1986); caudillist, insofar as it is believed that the leader is invested with extraordinary management powers and influence to defend jobs obtaining economic or political benefits; clientelist and patrimonial, insofar as it considers normal the exchange of favors and loyalties between workers and managers, or taking the leader as the boss of the trade union, without claiming, but asking him for favors (Novelo, 1991); terrorist and gangsterist due to a strong belief about fear culture, making people feel they can be fired or physically affected (Quintero, 1995).

(2)   *Trade union relations with work and the company.* The union can be autonomous in considering the company as an enemy to hold discussions with (de la Garza, 1995); it can passively subordinate itself to the company in the work process or become active in its favor, but these positions do not have very precise limits. In terms of a privileged arena for action, a trade union can be one 'of circulation', that is, it concentrates on negotiating the purchase–sale of the labor force as merchandise (employment, wages and benefits); or it can be one 'of production' focusing on intervention in the productive process. Within this last option there are four possibilities: workman (the space of the work process is defined as a struggle for power in productive decisions relating to capital); conciliation of interests (the labor relationship is negotiated in the work process with union positions, without seeking confrontation); defense (against erosion of the labor force); and subordination to the company (co-operating or not in tasks of human resources management).

This issue includes the concept of microcorporatism or company corporatism, different from that of State, although they can be combined. In international theory this concept is reserved for the trade union that, representing the workers, negotiates the problems of production with the company (Standing, 1999). In the case of Latin America, however, it would be necessary to open up the spectrum of corporate trade unions to the types of enterprises, as well as those of the State, which has also included several approaches: from those unions which not only negotiate but also perform management tasks, to liabilities in workers' control and even those of yellow Unions, appearing on the public scene only when there is a danger of creating alternative unions (de la Garza and Bouzas, 1998). Company corporatism may have specific union and labor cultures associated with it, such as employer paternalism and employer–employee patronage, in which jobs are seen as a gift from the chief which have a component of moral commitment to him; or productive instrumentalism plus productivity in return for bonuses and incentives, without any other moral commitment to the company.

(3) *Relations between trade unions and the State.* The union may cooperate with the State, being co-responsible for design and operation of state policies, or politically opposite to the State, or a critical partner; or it can be absent from the State arena. On the other hand, the trade union can be protected by the State through legal and extra-legal mechanisms; be hostile to it, as some cases with many independent trade unions; or establish a modus vivendi with it, without invading its spheres. These relations with the State have led to the creation of trade union cultures: statalism, believing that labor is a matter for the State and it is resolved by statal influence and politics; opposition – as a principle – to everything that comes from the State; enterprise, seen as a large family run by the patriarchal entrepreneur where the State does not have to interfere.

(4) *Trade union and company relations.* There may be many trade unions that are only interested in their labor problems with the company, participating in federations or confederations, as well of those composing broader fronts with NGOs and social movements to address problems transcending the labor context, including those of intervention in labor reproduction, such as public, urban or rural services.

In other words, a *trade union model* should at least include the articulations between its internal structure and its functioning with work and other companies, with State and society. They do not have to be fully coherent, which implies contradictions, and they are historically constituted and embedded in culture, with the manner of interpretation and social action giving them content, levels and processes. Trade unionism, in a given country and time period, not only came to recognize one or more trade union models, they were able to define and establish privileged spaces for action and intervention (Di Tella, 1970). These spaces were built through unionism, but according to conditions that they did not choose. Besides, the definition of scopes for action is also defined in functions of who are friends or enemies, where the strongest is usually in a position to determine the place of conflict or negotiation (Burawoy, 1985). Prior to neoliberalism, the privileged spaces for the corporate union were the State arena and the circulation of the labor force, understood as buying and selling – at most a defensive attitude regarding work positions (Bizberg, 1990).

Negotiations for purchase-sale were carried out within the company order (wage increases and the benefit system), but general parameters for the whole labor relations system were set by the State, the company and trade union leaders. The classist unions were indirectly favored by those national negotiations, without proper intervention, and they also took part in the negotiations at company or employment institution level on issues such as wages and benefits, although the questioning of State policies was the axis of their action. That is, both within the corporate and the classist modes, State space had a privilege in the support or opposition to the Unions.

Even though certain aspects of social relations were privileged, trade union action can be organized with others in different spaces: from the relationship of the State to that of labor relations in the company, to that of social reproduction in the territory, or following the politically opposite road (Sariego, 1988). Historical genesis is also important in the shaping of areas for union action, because previous stages leave their traces in later ones and because deciding on a historical trajectory sometimes cancels out other options that might have been undertaken. In the nineteenth century craft unions prevailed, but they were repressed by dictatorships; therefore in the beginning of the twentieth century the new unions were not their heirs, they were born not by crafts as in England, but by enterprises in the most modern companies of that time: mining, railways, textiles and electricity. In this way, company unions were born outside the institutional framework and turned institutionalism into corporatism, this was the most important historical change in the twentieth century. It was not the centrality of the craft in manufacturing processes (in Marx's sense, as unmachined productive processes). However, the main feature of this great transformation was the submission of labor relations to State ones, instead of drawing up a system of norms, values and actors committed to chasing collective bargaining. In turn, part of the 'labor relations system' has been constitutive of the 'political system'. Corporatism has also been permeable to nationalism, anti-imperialism, populism and socialism.

The possibilities for reconstitution at the current juncture are framed by processes and structures that are wider than those of internal trade union life. On one hand, such processes and structures fulfill the function of parameters that set limits for viable action. On the other hand, they are also subject to change by action. The most important would be the following.

(1) *The neoliberal model.* This model has meant opening up the economy and subjecting companies to competition in the international market, as exporters, and in the internal market itself. This is an economic policy

that has forsaken public productive investment and industrial promotion to combat inflation in favor of macroeconomic balance. The opening of the economy and its complementary partial process of productive reform have meant the polarization of the productive landscape, particularly the industrial one, between a minority group of companies, restructured mainly in terms of labor organization and flexibility, which is competitive and exporting, and the world of small and medium-sized microenterprises, with opposite conditions to the former but quite important as a source of employment (de la Garza, 1993). Polarization should not be understood as without links between the poles, different to the conception of Theory of Marginality of the eighties. Rather than segments, these are constellations with a restructured central core, satellites in successive orbits and, at the end, a morass without a core. Associations between these extremes as productive chains, are scarce; services become more profuse and reproductive chains between reservoirs of micro and small enterprises and workers within a restructured pole become denser.

In the restructured pole, large industrial and service companies predominate, with intermediate technologies, new figures of work organization and Toyotist flexibility; with the presence of this new working class (composed of young people and women, semi-skilled and low-wage), with high external rotation, intense work processes in terms of the labor force (which should not be confused with the economic concept of labor-intensive rather than capital-intensive jobs), low labor, business or trade union identity, little union interference in production decisions, little delegation of decisions by management to workers, which reproduces the separation between the work of technicians and engineers regarding that of workers, easily replaceable with scarce training investment. This is the model of precarious Toyotist production, which has increased productivity but based on the degradation of the workforce. This model faces physical limits in the workers and social resistance represented by high turnover and little identitification with the company, having an impact on participation and constraining the capacities of the model itself to raise productivity. Within this context in which the new working class participates above anything else, it is not yet possible to speak about the constitution of one or more subjects. So far, it is a stratum with no specific identity or broad collective actions, even though it has high rates of formal union and workers may have a potential that starts from similar working and living conditions.

On the opposite side there is a swamp – not a pole – of micro and small enterprises, with self-employment and family work, non-capitalist agricultural work, door-to-door and street sales. Their technologies are low-level and their ways of organization are not based on any science of business management; unionization rates are very low, leadership styles are authoritarian and patriarchal and their identity, when there is one, is built through patronage, familiarity or buddy relationships. Wages in this sector are low and instability is not only due to voluntary rotation but also to the failure of micro-units; their average lifespan is short. This sector is concentrated in a few activities: manufacturing/repair garment shops, services and commerce, personal services, street food cooking and sales, urban transport and small construction. The new working class also takes part in this category and it is not a subject either, only a stratum hard to organize because a significant part of its members are not salaried. Among these poles is the old working class of the export substitution model, which has diminished quantitatively, located in what is left of State-owned enterprises, public universities and some large restructured private companies. The productive processes can be sophisticated, with production models swinging between Taylorism-Fordism and the partial application of Toyotism, with flexible labor relations but without reaching extremes. The labor force is mainly male, mature, relatively highly skilled, with higher wages and benefits, despite the fact that many of its contracts changed between the 1980s and 2000s; the unionization rate is very high and the union, though its protective capacity has been reduced, still defends employment and production process practices. Until the 1970s, this working class was the central nucleus of the workers' movement and was the one that offered the greatest resistance during the 1980s and 1990s to labor flexibilization.

It is possible that in this old working class there are several subjects at stake: the decadent remains of the populist worker, the 1960s substitution of workers of the economic model directed to internal market for workers of large export corporations. However, it should be doubted that the labor culture has changed so much among these workers; it probably moves between the complicit consensus[4] with the union (a union that overlaps with the relaxation of work) (Leyva, 1995) and productive instrumentalism (intensive work for the bonus of productivity, not for identification with the company). In short, trade union options will have to take into account the heterogeneity of workers, which is not entirely assimilated to international theorizations (Hyman, 1996). In the informal sector the differences between manufacturing and services are less important than in large companies because in both cases face-to-face contact with the customer is frequent; because there is a shift between production and reproduction in the domestic unit, in terms of time, space and activity itself, due to the importance of unpaid work; because their fragmentation is not by areas of life, but between small units with similar production and reproduction conditions, where differences in terms of production and services are less important than in large companies.

In this sense, the meaning of work and its confusion with the world of reproduction can be similar between units, despite its separation and the diffuse identity of precarious workers, where the potential enemy may not be the small boss but the global society of winners (de la Garza, 1997). In the structured sectors, stating a difference between the restructured pole and the one where the former working class is included, the world of social reproduction and work can be stricter. In the old one, there is a greater labor identity and even trade pride remains, while in the new one there is still the potential identity of those who share working conditions, labor and life trajectories that are mostly very similar.

(2) *The system of industrial relations and its changes.* In Latin America, the previous system of labor relations was characterized by the assumption that society was divided into classes with contradictory interests, and in front of them the State was erected as the guardian of the weakest. The State arena was the main space for settling conflicts and labor negotiations, that is, labor relations were subsumed in the political-state, and the agents of negotiation and exchange were the organizations – union and business – in some cases co-responsible for the State's progress and its economic policy, while in others they stood aside from State policies. In the case of corporatism, there was an interweaving of State corporate relations with the political party and electoral system, and the stratified exchange system with unionized workers was established, based on negotiations between unions and the State. There was a monopoly on representation, guaranteed by the State in charge of corporate unions, an authoritarian corporatism within the State with the establishment of union oligarchies, a low turnover of elites and repression of the opposition based on clientelism and patrimonial cultures. Trade unions exercised a stratified protection of employment, wages (the wage concept according to reproduction costs was not linked to productivity) and working conditions (defensive intervention and clientelism in the work process).

This model of labor relations has changed since 1980 in most Latin American countries. This change was brought about by flexibilization in the labor legislation, by collective employment contracts for large companies and by loss of power of corporative unionism: a drop in economic benefits, a reduction of salary scales with an increase in job functions, a loss of importance in seniority scales, wage approximation towards minimum wages, the appearance of bonus systems and incentives for productivity and large cuts in companies staff when privatized. But above all, the main reason for change was the loss of power of the trade unions in the direction of economic and labor policy.

(3)  *Workers' organizations.* The trade union cultures in Latin America move between corporate statalism (a belief in the omnipotence of the State), which leads them to seek a restoration of their leadership – the restructured ones who privilege the company space – and the nationalists/classists who fight at the same level. Within the trade unions 'patrimonialism', delegation to the leader, authoritarianism and *caudillism* still persist. Accordingly, the renovation of unionism entails taking the following into account:

- Abandonment of the State as a benefactor for the upper layer of organized workers and polarization between companies. One part of the companies are pressured for quality competition in the international market; the other part of the companies participate in the internal market for poor people.
- Capital accumulation with production models based on labor intensification and low wages.
- A heterogeneous working class – not just salaried – going from the old to the new working class, settled in modern industry and services, without work, company or union identity, as if it were a swamp of the informal sector in which production and reproduction are often confused. In both areas, most of the potential identities do not come from subjectively shared collective experiences and memories, but from similar working and living conditions.
- A modified system of labor relations and the flexibilization of large collective employment agreements, which have weakened union influence on state policies.
- Entrepreneurial cultures carrying unilateral – not shared – concepts of ownership and direction, of work as a production factor and employment operating like a favor; union cultures without production proposals, with authoritarianism regarding the internal life of workers' organizations and worker cultures going from the employer in the informal sector to the productive instrumentalism of the modernized employer.

## Conclusion: From Corporatism and Classism to Post-Corporatism

The changing content of the trade union concept is a narrative on how the concept of social work itself has been built. During the nineteenth century, trade union work referred to the industrial area, since agriculture and services had not changed at that time. This situation continued until the 1950s, although it should be noted that some services such as transport and telecommunications were engineered early and have traditionally been highly organized. However, in the following decade, modern services were Taylorized (machining was limited until computers burst into offices), so that unionization spread to these white-collar sectors, bank employees and university professors. In Europe the 1970s also saw the spread of what some authors called the 'thirdarization of the conflict' (where the conflict passes from manufacturing to services). In any event, services have grown more than industry – although falling in some countries as a place of work – and by this measure industrial work is no longer the model of productive activity, with sectors such as telecommunications and computers in particular competing with the expanding automobile industry in terms of jobs and, above all, the capacity for technological change. Simultaneously administration, sales, finance and purchasing work involves more and more staff in contrast to work in direct production, and their work resembles that of modern services.

Despite the existence of large corporations, maintenance is one of the additional modifications changing the sense of work in small and medium sized companies, which become possible subcontractors for large ones with different working conditions; and also noticed in Latin American countries is a growing presence of precarious informal jobs and self-employment. In other words, the centrality of industrial work has been replaced by heterogeneity in powerful numerous productive areas (automobile, telecommunications, computers, banks and finance, education and electronics).

Will trade unions be able to change from organizations focusing on collective employment contracts, wages and economic benefits to those focusing on production in a variety of ways? From organizations negotiating with the State, obtaining benefits for their members, to more autonomous figures of political participation with new social forces? From one industry-focused trade union to another entering into the area of new services and precarious employment? Will the union change from a nationally based one to a globalized organization? Answering these questions would help to define the future of trade unions.

However, the following clarification should be made: the concept of the *world of work*, separated from other spheres of life (family, leisure time, study, etc.), is in part a social creation. For ancient societies, for example, there was no separation between work and religion. It would be necessary to think that productive restructuring, new subordination of ways of unpaid labor to capitalist production and a possible union between the world of production and that of non-wage labor would allow us to go back over the area of collective action of workers' organizations. Concerning micro-businesses, involving self-employment, linkages also extend through subcontracting with large corporations. When these small businesses have salaried workers, spaces for struggle are opened in order to improve their precarious working conditions, a kind of struggle that can be centered on legal changes, taking into account the dispersion of workers. Likewise, unequal relations in companies open options for alliances for workers and employers in small companies, seeking more equitable relations with large consortiums. Regarding relations between the *world of work* and the *world of life*, Toyotist companies proposed a link connecting enterprise and workers' families, their neighborhoods, religion, leisure time and consumption, in order to achieve the identification of workers with the company. However, these relationships create considerable uncertainty, they are new and voluntary, and may become a core area of dispute with trade union intervention.

Certainly the space of process production – so important now and subject to management restructuring – is essential in the workers' struggles, where new technologies, forms of work organization, labor relations and cultures are experienced. It is full of uncertainties and possibilities for a new 'negotiation of order' by workers and their organizations. At this time, trade union leaderships cannot be the best armed and most capable bodies for proposing negotiation and struggle, but rather there should be forms of organization similar to factory committees – whether or not they are part of the unions – which are decentralized in workplaces and can stimulate communication and growth within struggles. It is clear that decent employment and wages are not resolved with the free market, the field of the labor market should be a space for work action with new regulations and protections. In this sense, workers must insist on the concept of minimum labor standards, below which it is not worth working, regardless of the market.

Workers not only produce but also live in other universes, urban or rural, with educational and ecological problems, as inhabitants, consumers or debtors. These spaces are not naturally organized but can be organized. Some of them can be addressed through local actions, others will need to be converted from workers' organizations into political forces. This is where, facing the new heterogeneity, decompositions and globalization, multiple action is imposed, without hegemonic pretensions a priori by anyone; the 'guerrilla civil war' of the social movements, agile, multiform and re-articulable in different ways, which does not always involve the same actors, which knows how to make creative use of the national and international media, which creates and recreates symbols and speeches in a new seductive language. New types of organizations will be so because of the content of their discourse, their demands and struggle outlines, but we should not bet too much on their bureaucratic composition. The current time is one of flexibility and permanent recreation rather than one characterized by the creation of solid and definitive structures.

## Notes

1. Published originally in Spanish in Erique De la Garza Toledo (2004), en "Alternativas sindicales en América Latina", Documentos de la Escuela No. 53, ENS: Colombia, pp. 38–60. Translated by Marta Pierre (INCIHUSA, CONICET-Mendoza, Argentina) and revised by E. de la Garza Toledo.

2. We name the configuration between technology, organization, the labor relationship, workforce profile and labor culture, which characterizes a productive process, as the productive model.

3. We would rather use the concept of Toyotism, rather than post-Fordism, postmodern organization and flexible specialization, restricting the concept to production model characteristics originally inspired by the Toyota experience in Japan and involving a combination of 'total quality control' with 'just-in-time' processes, as well as the labor culture of worker participation and involvement in production problems.

4. In his research on the railroad workers' union, Marco Antonio Leyva names 'complicit consensus' as the relationship of complicity between the union and the workers to relax the pace and discipline of work.

## References

Bizberg, I., *El sindicalismo mexicano*, Mexico, El Colegio de Mexico, 1990.
Burawoy, M., *The Politics of Production*, London, Verso, 1985.
De la Garza Toledo, E., Reestructuración productiva y respuesta sindical en México, Mexico, IIEc-UNAM, 1993.
De la Garza Toledo, E., 'Cogestión, calidad total y sistema de relaciones industriales', in: *Competitividad vs Democracia industrial*, Mexico, Fundación F. Ebert, 1995.
De la Garza Toledo, E., 'Trabajo y mundos de vida', in: H. Zemelman (ed.), *Subjetividad: umbrales del pensamiento social*, Madrid, Anthropos, 1997.
De la Garza, E., *La Formación Socioeconómica Neoliberal*, Plaza y Valdés: Mexico, DF, 2001.

De la Garza Toledo, E. and A. Bouzas, *Contratación colectiva y flexibilidad del trabajo en México*, Mexico, IIEc, 1998.

De la Garza Toledo, E. and J.C. Neffa (eds), *El trabajo del futuro, el futuro del trabajo*, Buenos Aires, CLACSO, 2001.

Di Tella, T., *Estructuras sindicales*, Buenos Aires, Nueva Visión, 1970.

Hyman, R., 'Los sindicatos y la desarticulación de la clase obrera', *Revista Latinoamericana de Estudios del Trabajo*, 2, 4, 1996.

Leyva, M.A., *Poder y dominación en los Ferrocarriles Nacionales de México*, Mexico, UAMI, 1995.

Lipset, S., *Unions in Transition*, New York, ICS Press, 1986.

Novelo, V., *La difícil democracia de los petroleros*, Mexico, El Caballito, 1991.

Quintero, C., *Reestructuración sindical en las maquiladoras mexicanas*, Mexico, El Colegio de la Frontera Norte, 1995.

Sariego, J.L., *Enclaves y minerales en el norte de México*, Mexico, Ediciones de la Casa Chata, 1988.

Standing, G., *Global Labor Flexibility*, London, Macmillan, 1999.

## Enrique de la Garza Toledo, by Patricia Collado (Argentina)

Enrique de la Garza (1947–) is one of the most original and prolific researchers in the field of labor studies. His early concern with the issue dates back to his childhood in an industrial district of Monclova, San Buenaventura de Coahuila, a state on the US border, around the time of the region's import-substitution industrial development model. Afterwards, he moved to Monterrey, an important industrial city since the late nineteenth century, where he studied at the University of Nuevo Leon. He wanted to study philosophy but his family persuaded him to enroll in chemical engineering, the most legitimate profession in this highly industrial zone. In spite of this, he pursued his studies on sociology later on.

One of the most important strands in his intellectual formation occurred within the Mexican student movement during the 1960s. Far from being devastated by the Tlatelolco massacre (1968), these events strengthened his commitment to the students and workers who were actively questioning the authoritarian regime that dominated the State. Both topics – the student movement and authoritarianism – shape the raw material of his first published works. He was influenced by the Marxist debate on the exploitation of the working class and the generalized pauperization expressed in popular and urban movements during the 1970s. This perspective, linked to the observation of the experience of popular organizations, was consolidated when he applied to El Colegio de México. He carried out his doctoral studies in Sociology under the direction of the Chilean sociologist and epistemologist Hugo Zemelman. Additionally, his postgraduate studies in Italy brought him closer to Italian *workerism*, distanced from Structuralist Marxism.

From the 1980s he joined the Universidad Autónoma Metropolitana in Mexico City as a professor, where he started research on the labor movement from the critical perspective of the existing local literature – untying his links with the radical groups of the Mexican Left present in his youth. This rupture, and the defeats of the Mexican independent labor movement during the crisis of capitalism in the late 1970s, produced a breaking point in his trajectory. Thus, emerged his new studies centered on the mutation of labor and the type of worker forged under Keynesianism, the crisis of post-war models of production and the role of corporate unionism (especially the Mexican case). The 1990s were his most prolific period in terms of the consolidation of this research. At this time he started building his own school of thought in the field of labor studies that addressed the transformations that precipitated neoliberalism in Mexico.

In the course of his trajectory, De la Garza revised the methodological, theoretical and empirical paths of his original concerns. His initial configurationist position (following the ideas of Teodorno Adorno and Hugo Zemelman) was conjugated with heterodox Marxism, combining Critical Theory with the method synthesized in the tripod 'concrete-abstract-concrete'. These influences enriched the polyhedral forms of his focus. Theoretically, he advanced in this direction based on empirical research: models of industrialization, labor processes, productivity and working conditions, modernization, labor and industrial relations, and the role of the union. These were his privileged spots of observation. In the course of this process, he was projected as a regional and international point of reference, due to his challenging positions confronting postmodernity and the 'end of work'. In contrast, he focused on the complexity of the labor world and its subjects within the nonlinear stamp of the end-of-century global transformation in Latin America.

At the dawn of the twenty-first century, de la Garza once again defies the foundations of the field of study. This time turning on the Latin American question in order to seek theoretical answers and build knowledge around the more invisible aspects of work. Non-classical, atypical, non-formal work, its concrete forms of configuration and its impact on the living conditions of broad layers of the population shape the new agenda of Latin American labor studies. In parallel, the flexible forms of 'formalized' work, the loss of acquired rights, and the path taken by wage negotiations/labor relations set a broader perspective on the issue. The novelty of his work highlights the combining of split worlds, expanding labor focus, discovering new labor subjects and catching the totality in its complexity – for sure related to the commitment present at each stage of his prolific ouput.

# Part Five
# State, Society and Politics

## 23

# Politics, State and Society in Latin American Sociology: A Partial Introduction

*Manuel Antonio Garretón (Chile)[1]*

As has been widely recognized, let's recall that scientific sociology was born in this region to understand and intervene in the question of the transformation of society – what economics would call development (Trindade, De Sierra, Garretón, Murmis and Reyna, 2007). But a transformation of society does not depend on natural forces but on human action, and for that reason, from a sociological perspective, it must address politics as a central element and, in contemporary times, the fundamental agent for its direction, the State. Accordingly, sociology in these latitudes was born as sociology of development and as political sociology,[2] occupying with some exceptions the role that political science had occupied in other societies

The paradox is that, nevertheless, in the big paradigms of the time associated with the foundation of sociology, politics and the State were assigned the role of a dependent variable. Thus, from the approach of modernization, the processes of secularization, rationalization and differentiation would make it possible to overcome the intrusions of politics and the State in social and economic life – and democracy as a regime would be the effect of such modernization. From the perspective of Marxist views and dependency, State and politics were the result of economic processes and the capitalist feature of development (Marini, 1969). It would be unfair to consider that there were no perspectives that emphasized the more autonomous character of politics and the State to understand that the same insertion in the world capitalist system allowed a diversity of development paths or that political processes had been developed involving a certain autonomy of politics and the State.[3] In fact, studies on Nation-State building, thematically explored by Suzy Castor in this section of the book, point to its central role in the planning processes or in the relationships with social classes and have also shown important efforts to understand and analyze the non-total determination and relative autonomy of political and State phenomena (Kaplan, 1969; Jaguaribe, 1972; Solari, Franco and Jutkowitz, 1976; Graciarena and Franco, 1981).

But specific theories about the State and actors within the political sphere, such as political parties, will come later. And this is so because politics and State, as some have pointed out, were 'dampened' or penetrated by society when they ceased to be the exclusive game of the oligarchies and the military. Thus, in the so-called 'popular national' era, the State becomes the main reference for collective action and politics its main access route, either to satisfy demands, or to reorient the course of development. This last aspect will become more evident with the impact of the Cuban Revolution (1959). Politics had an instrumental nature, but was also conceived as the main meaning of collective life.[4] It was manifested in two forms, with many intermediate variants of course: the institutional policy of a democratic style, as in the cases of Uruguay or Chile, or authoritarian, as in the case of Mexico, or in a more personalized style in deep relationship with the masses that gave rise to populism – this latter studied by one of the authors included in this section Ernesto Laclau, but also by many others (Germani, Di Tella and Ianni, 1973; Laclau, 2004; de la Torre, 2017). We must recognize in this line the greater depth that sociological studies have regarding populism, compared to the economistic versions, especially the neoliberal oriented-, considering them as a form of collective action, even as a political culture that paradoxically had a modernizing effect. It is precisely this interrelation between politics and society that will posit the social movements as main social actors privileged over the parties, the latter subject mainly confined to Political Science.

A particular contribution in the founding times of Latin American sociology was to coin the concept of State of compromise (Weffort, 1966; Graciarena and Franco, 1981). Even lacking a systematic theory of the State, it pointed to a particular feature in the Latin American case, and especially in some countries. It referred to the transit through which the oligarchic State hegemony gives way to a pattern of unstable arrangements between various incorporated groups that include some oligarchic sectors, middle classes and organized labor sectors – excluding the peasant masses and the urban poor. The contradictions of this form of domination, which is defined politically but related to economic structures and development processes, will lead to the crisis of the sixties, marked by the confrontation between development, revolutionary or populist projects and the authoritarian project of capitalist recomposition that was incarnated in the military dictatorships – what were called new authoritarianism, military dictatorships of the Southern Cone, national security dictatorships or authoritarian bureaucratic State.[5]

## The Military Dictatorships

It was probably with the defeat of developmentist, populist or revolutionary projects and the triumph of dictatorships that there was a significant change in the analysis of politics and the State in relation to society. Within the framework of what could be called a shift in the social sciences, from the monocausality of the big paradigms to the theoretical perspectives of medium range, politics and the State acquired greater autonomy and academic interest. This was accompanied by a greater interdisciplinarity, with theorizations and methodological instruments coming from political science, mainly, and also from other disciplines. Thus, the analysis of these regimes that were implemented by blood and fire, highlighted political dimensions, while recognizing their origin in the type of development of society and in its particular feature of attempting to make capitalist revolutions from above.[6]

In the discussion about the nature of these regimes, perhaps one of the most valuable contributions has been the one that leads to the distinction, coming from political science, between State and political regime. Indeed, the consideration of these dictatorships as a new type of State associated with a specific type of capitalism posed the theoretical problem of how to operate change (from authoritarian to democratic) without necessarily implying leaving capitalism or making a revolution (O'Donnell, 1985). So, from provisional elements of State theory and the study of the types of classical political regimes in political science, the State appeared in all its characters, as a set of institutions and public organizations with a legitimate monopoly of violence, a crystallization of the relations of domination, an agent of national unity, a reference of collective action and development. The political regime, on the other hand, appeared as the set of institutional mediations between State and society that solve the triple problem of: (a) how and who governs; (b) the relationships between the individuals and the State; and (c) channeling demands and solving conflicts.[7]

Through this distinction, it was possible to think about both the new dictatorships of the Southern Cone and this type of authoritarian regime in a context of recomposition of capitalism, alongside the change of regime from a dictatorship to democracy, without implying the revolutionary change of the State. This meant at the same time accepting the intertwining between the social conditions of a political regime and the possibility of its autonomous transformation, leaving open the question of the change of the mode of production. Precisely the distinction between State and political regime allowed us to think about the possibility of what would be called from then on the transitions to democracy.

Beyond the characterization and nature of these dictatorships, the sociological analysis, hand in hand with more political perspectives, addressed, among other aspects, the transformations that dictatorships produce in the forms of operation of the State, such as the 'bureaucratic rings' (Cardoso, 1972; De Castro Andrade, 1964), the relationship with the capitalist sectors and the particularity of the military actor in the State in relation to the repressive tasks and the violations of human rights. The specificity of the sociological perspective was to look at the relationships of these regimes with the socio-economic models that they implant as political options of the actors involved and not only as a requirement of the laws of capitalist accumulation, which allows different paths according to the differences between these regimes and within the countries.

The importance of social actors and the perspectives of ending these regimes is at the heart of the studies on oppositions to dictatorships. These oppositions could come from social movements, often described as 'new' social movements and corresponding to an 'awakening of civil society', as well as the political actors themselves, the parties, in a complex relationship with a more social moment during the dictatorships and a more partisan moment at the time of the transitions and their subsequent tension in the new democratic regimes.[8] Their horizon was to conquer a new regime: democracy.[9]

## Democracy and Democratizations

The issue of democracy in its political dimension was not always a priority in sociology insofar as, in part, its permanent absence in many countries, as well as its relatively permanent validity in others, did not make it a central object of questioning or analysis, also due to the predominance of the sociologizing or *societalist* perspective (Garretón, 2000). In this sense it can be affirmed that democracy was seen and valued, more than as a political regime, as a feature of society that defined not a set of rules but a process of social democratization, in terms of inclusion or equality, in the style of the concept of Mannheim (1950) as 'fundamental democratization'.

And this bias not only predominated in the political field, where progressive ideas proclaimed a substantive democracy versus a formal democracy, but was also present in the academic world and in the big paradigms already mentioned. With the establishment of dictatorships, the central problem of these societies until then defined in terms of development – whether as modernization or change or revolution of the model of capitalist development – was transformed into the way out of dictatorships. In the historical context generated by the democratic transitions of Portugal and Spain, the concept of democratization was transfigured into political democratization.[10] Probably theorizing about transitions is one of the greatest achievements of sociology and, in general, the social sciences in Latin America, after its contribution to the issue of development and dependence. Although democracy was transformed into what we have called the new limit concept, the central object of study and normative principle that guided such studies and the action that derives from it, was the change of regime. The idea of transition, thus, provided in several countries a field of rapprochement between the political actors themselves and the actors of the intellectual and academic world.[11]

In fact, both the emphasis on the transition processes and the success of these processes that ended with the military dictatorships obscured the discussion on the subject of democracy as such. To put it succinctly: there was strong theorization about democratization but there was weak or little theorization about democracy itself, to which the image of democratic waves as a historical context contributed. In fact, the concept of democracy was not discussed, but it was assumed to be common sense: democracy was representative democracy, prevailing in most Western societies.

Along with recognizing the great historical conquest by which for the first time the great majority of the countries of the region were governed by democratic regimes, the deficits of these same transitions appeared. They were formulated in terms of authoritarian enclaves, the impact of neoliberal reforms, the processes of dependent globalization or the so-called democratic disenchantments. All this will lead to consider theoretically and politically the question of democracy itself.[12]

Perhaps the fundamental text in this matter for its interpretation of what happened at the Latin American level once the transitions are over and the issue of the so-called consolidation of democracy has been largely solved, is the 2004 UNDP Report.[13] A new field of reflection is here opened, regarding the meaning of democracy in countries with a high level of inequality, in the midst of neoliberal reforms and in a globalized world that affects not only the quality but also the very relevance of democracy. This report analyzed the deficit of citizenship that was observed in democratic processes which had a mainly electoral stamp in which the subject was not the citizen but a voter. Thus, there was a warning against a definition of the democratic subject as the elector and not as the subject of civil and social rights, stressing only the political rights. The importance of this perspective was its emphasis on the rights themselves, thus moving from a democracy of freedoms and elections to the concept of a democracy of citizen rights.

A product of the indicated deficits and within the framework of a more global current of expressions of disenchantment and criticism, both on the intellectual level and on that of social demands, is that democracies will be judged not for their validity but for their quality (O'Donnell et. al., 2003; Morlino, 2012; Morlino et al., 2014). Indicators and quality indices were developed that lead to comparisons and rankings between countries and regions. The paradox is that in the Latin American case, democracies that appeared in situations of greater or lesser ranking in terms of indicators showed contradictory situations, when each case was analyzed in terms of the fundamental concept of democracy of popular sovereignty ('government of the people, by the people and for the people') and not only the most procedural, indispensable but insufficient issues in a quality democracy.

The academic debate and political proposals then aimed to go beyond the representative character of democracy, which was considered in crisis, by the transformations of society that left the political parties in an ambivalent situation, considered indispensable but scarcely related to the 'People's interests and aspirations'. The question of the participation of civil society was raised, which will lead to the introduction of the concept of participatory democracy with the creation of new indicators (Panfichi, 2002; Dagnino et al., 2006; Lissidini et al., 2014). The concept of participatory democracy appears, thus, as an element of the redefinition of democracy insofar as it implies the active presence of demos in the affairs of the polis. But both aspects, the representative and the participative, are part of the strictly institutional definition of the regime.

### Politics and State in a New Context

At this point the question of the structure of society became critical to ensure the possibility of democratic rooting. That is, the issues of equality and cohesion, without which the democracy of citizens and rights risks its social realization. These will be the predominant issues in the political, intellectual and technical debate since the late nineties.[14] These issues enter the debate along with what can be called the subjective dimension of democracy that incorporates citizenship and civil society – democracy understood as a personal and collective experience that goes beyond institutional processes. This 'mutation' of democracy leads to its definition more as a process and experience than as an institutional regime. Thus, a new ethos linked to the experience of a mobilized subject is recognized, in which the demos is no longer just the people of the national-popular era nor the citizens of a diversified and complex society, but a subject that moves between rights, consumption and diverse identities, with high levels of information but moving away from the classic political expressions (Cheresky, 2006, 2011, 2012, 2015; Rodotá, 1999; Rosanvallon, 2007).[15] The problems faced by democracies refer to an even deeper question: the crisis of politics itself. During the 1980s, in other contexts, it emerged as a decentering or emptying of politics, as a sort of subpolitics (Beck, 1998). In Latin America this reflection arises by the end of the last century as a change of direction in politics (Lechner, 1994).

We have pointed out that in the period of the developmentalist, revolutionary or populist political projects, politics was at the same time the main instrument of claims and demands, and also the link between collective life, the project of society and subjectivities, acting as a producer of identities, whether in its more institutional forms such as parties or through the link with charismatic leaderships. Today it seems that this sense of politics has radically changed through phenomena such as the corruption that permeates the entire political sphere, the presence of factual powers that tend to make it irrelevant, the loss of representativeness of political parties and electoral volatility.[16] Politics seems to revolve around itself and loses its sense of linking collective projects and subjectivities. Of course in degrees and different ways in each country, this activity is losing prestige and begins to be rejected by many sectors that previously were expressed through it – becoming increasingly distant from the demands and concerns of the social actors. On this level, the phenomenon of the expansion of so-called 'social networks' (actually more virtual than social), as Sorj's article points out in this Part, oscillates between its ability to contribute to the renewal of politics and generate participation, or to radically change its meaning, becoming an expressive vehicle of purely individual or corporatist short-term aspirations.

These political phenomena also generated new concerns about the State. In the era of the great paradigms of modernization and dependence, it appeared fundamentally as either the space of the processes of containment or promotion of development, or as a space of capitalist domination. In the period of dictatorships, the State appears in all its dimension of domination and as a repressive apparatus. But it is precisely here that concerns about the various dimensions of the State will begin to emerge, which will continue in recent times. At the height of neoliberal theories against the State, the problem of size arose, it was advocated by its subsidiary function and only responsible for targeted policies, or the need for its purely managerial modernization was pointed out. But, in a different direction, there was also a concern about the ability of the State to face the challenges of globalization (Calderón, 2004a, 2004b) in its double role of a globalization space crossed by external forces and a negotiating agent of globalization, for which it requires its internal relegitimation in the democratic context; that is, the overcoming of poverty and the promotion of equality, the elaboration of public policies in new fields such as the environment, cultural diversity, the problem of crime, corruption and citizen security.

Thus, the question of the State was once again put in theoretical terms and in its complexity as a referent of national unity and collective action, which will lead to the idea of plurinational States and to the analysis of the crystallization of the various relations of domination – not only class but also gender and race (O'Donnell, 2010) (see also the pieces by Castor and O'Donnell in this volume). We are facing a State that must be analyzed, far beyond its character of public bureaucracy, in terms of agency or actor, which leads to debate against those partial approaches, generally coming from political science, that reduce the problem to a question of efficiency, or response to demands of a regulated market through public policies. To a large extent, the administrative reforms or modernizations of the State in the last decades were inspired by a managerial vision. Undoubtedly, such policies and the studies from which they were inspired in many cases contributed to the improvement of State action; but with a double risk. On the one hand, there is the risk of reducing administrative reforms to mere efficiency, confusing modernity and modernization, and without having a model of a new State project that implies a transformation at the same time of the State and its relations with society. On the other hand, there is the risk of conceiving public policies only as expert or technical responses to specific demands devoid of general sense (Schneider and Heredia, 2003).[17]

## Towards a Renewed Perspective on Politics and Society

Precisely to overcome approaches that lead to abstracting and taking out of context the problems and political processes of the society as a whole but at the same time to promote analysis of the autonomy of the different dimensions and processes, in the 2000s attempts reappear to rethink Latin America from a more integral theoretical perspective, including society, State, socio-economic models and social and political actors; that is, to relate the set of social phenomena and their actors and processes, without neglecting to consider their autonomous dynamics and logics.[18]

In this framework, together with other authors, we proposed the concept of a socio-political matrix understood as the problematic articulation of four components, produced by and at the same time constituent of the social actors (Garretón et al., 2004).[19] These four components are: the State; the system of representation; the socio-economic base (development model); and the cultural orientations mediated by the political regime. The basic hypothesis is that in Latin America the decomposition of the State-national-popular matrix, dominant from the mid-twentieth century up to the military dictatorships, is a result of the processes of globalization as well as changes in politics and the State, as indicated before. The attempts to establish a neo-liberal matrix that introduces the commodification of all social relations as a principle were rejected by social struggles and movements (Garretón, 2014). The overcoming of such attempts can be expressed in terms of the search for the autonomy, strengthening and mutual complementarity of the various components.

Democracy seems consolidated as a relatively stable regime, but the rest of the components remain without solid definitions, as we have indicated regarding State reforms and the absence of a new autonomous production model within globalization. The same happens with the political dimension of the new actors and identities.

Perhaps one of the most important issues in this approach is to conceive the interrelation and autonomy of the components of the matrix not only as an articulation of parts, but as a structural-historical problem, in the classic CEPAL's language. And this problem can be defined today in terms of the recomposition of relations between State and society with a horizon that includes, among other dimensions, the autonomous insertion in the process of globalization, sustainable development, democratic deepening and equality, inclusion or social cohesion.[20]

The greater productivity of these approaches, which try to understand politics in a wider frame than itself, however, until now seems to be found in the study of past sociopolitical models or matrices. With the exhaustion of the so-called State-national-popular matrix and the attempts to impose a neoliberal matrix, what occurred was a disarticulation between the components and the appearance of new actors seeking a recomposition of the relations between State and society and the emergence of a new limit concept, which gave rise to the phenomenon of the so-called 'left turn' (Chiroleu, 2010; Ominami, 2017).

We face, then, the task of analyzing an exploded socio-political matrix in which politics is split from society, including political parties and electoral processes that seem no longer to respond to historical projects. The appeal to the State appears more often for solving private problems than related to general interest.

In this context academic sociological contributions will be very important to emphasize structures and processes, endowing politics with its own theoretical statute, along with reflections on fragmented processes and the emergence of new subjects – contributions eager to explain the relations between the dimensions of gender, race, territory, culture and civil society, as well as the problems of coloniality, Eurocentrism, good living, emancipation and new styles of politics.[21] If in the sixties we were in front of paradigms that sought to replace each other, today we can think of the indispensable convergence and feedback of the diverse voices that analyze politics from a sociological perspective.

## Notes

1. Translation revised by Fernanda Beigel.

2. It is worth remembering that one of the founding works of scientific sociology in Latin America is entitled *Politics and Society* (Germani, 1964).

3. See the classic text by Enzo Faletto and Fernando Henrique Cardoso (1968). Among the most important texts that summarize the political debates from the sociology of the sixties to the eighties, are those that took place in the workshops of UNAM's Institute of Social Research: the first in Mérida in 1971, focusing on social classes studies (Instituto de Investigaciones Sociales, 1973); the second in Oaxaca in 1975 where, from the classes perspective, the theme of the political crisis was addressed, especially that produced by the new dictatorships of the Southern Cone (Benitez Zenteno, 1977); the third in Morelia in 1980 and the fourth in Oaxaca in 1981, both already under the military dictatorships of the Southern Cone, and in which the political alternatives and the perspective of democratic transition are directly examined (respectively Julio Labastida, (Ed.) 1985, 1986) It is interesting to note that

in all these debates there is a discussion about the autonomy of political processes in relation to their determination by social structures and where the hegemony concept appears as one of the solutions.

4. Perhaps the most important sociological text about the relations between politics and society is the one by Alain Touraine (1989), who despite not being a Latin American author, reviews all Latin American literature up to that time.

5. These *coups d'état* were implemented in Brazil (1964), Argentina (1966 and 1976), Uruguay (1973) and Chile (1973), sharing some features also with other dictatorships in other countries. Some of the initial debates on these regimes are found in Collier (1979).

6. This perspective has its main base in Barrington Moore (1966), and which was developed among others by F.H. Cardoso (see his contributions in Benitez Zenteno, 1977); M.A. Garretón (see his contributions in Labastida, 1985 and 1986); Florestan Fernández (1978) and later for the Chilean case T. Moulian, (1997).

7. These definitions are based also on the intuitions by O'Donnell (1978). Even when he will name 'political regime' to the form of government (his classic phrase 'democracy is not only a political regime', illustrates the point) and he will keep on naming it Bureaucratic-Authoritarian State, I would prefer to speak of an authoritarian or dictatorial regime and democratic regime, in the sense given to political regime by Juan Linz (2000), distinguishing this from the concept of State.

8. The conceptualization of 'new' social movements occurs in the sixties in European and North American contexts when cultural, pacifist, ecologist and feminist movements appear, for which a character less directly linked to politics and class is pointed out. In Latin America, they are new because of their unprecedented character, arising above all in the dictatorships to which we have referred, and addressing issues such as human rights, urban and population topics, and others, but also relating as much to classes as politics. For the Chilean case, see Gonzalo de la Maza and Mario Garcés (1985). For Brazil, Paulo Singer and Vinicius Caldeira Brant (eds) (1980); Elizabeth Jelin (1989); Susan Eckstein (2001)). Regarding the rebirth of parties in the processes of democratic transition, Manuel Antonio Garretón and Marcelo Cavarozzi, (1989). And for later periods already in democracy, see Marcelo Cavarozzi and Juan Abal Medina (eds) (2002).

9. The project of the Wilson Center Latin American Program in Washington DC on democratic transitions carried out workshops on democratic transitions in Latin America between 1980 and 1981, the upshot of which were four emblematic volumes on the subject: Guillermo O'Donnell, Philippe Schmitter and Laurence Whitehead (eds) (1988 [1986]). In Latin America itself, the workshop organized by FLACSO and the University of Guadalajara in 1991 that gave rise to the book by Carlos Barba Solano, José Luis Barros Horcasitas and Javier Hurtado (1991).

10. Both in the literature and in the political debate, there was a strong presence of the Spanish model, which was not exempt from criticism.

11. A critique of the dominant approaches is developed in C. Franco (1998).

12. Regarding authoritarian enclaves, the concept was created in 1988 to account for the presence of typical elements of the authoritarian regime in the subsequent democracy, and it has institutional, ethical-symbolic, actoral and cultural dimensions, giving the emerging democracies an incomplete character (see Garretón, 1995). The common-sense critical phrase to indicate the democracy deficits was 'low intensity democracies'. Among

other concepts used to characterize them were: 'incomplete democracies', M.A. Garretón, (2003), 'half-sovereigns', Carlos Huneeus (2014); 'neoliberals', Paul Drake, (2009), and the most influential, 'delegative democracies', Guillermo O'Donnell (1997).

13. The report is based on a series of seminars and works led by Dante Caputo and the intellectual orientation of Guillermo O'Donnell, PNUD (2004a), and is accompanied by a book with various analyses, United Nations Development Program, (2004b).

14. It is worth mentioning the important contribution to this issue by LATINO BAROMETRO through its surveys.

15. The idea of citizenship restricted to rights whose owners are individuals, neglects the other dimension of citizenship that corresponds to the belonging to the polis, from which emanate duties and responsibilities, which imply participation and involvement in public affairs. Thus, the question of the reconstruction of the polis or the society and, therefore, of the relations between it and the State, which raises the issue of cohesion and equality and the need for new social pacts, will be central for the political debate that somehow began with the Chiapas movement in 1994 (see an analysis of the movement in the context of Mexican society at the time, in Sergio Zermeño (1996)) and continues with the so-called turn to the left of governments in the 2000s (for a general perspective, see the studies presented in Chiroleu (2010)). Concerning the intellectual debate of the socio-historical *problematique* opened at that time and the themes of the new social pact, see Manuel Antonio Garretón, (2014); CEPAL, (2007, 2010).

16. When we speak of factual powers we refer to those organizations or institutions that use their influence or power outside their own fields of action (the transnationals, the media, the churches, military sectors, trade associations, etc. can act as factual powers; drug trafficking, when it is introduced into political decisions at the local, State or transnational level, beyond its intrinsic criminal dimension, becomes a factual power). It can also be spoken of as *de jure* factual powers, when institutions such as the judiciary, the executive or legislative surpass their attributions and use their legitimacy to intervene in spheres that are not their own (for example, the issue of the judicialization of politics, the so-called 'Presidential decisionism', etc.). This is a subject whose theorization and empirical study is, in our opinion, overdue. Regarding corruption, see a general report in Alejandro Salas (2016).

17. A very important contribution to administrtaive reform has been made by the debates of the CLAD (Latin American Center of Administrartion for Development).

18. As an example of this, among many others, Francisco Delich (2004) analyzes the Latin American *problématique* at the beginning of the century through the interrelation between four dimensions State, nation, civil society and markets.

19. Currently, a review of the concept through five case studies has been prepared. For a discussion of this perspective see Aldo Mascareño, (2009).

20. We are dealing here with a new limit concept as an object of study and normative principle of collective action (see Garretón, 2014). Some call this limit concept *'vivir bien'* (good living) (see Farah and Vasapollo, 2011); others retake the concept of development as human development (UNDP, 1990); Castells and Himanen, (eds) 2014, based on Amartya Sen use the concept of dignity as the goal of human development in the informational era and Calderón and Castells (2014) apply the concept to Latin America. See also CEPAL 2007, 2010.

21. This perspective is partly illustrated in this volume by Suzy Castor's text. See a compilation of this perspective in Alberto Bialakowsky and Pablo Gentilli (eds), and Farah and Vasapollo (2011).

# References

Barba Solano, C.C., Barros, J.L. & Hurtado, J. (eds) (1991) *Transiciones a la democracia en Europa y América Latina*. Universidad de Guadalajara, FLACSO–México: Grupo editorial Miguel Ángel Porrúa, Mexico.

Beck, U. (1998) *La invención de lo político. Para una teoría de la modernización reflexiva*. (1st edition in German, 1993). Buenos Aires: F.C.E.

Benitez Zeneto, R.Z. (ed.) (1977) *Clases sociales y crisis política en América Latina*. Mexico: Siglo XXI.

Bialakowsky, A. & Gentilli, P. (eds) (2012) *Latin American Critical Thought*. Buenos Aires: CLACSO.

Calderón, F. (ed.) (2004a) *¿Es sostenible la globalización en América Latina? Debates con Manuel Castells*. Fondo de Cultura Económica.

Calderón, F. (2004b) 'Una discusión sociológica sobre el tema de la globalización', in *Debates con Manuel Castells*. Fondo de Cultura Económica.

Cardoso, F.H. (1972) *O modelo político brasileiro e outros ensaios*. São Paulo: DIFEL.

Castells, M. & Himanen, P. (2016) *Reconceptualización del desarrollo en la era global de la información*. Fondo de Cultura Económica.

Cavarozzi, M. & Abal Medina, J. (eds) (2002) *El asedio a la política. Los partidos latinoamericanos tras la década del neoliberalismo*. Rosario: Homo Sapiens.

CEPAL (2007) *Cohesión social: inclusión y sentido de pertenencia en América Latina y el Caribe*.

CEPAL (2010) *La hora de la igualdad. Brechas por cerrar, caminos por abrir*.

Cheresky, I. (ed.) (2006) *Ciudadanía, sociedad civil y participación política*. Buenos Aires: Miño y Dávila Editores.

Cheresky, I. (ed.) (2011) *Ciudadanía y legitimidad democrática en América Latina*. Buenos Aires: CLACSO-Prometeo.

Cheresky, I. (ed.) (2012) *¿Qué democracia en América Latina?* Buenos Aires: CLACSO-Prometeo Editores.

Cheresky, I. (2015) *El nuevo rostro de la democracia*. Buenos Aires: Fondo de Cultura Económica.

Chiroleu, A. (ed.) (2010) 'Contrapuntos en torno a los nuevos gobiernos progresistas de América Latina'. *Revista Temas y Debates*. No 20 Rosario, Argentina.

Collier, (ed.) (1979) *The New Authoritarianism in Latin America*. Princeton: Princeton University Press,

Dagnino, E., Rivera, A.O. & Panfichi, A. (2006) *La disputa por la construcción democrática en América Latina* (Vol. 3). CIESAS. FCE, Universidad Veracruzana.

De Castro Andrade, R.S. (1964) *Política social y normalización institucional en Brasil*.

De la Maza, G. & Garcés, M. (1985) *La explosión de las mayorías. Protesta nacional 1983–1984*. Santiago: Eco.

De la Torre, Carlos (2017) *Populismos, una inmersión rápida*. Barcelona: Ediciones Tibidabo.

Delich, F. (2004) *Repensar América Latina*. Barcelona: Gedisa.

Drake, P. (2009) *Between Tyranny and Anarchy. A History of Democracy in Latin America*. Stanford University Press.

Eckstein, S. (2001) *Poder y Protesta Popular, Movimientos sociales latinoamericanos*. Mexico: Siglo XXI.

Faletto, E. & Cardoso, F.H. (1968) *Dependencia y desarrollo*. Mexico: Siglo XXI.

Farah, I. & Vasapollo, L. (2011) *Vivir bien: ¿Paradigma no capitalista?*. La Paz: CIDES-UMSA and Sapienza: Oxfam.

Fernández, F. (1978) *La revoluición burguesa en Brasil*. Mexico: Siglo XXI.

Franco, C. (1998) *Acerca del modo de poensar la democracia en Améric Latina*. Argentina: Friedrich Ebert Stiftung.

Garretón, M. A. (1995) *Hacia una nueva era política. Estudio sobre las democratizaciones*. FCE.

Garretón, M.A. (2000) *Política y sociedad entre dos épocas: América Latina en el cambio del siglo*. Santa Fe, Argentina: Homo Sapiens Ediciones.

Garretón, M.A. (2003) *The Incomplete Democracy. Studies on Politics and Society in Latin America and Chile*. North Carolina University Press.

Garretón M.A (2014) *Las ciencias sociales en la trama de Chile y América Latina*. Estudios Sobre Transformaciones Sociopolíticas y Movimiento Social LOM Santiago.

Garretón, M.A. & Cavarozzi, M. (1989) *Muerte y Resurrección. Los partidos políticos en el autoritarismo y las transiciones del Cono Sur*. Santiago: Ediciones FLACSO.

Garretón, M.A., Cavarozzi, M., Cleaves P., Gereffi, G. & Hartlyn, J. (2004) *América Latina en el siglo XXI. Hacia una nueva matriz socio-política*. Santiago: Ediciones LOM.

Germani, G. (1964) *Política y sociedad en una época de transición*. Buenos Aires.

Germani, G., Di Tella, T.S. & Ianni, O. (1973) *Populismo y contradicciones de clase en Latinoamérica*. Mexico: Era.

Graciarena, J. & Franco, R. (1981). *Formaciones sociales y estructuras de poder en América Latina*. Madrid: Centro de Investigaciones Sociológicas.

Huneeus, C. (2014) *La democracia semisoberana*. Santiago: Taurus.

Instituto de Investigaciones Sociales Universidad Nacional Autónoma; (1973) *Las classes sociales en América Latina*. Mexico: Siglo XXI.

Jaguaribe, H. (1972) *La dominación de América Latina*. Amorrortu Editores.

Jelin, E. (1989) *Los nuevos movimientos sociales*. Buenos Aires: Centro Editor de América Latina.

Kaplan, M. (1969) *La formación del Estado nacional en América Latina*. Santiago: Editorial Universitaria.

Labastida, J. (ed.) (1985) *Hegemonía y alternativas políticas en América Latina*. Mexico: Siglo XXI.

Labastida, J. (ed.) (1986) *Los nuevos procesos sociales y la teoría política*. Mexico: Siglo XXI.

Laclau, E. (2004) *La razón populista*. Buenos Aires: Fondo de Cultura.

Lechner, N. (1994) 'Los nuevos perfiles de la política', *Nueva Sociedad*, *130*, 32–43.

Linz, J. (2000) *Totalitarian and Authoritarian Regimes*. Boulder, CO: Lynne Rienner Publishers.

Lissidini, A., Welp, Y. & Zovatto, D. (eds) (2014) *Democracias en movimiento: mecanismo de democracia directa y participativa en América Latina*. Universidad Nacional Autónoma de México, Instituto de Investigaciones Jurídicas.

Mannheim, K. (1950) *Diagnosis of Our Time: Wartime Essays of a Sociologist*. London: Routledge.

Marini, R.M. (1969) *Subdesarrollo y revolución*. Mexico: Siglo XXI Editores.

Mascareño, A. (2009) 'Acción y estructura en América Latina. De la matriz sociopolítica a la diferenciación funcional', *Persona y sociedad* / Universidad Alberto Hurtado Vol. XXIII, No. 2.

Moore, B. (1966) *Los orígenes sociales de la Dictadura y la Democracia. El Señor y el campesino en la formación del mundo modern*. Argentina: Ariel.

Morlino, L. (2012) *Changes for Democracy: Actors, Structures, Processes*. New York: Oxford University Press.

Morlino, L., Katz, G., Sottilotta, C. & Rial, J. (2014) *La calidad de las democracias en América Latina*. San José de Costa Rica: International IDEA.

Moulian, T. (1997) *Chile actual: Anatomía de un mito*. Santiago: LOM.

O'Donnell, G. (1978) 'Apuntes para una teoría del Estado', *Revista Mexicana de Sociología*, Vol. 40, No. 4, Estado y Clases Sociales en América Latina.

O'Donnell, G. (1985) 'Las tensiones en el Estado burocrático-autoritario y la cuestión de la democracia', in D. Collier (ed.), *El nuevo autoritarismo en América Latina*. Fondo de Cultura Económica. Original English version: (1979) *The New Authoritarianism in Latin America*. Princeton: Princeton University Press.

O'Donnell, G. (1997) *Contrapuntos. Ensayos escogidos sobre autoritarimo y democratización*. Buenos Aires: Paidós.

O'Donnell, G. (2010) 'Democracia, agencia y Estado'. *Teoría con intención comparativa*. Buenos Aires: Prometeo Libros.

O'Donnell, G., Schmitter, P. & Whitehead, L. (eds) (1988) *Transiciones desde un gobierno autoritario*. Buenos Aires, Paidós (*Prospects for Democracy and Transition from Authoritarian Rule* (1986) Johns Hopkins University Press).

O' Donnell, G., Iazzetta O. & Vargas Cullellcomps, J. (2003) 'Democracia, desarrollo humano y ciudadanía'. *Reflexiones sobre la calidad de lademocracia en América Latina*. Rosario: Homo Sapiens/PNUD.

Ominami, C. (ed.) (2017) *Claroscuro de los gobiernos progresistas: fin de un ciclo histórico o proceso abierto?*. Santiago: Editorial Catalonia.

Panfichi, Aldo (Ed.) (2002) *Sociedad civil, esfera pública y democratización en América Latina: Andes y Cono Sur*. Mexico: Fondo de Cultura Económica.

PNUD (2004a) *Democracia en América Latina. Hacia una democracia de ciudadanas y ciudadanos*. Argentina: PNUD.

PNUD (2004b) *La democracia en América Latina. Hacia una democracia de ciudadanas y ciudadanos. Contribuciones para el debate.* (Aguilar, Altea, Alfaguara, Buenos Aires).

Rodotá, S (1999) *Tecnopolítica: la democracia y las nuevas tecnologías de la comunicación*. Buenos Aires: Losada.

Rosanvallon, P. (2007) *La contrademocracia: la política en la era de la desconfianza.* Buenos Aires: Ediciones Manantial.

Salas, A. (2016) 'Un análisis de la corrupción en América Latina Revista Internacional', *Transparencia Internacional*, No. 2, September–December.

Schneider, B.R. & Heredia, B. (eds) (2003) *Reinventing Leviathan: The Politics of Administrative Reform in Developing Countries.* Miami, FL: North–South Center Press.

Singer, P. & Caldeira Brant, V. (eds) (1980) *São Paulo: O povoem movimiento.* Vozes-CEBRAP.

Solari, A., Franco, R. & Jutkowitz, J. (1976) *Teoría, Acción Social y Desarrollo en América Latina.* Mexico: Siglo XXI.

Touraine, A. (1989) *América Latina política y sociedad.* Espasa.

Trindade, H., De Sierra, G., Garretón, M.A., Murmis, M. & Reyna, J.L. (2007) *Las Ciencias Sociales en América Latina en perspectiva comparada.* Mexico: Siglo XXI.

Weffort, F. (1966) 'Estado e massa no Brasil', *Revista Civilizao Brasilera*, No 7, Mayo.

Zermeño, S. (1996) *La sociedad derrotada. El desorden mexicano del fin de siglo.* Mexico: Siglo XXI Editores.

# 24

# The Secular Roots of a Difficult Nation-building[1]

*Suzy Castor (Haiti)*

The evolution of Haiti during the last half century raised many questions without answers or answers based on all kinds of subjectivisms. The deep contradictions within its society has led many to claim Haitian exceptionalism, rather than contemplating its particularities. In essence, the Haitian process is in fact similar to other processes that developed at different times throughout Latin America, sharing common characteristics, *mutatis mutandis*, with varying intensities. To consider its current predicament as an isolated event, without putting it into a historical context, encourages the vision of Haiti as a 'failed state', 'non-viable' or a 'pariah nation with no future', largely hindering understanding of its continuities and ruptures. We cannot build the future without questioning the past, which shapes the present with its inconsistencies and ambiguities. In order to understand Haiti's current trends and features it is necessary to refer back to the historical factors that have shaped and influenced its evolution as an independent nation since 1804. Through a brief overview of the past century, I will attempt to identify the roots of the difficult problems the country has faced since the earthquake of January 12, 2010.

In the late eighteenth and early nineteenth centuries, Haiti's foundational century, the country wrote its first heroic page in universal history. In an international context of widespread slavery, colonialism and racism, the newly emerging State had to cope with defense, sovereignty, development and integration issues. The military-oligarchic power reproduced the colonial domination system, this time around coffee, and established a scheme of exclusive appropriation of political power and natural resources, while peasant revolts, some of them on quite a large scale, persisted stubbornly. Thus, at the end of the nineteenth century, critical voices, among them some of the most sensible representatives of the existing order, demanded industrialization, agricultural promotion and more social justice, while highlighting the need for a political force that would ensure national integration, help overcome economic obstacles and re-establish the balance among social forces. The oligarchic Republic, with its lack of coherence and unity, prevented economic and social development. Polarized struggles for power were waged between the two oligarchic sectors. This polarization was supported by vindictive farming groups and fueled by foreign powers' interferences and conspiracies, resulting in constant unrest and evident lack of governability. A deep, political, economic, social and moral crisis shook Haitian society.

Four major demands prevailed throughout the period: a State that would ensure modernization; integration of all citizens; a country with the capacity to satisfy the needs of its population; and a sovereign Haiti within the concert of nations. The solutions to political, social and ethno-cultural contradictions did not manage to get modernization underway since, on May 28, 1915, American marines landed in Haiti to impose their logic and their own solutions by force of arms, altering the historical course of Haitian people's life.

### The US Occupation and Aborted Modernity

Like other countries in the Caribbean and Central America, the 'big stick' policy imposed on Haiti entailed losing its political independence and adjusting its national structures to the interests of the occupying power.

At first, the expansion of very popular peasant guerrillas led by Charlemagne Péralte stood as an obstacle; however, until actual pacification in 1920, 'exemplary' violence led to 11,000 victims. Despite the use of unlimited coercive power, the dream of turning Haiti into a huge sugarcane plantation faltered over a scheme based on small land holdings, the lack of adequate infrastructure and a weak development of production forces. The plantation then merged into the local, archaic scheme. Thus, incorporation into the capitalist economy was reduced and farming production was not diversified nor did it increase substantially. Social relationships remained unaffected. Capital opted to exploit Haitian laborers, who were sent to work on American plantations in Cuba and the Dominican Republic. The occupation also failed to lay the foundations for industrial development or to significantly propel the internal market. However, representative democracy and the creation of an army, the backbone of the new political system, brought with it institutional modernization. A modern administrative apparatus, renewal of bureaucratic officials, expansion of the middle class, execution of large urban works and introduction of certain technological advances in daily life created, for many, the illusion of modernization.

In fact, this façade did not respond to development imperatives or real democratization. Large landowners, merchants, the military, prominent rural lords, etc., under the 'mulatto'[2] hegemony, became the dominant-dominated elite, thus securing the marginalization of the peasantry and urban masses, the removal of the provinces from the political scene and the excessive centralization of the 'Port-au-Prince Republic'. In addition, the occupation had aggravated the fundamental contradictions in the socio-economic structure, reinforcing other dimensions: urban/rural, Port-au-Prince centralization/weak provincial cities, black/mulatto, citizens/non-citizens, and occupation/sovereignty. A growing, peaceful nationalist movement demanded the end of the occupation, and, in 1930, elections opened up a new phase for the country. The army was ready to take over and ensure the status quo. On August 11, 1934, the last US marine left Haiti.

The apparatus deployed by the American system operated in a calm environment. However, it is worth noting that representative democracy adjusted very well to presidential absolutism, disputes with Parliament, army-dominated elections and even public liberties were sporadically despised.

With the end of the Second World War, the fall of fascism and the struggles against dictatorships, the post-occupation system underwent its first turmoil: the 1946 movement. Led by radical university students and promoted by socialist forces, this movement had a strong democratic content. It involved large popular sectors, mainly the masses in Port-au-Prince and provincial cities. Peasant struggles in the nineteenth century gave way to the urban movement. With few exceptions, the latter did not question the post-occupation system but rather demanded, based on the *noirisme*[3] doctrine, inclusion of black people into the state apparatus. This contributed to broadening and reinforcing the system's base of support. High raw materials and agricultural prices on the international market, financial support and an increase in foreign investments triggered an economic recovery, inducing a certain euphoria in dominant circles.

In fact, during the 1930–1956 period of 'democratic' rule, except for the war period, modernization became visible in a variety of ways and domains, such as: the urbanization of the capital city and other provincial cities; infrastructure works, like the International Exhibition commemorating the bicentennial founding of Port-au-Prince; significant production of scientific, literary, artistic, historical and economic works; and the implementation of education and health policies. It was a time of capitalist euphoria, backed by a monolithic army. Over this period, Latin America saw the rise of military power and McCarthyism, bent on fighting communism at all costs.

In the mid-1950s, the end of the Korean War and a natural disaster, tropical storm Hazel, brought this cycle of circumstantial prosperity to an end. All the dormant contradictions re-emerged, and new conflicts fueled military ambitions. Actually, favorable conditions had facilitated the effective functioning of a modernized political system, while concealing archaic economic structures. The deep structural crisis that could be retraced to the beginning of the century and increasing social demands gained strength in 1957. Thus came the dictatorial solution.

## The Dictatorial Solution: The End of the Post-occupation Model

The Duvalier regime introduced new methods of political domination through a power system based on institutionalized violence and State terrorism. Control mechanisms were reinforced, political opponents were eliminated and institutions were dismantled. As Michel Rolph Trouillot (1986) stated, François Duvalier 'formalized' the crisis. The regime, that had its own logic, meant the collapse of representative democracy as established by American occupation. Using an obscure, manipulative, doctrinal arsenal, Duvalier's dictatorship managed to disband the army, presented itself as the flagship of the middle classes and sought to broaden its base of support through the false inclusion of peasants into the political scene. The regime attempted to systematically destroy all sources of resistance and suffocate heroic struggles for democracy, extending to certain oligarchic segments particular forms of repression and domination it had thus far reserved for peasants and the masses. It is worth noting that during this extremely difficult time, many foreign nations supported Duvalier, particularly the United States, with its obsession with the Cuban Revolution.

For more than ten years, the country experienced an economic breakdown, which, according to Gérard Pierre-Charles (1997), led it towards a spiral of 'development of the underdevelopment'. This collapse occurred at a time of great human advancement: the first man on the moon, the third technological revolution, and people's rising aspirations for greater social justice and more democracy. Those were the days of the Cuban Revolution and the independence of African and Caribbean countries.

In 1971, Jean-Claude Duvalier inherited the title of president for life. Modernized repressive methods, the reconciliation of the black and mulatto bourgeoisies and the logic of absolute power varnished with a technocratic sheen marked a stage of continuity that promised to bring an 'economic revolution'.

After over fifteen years of setbacks, economic recovery was feeble. Opening the door to 'wild capitalism' attracted foreign investments towards the assembly industry or mining, as well as developing an embry-onic, internal market-oriented industry, with the introduction of private monopolies. High essential oils and pita prices on the international market, added to the rise in foreign debt and bilateral and multilateral donations, ensured a relatively large quantity of money in circulation that concealed the drop in coffee production, rapid environmental degradation by tra-ditional farming, impoverishment of the peasantry, emergence of shanty towns and the 'boat people' phenomenon. In the context of the Duvalier regime, this was the mirage of modernization and of new forms of increas-ing dependency.

In short, the Duvalier era constituted, at a huge cost to our people, a violent attempt to expand the bases of the oligarchic State through rec-onciliation between the old and the new black and mulatto oligarchies, incorporation of middle sectors and false inclusion of the peasantry. Its extended time period, twenty-nine years, enabled its practices and ideas to anchor themselves deeply into our society, shape its institutions and dis-rupt all national structures. It deepened contradictions in society, widened the gap between the rich and the poor, intensified social exclusion and the breaking of social bonds and reinforced the two-way society. At the end of the day, the son of a US occupation, Duvalier was unable to guarantee social and political stability and the survival of the post-occupation sys-tem. The effects of the US economic crisis, the decline in coffee prices and rising popular struggles exposed the fragility of the Duvalier regime and the limits and contradictions of its dictatorial project.

Dictatorships, such as Alfredo Stroessner's in Paraguay or Ferdinand Marcos's in the Philippines, were coming to an end. In Haiti, the crisis, nurtured by old and new problems, demanded an urgent and firm solution to answer people's clamor for an integrated nation that could meet the needs of its citizens in terms of development and democracy. The Haitian elite had, once again, failed to promote democratic ideals and deploy mod-els for progress and development fitting for a modern community. There was also the failure of the politics by its powerful supporters.

## The Transition: From Consensus to Polarization

The fall of the Duvaliers, on February 7, 1986, gave way to a long transition period during which renewed contradictions resurfaced. The consolidation of a large social movement, the struggles against restoring Duvalierism without Duvalier, and elections in December 1990 ushered in a new stage laden with illusions of change. For the first time since the US occupation, the army did not hold the power and the traditional political class seemed overwhelmed. The crisis of hegemony appeared to have found a way out, but this was nothing more than an illusion that ended with a bloody military coup seven months later. Despite a few advances from the legal perspective and an improvement in the living conditions of citizens, beyond objective reality, the feeling of access to citizenship and sovereignty could have turned into a powerful leverage to advance towards building an integrated nation. Popular resistance strengthened, the army lost its traditional allies and American troops had to restore democratic government. Except during the coup period (1991–1994) and the interim government period (2004–2006), the Lavalas[4] movement dominated the transition. This second stage, despite everything, brought new hopes and opportunities, but also ruptures, displacements and perversions. Populist content and lack of projects affected the legitimacy of the regime, particularly as the government reproduced previous schemes that had supposedly been overcome, aggravating economic and social distortions. Deinstitutionalization did away with all reference points, both in society and in power spaces, and contributed to growing social disintegration, a crumbling economy and the nation's dismantlement.

The Lavalas movement wanted to destroy the old power establishment but failed to build a new one. The hybrid representative democracy model grafted onto Duvalierism did not work out, entangled in its own contradictions and, mostly, fought off by the population's advanced awareness of citizenship and the international evolution of transparency demands. An authoritarian State tried to find its way with more or less strength and nuances, and, adjusting to the new domestic and international realities, it enriched its modus operandi with new instruments. Thus, institutions performed poorly and, later, fell apart: a weak State in terms of national leadership and construction, unable to perform its sovereign duties. In 1994, a major change took place: the de facto army, the backbone of the post-occupation system, was disbanded.

Haiti, in its capacity as the most underdeveloped country in the continent in terms of human development, saw the decline of traditional production and reproduction mechanisms as well as a lack of dynamism in emerging sectors of the economy. The assembly, craft or agricultural production industries oriented towards exports or the internal market failed to consolidate themselves. However, new distortive factors facilitated monetary circulation and helped keep the country going: significant international bilateral or multilateral aid, migrant remittances, drug trafficking, smuggling and speculations of all kinds. There was a fact that could not be ignored: Haiti had stopped producing while its population and consumption continued to grow. The farming sector laid bare the structural weaknesses of the production system: collapsing rural structures, the expulsion of peasants to cities, expanded shanty towns, the higher number of emigrants, wild urbanization, decline of the shrinking industrial sector, and the central significance of informal employment in the economy. Economic disintegration strongly affected all sectors, except for the system's beneficiaries and protégés. The traditional bourgeoisie displaced itself, middle classes shrank, and the living conditions of the working classes became inhumane. However, as compared with previous periods, major changes had taken place.

The assertion of free speech enabled individual and collective expression of claims, complaints and critiques of power. Numerous actors, until then invisible, came onto the stage. The forever excluded groups, the peasantry and the provinces, which had undergone repression since the 1915 occupation, reappeared to claim their rights. Slum dwellers and the middle classes challenged the power of the State, the bourgeoisie and the traditional political class who failed to perceive the changes underway in society. Popular classes made strong claims for integration, demanding, for the first time, not only social but political inclusion, a political system with a well-defined set of rules of the game, and a new institutional framework to facilitate the implementation of a national project that would include all social classes.

Against this backdrop, the support, coopting, domination and even repression and violent methods of traditional power became less effective, just like populist demagogy. Faced with the demands of these new collective actors, the political regime withered, unable both to satisfy the population's demands for well-being and participation, and to ensure adequate governance, social cohesion and legitimacy. At the same time, the social movement, through its renovated struggles, with equally significant advances and setbacks, powerful in essence but weak at the organizational level, and particularly lacking support from well-organized political parties and solid well-structured civil society organizations, still failed to resolve the issue of political and economic management. The problem of hegemony already raised at the end of the nineteenth century and the exacerbated polarization evidenced throughout this stage shook the destitute Haitian society with contradictions and confrontations.

Throughout this period, the very notion of sovereignty vanished against the overwhelming magnitude of military intervention and a military force of over 12,000 soldiers.

The earthquake of January 12, 2010 became a melting pot, highlighting the features already outlined, deepening contradictions and blending old and new challenges, as well as possibilities, opportunities, resources and leverages that could prove useful to reconstruct and re-found the nation.

This catastrophe exposed the State's inability and lack of organization to lead and build the nation, emphasizing its collapse. Although alleviated by emergency aid, and despite its perverse effects, the already precarious living conditions of the population took a turn for the worse. Daily life became more and more difficult for all social sectors, from the poorest strata to the needy bourgeoisie. Growing frustrations fueled potential outbreaks which were difficult to predict. A fragile State apparatus and loss of government authority led to an all-pervasive, all-powerful international presence that replaced the Haitian State in a straightforward way. Therefore, in this scenario, the process of national reconstruction was shaped without a real government vision and without the participation of its population. More than ever, on account of its historical-structural character and its level of maturity, the global Haitian crisis denied any attempt at recomposition.

## Will the Twenty-first Century Be the Color of Hope?

This brief outline seems to lock ourselves in a closed circle of thwarted experiences, disappointments, frustrations and struggles, but also of success, within an endless historical search to build the nation on a consensual basis. This process of beginning anew once again raises issues and signals contradictions when confronting our political imaginary with reality. Rather than being solved, problems seem to get more complex. Haiti seems to have missed the train of development. Today, we take pride in our historical past and our peoples' determination; they are our greatest assets. Therefore, we must learn from our experiences in order to 'regain our history', to open up original paths in tune with our past itinerary and our current state of extreme underdevelopment and to create a society governed by organized leaders with the ability to build trust in order to overcome obstacles to progress, and where efficiency, solidarity, collective interest, ethnic consistency and a national project are among the most cherished values. It is a difficult task, particularly when the present compromises the future: to build the nation at a time when globalization dominates the world scene, and with its rigid laws and ruthless social Darwinism strips poor countries of essential tools that have contributed to forging the founding states.

This severe crisis requires major changes. The current situation calls for an alternative to lay the material, intellectual and moral foundations of the country and re-found the nation. Whether we like it or not, this alternative involves improving and modernizing the current political system, which bears an enormous weight at the present time. Only a dispassionate view of the past can provide an understanding of present difficulties and ambiguities and contribute to activating our culture, the guarantor of a world of justice and well-being that inspired a century-old fight and a dream. To untie the historical knots of the four great demands that prevailed throughout the last century is the great challenge that all fully self-aware Haitians have to assume.

## Notes

1.   Originally published in French as 'Les racines séculaires d'un difficile construction nationale', in S. Castor (2010) *Haïti, Réinventer l'avenir*, Éditions de la Maison des Sciences de l'Homme: Paris. Translation by Mariana Donadini, revised by Fernanda Beigel and annotated by Nadine Berger.

2.   'Mulato/a' is a Spanish term used to refer to a person of mixed white and black ancestry.

3.   A political ideology sustained by François Duvalier which allegedly aimed to promote the blacks.

4.   The Lavalas movement created a political party called the Struggling People's Organization and, in 1996, the more conservative members split from the party forming their own Fanmi Lavalas. ('Lavalaś' in créole means avalanche.)

## References

Castor, Suzy (1999). *L'occupation américaine d'Haïti*, Port-au-Prince, Éditions Résopresse.

Pierre-Charles, Gérard (1997). *Haití pese a todo, la utopía*, Porto Rico, Universidad de Puerto Rico.

Trouillot, Michel Rolf (1986). *Les racines historiques de l'État duvaliérien*, Port-au-Prince, Éditions Henri Deschamps.

## Suzy Castor, by Patricia Funes (Argentina)

Suzy Castor (born in Port au Prince in 1936) is one of the most renowned intellectuals and activists in the Caribbean area. Her work analysing Haiti's historic and social processes has been pioneering in the field. She studied social sciences at Haiti's École Normale Supérieure (1955–1958) and doctoral studies in History at the Universidad Nacional Autónoma de México (National Autonomous University of Mexico, UNAM). Castor's decision to study in Mexico was exceptional, as Haitian intellectuals in the 1960s generally opted to travel to Europe, and mainly to French universities. After completing her degree, it was impossible for Castor to return to Haiti during the regime of the Duvaliers. François Duvalier was elected president in 1957 but later established a dictatorship (1964–1971). He was succeeded by his son, Jean-Claude Duvalier, who ruled the country until 1986.

From 1968 to 1989, Castor's years of exile in Mexico, she taught at UNAM's School of Philosophy and Letters and the School of Political and Social Sciences. Caribbean Studies was still a fledgling field, not only in Mexico but also across Latin America. In this regard, she made pioneering contributions to understanding the region. In 1972, she and her husband Gérard Pierre-Charles, also an intellectual and activist, founded the Centro de Estudios del Caribe (Caribbean Studies Centre) at UNAM's School of Political and Social Sciences; four years later, they started the journal *Caribe Contemporáneo* (*The Caribbean Today*), which is still published by the centre.

Two of Castor's books are fundamental for Caribbean Studies: *La intervención norteamericana en Haití y sus consecuencias* (*U.S. Intervention in Haiti and its Consequences*, Siglo XXI, Mexico, 1978) and *Migraciones y relaciones internacionales. El caso Haitiano-dominicano* (*Migrations and International Relations: The Case of Haiti and the Dominican Republic*, University Press of the Santo Domingo Autonomous University, Santo Domingo, 1987). She has edited and contributed to numerous anthologies on Haiti, the Caribbean and Latin America, and published more than fifty articles on the topic. In those studies, Castor addresses how Haiti has suffered the effects of slavery, colonialism, foreign interventions, dictatorships and natural disasters over the course of its history. These processes had frequently been analysed from perspectives like sociological singularity, naturalization and even magic or mystification. As Castor notes, a heroic feat in world history occurred in Haiti early in the late eighteenth century (1791) when a slave uprising culminated in the country achieving independence (1804). In Castor's sociological arguments, the socio-political dynamics of Haiti are explained in a dialogue with Latin American processes. In the text included in this volume, she describes the four biggest challenges facing Haiti today – modernization, integrated society, development and sovereignty – examining the historical roots that contribute to understanding the still incomplete construction of Haiti's state and nation.

In addition to her scholarly work, Castor is also a human rights activist. In Mexico, she collaborated with solidarity networks welcoming exiles from Southern Cone dictatorships; she also supported the cause of Guatemalan and Salvadoran refugees during the civil wars of the 1980s and the movements that protested the dictatorship in her homeland, Haiti. After the overthrow of Jean-Claude Duvalier in 1986, Castor and Pierre-Charles returned to Haiti and founded the Centre de recherche et de formation économique et sociale pour le développement (Economic and Social Research and Training Centre for Development, [CRESFED]). This NGO conducts collaborative research for the consolidation of democracy, human rights, education, de-centralization, local development, women's rights, migrant conditions and rural development.

Castor holds an honorary doctorate from the Santo Domingo Autonomous University, she is a member of the board of directors of the Consejo Latinoamericano de Ciencias Sociales (the Latin American Council of Social Sciences, or CLACSO) and of the Permanent People's Tribunal. She has received many awards for her work, including the *Ohtli* ('path' in Náhuatl) award from the Institute for Mexicans Abroad (2015), the UNESCO Mahatma Gandhi Medal (2009), the IV Premio Juan María Bandrés from the Comisión Española de Ayuda al Refugiado (Spanish Commission for Refugee Assistance [CEAR], 2005), and the Casa de las Américas prize (2004), among others. Currently she is Professor at the State University of Haiti and has been Director of the CRESFED since 1995.

# 25

# The Populist Turn and the Center-Left in Latin America[1]

*Ernesto Laclau (Argentina–UK)*

When does a populist rupture emerge? It inevitably occurs with the dichotomization of the social space, wherein actors see themselves as participants in one or the other of two opposing camps. Constructing the people as a collective actor implies appealing to 'the underdogs', set against the established institutional order. This implies that, one way or another, existing institutional channels for satisfying social demands have lost their efficacy and legitimacy and that the new hegemonic configuration – the new 'historical block', to use a Gramscian term – will suppose a regime change and a restructuring of the public space.

Of course, this does not anticipate the ideological content of the populist turn. Ideologies of most diverse kinds, from communism to fascism, may adopt a populist bias. However, in all cases, there will be a more or less profound rupture with the current status quo, depending on specific circumstances. Two French authors, Yves Meny and Ives Surel (2000), have argued, from this point of view, that all policies have a populist dimension. The corollary is that, from my perspective, the category of populism does not necessarily imply a pejorative assessment. Of course, this does not mean that all populism is by definition good. If the most diverse political contents are liable to a populist mode of articulation, our support for a particular populist movement will not depend on its populist discourse but rather on content analysis.

In my work on the subject, I have drawn the distinction between the social logic of difference and the logic of equivalence. The former is an eminently institutionalist logic, in which social demands are individually satisfied and absorbed by the system. The exclusive prevalence of this institutional logic would lead to the death of politics and its replacement by mere administration. Saint-Simon's formula 'from the government of men to the administration of things' perfectly expresses this utopia of a reconciled society, devoid of antagonism. No wonder Marx adopted it to describe the classless society that would follow the extinction of the State.

In the logic of equivalence, things happen differently, and its prevalence hinges on unmet demands among which a certain kind of solidarity arises. If a group of people with unmet housing needs, for example, starts to perceive that their neighbors have other, equally unsatisfied claims at the levels of transport, employment and essential public services, an equivalential relationship is established between them. All demands are then perceived as elements of a common popular identity, individually and administratively unsatisfied within the current institutional system. This plurality of demands then begins to express itself through common symbols and, at a given time, some leaders start to interpellate these frustrated masses outside the existing system and against it. This is the time when populism makes its entrance, linking these three dimensions: equivalence among unsatisfied demands, their crystallization around certain common symbols, and the emergence of a leader whose word embodies this popular identification process.

As you can see, populism is a matter of degree, of the extent to which equivalential logic prevails over differential logic. But the prevalence of one over the other can never be total. No popular dichotomous logic will ever dissolve one hundred percent the institutional apparatus of society. And no institutional system will ever operate with such clockwork precision as to avoid giving rise to antagonism and equivalential relationships between heterogeneous demands. Any political analysis must first determine the dispersion of demands, both in civil society and in the public space. It is no coincidence that populism has always been a primary target of criticisms by supporters of the status quo, since their biggest fear is the politicization of social demands. They hold the ideal of a public sphere entirely dominated by technocracy.

The current situation in Latin America must be considered within this perspective. Our countries have inherited two interrelated and traumatic experiences: military dictatorships and the destruction of the continent's economies by neoliberalism, best epitomized by the International Monetary Fund adjustment programs. I describe these experiences as interrelated because the reforms implemented by the Chicago Boys in Chile or the suicidal economic plan carried out by José Alfredo Martínez de Hoz in Argentina (the adjective 'suicidal' has been used by English author Duncan Green (2003) to refer to the elimination of import tariffs and controls while maintaining an overvalued peso, resulting in the

Argentine market being flooded with cheap foreign goods and leading to the collapse of local industrial production) would not have been possible without military dictatorships in power.

The consequences of this double crisis are clear: a crisis of institutions as channels for satisfying social demands and a proliferation of such demands in horizontal protest movements that were not vertically integrated into the political system. The *Piquetero*[2] movement in Argentina, the Landless Rural Workers in Brazil and Mexican Zapatism (at least in its initial stages) are clear expressions of this trend, but comparable phenomena can be found in almost all Latin American countries. They illustrate the full operation of the distinction between 'equivalence' and 'difference' that I mentioned earlier. Mere individual satisfaction of social demands by the institutional system is replaced by a rising mobilization and politicization of civil society. This is the real challenge facing the democratic future of Latin American societies: to create viable States, which can only be achieved if the vertical and horizontal moments of politics reach a certain kind of integration and balance.

It is well known that, during the 1990s, social repression and deinstitutionalization were the conditions for the implementation of social adjustment policies. We need only consider Carlos Menem's abuse of 'necessity and urgency decrees'; the state of siege followed by violent repression of labor unions in Bolivia in 1985; the use of antiterrorism legislation for the same purposes in Colombia; the dissolution of the Peruvian Congress by Alberto Fujimori; or the brutal repression of popular social protest by Carlos Andrés Perez following an astronomical rise in the price of gasoline in 1989. The failure of the neoliberal project in the late 1990s, together with the need to elaborate more pragmatic policies that would combine market mechanisms with larger degrees of public regulation and social participation led to more representative regimes and to what is now called a general turn to the center-left. In other words, the viability of these new regimes called for a change in the form of the State so as to articulate the above-mentioned two dimensions in a new way.

At this point, several regional variants arise, whose comparison particularly brings into light the specificity of the Venezuelan experience. In the cases of Chile and Uruguay, the institutional dimension has prevailed over the rupture moment in the transition from dictatorship to democracy, thus few populist elements can be found in these experiences; whereas in the Venezuelan case, the moment of rupture is critical. Argentina and Brazil hold an intermediate position. In Chile, the transition towards democracy entailed a rather peaceful and gradual process, dominated by the theme of reconciliation; while in Uruguay no public action was taken against oppressors, as Nestor Kirchner did in Argentina.

In Venezuela, the transition towards a more fair and democratic society required the displacement of and radical rupture with a corrupt and discredited elite, lacking political communication channels with the vast majority of the population. That is, any advance demanded a regime change. But to achieve it, it was necessary to construct a new collective actor of a popular nature. It could be said, in keeping with our terminology, that there was absolutely no possibility of change without a populist rupture. We have already pointed out the defining features for the rupture of populism, all of which are present in the Chavez case: an equivalential mass mobilization; the constitution of a people; ideological symbols that reflect this collective identity (the *bolivarismo*); and, finally, the centrality of the leader as a binding factor. This factor arouses much controversy regarding Chavez's alleged tendencies to mass manipulation and demagogy. However, those who think along these lines do not question the centrality of the leader in all cases. Would the transition towards the Fifth French Republic have been possible without the centrality of the leadership of Charles de Gaulle? All our reactionaries, whether leftists or rightists, share this one characteristic: they condemn Mario's dictatorship but support Sila's.

A truly legitimate issue is whether there is a tension between the moment of popular participation and the moment of the leader; if the prevalence of the latter may limit the former. It is true that any populism runs this risk, but no iron law determines that yielding to it constitutes populism's manifested destiny. In Africa, for example, after the decolonization process, we have witnessed the bureaucratic decadence of populism in the case of Mugabe, but we have also seen a democratic and highly participative populism in Nyerere's government. However, nothing in the Venezuelan experience allows us to believe that a tendency towards bureaucratization will prevail. On the contrary, we are witnessing a mobilization and self-organization of previously excluded sectors which have considerably expanded the dimensions of the public sphere. The greatest danger to Latin America's democracy comes from neoliberalism and not from populism.

Hence the importance of consolidating Mercosur and definitively rejecting the Free Trade Area of the Americas (FTAA) project, which would have implied subordinating our countries to the dictates of North American economic policy (which does not hesitate to practice, against all neoliberal recipes, open protectionism when it comes to defending its interests). At present, Latin American political and economic perspectives are more promising than they have been for a long time, and Venezuela, together with other progressive regimes in the continent, is playing a critical role in this respect.

## Notes

1. Published originally in Spanish in Ernesto Laclau (2006), 'La deriva populista y la centro izquierda Latinoamericana', *Revista Nueva Sociedad*, No. 205, pp. 56–61. Translated by Mariana Donaldini and revised by Chantal Mouffe.
2. The term mainly refers to the Argentine unemployed workers' movement that unites impoverished workers in repeated waves of protest involving blocking and barricading roads.

## References

Green, D. (2003) *Silent Revolution: The Rise and Crisis of Market Economics in Latin America*. New York: Monthly Review Press.
Meny, Y. and Surel, I. (2000) *Pour le peuple, par le peuple*. Paris: Fayard.

## Ernesto Laclau, by Paula Biglieri (Argentina)

Ernesto Laclau (1935–2014) was the kind of philosopher whose theoretical intervention made a difference: it opened a whole path to a new kind of emancipationist thought that reoriented the political leftist position. His text, written together with Chantal Mouffe – *Hegemony and Socialist Strategy: Towards a Radical Democratic Politics*, first published in English in 1985 – gave birth to what has been known as Post-Marxism. *Hegemony and Socialist Strategy* was crucial for the left because it stood against the overwhelming conservative current which was delighted to celebrate the failure of the socialist project and with it the unsuccessfulness of Marxist theory. In an enormous effort – that could be interpreted as work to overcome their Marxist heritage – Laclau and Mouffe deconstructed Marxist theory in such a major way that they ended up dismantling its foundations. However, they persisted in the idea of social change and antagonism, but this time without any possibility of reaching a dialectical resolution. Once they noticed that antagonism inhabits the heart of the subject, the affirmation that a final complete coherent resolution that would not leave any residue turned out to be absurd. Thus, they posed the enigmatic phrase 'society is impossible', a metaphor to say that society lacks the ultimate foundations from which the totality of partial process could be established. Therefore, it will no longer be possible to maintain the argument that the subject of history could be determined a priori (the proletariat) and that it has a destiny that is pre-established (the reconciled society of communism). Nevertheless, they never surrender a sense of revolutionary spirit; they insisted on the idea of an emancipatory project, but now in plurality: emancipation(s), as effects of different struggles carried out by different subjects depending on diverse contexts.

In a sense, this theoretical intervention brought bad news for both academics and political activists who were still concerned about emancipation. There were no more certainties left standing to hold on to. However, at the same time, this bad news meant a breath of fresh air as it opened a new field for a leftist position, named Post-Marxism. *Hegemony and Socialist Strategy* obliged us to rethink what it is to 'be on the left' as we addressed the debate on the subject.

Laclau kept on developing his theory, usually known as the Theory of Hegemony. Gramsci, Althusser, Foucault, Derrida have served Laclau as background, as sources from which to draw nourishment. Nonetheless, Laclau's theory is more than a Theory of Hegemony, it is also a Theory of Antagonism. Furthermore, it is the centrality of that concept of antagonism that led him to go deeper into psychoanalysis – in particular in his Lacanian stream – and to take and 'make use' of certain fundamental categories from this field of knowledge, which ended up having a special place in his postulates. Not everything was deconstructing the Marxist Theory for Laclau. He constructed his own theory, taking into account some key elements coming from psychoanalysis. Laclau liked stating that he was not 'Lacanian', but a 'Laclausian'. Nevertheless, if we lose sight of how deeply psychoanalysis incarnates in Laclau's theory, we run the risk of flattening his concepts and nullifying their explanatory power.

*New Reflections on the Revolution of our Time* (1990), the collections of essays in *Emancipation and Difference* (1996) and *The Rhetorical Foundations of Society* (2014), published posthumously – which includes one of the greatest essays in Contemporary Philosophy, 'On the Names of God' – are some of his major works. Although it is *On Populist Reason* (2005) that needs to be considered separately because of the impact it had, especially in Latin America. This was the book that gained public recognition for Laclau, even outside the academic cloisters. *On Populist Reason* implies the most promising attempt to continue with the idea of a political subject, right there where many other thinkers ended up either with an open or veiled return to Marxism or with a dilution of the possibility of any organized political action. For Laclau it is the people – when it is able to articulate itself as such – the only figure capable of unleashing modifications on the status quo. That is to say, it is the people – as an effect of an equivalential chain that is formed with diverse demands, that crystallizes from the libidinal attachment to a leader – the figure capable of pushing emancipatory struggles. That is populism. However, Laclau also warned us that a populist articulation is a form, and the different modalities it might take depends on the correlation of political forces. The general political content of a populist articulation will depend on the result of political struggles within the context where it was formed. Therefore, it is possible to find leftist populisms as well as rightist populisms.

That is the moment when Laclau, the philosopher, allowed the militant political activist to arise. This is when decision acquires its whole dimension, since he is aware of standing on an undecidable ground without the reassurance of the political orientation that the figure of the people might take. It is that lack of guarantees which evokes a call to become involved in political struggles, since there is nothing guaranteed, as antagonism is inextricable and we do not know what its incessant irruption may generate in the Symbolic and Imaginary orders, as we do not know in advance how

*(Continued)*

(Continued)

things are going to turn out to be. Nothing ensures that the rights that we have today will still be there tomorrow, as the figure of the people does not have an emancipatory pre-established destiny – it is because of all these things that we do have to become political activists. In other words, it is a matter of becoming responsible. In any case, the best we can reach with a populist articulation are some political practices that will imply at the same time the experience of the possibility and the impossibility of emancipation because the reconciliation of society with itself is impossible.

This ethics of militant commitment was always practiced by Laclau because for him there was no possibility of thinking a political theory without a political position. He practiced this commitment when he was a young student at the Faculty of Philosophy and Arts in the University of Buenos Aires, Argentina. *New Reflections on the Revolution of our Time* is dedicated 'To Viamonte 430, where everything began', the old street address of the Faculty in downtown Buenos Aires. There, he combined political activism with his studies. In 1956 – only one year after a military coup had overthrown the populist government of Juan Domingo Perón – he became President of the Student's Union, representing the 'national left wing', which was the left involved in the Latin American popular movements (not the other one, the so-called and popularly known as 'Sepoy left', which expected that the Latin American workers' struggles would evolve along the same path as the European ones). Later he also became the editor of the National Left Party's newspaper, *Lucha Obrera* (Workers' Struggle). In those early writings of the student political activist we can find a lot of papers that show how Laclau was – in a way – thinking about the same topics from the very beginning: the non-correspondence of social class identity with a particular determined social class task as it was postulated by classical Marxism, all these problematics about the political subject were already taking him to the lectures of Antonio Gramsci, that would later emerge through his own notions of hegemony and antagonism.

During the last years, while many academics, particularly from Latin America, preferred the safe place of indifferent distance, Laclau reaffirmed his ethic of political militant commitment by strongly supporting the left-wing wave of populisms of Latin America. Although he obviously knew that his position-taking would not be an easy place, as we all know there will always be deficits and excesses, he decided to take the risk and supported the governments of Néstor Kirchner and Cristina Fernández de Kirchner in Argentina, Rafael Correa in Ecuador, Evo Morales in Bolivia, Luiz Inácio 'Lula' da Silva and Dilma Rousseff in Brazil, José 'Pepe' Mujica in Uruguay and Hugo Chávez in Venezuela, in their attempt to resist neoliberalism from a popular-democratic frame by promoting equality.

## References

Laclau, Ernesto (1990) *New Reflections on the Revolution of our Time*. London/New York: Verso.

Laclau, Ernesto (2005) *On Populist Reason*. London/New York: Verso.

Laclau, Ernesto (2014) *The Rhetorical Foundations of Society*. London/New York: Verso.

Laclau, Ernesto and Mouffe, Chantal (1985). *Hegemony and Socialist Strategy. Towards a Radical Democratic Politics*. London/New York: Verso.

# 26

# On Certain Aspects of the Crisis of the State[1]

*Guillermo O'Donnell (Argentina–US)*

There is enough evidence to show that the extraordinarily severe socioeconomic-economic crisis most newly democratized countries are suffering furthers the spread of brown[2] regions. The spread not only comes from various processes of social and economic disintegration; it also results from the profound crisis of the State – as effective legality, as a set of bureaucracies, and as a legitimized agent of the common interest. But the spread also results from the strong anti-statism of neoliberal ideas and policies,[3] especially the endeavor to diminish at all costs the size of the State bureaucracies and the fiscal deficit.

Many efforts are in train to reduce the fiscal deficit. On the expenditure side, the main actions have been privatizations and attempts to get rid of 'excessive personnel'. The latter has not been easy, in part because in most cases the tenure of those employees is legally protected, and in part because strenuous opposition from the unions has proven costly for fragile governments. More effective for reducing the fiscal deficit have been policies that resulted in the fast decline of the salaries of most public employees.

In addition to abrupt falling salaries, there are many indications of a severe degradation of the functioning and the very idea of public service. Many of the most capable officials have left the public service for the private sector. For those who have remained, their status has declined no less faster than their salaries: prevailing anti-statist ideologies prejudice their positions; at best they feel observed with mistrust, and the mass media as well as public opinion are full of anecdotes (too often true) of their idleness, lack of competence or interest in their jobs, and corruption. If some time ago to be a State official was a signal of high status, nowadays it is almost the opposite.

Probably worse still is the change in expectations. Before the present crisis, to become a public official was to be part of a career structure.

This meant working in a framework that provided a predictable path towards promotion, and receiving a monthly income and various benefits that allowed a solid middle-class lifestyle (usually including good housing and the capacity to afford university education for one's children). Except for some privileged salaries (typically the Central Banks) this is no longer true in the countries affected by the present crisis. A dark picture arises from the decapitation of the top and more specialized bureaucracies due to the outflow of the more qualified individuals, the politicization of those positions, the various and always failed 'rationalizations' and 'reorganizations', and the spectacular drop of the physical infrastructure. (There is perhaps nothing more discouraging than hammering at a worn-out mechanical typewriter in an office where the painting and furniture have not been renewed in decades.) This is propitious for the existence of a poorly motivated and unskilled bureaucracy, which, in turn, fits and feeds back into the innumerable anecdotes that support the direct attack on the State and erodes the political support that would be necessary for effecting a better balanced public policy towards its own bureaucracy.

Furthermore, under conditions of high and erratic inflation, in one month State employees may lose 30, 40 and even 50 percent of their real incomes. Under these circumstances they cannot but demand immediate readjustment. Strikes and demonstrations spread, sometimes violently. As a result, this leads to the paralyzation of essential public services. The consequences of these protests are harshest in the big cities, the center of power and politics. These protests make a large contribution to the feeling that democratic governments and leaders are incapable, and for demagogic reasons are even unwilling to prevent 'chaos' and further general economic deterioration. The rational – and desperate – behavior of State employees feeds the generalized image of an unruly public bureaucracy that is far more interested in defending its 'privileges' than in fulfilling its duties. Finally, even though the evidence on these facts is clear, the public employees' strikes and protests paralyze and cause further deterioration of essential public services, creating an antagonism between the popular sector and many middle- class segments. The anger of these sectors, who are more dependent on most public services than the higher classes, generates a split that favors the anti-statist offensive, which mixes up the (necessary) task of achieving a leaner State apparatus with the (suicidal) weakening of the State in all its dimensions.

Shrinking personal income, decreasing career prospects, bad working conditions and a hostile political environment added to the countless interventions that the State undertakes provide the perfect soil for an enormous growth of corruption. In many bureaus few things work without 'extra payments' that are insignificant for the rich but severely harmful for the poor. At the top and even middle levels of the bureaucracy, corruption involves huge amounts of money, which consumes scarce public resources. In addition, when some of these acts of corruption become public scandals, they undermine general trust, not only in the outcome and role of the State but also in governments that seem incapable of correcting this situation, when not active participants in it.

The temporary solution applied by these governments desperate for funds has been to increase indirect taxes and the prices of public services. But this feeds inflation and has serious distributional consequences. In terms of the income tax, the only way it can be easily applied is as withholdings from the salaries of the formal sector of the economy (including public employees). If we take into account, in addition, that the formally employed are the main contributors to social security, the result is a powerful incentive both for them and for their employers to leave the formal sector. In periods of uncertain employment and diminishing salaries, the acute deterioration of most social policies (observed both in Latin America and in post-Communist countries) comes to aggravate the misfortunes of vast segments of the population. Furthermore, the income and the social security taxes imposed on the formally employed entail an expensive tax rate which very few pay but which is nominally effective for the economy as a whole – this increases the incentives for tax evasion, it diminishes the relative cost of bribery. Finally, there are generalized protests about 'excessive taxes', at the same time as the overall tax income of the State is diminishing, along with direct taxes (those that, supposedly, a democratic government should reinforce), which are dropping rapidly. The long agony of the State-centered, import-substitutive pattern of capital accumulation has left us with a dinosaur incapable even of feeding itself, while the 'solutions' currently under way lead towards an anemic entity incapable of supporting democracy, decent levels of social equity, and economic growth.

## On Certain Economic Crises

I will discuss here a particular kind of economic crisis, the one suffered by countries such as Argentina, Brazil and Peru, which voluntarily locked themselves into a pattern of high and recurrent inflation[4] (eventually reaching hyperinflation), featuring repeated failed attempts to control inflation and performing the 'structural reforms' currently recommended by international financial institutions. This is, fortunately, a small set of countries; but several post- Communist and African countries seem to have already fallen, or are near to falling into this pattern. It can be argued that the longer and the deeper the crisis is, and the less confidence there is that the government will be able to solve it, the more rational it becomes for everyone to react (1) at highly disaggregated levels, especially in relation to State agencies that may solve or alleviate the consequences of the crisis for a given firm or sector, (2) with extremely short time-horizons, and (3) with the conviction that everyone else will act the same way. A giant national 'prisoner's dilemma' persists when a deep and prolonged economic crisis teaches all agents the following lessons: (1) inflation will continue to be high, and it is near impossible to predict in the medium run its fluctuations – not to mention in the long run; (2) among such fluctuations, periods of hyperinflation cannot be excluded (say, rates of 50 percent or above per month); (3) at some point the government will make some drastic interventions, aimed at controlling inflation, but these are likely to fail; (4) expectations about the future situation of the economy are strongly pessimistic; and (5) predictions about the future economic situation of each agent are contingent timely adaptations to the conditions imposed by the preceding points.

Although micro-level studies are scarce, anyone who has lived under these circumstances knows that this is a harsh world. Rationally, the most extended strategy is to do whatever is necessary to protect one another against the losses expected by high and erratic inflation. Remaining passive and/or not having the power resources for running at the speed of inflation guarantees huge losses – at the limit, for some, bankruptcy, and for others falling into abysmal poverty.

This is a world of *every man for himself*, and playing this game reinforces the very conditions under which it is played. The primary, basic phenomenon is a generalized de-solidarity. Every rational agent acts at the level of disaggregation and with the time horizon that is deemed most efficacious in his/her defensive moves. The time horizon is the very short term; what sense would it make to sacrifice short-term gains for the sake of longer-term ones, when the future situation of the world cannot be predicted with any accuracy and abstaining from maximizing short-term gains may provoke heavy losses? Some agents, difficult to identify topically from the data available, harvest big profits. The ways to achieve this are many, but the chances across classes are extremely skewed. Some of the more important of those ways entail the pillage of the State apparatus. For players of this game, broad long-run economic policies negotiated and implemented with the participation of highly aggregated interest representation associations are not important. As the government also has to dance to the rhythm of the crisis, its capacity for formulating those policies is very limited, and often their implementation is canceled or captured by the disaggregated strategies just described. What is truly important for defending oneself, and for eventually profiting from the crisis is (basically, but not exclusively for capitalists) open and get quick access to the State agencies that can deliver the resources hoped for. Privileges and favors of all kinds are procured by the minimum size of coalition that is able to obtain the appropriate decisions from a given public agency. Those advantages must be obtained fast – if not, continuing inflation would eat them up. In this situation, the rational strategy consists of a double disaggregation: first, act alone or allied to the minimum possible set of agents that can guarantee the desired outcome; second, colonize the State agencies that can provide the sought-for benefits, avoiding more aggregated and/or public arenas that would only complicate the attainment of the topical benefits. Various processes noted in the literature, such as the loosening of popular collective identities, the implosion of historically rooted parties, and the decreased importance of capitalist organizations, are expressions of the perverse collective consequences of this rational defensive behavior.

Capitalists in Argentina, Brazil and Peru have an important advantage. This is not a new game for them, only the urgency, the stakes, and the level of disaggregation have increased. In those countries, as well as elsewhere in Latin America, they have a long experience of living off the largess of the State, and of colonizing its agencies. They do not have to find many new counterparts inside the public bureaucracies, or to invent new ways to engage with them in manifold forms of mutual corruption. But, nowadays, the depth of the crisis has accentuated those ills. First, there is the evidence of a great increase in corruption; second, there is an enormous fragmentation of the State apparatus – or, equivalently, its acute decline of autonomy, not in relation to 'a' capitalist class but in relation to the many segments into which this class has disaggregated itself to the rhythm of the crisis. The problems noted in the preceding section are multiplied by these consequences of the economic crisis, at the same time that the resulting disintegration of the State apparatus makes it even more incapable of solving that crisis.

Every spiral of the crisis is unlike the preceding one. Actors learn. Those who were astute enough to survive, and even get ahead, can buy at bargain prices assets the losers had. The fast concentration of capital in these countries reflects the gains of the Darwinian survivors. Agents assume that as the previous stabilization efforts failed (and as the government was further weakened by that failure) the future efforts of the government will also fail. Thus those agents make their bets on the high estimated probability of future policy failure, which of course increases the likelihood of that same failure.

As for governments, the more spirals occur, the more desperately they try to find a way out of the crisis. But the accompanying disintegration of the State apparatus, increasing fiscal deficits, hostile public opinion, political parties that anticipate future electoral gains by harshly criticizing the government (including leaders of the governing party, who see themselves dragged into the abyss of the unpopularity), and the anticipatory hedging of powerful economic actors all diminish the probability that the next policy will succeed. This also means that, for an economy with increasing levels of immunization, the next stabilization attempt will be more radical than the preceding one. The stakes of the game become higher at every turn of the wheel.

The repetition of policy failures continues the process of Darwinian selection, at each turn made easier by the decreasing ability of the government to control the distributional consequences of these policies. In particular, since many segments of the middle sectors are, in relative terms, impacted most severely, widespread cries of 'the extinction of the middle class' are heard, sometimes with overtones that are not exactly consistent with the rooting of democracy. In this situation, the government projects a curious image that mixes omnipotence with naked impotence. On one hand, every attempt at solving the crisis is resonantly announced as the one that this time will succeed, hence justifying the further sacrifices required of the population. On the other hand, aside from the welcome relief of a temporary fall in inflation (usually at a high cost in terms of economic activity and distribution), it soon becomes evident that the government will not be able to implement other necessary, policies. This is another factor in shortening the time horizons and in worsening the expectations that give dynamics to the overall game.

In these conditions, a society sees itself in an ugly image. One could collect thousands of expressions of the deep malaise that follows. The evidence of widespread opportunism, greed, lack of solidarity, and corruption is not a happy reflection of society. Furthermore, many of those actions entail obvious disregard for the laws. When it becomes clear that many violate the law and that the costs of doing it are usually null, the lesson learnt further erodes the predictability of social relations; widespread opportunism and lawlessness increase all sorts of transaction costs, and the texturing of society by the State-as-law weakens at every turn of the spiral.

Bitter denunciations and desperate appeals to overcome the 'moral crisis' follow. The media and daily conversations become full of exhortations for 'restoring national unity', for the panacea of socioeconomic pacts (that under these conditions no rational actor would enter into in good faith), for 'moralizing' public administration and business, and the like. Moralizing critiques and pious exhortations – however valuable they are as indications that basic values of public morals somehow survive – ignore the locking in of social action into a colossal prisoners' dilemma.[5] Moreover, such statements can easily escalate into a full-fledged condemnation of the whole situation, including a democracy that performs poorly in so many aspects.

The angry atomization of society is the other side of the same coin in the crisis of the State, not only as a set of bureaucracies but also – and even more so – as the lawful source of social predictability. Besides, the crisis leads to the decreasing plausibility of the State as an authoritative agent of the country's interests; it looks more and more like a burdensome apparatus allowing itself to be plundered by the powerful. The disintegration of the State apparatus and the decreasing effectiveness of the State-as-law make governments incapable of implementing even minimally complex policies. It is no easy matter to decide what segments of the State should be given priority for making them more effective; or to implement an industrial policy; or to decide the degree and sequencing of the financial and commercial opening of the economy; or to agree on salaries and employment policies, etc, etc. Without this 'restructuring' neither the current neoliberal policies nor alternative ones may succeed.

In order for those policies not only to be stated (the easier part, obviously) but also to be implemented, three conditions must be met:

1.  Both private and State agents must have at least the medium run as their time horizon. But in the conditions we discussed this is unlikely to happen. Even government leaders are unlikely to have anything other than a short time horizon because the crisis means, first, that they must focus their attention on

extinguishing the fires that pop up everywhere and, second, that their jobs are in perpetual risk.

2.   If stabilization and especially structural policies are going to be something more than a crude translation of whatever interests have access to them, the relevant State agencies must be able to gather and analyze complex information. They have to be sufficiently motivated in the pursuit of a definition of the public interest, and see their role in putting up such policies as a rewarding episode in their careers. As we saw, except for some organizational areas, these conditions are nowadays inexistent.

3.   Some policies can be successfully implemented only if they go through complex negotiations with the various organized private actors that claim legitimate access to the process. However, the extreme disaggregation with which it is rational to operate under the present crisis erodes the representativeness of most organized interests. Who can really speak for someone else in these countries? What ego can convince an alter that what he agreed with the alter will be honored by those he claims to represent? The atomization of society mirrors and accentuates the disintegration of the State.[6]

How can this world of actors behaving in extremely disaggregated, opportunistic and short-term ways be politically represented? What can be the anchors and links with the institutions (of interest representation and the properly political ones, such as parties and Congress) that texture the relationships between State and society in institutionalized democracies? What representativeness and, broadly, which collective identities can survive these storms? The answer is that very little, if any, progress is made towards the accomplishment of institutions of representation and accountability. On the contrary, connecting with historical roots that are deep in these countries, the atomization of society and State, the spread of brown areas and their peculiar ways of pushing their interests, and the enormous urgency and complexity of the problems to be confronted feed the delegative, plebiscitary propensities of these democracies. The pulverization of society into countless rational/opportunistic actors and their anger about a situation that everyone – and, hence, apparently nobody – seems to cause, has a major scapegoat: the State and the government. This common sense is, on one hand, fertile ground for simplistic anti-statist ideologies. On the other, it propels the loss of prestige of the democratic government, its shaky institutions, and most of all politicians. Of course, these evaluations have good groundings: the policy failures, the blunderings and vacillations, the impotent omnipotence, and too often the evidence of corruption, as well as the dismal spectacles too often offered by politicians (in and out of Congress) and parties, give the perfect occasion for the projective exculpation of society into the manifold ills of State and government.

The least that can be said about these problems is, first, that they do not help in advancing towards a consolidated, institutionalized democracy. Second, they make it extremely difficult to implement the complex, long-term and multi-sided negotiated policies that could take these countries out of their turmoil. Third (not only in Latin America, indeed), these problems powerfully interact with a tradition of conceiving politics in a Caesarist, anti-institutional and delegative fashion.

At this point a pending question must be posed: Is there a way out of these downward spirals? Or, more precisely, at what point and under what conditions might there be a way out? We must remember that we are dealing with countries (Argentina, Brazil and Peru) that were unfortunate to suffer a pattern of recurrent high inflation periods, featuring periods of hyperinflation or very close to it (depending on definitions I need not argue with here), and that suffered several failed stabilization programs.

One country that recently suffered these problems but that does seem to have found a way out is Chile. The policies of the Pinochet government accomplished, with an effectiveness that Lenin would have admired, the destruction of most of what was left of the national bourgeoisie oriented to import-substitution, after the Allende government – which was too grateful for having been rescued as a class to organize any concerted opposition. Of course, the Pinochet government also brutally repressed the labor organizations and the political parties that could have mounted an effective opposition to its policies. In this societal desert, huge social costs were incurred, and, although with various changes and accidents, the neoliberal program was mostly implemented. The new democratic government in this country still has the serious problem of preserving low inflation, reasonable rates of economic growth, and a favourable international climate. That government also faces the problem of how to alleviate the inequalities that were accentuated by the preceding authoritarian regime. But the crude reality is that the distributional consequences of more ambiguous and less harsh policies in countries such as Brazil, Argentina and Peru have not been better than those under Pinochet's government. Furthermore, the resources presently available to the Chilean government for alleviating equity problems are relatively larger than those available to Brazil, Peru and Argentina. Finally, the fact that Chile was but is no longer trapped in the spirals depicted here means (although this is not the only reason – there are other more historical ones which I cannot elaborate here) that its State is in better shape than in the countries discussed above for dealing with the equity and developmental issues it inherited.

Another case could be Mexico, although inflation and its manifold social dislocations were never as high in Mexico as in Argentina, Brazil and Peru (or, for that matter, as it is today in most of the former Soviet Union). The PRI (Partido Revolucionario Institucional – Nationalist Revolutionary Movement) provided a more effective instrument for policy implementation than anything available to the latter countries, while the geopolitical interests of the border with the United States are helping the still painful and uncertain navigation of this country towards the achievement of the long-run goals of its current policies. Another country is Bolivia, where the implementation of policies that were successful in controlling inflation and liberalizing trade and finance (but not until now in restoring growth and investment) was accompanied by a brutal repression which can hardly be seen as consistent with democracy. A more recent candidate to be part of this list is Argentina.

Focusing on the South American cases, what do Chile, Bolivia, and Argentina have in common? Quite simply, that the crises in these countries – in the first under authoritarian and in the latter two under democratically elected governments – reached the very bottom. What is this bottom? It is the convergence of:

1. A State that as a principle of order has a tiny hold on the behavior of most actors, that as a bureaucracy reaches extreme limits of disintegration and ineffectiveness, and at some point in time becomes unable to support the national currency;
2. A workers' movement that is thoroughly defeated, in the sense that is no longer able to oppose neoliberal policies except by means of disaggregated and short-lived protests;
3. A capitalist class that has devoured itself to a large extent, with the survivors metamorphosing into financially centred and outwardly oriented conglomerates (together with the branches of commerce and the professionals that cater to luxurious consumption); and
4. A generalized mood agreeing that life under continued high and uncertain inflation is so intolerable that any solution is preferable, even if that solution ratifies a more unequal world in which many forms of solidarity are lost.

At this point whoever tries to control inflation and initiate the 'restructuring' advised by neoliberal views does not confront powerful blocking coalitions: the more important fractions of the bourgeoisie no longer have interests antagonistic to those policies. The various expressions of popular and middle-class interests are weak and fragmented, and the State employees who have survived their own painful experience can now have hope of improving their situation. The pulverization of society and of the State apparatus, together with the primordial demand to return to an ordered social world, wind up eliminating the resistances that, unwillingly but effectively, fed the previous turns of the spiral. In Chile this happened through the combined effects of the crisis unleashed under the Unidad Popular government and the repressive and determined policies of the Pinochet period. In Bolivia and Argentina it is no small irony that, after hyperinflation, the (apparent, far from clearly achieved yet) end of the spirals came under presidents originating in parties/movements such as MNR – Movimento Nacionalista Revolucionaria (Nationalist Revolutionary Movement) and Peronismo. Probably it was incumbent on such presidents, and only on them, to complete the defeat of the respective workers' movements.

What about Brazil? It was the last of the countries discussed here to get itself into this type of crisis. This was closely related to the larger size of its domestic market and to its more dynamic economic performance, which have created a more complex and industrialized economy than that of its neighbours. In a 'paradox of success'[7] this advantage may turn out to be a severe curse. In Brazil there are many powerful agents capable of blocking the more or less orthodox neoliberal policies that have been tried already and will be attempted again. Conversely, if there is no way other than continuing the spirals until the bottom of the pit is reached, the degree of economic destruction would be much larger than that of the countries mentioned above. Furthermore, in contrast with the situation of the Southern Cone countries before their own spirals, socially, in Brazil there is already a vast part of the population that has nowhere lower to fall. The Brazilian capacity for resistance would be an advantage if there was a better alternative to the given course of events. But the only alternative on the table is doing more of the same in a pattern of State-led capital accumulation that seems exhausted. Of course the players of this game can further plunder the dinosaur, but this only accelerates the spirals, cannot continue indefinitely, and has perverse distributional consequences.

## A Partial Conclusion

What alternatives are there to the crises I have described? The prisoner's dilemma has a powerful dynamic: invocations to altruism and national unity, as well as policy proposals that assume wide solidarities and stable identities, will not do. If there is a solution, it probably lies in finding areas that are important in their impacts on the overall situation and in which a skilled action (particularly by the government) can lengthen the time horizons (and, consequently, the scope of solidarities) of crucial actors. The best known invention for such an achievement is the strengthening of social and political institutions. But under the conditions described above, this is indeed a difficult task. In the contemporary world, the joyful celebration of the advent of democracy must be complemented with the sober recognition of the immense (and, indeed, historically unusual) difficulties for its institutionalization and its rooting in society. As Haiti, Peru and Thailand have shown, these experiments are fragile. Also, against some rather premature proclamations of the 'end of history', there are no immanent forces that will guide the new democracies towards an institutionalized and representative form, and to the elimination of their brown areas and the multiple social ills that underlie them. In the long run, the new democracies may split between those that follow this felicitous course and those that go back to all-out authoritarianism. But delegative democracies, weak horizontal accountability, schizophrenic States, brown areas, and low intensity citizenship are part of the predictable future of many new democracies.

## Notes

1.  This is a fragment of the article published originally in Spanish by Guillermo O'Donnell (1993), 'Estado, democratización y ciudadanía', in *Nueva Sociedad 'Gobernabilidad ¿sueño o democracia?'* No. 128, Caracas, Venezuela. Translation revised by Fernanda Beigel.

2.  [Translation Note: In the first part of this article, O'Donnell argues that a map of each country can be built where the areas covered in blue would designate those where there is a high degree of presence of the State (in terms of a set of reasonably effective bureaucracies and of the effectiveness of properly sanctioned legality), both functionally and territorially. The green color indicates a high degree of territorial penetration but a significantly lower presence in functional/class terms; the brown color a very low or null level in both dimensions.]

3.  By 'neoliberal' policies I mean those advocated by international financial institutions and mainstream neoclassical theories. These policies have been through some changes, presumably driven by the very mixed styles of application. But a very strong – and indiscriminate – anti-statist bias continues to be at the core. For a critique of these policies, see especially Adam Przeworski et al. *Sustainable Democracy*. Even though I agree with the critique and I am one of the co-contributors of this book, it is ethically necessary to say that I didn't participate in the part of the volume containing this analysis. See also Przeworski (1992).

4. By this I mean periods of at least three years or more with monthly inflation averaging above 20 percent, along with peaks of three-digit figures per month.

5. Although I cannot extend the argument here, none of the conditions identified by the literature as conducive to cooperative solutions hold in the situation I am depicting.

6. One should not forget the longer-term effects of the crisis, and of the indiscriminate anti-statist ideology that underlies the current economic policies, on factors crucial for sustaining economic growth. I refer in particular to education, health, and science and technology policies, and to the modernization of the physical infrastructure. These areas are being grossly neglected, in spite of many warnings and complaints. But to undertake those policies a reasonably lean and effective State apparatus is required.

7. I have discussed Brazil's apparent paradoxes of success in O'Donnell (1991).

## Reference

Przeworski, A. (1992). 'The Neoliberal Fallacy', *Journal of Democracy*, *3* (3) (July), 45–59.

## Guillermo O'Donnell, by Maria Hermínia Tavares de Almeida (Brazil)[1]

Guillermo O'Donnell (1936–2011) occupies a unique position in Latin American social sciences due to the breadth and importance of his work, the influence of which goes far beyond the region. O'Donnell dealt with the three most important political phenomena in contemporary Latin America: authoritarianism, transition to democracy and the democratic experience over the last quarter of a century. In all three cases, by seeking the specific form of these phenomena in the region he ended up offering an original and universal theoretical contribution. Let's take a closer look at his seminal contributions.

For a long time, the dominant autocratic forms of government in Latin America did not have adequate denomination and theory. Different modalities of non-democratic regimes, at different times, were classified as *caudillismo*, fascism or simply as dictatorships. Conceptual imprecision made it difficult to capture the particular nature of the various expressions of autocracy in the region. Thanks to Juan Linz (1926–2013) there was an important advance in the theory of autocratic rule when – analysing the case of Franco's Spain – he proposed to distinguish between totalitarianism and authoritarianism. This distinction emphasized political dimensions: the nature of the institutions that defined limits to the discretionary behavior of rulers, the presence or absence of an official ideology and the relations between leaderships and masses. Linz's distinction between totalitarian and authoritarian regimes allowed much progress to be made in understanding different forms of autocracy.

*(Continued)*

(Continued)

However, in a region where, for many decades, those were the mode rather than the exception, the notion of authoritarianism continued to encompass very different realities: the personal rule of *caudillos*, regimes of populist leanings, civilian dictators or right-wing governments in the hands of the military. On the other hand, the theory of modernization at the end of the 1950s foresaw that the socioeconomic changes induced by industrialization would end up opening the way to democracy in developing countries.

The concept of bureaucratic authoritarianism was Guillermo O'Donnell's specific contribution to autocracy theory, while investing against the optimistic illusions of the modernization theory. The study of the military dictatorship in Argentina, under the government of Juan Carlos Ongania and successors (1966–1973), revealed a particular form of authoritarianism based on the rule of the Armed Forces as an institution in alliance with public and private technocracies typical of the modern economic sectors. Bureaucratic authoritarianism actually occurred at an advanced stage of industrialization by import substitution, an approach of deepening the industrial development by internalizing the production of capital and intermediate goods. In fact, bureaucratic authoritarianism, according to O'Donnell, was a consequence of the economic and State structures' modernization, as well as the social tensions it provoked, occurring, therefore, in the countries that had advanced the most along the path of industrialization – Argentina and Brazil.

His second original contribution was the study of transitions to democracy. With Philippe Schmitter and Laurence Whitehead, O'Donnell organized, within the scope of the Latin American program of the Woodrow Wilson Center for Scholars in Washington DC, then under the leadership of political scientist Abraham Lowenthal, an ambitious research project that tried to assess where contemporary authoritarian regimes were or might be heading. The project evolved around three conferences in 1979, 1980 and 1981 and mobilized leading academics from the Americas: Robert A. Dahl, Juan Linz, Adam Przeworski, Fernando Henrique Cardoso and Albert Hirschman. The result was their collective work, in four volumes, first published in 1985. It is important to underline the intellectual boldness of the project that began when democracy had barely reached southern Europe and there was no prospect of its arrival in Latin America. However, this was not the only expression of O'Donnell and Schmitter's intellectual courage. The proposed analytical framework radically broke up with the predominant models of analysis in the Latin American social sciences, largely inspired by structuralist paradigms, which sought the explanation of political events in socioeconomic structures. Breaking with their own analytical schemes, used in the study of bureaucratic authoritarianism, O'Donnell and Schmitter adopted an intentional explanation framework, looking at the preferences and contingent strategies of decisive political actors, e.g. 'hawks' and 'doves' from the authoritarian and the opposition sides. In doing so, they definitely changed the predominant political science paradigm in the region.

O'Donnell's third major contribution was the analysis of the democratic regimes that replaced the various types of authoritarianism in Latin America. In a series of intellectually challenging articles he examined with cunning analytical sensitivity the obstacles to rooting competitive and fair political regimes, based on the rule of law, in a social ground undermined by extreme inequalities and entrenched privileges. Among the different aspects submitted to dour scrutiny in his writings, those related to the concentration of decision-making powers in Presidents' hands and absence of mechanisms of accountability and control available to the citizens stand out. He has also highlighted the unequal and incomplete process of enforcing the rule of law and citizens' rights. The notions of delegative democracy and brown zones of democracy attempted to capture the actual shortcomings of competitive systems in Latin America. These ideas were developed in numerous articles published in academic journals and in now classic books. The text published here is an outstanding example of that effort on theoretical elaboration that could account for a critical understanding of our recent democratic experience. O'Donnell's writings on democracies in Latin America condense, like nowhere else in his work, the tension between the discipline of the scientist and the ethical passion of the intellectual committed to the travails of his time.

Educated as a lawyer at the University of Buenos Aires (1958), O'Donnell received a PhD from Yale University (1987). He belonged to a generation of Latin Americans who lived for long periods under authoritarian oppression and, in those circumstances, nurtured strong democratic values and pulsating intellectual indignation at power abuse and the wealth concentration so typical of Latin American societies. Producing social sciences under authoritarianism often required building research institutions and protecting them from governmental onslaught. In 1975, with other Argentine opposition intellectuals such as Elizabeth Jelin, Roberto Frenkel, Marcelo Cavarozzi and Oscar Oszlak, he committed himself to the creation of the Centro de Estudios de Estado y Sociedad (CEDES), an independent research institute of major importance for Argentine intellectual life in the hardest moments of its history. Between 1983 and 1997, O'Donnell led the Helen Kellog Institute for International Studies at the University of Notre Dame, which became an academic hub for Latin American and North American intellectuals and an important locus of academic research on Latin America.

Guillermo O'Donnell passed away in 2011, but his works continue to be an inspiration and a mandatory starting point for all those who wish to understand the troubled paths of politics in contemporary Latin America.

## Note

1.   Translated by Marta Pierre (INCIHUSA-CONICET, Argentina) and revised by Maria H. Tavares de Almeida.

## References

Collier, David (ed.) *El nuevo autoritarismo en América Latina*. Mexico: Fondo de Cultura Económica.

O'Donnell, G. (1991) 'Argentina, de nuevo'. Kellogg Institute, Working Paper No. 152.

# 27

# Political Activism in the Era of the Internet[1]

*Bernardo Sorj (Uruguay–Brazil)*

Sociologists navigate using two compasses. One points to social transformations and emerging processes, in sum, all that is new. The other focuses on the permanence of social structures and actors that possess an enormous capacity for survival by appropriating and/or accommodating to changes. A large number of the studies regarding the impact of new communication media tend to use either one compass or the other, which generally results in dismissing the importance of social transformations or only focusing on the novelties. The challenge is to identify what mutates without disregarding how the old reconstructs and inserts itself into the new, and from a normative perspective staying away from both nostalgia for an idealized past and uncritical celebration of the latest social innovations.

In this article we present the hypotheses and main conclusions of a research project that analyzed 19 case studies in six countries (Argentina, Brazil, Chile, Colombia, Peru and Venezuela).[2] Our focus is on political cyberactivism initiatives in civil society; therefore, it does not include Internet uses by political parties or cyberactivists groups who operate at the margins of the legal system, such as Anonymous.

## Main Hypotheses

This research was based on the following hypotheses:

1. There were three major waves in the formation of civil society in Latin America in the twentieth and twenty-first centuries. The first wave comprised organizations that represented broad social sectors, generally grouped around socio-economic or professional interests, whose leaders, in democratic regimes, were chosen by their members. The second wave, whose typical format was that of the NGO, consisted of myriad organizations, mostly small, whose legitimacy is sustained by the moral value of the causes they advocate (such as human rights, gender identity, race, sexual orientation,

environment, etc.) and not by a mandate granted by a determined audience. Lastly, the third wave was constituted within the virtual public space, comprising citizens who issue opinions, mostly of a personal nature, on social networks. None of these waves eliminates their predecessor; they overlap and influence each other mutually, with each new wave tending to occupy the spaces of the previous ones, both in terms of organizational format and in the content of the messages they convey.

2. The impact of the new virtual world should not be dissociated from broader social processes in society and in the political system, which, in turn, are affected by the new forms of communication. For example, social transformations – in the world of work and consumption, individualization, the crisis of the ideological frameworks which structured political life in the twentieth century, the weakening of political parties – date from before the emergence of communication via the Internet, which is influenced by these pre-existing trends, while at the same time modifying them.[3]

3. The bibliography on the effects of the virtual world counterposes 'pessimists' and 'optimists'. The optimists stress that the communication technologies open up new possibilities for horizontal communication among citizens, diminish communication transaction costs in the public space and accelerate the speed of communication – enabling people and groups to issue opinions and establish dialogues on an unprecedented scale – reducing the relative importance of the old communication media and opening up new alternative information channels for citizenship. The pessimists believe that the Internet produces an impoverishment and polarization of political culture and debate, destroys privacy – providing the State and companies with access to databanks which enable the manipulation and control of individuals – and creates the illusion of click activism, a form of catharsis which results in little of consequence. They also state that the basic power structures, be it in the offline or online world, remain the same as in the past, dominated by large companies and by political power. We consider that both positions indicate real phenomena, and that cyberactivism is influenced by both tendencies.

4. Online and offline worlds cannot be dissociated. The offline world plays a key role in the virtual space, whether through its capacity to intervene directly in the social networks, or through the appropriation of movements of opinion and mobilizations generated and/or promoted by the virtual world. As such, the virtual world and the offline world are profoundly interlinked. The analysis of how they relate, be it through offline actors who initiate virtual movements or intervene in virtual communication, or be it at later phases, when the political dynamic is redirected to the streets should consider the particularities of each case.

5. In a way, the virtual public space has deepened but also modified certain tendencies, already present in the second wave of civil society, of political

fragmentation and the distancing of society from party political life. The new forms of communication tend to eliminate the separation between the public and the private, merging the subjective and the commons, the personal and the collective, and valuing messaging in which personal malaise and denunciation predominate. If the first wave of civil society was built on political ideologies with visions of the whole of society, and the second around the defense of the most diverse rights, both were sustained by the arguments and worldviews of a desirable society. In the new communication format dominant in the virtual world, there is a predominance of short messages (or images) related primarily to contextual situations that mobilize essentially reactive feelings and attitudes.

6.  One of the major challenges for the Internet as a public space based on standards of civility is its anonymous nature, that is, the difficulty or impossibility of identifying the authors of messages. An ever-growing number of messages circulate on the Internet produced by fake profiles (generally professional agents, provocateurs, who do not present themselves as such) and disseminated by robots and trolls. They are specialized in producing distorted or false 'information' which is presented as if having being written by an ordinary member of the public. These messages are highly effective because they are elaborated based on the existing preconceptions, affinities and sensitivities of the readers, previously profiled.

We critically confront these hypotheses by means of the analysis of 19 case studies in six countries (Argentina, Brazil, Chile, Colombia, Peru and Venezuela) in order to develop and modify them in the light of new experiences.

One particularly interesting case is that of the Partido de la Red (Web Party) in Argentina. Organized in 2012 and based on a small group of people – from the technology and human sciences areas – the party's proposal was to promote the web as an instrument for deliberation and decision making to which representatives elected for legislative mandates should be submitted. The party does not have a program of substantive proposals, with the exception of promoting use of the web for citizens to deliberate and decide. Therefore, the Partido de la Red may be considered both an organization whose mission is the reform of the political system by means of promoting a democracy with plebiscitary characteristics (although its website speaks of a 'hybrid between direct democracy and representative democracy') and a political party which seeks to occupy positions of power and whose representatives will define their positions on an ad hoc basis, according to the decisions of the majority of all citizens, case by case.

The Partido de la Red is discovering the offline world and local realities, where concrete problems known to the public may generate interest and mobilize more immediate responses, as well as the importance of face-to-face sociability. The party is undergoing an internal process of reflection on the limitations of the experience. However, it is far from reaching conclusions on all of its questions: ad hoc voting on a case-by-case basis mainly mobilizes the militant or those directly affected by each specific issue. Furthermore, political parties are based on programs and priorities. Decision making, and even more so the elaboration of programs, requires a process of deliberation on disparate and many times opposite proposals, that involves negotiations and producing a coherent narrative. Therefore it is not possible to eliminate the intermediary levels of representation, at the risk of subjection to authoritarian manipulation.

The idealizers of the party, which was to be organized around decisions based on virtual consultations, more recently created an independent Foundation, with a professional management and structure, which develops technological resources (software) that promote civic participation. These resources are made available to all interested parties and politicians.

The Partido de la Red has a small number of members and has only participated in one election, in the city of Buenos Aires, without any representatives being elected. Perhaps the fact that no representatives were elected may be positive, because it gives them more time to further develop and refine, through their Foundation, technological instruments aligned with the party's mission. The new technologies may be important instruments for democratizing and strengthening existing political parties, and not just for bypassing them.

The Partido de la Red is an interesting case because it sought to radicalize the idea of direct democracy and soon came up against the limits imposed by political life in complex societies. From a practical standpoint, the party's proposal as an organization seeking to occupy positions in institutional power continues to raise questions about how it would function in practice. Might a party which does not have a substantive program, except for the public consultation process, be considered viable or desirable by electors (and, according to the Partido de la Red, the consultation would involve all citizens, not just party members)? What degree of discretion would the party representatives have in the formulation and negotiation of laws with other parties? What would happen in cases in which participation in the online consultations was very low? Even if they decide that the party should have a substantive platform, could this be formulated by grouping the proposals receiving the most votes online, without concern for internal coherence and the practical feasability of the result obtained? In addition, if party members do assume executive positions in the government, what will happen when they have to take decisions that are not approved by the majority of the public but which are fundamental to ensuring governance or the protection of minority rights? Is it possible to organize a mass party without intermediary institutions that have decision-making power? Is it viable, at least given the current state of technology, to organize a party without offline forums for deliberation? How should the formation of party leaders be guaranteed? Is there a risk that the founders will end up constituting an oligarchy and, directly or indirectly, becoming the controllers of the party?

Setting up a 'hybrid' format, with elements of direct participation and representation, is the major challenge for the virtual world in its relationship with the world of politics. By not recognizing this challenge, there is the risk that forms of direct participation will obscure rather than improve the transparency of decision-making mechanisms. The lack of answers to the questions above does not diminish the relevance of the Partido de la Red's experience, which is posited as an experiment rather than a finished project. Moreover, some of its directors do recognize its limitations, and the contribution made by its Foundation to the development of tools can benefit all the parties and politicians.

## Online Support Campaigns

Online support campaigns for specific causes represent the continuation of a long democratic tradition of support for manifestos or petitions requesting changes in legislation. The use of signatures collected online is still not recognized legally in any of the countries in the region. Alternative ways of using this means of online participation to obtain effective results, must, therefore, be explored. We did analyze three case studies of online campaigning organizations: Avaaz in Brazil, Change.org in Argentina and YASunidos in Ecuador. Avaaz in Brazil and Change.org in Argentina are global organizations of foreign origin and have existed for a number of years. In these countries they have the largest number of followers (people who have signed at least one petition), in absolute numbers in the case of Brazil and relative to the size of the population in Argentina. YASunidos is an isolated experience related to a specific problem.

Avaaz has as its mission the creation of 'a better world' and proposes themes such as combating corruption, poverty, armed conflict and climate change.[4] Run in Brazil by a small team of professionals, its principal modus operandi is to seek the highest possible number of supporters for its causes and then to send petitions to public authorities. In general, questions of global reach or related to international events predominate on the home page of its website. The petitions, written in the form of arguments in defense of a cause, may be proposed by community members, but the internal team has the power to decide on the priority causes and, most importantly, on the ways to use its email database, which is not open to the public.

Avaaz's modus operandi has generated controversy. It is criticized by some for its 'click-activism' (a lazy way of engaging in politics) and for being more concerned with garnering a large number of supporters than obtaining practical results. The Brazilian case study indicates that these criticisms are partial. Although for some people supporting a cause through Avaaz may produce a cathartic sensation of having done their duty, for others it is a way of getting in touch with and becoming aware of current events, and for many activists it offers another field of action for issues of public interest. The Brazilian case shows that at moments of great mobilization, such as the street protests in June 2013, Avaaz constituted an additional resource available on the Internet. In another case, involving the Ficha Limpa Law (which excludes candidates with criminal records from elections), Avaaz obtained offline signatures to support a publicly generated bill of law to be considered by Congress and provided significant backing in the mobilization to get the law approved.

Analysis of Change.org in Argentina shows a very different modus operandi to that of Avaaz, although they both have a professional team with the power to prioritize each petition on their websites and control the use of their email lists to promote causes. Change.org does not propose the pursuit of a specific agenda. It may carry multiple petitions related to the same subject or even petitions presenting opposite viewpoints. Instead of major international causes, the Change.org petitions are related to local problems faced by individuals or by groups, and are presented in the form of testimonies of the event experienced. Another key difference is the way the petition is processed. Instead of sending a petition at the end of the signature collection process as Avaaz does, normally to a national or international high-level authority, each manifestation of support generates an email, which is sent directly to the decision maker responsible for the possible solution of the problem, frequently a mid-level employee.

Change.org's large number of successful campaigns may be attributed to a variety of factors, such as the concrete nature of its demands, the format of its petitions, which includes the actual experiences of people living with the problem, and the effectiveness with which it applies direct pressure on those in a position to provide a solution by sending them emails. Although to an extent they deal with varied audiences, since Change. org does not promote a specific agenda, the effectiveness of its model is unquestionable. In dealing with themes based on the daily dramas faced by individuals or groups, identification occurs more through emotional appeal than through universal principles and values. This, however, may also constitute Change.org's most vulnerable point. By promoting solutions for situations that frequently deal with personal cases, the success of a petition does not always resolve the problem for all the people affected. Rather individual cases are prioritized to the detriment of others, thus tending to favor individual rather than collective solutions.

Both cases also reveal an important characteristic of the political culture of the virtual world. In a manner similar to practices in private companies and in political marketing, large online campaign organizations work with profiling. In other words, in order not to overload their followers with an excessive number of emails on the most diverse subjects, these organizations seek to profile the thematic affinities demonstrated by their public on previous occasions. Therefore, just as in commerce or in political marketing, use of these profiles results in the segmentation of the internauts, who only receive information (or advertising) based on their preferences, restricting their contact with other issues.

The third example of online campaigning organizations, the YASunidos collective, is focused on mobilizing support in Ecuador to ban the exploitation of oil in the Yasuní National Park. This position was supported initially by president Correa, on the condition that the international system would compensate the country financially for forgoing exploitation. Later, when this proved unfeasible, the president changed his position to one of support for the exploitation of natural resources in the region. When YASunidos conducted a wide-reaching online and offline campaign to collect signatures in support of a public consultation on the issue, it had to face opposition from the Presidency of the Republic and government members. The National Electoral Council invalidated a large number of signatures collected offline and the public consultation was invalidated.

## Consultation Platforms

Consultation platforms are dedicated to promoting debate and proposals on specific themes. In this article we present two experiences: one from Brazil, referring to the formulation of legislation for regulating the Internet, and another from Chile, related to the country's new constitution.

The proposal of a Brazilian member of Congress to regulate the Internet unleashed a negative reaction among users and civil society organizations, that considered it repressive and at the service of economic groups. In 2009, the Ministry of Justice commissioned a university research center to elaborate a platform to receive inputs from the public, civil society organizations and businesses. The participants in the platform numbered a few thousand. The new proposal, elaborated by the Ministry of Justice based on the platform contributions, called the 'Internet Civil Framework', was approved by the Brazilian Parliament in 2014 and is currently awaiting regulation.

The Brazilian case of the Internet Civil Framework is an example of productive collaboration between the government and civil society. It was a mechanism that was effective in diminishing the weight of the lobbies which exert direct influence on the Executive and members of Parliament in the formulation of public policy. However, it would be an exaggeration to say that the document represents society's opinion. The consultation served to redistribute the power of influence among the elite groups. Due to the mobilization of alternative groups, the government expanded its room for maneuver, elaborating a more legitimate proposal.

In the context of discussing a new constitution for Chile under the Bachelet government, a series of platforms have been created to inform, educate, promote and stimulate public debate and support for various causes. None of these was aimed at elaborating a proposal for the constitution. These activities are complemented by offline actions, such as seminars and activities within the education system. The government, universities, think tanks, foundations and civil society sectors were responsible for the diverse platforms. The impact of these efforts is not clearly measurable and, if we take as a reference one of the main initiatives, *#TuConstitución*, promoted by former President Ricardo Lagos's Fundación Democracia y Desarrollo, the number of people involved was rather limited. Another element which fragmented the efforts was the diversity of initiatives, which, to a certain extent, have common goals.

The limitations presented by the platforms do not diminish their role in diffusion and experimentation – each presents architectures that use new formats aimed at facilitating participation in virtual spaces. It should also be remembered that the process of elaborating the Chilean constitution, at the time of the research, was at an early phase.

## Street Protests

The street protests that have occurred in recent years, in the United States, in Spain, in the Middle East and in Brazil, have given rise to an extensive bibliography on a new generation of 'the outraged', who, thanks to the new communication media, can communicate freely, horizontally and instantaneously, at times generating protests that put thousands of people on the streets.

The Internet certainly enables instantaneous, horizontal, mass communication calls to action via hashtags and viral messages and images spread in real time across social networks. Nevertheless, we should not forget that social explosions have permeated human history and their main characteristic is their unpredictability. Explanations for their possible causes are only encountered afterwards. In the case of the street protests in recent years, the novelty, that is the use of the Internet, has made it difficult or prevented many analysts from understanding the dynamics of the processes that precede and, principally, follow the protests, in part due to the lack of a greater historical time horizon. It is worth emphasizing, therefore, and this is valid for the theme as a whole, that the historians of the present, that is, the sociologists and political scientists, should certainly be attentive to the new, but without forgetting the lessons of the past. The surprise of many analysts regarding the ramifications of the Arab Spring, or the limited immediate consequences of Occupy Wall Street, which had been hailed by some as the beginning of a new era of democratic participation and which others today disparage as movements incapable of changing history, is the result of a vision that no longer takes into account historical experience nor the relation between offline and online social processes. Social explosions recur in all societies, and their developments have always been controlled by organizations that have known how to take advantage of or neutralize new situations.

The cases analyzed in this article highlight the variety of factors which have preceded protests, the events themselves and, where possible, their consequences. The case of the Chilean student movement shows the existence of a group that worked hard on offline organization before going to the streets. In Chile, the movement's demands were incorporated into the program of the Concertación, the center-left coalition, and a number of leaders of the movement, which declined sharply in size after the elections, were integrated into the political system as candidates of political parties or members of the government.

In Brazil, the dynamics of the protests in June 2013 were very different. Initiated by a group organized offline comprising mostly students, the Movimento Passe Livre took its first steps in 2005, advocating improved urban mobility and free public transport. The protests in June 2013 in São Paulo, initiated by the Movimento Passe Livre, spread rapidly throughout the country and, during this process, incorporated other causes defended by the protesters. Denunciations against corruption, the waste of public money on organizing the World Cup and the poor quality of public services became the main motifs of the protests, carried out without the involvement of political parties and with frequent abuse directed at politicians. Although the text here concentrates on the events in 2013, they may be considered a first phase, which had its continuation in the protests of March and April 2015, directed fundamentally against President Dilma Rousseff and in favor of the impeachment process. In this new phase, greater space is occupied by organized offline nuclei with a political identification, in general conservative and/or pro-market, who seek to present themselves as their spokespersons of the street mobilizations.

In Venezuela, the protests in 2014 occurred within an extremely polarized political context. Driven by growing ill-feeling towards the Bolivarian government, the protests were convoked via social networks in a decentralized manner. Without the participation of established NGOs and in a context of strong government repression and internal divisions among the opposition, they gradually lost momentum. The political polarization and the street protests reached the Venezuelan diaspora, leading to the emergence of a website and a Facebook page entitled SOS Venezuela. This initiative by Venezuelan activists, many of whom are based outside the country, was aimed at attracting international attention to the disorder provoked by the government. With the end of the protests, this activity declined, but the SOS Venezuela brand remains active on social networks.

**New Forms of Civil Society**

There is no single format for defining the relationship between the first and second waves of civil society and the new one under configuration in cyberspace. At the risk of simplification, we may identify a number of different models.

In some of the cases presented in this article, such as the student and the Alto Maipo movements in Chile, the peasant movement in Colombia, the protests in Venezuela and the various platforms related to the elaboration of the Chilean constitution, the actors are first- and second-wave organizations which use virtual media to reach a broader audience.

A different format combining 'old' and 'new' politics is provided by the Marcha pela Vida (March for Life), promoted by the Colombian politician Antanas Mockus, involving a call to action via social networks to participate in an event defined as super-partisan. This call, made by a politician to the population as well as to other party leaders, achieved only relative success because, despite its repercussions in the social networks, the pubic probably didn't fully differentiate the personal figure of Antanas Mockus, from a message intended to be ecumenical.

Many of the case studies demonstrate a certain incapacity on the part of the traditional NGOs and/or an active effort not to get them involved. In the case of the Marcha de Las Putas (Slutwalk) in Colombia and Ni Una Menos in Argentina, we see the emergence of a feminist mobilization that takes place without the involvement of the established organizations dedicated to this cause. Evidently building on a century of struggles for women's rights, the new activists have taken to the streets to defend their 'human rights' within a vision that is no longer part of a 'feminist' discourse, but of individuals demanding respect as autonomous human beings.

In the case of the Ni Una Menos march in Argentina, the mobilization originated with female journalists opposed to femicide and violence against women, receiving support from known figures in the fields of communication, culture and politics, but NGOs as institutions did not play a relevant role. The success of this mobilization led politicians to try to capitalize on the event for their own benefit, associating themselves with it through declarations and images of support.

The origin of the Slutwalk in Colombia was more unusual. Promoted by a little-known female human rights militant and inspired by a protest held in Canada, it unleashed a movement in the social networks, gaining widespread adhesion and promoting a protest in which a varied range of slogans focused on freedom for people. Held without support from feminist organizations, it was only on a second march that the movement gained the adhesion of one NGO, which incorporated causes of its own interest (the treatment of prostitutes), but participation was now lower. In a later development, the promoter of the marches created her own NGO to ensure the continuity of the initiative after her public visibility waned.

The last of these case studies, Quito, Yo me Apunto, presents the experience of a virtual space created in the social networks, with the later inclusion of offline encounters, aimed at developing proposals to improve the quality of life in the Ecuadorian capital, and which, through contacts with city authorities, has obtained tangible results. The initiative came to an end after a change in command in the local government and the systematic disruptive actions of trolls aimed at its Facebook page, possibly associated with political interests.

These new forms of organization present strengths and weaknesses. In the case of Quito, Yo me Apunto and the Slutwalk, worthy of note is the role played by a single person, who kept control of the initiative, and the organizations were mainly dependent on her decisions. In the case of the peasant march or Alto Maipo, the support received from civil society proved important, but to a large extent, the movement tended to dissipate rapidly.

**The Role of the Traditional Communication Media**

The case studies show that the cyberactivists make an effort to ensure their causes have repercussions in the traditional communication media, although many of them are at times extremely critical of the commercial press. To a certain extent, the traditional media maintain a capacity to legitimate (or not) the information that circulates in the social networks and/or the social mobilizations unleashed by them. At least two factors explain the ongoing importance of these media: (1) for a large part of the population, the traditional media continues to be the most reliable source of information; and (2) however broad its reach, communication via cyberspace still affects a limited audience.

Relations between the new virtual space and the traditional media are sometimes tense, in some cases, cross-pollination occurs and in others, divergence may prevail. In some of the case studies the traditional media are overtaken by events, and dissatisfaction with them makes room for new formats of professional journalism. In Venezuela, government repression of the communication media led groups of professional journalists to create the digital news vehicles Efecto Cocuyo and Crónica Uno. During the June 2013 protests in Brazil, Mídia Ninja, formed by a group that promotes alternative journalism, was transformed into a channel for transmitting images, in particular of police repression, influencing broad sectors of society, in particular young people. Lastly, analysis of the events of September 30, 2010 in Ecuador during a police revolt, show how the public started using social networks, in particular Twitter, to obtain real-time information about events when traditional media websites went off the air, ultimately due to government media control measures.

## Dependence on Commercial Social Networks

All the case studies indicate that cyberactivism occurs fundamentally through social networks, in particular Facebook and Twitter, and by means of the transmission of images, principally via YouTube.[5] Even the most ardent critics of these networks use them systematically. Facebook is the main medium for disseminating rather more elaborate messages and contents, and Twitter is particularly useful for transmitting specific information on events and for disseminating watchwords.

The traditional criticism of traditional mass media claimed that communication was monopolized by the owners, which influenced their agendas. On the other hand, face-to-face communication has traditionally played an important role, frequently in opposition to the traditional media. To the extent that a large part of the communication taking place in today's world occurs via the virtual networks, a new conformation of the public space emerges. A great part of communication, including communication that was formerly conducted face-to-face, now takes place via social networks, which do not control the content of the messages, but define the rules under which information is transmitted, and its content is later used for commercial purposes. In this way, the format of the networks is directly related to the commercial goal of obtaining as much information as possible about people and their preferences, building user profiles that have great commercial value. In the case of Facebook, for example, this means that the 'time line' is a mosaic composed of the most diverse messages, the subject of which changes from second to second and which, in the best of hypotheses, leads to variations around 'likes' and banal comments.

Twitter, on the other hand, with its short messages, is far from being a space for public debate.

In short, if on the one hand the social networks enable horizontal communication, on the other, they are structured in a way that does not favor debate based on argumentation, with simplification and polarization predominating. As we have seen, platforms that pursue the development of a more serious exchange are still taking their first steps and have not yet reached a broader public.

## Conclusions: New Technologies and the Future of Democracy in Latin America

The public arena is not an empty 'space' which precedes its occupation by social agents. On the contrary, it is constituted – in both form and content – by political and social organizations and the diverse forms of social participation and political communication. As we have argued in this article, we are confronting a moment of inflection in which this public space is assuming new forms, as the product of the shifts in sociability produced by the new means of communication. What is happening in Latin America, with its different national variations and peculiarities, is part of a global phenomenon. In many countries around the world new actors and forms of participation, self-defined as the 'outraged' and 'collectives', are emerging and their profile no longer fits into the traditional sociological categories of class, identity groups and social movements.

The case studies indicate that in regimes with authoritarian tendencies (such as the Venezuela of President Maduro or the Ecuador of President Correa), the State interferes directly in the virtual world, using both legal and discretionary instruments, restricting freedom of expression and resorting to underhand means (such as bots and teams of communication professionals dedicated to sabotaging opponents' websites, blogs and pages on social networks). It is also in authoritarian situations that the libertarian potential of the web plays a more decisive role.

Nonetheless, it is not only in authoritarian regimes that the State attempts to control or interfere with the virtual world. Democratic governments are also present in the virtual public space. The financing of 'friendly' online news vehicles and blogs with public funds, the monitoring of what happens on the web and the use of bots to inflate the number of followers of presidential tweets and disseminate messages of support have also become widely used tactics.

The expectation that the online world would constitute a space in which citizens empowered by the possibility of directly accessing the public space and communicating in horizontal networks would be more motivated to participate is not yet confirmed. Certainly, during moments of 'social explosion', events that mobilize an entire society, direct, horizontal online communication en masse reaches a wide audience and can have important political effects. In general, however, political communication continues to be a subject of interest only to a minority. In the social networks, not only do personal messages predominate, but also the opinion makers and formers are the pop stars. Regarding political topics, few people relate to and comment on more complex subjects, and normally the reactions are limited to 'likes' and short comments, the majority accusatory in nature. Meanwhile consultation platforms dedicated to specific subjects reach very limited segments of society.

The Internet was, and for many still is, considered an alternative capable of substituting representation with direct participation or, in other words, enabling the elimination of intermediary institutions between the public and government decisions. Our study, whether looking at new formats of political parties, of consultation platforms or online campaigns, shows the potential and the limitations of the new systems of consultation, direct communication and political participation. The social networks are extremely effective in sending clear and simple messages during moments of mobilization or in addressing isolated questions that demand a binary response. However, as yet, no one has developed platforms capable of enabling the broader public discussion of complex themes that require efforts of negotiation and synthesis.

In certain visions of virtual democracy, political life would constitute a permanent consultation of the public. This implies that politics is the aggregate of personal opinions, rather than a collective construction, the product of an argumentative effort and of negotiations that permit not only the creation of consensus, but also proposals and visions of the possible and the desired society, all of which requires stable organizations capable of processing the debates and ensuring the continuity over time of currents of public opinion. This vision has proven to be unrealistic, if not detrimental to democracy, at least so far.

To date, virtual political communication, to a great extent, has played more the role of a 'counter-democracy',[6] expressing ill-feeling related to the core problems afflicting democratic societies, such as social inequality. If it is to evolve beyond being an instrument for social catharsis, it should become capable of transforming democratic institutions and government policies. The great challenge is to articulate the possibilities of virtual participation in conjunction with representative forms, and of ephemeral protests with organizations that are sustained over time. A virtuous relationship between the different forms of communication and organization can overcome the distortions in the political culture that currently predominate in the virtual world. This requires organizational innovations on the part of political parties and NGOs that will enable the integration of virtual communication into the forms of organization, participation, mobilization and contact with the public. On the part of the public, this requires learning about the critical use of the Internet, which should start in school, as an instrument for information and political participation.

Each wave of civil society has transformed political institutions and forms of social participation. The first wave promoted workers' rights and access to goods and social services (such as healthcare, education and pensions), leading to a decrease in social inequality and to the social welfare state. The second wave was successful in advancing questions to a certain extent overlooked in the first wave, such as gender relations and 'racial and indigenous minorities, state violence and environmental awareness. While it expanded and deepened expectations of equality and the pursuit of recognition and dignity for each citizen, it also proved to be impotent against the increase in social inequality.

Still, in spite of the online/offline linkages, the virtual universe has its own distinctive characteristics, which profoundly transform traditional forms of communication and sociability. It also creates new opportunities for civic communication, which are particularly attractive to the young. Furthermore, it opens up space for a new generation of communicators and journalists, transforming the dynamic of the public space and enabling new forms of activism and political culture. To ensure the democratic nature of these new forms of participation, these instruments need to be transparent, minimizing the effects of anonymity by increasing the public's critical capacity and discernment.

The third wave, and here again we insist on repeating ourselves, is still in its infancy. Increasingly the web is permeating all human activities and one of its consequences, the creation of a new format of the public space, results in new forms of communication and organization of social relations that affect the diverse types of political activism and their content. This text is an effort to map some aspects of these transformations, showing the diversity, the contradictions and the virtuous possibilities and risks that Latin American democracy is confronted with in the twenty-first century.

## Notes

1. This text was translated by the author into English especially for this volume. It was originally published in Portuguese as Bernardo Sorj, 'Online/off-line: o novo tecido do ativismo político', in Bernardo Sorj and Sergio Fausto (Eds), *Ativismo político em tempos de Internet*, São Paulo: Plataforma Democrática, 2016. Available at: http://www.plataformademocratica.org/Arquivos/Ativismo_pol%C3%ADtico_em_tempos_de_internet.pdf.
2. See Sorj and Fausto (2016), ibid.
3. For an overview on the recent transformation of Latin American societies see: B. Sorj and D. Martuccelli, *The Latin American Challenge*. São Paulo: Plataforma Democrática, 2008. Available for free download at: www.plataformademocratica.org/PDF/Publicacao_57_em_06_05_2008_23_20_53.pdf
4. See www.avaaz.org/po/about.php
5. Possibly future studies will indicate the importance of new tools such as WhatsApp.
6. Characterized by Pierre Rosanvallon as complementary mechanisms to elections, involving criticism and denunciation based on a healthy distrust of politicians and institutions, but which may result in distance from the political system expressed in an 'apolitical' or 'impolitical' citizen, leading to the stigmatization of the representative sys-tem and ultimately to destructive populism, *La Contre-démocratie: La politique à l'âge de la défiance*. Paris: Seuil, 2006.

## References

Rosanvallon, P. (2006) *La Contre-démocratie: La politique à l'âge de la défiance*. Paris: Seuil.
Sorj, B. and Fausto, S. (2016) *Ativismo político em tempos de Internet*. São Paulo: Edições Plataforma Democrática.
Sorj, B. and Martuccelli, D. (2008) *The Latin American Challenge: Social Cohesion and Democracy* [online]. Rio de Janeiro: Centro Edelstein de Pesquisa Social.

## Bernardo Sorj, by Carlos Ruiz Encina (Chile)

Bernardo Sorj (1948–) is a sociologist and retired Professor of Sociology at UFRJ (Universidade Federal do Rio de Janeiro), current Director of the Centro Edelstein de Pesquisas Sociais and the Plataforma Democrática project. His research has delved into several issues, such as political development, international relationships, the social impact of new technologies, social theory and Judaism. He is Director of the Edelstein Social Investigation Center and of the Democratic Platform Project, from which he promotes research that connects civil society's use of the Internet, political participation and the strengthening of democracy in Latin America.

'Political activism in the Internet era' is an inquiry that delivers social and political references to understand the phenomenon of 'cyberactivism' in Latin American civil society during the past decade. For Sorj, the main issue resides in what he refers to as a possible 'online/offline imbrication', that is, in how the new civil society is capable of articulating both virtual participation and social activism with representative forms, as well as in the effective bond between the ephemeral use of the social networks and the establishment of social and political organizations that strengthen with time.

In his research he distinguishes three formation periods of Latin American civil society and relates them to the broadening of specific social rights. The first period, is one in which civil society is constituted by organizations that represent social interests related to production, whose leaders are elected democratically by their associates, and where labor rights and access to public goods are promoted. The second period is forged mainly by NGOs that validate themselves because of the causes they advocate, not by any sort of popular mandate, and that pursue egalitarian expectations and the search for personal liberties. Finally in a third period, which is still in an embryonic gestation phase, the virtual world is constituted by 'citizens' that broadcast their opinions through social networks. These three constitutive movements coexist historically and influence each other.

Through the study of specific cases in Latin American countries, Sorj distinguishes a series of elements the make it difficult to conclude that online political activism permits the constitution of a new citizenship: first, because the deliberation spaces promoted on the Internet have not given rise to political alternatives that challenge the existing ones; second, because online campaigns have been more effective when it comes to solving concrete issues than those which involve the general interest of society (i.e., public interest); third, because the platforms for online participation and polling lack the institutional framework that validates them in terms of formal power; fourth, because the impact of social networks still depends on the use of commercial platforms (such as Facebook or Twitter) or on the impact that online debate generates in traditional media, which are still those used by the vast majority of the population; finally, because governments have managed to counteract the role of alternative media through the active use of the same social networks.

Nonetheless, these studies shed light on the elements that have impacted positively on the democratization of social processes: first, they have allowed a broader participation of citizens in terms of social protest and the spreading of their demands; second, they have made possible the increase in alternative information media that strengthens the coordination and communication between subordinate social actors during the noted periods; and finally, because social networks allow the playing down of the power of official communication media controlled by governments or the large national and international corporations.

Ultimately, the author reveals the impossibility of dissociating current social and political processes from the new digital communication forms. This allows him to assert that the structural transformations registered in Latin America were previous

*(Continued)*

(Continued)

to the rise of the Internet, but their evolution is influenced by it. In that sense, his research challenges those optimistic views that idealize the political use of the Internet as a privileged medium to promote political participation and to strengthen Latin American democracy, that is to say, that its impact depends on historically constituted actors; but also challenges pessimistic perspectives that criticize the political deliberation deficits and immediacy that characterizes people's interactions online. Lastly, Sorj equates several types of 'cyberactivism' which are expressions of very different social interests (some even contradictory) which would be worth distinguishing in future research.

# Index

Page numbers in *italics* refer to tables.

agrarianism/agriculture
    and capitalism 188–9, 192
    Haiti 372, 377
    periphery and industrial center 76–7
    reform 52, 225–6, 227
    social movements 280–1, 283
    *see also* coffee production; feudalism; land
ALAS *see* Latin American Sociology
    Association (ALAS)
Allais, M. 124
Althusser, L. 243
Alto Maipo movement, Chile 414, 415
Álvarez, E. 327
Álvarez, S. 324
'American' modernity 157–8
    and 'American progressivism' 166–8
    and European modernity 158–67
    success of 169–70
    use value and consumerism 168
anti-dictatorial struggles 91–2, 322, 358
    1946 movement, Haiti 373
anti-racist social movements 279
Arab/Islamic occupation, Spain 66–7, 108–9
Arendt, H. 95
Argentina
    households, families and social inequalities
        249–65 *passim*
    military coups 12, 13, 38, 40
    military dictatorships and neoliberalism,
        relationship between 383–4
    political activism in Internet era 404
        Change.org (online support campaign)
            408, 409–10
        new forms of civil society 414
        Partido de la Red (Web Party) 406–8
    sociology 9, 36
    State and economic crises 398–9
    surpluses 131
aristocratic regime, Spain 66, 67
aristocratic and rentier class, Mexico 295

Aristotle 120, 186
authoritarianism 81, 85, 92–3
    State terrorism/repression and resistance
        91–2, 309–11
    *see also* anti-dictatorial struggles;
        dictatorships; military dictatorships
autonomy
    academic 37, 40, 43
    feminism 324–6
Avaaz (online support campaign), Brazil 408, 409

Bagú, S. 11, 108–10, 116–29
    career 126–8
baroque, originality of 113–14
Barrig, M. 328
Barthes, R. 243
Bedregal, X. 327
Beigel, F. 1–28
    et al. 37, 40, 43
Biglieri, P. 386–8
Black community
    *see* Negroes and Mulattos,
        São Paulo; race; slavery
Bolívar, S. 4–5
Bolivia 24–5
    constituent moments in history 111
    decolonization practices and discourses
        290–302
    populism 384, 385
    State and economic crises 398–9
Bolivian Revolution 21–2
bourgeoisie *see* elites; middle class/bourgeoisie
Brazil
    BRICS nations 144
    economic crisis 399
    feminist movement influence on State 328
    households, families and social inequalities
        250–65 *passim*
    military coups 12, 38, 309
    political activism (Internet era)

Avaaz (online support campaign) 408, 409
Internet Civil Framework
(consultation plaform) 411
street protests: Movimento
Passe Livre 413
political activism (workers) 307–14
race, racism and racial studies 15, 19–20, 22
*see also* Negroes and Mulattos, São Paulo
sociology
canned vs dynamic 47–54
foundational period 36
and US development strategies 53
Bringel, B. 273–89
*Buen Vivir* (BV) 146–7, 148, 150–1
Bukharin (Marx) 190–1
Burki, S.J. 123–4
Butler, J. 15

Calderón, F. G. 10
Cangiano, M. and Dubois, L. 15
canned vs dynamic sociology 47–54
capitalism
global expansion 76, 118
and Indigenous agrarianism 188–9, 192
and inequality 177–9
in less developed countries 51
oligopolized (internationalized) and
competitive (local) 178–9
present-day Spain 68
surplus value 132
*see also* development (and modernity);
globalization
Cardoso, F.H. and Faletto, E. 39, 78, 178
Casanova, P.G. 295–6, 297, 298
Castor, S. 371–9
career 380–1
Catholicism
and marginality 242
modernity 160
and slavery 210–11
theology and ethics 120, 121
center-left and populist movements 382–6
center–periphery relations 2, 34, 39, 45
Central American Program of Social
Sciences 34, 38
CEPAL (Economic Commission for Latin
America) 50–1, 177, 249, 250
Change.org (online support campaign) 408,
409–10
Chavez, H. 24, 385
Chile 11–13
democratic transition 384–5
feminist movements 95–6, 322, 325, 327, 329
institutionalization of sociology 34, 36, 37–9
military coup (1973) 12, 40

political activism in Internet era 404
new forms of civil society 414
online consultation platforms 411–12
student movement 413
State and economic crises 397–8, 399
surpluses 131
*ch'ixi*
areas 301
notion of 299–300
Christianity
European and American forms 160–1,
163–5, 167, 169
*see also* Catholicism
Churata, G. 301
Ciriza, A. 15
and Fernández 14
citizenship 94–5, 96–7
deficit of 360
indigenous 292, 294
civil society
Internet era 414–15
neoliberalism (1990s) 96
and State terrorism 309–11
*see also* social movements
civilizing project of capitalist modernity
158–60
CLACSO (Latin American Council of Social
Sciences) 8, 12–13, 44, 92, 106
CLADEM (Latin American and Caribbean
Committee for the Defense of Women's
Rights) 332
class
aristocratic and rentier class, Mexico 295
ethnicity and colonialism 182
*see also* Indian-Ladino relations, Mexico;
Negroes and Mulattos, São Paulo
working/popular class movements 307–14,
382–6
*see also* elites; middle class/bourgeoisie
coffee production
Brazil 201, 202, 203
Mexico 226, 227
Colombia
foundational period of sociology 36–7
political activism in Internet era 404, 414
populism 384
colonialism 4–5, 107
Arab/Islamic occupation, Spain
66–7, 108–9
Haiti 371
internal *see* internal colonialism
and race/ethnicity 182
*see also* Indian-Ladino relations, Mexico;
indigenous community/population;
Negroes and Mulattos, São Paulo

coloniality
 and dependency 23–4
 of knowledge 298
 and modernity
  -decoloniality (MCD) perspective 149–50
  resistance 275–8
  Spain 64, 67, 70
 of power 70, 298
communism *see* Marxism; socialism/
  communism; Soviet Union
company and trade union relations 340–1
corporate community 226, 231–2
corruption 105, 393, 396–7
Cortés, F. 40
'Cost-of-Living Movement', São Paulo 307
Costa, S. 4
Costa Pinheiro, C. 70–2
Costa Rica: CLACSO seminar (1978) 92
Crevenna, T. 11
'critical' sociology 25–6
 and academic autonomy 43
critical thinking 110–12
Cuba: surpluses 131
Cuban 38, 42, 80, 356, 374
Cuban Revolution 38, 42, 80, 356, 374
Cueva, A. 13
cultural anthropology 121–2
cultural factors and development
  strategies 53
cultural movements 286
cultural values 119
Cusicanqui, S.R. 290–304
 career 304–5

Dagnino, E. 96
'Day of Race'/'Day of cultural diversity' 5
de Arnoux, N. 5
De la Garza Toledo, E. 338–50
 career 350–1
De Marinis, P. 126–8
De Tocqueville, A. 130
debt crisis (1980s) 81–2
decolonization
 Asian and African movements 20–1
 epistemic 146–7, 149–50
 modernity-coloniality (MCD) perspective
  149–50
 practices and discourses, Bolivia 290–302
democracy 75, 92–3
 and democratization 358–60
 and feminism 322, 323–4, 326
 populist rupture and transitions 384–6
 racial 216–18
 social sciences and sociology 41, 43
 virtual world and future of 417–20

*see also* citizenship; civil society; Internet/
  information technology; social
  movements
demographic changes 250–2
demographics and census surveys 122
dependency analysis/theories 7, 23–4, 25, 39,
  40, 41–2, 44–5, 77–9, 140–1, 177–8
developed countries vs developing countries
 economic/development strategies 50–4
 'First World' and Latin American
  inequalities 180–1
development (and modernity) 112–13, 139–40
 alternatives to 'development' 150–1
 crisis of 'globalization' 143–5
 and dependency 23–4, 39, 177–8
 free-market based 123–4
 genealogy of 'development' (1951-2000)
  140–2
 and independent centers 41
 Latin American perspective 145–6
 and marginality 242–4
 modernity-coloniality-decoloniality (MCD)
  perspective 149–50
 post-development as concept and social
  practice (1991–2010) 142–3
 as sociological issue 36, 38–9, 44
 transition discourses and post-extractivism
  151–2
 trends in 'development' studies 146–9
 *see also* modernization/modernity
Dewey, J. 116–17
dictatorships
 Duvalier regime, Haiti 374–5
 *see also* anti-dictatorial struggles; military
  dictatorships
difference and equivalence, logics of 382–3, 384
Durkheim, E. 1, 33, 83
Duvalier, F. 374
Duvalier, J.-C. 375
dynamic vs canned sociology 47–54

Echeverría, B. 113–14, 157–72
 career 170–2
Economic Commission for Latin America
  (CEPAL) 50–1, 177, 249, 250
Economic Commission for Latin America and
  the Caribbean (ECLAC) 7, 11, 34, 36, 39,
  40, 77–8, 79, 123
economic crises 391–9
 1980s 81–2
 2007 145
economic restructuring 250–2
economic theory 119–20, 121, 122–3, 125
 critical attitudes 123–4
 struggle for surplus 130–4

*Economy of the Colonial Society* (Bagú) 108
Ecuador
  police revolt 416
  Quito, *Yo me Apunto* 415
  YASunidos (online support campaign)
    408, 410
elites
  Bolivia 290, 292, 293, 294, 295, 301–2
  *see also* middle class/bourgeoisie
employment *see* labor/employment
environmental crisis 144
epistemic decolonization 146–7, 149–50
Escobar, A. 112–13, 139–56
  career 154–6
Esteva, G. 139, 143
Eurocentrism 33, 45, 69, 70, 149–50, 176–7,
    275–6
Europe
  cultural traditions 109
  post-war development model 112
  social sciences 3–4, 33, 45, 121
  *see also* Spain
European and 'American' modernity 158–67
Europeanization
  urbanization as 208
  *see also* modernization/modernity
Evers, T. 326

Facebook 416–17
Faculty of Latin American Social Sciences
    (FLACSO) 7, 11–12, 36, 37–8, 44, 106
Fals Borda, O. 36–7, 42, 57–63
  career 62–3
families *see* households, families and social
    inequalities
Feijoo, M.C. 321, 331
feminism
  actors, strategies and performance spaces
    319–24
  continuity and change 324–31
  gender and women 14–16, 27
    *see also* gender; women
  human rights and memory, history
    of 89–98
  natural resources struggles 285
  as political-ideological matrix 281–2
  transformations and trends 331–3
Fernandes, F. 22, 36, 201–21
  career 219–21
fertility rates 90, 252
feudalism 187–9, 192, 223
  feudal-mercantile alliance 193
  Spain 66, 89
Fiat Brazil 307
fiscal deficit reduction 389–91

FLACSO (Faculty of Latin American Social
    Sciences) 7, 11–12, 36, 37–8, 44, 106
Fossaert, R. 125–6
Franco, R. 25, 35, 36, 38
Free Trade Area of the Americas (FTAA)
    385–6
functionalism 243–4
  structural-functionalism 39
Funes, P. 380–1

Gamonalismo 188, 190, 193–5;
    *see also* Indio struggles
García Canclini, N. 300
Garretón, M.A. 355–70
gender
  feminism and women 14–16, 27
    *see also* feminism; women
  human rights and memory, history of 89–98
  inequality 183
  notions of identity 301
Germani, G. 9, 11, 36, 39, 44, 76, 81
Gini coefficient 175
globalization
  'Americanism' as 'common identity' 157
  of capitalism 76, 118
  crisis of 143–5
  and democracy 359–60
  and economic restructuring 250–2
  and feminist movement 323, 329–30, 331
  politics and State 362, 363
  *see also* neoliberalism
Godfrey, M. 244
Gohn, G. 316–17
González, L. 15
González Casanove, P. 21, 45
governments
  loss of legitimacy 105
  *see also* State
Greco-Roman era 120–1
Guatemala 230–1
Gudynas, E. and Acosta, A. 146, 148–9, 150–1
Guerreiro Ramos, A. 36, 43, 47–56
  career 55–6
Guimarães, A.S.A. 219–21
Guimarães, N.A. 175–85

Haiti 279
  American occupation and aborted modernity
    372–4
  colonialism and Republic 371–2
  Duvalier regime 374–5
  military coups 376, 378
  slave revolution 279
  transition: from consensus to polarization
    376–8

twenty-first century challenges 378–9
health services, Brazil 52–3
Heilbron, J. 3
hermeneutic techniques (Participatory Action
    Research) 59–61
Herodotus 120
hierarchization in theory building 122–3
Hispanic-American Modernism 5
historical and contemporary debate 105–6
    critique of development and modernity
        112–13
    learning to observe 108–10
    learning to think critically 110–12
    originality of the baroque 113–14
    roots 106–8
historical recovery (hermeneutic technique) 60
Honduras: households, families and social
    inequalities 250–65 *passim*
households, families and social inequalities
    183, 248–50, 265–7
    household characteristics, socioeconomic and
        demographic changes affecting 250–2
    household composition, continuities and
        changes 252–8
    household poverty levels 261, *262*
    male breadwinner family model, loss of
        importance of 258–9
    two-parent nuclear families with children
        261–3
    woman headship 256–8, 263–5
human geography 122
human rights activism 91–7, 98
hybridity, discourse and notion of 295, 300–1
hyperinflation 391–2, 397

identity, indigenous notions of 301
identity politics 286, 322
ideology
    political–ideological matrices (social
        movements) 278–82, 283
    surplus as transmitter of 134
import-substitution 391, 397
income
    inequality 175–6
    levels and household types 253, *254*
    tax 391
independence revolutions and narrative 4–5
independent centers 41
Indian-Ladino relations, Mexico 222–31
    class relationships 233–5
    colonial relationships 231–3
    social stratification 235–6
Indigenous community/population
    Bolivia: decolonization practices and
        discourses 290–302

colonial and class relationships 182
Peru
    exploitation of 187–9, 193
    'indigenous libertarian' movement 279
    rebellions and socialist struggles 193–5
    tasks involved 195–7
    race, nation and class (RNC) 14–25
    social movements 278–9, 283
Indio struggles 188, 190, 193–5; *see also*
    Gamonalismo
industrial center and agricultural periphery
    76–7
industrial contamination 123
industrialization 38
inequality/ies 175–83
    and feminist movement 332
    industrial center and agricultural periphery
        76–7
    measurements 175
    multidimensional and multilevel 176, 181–3
    *see also* households, families and social
        inequalities; marginality
inflation 390, 391–2, 397, 398–9
informal employment sector 338–9, 344–5
institutionalization and autonomy
    academic 37, 40, 43
    feminism 324–6
institutionalization of LAS 33–41, 74, 105–6
    fundamental themes 44–5
    inequalities and critique of Eurocentrism
        176–7
    tensions 41–4
Intergovernmental Panel on Climate Change
    (IPCC) 144
internal colonialism 19, 21, 45, 182
    Andean region 295–6
    Mexico 226, 230
    Spain 67
international inequalities 177–80
international migration 252, 256, 258
internationalization of social sciences 3–4, 12
Internet Civil Framework (consultation
    platform), Brazil 411
Internet/information technology 82–3, 144–5
    political activism 404–8
        consultation platforms 411–12
        dependence on commercial social
            networks 416–17
        new forms of civil society 414–15
        online support campaigns 408–10
        street protests 412–13
        traditional communications media, role
            of 415–16
        virtual world and future of democracy
            417–20

Jelin, E. 89–102

Katarista-Indianista uprising (1979), Bolivia 292
Kirkwood, J. 96
knowledge
   'political economy' of 297
   return (hermeneutic technique) 60
   types 82–3
knowledge production
   changes 147–8
   feminist 321, 331
   see also institutionalization of LAS

labor market: globalization and restructuring
   250–2
labor movements 284–5
   São Paulo workers, Brazil 307–11
   see also trade unions
labor/employment
   Indian, Mexico 227
   men 256
   Negroes and Mulattos, São Paulo 203–4,
      205, 208–10
   State officials 389–91
   women 205, 251–2, 259, 260
Laclau, E. 382–6
   career 386–8
Ladinization 228, 232
Ladino-Indian relations; see Indian-Ladino
   relations, Mexico
land
   and agrarianist social movements 280–1
   communal 195–6, 225–6, 227
   European 'land rent' and American 'rent of
      technology' 164
landholders
   and abolition of slavery 203
   Gamonalismo and Indio struggles 188, 190,
      193–5
Latin American and Caribbean Committee
   for the Defense of Women's Rights
   (CLADEM) 332
Latin American Council of Social Sciences
   (CLACSO) 8, 12–13, 44, 92, 106
Latin American Sociology Association (ALAS)
   1, 7, 9, 35, 105–6
   Second Congress 43, 47–8, 51
Latin-Americanism 5–6, 23, 24, 107
Lavalas movement, Haiti 376
Lechner, N. 94, 329–30, 331
liberal paradigm of development 141
life expectancy at birth 252, 253, 258
logic of difference and logic of equivalence
   382–3, 384
logos mythos technique 60

Malinvaud, E. 124
Marcha de Las Putas (Slutwalk), Colombia
   414–15
Marcha pela Vida (March for Life),
   Colombia 414
marginality
   and social exclusion 240–5
   theory of 178
Mariátegui, J.C. 9–11, 16–19, 21, 26, 182,
   186–7, 279
   career 198–200
Mariátegui Ezeta, J.-C. 198–200
Martínez de Hoz, J.A. 383–4
Martins, P.H. 25
Marx, K. 76, 119, 120, 134, 159, 179–80, 241,
   243, 382–3
   and Engels, F. 69
   and founding fathers of sociology 1, 33, 83
Marxism 10, 11, 39, 42, 79–80
   critique of neoliberalism 144
   development model 141
   and feminism 14, 15, 89–90
   Mexico 13
   and race 18–19, 190–1
   see also socialism/communism
Mayan region 230, 231
Medina Echavarría, J. 36, 44, 123
memory 286
   feminism and human rights 96–7, 98
Mercosur 385–6
Mexico
   First Intergovernmental Conference on
      women (1975) 91
   history of state receptivity and surplus 131
   households, families and social inequalities,
      250–65 passim
   inflation 398
   Marxism 13
   rentier and aristocratic class 295
   see also Indian-Ladino relations
micro/small enterprises 338–9, 344, 348
microcorporatism/company corporatism 340–1
middle class/bourgeoisie 10–11, 22, 79
   colored, Brazil 210, 214, 217
   and development 76, 81, 230–1
   Haiti 377
   racist attitudes 188–9, 210
   State employees 389–91
   see also elites
Midia Ninja, Brazil 416
Mignolo, W. 296–7, 298
   et al. 293, 299
migration
   and abolition of slavery 203, 204, 205,
      207–8

international 252, 256, 258
military coups/coups d'état 12–13, 38–9, 40–1,
    91, 309
    Haiti 376, 378
military dictatorships
    and neoliberalism, relationship between
        383–4
    Pinochet regime, Chile 397
    social memories 357–8
    *see also* anti-dictatorial struggles;
        Southern Cone
Mockus, A. 414
modernization/modernity
    -coloniality-decoloniality (MCD)
        perspective 149–50
    baroque 114
    failures of 80–3
    pessimism in social science 83–5
    promises of 74–5
    and race relations 218
    theory 36, 37–8, 42–3, 44, 74, 140
        vs Marxism 89–91
    triumphant reason 75–80
    *see also* 'American' modernity; coloniality,
        and modernity; development (and
        modernity)
'moral crisis' 395
Morales, E. 24
mortality levels 252
Mothers of the Plaza de Mayo 92
Movimento Passe Livre, Brazil 413
multiculturalism, discourse and notion of
    293–4, 295, 299, 302

nation-building *see* Haiti
national approach *see* regional tradition
national revenue 51
nationalism
    Indians, Mexico 232–3
    peripheral nationalism social movements
        279–80, 283
natural means of production 163–6
natural resources struggles 285
nature, rights of (RN) 150–1
Negroes and Mulattos, São Paulo
    inequality and social stratification 201–10
    prejudice, discrimination and phases of race/
        class relations 210–19
neoliberalism
    human rights and memory 96–7
    indigenous protests against 293–4
    and military dictatorships, relationship
        between 383–4
    military intervention in universities and 40–1
    and 'open regionalism' 6

reforms 43, 44, 144
    and trade unions 338–9, 342–5
    *see also* globalization
'New Negro' 214–16
NGOs
    feminist 324–5
    *see also* civil society
Ni Una Menos, Argentina 414
Nicaragua
    households, families and social inequalities
        250–65 *passim*
    Sandinista revolution 13, 40
non-transferability of economic/development
    strategies 53
North American Free Trade Agreement
    (NAFTA) 6
North–South international labor division 276
Nun, J.L. 178–9, 240–5
    career 246–7

observation
    learning to observe 108–10
    participant 58
O'Donnell, G. 389–401
    career 401–3
Oliveira, M.A. and O. 248–69
*Oppressed but Not Defeated* (Cusicanqui)
    291–2
oral history studies 296–7
Organization for American States (OAS)
    Convention on Sexual and Reproductive
        Rights 332

Pareto, V. 186–7
Participatory Action Research (PAR) 37, 42
    hermeneutic techniques 59–61
    vs scientific/logical empiricism 57–9
participatory and representative democracy 360
Partido de la Red (Web Party), Argentina
    406–8
peasantry; *see* Haiti; Indian-Ladino relations,
    Mexico; Indigenous community/
    population
Péralte, C. 372
'peripheral Fordism' and 'Brazilianization'
    180–1
peripheral nationalism social movements
    279–80, 283
Peru 9–11
    feminist movement 328
    political activism in Internet era 404
    populism 384
    race, Indigenism and Marxism 16–19
    *see also* Indigenous community/
        population, Peru

Piedrahita Arcila, I. 154–6
Pinochet regime, Chile 397
Pisano, M. 327
place: centrality in social practice 113
political ecology 113
politics and State *see* State and politics
'popular national' era 356
popular/working class movements 307–14,
    382–6
post-corporatist model of trade unions 346–9
post-development (1991-2010) 142–3
post-extractivism 152
post-structuralist critique of development
    141–2
postcolonial/decolonial studies 6, 292–3
Poviña, A. 9, 11
Prebisch, R. 51, 76, 77, 123
productive restructuring 250–1, 338, 339,
    343–5, 348
Puritan/Protestant colonists *see* Christianity

Qhispi, E.N. 301
qualitative description vs quantitative measures
    57, 118–19
Quijano, A. 23–4, 45, 64–73, 177, 178–9,
    291, 298
    career 70–2
Quito, Yo me Apunto, Ecuador 415

race 15, 19–20, 22, 182
    and feminist movement 332
    nation and class (RNC) 14–25
    *see also* Indian-Ladino relations, Mexico;
        Indigenous community/population;
        Negroes and
        Mulattos, Brazil
racial democracy 216–18
racial inferiority, idea of 186–91
Rainho, J.F. 307–8
rationality/reason
    modernity 75–80
    research vs political 59
    scientific vs political 74
Regional Indian Workers Federation 194–5
regional tradition 1–3
    'critical' approach 25–6
    global projection 26
    history and laboratories 8–13
    Latin American perspective 3–8
    national diversity and gender balance 26–7
    race, nation and class (RNC) 14–25
relative overpopulation 243, 244
    *see also* surplus
representative and participatory democracy 360
reproductive rights 286, 332

revolutions
    Bolivian 21–2
    Cuban 38, 42, 80, 356, 374
    independence 4–6
    Marxist theory of 79–80
    Sandinista, Nicaragua 13, 40
    slave, Haiti 279
Richards, N. 321, 325, 329
rights of nature (RN) 150–1
Roman Law 121, 211
Rousseff, D. 413

Sader, E. 307–18
    career 316–17
Sandinista revolution, Nicaragua 13, 40
Sanjinés, J. 299
Sapiro, G. 4
Sarlo, B. 329
Schumpeter, J. 120
'scientific sociology' 35–6, 39, 42
    *vs* 'chair sociology' 9, 35
    *vs* 'critical sociology' 25
scientific/logical empiricism vs Participatory
        Action Research 57–9
scientific vs political reason 74
Segato, R. 23
self-employment 338–9, 348
Shumaher, M. and Vargas, E. 328
slavery
    abolition
        and consequences 202–10
        revolutions 279
    black and anti-racist social movements 279
    prejudice and discrimination as consequence
        of 210–12
    and race 186–7
Slutwalk (Marcha de Las Putas), Colombia
        414–15
Smith, A. 119–20
social accountability imperatives 53
social inequalities 179
    *see also* households, families and social
        inequalities
social memories 97
social movements
    feminism and human rights 93–4
    Haiti 377–8
    Negroes and Mulattos 206–7
    research 273–5
        modernity, coloniality and resistance
            275–8
        political-ideological matrices 278–82, 283
        territory, regional imaginary and disputes
            over development 282–3
        twenty-first century 284–6

*see also* civil society; Internet/information technology, political activism; *specific causes*
social rights struggles 285–6
social security taxes 391
social stratification
and class relations 225
*see also* Indian-Ladino relations, Mexico
and inequality (Negroes and Mulattos, São Paulo) 201–10
social theory, changes 147–8
*Social Theory and Political Catastrophe* (Bagú) 110
social traumas 111–12
socialism/communism
fall of 82–3, 144
Indigenous population 16–19, 193–5, 196–7, 279, 297–8
revolutions 6
social movements 281, 283
*see also* Marxism
Sorj, B. 404–20
career 420–2
Southern Cone 13, 37, 40, 91, 97, 357–8
Soviet Union
economic policy and theory 123
fall of 118
Spain
Arab/Islamic occupation 66–7, 108–9
economic theory 120
history and Latin American parallels 64–70, 108–9
State
and feminist agendas 327–9
form transformation struggles 285
and free market (1980s) 81–2
modern capitalist 132–4
terrorism/repression and resistance 91–2, 309–11
trade union relations 341, 345
State crisis
economic crises 391–9
employees and fiscal deficit reduction 389–91
State and politics 355–7
democracy and democratization 358–60
military dictatorships 357–8
new context 360–2
new perspective 363–4
Stavenhagen, R. 21, 222–37
career 237–9
street protests 412–13
structural reforms *see* economic crises; economic restructuring; productive restructuring

structuralism 7, 34, 40
post-structuralist critique of development 141–2
structural-functionalism 39
student movement, Chile 413
*Subaltern Studies* (journal) 292–3
subjectiveness 114
subjectivity
feminist perspective 94–6
and objectivity (Participatory Action Research) 59
Summers, L.H. 123
surplus
struggle for 130–4
*see also* relative overpopulation
Svampa, M. 26, 146, 148, 277–8, 304–6
system, notion of 117–18
Sztompka, P. 111–12

Tanizaki, J. 64
Tavares de Almeida, M.H. 401–3
Tawantinsuyu Indigenous Rights, Committee for 194–5
taxation 391
national revenue 51
Taylor-Fordism and Toyotism 338, 344
technological revolution *see* Internet/ information technology
territory
identity as 301
social movements 282–3, 285
theory building 116–17
antiquities 120–1
beginnings/gestation in modern times 121–2
contribution of social sciences 125
critical attitudes 123–4
European roots 119–20
heterogeneity of homogeneity 117–19
hierarchization 122–3
scheme: producing, organizing and reasoning 125–6
*Time, Social Reality and Knowledge* (Bagú) 108–9
Torres Rivas, E. 38, 39, 42–3, 74–88
career 87–8
Toyotism 338, 343, 344, 348
trade unions
influences on 338–9
model 339–42
corporative and classist 339, 346
possibilities for reconstitution 342–6
post-corporatist 346–9
*see also* labor movements

transition discourses 151–2
Truman, H.S. 139
Twitter 416, 417

United Nations (UN) 11, 34, 323
  UNDP Report (2004) 359–60
  UNESCO 11, 12, 19, 20, 36, 37
  *see also* Economic Commission for Latin
    America and the Caribbean (ECLAC)
United States (US)
  counter-insurgency ideology 12, 40
  Department of Defense funded
    research 12
  failure of mathematical economists (1985) 124
  national tradition 3–4
  occupation of Haiti 372–4
  Pan-Americanism 5
  post-war development model 112
  sociology 33, 35, 40, 41–2, 52, 53
  Truman: 'Fair Deal' doctrine and Four Point
    program 139
  World Trade Center (September 11, 2001)
    attacks 144
  *see also* 'American' modernity
Ungo, U. 326
urban migration, Negroes and Mulattos 205
urban settlements, peripheral 241
Uruguay
  and Chile, populism 384–5
  coups d'état/military coup 13, 40
  households, families and social inequalities
    249–65 *passim*
use value
  and consumerism 168
  nature and 'naturalness' of 164–6

Valenzuela, M.E. 328, 331
Van Gunsteren, H. 95
Vargas, V. 319–35
  career 335–7
Vega Camacho, O. 137–8
Venezuela
  oil surplus 131
  political activism in Internet era 404
  street protests 413
  and traditional communications media 416
  populist rupture and democratic transition
    385–6

Walsh, C. 296–7
Washington Consensus 143–4
Weber, M. 1, 33, 42, 83, 177, 183
Weffort, F. 308, 309–10
women
  employment/labor 205, 251–2, 259, *260*
  feminism and gender 14–16, 27
    *see also* feminism; gender
  headship of households 256–8, 263–5
  identity and practices 301
work and life, worlds of 247–8
working/popular class movements 307–14, 382–6
World Bank 123–4, 140, 145
World Trade Center (September 11, 2001)
  attacks 144

YASunidos (online support campaign),
  Ecuador 408, 410

Zapata Schaffeld, F. 237–9
Zavaleta Mercado, R. 110–11, 130–7
  career 137–8